MORE... Frozen Memories
Celebrating a Century of Minnesota Hockey

By
Ross Bernstein

Nodin Press

"MORE...Frozen Memories"
Celebrating a Century of Minnesota Hockey

by Ross Bernstein
(www.bernsteinbooks.com)

ISBN: 1932472495

Nodin Press (a division of Micawbers, Inc.)
530 North Third Street (Suite #120) • Minneapolis, MN 55401

Distributed by ADVENTURE PUBLICATIONS
820 Cleveland St. South, Cambridge, MN 55008 • (800) 678-7006

Printed in the USA by Bang Printing (Brainerd, MN)
Cover Painting by Artist Tim Cortes

Photo Credits:
Donald M. Clark Collection: 50-57, 59-60, 62-63, 71, 175-176, 251
U.S. Hockey Hall of Fame: 12, 14-27, 29-39, 41-45, 47, 73, 184, 187-189, 192
Bruce Kluckhohn: 6, 7, 76-77, 79-82, 84-87
TPG Sports: 65-70
USA Hockey: 51, 60, 106, 108, 180-183, 241, 245
Minnesota State High School League: 188-191, 193-229, 233-237
Herb Brooks Foundation: 67, 107, 175
Dallas Stars: 68, 70, 72, 103, 180
Minnesota Wild: 74-75, 78, 83, 88-89, 99
LeRoy Nieman: 73
Charles M. Schulz: 109
Minnesota Historical Society: 232
Jamey Guy Photography: 184
Murray Williamson: 179
Tim Cortes: 4
Pioneer Press: 8, 61, 64
Mike Lamey: 10, 58, 90-93
USHL: 175-179
University of Minnesota: 15, 40, 41, 43, 94-105, 109-126, 128, 176, 238-241
University of Minnesota Duluth: 9, 128-135, 231, 242-243
St. Cloud State University: 136-143, 244
Minnesota State University, Mankato: 144-149, 246
Bemidji State University: 150-157, 247
Augsburg College: 158-160, 248-250
Bethel College: 160-161
Concordia: 161
Crookston: 172-173
Gustavus: 162, 249
Hamline: 164
St. John's University: 165-166
St. Mary's University: 167-169
St. Olaf College: 169
St. Scholastica: 174
St. Thomas University: 170-171
Christian Brothers: 28, 181
Lynn Olson: 232
Roger Buck: 31
U.S. Pond Hockey: 10
Shattuck-St. Mary's: 230
U.S. Air Force Academy: 93
Hobey Baker Memorial Award: 128

Acknowledgements:
I would like to thank all of the people who were kind enough to help me in writing this book. In addition to the countless college and university sports information directors whom I hounded throughout this project I would like to sincerely thank all of the men and women who allowed me to interview them. In particular, I would especially like to thank my publisher and friend, Norton Stillman.

For Sara & Campbell

COVER PAINTING by TIM CORTES

One of the nation's premier photo realism artists, Tim Cortes uses colored pencils as his preferred medium. Hundreds of his collectible lithographs have been sold throughout North America and his clients are a venerable who's-who of American sports. From Shaquille O'Neal to Mark McGwire and from Wayne Gretzky to Troy Aikman, Cortes has been commissioned to create countless commemorative works of art over the past two decades.

Cortes' paintings have been featured in numerous venus around the world, including: the U.S. Hockey Hall of Fame, Franklin Mint, Kelly Russell Studios and Beckett's Magazine, as well as on trading cards, pro sports teams' game-day programs, and in various publications. Known for his impeccable detail, Cortes has dedicated his life to the pursuit of celebrating the life and times of many of the world's most famous athletes and the sporting events in which they play.

Cortes grew up in Duluth, where he later starred as a hockey goaltender at Duluth East High School. After a brief stint in the United States Hockey League, Cortes went on to play between the pipes for two seasons in the mid-1980s for the University of Minnesota's Golden Gophers. Cortes then decided to pursue his passion of art and sports full-time, and enrolled at the prestigious Minneapolis College of Art and Design. He has been painting ever since.

Presently, Tim lives in Duluth with his wife Kathy and their two children. He continues to play senior hockey and also gives back by coaching both youth football and hockey. In addition, he also served as the goalie coach for the three-time NCAA champion University of Minnesota-Duluth Women's Hockey program in the mid-2000s.

"Nagano Gold..."

"Prized Possessions..."

Brett Hull

TABLE OF CONTENTS

6.	Foreword by Marian Gaborik
7.	Foreword by Mark Parrish
8.	Foreword by Neal Broten
9.	Foreword by Brett Hull
10.	Introduction
12.	In the Beginning...
29.	Senior Hockey in Minnesota
32.	Cal Marvin's Warroad Lakers
35.	Eveleth: The Capital of American Hockey
45.	The United States Hockey Hall of Fame: Eveleth, MN
48.	Native Minnesotans Who Have Played in the NHL
49.	Minnesota's Olympians
50.	The Minnesota North Stars (1967-1993 R.I.P.)
74.	The Minnesota Wild
70.	St. Paul's Fighting Saints
93.	The Minnesota Moose
94.	University of Minnesota Hockey
104.	Remembering Herb Brooks
127.	The Hobey Baker Memorial Award
129.	University of Minnesota-Duluth Hockey
136.	St. Cloud State University Hockey
144.	Minnesota State University Hockey
150.	Bemidji State University Hockey
158.	Division III College Hockey and the MIAC
172.	Minnesota's Other D-III & Junior College Programs
175.	Junior Hockey in Minnesota
181	The 1960 Gold Medal Winning U.S. Olympic Team
182.	The 1980 Gold Medal Winning U.S. Olympic "Miracle on Ice" Team
184.	In-Line Hockey in Minnesota
186.	High School Hockey in Minnesota
189.	Tourney Time!
232.	Women's Hockey in Minnesota
252.	Index

Foreword by Marian Gaborik

"The fans here in Minnesota, they are the best. I can't thank them enough for all of their support. The Wild has had a sold out building since day one and that has always meant a lot to me. Our fans have been with us through the good times as well as through the bad times, and they are extremely loyal to their team. When I see them out there when I come out onto the ice, it just makes me want to work as hard as I can."

"The Xcel Center is a big home-ice advantage for us, it really is. The fans are so loud in there and so supportive of us. They are very smart too. They really understand what is going on and get behind us at just the right times to give us the lift that we sometimes need. Overall, our fans are unbelievable and their support for us is huge. They have shown me so much support over the years and I just can't tell them enough how much I appreciate that.

"Being the team's No. 1 overall pick back in 2000 has meant a lot to me. The organization has been very loyal and committed to me over the years and has shown me a lot of respect. The Wild has been the only team that I have ever played for in the NHL and I feel very fortunate to be a part of such a first class organization. It is crazy to think that I have been on the team longer than just about anybody now. I guess with Manny leaving, it is just Wes Walz and I who have been here since the very beginning. I have seen a lot of teammates come and go over the years. It is always hard to see your friends go, either through free agency or through trades, but that is just the business of hockey and something you just have to deal with.

"I really enjoy playing for this team and with my teammates though. It is a lot of fun, especially now to play with Pavol (Demitra), who is one of my best friends from Slovakia. We click very well together out on the ice and have a lot of fun playing with each other. I was very surprised that the Wild traded for him and that made me very happy. We had played together on the Slovakian National team and found that we had a lot of chemistry together. So, it was a great move for the Wild to bring him in. He is a fabulous player and somebody whom I look up to a great deal.

"As for my biggest assets on the ice, I would have to say that I am most proud of my skating ability. Skating is for sure my biggest weapon. I take a lot of pride in being a fast skater and really enjoy flying around out there trying to score goals. That is so much fun to me. Really though, I just try to do whatever I can to help my team win. If that means passing or playing defense, or whatever, then that is what I will do. I just want to be a good professional and do my part for the good of the team.

"There have been so many good times and so many memories here in Minnesota. I remember scoring my very first goal in our first ever game against Anaheim, it was such a great feeling. I will never forget beating Colorado back in 2003 in the first round of the playoffs. That was just unbelievable. When Bruno scored the game-winning goal we all went crazy, we couldn't believe what we had done. It was for sure the biggest upset in the team's history, without a doubt.

"Playing for Jacques (Lemaire) has been great too. He has been my only coach in the NHL and I have a lot of respect for him. He understands the game so well and is very respected by the players. He has won a lot of Stanley Cups, so he has a lot of credibility with us. His coaching style is unique and he is very demanding, but that is why he is so successful. Without him this team would not be where it is right now, that is for sure. It is only a matter of time before he finally wins a Stanley Cup here in Minnesota. He is a tremendous teacher.

"Overall, I just really enjoy working and living in Minnesota. I have been here for eight years now, so I guess I am a Minnesotan too. I love living here, it is a beautiful place. I live in downtown Minneapolis and have a lot of fun here. The people are very nice and friendly to me, which I really appreciate. Maybe if it wasn't quite as cold in the winter, that would be my only wish. Other than that, it is great.

"Living in Minnesota for as long as I have now, I have also really gotten a taste for just how much hockey is a part of the culture here. So many people love the game here, it is amazing. I will never forget the first time I saw the high school tournament and how they were selling out games at the Xcel Center. That kind of stuff doesn't happen back in Slovakia, so that is pretty neat. The Gophers are a big deal here as well, and they are a lot of fun to watch too. All of it, from the youth levels to girls hockey, it is all fantastic. I love it. What a fantastic place Minnesota is for hockey, at all levels. I am just happy to be a small part of it. It truly is the state of hockey.

"I especially love to see all of the young kids come to our games. They wear their jerseys and are so proud of

their home towns and of their teams. That is great to see. They all dream of playing in the NHL, just like I did when I was a young boy in Trencin (Slovakia). Whenever I see kids and they ask me about hockey, I just tell them to have fun and to try their hardest. Kids nowadays need to play all kinds of sports and to have a good time. Everything else will take care of itself in the long run.

"I was fortunate in that my parents never really pushed me too hard in hockey. They saw that I had potential and that I liked the game, but they didn't make me do it. I developed my own love for the game and that was great. I played other sports during the school year and would always look forward to getting out on the ice with my friends. At a certain point I knew that it was what I wanted to do though, and I wound up turning pro when I was 16. My family was very supportive of that decision and I am grateful for that.

"You know, when it is all said and done for me, I would just like to be remembered as a hard working player who did his best to help his team win. I hope that people will think of me as someone who was exciting to watch and who was a good teammate. It has been a great experience to be here in Minnesota and I am grateful for the opportunity. I don't take anything for granted. Most of all I want to be remembered as a winner. My hope is that I can one day win a Stanley Cup for the fans of Minnesota. That would be a dream come true."

In six seasons in the NHL, Marian Gaborik has tallied 164 goals and 167 assists for 331 points in 408 career games.

Foreword by Mark Parrish

"For me to be able to come home and play for the Wild is really a dream come true. I feel so lucky and blessed. I grew up playing hockey on the ponds of Bloomington pretending to be Neal Broten and Dino Ciccarelli, imagining myself scoring the game-winning goal to win the Stanley Cup for the North Stars. So, for me to now be able to play for my hometown team, that is really something special. I have to pinch myself every now and then, I really do."

"I grew up like most kids in Minnesota, loving hockey. For myself as well as for most of my buddies, it was all about playing for the Bloomington Jefferson Jaguars. I was so fortunate to win a pair of state titles along the way and that was such a thrill for me. We beat Hill Murray in 1993 and Moorhead in '94 and that was something I will never forget.

"Playing for Coach Saterdahlen was great and we had some pretty good teams in those days. I mean I only lost three games in my entire high school career. That was back in the day when the players stuck around and didn't go off to play junior hockey, so we were able to keep our best guys around. I think there were about a dozen players from those teams who went on to play Division One hockey, that was how good our program was at the time. And it wasn't just the players either, there were so many outstanding coaches, parents and volunteers who were a part of all that as well.

"From there, I was lucky enough to go on to play college hockey at St. Cloud State University. I had so much fun playing for Huskies, what a great program. I met so many neat people while I was there, many of whom are my best friends even to this day. I also got to play hockey with my big brother Geno up there, which was really cool. We had a ball playing together. Coach Dahl was a fantastic guy and I learned a lot from him as well.

"Seeing St. Cloud State go Division One after Herb Brooks came up there back in the mid-1980s, that was wonderful not just for the Huskies, but for all of Minnesota hockey. Then, to see Mankato and Bemidji State go Division One as well, that just means more opportunities for more Minnesota kids. That is what it is all about. Overall, I would say that the state of the state of hockey here in Minnesota is fantastic. To see how far things have come for both the boys as well as the girls over the years is just awesome. More and more kids are advancing on to the next levels and I am living proof that a kid with marginal talent can actually make it through a lot of hard work and dedication.

"As for being with the Wild, it is amazing. To the Wild fans all I can say is thank you from the bottom of my heart. After playing in Florida, New York and L.A., to finally get the chance to come home and play in front of such unbelievable fans means the world to me. The fans here truly get it and really understand the game at a high level. The atmosphere at the Xcel Center is incredible and the fans in there just make us want to work as hard as we can for them.

"You know, the Xcel Center is a very intimidating place to play. The fans are on top of you and they can sense when the momentum and energy is changing out there. They respond and react to that and are all over that kind of stuff. They are the reason we have such a great home ice advantage. I mean as a player when you are out there and are just dead tired, or you need to get a goal, or need to stop a goal, our fans can give us that extra little bit of adrenaline to push us over the top and keep us going. It is an amazing thing, it really is.

"I have only been with the Wild for one season so far, but have already had so many great memories. I will never forget the first time I stepped onto the ice at the Xcel Center for my first home game. I was so nervous and so excited, it was just exhilarating. I literally couldn't stop my legs from shaking, it was a feeling I cannot even describe. I don't think my skates even touched the ice on my first shift, I was so pumped up. I remember scoring my first goal, getting my first hat trick against Chicago, and then winning Game Four of our playoff series against Anaheim. Winning that game was just intense, I don't think I have ever been in a louder arena in my entire life.

"The Wild is such a first class organization. From the front office to the coaching staff on down, everybody is so professional and so dedicated to the team's success. As for the players, we love playing here and we love playing for Jacques Lemaire. I don't think that there is a coach in hockey today more revered and respected than he is. Players want to play for him because he is such a legend.

"I am so proud and happy to play for the Wild. I just hope like crazy that I can one day hoist the Stanley Cup above my head at the Xcel Center. That is my ultimate goal and one that I promise to work hard at for the fans of Minnesota. I signed a long term contract with the team and hope that when the time finally comes, that I can retire as a member of this team.

"My wife and I really love being back in Minnesota. We are both from here originally and had always planned on retiring back here when I was done playing; so to get back at this stage of the game is fabulous. We both have a lot of family here and look forward to raising our own family here as well. As a player, knowing that my family and friends are up in the stands supporting me night in and night out, it doesn't get much better than that.

"As for my legacy, I would hope to be remembered as a hard working player who was willing to do whatever it took to help his team win. That is what it is all about in my eyes. I am certainly not the best player out there, but I pride myself in being not only a hard worker but also a good teammate who can be counted on.

"Just to be a part of Minnesota hockey is such an honor. I have such a great respect for the game and how it is played here. The traditions that we have all built up over the years are what it is all about and I am humbled to be able to say that I have played a small part in that. I have certainly had a ball spending my lifetime in hockey, that is for sure. From mites to squirts to peewees to bantams to winning the state tourney, to playing at St. Cloud State, to playing in the NHL with the Wild — it has been an amazing journey so far. I just hope that I can bring a Stanley Cup home for the fans of Minnesota before it is all said and done, that is my ultimate goal."

In his 10 seasons in the NHL, Mark Parrish has tallied 192 goals and 150 assists for 342 points in 594 career games.

Foreword by Neal Broten

For the kid legendary coach Herb Brooks called "the best player I ever coached at the University of Minnesota," the circle is complete. Three trips to the Minnesota State High School Tournament for the Roseau Rams, an NCAA National Championship and Hobey Baker Award with the Gophers, an Olympic Gold medal, two Stanley Cup runs with the North Stars, and finally, winning a Cup of his own with the New Jersey Devils in 1995. At 5-foot-9 and only 170 pounds, Neal Broten was not a physical giant out on the ice, but he lived out a hockey dream as only John Mariucci might have dared to imagine it. Known and loved by nearly every hockey aficionado in the state, Neal will forever be the measuring stick, the hockey player against whom all others will be judged. Neal Broten truly represents everything that is good about Minnesota hockey. Neal hung up the skates back in 1997 and currently resides in River Falls, Wis., where he and his wife run a 75-acre horse farm.

"I originally met Ross back in 1992, when we got together for dinner to do an interview for his first book entitled "Gopher Hockey by the Hockey Gopher," said Neal. "I was skeptical about just what this kid was up to back then, after all his most prominent hockey credential at the time was being the mascot, 'Goldy the Gopher' for goodness sakes! But we hit it off right away and have since become good friends. I was flattered to be included in his second book, "Fifty Years • Fifty Heroes" as well, and when we did a book-signing together at the high school hockey tournament, I could see that people really, genuinely enjoyed reading his books. So, when he called me to tell me that he wanted me to write the foreword for his new book about the history of Minnesota hockey, I was not only flattered... I was honored."

"When I first saw 'Frozen Memories,' I was immediately taken by all of the incredible pictures. There are hundreds of them, going way back to the 1800s, all the way up to today. Hockey is such a part of our culture here, and this book has somehow captured it all. It was so fun to read about all of the old teams that played here through the years as well, from the Duluth Hornets, to the Eveleth Reds, to the old St. Paul Athletic Club. And being from Roseau, I loved reading about the history of the high school tournament. Just to be able to read about so many of my childhood heroes, and to learn about all of the people who worked so hard, so that guys like myself could make a career out of hockey was incredible.

"Some of my first memories of hockey were when the Warroad Lakers would come down the road to Roseau to play in tournaments. I remember as little kids we would run down to the penalty box during the games and grab the broken sticks that the players had thrown over the boards. We would run home and have our dads glue them back together so we could pretend we were North Stars.

"Growing up, my heroes weren't the NHL guys though, they were the Roseau High School hockey players. I feel really lucky to have grown up in such a wonderful hockey town, where the tradition runs so deep into the community. I mean hockey is what that town is all about for basically eight months out of the year. It's pretty amazing, and to be a part of that is something special. In small towns like that, you start playing with the same group of guys from when you first get on skates, all the way through pee wees and finally through high school. So when its over, its like saying good-bye to family. I was lucky though. We got to play in the state tournament, and I even got a chance to go to the University of Minnesota.

"The way I feel about the Gophers can be summed up in two words, Pride and Tradition. There is just so much class there, and to be a part of that was really a humbling experience. Just the feeling of putting on that big 'M' sweater with all those other Minnesota kids, and to play in front of such great fans was something I will always cherish. Then, getting the chance to play on the 1980 Olympic team was an experience I will never forget as well. Just making that squad was an accomplishment. It's something that I always look back on proudly, because there were 12 of us Minnesotans on the team. That just showed the world what kind of kids come from Minnesota, and we were all really proud of the way we represented our state.

"From there, I got to spend 13 glorious seasons with my hometown team, the North Stars. What more could a guy ask for? I mean, I could've wound up in Edmonton, or somewhere like that, and who knows what my life would be like today. In retrospect, sometimes I think I took it for granted, just how great it actually was to play for so long in my own backyard. Having the privilege of playing near your friends and family, without having to move around all the time was wonderful. I feel spoiled that I got to be here for so long, and that the fans for some reason treated me like a king. I just can't thank them enough. To come home and retire, and to be treated so well by the people here is something I can't explain. I am so humbled by everyone's generosity and am just proud to have been able to have brought joy to their lives through the game of hockey.

"The state-of-the-state of Minnesota hockey is strong today, and the fact that there are five Division-I schools here now is proof that our youth programs are second to none in the nation. I know what hockey means to the people up here, and from all my traveling throughout North America and Europe, I have seen first hand that we are well known as one of the premier hockey hot-beds in the world.

"Frozen Memories is about celebrating our past, and getting excited about our future. So many great things are happening right now at the youth levels, with women's hockey, the college scene and with the Wild. Ross spent the better part of a year researching, interviewing, and preserving our rich hockey heritage in this book. And for that, we all should be grateful, because the final product is awesome. If you enjoy reading about history, biographies, nostalgia and great, funny stories — then you'll love it, because it's all here."

In 17 seasons in the NHL, Neal Broten tallied 289 goals and 634 assists for 923 points in 1,099 career games.

Foreword by Brett Hull

Being the son of NHL Hall of Famer Bobby Hull and nephew of ex-NHLer Dennis Hull, Brett Hull was born into some pretty amazing "thoroughbred" hockey lineage. Add to that the fact that his mother was a professional figure skater and it is no wonder that Brett would develop into one of the game's all-time great ones. After playing in the Junior ranks up in Canada, Hull came to the Land of 10,000 Lakes in 1985, when he joined Mike Sertich's University of Minnesota-Duluth Bulldogs. In his first year with the Dogs, he won WCHA Rookie of the Year honors, and led the team to the NCAA Final Four. Deciding to join the NHL's Calgary Flames in 1987, Hull finished his incredible career in Duluth with an amazing 84 goals and 60 assists for 144 points in just 90 games.

From there, Hull went on to play in the NHL, where, over the next 20 years, he would become a nine-time All-Star, a three-time NHL goal-scoring champion, a 1991 league MVP, and even win a pair of Stanley Cups with the Dallas Stars in 1999 and the Detroit Red Wings in 2002. Hull retired from the game in 2005 and got into broadcasting with NBC Sports. In 2007, however, he left the booth to take a front office position with the Dallas Stars. On December 5, 2006, Brett's No. 16 sweater was retired by the St. Louis Blues. Along with his father, they are the only father-son combo in any professional sport to have their respective numbers retired. The future Hall of Famer still has a lake place near Duluth and remains a living legend in Northern Minnesota. One of the nicest, and most down-to-earth guys you will ever meet, Brett Hull is truly Minnesota hockey royalty.

"When Ross first called me to tell me about his new book project, I was flattered that he considered me to be a part of it," said Brett. "I told him that there were probably a lot of other people much more worthy of doing the foreword than myself though. I explained to him that I really only played in Duluth for two seasons, and that surely I couldn't have that much to say about the future of Minnesota hockey. But after he told me how much the fans and all the little kids back there had been following my career, it made me feel really proud to say that I am a Minnesotan."

"All in all, I think hockey in Minnesota is going great, and the future of the game is in good hands. The fans there truly know and understand the game. I have played in a lot of places over the years, including at the old Met Center against the North Stars, and I can tell you that those are some of the most loyal fans in the world. Some of the greatest hockey minds in the game are there as well, because the state wreaks of hockey tradition. The kids are born into it, much like they are in Canada, and it is really a special place to learn the game. I see kids up there roller-blading and playing constantly, and that's why Minnesota continues to be the top hockey state in the country. Even to see where it has gotten to since the mid-1980s, when I was at UMD, has been great. There are five Division I college programs there now, the women's game is strong and the high school tournament is still the best in the country. The sport has continued to move onward and upward and Minnesota just continues to raise talent for the next levels."

"From Mr. Mariucci on down, Minnesota has produced a lot of great players over the years, and that is well known throughout the ranks of pro hockey. The people there know hockey and respect the game. I learned that right away from playing there, and as I spend more and more time there, I can see how important it is to all of the communities. It is obviously a great source of pride for the people there, and I am honored to be a part of the great tradition. I mean, just look at the little town of Cloquet. The fact that Derek Plante and Jamie Langenbrunner were both on the Dallas Stars team that won the Stanley Cup in 1999 is amazing. That community must be so proud of those guys.

"I feel very lucky and very fortunate to have had the success that I have had in the game of hockey. I know that even when I have retired from the game though, that I can always become a bar-league star up in Duluth! I can play golf at Northland Country Club during the day, and then play hockey at night, it'll be great! But seriously, I am really honored and humbled that the people and fans of Minnesota have treated me so well through the years, and I can't thank them enough.

"The people of Duluth and from all over Minnesota have been fantastic to me and my family. I remember bringing the Stanley Cup back to Grandma's and Norman's (bar) and seeing all of the people who were just genuinely excited about hockey. That is so awesome to see. That is what life is all about up there, hockey and family. They work hard and they play hard. I was so humbled to be able to let them share in one of my proudest moments in hockey, it was a real thrill. That is why I still love coming back to Minnesota in the Summers, the people are so great up there.

"I would also say that the state of the state of hockey in Minnesota is probably better than it has ever been. I mean there have been so many kids from there who have been drafted in the last several years, it is amazing. I think that is a direct result of all of the youth programs that have been going on there for so long and because of all of the great coaches who teach those kids. You can't have success on the ice without good coaches and good parents who teach their kids how to play the game with respect.

"I enjoyed Ross' recent book, "The Code," because it really got into how important respect is in the game, at all levels. When kids learn about playing the game the right way, and they can learn those lessons and values from people who share those same philosophies, then that is when good things happen. I think that is where a lot of kids in Minnesota are right now, they are products of a good system that teaches them about playing the game hard and with respect. That is what it is all about in my eyes.

"I am just glad that I was able to have played the game that I loved for as long as I did. I was so fortunate to have been able to play alongside so many outstanding players too. I just worked hard and tried to be a good teammate. Beyond that I tried to play the game with respect and just have fun. That was the key, having a lot of fun."

In 20 seasons in the NHL, Brett Hull tallied 741 goals and 650 assists for 1,391 points in 1,296 career games.

Introduction by Ross Bernstein

Welcome to *"More...Frozen Memories,"* the updated and expanded sequel to the 1999 regional best-seller, *"Frozen Memories."* Back by popular demand (I have always wanted to say that), I am thrilled to be able to revisit a subject that is so near and dear to so many Minnesota hearts — the sport and lifestyle of hockey.

As luck would have it, millions of years ago when the glaciers melted across Minnesota, tens of thousands of lakes and ponds were left in their wake. In fact, our state's name is derived literally from the Native American words *"minne"* and *"sota"* which mean *"land of sky-blue waters."* In the summertime Minnesotans purchase more fishing and boating licenses than any other state in the country, and in the wintertime, when all those bodies of water freeze, most of us can't wait to get out there and play hockey on them. It has been that way in the Gopher State for more than a century, and the epiphany behind this book is to celebrate that wonderful heritage of hockey that we so dearly love and respect here.

Minnesota has such a rich and storied hockey tradition, and I am truly honored and humbled to be able to bring so much of it to life for everyone to enjoy. When I first began the arduous task of researching all of the history and interviewing the hundreds of men and women who are included in the book, I was floored by just how much information was actually out there. As such, this led to a rather interesting dilemma on just how I was going to disseminate it all. I mean there are literally thousands of players, coaches, administrators, media personalities and others who are deserving of being included in a book like this, and as a result it was extremely difficult to pick and choose just which players and teams would be featured.

Because of this, I have to issue a caveat of sorts to explain my rationale for how I chose to tackle a subject that is so passionate to so many Minnesotans. For starters, this book is not the definitive history of hockey in Minnesota. Rather, it is intended to be a fun sampling of many of our state's best and brightest, from all different eras and levels of the game. Some chapters, such as the Wild or the High School Tournament, will read like condensed *"Reader's Digest"* stories that are intended to cover the basics. Others will go way in depth — it just varies. I also chose to focus primarily on the historical side of the game and tried to chronicle the big games and memorable teams from the past century or so. There is a ton of info crammed in there. So, if you find an error, please accept my humble apologies. And, if a forgot or misspelled a name, again I am sorry. Between the more than 500 sources of information, coupled with the several hundred interviews that I was able to conduct, occasionally facts became convoluted. I want to get it right though and regard this project as a *"work in progress"* that will continue to grow and expand over the years to come.

Undoubtedly, and expectedly, whenever a book such as this is written, people tend to get bent out of shape when they realize that so-and-so wasn't mentioned, or that he or she got more ink than so and so. I guess that is just the nature of the beast with something like this, and all I can say is that I tried to be arbitrary and objective in my research, and hopefully the vast majority of people who *"should be in here,"* are in here. Believe me, it was a difficult process to have to eliminate so many wonderful biographies and funny stories because I simply did not have the space. My main objective was to celebrate the positive aspects, i.e. the people, the epic games, the history, and the drama of hockey in Minnesota, and hopefully I have succeeded in my mission.

I would also add this, there is a ton of information in the book about the Gophers. Yes, more so than other schools. I am a huge Gopher fan and a complete and unapologetic homer in that regard... so I make no apologies. I will say this though, I root for all Minnesota teams come playoff time... just as long as they aren't playing my Gophers. So, just where does that Maroon and Gold love come from? To fully understand this, we have to go back, way back, to the very beginning — all the way back to the small southern Minnesota town of Fairmont.

My hockey story is a rather unique one to say the least. Growing up in Fairmont was, as the Hanson Brothers so eloquently put it *"Old time hockey... you know Eddie Shore, Toe Blake...".* I learned how to skate behind my house on Hall Lake. It was beautiful, like a scene right out of a Norman Rockwell painting. Despite playing on outdoor rinks, usually getting pummeled by our competition (and having to be sponsored by Domino's Pizza because our high school wouldn't sanction us), I grew to love the game with a real passion. It was old school. We couldn't even buy skates in town. Coast-to-Coast Hardware had sticks and tape, but no skates. So, we had to drive an hour to Mankato to get them.

To say we were off the hockey radar would be an understatement to say the least. After all, this was wrestling and basketball country, but we didn't care. Through it all I persevered though, and was even able to make the varsity team as a freshman. Now, it wasn't as if I was a particularly good player either, we just needed warm bodies out there. Luckily I had a pulse and therefore qualified to start as a left defenseman for the mighty Cardinals. We played on outdoor ice all the way through my senior year, until we finally convinced the city to build us an arena. Well, it was a hog barn at the Martin County Fairgrounds, but you could put boards up in there and freeze the floor. Given our options at the time, we gladly took it.

We would travel around southern Minnesota playing teams like Luverne, Windom, Sleepy Eye, Marshall and Worthington. We were all in the same boat. All of the coaches were volunteers and none of them had any formal coaching experience whatsoever. They just did it for the love of the game and to give back to their communities. Our parents shoveled the rink between periods and we cleaned up at the local McDonald's afterwards. We didn't know any better. Most of the fans who came out to see us didn't know the difference between blue lines and clothes lines, but we didn't care. We just loved playing hockey. None of our equipment matched, and we were sporting some pretty ugly mullets to boot.

I remember having my mom order cases of White Castle cheese burgers for all my buddies so that we could watch the state high school tourney in my basement. We loved rooting for the underdogs: Roseau, Warroad, Greenway, Grand Rapids — that was what it was all about for us. We knew that we would never be able to make it there in a million years, so we just ate Sliders and lived vicariously through those kids.

Well, I graduated in 1987 and went on to attend the University of Minnesota. There, I joined a fraternity and wound up becoming buddies with some Gopher hockey players. Before long, they convinced me that I should walk-on to the team. I figured why not? After a brief "cup of coffee," (as a practice pylon nonetheless), Coach Woog politely informed me that it just wasn't going to work out. I knew it was coming, but it was still a thrill of a lifetime for me. It turned out that there was another opening on the team, however, as the team mascot — *"Goldy the Gopher."* Supposedly, they were tired of "Bucky the Badger" coming to town and kicking Goldy's ass out on the ice and something had to give.

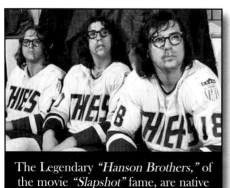

The Legendary *"Hanson Brothers,"* of the movie *"Slapshot"* fame, are native Minnesotans who absolutely wreak of *"Old Time Hockey...".*

You see, up until then, Goldy had always been a member of the U of M's Marching Band. Well, they needed a *"ringer."* Their were two basic criteria for the job: first, you had to be a pretty good skater; and secondly, you had to be a complete idiot. I apparently fit on both accounts and got the gig.

So there you have it, the extent of my hockey experience came from wearing a giant rodent costume and making a fool out of myself in front of thousands of people. Needless to say, I had a ball. I wound up commandeering this TV platform, or perch, just under the scoreboard at the arena. In between periods, when I wasn't skating out on the ice with the cheerleaders, I climbed up there and had the best view in the house. I wound up doing this shtick where I would hold up signs all the time to get both sides of the crowd to basically yell stuff at each other, much like the old Miller Lite commercials: *"Tastes Great!"* vs. *"Less Filling!"* It was hilarious. Soon, I was branching out and making signs of people such as Larry Olimb, or Doug Woog, or even Frank & Wally, the TV announcers. The fans at it up: *"Fraaaank! — Waaaalllyy"* Eventually, I started bringing toys up there with me, such as Gumby, Pokey, Fred Flintstone, Cookie Monster, Mr. Potato Head, Godzilla, Ken & Barbie, and even a three foot alligator — which I used to lower down onto the ice with a rope to taunt unsuspecting opposing players. It was affectionately called *"Goldy's Toy Box"* by various members of the media, and it brought out the little kid in everybody I think.

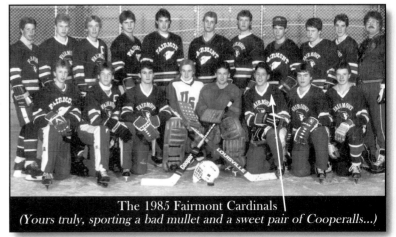

The U.S. Pond Hockey Championships, out on *"The Lakes,"* are yet another indication that the state of the state of hockey in the *"State of Hockey"* is stronger than ever...

Now, I used to live in a frat house, just a half a block away, and would literally walk over to the arena all dressed in my costume, ready to go. Coincidentally, most Friday and Saturday afternoons, our fraternity had kegs tapped for all the brothers to get a jump-start on the evenings' festivities. So, once in a while I would partake in the social goings-on before a game, which sometimes made for some interesting fodder. Well, one time after a few cocktails, I came over to entertain the masses at the arena. No sooner than I had gotten my skates off after the first intermission to climb back up onto my perch, nature called and I had to relieve myself. So, I climbed down and went out into the hall to use the bathroom. Luckily, because the game was going on, it was empty. The coast was clear, and I could now take off my head to take care of the business at hand. No pun intended. I had to be very careful that no little kids saw me though, otherwise it could mean big trouble. You see, little kids believe in Goldy the same way they believe in Santa Clause and the Easter Bunny, so Rule No. 1 of mascoting is and always will be: *"NEVER BE SEEN WITHOUT YOUR HEAD ON!"*

For those of you who may not remember the posh lavatory facilities at the old barn, let me refresh your memories, they were a dump. I had to choose between the ever-popular urinal trough, or the more private, luxurious stalls in the rear. I chose the latter. Realizing that my giant head would not fit in the stall with me, however, I took it off and put it on the toilet in the next stall over, closing the door behind me. I then went back into my stall and started to undo my breezers so that I could relieve myself.

Then, I heard a sound. Someone had come in. I quickly jumped up on top of the stool so that I wouldn't blow my cover. That's when I heard it, a noise I will never forget. It was a horrifying, blood-curdling scream that could set off car alarms and drive dogs mad. As I peered through a crack in the stall door, I could see a little boy just standing there horrified, perplexed, and confused — pointing at the Gopher-less head which was sitting on the potty before him. Figuring that the rest of Goldy had been whooshed away like so many poo-poos before, he yelled out in sheer terror: *"Daddy, Daddy, help, quick! Goldy's flushed down the toilet!"*

I nearly fell off the can at this point, trying not to laugh. As dad came over and saw the situation, I knew that young junior had been emotionally traumatized. Daddy just shuttled his son away and tried to reason with the little fella, but to no avail. I could hear him screaming *"GOLDEEEEEEEE!"* out the door and all the way down the hall. I only wish I could've heard the conversation that took place in the wagoneer family truckster on the way home from the game. That kid may wind up as a serial killer one day, and it will probably be my fault. We'll never know.

Anyway, after three glorious years as a giant rodent, I was approached by a publisher after a game one night who told me that he wanted to write a book about all of the trouble I had gotten into over the years. I told him I was flattered that he enjoyed my shtick, but that other than my mother, I wasn't sure anybody would ever want to read his book. So, I politely said thanks but no thanks. Now, at the time I was a senior and wasn't really sure what I wanted to be when I grew up. So, I got to thinking. What if I wrote a book about the history of Gopher Hockey, but with a twist — what if it featured interviews and stories from hundreds of former players, coaches and media personalities? And, most importantly, what if it was ghost-written with an inside slant from Goldy's perspective? Hey, that's not bad. I had never written a book before, but I thought this could be pretty fun. And, it would certainly help divert my attention away from the scary specter of entering the real world for at least one more year while dad's cash was drying up.

With that, I jumped in head first and started interviewing anybody and everybody who had ties to Gopher Hockey. I was buzzing around the Twin Cities in my little Plymouth Horizon, meeting up with the likes of everybody from Herb Brooks to Lou Nanne to Neal Broten to Stanley Hubbard to Glen Sonmor. It was a riot. If they had stories to tell, I was going to record them and put them in my book. What started as a "neat" project, completely took off. Soon, guys were looking me up and taking me to lunch, just to make sure that they got in the book. It was amazing. They were thrilled that Gopher Hockey was finally going to be chronicled, and they were even more thrilled that if somebody was going to be doing it, that it was one of their own. The book, appropriately titled *"Gopher Hockey by the Hockey Gopher,"* came out in the Fall of 1993 and was an instant regional best-seller. Who knew?

From those humble beginnings, I am proud to say that I will soon be working on my 40th book. Go figure. My passion is hockey, and through that medium I am just so happy and lucky to be able to make my career doing what I love — chronicling the history and heroes of the *Land of 10,000 Lakes.* Hockey is such a part of our fabric of life here, and seems to touch nearly everyone in some way or another. I am truly honored and humbled to be able to share this wealth of information with you in my new book. Hopefully you will have half as much fun reading about and celebrating this amazing tradition as I did in getting the opportunity to bring it all to life. See you in the "NE" section. Cheers!

The 1985 Fairmont Cardinals
(Yours truly, sporting a bad mullet and a sweet pair of Cooperalls...)

IN THE BEGINNING...

To truly understand the modern game of ice hockey today, you have to go back — way back to the very beginning. There, you can get to the root of the game's most fundamental origins: ice skating. Now, where and when that beginning actually is, makes for some very interesting debate. We do know, however, that what most likely first started out as a more convenient mode of winter transportation across the slippery ice and snow of frozen lakes and rivers, has evolved over time into what we now know today as hockey.

It seems that most every country through the ages has laid claim to the creation of one form or another of an athletic game. And, the history of advanced games, which involved using a stick to strike an object of some sort, can be traced back for thousands of years. For instance, wall-murals nearly 2,500 years old have been found in Greece which contained carvings portraying two people holding sticks in an athletic-like face-off position, very similar to what we now know as field hockey. Perhaps it was war-like in nature, possibly portraying hand-to-hand combat? Nonetheless, this is one of the ways that sports have evolved.

One such ancient game that may have led to the creation of hockey, was an old British past-time called "camp." Created in the 11th century following the Norman invasions, the game was

Hockey's roots can be traced back more than 1,000 years...

supposedly started when the local villagers began to imitate how they booted out their intruders, by kicking rocks amongst one another for amusement. Various new games began to develop from this, and not long thereafter different sporting games that involved striking a ball or object with a stick began to emerge. Among them that may have played a part in the genesis of ice hockey over the upcoming millennium would be an amalgam of many different ice and field games including: Shinny, Hurley, Bandy, Baggataway, Ho-Gee, Oochamkunutk, Field Hockey, Lacrosse, Ice Polo and Kolven.

It All Started With Skating...

In as early as the 1400s, Northern Europeans and Scandinavians were using not only snowshoes, but also snow skis to get around in their harsh winters. It was not too long after that someone invented the ice skate. It is believed that the first form of ice skates were made of small animal bones, which were crudely fastened to one's boots. Later, they evolved into wood, which was easier to carve into shape.

There are also many theories as to where the word "skate" came from. Some historians believe that it might be a derivative of the Dutch word "schaat," but there remains a controversy as to who was the first to actually use the new device. Along with the Dutch, all of the Scandinavian countries, as well as the Russians, English, Scottish and Irish, have also laid claim to skating's origins.

In the mid-1500s, the iron skate was perfected by a Scottish blacksmith. Soon after, skating became not only a popular form of transit, but also entertainment. In the mid-1600s, the Skating Club of Scotland was established, and other countries followed suit not too long after. When many of these people emigrated to North America in the 1800s, they brought their skates with them. Once ice skating became popular, ice games naturally began to emerge.

Hockey's Evolution...

The word hockey seems to be as complex as the game itself. Despite all of the historical research and speculation, nobody really knows for sure who actually invented the game. The most likely scenario is that wherever there were frozen lakes, ponds, rivers, and streams; there were most likely Europeans, Scandinavians, Asians, and North American Indians who probably conceived and played some crude form of ice hockey.

One school of thought on how the game got its name came from Great Britain. As early as 1400, the word hockey was being used in England to describe a field game that was being played by young boys who hauled produce in "hock carts" during harvest festivals. Another theory claims that the word is an English form of the French word "hoquet," which was a shepherd's cane that resembled a modern looking hockey stick.

Others claim the word had Native American origins. As far back as the mid-1700s, French explorers who voyaged up the St. Lawrence Seaway, claimed to have seen Iroquois Indians playing a primitive game which entailed using a stick to strike a ball on the ice. When a player hit the ball he would shout out "Ho-Gee," which apparently meant, "it hurts." Yet another school of thought on how hockey got its name came from Canada in the mid-1800s. As the story goes, an English Colonel in the military whose common English family name was "Hockey," had his troops playing shinny near Windsor, Ontario, as a form of winter exercise. Supposedly, the game that they were playing became known as "Hockey's game."

THE EVOLUTION OF SKATES

What were first hand-carved out of small animal bones, and then into wood, the evolution of ice skates has come a long way. Skates used in the early 1800s had been either hand-made out of whatever materials a person could find, or else imported from Great Britain or Holland. Called block or stock skates, because of the heavy wooden blocks that were used to hold the metal blade to the boot, the skates featured ropes or leather straps to fasten a person's foot into his skate. Those tight straps, which were necessary to hold the skates onto the boot, often times wound up cutting off the skaters circulation to his already cold feet.

A major breakthrough in the advancement of skating occurred in 1850, when E. W. Bushnell of Philadelphia invented the steel hockey skate blade. Bushnell's invention allowed skaters much more agility on the ice, and in addition, they did not have to sharpen them as frequently as they did those with the older iron blades. Bushnell manufactured and sold his new "practical" ice skates around the world.

Then, another competitor began providing an even better skate in 1861. That's when the Starr Manufacturing Company of Dartmouth, Nova Scotia, began making superior quality ice skates from high quality steel. In 1863, another advancement was made when the self-fastening "Acme Club Spring Skate" was invented. Now, with just a flick of a lever, a skater could securely and quickly clamp his skates to the soles and heels of his boots. However, this trigger-type fastener often-times got hit inadvertently, which would in-turn release itself, and fly off the skater's foot in mid-stride.

For an encore, the company then developed and sold what would become the most famous hockey skate in the world, the "Starr Skate." Best known for revolutionizing skating and ice hockey, the Starr Skate featured a wider, rocker-shaped blade. The blade was rounded in both the front and back, which made instant stops and starts, as well as sudden turns, much easier for the skater.

Hockey's roots can also be traced back to Europe, where in the 1600s the Scottish played a field hockey game called "Shinny," while the Irish played a game known as "Hurley." An additional pastime of this era was a Dutch game played on ice called "Kolven." Played with a ball, and stick that resembled a golf club, one would score a point by hitting the ball between two poles that had been stuck in the ice. Yet another game that was witnessed by French explorers in Canada in the mid-1700s, was an Indian game similar to lacrosse, called "Baggataway."

In the early 1800s, a game called "Bandy" was being played on icy rivers and lakes throughout the marshy Fen region of England. The village of Bury Fen, credited with starting the game, fielded a legendary team that supposedly went more than 100 years without ever losing a match. The game was played on skates with a short curved sticks, called "bandies." They were typically willow tree branches which were cut to the shape of a curved stick. Players used their sticks to strike a "cat," or ball, which was made of wood or cork, and eventually of rubber. Teams consisted of 11 players, and the games began when a referee threw the cat up in the air. The players would quickly fight to grab the cat and dribble it down the enormous 450' x 300' playing surface, and try to shoot it into a large 12-foot-by-7-foot goal. (Incidentally, bandy, which is considered to be the fastest team sport in the world, is currently being played in several places throughout the world including: the former Soviet Union, Scandinavia and also Minnesota. In fact, Minnesota has one of the only bandy programs in the United States, with several leagues and teams playing at rinks in Edina, Roseville and Bloomington.)

The Evolution of Hockey in North America...

As more and more Europeans and Scandinavians emigrated to Canada, variations of these games slowly became popular on this side of the Atlantic. The Irish game, hurley, was perhaps the first to be played competitively. One of the ways that the game was brought overseas was from Irish immigrants, who had come to work on the Shubencadie Canal near Dartmouth, Nova Scotia, in the early 1830s. Hurley was a game that was originally played on the grassy fields of Ireland with a brass ball and heavy wooden sticks called "shillelaghs." However, the fields of Eastern Canada's Nova Scotia region were much too rugged to play on, so instead they decided to play the game on ice. Soon "ice hurley" became the rage at Canada's first college, Windsor's King's College, which was established in 1788. There, students began playing the game competitively on both Long Pond and at Chester Lake.

Located on the shores of the Avon River in Nova Scotia, the region was first settled by French Acadian's. The Acadians, many of whom were farmers, lived harmoniously with the Mi'kmaq Indians, who were native to the territory. According to the Dictionary of Language of the Mi'kmaq Indians, which was published in 1888, the Micmac's, as they were known, had invented an ice game which involved using a stick and a ball, called "Oochamkunutk." The Micmac's, who were known for their superior wood-carving abilities, had mastered the art of crafting a one-piece stick. From hornbeam trees, and later from second-growth yellow birch trees, these craftsmen could carve powerful, yet durable sticks, or "hockey's" as they became known, from a single piece of the tree's root. (Later, throughout the early 1920s-30s, the "MicMac" brand evolved into a very high pedigree style of hockey stick. It become the most popular manufactured stick of its kind in hockey, and by 1925 it was being advertised and sold around the world for a whopping 50¢ to 75¢ apiece.)

The Micmac's, who referred to ice hurley as "Alchamadijik," would gradually join with both the Acadians as well as the British soldiers in playing pick up games. Slowly their games began to rub off on each other and melded together. With an unlimited number of players out on the ice, some of them competed in wooden skates, while others simply wore moccasins. The games got rough, and for protection, the Micmacs used moose skin for padding on their shins and arms. Their new Canadian style of hurley featured sticks which they called "hurleys" to hit a square wooden block, through a goal. As time went

THE EVOLUTION OF THE PUCK

The word "puck" was probably derived from the game of hurley. When a hurley ball was struck with a hurley stick, it was referred to as being "pucked." Cherry wood was the preferred material because its dark color would show up well against the white snow and ice.

The origins of hockey have clearly stated that the game began with the use of a round ball. One can only speculate as to why the flat puck evolved into what we know today, but a pretty good guess might entail the fact that people probably got tired of chasing after that damn ball down the river or across the lake after an errant shot. One can speculate that someone probably got smart and chopped the top and bottom off of the ball to make a puck. In the interim, between the ball and the flat disk, there were many items that were used as pucks, including: frozen manure, blocks of wood, chunks of coal, various pieces of fruit and vegetables, rocks and even tin cans.

It is believed that the puck first surfaced as a flat disc in 1860, at Kingston Harbour, Ontario. It apparently made its big league debut during a game in Montreal, in 1875. There, the game program prophetically described the puck as follows: "Some fears have been expressed on the part of the intending spectators that accidents were likely to occur through the ball flying about in a too lively manner, to the imminent danger of lookers-on... but we understand that the game will be played with a flat, circular piece of wood, thus preventing all danger of it leaving the surface of the ice."

By the late 1890s, the flat rubber puck was the standard at hockey games. But they weren't always made of rubber, rather the first pucks were made of wood. The evolution into vulcanized rubber is an interesting story in itself. Once during a game, a player shot a puck into the net. As it hit the post, it split in two. One half went in the goal, while the other half rolled out. During the mayhem which ensued as to whether or not it was in fact a goal, the referee consulted his trusty rule book. In it was stated that the puck must be one inch thick. He deduced that because the piece that was in the net was only half that width, it was ruled a no-goal. This ultimately led to the creation of a one-piece rubber puck, rather than two disk-like pieces that were glued together.

Made from carbon, sulfur, and rubber, today's NHL pucks adhere to strict guidelines. They are made of vulcanized rubber, are 1"x3" in dimension, and weigh no more than six ounces. In addition, teams freeze "les rondelles," as they are known in their native Canada, before games, in order to take some of the bounciness out of them.

by, ice hurley was referred to by many names, including: hurley, ricket, cricket and wicket.

Long considered to be hockey's predecessor, "shinny" was yet another informal ice game of the mid-1800s to evolve from the United Kingdom to North America. The game's rules were directly related to English field hockey, hurley, and lacrosse. The object of the game is very similar to today's hockey, in which opposing players tried to shoot a block of wood or a rubber ball into a goal, commonly made from two rocks, which served as markers. With no set time limits, games were played on huge rinks that were formed in rivers, lakes, ponds and creeks. Spectators could oftentimes be seen cheering for their teams by running up and down the river banks. There were no side boards of any type, so much of the games were spent chasing after the ball. One of the game's most prominent rules was taken directly from field hockey, in which during a face-off, or "bully" as it was called, players had to "shinny on their own side," which meant they had to take the draw right-handed.

Considered by some to be the greatest winter sport in

North America, shinny, or shinty, became quite popular throughout Canada and parts of the northern United States in the mid to late 1800s. Many kids played in their boots if they didn't own a pair of ice skates. Kids used to scour the forests to find a good "shinny stick" to play with. They would look for a solid branch from an old maple, oak, or ash tree, which might have a slight crook or growth at the end of it which would form a blade. (A good shinny stick was so durable that players would occasionally pass their sticks down generationally to their own kids.) And, getting whacked on the shins, or anywhere else for that matter, was just part of the game. The referees typically ignored slashing, roughing, high sticking and cross checking. Rather he would holler out the cry, "Shinny on your own side!" which was also a warning to settle down. Sometimes if a player didn't cool off, the ref would simply whack him across the shins. Most kids came home with torn trousers, and most likely, bruised shins.

While there is much debate as to whether or not the first ever hockey games played in Canada, were in fact shinny games, yet one more ice game evolved in the late 1800s after shinny and before ice hockey, called "ice polo." Besides shinny, it is believed that the forerunner to ice hockey in the United States was ice polo, an American conception that was probably adopted from the popular fad-sport of roller polo — which was played on indoor roller rinks. Played much like football on ice, only with a hard rubber ball, ice polo teams featured a goaltender, a halfback, a center and two rushers. Ice polo was being played on outdoor ice by the late 1870's in parts of Minnesota, New England and Michigan. Beginning in 1883, there was even a four-team ice polo league playing in St. Paul which sponsored annual tournaments at the infamous St. Paul Winter Carnival. But, by the early 1900's ice hockey had replaced ice polo in the U.S.

The Modern Game...

As the present-day game of ice hockey started to take shape from bits and pieces of its many unique predecessors, it can safely be said that Canada is the modern game's originator. It is believed that a refined game of shinny, which included many of modern hockey's rules and characteristics, was first played in 1855 on a harbor just outside Halifax, Nova Scotia, by members of an Imperial Army unit known as "Her Majesty's Royal Canadian Rifles."

Much of the credit for the rules of the modern game have been credited to a gentleman named, J.G.H. Creighton, of Halifax, who, in the 1850s, combined the rules of British field hockey, shinny, and ice lacrosse to form the basis of ice hockey. Several rule changes were starting to be introduced to the game, including: reducing the number of players on the ice from eleven to seven players, incorporating a standard 3" x 1" puck — instead of a ball, and also creating short side-boards around the ice surfaces. In addition, ice rinks were popping up all around the countrysides. (The term rink, which referred to the designated area of play, and also meant race-course, was originally used in the game of curling in 18th-century Scotland.)

Others debate that the first real hockey game, with more defined rules and with a limited number of players, was actually played in 1875 at the indoor Victoria Skating Rink, by McGill University students in Montreal. (Incidentally, for this game, J.G.H. Creighton ordered and shipped two dozen MicMac hockey sticks to his friends in Halifax for their big game against McGill in Montreal.) Here, hockey grew and prospered. The early playing style seemed to accentuate a more rugged playing style, versus a finesse game. But, as time went by and more and more people began playing, stickhandling, passing and skating became much more refined. During this period at the University, there is also speculation

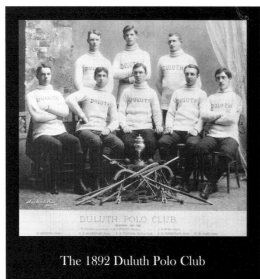

The 1892 Duluth Polo Club

that several football coaches incorporated many of the rules of rugby into the game — which may explain for the game's rough style of play.

By the mid-1880s, hockey leagues were being played between both coasts throughout Canada. Nearly every small town had teams which played against one another, and kids began to learn how to skate as soon as they could learn how to walk. Ice hockey became a recognized sport, and in 1883, also an official event at the Montreal Winter Carnival. The carnival committee even issued a challenge for the "world championship" of ice hockey, as teams from Quebec, Ottawa, Toronto, and Montreal answered the call to play in what is believed to be the first ice hockey tournament in the world. An interesting refinement even came to the game by way of the Winter Carnival a few years later. That was when one of the teams showed up for the tournament short a pair of players. The other team felt compelled to help out their opponents, and thereby agreed to drop two of their skaters to make it even. The teams found that with four less men on the ice, they could open up play and spread things out. And with that, the nine-man game finally gave way to the seven-man game.

Shortly thereafter, in 1886, representatives from several Canadian teams gathered together to finally establish a formal set of rules for consistent play. What they came up with would become known as the "Montreal Rules." A governing body was formed, and they called themselves the Canadian Amateur Hockey League (the predecessor to today's Canadian Amateur Hockey Association). They called for seven-man hockey, which featured a goaltender, two halfbacks (who played close to the goal like a modern defenseman), a rover and three forwards. Players became quite proficient in stickhandling, because back then there was no forward passing allowed. Any forward pass was immediately ruled off-sides. Games consisted of two half-hour periods, with a ten minute breather inbetween to shovel the ice.

Hockey America...

America's hockey roots are not quite as complicated as those of Canada's, but nonetheless, there is some debate as to where and when the game migrated southward below the 49th parallel. The American concoction known as ice polo, muddied up the waters with regards to determining the exact origins of the game in the U.S. While some say the game started officially on the East Coast, an argument can be made that the game was also being played at the same time right here in Minnesota. One of those theories, however, takes us back to the summer of 1894, to Niagara Falls, N.Y.

There, a group of American tennis players from Yale University were competing in a tournament with some players from Canada. In between the competition, some of the players began socializing, and talking about winter ice games. Upon learning that the Americans were still playing ice polo, the Canadians, who were playing ice hockey, invited their new American friends to play a friendly exhibition of both sports.

They agreed, and played a series of two-period, doubleheaders of each game throughout several major Canadian cities in front of capacity crowds. Upon the conclusion of the contests, the Canadians had swept the hockey games, while the Yanks won two and tied two of the ice polo games. When it was all said and done, the Americans agreed that ice hockey was a much better game to play. Instantly enamored with their new-found game, the American boys bought up all of the sticks and skates that they could carry and returned home. Upon their arrival, they began to play hockey full-time, which included switching over to using flat-bottom skates, a puck instead of a ball, and a longer hockey-styled stick instead of the field hockey kind. Within a couple of years, most of the universities and club teams on the East Coast had switched from ice polo to the faster and more exciting sport of ice hockey.

At about the same time that the East-Coaster's were getting indoctrinated to the game of ice hockey, the game was also being spread southward into the U.S. from other points of Canada as well. Which is why at about the same time during the late 1890s, the game was also being played in Minneapolis and St. Paul, and in Northern Minnesota at such places as Hallock, Eveleth and Duluth. In addition, the University of Minnesota began playing ice hockey in 1895 against several teams from Canada, including Winnipeg.

America's first big-time league, the Amateur Hockey League, began play in New York City in 1896, and just months later the Baltimore Hockey League got started. In 1899 the Intercollegiate Hockey League was formed with teams from Yale, Columbia, Brown, Harvard and Princeton. In addition, high school and prep school hockey was being played by the early 1900's in Minnesota, New York City, New England, and in Michigan's upper peninsula. The sport continued to grow in America to cities throughout the East Coast and Midwest. In 1903, the International Pro Hockey League became the country's first professional circuit. Michigan's Upper Peninsula mining town team of Houghton, called the Portage Lakers, became the first professional team in the U.S. Now legendary, this club often-times whipped their Canadian counterparts, and helped to put American hockey on the map.

Then, a forerunner of the National Hockey Association, which began play in 1909, the present-day (six-man style) National Hockey League was created in 1917. That same year the Seattle Metropolitans, members of Canada's Pacific Coast League, became the first U.S. team to win the Stanley Cup in its 24-year-old history, greatly embarrassing the Canadian clubs who didn't give the American teams much respect.

Hockey's Early Beginnings in Minnesota...

In Minnesota, where the Scandinavians and European descendants loved their winters, shinny had been played on the frozen rivers and lakes since the Civil War. However, the more evolved ice game of ice polo was gaining popularity in the land of 10,000 lakes by the late 1800s. In the early 1880s, ice polo was the rage in both St. Paul and Minneapolis. The sport is believed to have evolved from the short-lived 1880s fad of roller polo, which was played on roller skates. So popular was roller polo that in 1885 Minneapolis alone had 14 indoor roller rinks, but two years later interest had died out and only two remained.

In 1883, Minnesotan, Frank Barron, an accomplished ice and roller polo player, formulated what is believed to be the first set of ice polo rules. Six (or sometimes seven) players formed a team which included the following positions: goal, coverpoint, cover goal, first rush, second rush and center. Short curved sticks similar to a present day field hockey stick were used to hit a ball into a goal cage similar to, but smaller than a soccer goal. Barron organized the St. Paul Polo Club in 1883 and for the next four seasons they held a monopoly in the Twin City area. Members of that team were: Gus Zenzens, Con Zenzens, Frank Barron, Charles Robertson, W.J. Murnane, Paul Kleist and Charles Trot. The club also built the first lighted outdoor rink in West St. Paul.

On January 22, 1887, the first ice

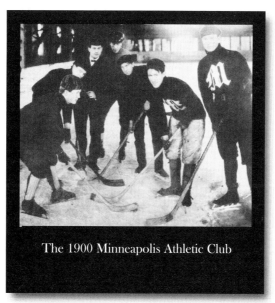

The 1900 Minneapolis Athletic Club

Bobby Marshall, who starred for the Minneapolis Wanderers, was also an All-American End on the 1906 Gopher football team.

polo tournament was held in conjunction with the St. Paul Winter Carnival at the Palace Grounds. The St. Paul Winter Carnival has an amazing history in itself. The annual event celebrated winter and all of its icy pleasures, which showcased several forms of ice skating, including: figure, speed, novelty, and trick skating, as well as long-jumping contests over barrels. Ice polo flourished here because of the number of people who became exposed to it.

Once again Frank Barron led the way that year. His squad, the Junior Carnival Club was awarded gold medals by beating the Royal Route Club of Omaha, and the Carnival Skating Club. The four team tournament featured two teams from St. Paul, and one from both Minneapolis, and Stillwater. The Minneapolis "Lelands" team was led by the infamous football star Walter "Pudge" Heffelfinger, who earned All-American honors as a guard at Yale from 1889 to 1891. He is still considered to be one of the greatest football players of all time.

The Barron and Murphy families, each with several members playing ice polo, played an important role in helping to promote the sport in the Twin Cities. Incidentally, there were two Edward Murphys involved in St. Paul ice polo and ice hockey. "Big" Ed Murphy was a Canadian hockey and lacrosse player, while the other Ed Murphy was an American who did not care for the ice polo sport, but was instrumental in starting ice hockey in St. Paul. The Barron brothers, the Murphy brothers, and the fast skating Harley Davidson, who was a world reknowned speed skater (no relation to the motorcycles), were among the best players during the heyday of ice polo in St. Paul.

Ice polo was also being played in Duluth, as the following article from the Duluth News-Tribune, on January 14, 1893, entitled "Polo on Ice," attests to: "A match game of polo has been organized between the Duluth Polo Club and the Zenith City Club. It will take place at the Central Skating Rink, foot of Fifth Avenue West, Friday night. The Zenith City team is a good club. Polo is a very popular winter sport and considerable interest has been aroused here among the fans. The attendance at this initial game of the season promises to be large. F.B. Taylor will captain Duluth and T. Moore will direct the Zeniths. Duluth: Berg, Morrison, McLennon, Thompson, Taylor (captain), Vincent, Paine, Carey, and Meining. Zeniths: Calvary, Buxton, McDonald, McIllhargie, Moran (Captain), Michaud, Maloney, Mitchell, and Grachau."

On February 7, 1893 the St. Paul Henriette's defeated the Duluth Polo Club 2-1 for the first Minnesota ice polo title. But the next year, in 1894, Duluth beat the Henriettes in a three game series for the state championship, which was held at Duluth's enclosed Glen Avon Curling Club rink. These games are believed to be first ice polo games played on an enclosed rink in the United States.

As ice polo grew in popularity The Twin City Ice Polo League was organized, with the championships tieing into the St. Paul Winter Carnival. Minneapolis and St. Paul turned up the heat on their cross town rivalry. Minneapolis teams such as The Polo Club, Acorns and Lelands would battle St. Paul teams such as the St. George's, St. Paul's, Centrals, Summits, Henriette's, Fort Snelling, Mascots and Gophers. St. Paul had a more extensive program than Minneapolis. Huge crowds followed many of the games in St. Paul which were played on several popular outdoor rinks, including: Broadway, Como, Aurora, Edgerton, Central, Ramsey, Hill, Palace and Victoria. In 1894 four covered roller rinks: Jackson, Summit, Wigwam and Exposition were flooded in the winter and used for ice polo contests.

The Army Companies at Fort Snelling even formed a four-team league. In addition, several youth teams were playing the game, including: St. Paul High School, Spauldings, Summit Juniors, and Interurbans. Other cities such as: Owatonna, Stillwater and Superior (Wis.), were also playing the game at this time.

Ice polo continued to be played in the large cities of Minnesota, but by 1895, ice hockey, which had recently been introduced to the area by our neighbors from Manitoba, had quickly become the preferred sport of choice. The game was actually brought down via James J. Hill's rairoad, which came through northwestern Minnesota to get to Minneapolis and then on to Chicago, before heading back up to Toronto. A game much better suited to the smaller ice surface and indoor rinks, hockey took over by the turn of the century. The last state ice polo tournament was won by Duluth in 1899.

A Hockey State of Mind...

During February, 1895, this article appeared in the St. Paul Pioneer Press: "Game of ice hockey started by Ed Murphy in 1894 as an outgrowth of the game of ice polo which flourished for years previously. Ice polo was the main winter sport in St. Paul when Ed Murphy moved in as a youngster of twenty-one years of age. Murphy, an American, had watched ice hockey in Canada. He did not care for ice polo and after several attempts he finally got the game changed to ice hockey and the first St. Paul club was organized in 1893, for the season of 1893-1894."

The evolution was complete, and hockey was now gaining recognition all across our state — especially in the Twin Cities as well as throughout Northern Minnesota (especially in Hallock), and throughout the Iron Range area. Kids and adults alike began to learn about the rules and style of this new game. All they needed now was to actually see it in action. It appears that Minnesota's first game of organized ice hockey was played between two Minneapolis teams in January of 1895. They met at an outdoor rink located at 11th Street and 4th Avenue South for a series of games against each other. These games were not only among the very first to have ever been played in Minnesota, but also in the United States.

Hall of Famer Coddy Winters starred for the 1908 Duluth Northern Hardware senior team

Later in January and early February the Minneapolis Hockey Club met the newly formed University of Minnesota team in a series of games. The first University of Minnesota team, unsanctioned by the school, was organized in January of 1895 by Dr. H. A. Parkyn, a quarterback on the Gopher football team who had played the game in Toronto. Parkyn coached the U of M team, comprised mainly of kids who were experienced ice polo players. These games would serve as a

The St. Paul Phoenix were an early senior team of the 1910s

warm-up for an upcoming contest against one of Canada's best teams of that era, the Winnipeg Victorias. A main reason why the Gophers were able to schedule a game with the Manitoba team was because at that time, there was no railroad connection between Eastern and Western Canada. So, the Victorias had to travel through the Twin Cities on their way out to play Ontario and Quebec. On February 18, 1895, the Gophers beat the Victorias by the score of 11-3. The game was played at Minneapolis' Athletic Park, which was located at Sixth Street and First Avenue North (the present sight of the Butler Square Building, next to the Target Center). The park was also the home of the professional Minneapolis Millers Baseball Club, before they moved to Nicollet Park.

On January 24-25, 1896, the St. Paul Winter Carnival played host to a four-team international tournament which took place at St. Paul's Aurora Rink. It was probably the first international ice hockey tournament ever held in the United States. The teams included the Minneapolis Hockey Club, two teams from St. Paul: St. Paul I & St. Paul II, and a squad from Winnipeg. In the first round, Minneapolis beat St. Paul II, 4-1, while Winnipeg whipped St. Paul I, 13-2. Winnipeg then trounced Minneapolis, 7-3, for the title. On January 26, the St. Paul Globe reported: "The games were attended by large crowds. The Winnipeg team received a silver stein for winning the carnival championship while the Minneapolis team members were given sticks."

By 1896-97, there were several hockey teams, including youth teams, competing in both St. Paul and in the Mill City. In addition, informal hockey was being played throughout Northwestern Minnesota in communities such as: Argyle, Hallock, Warren and Stephen. In 1899 the St. Paul Hockey Club was organized. The Club played several games that year, one of them against St. Cloud Normal School at the Virginia rink in St. Paul before some 400 fans. St. Paul won 6-0 with Patterson, Elliot and Newsom each scoring two goals. The team even planned a trip to the East Coast to play teams from New York City, Washington D.C. and Philadelphia. However, the trip was canceled due to a lack of participation and quality practice time.

By the turn of the century, grade school and high school hockey programs were taking off throughout the state. By now the sport had spread to communities such as Warroad, Roseau, Thief River Falls, Crookston, Baudette, Eveleth, Virginia and Duluth. At this same time, men's and youth leagues were growing throughout the metro area. Fueling this growth were several industrial and utility companies who sponsored these clubs. The culmination for all of the teams came down to an annual tournament which determined the Twin Cities championship. With this organized sponsorship, hockey soon became accessible to a wide variety of men and boys alike who wished to play the game. Rinks sprouted up everywhere as the game began to take off.

As the 20th Century began to unfold, hockey continued to grow and prosper. Minneapolis even got its first indoor rink, in 1900 when the old Star Roller Rink, located on 4th Avenue South and 11th Street, was retrofitted for ice hockey. The Minneapolis Hockey Club, Central High School, and North High School would all use the "Star" on a regular basis for games as well as for practice.

"Senior" Hockey at the Turn of the Century...

Men's senior leagues began to pop up throughout Minnesota in one form or another around the turn of the century. They have played a vital role in the development of amateur hockey in the state. By the early 1900s, there were countless men's senior hockey circuits which had sprouted up throughout the Twin Cities and Northern Minnesota. It was a social movement phenomenon, which Joseph Shipanovich, author of the book "Minneapolis," called "industrial paternalism," wherein business and corporations began the tradition of sponsoring athletic teams comprised of their employees. The first big-time league that came to fruition during this era was the Twin City Senior Hockey League.

Late in the winter of 1901, to accommodate the growing desire for organized hockey in the Gopher State, the Twin City Senior Hockey League was formed with the following four teams: Minneapolis Hockey Club, St. Paul Hockey Club, St. Paul Mechanic Arts High School, and St. Paul Central High School. During the next season of 1901-1902, the league became a six-team union when the St. Paul Virginias and the St. Paul Mascots were added. To make it official, the world famous curler, Robert H. Dunbar, presented a silver cup which would be awarded annually to the league champion. The Virginias went on to win the inaugural Dunbar Cup.

During the 1902 season, after losing two out of three to the St. Paul Hockey Club, the Minneapolis Hockey Club withdrew from the league, leaving the alliance with only five St. Paul teams. Minneapolis HC would play a very significant game later that season though. On January 23, 1902, the world famous Portage Lake Lakers, of Houghton Mich., defeated Minneapolis HC, 8-4, in a contest played at the Star Rink.

At the end of the season, the St. Paul Virginias traveled to Houghton to face the mighty Lakers, who were for the most part Canadian imports. Considered by most to be the best team in the world, Portage Lake whipped the Virginias 11-2 before a crowd of more than 700 at the Amphidrome Arena. The Lakers enjoyed the great competition that Minnesota offered, and came back again that season to face St. Paul one more time. This time they won only 2-0. The star of the Victorias was a goaltender named Joe Jones. So impressed were the Lakers with his performance, claiming that he was the best that they had ever faced, they hired him to come tend goal for them the following season. (Later Jones would go on to play for the American Soo team of the International Hockey League, the world's first professional circuit.)

In 1903 the University of Minnesota was invited to participate in the league. Using Como Lake in St. Paul (rather than Northrop Field), as the team's home rink, the Gophers defeated both Central High School, 4-0, and the St. Paul Virginias, 4-3. A highlight of the era occurred in 1904, when a St. Paul all-star team was formed and sent to St. Louis, where they competed in the World's Fair Tournament against teams from Missouri and Michigan.

Over the nine-year history of the Twin City League, which was comprised of all Minnesotans and no imports, St. Paul teams dominated the circuit with the Gotzian Victorias, winning the Dunbar Cup six consecutive seasons from 1902-07. Among the many Minneapolis teams that joined the TCL included: AAA, the Lake Shores, the Harriets, the YMCAs, the Eagles, the U of M and the Wanderers. (The Minneapolis Wanderers were led by one of Minnesota's greatest athletes, Bobby Marshall. Marshall, one of the first African Americans to play hockey at this level in the U.S., was also a 1906 All-American end for the University of Minnesota football team.)

After the 1911 season, when the St. Paul Chinooks and Minneapolis Wanderers withdrew from the organization, the league ceased operations. As a result of the league break-up, teams expanded their schedules in order to play a more diverse schedule. That same year, the Phoenix went on to play a series of exhibition games against several local high schools, Minneapolis Lake Shores, Duluth and Fort William. In addition, the team trav-

MOOSE GOHEEN

White Bear Lake native Moose Goheen joined the St. Paul Athletic Club in the fall of 1915, and from there went on to become one of Minnesota's greatest hockey superstars. The crowds at his games would chant "Moose" "Moose," to which Goheen would reply by first circling his own net several times to pick up speed, and then make an end-to-end rush, usually scoring. In addition to leading the AC to several McNaughton Cups, Moose also played on the 1920 silver medal-winning U.S. Olympic Hockey team. He continued to play with the St. Paul team through 1926, when it turned professional, and then on through 1932. He was offered several pro contracts from both Toronto and Boston, but opted instead to stay in Minnesota and continue working at the Northern States Power Company. In 1952 Moose was selected to the Hockey Hall of Fame in Toronto, becoming one of the few Americans ever to have done so. In 1958 he was voted by the Minnesota Hall of Fame as the finest player ever produced in the state.

eled to Cleveland and Chicago to play a series of games. Incidentally, the last two games of that season against Duluth and Fort William were played at the newly constructed St. Paul Hippodrome, located in the Livestock Pavilion at the state fairgrounds. The "Hipp," as it was known, with its natural ice, had the honor of having the largest sheet of ice in North America. The ice sheet measured a whopping 270 feet long by 119 feet wide, and covered an area of more than 32,000 square feet — more than twice as big as a normal hockey rink, which measures only 100' x 185'. Opponents who played there said it was like playing on Lake Superior! Not to be outdone, that same year the Curling Club of Duluth was built — giving the northerners their own hockey Mecca to compete in.

During that first decade, a series of games were played against teams from Minneapolis, St. Paul, Duluth and Two Harbors to determine the State Senior champion. By no surprise the St. Paul Victorias continued their dominance in the world of Minnesota hockey, by winning the title from 1904-07. In 1908 the Duluth Northerns won the title, and also went on to claim the U.S. Amateur championship as well. The St. Paul Phoenix won the championship in 1909 and 1910, and in 1912 the team was invited to play games in Chicago, Cleveland and Detroit.

The State's Dominion League...

Another league that got underway around the turn of the century was called the State's Dominion League. This men's senior amateur league ran from 1900 into the early 1950s, with teams from all over the state competing. Included were: the Duluth Northerns, the Hallock Legionnaires, the Thief River Falls Thieves, the Grand Forks Flickertails, Roseau, Baudette, Hibbing, Eveleth, Warroad, Two Harbors, Crookston, the St. Paul Victorias, the St. Paul Mic Macs, and the St. Paul Koppys.

Among the leading players during the first decade of the 1900's were: Carl Struck, Cleve Benowicz, W. Lalond, Ray Hodge, Kimball Hodge, Jack Bradford, Cornell

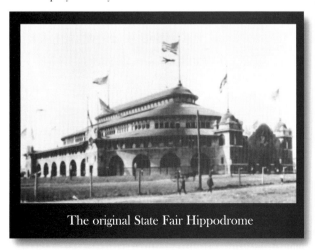

The original State Fair Hippodrome

Lagerstrom, P. K. Labafle, A. Raymond, C. Fairchild, Bobby Marshall, Fred Cook, Ed Murphy, Harry and Bert Clayton, Joe Jones, Roy Sanders, Jack and Matt Taylor, Charles Kenny, Roy Moritz, Ray Armstrong, George Patterson, Bob Barron, Tom Newson, Ed Fitzgerald, Harvey McNair, Jack Ordway, Leo Leonard, Port Palmer, Fred Minser, Walter Seeger, John Foley, Charles Driscoll, Fred Bawlf, and Art Larkin (who was a quarterback for the Gopher football team in 1906 and 1907).

Minnesota Hockey from 1910-20...

Following the break-up of the Twin City League after the 1911 season, the Minneapolis Senior League was formed with teams playing many of their games on the ice of Lake Harriet. Members of the league included: the ABC's, the Simokins, the North Commons and the Lake Harriets. The Lake Harriets emerged as the team to beat during this era and were considered by most to be among the best in the city. The Harriets would also play teams from not only St. Paul, but also from Duluth and even the tiny Northwestern Minnesota town of Hallock, where they would play the Lions.

The American Amateur Hockey Association...

In 1914 the St. Paul Athletic Club, one of the greatest organizations in the history of Minnesota hockey, was formed and competed in an independent schedule against some tough opponents. Among them were Duluth, Grand Forks, Fort William, Port Arthur, and the Ottawa Aberdeens. The team's only two losses came from a very experienced Ottawa squad. Among the players were: Weidenborner, Goheen, Conroy, Peterson, Henderson, Kahler, Fitzgerald, McCourt and LeClaire.

Only one year earlier, in 1913, the American Amateur Hockey Association, or AAHA, was created. Many of the players in the league were imported Canadians. The inaugural teams in the league included: Portage Lake, Calumet, Sault Ste. Marie, American Soo, Cleveland Athletic Club, Boston Athletic Association, and the Boston Arenas. In 1915, the St. Paul Athletic Club joined the league. The teams competed for the coveted McNaughton Cup, which was donated by James McNaughton, president of Upper Michigan's Calumet and Hecla Copper Company, and big-time supporter of amateur hockey. The cup, which weighs some 40 pounds and towers nearly three feet tall, is hand crafted of pure silver. (Years later, in the 1940s, the cup was passed down to the newly-formed Western Intercollegiate Hockey League which later became the Western Collegiate Hockey Association, or WCHA.)

From 1913-15, the Cleveland Athletic Club, led by Duluth-born speed skater Frank "Coddy" Winters, won three consecutive titles. Then, in 1916, ironically in the league's last year of existence, the St. Paul Athletic Club beat the American Soo (Sault St. Marie, Mich.) three games out of four, to win the cup. St. Paul AC was led by a high-scoring defenseman named Francis "Moose" Goheen, of White Bear Lake. Crowds at the "Hipp" in St. Paul absolutely loved the Moose. He was probably as popular back then as Kirby Puckett was in his heyday. At 200 pounds he was a bruiser, and could get the 8,000-plus fans to their feet in a hurry with one of his legendary body checks. At the time he was considered by most to be the best American developed player in the western United States.

The other stars of that St. Paul squad included the high-scoring center Nick Kahler, Cy Weidenborner, Eddie Fitzgerald and Tony Conroy. And, all but Kahler, who had work obligations, would go on to represent the USA on the 1920 Olympic team in Antwerp, Belgium. Playing under the guidance of the International Skating Union, the Americans lost to the Winnipeg Falcons (who represented Canada), for the gold medal, in the first-ever Winter Olympic

games. After winning the AAHA crown, St. Paul traveled to Montreal in March of 1916, where they beat Lachine, Quebec, 7-6, for the International Art Ross Trophy, which was emblematic of the world's amateur championship. The people of Canada were shocked that a U.S. team was that good. By the spring of 1917 World War I was underway, and the AAHA ultimately dissolved.

The St. Paul AC played an independent schedule for the season of 1916-17. Several key players were added to the club that year. Dick Conway, a star football and baseball player at St. Thomas College from White Bear Lake; Herb Drury, a speedy winger from Midland, Ontario, who would later go on to play in the National Hockey League with Pittsburgh; and Everett McGowan, a nationally known speed-skater. In addition to playing the American Soo, Duluth, Pittsburgh, and several Canadian teams that season, the AC also played a new team from Minneapolis, which featured a familiar face.

The Minneapolis Millers are Born...

An interesting thing happened in 1917, when Nick Kahler, one of the great young hockey players of the time who had been captain of the St. Paul AC team, crossed the river to Minneapolis and formed a new team comprised mostly of Canadian imports. His new squad, the Minneapolis Millers, played the St. Paul AC and split a two game series. The first game, played at the Hipp, resulted in a 9-2 rout for the St. Paul seven, while the second, which was played at the smaller Coliseum Rink located on Lexington Avenue near University Avenue in St. Paul, ended in a 9-0 loss for the Millers. Kahler's Mill City team even sought entry in the National Hockey Association (The NHA precluded the NHL), as a replacement for the defunct Pittsburgh team, but was unsuccessful. The Millers played several of the teams in that league, which was based mostly in the East and from Canada, and fared well. The roster of that early Minneapolis hockey club included such stars as: Babe Elliott, goaltender; Jack Chambers, Fosdale and Alex Dunlop, defense; Lyle Wright and McPherson, wings, and Nick Kahler, center. The Millers became the orphans of the hockey world though, with no league affiliation and no permanent home rink. After playing the 1919 season on a flooded roller rink at Plymouth and Washington avenues north, the team moved into the luxurious confines of the Hippodrome in St. Paul.

The War finally came to an end on November 11, 1918, and with that, the American Amateur Hockey Association resurfaced for the 1919-20 season. The St. Paul AC again won the McNaughton Cup, this time sharing the title with Canadian Soo, because they could not agree on a neutral sight to play the championship. (It is important to note that up to this point, hockey in the United States was changing from being played with seven players to six, thus eliminating the position of rover. There was also no forward passing either. Players could skate the puck up and pass laterally or back, but not ahead. Another key rule change of this era was the allowance of a substitute for a penalized player, so there was always a full complement of players.)

Other significant events in the world of Minnesota hockey during this decade included the growth of intramural hockey at the University of Minnesota. By 1915 some 16 fraternities were playing organized hockey on campus. Their league games were played on the flooded Northrop Field, with the playoffs taking place at the Hipp. The Bros brothers, Chet and Ben, who would later dominate for the Gophers, were the stars of that Greek league. In addition, a women's league got underway at the U of M that next year as well.

The late Carl F. Struck, considered the father of the ice sport in the Mill City, organized park league teams in 1916 and 1917. Two of the better known teams of that era were the Vertex and the Camdens, bitter championship rivals.

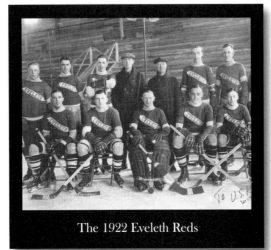

The 1922 Eveleth Reds

During this period, not only were college and amateur teams playing at the Hipp, but also several high school teams as well. High school hockey was really gaining in popularity. The Mechanic Arts High School team was consistently one of the strongest of the Twin City high schools. The same was happening in both Duluth, at the Duluth Curling Club, and also in Hibbing, where the Hibbing Curling Club had recently opened. In addition, Duluth and Eveleth amateur teams were playing an independent schedule against Canadian and Michigan Copper-Country teams.

The U.S. Amateur Hockey Association...
In the fall of 1920 the United States Amateur Hockey Association (U.S.A.H.A.) was formed, and the A.A.H.A. decided to become an affiliate of the new league. The U.S.A.H.A. (by virtue of an agreement with the International Skating Union, Canadian Amateur Hockey Association, and the Amateur Athletic Union) was now recognized as the sole governing body for amateur hockey in the U.S., and over the next several years its league champion was acknowledged as the national champion.

During that first season of league play in 1920-21, there were three groups that made up the new association — one in the East and two in the Midwest. The clubs that played in the league included: the Duluth Hornets, St. Paul AC, Eveleth Reds, Boston AA, Boston Westminster HC, Pittsburgh Hornets, Pittsburgh Yellow Jackets, Cleveland HC, New York, Philadelphia, Cleveland, Calumet, Portage Lake, and both the American and Canadian Soo of Sault St. Marie. They were all playing a uniform version of six-man hockey as well, having eliminated the "rover" position.

Eveleth got off to a great start that inaugural season. The Reds, who were playing their home games in the newly constructed Eveleth Recreation Building, finished the season by winning the Group Three Division with a record of 14-1-1. Eveleth then faced Cleveland, the Group Two champ which had beaten the Group One champ, Boston AA, in the finals. On April 2-3, in Cleveland, the Cleveland Hockey Club beat Eveleth by the back-to-back scores of 6-3, and 6-3. Then, because of the lack of ice in Northern Minnesota at the time, the series shifted to Pittsburgh, where there was artificial ice to play on. There, the Reds beat the Clevelanders by the scores of 2-0, and 4-2 to tie it up at two games apiece. But, Cleveland was declared the winner of the four-game series on total goals (14-12), and was awarded the league's championship trophy, the Fellowes Cup. As for the other Minnesota teams that season? St. Paul skated to a modest record of 3-5, while Duluth finished 1-7.

At the end of the 1921-22 season, Eveleth, winners of Group Three, had finished with an impressive 12-4 record. The Reds then went on to face the St. Paul AC, the winners of Group Two who posted an 8-4 record. Eveleth had a very strong team with the likes of Monette, Ching and Ade Johnson, Seaborn, Grey, Des Jardins, Galbraith, Breen and Nicklin. With the exception of Des Jardins, the entire roster was Canadian. St. Paul beat Eveleth, 3-1, only to lose 4-2 the following evening. The series then shifted back to St. Paul, where the teams skated to a pair of 0-0 ties, in addition to a 2-1 nail-biter victory for the AC. St. Paul wound up winning the series 7-6 on total goals. In so doing, St. Paul then went on to face Boston Westminster in the finals, only to lose 3-0, 2-1, 0-0 and 2-0. Although the AC lost the championship, the playoffs proved that Minnesotans indeed loved their hockey. That's because St. Paul, with a rink that held 7,800, drew in excess of 51,000 fans for the two (seven-game) playoff series' against Eveleth and Boston.

For the 1922-23 season and

thereafter, the league decided to split into two divisions — the Eastern and Western. St. Paul along with Duluth, Eveleth, Pittsburgh, Cleveland and newcomer Milwaukee, formed Group Two of the USAHA. Again St. Paul won the Western Division with an impressive 35-5 record that year, three games in front of Cleveland and four games ahead of Eveleth. Playing a big part in those wins were the addition of several new faces to the line-up that included: Taffy Abel, Dennis Breen, George Clarke and Joe McCormick. By season's end the only two teams left standing were once again St. Paul AC and Boston Westminster. Boston went on to win the Fellowes Cup for the second straight season by winning the series in four, with St. Paul winning only Game Three by the score of 2-1. Incidentally, all four games, which were decided by one goal margins, were played in the newly constructed Boston Arena. The leading scorers in the league that year included St. Paul's Clark, who scored 15 goals, Moose Goheen, who tallied 11, and Duluth's Seaborn, who added 10.

During the 1923-24 season, the upstart Minneapolis Rockets replaced the struggling Milwaukee franchise as the sixth team in the division. The team played in the brand new Minneapolis Arena, which was located at 2800 Dupont Avenue South. Not only did the new facility have an artificial ice surface, it also had a seating capacity of some 5,400. That year Minneapolis was blessed with some of the best hockey that the Mill City would ever know. Two Winnipeg natives named Ching and Ade Johnson, who had previously played for the Eveleth Reds, joined the Rockets for their inaugural season. Ching, who, at more than 200 pounds was considered to be a giant, was an incredible crowd favorite not only back up on the Range in Eveleth, but also most everywhere around the league. His big bald head, huge grin, and rough antics on the ice made him an instant hero to hockey fans everywhere.

Minneapolis, despite having the Johnson brothers as well as another star named Taffy Abel on their team, wound up in the league cellar that year tied with Duluth at 6-14-0. St. Paul, who added Wilt Peltier to their line-up that season, would end up finishing the season at 14-6. Pittsburgh, who edged St. Paul for the group title by one game, went on to beat the AC in a round robin playoff with Cleveland. Pittsburgh then went on to beat Boston for the national title. At the end of the season the Duluth News Tribune selected an all-star team. Included as the best of the best that year were the Rockets' Ching Johnson, as well as St. Paul's Moose Goheen and Wilt Peltier. Leading scor-

The 1930 St. Paul Athletic Club

Vic Des Jardins

Vic Des Jardins starred for the USAHA's Eveleth Rangers from 1921-26, before heading south, to lead the AHA's St. Paul Saints. He captured the league scoring title in 1928 before going on to play in the NHL with both the Chicago Blackhawks and New York Rangers. He would later take over as the head coach of the AHA's Tulsa Oilers.

ers that year included St. Paul's Nobby Clarke, who finished as the league's second leading scorer with 18 points. Moose Goheen added 14 points, Duluth's Goodman netted 13, Peltier and Ching Johnson tallied 12, Eveleth's Galbraith and Rodden each scored 11, while St. Paul's Conroy added 10.

The 1924-25 season would prove to be an important one in for Minnesota hockey. St. Paul, coached by Ed Fitzgerald, finished its 40-game schedule with a 16-22-2 record, not good enough for the post-season. The Rockets joined the AC on the sidelines that season with an equally brutal record of 16-19-3. The last of the Minnesota contingent, Eveleth, which came on strong to finish the second-half of the season at 13-6-1, was defeated by Pittsburgh in four straight in a playoff series. Interestingly, the series was played in both Pittsburgh and Duluth, because the temperature got too warm and Eveleth did not have artificial ice. The Yellow Jackets then went on to defeat Fort Pitt, which represented the East, in the national finals. Eveleth's Vic Des Jardins was second in the league that year with 14 goals in 39 games.

Unfortunately, after running for five glorious seasons, 1925 was the last year of operation for the USAHA. The league was vital for jump-starting the game of hockey throughout the United States. Many of the game's best and most talented players suited up for a USAHA squad over its brief history during the early and mid-1920s, many of whom would go on to play in the NHL. Dozens of the league's elite came from the Minnesota contingent which included: Cooney Weiland (Minneapolis), Ching Johnson (Eveleth & Minneapolis), Tiny Thompson (Duluth & Minneapolis), Taffy Abel (Minneapolis & St. Paul), Herbie Lewis (Duluth), Mike Goodman (Duluth), Moose Goheen (St. Paul), Coddy Winters (from Duluth but played for Cleveland), Vic Des Jardins (Eveleth), Perk Galbraith (Eveleth & Minneapolis), Gus Olson (Duluth), Joe Bernardi (Duluth), Jim Seaborn (Eveleth &

Duluth), Tony Conroy (St. Paul), Babe Elliott (St. Paul), Nobby Clarke (Eveleth & Duluth), Iver Anderson (Duluth), Ade Johnson (Eveleth & Minneapolis), Ed Rodden (Eveleth), Emy Garrett (St. Paul), George Clarke (St. Paul), and Bill Hill (Eveleth).

Hockey in the Early 1920s...

Hockey was going through its share of growing pains during the early 1920s, and the USAHA helped to define the game's identity. During this period, a total of seven to nine players would typically see action in a game, and often times a player might play an entire contest without taking a breather. By the mid-1920s, as many as a dozen players made up a team's roster. Goalies were a different story. For a team to carry a spare keeper was a luxury which was unheard of. However, because they didn't wear masks, and often times got injured, this became a problem. So, in an emergency situation an extra forward or defenseman might have to strap on the pads. Or sometimes, if the team was lucky, a goalie who might be in attendance at the game would be permitted to suit up if he so desired.

Refereeing was also an enigma, especially in the early years of the association. One time, during a game in Sault St. Marie, St. Paul's coach, Ed Fitzgerald, protested a referee's call and proceeded to inform the official that the rule was not in the rule book. The referee took the book and said, "There ain't any rule book. Up here it is played the way I say." He then tore the rule book in half and threw it into the crowd. The term "Homers" came about from the fact that referees were usually from that particular home-town, and were easily swayed in their decision making. Time-keepers were also locals who sat on the home team's bench and often adjusted things to their team's favor.

Playing facilities also posed big problems back then. Because the East Coast teams, along with Pittsburgh, Milwaukee, and Cleveland, had artificial ice, and the teams such as Duluth, Eveleth, and St. Paul had natural ice, they had a huge advantage. They not only got an earlier start, but they also got to play later into the Spring as well. At times some of the home playoff games of Duluth, Eveleth, and St. Paul had to be moved to their opponents home ice or to a neutral rink. But this also sped up the process of getting more arena's built in Minnesota, such as Duluth's Amphitheater and the Arena in Minneapolis, which both opened in the mid-1920s.

The rules of the early 1920s were quite a bit different, too. Gus Olson, the legendary Duluth coach and player, helped to better explain them in an article that appeared in the Duluth Herald and News Tribune in April of 1945:

"The rules of hockey have seen many changes. Originally the team was composed of seven players. A goalie, point, cover-point, center, left and right wing, and a rover. The cover-point played in front of the point, who was directly in front of the goalie, and the rover played on the forward line, backing up the three forwards. Shortly after WWI, the line-up was changed to six men: a goalie, left and right defense, and three forwards. This was a big improvement, as it made for more open hockey with two less players on the ice. Often times I thought this was a great deal too many, the way I was checked."

"Under the seven-man lineup, forward passing was prohibited. Passes had to be made straight across the ice, which was later changed to permit the puck to be passed forward, but the player taking the puck had to be even or on side when the puck was passed. This sped up the game a little and later the first blue line appeared. This was 20 feet out from the goal line and permitted the defending team to pass from its end of the rink up to the blue line, but from there on it had to be played on-side. About 1927, the blue lines were moved out 60 feet from the goal mouth and forward passing was permitted in each of the three zones between the different blue lines.

Nick Kahler

Nick Kahler was an early star on the 1913 Duluth Curling Club Team, and later for the St. Paul Athletic Club, where he served as manager, coach, and player. Later, in 1920, Kahler launched the Minneapolis Millers in the United States Amateur Hockey Association, where his 1925 team won the league title.

In 1942, the red line was added to the others, being put in the center of the rink and permitting the defending team to pass from its end of the rink up to the red line. If a defending player was over his own blue line, he had to touch the puck before it crossed the red line. But if he was behind his own blue line when the puck was passed out, he was permitted to take the puck past the red line."

Travel during this era often proved to be a difficult undertaking as well. Because there were few hard surfaced highways and they were not maintained properly during the winter months, most of the travel was done by train. Here, Gus Olson explains the problems they encountered in 1923 on a road trip to Milwaukee, Canadian Soo and Marquette:

"We had some tough road trips in the early days. The year Milwaukee was in the league we did not have too many players, and on one road trip we were to go to the Copper Country for some exhibition games after playing Milwaukee. We left Milwaukee at 5:30 p.m. for the Canadian Soo, where we were to play on Monday morning between Milwaukee and the Soo, but due to a snow storm we missed connecting and as a result, we did not get anything to eat until we reached the Soo Monday at 6:00 p.m.

"Then as we had missed the regular train across the Straits, we climbed into a caboose and put our trunks on the back of the engine. We arrived at the Soo and started our game at about 10:00. We played again Tuesday night and after the game rented two toboggans and hauled our trunks across the ice as we had to catch a train out of American Soo at 5:30 am for Marquette, where we were booked for Wednesday night. We ran into more snow and did not get our game underway that night until after 10:00 p.m. Then we sat up until 4:00 a.m. to take the train back to Duluth where we were playing a team from Winnipeg on Thursday and Friday nights. That was five games in five days with all the train travel thrown in. Incidentally, we won four of the five games."

One thing has remained a constant through the years, the fact that hockey is an extremely rough sport. Many an old timer would tell of playing in games when they had injured elbows and knees and had dozens of recent stitches. The legendary hockey historian Don Clark remembered reminiscing with a couple of ice legends about what it was like back then. Emy Garrett, St. Paul forward, stated: "When we started on a road trip to the other rinks it was like going to war. Visiting teams often lost and had to be escorted off the ice by the police." Eveleth, St. Paul and Duluth dreaded visiting the small rinks in Upper Michigan. Moose Goheen thought about all of the rough and rowdy games in which he had played in during his 19-year career and said that the toughest was the 1922 playoff series between St. Paul and Eveleth, when the penalty boxes were usually filled up to the brim. With large crowds attending games at both home rinks, St. Paul edged Eveleth three games to two, scoring seven goals to Eveleth's six, with two of the contests ending as scoreless ties.

Although the USAHA only lasted for four years, it was responsible for generating incredible growth in the popularity of the game. As a result, more leagues popped up across the country, and with them came more rinks. The level of play at this time would probably have been considered to be just below the level of Canada's top circuit — the National Hockey League.

The Central Hockey Assoc. & the Saints...

With the senior leagues going gangbusters, Minnesota's appetite for hockey kept growing and growing. So, it was only natural that the hockey braintrust put their heads together to form a new league, and that's just what they did. Deciding to disband the USAHA's Eastern Division, it was decided that the USAHA's Western Division would be reorganized as the Central Hockey Association for the 1925-26 season. Pittsburgh and Cleveland withdrew from the Western Division and were replaced by two teams which were closer in proximity to

the Midwest — American Soo and Winnipeg. Pittsburgh then promptly joined the National Hockey League. (To personify just how good the USAHA was, the Yellow Jackets -- using nearly the same lineup from the year before — finished third in the then seven-team NHL, which was the highest level of hockey in the world at the time.) The new league featured the following teams: the St. Paul Saints, the Minneapolis Rockets, Duluth Hornets, Eveleth-Hibbing Rangers (Eveleth joined forces with their Iron Range neighbors from Hibbing to form one team), Winnipeg, and the American Soo. The league had great parity, and each team

Cooney Weiland

Ralph "Cooney" Weiland played for four seasons during the 1920s with both the Minneapolis Millers and Rockets before going on to superstardom in the NHL. Weiland would win several Stanley Cups as a member of the Boston Bruins famed "Dynamite Line."

had its share of stars. St. Paul was blessed with the talents of Moose Goheen, Tony and George Conroy, and Emy Garrett; Duluth had the amazing Herbie Lewis, Jim Seaborn, Mike Goodman, and Moose Jamieson; Eveleth featured Vic Des Jardins and Goalie Pat Byrne; Winnipeg showcased Artie Somers, Murray Murdoch, and Chuck Gardiner; and The Soo of Sault Ste. Marie, Ontario, enjoyed a smorgasbord of Canadian superstars.

That season Minneapolis, under the tutelage of Lloyd Turner of Calgary, finished on top of the regular season standings with an impressive 22-10-6 record, while Duluth was the runner-up finishing at 18-14-8. This outstanding Minneapolis team was put together by several prominent Mill City businessmen, including Paul Loudon, George Drake, and Louis and George Piper. That season also gave Minneapolis an identity of their own in the Twin Cities. They said good-bye to playing in St. Paul's Hippodrome, and said hello to their new home, the Minneapolis Arena, complete with an artificial ice surface. St. Paul placed

Ching Johnson

Ching Johnson was one of Minnesota hockey's first superstars. First recruited to Eveleth from his native Winnipeg to play for the semi-pro Rangers in 1920, Ching went on to play three seasons in Eveleth before moving to Minneapolis, where he starred for the Millers and Rockets from 1923-26. From there, Ching signed with the NHL's New York Rangers, where he was a perennial all-star for more than a decade during the 1920s and 30s. In 1938 Ching returned home to the Millers, where he played until 1940. With his shiny bald head and hulking 200-pound frame (which was considered to be a giant back then), the hard-hitting bruiser was one of the leagues's biggest fan-favorites. He was elected to the Hockey Hall of Fame in 1958.

fourth behind Winnipeg with a 15-17-6 record, while Eveleth-Hibbing wound up in fifth place at a respectable 15-16-7. In the playoffs, Duluth beat Winnipeg in a five-game series, only to meet the red-hot Minneapolis Rockets in the finals. After blanking the Hornets in the first two contests by the scores of 3-0 and 4-0, the Rockets then ventured north to Duluth, where, on April 6, 1926, they won the final game of the series by the score of 2-1. The CHA crown was theirs. Some of the greatest players in the game were members of that Minneapolis team. Among them were Tiny Thompson, Cooney Weiland, Taffy Abel, Ching Johnson, Mickey McQuire, Bill Boyd, Denny Breen, Vic Ripley and Johnny McKinnon. Many would go on to star in the NHL.

That year would also mark the end of a Minnesota hockey institution, the St. Paul Athletic Club. The AC ended that year and became the St. Paul Saints. Hockey fans were blessed with the likes of countless stars that donned the AC sweater including: Abel, Goheen, Tony Conroy, George Conroy, Fitzgerald, Weidenborner, Garret, Gehrke, McCarthy, Breen, McCormick, Romnes, Shea, Wellington, Adams, Whalen, Mohan, Elliott, Clarke, Drury, Nichols, Ching Johnson, Nick Kahler, Galbraith, Weiland, Des Jardin, Somers, Gottsleig, Stewart, Worters, Jamieson, and Thompson, to name a few.

The American Hockey Association...

The year of 1926 was somewhat of a tumultuous year of hockey for Minnesota. You see, because the Central League was amateur in status, it had become the target of raids by the upstart Eastern professional leagues. As a result, the Central League lasted just that one season. This article about the Central Association's woes appeared in the St. Paul Pioneer Press on February 13th, 1926: "The Central Hockey Association is on the verge of going professional. For the past several seasons the league has been amateur in name only. The league had to spend money liberally in order to secure good players. Now they face a new danger — the growth of pro hockey in the East and the constant threat of raids on Central League players, which has made it mandatory that teams in the league protect themselves from wholesale raids. The league has acted slowly to protect the smaller cities in the circuit who could not afford to turn pro."

Ultimately the success of the league proved to be its undoing. Apparently, at the time, plans were in the works to add a new "American Division" to the professional NHL's already existing Canadian group. The talent on the U.S. side of the border was an apparent green pasture for the eastern promoters who wanted to fill their rosters. Tired of being the main suppliers of NHL talent for nothing in return, a new league was formed that next season, the American Hockey Association. It would be the first outright professional league in the Midwest at the time. They figured if they paid their players, it would prevent them from packing up and heading East.

However, it was too late for a few Minneapolis stars who opted for the big bucks. The infamous Colonel John S. Hammond of the New York Rangers, who was at a Duluth Hornets vs. Millers game near the end of the 1926 season, plucked Ching

The Duluth Hornets were led by superstars Herbie Lewis and Mike Goodman

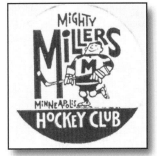

Duluth Hornets goalie Alfie Moore

Johnson, Taffy Abel, Billy Boyd and Johnny McKinnon from the Millers right after the game with the allure of large sums of money as bait. Ching Johnson, after three years with Minneapolis and three years prior with the Eveleth Rangers, and at the relatively old age of 29, succumbed to the intense recruiting and joined the NHL's New York Rangers. He reportedly signed a three-year contract for the then unprecedented sum of $30,000. Ching went on to star in the NHL for 11 years, before returning to his Millers for a final stint from 1938-40. He was joined by another very popular player, Taffy Abel, who played for St. Paul AC from 1922-25, and also with the Millers in 1926. (Both are members of the U.S. Hockey Hall of Fame.) In addition, the Boston Bruins later lured away Cooney Weiland and Tiny Thompson.

Due to high operating costs, the Eveleth-Hibbing franchise, along with the Soo, opted to drop out of the league to play independent schedules for the 1926-27 season. This left the Minneapolis Millers, St. Paul Saints, Winnipeg Maroons, and Duluth Hornets, along with newcomers Detroit Greyhounds and the Chicago Cardinals, to form the upstart AHA. Detroit's franchise then folded after only six games, leaving it to be just a five-team league. Because the league wanted to be different from the Eastern pro leagues, that were made up of mostly Canadian players, they decided to stockpile as many American-born players as possible and ultimately challenge for Lord Stanley's Cup. This strategy was, in part, thanks to a couple of Minnesota boys named A.H. Warren of St. Paul, who served as the league's first president, and also Duluth's William Grant, who acted as secretary-treasurer.

For the 1926-27 season, the Hornets won the regular season title by finishing 20-10-8. The Millers finished second at 17-11-10, while the Saints came in fourth behind Winnipeg with a 17-15-5 record. Chicago, which finished in last place, changed their name on March 8th that year to the "Americans." The Millers went on to beat the Maroons in a three game playoff, and then met Duluth in the finals. The Hornets crushed Minneapolis by winning three straight, thus capturing the first-ever AHA championship.

The next year Chicago was replaced with a new franchise from Kansas City, called the Greyhounds. Duluth's William Grant served as the new club's president, general manager, and coach. The Hornets again finished on top of the 1927-28 regular season standings with a 18-9-13 record, followed by Kansas City, Minneapolis, St. Paul, and Winnipeg. St. Paul's Vic Des Jardins was the league's leading scorer with 28 points, followed by Minneapolis' Cooney Weiland who tallied 26, and St. Paul's Moose Goheen who added 24. In the semifinals, Minneapolis defeated the Greyhounds, and then went on to beat the Hornets for the championship. They were led by future hall of famer Tiny Thompson, who had an amazing 0.35 playoff goals-against average for the Millers that year.

Winnipeg withdrew from the league in 1928, and was replaced by both Tulsa and the St. Louis Flyers to once again make it a six team league. Tulsa went on to win the league crown that season with the Millers finishing as the runners-up. The Saints came in third, followed by Duluth and St. Louis. Turner resigned as the Millers head coach after that season to join with Seattle, of the Pacific Coast Hockey League. Lyle Wright, the manager of the Minneapolis Arena, took over the reigns for the Millers.

By 1929 the AHA was booming in popularity. Attendance was strong throughout the league and particularly in Minnesota. Duluth finished second with a 18-13-17 record that season, only to lose to Tulsa in the opening round of the playoffs. The Hornets won the opener 2-1, but then lost two heartbreakers by the scores of 1-0 and 2-1 to end their season. KC then beat Tulsa for the title that year. St. Paul's Vic Des Jardins finished second in the league scoring race with 35 points, while Corb Denney of Minneapolis wound up third with 34, and Laurie Scott, the Hornet's speedy winger, was fourth with 32 points.

Duluth again finished strong at the end of the 1930-31 season, with a 28-19-1 record. Led by Scott, who finished third in the scoring race with 40 points in 48 games, the Hornets lost in the playoffs to KC in four games. Tulsa then beat KC for the title. In 1931-32 Duluth finished third in the regular season with a record of 21-24-3, and finally beat Kansas City in the playoffs. Although each club won two games, the Hornets advanced on the total goals by the score of 6-5. They then met the Chicago Shamrocks (they had changed their name) in the finals, where they lost three games to one. The Hornet's Forslund finished fourth in the league scoring race with 27 points. By this time the AHA was developing its own players at the minor professional level. It was also a breeding ground for future NHLers, and as a result it too was often raided by the big-six NHL teams. So, during that season, the AHA and the NHL made an agreement of sorts which ultimately resulted in both leagues respecting one another's player contracts.

Hockey and the Great Depression...

Meanwhile, as the Great Depression started to set in, times became tough for everyone across the country. Teams were finding it hard to make ends meet, because the fans had to save their money for more important things, such as food. That year proved to be a turning point for the AHA's Minnesota contingent. Both the Saints and Millers dropped out of the league and became members of the upstart "Senior" Central Hockey League, which began as an amateur league in 1931-32, but changed to professional in its second season.

The genesis of the league is quite interesting. In 1930-31 there were two strong amateur leagues operating in Minnesota: The Twin City League, and The Arrowhead League. The Twin City League featured the Minneapolis Americans, Minneapolis Phantoms, St. Paul and White Bear Lake. While the Arrowhead League, which had been in operation since 1927, had teams from Eveleth, Hibbing, Virginia, and Fort Frances. In 1931 Minneapolis, St. Paul, Hibbing, Eveleth, and Virginia joined forces to form the Central Hockey League. (Incidentally, the Eveleth Rangers earned a unique nickname during the league's inaugural season. Because their rink had been condemned, they had to play their entire schedule on the road. With no home ice that year, their fans dubbed them as the "Eveleth Orphans." And, even though the Millers won the championship that season, Eveleth did manage to win the regular season crown.)

Comprised almost entirely of native Minnesotans, the league consisted

Tiny Thompson was an early star for the Minneapolis Millers

of the following teams: St. Paul Saints, Minneapolis Millers, Eveleth Rangers, Virginia Rockets, and the Hibbing Maroons (who changed their name to the Hibbing Miners in 1933-34). Virginia dropped out of the league after the first season, but the Duluth Hornets, who had been playing an independent schedule, were invited to join in their place in 1933. The NHL viewed the Central as a legitimate professional circuit, and its teams played a tough 48-game schedule.

The 1932-33 AHA season was an ugly one, but did manage to feature two more Minnesota teams that "briefly" made it to the big time. That year the St. Paul Saints were replaced with another team from Pig's Eye, called the St. Paul Greyhounds. In addition, the Duluth Hornets were replaced by the Duluth Natives. During the first half of the 1932-33 season, both St. Paul and Duluth finished behind St. Louis and Kansas City in the basement of the now fledgling four-team league. The economic turmoil was affecting the league's profitability, and as a result, the St. Paul Greyhounds franchise moved to Tulsa, and the Duluth Natives moved to Wichita.

The Rangers finished at the pinnacle of the regular season standings during the league's first year of 1931-32 with a 25-10-0 record, followed by the Millers at 22-11-3, the Saints at 17-17-2, the Maroons at 16-18-2, and the Rockets at 5-29-1. The Millers went on to tie St. Paul in the playoffs at one game apiece, but won the series 5-4 on total goals. They then went on to face Eveleth in the finals, where they beat the Rangers two games to one, winning the CHL title.

In its second season of 1932-33, the league changed from "amateur" status to "professional." Players were now signing contracts and were being paid weekly salaries. Eveleth won the regular season crown that season with a 26-12-2 record. The Rangers then went on to beat the Millers in the playoffs in three straight to capture their first CHL championship. The league's leading scorers that year were as follows: St. Paul's Oscar Hanson (a former Augsburg College star and part of the original "Hanson-Brother" trio), led with 39 points, Minneapolis' Flood scored 36, while the Hibbing tandem of Lilly and Andrews each tallied 29 points.

Minneapolis won the regular season crown in 1934 with an impressive 28-11-5 record. The Millers then faced Hibbing, which had defeated Eveleth two games to one, for the title. Minneapolis went on to sweep the Miners in three straight to recapture the championship. The league's leading scorers that year were as follows: Hibbing's Lilly led with 35 points, Eveleth's Brink scored 34, while Hibbing's Andrews punched in 34 total points. Tragically, that spring Hibbing's rink burned down. So, they along with Duluth, which was in financial trouble, decided to withdraw from the league, leaving just three teams for the 1934-35 season.

Former Duluth Hornet Gus Olson

At the end of that season, tired of beating up on each other, the Central League's "powers that be" got together to round up some more competition. They didn't have to look too far. That's because that next season of 1934-35, the AHA and the CHL, both of whom were short on member teams, decided to play an adjoining schedule against each other. It was decided that each of the seven teams in the circuit would play each team in each other's leagues twice. The St. Paul Saints won the regular season crown for the 1934-35 season by going 28-10-9. Minneapolis finished second at 21-19-8, while Eveleth finished in the basement at 9-30-8. St. Paul then faced the Millers for what would prove to be the last ever CHL title. In the best-of-five series, the Saints barely beat their cross-town rivals, three games to two, to win it all. Each game alternated winners, with the Saints holding on to take Game Five by the score of 4-2. The St. Louis Flyers, champs of the AHA with a record of 29-15-4, then met St. Paul for the Inter-League title. There, the Saints promptly swept the Flyers in three straight to win it all. Eveleth then defeated the AHA's Kansas City franchise to finish in third place. Crowds of more than 7,000 were commonplace for the league's games. Leading scorers in the league that year included: St. Paul's Oscar Hanson who poured in an amazing 59 points, followed by Minneapolis' Cully Dahlstrom who scored 45, and the Saints' Emil Hanson, who added 40.

Yet Another Merger of Sorts...

Things went so well during that interlocking schedule, that for the 1935-36 campaign the two leagues decided to merge. However, due to financial constraints, only St. Paul and Minneapolis were able to rejoin Tulsa, Kansas City, St. Louis, and Wichita to form the "new" AHA. As a result, the Central, after four glorious years of big-time hockey in Minnesota, was no more. The Central would play an important role in the development of American hockey though, with many of its players going on to compete in the AHA, AHL and NHL. One silver lining in all of this was the fact that after the league's break-up, some three dozen former CHL players, most of them Minnesota-born and developed, were able to join one of the six AHA squads.

In 1936, another league was formed in Northern Minnesota, called The International Amateur Hockey League. The North American circuit was comprised of teams from both the Iron Range and Ontario. Its members included: Eveleth, Duluth, Virginia, and Hibbing, as well as the Canadian teams of Port Arthur, Fort William, and Fort Frances. The Duluth Zephyrs would prove to be one of the most popular teams in Duluth hockey history, consistently playing to a full house at the Duluth Amphitheater, or "Amp" as the locals used to call it.

Under the new "combined league" system, the Saints went on to capture the league title with a record of 32-13-3 and were followed by St. Louis. Minneapolis, which finished third in the standings, was involved in a merger of their own. On March 12th that year, the Oklahoma City Warriors franchise moved to Minneapolis, to join forces with the Millers. The Saints once again met up with St. Louis in the finals, but this time the Flyers beat St. Paul three games to two to win the cup. St. Paul's Oscar Hanson won the league's scoring title with an impressive 60 points in just 49 games, and was followed by his teammate Cully Dahlstrom, who finished second with 43. Most impressive about the Saints victory that year was the fact that they did it with a line-up composed

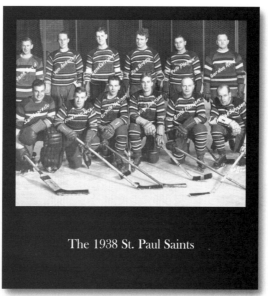

The 1938 St. Paul Saints

Hibbing and the Hawks

During the 1930s, Hibbing became the first city on the Iron Range to install artificial ice, when it retrofitted Memorial Arena. As a result, Hibbing's Memorial Arena played host to the NHL's Chicago Blackhawks for their off-season training camps. This was quite a spectacle for the locals to be able to watch hockey's elite in their own backyard.

In fact, several Minnesotans got to be a part of that history with the Hawks in 1938, the year the team won the Stanley Cup with a roster of mostly Americans. The Hawks, thanks to Major Fred McLaughlin, the team's eccentric owner, wanted to have an all-American roster. Now, by the mid-'30s there were only a handful of American-born players in the NHL, but that didn't deter the Major. Five Minnesotans: John Mariucci, Mike Karakas, Cully Dahlstrom, Virgil Johnson and Doc Romnes, all played for the Hawks during this era, and in 1938 the team shocked the world by beating the powerful Toronto Maple Leafs to win the Stanley Cup.

entirely of Minnesota players. Beef Munson and Julie Matschke were St. Paul natives, while the bulk of the Saints line-up came from both Eveleth and Minneapolis. They included: coach Emil Hanson, Oscar Hanson, Emory Hanson, Oscar Almquist, Jack Flood, Virgil Johnson, Hodge Johnson, Pete Pleban, Bill McGlone and Cully Dahlstrom.

The Saints wound up finishing third overall in 1936-37, but were swept by the Millers three games to none in the play-offs. Minneapolis was led that year by a Minnesota hockey legend, Nick Kahler, who re-emerged as the owner and promoter of the team. He hired Joe Simpson as his coach, and under the leadership of players such as Phil Hargesheimer, George Patterson and Bob Blake, the Mill City squad went on win the title by sweeping St. Louis in three straight. The Millers put the final explanation point on the season by crushing the Flyers, 6-0, in the last game to seal the deal. In that series they had to face the legendary Oscar Hanson, who was traded to St. Louis in the off-season. Hanson again won the scoring title with 62 points, followed by Minneapolis' Hargesheimer, who tallied 49. The league was faring reasonably well at this point, but the fans weren't flocking to see the games as they had back in the 1920's when they lined up to see Ching Johnson.

An example of just how good the level of play was in the minor pro AHA at that time, however, occurred that season when Ottawa transferred its NHL franchise, the Eagles, to St. Louis. There, the Eagles were beaten soundly by the AHA's other St. Louis team, the Flyers. Incidentally, the Eagles folded after just that one season.

In 1938 the Millers finished second in the regular season standings and then defeated Wichita three games to one in the playoffs. It was then off to "old Saint-Louee" to meet their old nemesis, the St. Louis Flyers, which had beaten Tulsa to advance to the finals. The teams had developed quite a rivalry, and it was fueled by the fact that many of the players knew one another from their playing days together back in Minnesota. The Flyers didn't get too sentimental over seeing their old pals though, and trounced Minneapolis in three straight to win the championship.

By 1939 St. Louis had become somewhat of a dynasty in pro hockey. That season the Millers were blessed by the return of their star centerman, Oscar Hanson, who was reacquired from their arch rivals from St. Louis. Oscar went on an unbelievable scoring barrage that season, scoring 89 points in a 48 game schedule to set a long-time standing single season record for all of professional hockey. However, despite Hanson's heroics, the Millers again finished second in the regular season standings to the Flyers with a 31-17-6 record, only to lose to Tulsa in the playoffs four games to two. It was now up to the Saints, who finished the regular season in fourth place with a 24-24-6 record. After defeating Wichita, St. Paul went on to face St. Louis in the finals, only to get swept in three games.

As the new decade of the 1940s loomed in the horizon, the Saints and Millers found themselves pitted against one another for their playoff lives. The Saints, under the tutelage of Perk Galbraith, a former Eveleth and Boston Bruins star, finished second in the regular season chase behind the Flyers with a 29-18-0 record, while the Millers placed third at 26-22-0. The teams faced off in the playoffs to huge crowds. Oscar Hanson couldn't work his magic this time though, as St. Paul, which was led by Jack, Saunders, Carrigan, Connelly, Virgil Johnson and LoPresti, swept their neighbors in three straight. The Saints didn't stop there, going on to whip the upstart Omaha franchise (which had upset St. Louis in the other playoff match), three games to one, to win their only playoff championship in the history of the AHA.

The Millers and Saints finished tied for third in 1940-41, with records of 25-23. St. Paul lost three games to one to the Flyers, while Minneapolis, which was led by Tustin's 50 points that season, lost in an extremely close and controversial three games to two thriller to Kansas City. St. Louis then beat up Kansas City to win the league crown. That year a Minneapolis radio announcer and sports official named George Higgins took over the reigns as league president. In addition, that spring the league introduced its first all-star game. Held in St. Louis, the game drew more than 9,000 to the star-studded affair – a huge accomplishment at the time.

By 1941 the United States was mired in politics and the threat of war was fast becoming a reality. The league pressed on that year though in what would ultimately be its last. Dallas and Fort Worth both joined the league for its final season of 1941-42. The league opted to divide up into two divisions that year, the Northern and the Southern. The Northern featured St. Paul, Minneapolis, St. Louis, and Omaha, while the Southern consisted Kansas City, Tulsa, Fort Worth and Dallas. St. Paul finished second with a 28-17-5 record, while the Millers ended their season in the cellar at 22-25-3. The Saints advanced to the Northern playoffs, where they were then swept in two straight by Omaha. Kansas City advanced to the finals where they blitzed Omaha in three straight to win the last ever AHA championship. For the young men who clashed so hard on the ice, it was now off to Europe and the Pacific to fight in a real battle, World War II.

For 16 years the AHA proved to be a solid league which greatly helped advance the hockey prowess of countless Minnesotans, who were able to play big-time hockey throughout the country. At one time or another, 14 different cities held franchises in the circuit including: St. Paul, Minneapolis, Duluth, Winnipeg, Chicago, Kansas City, Tulsa, St. Louis, Buffalo, Wichita, Oklahoma City, Omaha, Dallas and Fort Worth. Because of this, there were as many American-born pro players in the 1920s and 1930s as there were at any time until the 1980s. Countless star players such as Doc Romnes and Cully Dahlstrom would likely never have had the opportunity to play in the NHL without first getting their chance in the AHA.

More than 50 different Minnesota players competed in the AHA during its 16 year history as well. Players from Eveleth included: Tom and Mike Karakas, Alex McInnes, Paul Schaeffer, Milt Brink, Andy Toth, Joe Papike, Hodge Johnson, Peter Pleban, Joe Kucler, Rudy Ahlin, Art Erickson, Mike Kasher, Oscar Almquist, John Phillips, Sam Lo Presti, John and Tony Prelesnik, Glee Jagunich and Billy De Paul. Minneapolitans included: Oscar, Emil and Emory Hanson, Manny Cotlow, Virgil Johnson, Don Olson, Phil Perkins, Burr Williams, Bill McGlone, Cully Dahlstrom, Ted Breckheimer, Bill Oddson, Jack Flood and Hub Nelson. St. Paulites included: George and Tony Conroy, Doc Romnes, George Nichols, Bob McCoy Beef Munson, Emy Garrett, Julie Matscke, Bill Galligan and Bob Graiziger. Hibbing furnished Bill

Bobby Dill

Bobby Dill starred for Cretin High School in the 1930s and went on to become one of Minnesota's best ever. In 1944, after playing in the minors, Dill was called up by the NHL's New York Rangers. One of the toughest men ever to lace em' up, Dill was the nephew of former prize fighter, Mike Gibbons. During the late 1940s and early '50s Dill played for the St. Paul Saints, where he and John Mariucci used to mix it up on more than one occasion. Dill later worked as a scout for the North Stars, and was inducted into the U.S. Hockey Hall of Fame in 1979.

Mickelich, Bob Blake and Joe Bretto while Nobby Clark, Iver Anderson and Gus Olson hailed from Duluth. Moose Goheen, Pat Shea and Doc Romnes came from White Bear Lake, while Don Anderson who played for St. Paul called Lindstrom his home. Amazingly, only five other Americans played in the league: Curley Kohlman, Muzz Murray and Vic Des Jardins came from Upper Michigan while Fido Purpur was born and reared in Grand Forks, and Bob Nilan called Philadelphia home.

The United States Hockey League (1945-51)...

When the war was over in the mid-1940s, countless men were anxious to get back on the ice. So, in its first season of 1945-46, the AHA resumed playing under the new name of the United States Hockey League with the following teams: Minneapolis Millers, St. Paul Saints, Kansas City Pla-Mors, Omaha Knights, Tulsa Oilers, Fort Worth Rangers and Dallas Texans. Kansas City finished on top of the USHL standings during that first year with a record of 35-17-4. The Saints came in thrid at 28-26-2, while the Millers brought up the cellar at 20-33-3.

Over the next couple of seasons teams from Louisville, Milwaukee, Houston, and Denver would join the USHL. The league was a viable professional outlet for players both on their way up the ladder and also for those on their way down. Hockey fans in many of the cities now had the opportunity to enjoy a quality brand of hockey at an affordable price, all while receiving an education about this new sport which was foreign to them. In 1945 the International Hockey League was also organized as an outgrowth of the Windsor City Senior League near Detroit. The "I" as it is known, was, and still remains today as one of the top

Virgil Johnson

Virgil Johnson starred on the ice as well as on the gridiron as a quarterback at Minneapolis South High School. Johnson was a member of the St. Paul Saints prior to making his NHL debut with the Chicago Blackhawks in 1938, the same year they went on to win the Stanley Cup. Johnson played with the Hawks until 1946, then spent several years with Minneapolis in the USHL, and then with the Minneapolis Jerseys and St. Paul Saints of the AAHL.

Cully Dahlstrom

Cully Dahlstrom played high school hockey at Minneapolis South and then went on to play for both the Minneapolis Millers and St. Paul Saints in the American Hockey Association. He won the Calder Trophy as the NHL's rookie of the year 1937-38 as a member of the Chicago Blackhawks and played a big role in leading the team to the Stanley Cup championship that year. He would play for a total of seven seasons in the NHL, all with Chicago, from 1937-45.

professional leagues in all of hockey with teams in both the U.S. and Canada.

The USHL divided into two divisions from 1946-49 with both St. Paul and Minneapolis playing in the Northern Division. The league, which was very popular, lasted in Minnesota until 1951. The Millers dropped out in 1950, and the Saints followed suit after that next season. (The USHL would reemerge in the state several years later with a group of new teams.) The Millers' best season came in 1947-48 when the squad went 34-36-6, while St. Paul's best year was in 1948-49, when they finished 36-20-10.

During those years the Saints were led by dozens and dozens of great players, among them was the legendary Bobby Dill, who, from 1945-50 scored 163 points, while racking up an amazing 567 penalty minutes. Hall of Famers John Mariucci and Gump Worsley also played on the team from 1950-51, and Gus Schwartz wound up as the team's all-time leading scorer with 238 points. Others who made major contributions included Lloyd Ailsby, Harry Bell, Lin Bend, Harold Brown, Armand Delmonte, Joe Levandoski, Ian MacIntosh, Jack McGill, Mitch Pechet, Cliff "Fido" Purpur, Gino Rozzini, Alex Sandalack and Joe Shack.

The Millers were blessed with the talents of several greats as well, including John Mariucci (who played from 1949-50), Virgil Johnson (1945-47), and Tom Karakas, who played in 1947-48. Others who made major contributions included: George Agar, Earl Bartholome, Tom Forgie, Ian Fraser, Wally Hergesheimer, Carl Kaiser, Harry McQueston, Walter Melnyk, Billy Richardson, Gordon Sherritt, Stanford Smith, Art Strobel and Nick Tomiuk.

The Western & Central Leagues...

After a pretty lengthy absence, professional hockey finally returned to Minnesota in 1957. That year St. Paul formed a combined team with Saskatoon in the professional Western Hockey League. The St. Paul/Saskatoon Regals, as they were known, posted a 25-45-0 record during the 1957-58 season. The league lasted just one year. Some of the players who starred on this "international" team included: Ken Yackel, Doug Bentley, Bob Chrystal, Les Colwill, Gerry Couture, Lucien Dechene, Robert Kabel, Vic Lynn, Reginald Primeau, Don Raleigh, Ray Ross and Lyle Willey.

The next year the Minneapolis Millers and Rochester Mustangs played in the "on again - off again" Central Hockey League, then a senior professional circuit. It lasted only a season before folding.

The International Hockey League (1959-63)...

Big-time pro hockey came back for good in 1959 when the St. Paul Saints joined the upstart International Hockey League. Later that season, the Denver Mavericks moved their struggling franchise

to the Twin Cities, where they became the "new" Minneapolis Millers. Both teams played in the IHL's Western Division. The IHL featured many of the same cities from the former USHL, in addition to several more from out East. The league played a vital role in advancing the game throughout the country, and offered a quality brand of hockey to many areas that weren't yet familiar with the game.

During that first season of 1959-60, the Saints posted a league-best 41-21-6 record. St. Paul then cruised through the playoffs by beating among others, Minneapolis, which had finished the year with a very modest 39-27-2 record. The Saints kept on rolling and won the coveted Turner Cup, given annually to the league's playoff champion. That next year Minneapolis posted a whopping 50-20-2 record, only to get beat again by the defending champion Saints, who went 46-22-4. St. Paul cruised to the finals, this time defeating Muskegon four games to one, for their second consecutive Turner Cup.

In 1961-62 the Millers went 41-26-1, while the Saints finished at 42-25-1. Both were eliminated in the playoffs. The next season Minneapolis went 36-32-2, finishing just one point behind Fort Wayne, while St. Paul slumped all the way down to sixth place. The Millers went on to beat Omaha in a tough seven-game semifinal contest, only to lose to Fort Wayne in the finals. That would prove to be the last season for the IHL in Minnesota, as both the Millers and Saints dropped out of the league that following season.

The IHL provided a lot of excitement for Minnesota fans during this era, and many great players came through the league throughout its existence. For the Saints, many of those players included: Elliot Chorley, (the team's leading scored with 242 points in 215 games), John Mayasich, John Bailey, Dick Bouchard, Fred Brown, Rich Brown, Nelson Bullock, Jean Denis, Brian Derrett, Dick Dougherty, Ted Hodgson, Howie Hughes, Mickey Keating, Aggie Kukulowicz, Wayne Larkin, Joe Lund, Jacques Marcotte, Paul Masnick, Bud McRae, Art Miller, Reg Morelli, Danny Summers, and Gilles Thibeault.

For the Millers, those players included: Ken Yackel (the team's leading scorer with 312 points in 208 games), Dick Meredith, Ed Bartoli, Bob Currie, Larry Hale, Paul Johnson, Marv Jorde, Aggie Kukulowicz, Guy LaFrance, Laurie Langrell, Bruce Lea, Bill LeCaine, Dennis Maroney, Murray Massier, Bud McRae, Jerry Melynchuk, Ray Mikulan, Harry Ottenbriet, Ed Pollesel, Joe Poole, Billy Reichart, Ken Saunders, Jack Turner, and Cy Whiteside.

The Central Professional League...

In July of 1963, with the slogan: "The Fastest Version of the World's Fastest Game!", the Central Professional Hockey League was formed. It would also be the final stop for both the Saints and Millers, as they would each be transformed into minor league affiliates of the then six-team National Hockey League. The Millers became the upstart Minneapolis Bruins, whose parent club was the Boston Bruins, while the Saints would become the St. Paul Rangers, whose parent club was the New York Rangers. The CPHL featured five teams that first season, the three others included: the Omaha Knights (minor league affiliate of the Montreal Canadiens), St. Louis Braves (minor league affiliate of the Chicago Blackhawks), and the Cincinnati Wings (minor league affiliate of the Detroit Red Wings). Formed as a developmental league for younger players who needed more ice-time and game experience before embarking on a career in the NHL, the CPHL was just one step removed from hockey's elite. The league rules stated that each team's roster had to be made up of 10 players under 23 years of age, five could be over 23, while the goaltender could be any age. So, with all of that youth came speed — and that's what the fans of the CPHL got.

The Bruins played their home games in the Minneapolis Arena which had a 5,000 seating capacity. The club was owned jointly by both the Boston Bruins and three local Minneapolis businessmen: Walter Bush, Jr., attorney, Robert J. McNulty, contractor, and Gordon Ritz, a Time-Life executive. The general manager was Wren Blair, while Harry Sinden served as the team's first player-coach.

The St. Paul Rangers played in both the St. Paul Auditorium, which had a more than 6,000 seating capacity, as well as at Aldrich Arena. The Rangers were headed by George Cobb, of Brown & Bigelow. Jake Milford was brought in to serve as the team's general manager, while Fred Shero, who formerly coached the then IHL St. Paul Saints for four years, was brought back to serve as the team's first coach.

The first season of 1963-64 saw both the Rangers and Bruins playing to packed houses as the fans immediately took to this high calibre of play. The Rangers finished second behind Omaha with a 38-30-4 record, while Minneapolis placed third at 36-29-7. Omaha then defeated Minneapolis in the semifinals, and went on to face the Rangers in the finals. There, the Knights beat St. Paul in the best-of-seven series to win the inaugural Jack Adams Cup. St. Paul also featured two all-stars that season — goaltender Marcel Pelletier and defenseman Bob Woytowich.

In 1964-65 the league increased to six teams, with the newest member being the Tulsa Ice Oilers (minor league affiliate of the Toronto Maple Leafs). In addition, the Cincinnati franchise moved to Tennessee, where they became known as the Memphis Wings. Dressed in their gold, black, and white jerseys, the Bruins finished 36-29-7 in 1964-65. Their crosstown rival Rangers, dressed in their patriotic red, white and blue sweaters, finished at 41-23-6, good enough for first place in the regular season. The Bruins, who finished third during the regular season, wound up losing in the semifinals. The Rangers, on the other hand, went on to win the CPHL Championship. Both squads featured all-stars that year. Minneapolis had future North Star goalie Cesare Maniago, while St. Paul had the speedy right-winger Marc Dufour.

1965 would prove to be the last year of operation for the Minneapolis Bruins, as they packed up and moved their operation to Oklahoma City, where they became known as the Oklahoma City "Blazers." With St. Paul left as the only club in town, the team decided to changed its name to the "Minnesota Rangers" in order to unify the Twin Cities' hockey faithful. It worked, because that year the team went 34-25-11, finishing first in the regular season standings. In April of 1966, more than 6,000 fans jammed into the Saint Paul Auditorium to watch the Rangers battle the Tulsa Oilers in the playoff semifinals. Unfortunately, Minnesota lost in a heartbreaking seven game thriller. Tulsa then went on to lose to the former Bruins team, the Oklahoma City Blazers, made up primarily of the Minneapolis club from the year before, who went on to win the Adams Cup championship in their first season.

The Rangers attracted more than 130,000 fans during that season, the highest attendance in the Twin Cities since the league's inception. The team also placed three players on the CPHL all-star team that season: Paul Andrea, Al Lebrun and goaltender Wayne Rutledge.

However, that would also be the last season for the CPHL in Minnesota. With the Met Center Arena under construction for the NHL's expansion Minnesota North Stars, which were hitting the ice that following year, the Rangers decided not to return to the league for the 1966-67 season. The club was then relocated to Omaha, which had lost its franchise the year before to Houston. (Incidentally, after playing in 25 cities in 17 different states for some 21 seasons, the league disbanded in 1984.)

There were countless stars who played for both the Bruins and Rangers over the years. Among the Bruins stars were: Don Awrey, Ed Bartoli, Terry Crisp, Gary Dornhoefer, Jean Gilbert, John Gravel, Brenton Hughes, Ted Irvine, Bill Knibbs, Skip Krake, Mike Mahoney, Cesare Maniago, Wayne Maxner, Gerry Ouellette, Pete Panagabko, J.P. Parise, Wayne Schultz, Harry Sinden, Ken Stephanson and Joe Watson.

Among the Rangers stars were: Paul Andrea, Bob Ash, Terry Ball, Ron Boehm, John Brenneman, Bill Collins, Bob Cunningham, Buzz Deschamps, Marc Dufour, Trevor Fahey, Sandy Fitzpatrick, Wayne Hall, Howie Hughes, Jim Johnson, George Konik, Al LeBrun, Dave McComb, Mike McMahon, Larry Mickey, Jim Mikol, Wayne Muloin, Mel Pearson, Bob Plager, Tracy Pratt, Barrie Ross, Gary Sabourin, Bob Stoyko, Ted Taylor, Bob Woytowich, Marcel Pelletier, and Wayne Rutledge.

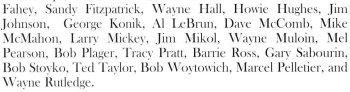

The 1962 Minneapolis Millers

The U.S. Hockey League...

Another league that arrived on the scene about this time was the "revived" USHL, which began in 1961 and lasted in Minnesota until 1970. This league, different from the one which ended in 1951, was a senior semi-pro circuit that featured several Minnesota teams, including the Rochester Mustangs (1961-70), Minneapolis Rebels (1961-62) St. Paul Steers (1962-65), and later the Minnesota Nationals (1967-68) and Duluth Port Stars (1968-69). Other teams in the league would include the Green Bay Bobcats, Des Moines Oak Leafs, Milwaukee Metros, and Waterloo Black Hawks. Teams in the league typi-

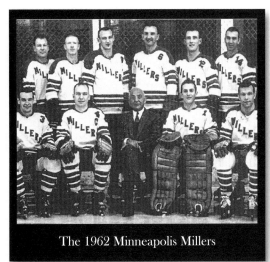

CHRISTIAN BROTHERS HOCKEY STICKS

Bill Christian, Hal Bakke
and Roger Christian

Billy and Roger Christian grew up as most kids did on Warroad's south-side, playing hockey on the river. The pair would go on to make up the "brothers" part of Christian Brothers, Inc., at one point, one of the world's largest manufacturers of hockey sticks and equipment. Today, the brothers only help to add to the mystique of the tiny town of Warroad, which lies on the shores of Lake of the Woods on the Canadian border, and is known by most simply as "Hockey Town, U.S.A."

Billy and Roger led the Warroad Warriors the 1953 State High School Hockey Tournament, where they finished runner's up to the St. Paul Johnson Governors. That team was coached by the legendary Cal Marvin. Both graduated from high school in 1956, and both played for Warroad's amateur Lakers senior team as well. They then earned spots on the U.S. National team, also coached by Marvin. That team was the first to play behind the Iron Curtain, playing both in Moscow and Prague, ultimately finishing fifth in the World Tournament, in Oslo. (Their other brother, Gordon, had played on the 56' Olympic team that won a silver medal in Cortina, Italy.) After that, the brothers returned to Warroad to work with their father as carpenters. The next year, Roger skated for the Warroad Lakers, while Bill played on the University of Minnesota freshman team.

Both brothers made the 1960 U.S. Olympic team that won a gold medal in Squaw Valley, Calif. In that fabled tournament, Billy scored the tieing and winning goals in the 3-2 pivotal win over the Russians. Roger and Duluth's Tommy Williams were his linemates. Roger also had a four-goal game against the Czech's, in what may have been the most memorable contest of the Winter Games. With the U.S. down 4-3 going into the third, Roger scored a hat-trick in the final period to ice the game and give the team the gold medal. The two brothers continued to play on U.S. National teams and again made the 1964 Olympic squad in Innsbruck, Austria.

With the family's construction business prospering, Roger's brother-in-law, Hal Bakke (they're married to twin sisters), came up with a business proposition for the two brothers to manufacture hockey sticks. The idea sounded good, so they dove right in. The three of them started their company at the old creamery in Warroad. With no money, they scraped to get by, all the time working like dogs to get the company off the ground. Then, in the 1965 World Tournament in Finland, which was coached by former Gopher Ken Yackel, and managed by Cal Marvin, the brothers got to show off their custom-made sticks to their teammates. They got a lot of great feedback, reinforcing the belief that their idea was a good one.

Meanwhile, back in Hockey Town, they continued to work nights and weekends, with little or no pay for several years, hoping to catch a break. Then, in 1969, after deciding to raise capital by selling stock in their company, they constructed a new manufacturing facility along Highway 11 that would allow them to ramp-up and become a profitable corporation. When the company started in 1964, Northland Hockey Sticks was their main U.S. competitor, while CCM, in Canada, got out of the stick business shortly thereafter. A merger soon followed.

"We were basically copying the Northland Stick," said Bakke. "We even toured their plant, and I think they were sorry they ever allowed us to do that. But little did we know then that we would end up owning Northland."

The company would go on to become one of the preeminent equipment manufacturers in the world, with hundreds of NHL players using their sticks over the ensuing years. Even players who were paid to endorse other competitors still remained loyal. Such was the case with Brett Hull, who endorsed Easton stick shafts, but refused to use it with anything other than a Christian Bros. replacement blade. With their trademarked Diamond Design stick blades, Christian Brothers sticks were among the best in the world. Eventualy, in 2004, the company was sold to a Denver-based manufacturer of sporting goods.

The Christian name synonymous with hockey in Minnesota. Billy and Roger (along with Cal Marvin), have all been inducted into the U.S. Hockey Hall of Fame in Eveleth. In addition, Bill's son Dave, who skated for two years at the University of North Dakota, was also inducted into the Hall of Fame. Dave made history when he won gold as a member of the 1980 U.S. Olympic Hockey team, and then went on to play for 14 years in the NHL — becoming one of the highest scoring American born players in league history. The entire family wreaks of hockey tradition and has certainly made Minnesota proud.

cally played a 30-35 game schedule against one-another.

One of the most influential founders of the league was Walter Bush. For some 15 years the league served as a feeder system for the U.S. National and Olympic teams. It was considered by many to be the first real attempt at a major senior hockey league which was built primarily for the advancement of Americans. The USHL quickly evolved into a very high calibre league for graduates of major U.S. college hockey programs from around the country, particularly those from Minnesota. This was important because back then there were not a lot of opportunities for American college kids to have a chance to play professional hockey. That's because in those days both the minor and major leagues still had less than 20 teams. To put that in perspective, from the period of 1951 to 1961 there were no Americans developed in the NHL. (Duluth's Tommy Williams signed with Boston in 1961.) As a result, the league became a haven for young U.S. players who were leaving college and were aspiring to make it on a U.S. National or Olympic team. For players such as John Mayasich, arguably the greatest Gopher ever to wear the Maroon and Gold, this league became a wonderful opportunity for him to not only play semi-professionally, but also to represent his country at the National and Olympic levels.

The league also served as a sort of collegiate minor league as well. Take Murray Williamson for example. Then a Gopher freshman in 1955, he played in the league because freshmen were ineligible for NCAA competition. His experience in the USHL helped him hone his skills, which ultimately led him to become an All-American by his senior year at Minnesota. Urged by Walter Bush, Murray later became player/coach of the USHL's St. Paul Steers in 1962, and that next year assumed ownership of the team. Under his tutelage, that Steers club became such a power in the league that by 1965 the team was converted into the U.S. National team. (Murray, the youngest man to ever coach a U.S. Olympic hockey squad, would become an icon in the world of U.S. National and Olympic coaching, leading the 1972 Olympic team to the Silver medal in Sapporo, Japan.)

The team probably the most synonymous with the old USHL would have to be the Rochester Mustangs, which won the league title during that first 1961-62 season with a 19-6-0 record. The Mustangs would play hockey in Rochester in one form or another for nearly a half century. An organization rich in tradition, they got their start in the 1950's as a senior team in the

American Amateur Hockey League (AAHL), and then played in the old Central Hockey League (CHL) from 1952-60. Then, from 1961-70 the team played in the USHL. The USHL later converted over to an all-junior circuit in the late 1970s (21-and-under), and remains that way to this day.

The Mustangs used to play at Rochester's old Mayo Civic Auditorium, infamous for being such a short sheet of ice that the players used to claim that the blue lines almost overlapped! Among the players who starred for the Mustangs over the years included: Herb Brooks, Lou Nanne, Bob Fleming, Ken Johannson, Bill Reichert, Gene Campbell, Craig Falkman, Gary Gambucci, Len Lilyholm, Oscar Mahle, Gary Schmalzbauer, Larry Stordahl, Murray Williamson, Tom Yurkovich, and of course, No. 9 — Arley Carlson.

Among the players who starred on some of the other teams in the league included: former Gopher's Larry Alm, Dick Burg and Dick Meredith, who played for the Rebels; Larry Alm, Herb Brooks, Dick Burg, Marv Jorde, Bill Masterton, Jerry Melynchuk, Wayne Meredith, and Murray Williamson, who played with the Steers; and Doug Woog, Jerry Melynchuk and Jack Dale, who played for the Nationals.

SENIOR HOCKEY IN MINNESOTA

Men's senior leagues have been around in one form or another since the turn of the century, and have played a vital role in the development of amateur hockey throughout Minnesota. By the 1920s, there were countless men's senior hockey circuits which had sprouted up throughout the state. Corporations big and small began sponsoring teams. Some even went as far as to recruit "ringers" in their pursuit of state-wide braggin' rights. This often-times meant that good hockey players could now get high paying jobs with companies that they never would have dreamed of working at previously.

By 1920 municipal hockey in Minneapolis fell under the jurisdiction of the Recreation Department of the Board of Park Commissioners. They established and maintained some two dozen skating rinks in the city (in addition to providing hockey rinks at Logan Park, North Commons, Lake of the Isles and Powderhorn Park), and made sure that there were warming houses at each of them for the skaters and spectators alike to stay out of the cold.

According to W.W. Fox, the Director of Municipal Athletics at the time, that year was one of the most memorable ever for the sport of hockey in the Mill City. Some 20 teams representing social and community center interests from all areas of Minneapolis were divided into both Senior and Junior Divisions, I & II, with little difference in playing strength between them. The teams competed for the "Struck" trophy, which was awarded annual to the winners.

In the Junior I Division the Logan Parks, Stewart A.C. and Powderhorn Parks competed against the Lagoons, Camden Juniors and Maple

The 1924 Virginia senior team

Hills. The Logan Parks won the championship from Stewart A.C. While the Junior II Division featured four teams, including the Deephavens, Raccoons, Heatherdale A.C. and the Ascensions. The Raccoons won the championship over the Ascensions in the final game. The Senior Division, on the other hand, featured several teams including the Vertex, Camden Seniors, Midway Merchants, East Side A.C., Lake Hennepin Merchants, North Commons and ABC. At season's end the Camden Seniors and Vertex were tied, so the two paired off for a playoff game which was played at Logan Park. There, in sub-zero temperatures, the contest went into extra periods and ultimately, because of the cold, finished as a draw. They met again that next Sunday, and this time the Vertex won the senior championship. The stage was set for the city championship between the aggressive Logan Parks, dual champions of Divisions I and II Junior, and the savvy veteran Vertex seven, champions of the Senior Division. The championship game was then played at the Logan Park rink with the Vertex capturing their fourth consecutive city title.

In the early 1920s there were eight teams which comprised the top St. Paul Senior League, they included: The Bilboas (a former junior team which won six straight league titles from 1916-1921), Tuxedos, Masters, St. Frances, Chinooks, Hook-Em-Cows, White Bear Legion and Phoenix. Among the other prominent Senior teams operating in St. Paul during the 1920's were: Armours, Sheriff Wegeners, Minnesota Mining, Fire and Marine, Van Guards, Gas Lites, Kennedy Arms, Northern Pacific, Palace, Hazel Park, Zimmerman, Sylvan and Fort Snelling.

In 1926, under the direction of both W.W. Fox of Minneapolis and Ernest Johnson of St. Paul, both city recreation department heads, the Minnesota Recreation Hockey Association was formed to create a statewide association which would promote hockey. The group elected Hibbing's George Ward to serve as president, and as their primary purpose they decided to hold the state's first ever senior (adult) hockey tournament.

U.S. Senior Champs	
1932	Genoa
1949	St. Paul
1951	Crookston Pirates
1952	Hibbing
1957	Minneapolis
1958	Rochester
1964	St. Louis Park
1966	St. Louis Park
1986	Minneapolis
1988	St. Paul
1989	St. Paul
1995	Minneapolis Bucks
1997	Minneapolis Green Mill

U.S. Senior Elites	
1986	Minneapolis Bucks
1987	Bloomington
1989	Bloomington
1997	Minneapolis Bucks

The tournament quickly grew in popularity and became every senior team's goal. The following year, in 1927, the four-team tournament was held at the Hippodrome, where the Minneapolis Buzzas defeated Nashwauk and the Duluth Aces for the State Recreation crown. In 1928, at Hibbing, the Minneapolis Buzzas lost to the Duluth Gateleys, the eventual champions, 4-3, in overtime in the first round of competition. The Minnesota Hockey Association continued to stage Senior state tournaments until the early 1930's. Ultimately, however, outside of holding annual state tournaments, the association did little to promote the youth game or

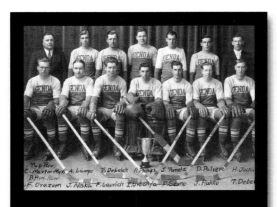

The 1934 Genoa national senior champs

extend the growth and popularity of the game in those areas of the state where the game was not being played.

By the end of the decade, senior leagues were sprouting up all over the state. In the late 1920s the Southern Minnesota League was formed with teams from Winona, North Mankato, Faribault and Owatonna. Over the next several years other teams such as Rochester, Northfield, Albert Lea, Austin, Red Wing, Kenyon, Marshall, Cottonwood, Worthington, Wabasha, Winona, Eden Valley, Cokato, Watkins, and Paynesville also played in the circuit. The league, which briefly disbanded for WWII, operated until the 1960s. The person who is credited with not only founding the league, but also for operating it diligently through the years, was legendary hockey historian, Don Clark, of Faribault. Another new senior league during this era was the Academy League, which was formed with teams from St. Paul Academy, Blake, St. Thomas, Cretin, and Shattuck of Faribault. (In addition, one of the stronger senior teams during this era was the American Legion Post in White Bear Lake, which lost only one game from 1927-29. They fared well against the very tough University of Minnesota squads as well.)

By the 1930s senior hockey was growing very rapidly throughout the state. Times were tough during the Great Depression, only fueling the popularity of the leagues, which proved to be an inexpensive form of entertainment for the fans. The advent of professional hockey in the area coupled with the construction of the Minneapolis Arena, all contributed to the growth of the sport in Minneapolis. Among the leading teams and programs during the period which played in the Minneapolis Arena League included: Logan Park, Vertex, Raccoons, Deephavens, Foshays, Buzzas, Federals, Flour-City, Lake Lyndale, Wheaties, Daytons, Munsingwear, Ewalds, Jerseys, Bankers, Aces, Ascensions, Americans, Midways, North Commons, Camden, Powderhorns, Norse, Vikings, Mitby-Sather, Pershing, Red Squirrels, Nolans, East Side, Cedar-Lake, Chicago-Lake, First National Bank and St. Lawrence.

Meanwhile, in St. Paul, the Recreation Dept. was operating a vast array of junior and senior hockey programs for players of all ages with scores of lighted outdoor rinks being maintained for their use. And just as the Mill City had their "Minneapolis Arena League," St. Paul too had its "Auditorium League," which featured the following: Fire and Marine, Wards, Midland Hills, Minnesota Mining, Fort Snelling and Barnes Cafe. Among the leading players in the circuit were brothers Howie, Al and Wylie Van, James Fletcher, Bill Toenjes, Lowell Booten, Bob McCabe, Al Trieble, Milo Gabriel, Don King, Bob Bates, Bob Meyers, Bobby Dill, Ray and Roy Schartin, Bill Galligan, Frank and Bill Haider.

From 1930 through 1940 the Minneapolis Recreation Department

The Roseau Cloverleafs

One of the more storied senior amateur teams in the state was the Roseau Cloverleafs, which, through the years participated in several Senior circuits, including the States-Dominion League and also the Canadian-American Border League of the 1930s and '40s (which included: Rainy River, Fort Francis, International Falls, Grand Forks Dragons, Hallock, Winnipeg Aces, Emerson, Fosston Chevrolets, Gretna, Mahnomen, Detroit Lakes, Fargo-Moorhead, Alvarado, Red Lake Falls, and the Fort Snelling Black & Tans). Years later, in 1978, the Cloverleafs won the Minnesota State Amateur Hockey Association championship under the direction of long-time skipper, Cap Nelson. The team disbanded in the early 1980s.

The 1940 St. Paul 7-Ups senior team

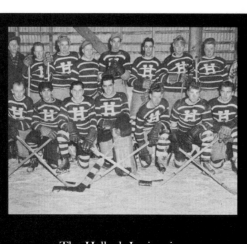

The Hallock Legionaires
played in the States Dominion League

sponsored the Northwest State AAU Hockey Tournament, a popular event which determined the outright champion from all the intermediate and senior winners throughout the Northwest. As many as 26 teams in two divisions participated in the annual tournament, which lasted for nearly a week. From 1936-37, the Wheaties and Jerseys, Minneapolis League teams, won the State AAU championships. From 1938-39 the Red Squirrels and Barnes Cafe, of the St. Paul Auditorium League, won the title.

Dozens and dozens of former Twin Cities high schoolers, as well as former University of Minnesota players, who had not turned professional, played in this popular indoor league. To put things into perspective as far as hockey growth during this era, there were some 435 teams, with nearly 6,000 players participating in Minneapolis Recreation Department hockey leagues by 1935. This was without a doubt the largest hockey program in the country and compared favorably in numbers with those in Canada's largest cities.

Senior programs were strong in northern Minnesota during this period as well. The Senior City League, which featured teams from Taconite, Virginia, Grand Rapids, and Duluth, was dominated by the Taconite Hornets, which had won five straight City League titles throughout the mid-1930s. (Several high schools played in this league as well, including: Two Harbors and Duluth Central.) Several northern Senior teams played big time hockey against some extremely good competition too, including the University of Minnesota — and often times won. These teams included: the Duluth Zephyrs, a very popular team that played to sell-out crowds at the Duluth Amphetheatre, M. Cooke & Sons, Superior Curling, Docks, Car Shop, Bullard Mills, M.P. Goodfellowship, Hibbing Veterans and others. One of the strongest teams of this era was the Eveleth Cubs, which dominated the senior circuit, winning six straight State Senior titles from 1929-35.

By the 1940s the Senior teams were also playing a vital role in the advancement of the sport at college and university levels. Because schools were limited in budgets, the fact that they could play these teams, who were loaded with older and more talented players, helped them to get better against their regular competitors. During this era, the University of Minnesota was playing against several senior teams including: Fort Snelling, Honeywell, Bermans, and the Park League All-Stars. Up north the University of Minnesota-Duluth was playing the West End Civic Club, Taconite Hornets, Warroad Lakers, and the Minneapolis Bungalows. Meanwhile, Bemidji State was playing against such teams as the Grand Rapids Raiders, Rainy River Legion, Bemidji Independents, Detroit Lakes Rangers,

International Falls, Crookston City, and Thief River Falls VFW. In addition, they also played against some of the local colleges and universities as well.

The American Amateur Hockey League (AAHL), another popular and successful Senior league, was formed in June of 1947 with the following charter member teams: Rochester Mustangs, Minneapolis Bermans, Minneapolis Jerseys, St. Paul Tally's, St. Paul Koppys, and White Bear 7-Ups. (Over the years the circuit expanded into neighboring states as well as into Canada before eventually becoming the semi-pro United States Hockey League in the early 1960s.)

The Advent of MAHA Fuels the Growth of Senior Hockey...

During this era, the Amateur Athletic Union (AAU) was solely conducting state and district Senior tournaments. In hockey circles, it was thought that the organization was failing to adequately promote the sport throughout the state, or even the country for that matter, in the manner that the hockey community was demanding. It was felt that what hockey needed at that time was a statewide organization that, in addition to conducting tournaments, would encourage, promote and improve the standard of play at all age levels throughout the state. So, in 1947, Robert Ridder, a native New Yorker who was associated with the Duluth Herald team, of the Duluth Industrial Hockey League during the early 1940's, got the ball rolling. Ridder, then a radio and newspaper executive, was well-suited to the task of forming a statewide amateur hockey association. An organization soon materialized in affiliation with the Amateur Hockey Association of the U.S. (AHAUS), the Minnesota Amateur Hockey Association, or MAHA.

The main activity of MAHA during its first year of operation was to conduct a state Senior tournament, the winner of which would represent the state at the AHAUS National tournament. So, in March of 1948, the seven best Minnesota Senior teams, one from each league in the state qualified and met at the St. Paul Auditorium to settle the score. Those leagues included: American Amateur, States-Dominion, Southern Minnesota, Arrowhead, St. Croix Valley, Twin City Suburban and St. Cloud Municipal. (Eight other Senior circuits operating in St. Paul, Minneapolis, Duluth and Hibbing did not join MAHA in its initial season of operation, and therefore did not compete.) In the tournament, Grand Forks, of the States-Dominion League, beat both Eveleth and the St. Paul 7-Ups to win the Class A championship, while North Mankato, of the Southern Minnesota League, beat St. Cloud and Frederic to win the Class B title. St.

The 1951 National Senior Champion Crookston Pirates

The 1938 Schmidt's Beer City Champion senior team

Paul 7-Up and Grand Forks then went on to play in the 1948 AHAUS National Senior U.S. Championship in Toledo, Ohio. There, in the first round of the four-team event, Grand Forks lost to Providence, R.I., 3-2, while St. Paul defeated Berlin, N.H., 7-2. Providence beat St. Paul in the finals, however, 3-2.

By the 1950s MAHA was in full swing, and senior hockey was as popular as ever. Minnesota was leading the way nationally and bringing home the hardware to prove it. The Crookston Pirates, led by Cal Marvin, Serge Gambucci and Pat Finnegan, defeated the New York Mets in 1951 to win the National Senior crown, while the Hibbing Flyers won the 1952 National Senior title that very next year.

One by one, new indoor rinks were being built throughout the state every year. More and more new senior leagues were popping up during this era as well. One in particular was the "international" Thunder Bay Senior League, which consisted of five teams: Eveleth Rangers, Hibbing, Fort William, Fort Frances and Port Arthur. Duluth promoter Len Naymark was influential in starting the league, which was essentially a semi-pro circuit featuring good young junior players combined with experienced veterans. Naymark would entice junior players to come play for him in return for scholarships at Eveleth Junior College. One such player who took him up on his offer was future Gopher and Olympic coach, Murray Williamson, who played for the Eveleth Rangers in 1954. The league offered a rough, entertaining brand of hockey for its Iron Range fans. However, in 1955, after only one season, the league folded due to financial problems.

Senior hockey went through its shares of ups and downs through the 1960s, '70s and '80s. However, the one fixture through that entire time was Cal Marvin's Warroad Lakers, which have been such an institution, that there is an entire chapter dedicated to them. The dominant Senior team of the 1980s and 1990s, however, is without question Minneapolis-based, Buck's Furniture. The elite team has been the home of countless former Division I and even pro players for years. Local icon Roger Buck has owned and operated the team for more than 30 years. The team won its first national senior championship in 1984, in Fairbanks, Alaska, and would go on to win a dozen more over the ensuing years, making them a true senior hockey dynasty. Among the stars of the team is Buck's living legend, Rodger Moy, who played for nearly a quarter century, winning no less than 13 adult elite national championships along the way.

The American Hockey Association

Another Senior Amateur league called the American Hockey Association (AHA), popped up in the early 90s. The circuit, which included the Minnesota Iron Rangers, Fargo-Moorhead Express, and even a reincarnation of the St. Paul Fighting Saints, played throughout the Midwest. Incidentally, the Saints, which finished with a 21-5-0 record in 1992-93, were led by several former Gopher stars, including: Grant Bischoff (who scored an amazing 69 points in 29 games), Jason Miller, Larry Olimb and Lance Werness.

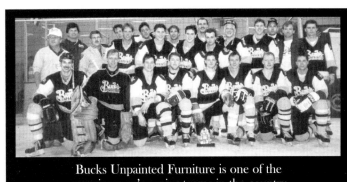

Bucks Unpainted Furniture is one of the premier men's senior teams in the country

CAL MARVIN'S WARROAD LAKERS

One of the biggest reasons why Warroad has been dubbed "Hockeytown, U.S.A.," is due in large part to the efforts of one man, Cal Marvin, and his passion for the game of hockey. Cal has become not only synonymous with the most successful senior amateur hockey team in the country, the Warroad Lakers, but also with Minnesota hockey in general. To fully appreciate just how amazing the Warroad hockey tradition is, you have to first understand the incredible story of one man's dedication to a town, and the sport it so dearly loves.

Warroad, a small town of some 1,700 people on the shores of the Lake of the Woods, is located just 10 miles south of the Manitoba border at the extreme tip of northwestern Minnesota. The town's biggest employer is Marvin Windows, which employs more than 3,000 locals to build and ship windows throughout the world. The owners of the company, the Marvin family, have been an intricate part of the fabric of the community for nearly a century. And luckily for Warroad hockey fans, Cal (one of five Marvin siblings), never wanted to get too involved with the day-to-day operations and management of his family's business, opting instead to pursue his love of hockey — something that would turn out to be a huge blessing in disguise.

The youngest of six children, Cal Marvin was born on April 29th, 1924, in Warroad, where he grew up playing hockey on the area lakes and ponds. After high school Cal joined the Marine Corps, where he served in the South Pacific during World War II. After returning home from the service in 1946, Cal, along with several of his buddies, including Dan McKinnon of nearby Williams, decided to approach the University of North Dakota about the possibility of starting a new varsity hockey program at the school. The administration thought it would be a good idea, and with that, the Fighting Sioux were born. (Incidentally, the Sioux would go on to capture a national championship within just their first decade of league play.) Cal spent the next several years recruiting players from around northern Minnesota to come to Grand Forks to play hockey. All the while, Cal decided to start another "senior" team back home in Warroad, which he called the Lakers. That way, Cal and his buddies could play hockey during the week at UND, and come home to play for the Lakers on the weekends.

That first Laker's roster was loaded with talent from the Lake of the Woods area, including Williams' Clarence Schmidt (who had a brief stint with the NHL's Boston Bruins in the early 1940s), Roseau's "Masked Marvel" himself, Rube Bjorkman (who played on both the 1948 and 1952 U.S. Olympic teams), as well as Gordie "Ginny" Christian (who played on the 1956 silver medal winning U.S. Olympic team in Cortina, Italy). The team, dressed in black and gold (like the Boston Bruins), played on outdoor rinks in the now defunct States-Dominion League with other local teams such as Emerson, Dominion City, Fargo, Grand Forks, Thief River Falls, Baudette, Crookston and Roseau. After graduating from UND, Cal returned home to play and coach full-time for the Lakers, as well as to

The Godfather of Warroad hockey, Cal Marvin

pursue business interests in the community. Later, after injuring his knee during a game, Cal opted to become the team's coach and manager.

In November of 1949, a significant event happened in Warroad hockey history when the indoor Memorial Arena was opened. Affectionately called the "Gardens" by the locals, the arena was a big boost for the community's hockey programs. Cal had started the fund-raising effort to get the arena built two years earlier, and got much of the labor donated for free. Although the rink had no locker room facilities (the kids used to shower across the street from the rink at the Warroad Creamery after games), it was nonetheless a huge improvement from being outside during the frigid Warroad winters.

By the early 1950s the Lakers were competing in the Northwest Hockey League with Crookston, Roseau, Hallock, Thief River Falls and Grand Forks. Not only were they dominating their own league play, they were also whipping the best college teams in the country at that time as well. They had become regulars on many college schedules, including Murray Armstrong's tough Denver teams, as well as Michigan Tech, North Dakota and Minnesota-Duluth. The one team he didn't play was John Mariucci's Gophers. That's because Maroosh would say: "Marvin, how dumb do you think I am? It doesn't do us any good if we beat you, and we look bad if we don't!" Marvin had a deep respect and admiration for Mariucci, someone he credits personally for the USA's Olympic gold medals in 1960 and 1980.

By 1953 Warroad had become a power on the high school scene, finishing second in the state tournament that year for the second time in five years. The stars of that team were a couple of brothers by the name of Billy and Roger Christian, two kids whose additional practice with the Lakers at night helped them to earn roster spots on the gold-medal winning 1960 Olympic team.

In 1955 the Lakers had reached the pinnacle of amateur success by beating the Grand Falls (Montana) Americans to win the U.S. National Intermediate Championship. In addition to winning the Northwest Hockey League title, something else happened that next year that really put Warroad on the map. John Mariucci, the coach of the 56' Olympic team, decided to have his squad play the Lakers before heading off to Italy. And, although Warroad lost the game (which was held in Eveleth) by the final of 6-2, nearly every U.S. Olympic team since then has kept that tradition alive by making the trek to Northern Minnesota to play the Lakers. Talk about respect.

That same year a new teacher by the name of Bob Johnson came to town to take over as the coach of the Warroad High School Hockey team. The U of M grad had originally signed a pro baseball contract with the Chicago White Sox, but instead had to go into the Service. When he was discharged, he opted instead to try his hand at coaching and teaching. Johnson wound up coaching the Warriors for three seasons, starring for the Lakers during that same time. He had quite a schedule going in those days, too. Playing with the Lakers on Wednesdays, Saturdays and Sundays, while coaching his Warriors on Tuesdays, Thursdays and Fridays. That left Monday as his only day to relax. Johnson left to take over the Minneapolis Roosevelt High School coaching position in 1959, and of course went on to achieve face as the skippers of several college and pro teams, including: Colorado College, Wisconsin, Calgary Flames, Team USA and finally with the Pittsburgh Penguins — where he won the Stanley Cup in 1991 against the North Stars.

(Johnson, who would earn the nickname "Badger Bob," after winning three national championships at Wisconsin, would later be inducted into the Hockey Hall of Fame in Toronto.)

In 1957 Marvin coached the U.S. National team to a fifth-place finish at the World Championships in Oslo, Norway. His club also became the first American sports team to play in the post-WWII Soviet Union. Marvin returned from Europe not to Warroad, but rather to a new locale that Warroad Mayor Morris Taylor had unofficially renamed "Hockey Town, USA." Cal, who was now coaching the team exclusively, guided his Lakers past the U.S. National team that next year by the final score of 7-1. Perhaps feeling somewhat patriotic, Marvin abandoned the team's black and gold colored uniforms in favor of red, white and blue ones.

In 1959 the Lakers, who were led by several future NHLers including: Sugar Jim Henry (a goaltender with the Rangers & Bruins), Ed Kryzanowski (a defenseman with the Bruins and Blackhawks), won the Ontario/Minnesota Hockey League's "Cranford Cup" title. The team went on to win two more consecutive league titles as they expanded into the international scene as well to seek out new competition. In 1960 the U.S. Olympic team (led by Billy and Roger Christian) came back to town, and this time they beat the Olympians by a 6-4 margin. Just a few weeks later, in Squaw Valley, Calif., that same team won the gold medal. The Lakers had become quite the test for college and Olympic squads. Soon other countries, including Sweden and Norway, were stopping in Warroad to take a crack at these kids.

The Christian brothers played again on the 1964 U.S. Olympic team, and returned home just in time to make history with their beloved Lakers. The Lakers, who, in 1962 began playing as the only U.S. team in the Canadian Amateur Hockey Association, defeated the British Columbia Kamloops to became the first American-based team ever to win a Canadian Amateur Hockey Championship. Shortly thereafter, opting to stay close to home rather than play pro hockey, the Christian brothers decided to go into business by launching a hockey stick manufacturing company under the slogan: "Hockey Sticks by Hockey Players." Their sticks would be used by countless pro's and kids alike from around the world over the ensuing years.

In addition to serving as the manager of the 1965 U.S. National team, Cal guided his Lakers to Western Canada's "Allan Cup" finals, where they ultimately lost to Nelson, British Columbia. In addition, the team jumped over to the Manitoba Senior Hockey League that next year, where they won titles in 1965, 1969 and 1970. From there, the team continued to play well throughout Canada, winning the Western Canadian Intermediate Championship in 1971, Central Canadian Hockey League title in 1972, and Manitoba/Thunder Bay Intermediate Championship in 1973.

In 1972 another Warroadite, Henry Boucha, who starred on the 1969 Warrior high school team that finished as the state's runner-up to Edina, won a silver medal as a member of the 1972 U.S. Olympic team that competed in Sapporo, Japan. (Boucha would go on to play professionally with the Red Wings, North

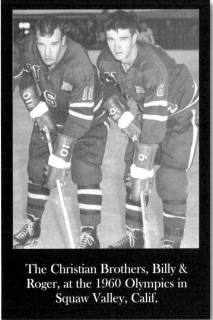

The Christian Brothers, Billy & Roger, at the 1960 Olympics in Squaw Valley, Calif.

LAKER OLYMPIANS:

1952	John Noah
1956	Dan McKinnon
1956	Gordon Christian
1960, 64	Bill Christian
1960, 64	Roger Christian
1972	Henry Boucha
1976	Blaine Comstock
1980, 84	David Christian
1992	Chris Imes

Stars and Fighting Saints before an eye injury prematurely ended his career.)

By 1974 the Lakers achieved another major milestone when they won their second Canadian Intermediate title by sweeping the Embrun (near Ottawa, Ontario) Panthers, in three straight games. With the win, the Lakers became the only U.S. team in history to ever win a "Hardy Cup," something reserved exclusively for the best Senior hockey team in all of Canada. Having to play all 17 playoff games on the road because the "Gardens" had only natural ice at the time, the Laker's long journey started in Manitoba, where they beat Thompson in five games. From there, the Lakers ousted the Saskatchewan champs from Rosetown, in four, followed by a five-game win over the British Columbia champs from Coquitlam, to win the Western title. With the win, the Lakers now had the home-ice advantage. But, with no ice of their own, Warroad had to suck it up and rent ice-time from their rival neighbors from 20 miles down the road in Roseau. (For those of you who may not know, Warroad vs. Roseau is without question Minnesota's most storied high school hockey rivalry. Bar none. For the locals, it is like religion. They take it that seriously.)

The team continued its winning ways through the 1970s, winning the Manitoba Eastern Hockey League Championships in both 1975 and 1976. In 1977 the Gardens was finally retrofitted with artificial ice and the Lakers responded by beating a couple of teams from Kindersley (Saskatchewan), and Vancouver (British Columbia), to win the Western Canadian title, but ultimately lost the Hardy Cup to Cambellton (New Brunswick). The team finished as Western Canadian Intermediate finalists in 1979 as well.

The Lakers roared into the 80s getting to see yet another native son win a gold medal. This time it was Billy Christian's son, Dave, a former UND star who was a member of the famed "Miracle on Ice" team of 1980. (Christian would go on to star in the NHL for 16 seasons with Winnipeg, Washington, Boston, St. Louis and Chicago.) And, although the U.S. team trounced the Lakers, 10-0, in Warroad that year, it was a thrill of a lifetime for Dave to get to play against his old man one last time. (Incidentally, Billy, then 42 years young, decided to finally hang em' up after that season with the Lakers.)

"It's a real tribute to our program," said Marvin," to think that the U.S. Olympic team will play in the Met Center on Tuesday, come to Warroad, and play a game on Wednesday and then play in Detroit before 20,000 fans a few nights later."

The U.S. National team came to Hockey Town a few years later in 1983, where they could only muster a 6-6 draw with the mighty Lakers. The Olympic team came back in 1984, the same year the Lakers hit the road for Europe, where they went .500 against national teams from Holland, France, Austria and West Germany. Another rink, named Olympic Arena, was constructed in Warroad that year, thanks to the efforts of Bill Christian and Cal Marvin, who helped raise the funds and arrange for all the volunteers to help build it.

In January of 1985 the Lakers ended their college competition when they lost to a tough Division One foe

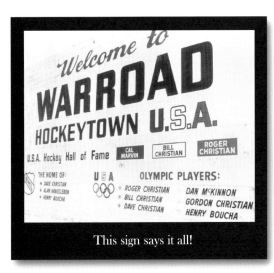

This sign says it all!

from Lowell, 7-3, in Warroad. The Lakers joined the Southeastern Manitoba Hockey League that same year, where they won titles in 1985, 1987 and 1989. In addition, they won Manitoba Intermediate championships in both 1989 and 1990.

In 1990 the Lakers finished third in the Southeastern Manitoba League, and then went on to beat Altona, Morden, and Portage to win the league title. (Eagan forward John Hansen scored five goals in the final game and was named as MVP of the playoffs.) Then, in 1991, the Lakers moved to the Central Amateur Senior Hockey (CASH) League, where they won the 1992 title en route to advancing to the Allan Cup final-four. In January of that same year, the Lakers took their second trip to Europe, where they finished with a 3-1 record against French, German and Austrian teams. That year also saw Chris Imes play on the '92 U.S. Olympic team in Lillehammer, Norway, thus becoming the ninth Laker player ever to wear a red, white and blue sweater.

In 1993 Cal's family stepped up to the plate big-time, when his brothers, Tot and Jack, donated more than a half-million dollars towards the price tag of the "new" Warroad Gardens arena. The state-of-the-art facility then played host to the 1994 Allen Cup finals (the Stanley Cup of senior amateur hockey), becoming only the second U.S. city ever to do so. (Spokane hosted it in 1980.) After advancing through the CASH playoffs, the Lakers, which had nearly a dozen Division I players on its roster (with several Warroad boys including: UND's Steve Johnson, Maine's Chris Imes, Gophers' Larry Olimb and UIC's Scott Knutson), made it to the finals with a 33-8 record. Then, with the new arena jammed, the Lakers, with a roster of entirely home-grown players, made history by beating Manitoba's St. Boniface Mohawks 5-2.

From there, the Lakers dynasty just continued to grow. They won the Cup that next year as well, this time beating the Stoney Plain Eagles (Alberta) on their home ice thanks to Gopher Wyatt Smith's third-period goal to give the team a 3-2 victory. Playing an independent schedule, Warroad faced the Eagles that next year in the finals as well, this time in Unity, Saskatchewan. Incredibly, the Lakers prevailed 6-1 to notch their third straight Allen Cup title, something that had never before been accomplished in nearly a century of Canadian competition.

Even though the Lakers were performing so well, men's senior hockey seemed to be going by way of the dinosaur. The rise of high school and junior hockey had taken its toll on the leagues, with most folding in the 1980s and '90s. It was also taking its toll on Marvin, who was constantly battling to find a new league to play in, combined with the ever-increasing expenses of travel throughout Canada. While the Lakers decided to play in the Hanover-Tache League in 1996-97, Marvin painfully announced that after 50

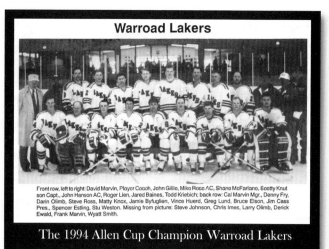

Warroad Lakers

Front row, left to right: David Marvin, Player Coach, John Gillio, Mike Ross AC, Shane McFarlane, Scotty Knutson Capt., John Hanson AC, Roger Lien, Jared Baines, Todd Kriebich; back row: Cal Marvin Mgr., Denny Fry, Darin Olimb, Steve Ross, Matty Knox, Jamie Byfuglien, Vince Huerd, Greg Lund, Bruce Elson, Jim Cass Pres., Spencer Estling, Stu Weston. Missing from picture: Steve Johnson, Chris Imes, Larry Olimb, Derick Ewald, Frank Marvin, Wyatt Smith.

The 1994 Allen Cup Champion Warroad Lakers

LAKERS IN THE NHL:

Dean Blais	Columbus
Henry Boucha	Detroit, Minnesota
David Christian	Winnipeg, Washington
	Boston, St. Louis, Chicago
Chad Erickson	New Jersey
Allan Hangsleben	Hartford
Jim Henry	New York, Boston
Bob Johnson	Pittsburgh, Calgary (coach)
Bill Juzda	Toronto
Ed Kryzanowski	Chicago
Clarence Schmidt	Boston
Wyatt Smith	Nashville, Minnesota,
	New York Isles, Colorado
Howard Walker	Washington, Calgary

tion alive.

Cal Marvin dedicated the better part of his life in the pursuit of helping others. He turned his entire community into a Laker's booster program and was fortunate to have the corporate backing from companies such as Marvin Windows and Christian

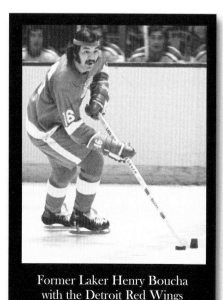

Former Laker Henry Boucha with the Detroit Red Wings

years, it would be the team's final season. Wanting to take their leader out in "Knute Rockne-like" style, the Lakers somehow fought, kicked and scratched their way past a tough Flin Flon team to get back to the Allen Cup finals one last time. There, regrettably, Warroad was beaten by the final of 7-3 by the Powell River Regals from British Columbia.

A 50-year reunion was held on March 15th, 1997, the same day that Governor Arne Carlson proclaimed "Cal Marvin Day" throughout the state of Minnesota. It was a fitting celebration to a man who had become the venerable Godfather of hockey in Warroad. The Lakers helped countless kids who were in transition from moving from high school to college, or from college to U.S. National or pro teams. Fully 19 U.S. Olympic and National teams have had former Lakers on their roster, and incredibly, the Lakers never had a losing season in their rich five-decade history. The man behind all of this... of course, was Cal Marvin.

Yes, Marvin had done it all in the name of hockey. The financial challenges had him doing everything from running community auctions, to bingo games, to turkey shoots, to fishing contests, and even a male style show to raise money for the kids. From coaching, to selling candy at games, to pouring cement, to writing weekly newspaper columns, to selling advertising, to serving on boards, he did it all so that each generation of children had it a little better than the one before. And most importantly, all he wanted in return, was for the kids to give back their time to help out the next crop of youngsters coming up after them in order to keep the wonderful tradition alive.

Brothers to keep his dream alive. Arguably no man has done more for his community with regards to promoting the game of hockey than has Warroad's Cal Marvin. Today the town boasts one of the most complete hockey programs in the country, with kids of all ages being able to play the game for free. That's right, free. No association fees, spendy ice-time payments, travel expenses, costly equipment or uniforms. It's all donated and paid for through fund-raisers and sponsors. The coaches volunteer and the community rallies behind them to give their kids the best opportunity it can have for success.

"Somebody did it for you, and you've got to pay it back," said Marvin about his town's amazing commitment to young people.

Among his many awards and honors, Cal was elected to the United States Hockey Hall of Fame as an administrator in 1982.

He is also a member of the Manitoba Sports Hall of Fame, the University of North Dakota Athletic Hall of Fame and the Warroad High School Athletic Hall of Fame. He also received the "Maroosh," an award presented in the name of the late John Mariucci for an individual's contributions to hockey. In addition to his Lakers, Cal operated various motels and restaurants in the community, including his Lake of the Woods Resort called "Cal's," which he ran for more than a quarter century as well.

Cal and his wife Beth had 12 children and numerous grandchildren. "We've quit, now," Cal once quipped in an interview with writer John Gilbert a few years back, "and we're not Catholic. But I always kept the thermostat down in the winter."

"I am grateful to have worked with and to have coached so many great people over the years," said Marvin. "It was a sad day when we had to shut the team down here a few years ago, after 50 years it had become a way of life for me. But, it was just too tough. We were the only senior team between Minneapolis and Winnipeg, and all that traveling takes a toll. I have no regrets though, and would do it all over again in a second. It was a wonderful ride!"

Sadly, Cal died in the Fall of 2004 at the age of 80. He will forever be remembered as one of the game's true pioneers though and as somebody who really did make a difference in life.

EVELETH: THE CAPITAL OF AMERICAN HOCKEY

Synonymous with the sport of ice hockey, Eveleth has come to be known around the country as the "capital of American hockey," because of its amazing ability to produce so many elite-level players in the first half of the 20th century. Arguably, no city in the United States has meant more to hockey than the tiny town of Eveleth. Located just 60 miles north of Duluth, and a mere 100 miles south of the Canadian border, this melting-pot mining community has an incredible history.

In 1890 a pioneer lumberman named Erwin Eveleth emigrated from Michigan to northern Minnesota with the intent of purchasing a plot of the region's rich pine forest lands. Three years later iron ore was discovered in the area, and as a result a townsite was surveyed and later incorporated. In 1893 the tiny settlement, located a mile southwest of the city's present location, near the Adams Spruce Mine, officially became incorporated as Mr. Eveleth's namesake. At first things were very tough for the community. There was a national financial depression that year that put a great burden on the people. As a result, the townsite, which consisted of only a few buildings, almost disappeared. During that harsh winter, food became scarce, and with the exception of occasional mail service by dog sled, the town was virtually cut off

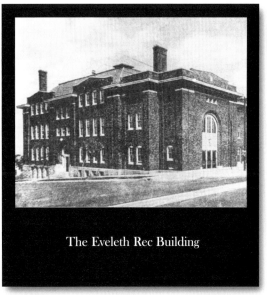

The Eveleth Rec Building

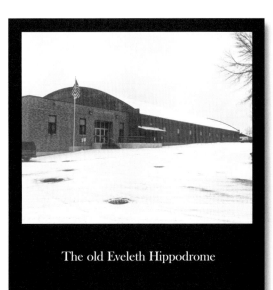

The old Eveleth Hippodrome

from the rest of the world.

Eveleth survived though, and soon people from all over the world were packing up their lives and making the trip across the Atlantic to start over there as miners. Immigrants, mostly from southern Europe and Scandinavia, came in droves to the east end of the Missabe Iron Range in search of a better life. Before long the Slavs, Croats, Slovenians and Serbians, found themselves living among the Italians, Irish, French, Fins, Swedes, Danes, Norwegians and English. And, because of Eveleth's cold climate, high altitude and hilly terrain, the new settlers seemed to feel right at home. In May of 1895, the Duluth, Missabe and Northern Railroad shipped its first load of iron ore from the Adams Mine, thus putting the town of Eveleth officially on the map.

By now the town was booming for these hearty people, who seemed to live by the adage "work hard — play hard." Working diligently in an open pit mine all day meant that at night and on the weekends, there was some steam that needed to be let off. Hockey would ultimately prove to be that perfect outlet. Many of the immigrants were already familiar with several ice games that were being played across the pond during the late 1800s, including shinny, bandy, ice polo and curling. So, it was just a matter of time before they started to incorporate these ice games, along with the relatively new sport of hockey (which was gradually spreading up to northern Minnesota from the Twin Cities, and at the same time down from Canada), into their new Iron Range homeland.

By best guestimates, the sport of hockey was first played here in 1902 at an outdoor rink on Fayal Pond. However, the first recorded game wasn't played until a year later, on January 23, 1903, between Eveleth and Two Harbors. The contest was played on the newly constructed O'Hares' skating rink (an indoor facility with a 75' x 150' natural ice sheet), which was located at the south end of Grant Street. That following day this article appeared in the January 24, 1903, edition of the Eveleth Mining News:

"The first hockey game of the season was played last evening at the Eveleth Rink between Two Harbors and the local seven. The local team was defeated, 5-2. The game was hard fought by both teams, as it was the first match game that either team had played in during the season. The visiting team did good team work and played a fast game. There was a great deal of offside playing by both teams. Hockey is practically a new game on the Range. With proper support, Eveleth can put up a good team, as there is plenty of first class material here. A return game will be played with Two Harbors."

Shortly thereafter, a hockey team was organized by a gentleman named John Herman, called the "City Hockey Club." The club played games against several area teams including: Two Harbors, Duluth, Biwabik and Virginia. Eveleth soon developed a great rivalry with nearby Virginia, where they played on what was then called Rainy Lake, but is now Silver Lake. Their games against one another, more often than not, usually ended up in a brawl, proving that fighting has been a part of the game since its early beginnings. Some of the "lads" who played on those early Eveleth teams included:

Alvin Skramstad, Victor Lundgren, Leonard Peterson, Tony Van Buskirk, Henry Lamier, Hart LaVigne, Ernest Baldi, Tom Dolan, "Foxy" LaVigne, Joe Haley, Fred Viger and James Clark.

By 1910 Eveleth's population had reached 7,000. Hockey continued to flourish in the community, as did other ice sports, including curling. In 1907 the first curling club was built on the west end of Jones Street, near the present sight of the Spruce Pit. It is readily apparent that Eveleth's ascendance as the hockey Mecca for which we know it today was clearly fueled by its mining riches. The mining companies, which were in some way responsible for nearly everyone in the town's income, figured

Eveleth High School 1922

that it was probably in their best interests to keep their employees and their families happily entertained in their new surroundings, always remembering that a happy worker was a productive worker. So, they, along with the city of Eveleth, decided to provide this entertainment in the form of constructing several new meticulously maintained public ice rinks. Recreational commissions were soon organized in conjunction with the local school board and ran by both parents and local citizens alike — all of course without pay, in order to give their kids the very best facilities.

Soon, kids from every neighborhood in the city were playing hockey. From October to March, Eveleth was transformed into an annual winter-wonderland. Kids began to expect a new hockey stick under the tree every Christmas, and couldn't wait to go out and show it off to their neighborhood pals. There were countless family teams, gang teams, and even rival groups from one neighborhood street who would challenge the boys from an adjoining street. Rinks were merely a formality, as nearly half of the streets in town had become make-shift ice sheets, complete with goals made of snow and ice. From dusk till dawn, kids could be seen passing pucks back and forth across the street to one another. Some kids used branches as sticks, and instead of wearing shin pads they put "Saturday Evening Post" magazines over their shins for protection. There even was a lot of pressure put on parents to get their kids new skates, which were a great expense for a family back then. Usually a kid would get his first pair by about kindergarten, and then hope to swap with another kid later on when he outgrew them. The result was the fact that most kids grew up on boot-hockey, perfecting their stick-handling skills way before they even learned how to lace up a pair of skates. Each generation of kids tried to emulate the one before them, and to no one's surprise, Eveleth soon became a spawning ground for some of the best hockey talent the world would ever see.

In 1918 the first formal hockey organization, called the Eveleth Hockey Association, was formed in Eveleth by several business and professional gentlemen, including Edward Hatch (who later became mayor of Eveleth and then mayor of Duluth), Victor Essling (also a mayor of Eveleth), Leonard Peterson (who later managed the Eveleth team), Charles Hale and Tony Van Buskirk (both pioneer residents of Eveleth). That next year the Eveleth Recreation Building was built at a cost of $125,000. Complete with six sheets of curling ice on the ground floor, and a hockey rink on the second floor, the building was state of the art for its day. The first organized senior league, called the "Hot Stove League," was sponsored that year by Helps-Shea Hardware. That next year an all-star team of sorts, called the "Reds," was formed to play in conjunction with the Winter Carnival at the new

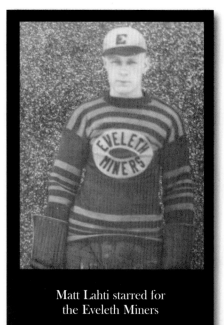
Matt Lahti starred for the Eveleth Miners

"Rec" Building. Eveleth beat Hibbing 5-2 at the first-ever game played there. Members of that squad, many or whom were from Two Harbors and Duluth, included: Clark, Hedberg, Stein, Couture, Toppula, Sullivan, LeFleur, Bastien and Seaborn (a Canadian import who played the seventh spot better known back then as the "rover"). Playing an independent schedule against several local teams including: St. Paul, Hibbing, Duluth, Calumet, Rainy River, Virginia and Winnipeg, the team finished that 1920 season with an 18-5-1 record. It was at about that time that the Eveleth Hockey Association, along with various executives from the mining companies, began importing top-notch Canadian hockey players to play for the hometown Reds, and in return, they would get them good jobs working in the mines.

The USAHA, Eveleth's Goes Big-Time...

The first high school hockey team was organized in the fall of 1920. The team was coached by hockey legend Ade Johnson, who was the brother of Hall of Famer Ching Johnson. Ade was also one of the stars of the Eveleth Reds, which had by this time a year later, graduated from playing an independent schedule, and joined the professional ranks of an upstart big-time national hockey circuit called the United States Amateur Hockey Association (USAHA). During that first season of league play in 1920, there were three groups that made up the new association — one in the East and two in the Midwest. The clubs that played in the league included the Duluth Hornets, St. Paul AC, Boston AA, Boston Westminster HC, Pittsburgh Hornets, Pittsburgh Yellow Jackets, Cleveland HC, New York, Philadelphia, Cleveland, Calumet, Portage Lake, and both the American and Canadian Soo of Sault St. Marie. Incredibly, the people of Eveleth now had the unique opportunity of viewing some of the greatest hockey players in the world on a regular basis. Seeing that tremendous brand of hockey no doubt inspired the youth of the Range to foster a tremendous love and respect for the game.

In 1920 the Reds were designated to play in the USAHA's Group Three along with Calumet, Houghton, American Soo and Canadian Soo. The Reds were led by several Canadian imports during that first year in the league, among them were: the brothers' Ching and Ade Johnson, Perk Galbraith (later a member of the Boston Bruins), Denny Breen, Percy Nicklin, Monette, Seaborn, Grey and Vic Des Jardins. Eveleth got off to a great start that inaugural season. The Reds, which finished the season with a 14-1-1 record, went on to win the Group Three division by beating the American Soo, 10-1, in a wild and crazy Group Three title game. This story describing that game later appeared in the Eveleth Mining News:

"Fully 600 fans came over from the Canadian Soo (Sault St. Marie) to the Eveleth — American Soo hockey game, and made themselves known by throwing coal, rotten eggs and other objects at the Eveleth players. At one time a piece of coal intended for one of the Eveleth players struck and seriously cut Stanley Skinner, a Soo player. Manager Peterson wired Eveleth that the treatment received from the American Soo management and players and local fans was fine, but the Canadians who came over to see the game were the meanest crowd of spectators he ever saw, and they abused our players so much that the two teams did not change ends, as is customary after each period, so that the Eveleth players could defend the goal farthest from the mob of Canadian soreheads during the entire game."

When asked about the game, rover Jim Seaborn reportedly said: "They liked us so much that they practically presented us with the sports arena... one board at a time!"

For their efforts the team was awarded the coveted McNaughton Cup. Now they would go on to face the champs of Groups One and Two for the USAHA's National Championship. They went on to play Cleveland (the Group Two champs who had beaten Boston AA of Group One), in the national finals. On April 2 and 3, in Cleveland, the Cleveland Hockey Club beat Eveleth by the back-to-back scores of 6-3 and 6-3. Then, because of the lack of ice in northern Minnesota at the time, the series shifted to the neutral sight of Pittsburgh, where there was artificial ice. There, the Reds beat the Clevelanders by the scores of 2-0, and 4-2 to tie it up at two games apiece. But, Cleveland was declared the winner of the four-game series on total goals (14-12), and was awarded the league's championship trophy, the Fellowes Cup. Even though they finished as the runner up, people from all over the country were now asking, "Just where the heck is Eveleth?" People from all over the Range, meanwhile, just couldn't get enough of their new team. There was even a crowd of more than 1,000 Reds fans, who stood outside in the cold at the local Western Union office awaiting details of the playoff games via telegraph.

As a result of this onslaught of interest in the new team, Mayor Essling, a St. Peter native who was also a lawyer, promoter and developer, decided to get cooking on building an arena suitable for his town's Reds. Now, by 1921 World War I was over, and hockey in North America was experiencing tremendous growth, especially on the Iron Range, where there were already four indoor ice arenas: Eveleth, Hibbing, Virginia and Chisholm. The competition was becoming fierce throughout the Range, and Eveleth, in a classic case of wanting to "keep up with the Jones'," needed to keep their edge. Because the Eveleth Recreational Building had become inadequate to handle the ever increasing crowds, the city decided to build an arena like no other. The result was a 3,000-seat 230' x 150' icy masterpiece, called the Hippodrome. The giant wooden structure located on the corner of Garfield and Adams Streets, known affectionately by the locals simply as the "Hipp," soon became recognized throughout the state as the "Madison Square Garden of the Northland." It opened on January 1, 1922, before a full house, as the Reds defeated the Duluth Hornets, 10-6.

This hockey shrine became so popular that before long it became the focal point of the entire community. To best capture what it might have been like to be a young boy dreaming of one day wearing an Eveleth Reds sweater, here is an excerpt from a story written by Chuck Muhich, longtime Eveleth recreation director, that appeared in the November 26, 1953, edition of the State Sports News:

"Many a boy who later wore a Ranger uniform can tell you how he got into the Hipp through the coal chute through an underground tunnel or by means of a ladder reaching to a window. A game night found everyone in the neighborhood busy stowing away their ladders out of reach of the youthful raiders. Frequently the Hipp caretaker would snap on the light switch only to find a group of boys perched like crows holding down an entire section."

Later many of these youngsters formed the nucleus for the strong Eveleth High School and Eveleth Junior College teams and continued on to become college, professional and Olympic performers. The big time hockey had fostered an intense interest in the game in Eveleth and soon most of the youths and many of the adults were playing some form of hockey. During the

Frank Brimsek

Frank Brimsek grew up playing hockey in Eveleth. After starring on the local high school team, Frank attended St. Cloud Teachers' College, where he starred as both a goalie on the hockey team, and also as a fullback on the football team. After playing for a couple of seasons with the Pittsburgh Yellow Jackets of the Eastern Hockey League and Providence of the International American League, Frank was called up to the NHL's Boston Bruins in 1938, where he replaced the legendary Cecil "Tiny" Thompson in goal. There, he became an immediate sensation, and soon earned the nickname "Mr. Zero" for his many shutouts. In fact, during his rookie season, he blanked the opposition in six of his first eight games, and 10 of 41 overall over that Stanley Cup-winning season. For his efforts, he was awarded the Calder Memorial Trophy as the league's top rookie and the Vezina Trophy as its leading goalie. A perennial all-star, Frank played for the Bruins for five years before joining the U.S. Coast Guard for a two-year term. He then returned to the Bruins for four more seasons before finally ending his hockey career with the Chicago Blackhawks in 1950. Over 10 seasons, Brimsek's goals against average was 2.74 with 42 shut-outs. He was elected to the Hockey Hall of Fame in Toronto in 1966, and the U.S. Hockey Hall of Fame in Eveleth in 1973. "Mr. Zero" is without question the greatest Minnesota goalie ever to play between the pipes.

depression years many Eveleth kids and adults spent their spare time playing hockey. In 1921 the Eveleth Recreation Commission organized teams and leagues and built and maintained several outdoor rinks. Scout troops, churches, lodges, clubs and neighborhoods formed teams of various ages. Chickentown would meet Fayal, and Adams would play Hayes in intra-city games. (Street names would identify your neighborhood team.) Adults competed in Class "A" or Class "B" leagues. It seemed that almost everyone in Eveleth was playing hockey. In addition, the various mining locations adjunct to Eveleth, such as

Sam LoPresti

Hall of Famer Sam LoPresti, born in Elcor but raised in Eveleth, went on to mind the nets at Eveleth High School. From there he went on to play at both Eveleth Junior College and also at St. Cloud Teachers' College. Sam broke into the big leagues in the fall of 1939, after coach Cliff Thompson pointed him out to a scout for the St. Paul Saints of the AHA. In 1940-41, LoPresti joined the NHL's Chicago Blackhawks. Although he only spent two seasons in the NHL, he might be most remembered for an amazing game in which he played on March 4, 1941, when, in a 3-2 loss to the Boston Bruins, LoPresti made a record 80 saves! (Incidentally, Boston's goaltender during that game was fellow Evelethian, Frankie Brimsek.) After the 1942 season, LoPresti entered the US. Navy. There, after having his merchant ship sunk by a torpedo, he spent 42 days alone in a lifeboat at sea before finally being rescued.

Mike Karakas

Hall of Famer Mike Karakas, though born in Aurora, was raised in Eveleth and went on to play goalie on the Eveleth High School team and later for Eveleth Junior College. He later led the Eveleth Rangers to the 1931 state championship. Karakas went on to star for the Chicago Blackhawks, where after posting a 1.92 goals against average and nine shut-outs in 1936, earned rookie-of-the-year honors. He dazzled the Windy City fans for more than a decade, and even won a Stanley Cup in 1938. He retired from the game in 1948 after an 18-year professional career between the pipes.

Leonidas, Genoa, Iron, Cherry, Sparta and Spruce, iced hockey teams with some of them having very strong adult and Senior teams. (Incidentally, Sparta won the 1930 Minnesota Senior Recreation title with a line-up composed entirely of players of Finnish nationality.)

Those same kids couldn't get enough hockey, and as a result, the Hipp was practically open all day and all night for all levels of play. So, it wasn't uncommon for people to wake up either at the crack of dawn, or in the middle of the night, by the sounds of kids running down the streets for a game or practice at the Hipp. Sometimes, if the streets were frozen, they would simply skate to their games, with their hockey bags draped over their sticks. One of those kids, who grew up in the 1920s playing hockey as a way to stay out of trouble, was John Mariucci. Maroosh learned the game on Hayes Street, playing with his neighbor's — the Brimsek's and Karakas'. Some people referred to it as "Incubator Street," because it was said that there were so many nationalities living there, and each house was filled to the brim with kids. (Later, in the 1940s, the next generation of kids, such as John Mayasich, played for Summit Street, while Willard Ikola played for Jackson Street.)

At the end of the 1921-22 season, Eveleth, winners of Group Three, had finished with an impressive 12-4 record. The Reds then went on to face the St. Paul Athletic Club, which posted an 8-4 record. Eveleth lost to St. Paul, 3-1, on that night, only to lose, 4-2, the following evening. The series then shifted back to St. Paul, where the teams skated to a pair of 0-0 ties, in addition to a 2-1 nail-biter victory for the AC. St. Paul wound up winning the series 7-6 on total goals. In so doing, St. Paul then went on to face Boston Westminster in the finals, only to lose, 3-0, 2-1, 0-0 and 2-0. The Eveleth fans proved to be road warriors as well, making the trip in droves to St. Paul to support their Reds. The games played at the St. Paul Hippodrome attracted more than 8,000 onlookers per outing.

For the 1922-23 season and thereafter, the league decided to split into two divisions — the Eastern and Western. This was largely due to the fact that Eveleth was not satisfied with the USAHA placing them in a league with the weaker Michigan teams, and consequently requested to be placed in a group with larger cities and stronger teams. As a result, Eveleth joined St. Paul, Duluth, Pittsburgh, Cleveland and newcomer Milwaukee, to form the realigned Group Two (Western Division) of the USAHA. The Reds finished the 1922-23 season in third place, four games behind St. Paul (who won the Western Group title but lost the national championship to Boston,

The Eveleth Rangers of the 1940s were led by Andre and Elio Gambucci.

in a close four-game series, six goals to four). Members of that Eveleth squad were: Bernie McTigue, Ching and Ade Johnson, Percy Nicklin, Billy Hill, Perk Galbraith, Vic Des Jardins, Bob Davis and Bob Armstrong.

During the 1923-24 season, the upstart Minneapolis Rockets replaced the struggling Milwaukee franchise as the sixth team in the division. And, unfortunately for Eveleth, Ching and Ade Johnson decided to move to the Mill City to join them. Eveleth finished fourth in the six team circuit with a 9-11 record. It was a sub-par season for the Reds, who were led by Galbraith and newcomer, Ed Rodden, who each scored 11 points. The 1924-25 season would prove to be the last for the USAHA in Minnesota. The Reds, who came on strong to finish the second half of the season at 13-6-1, were defeated by Pittsburgh in four straight in a post-season playoff series. The games were played in both Pittsburgh and (neutral) Duluth, because the temperature got too warm for the Hippodrome's natural ice. Incidentally, the Yellow Jackets went on to defeat Fort Pitt in the national finals. Red's forward Vic Des Jardins was second in league scoring that year with 14 goals in 39 games.

Unfortunately, after running for five glorious seasons, 1925 was the last year of operation for the USAHA. The league was vital for jump-starting the game of hockey throughout the United States. Many of the game's best and most talented players who suited up for a USAHA squad over its brief history went on to play in the NHL. The Eveleth contingent included: Ching and Ade Johnson, Vic Des Jardins, Perk Galbraith, Jim Seaborn, Nobby Clarke, Ed Rodden and Bill Hill.

The season of 1925-26 would prove to be the last in the world of big-time hockey for Eveleth. That year St. Paul, Minneapolis and Duluth, along with newcomers Winnipeg and Canadian Soo, formed the re-named Central Hockey Association, while Pittsburgh and Cleveland both withdrew from the USAHA. Pittsburgh, with almost the same line-up that they had used the previous season in the USAHA's Western Division, joined the National Hockey League, where they became an instant force. As for the Reds? Eveleth and Hibbing joined forces to form one team which was known as the "Eveleth-Hibbing Rangers." The Rangers got off to a good start in the upstart CHA, but floundered in mid-season before finishing behind St. Paul for fifth place. By season's end it was the Minneapolis Rockets who would win the title over Duluth and Winnipeg. High operating costs and the problem of protecting players from raids by professional hockey clubs ultimately killed the Central Hockey Association after just that one season.

So, after six glorious years of world class "semi-pro" hockey on the Range, it was the end of the line for the Eveleth franchise. No longer would fans of the Range be able to see the best players in the world right in their backyard, players such as: Tiny Thompson, Taffy Abel, Nels Stewart, Lionel Conacher, Herbie Lewis, Mike Goodman, Bill Cook, Bun Cook, Ching Johnson, Moose Goheen, Herb Drury, Vern Turner, Perk Galbraith, Roy Worters, Coddy Winters, Moose Jamieson, Mickey McQuire and Hib Milks.

Exit Semi-Pro Hockey and Enter Senior Hockey...

A new outright professional circuit that had a working agreement with the NHL called the AHA was formed that next year, but Eveleth opted to sit on the sidelines. Instead they focused on producing the state's top amateur teams. And that is just what they did in 1926, when the Eveleth Cubs (using only home-town boys) won the first State Senior Championship held in Hibbing, sponsored by the Minnesota Recreation Association. Among the players on the team were: Frank DeLeo, Bill Langen, Matthew Lahti, Andrew Jagunich, Tony and John Prelesnik, Bill DePaul, and Victor Machek. The Cubs, who later became known as the Eveleth Miners, became a dynasty of their own, winning four straight AAU State Senior titles from 1929 through 1932. Incidentally, while the tiny nearby town of Genoa, which no longer appears on Minnesota road maps, captured the state crown in both 1933 and 1934, the 1935 title was won by St. Cloud Teachers' College, a team made up almost entirely of Eveleth natives.

That Eveleth team even received an invitation to be the United States representative in the 1928 Winter Olympic winter games to be held in Amsterdam. But, because the club was unable to raise the necessary funds to cover the costs of the trip, it was called off, and ultimately the U.S. had no hockey representative for that Olympiad.

From 1927-31, another senior amateur circuit was formed in northern Minnesota called the Arrowhead League, which featured teams from Eveleth, Hibbing, Virginia, Duluth and Fort Frances. Eveleth's team, known as the Rangers, was comprised entirely of locals.

In 1931 a new amateur league, called the Central Hockey League, was formed with teams from Eveleth, Minneapolis, St. Paul and Virginia. Virginia withdrew from the league after the first season, and from that point on, the circuit changed over to a professional status. For the 1931-32 season, the Rangers earned themselves a new nickname, the "Orphans," because the Hipp had been condemned for renovations, and they were forced to play their entire 35 game schedule on the road. This didn't even phase the team though, as they went on to win the regular season crown. The league, which ultimately ran through the 1934-35 season, featured tremendous competition. An example of just how good the caliber of play was in the league was displayed in 1934, when the CHL and the American Hockey Association (a higher level professional league with teams throughout the Midwest and East Coast), played an interlocking schedule. That year the St. Paul Saints swept the AHA champion St. Louis Flyers for the title.

Amazingly, almost the entire Central Hockey League was comprised of Minnesota natives, and of them, more than 20 of the league's 65 total players were Eveleth natives. They included: Milton Brink, Glee Jagunich, Rudy Ahlin, Art Erickson, Andy Toth, Vance and Joe Papike, Hodge Johnson, Alex McInnes, Pete Pleban, Frank Cervance, Paul Schaeffer, Bill DePaul, Tony Prelesnik, P.I. Murphy, Al Soumi, Mike Kasher, Frank DeLeo, Oscar Almquist, Sam and John Phillips and Sandy Constantine.

By 1937 Eveleth found themselves without a league again. So, they formed a new senior circuit called the International Hockey League. They were joined by teams from Hibbing, Duluth, Port Arthur and Fort William. Later Fort William and Port Arthur dropped out and were replaced by Fort Frances. And, just like the CHL before, most of the players were from Eveleth. Unfortunately, due to the commencement of World War II in 1940, and the fact that so many of our boys were sent off to battle, the league disbanded. However, the league was soon replaced by a strong four-team industrial league which was based in Duluth during the war years.

In 1938 the Hipp was comple-

One of the greatest high school lines ever was Eveleth's 1945 trio of Neil Celley, Pat Finnegan and Wally Grant.

ly renovated, with brick replacing the old wooden walls. A new lobby was added along the south side of the building, additional seating was built, and locker rooms were added to the basement. The original steel beams and trusses were renovated, with everything else being replaced for the sum of $150,000. (The rink's natural ice remained though, until 1950, when artificial ice was finally installed.)

After World War II, Eveleth bounced around in several senior leagues. The first was the Northern Amateur League, a senior circuit, which was formed in the early 1940s with teams from Eveleth, Duluth, Hibbing, Virginia and Fort Frances. The league prospered through the decade, and finally disbanded in 1951. That same year Eveleth, along with Hibbing, Minneapolis, St. Paul, Rochester, and Sioux City, decided to join the American Amateur Hockey Association. The AAHA changed its name to the Central Hockey League for that next season of 1952-53. Eveleth, however, decided to withdraw from the CHL after only one year. Then, in the fall of 1954, the Eveleth Rangers joined the upstart "international" Thunder Bay Senior League, which consisted of five teams: Eveleth, Hibbing, Fort William, Fort Frances and Port Arthur. However, in 1955, after only one season, the league folded due to financial problems. This ultimately ended Eveleth's participation in Minnesota Senior Open competitions.

The First High School Dynasty

There are perhaps but a few things in Minnesota which are more synonymous than that of high school hockey and the town of Eveleth. It can claim, arguably, the greatest all-time high school hockey program in the history of our country. It's history is a fascinating story within itself.

High School hockey was first played informally in Eveleth around the turn of the century, but the first official Eveleth varsity high school team was organized in 1920. The townspeople had the foresight to see the potential of giving their youth as many opportunities as possible, and backed the program through extensive volunteering and support. They pressed for new rinks, and worked in harmony with the Recreation Commission, Eveleth's school system and the City of Eveleth, in order to provide their kids with the best facilities possible.

The team's first coach was Ade Johnson, a Canadian import from Winnipeg who also starred for the semi-pro Eveleth Reds. Members of that first high school squad who played under Ade's tutelage included: Matt Lahti, Aro Ellison, Pete Brascugli, Tito Muscatelli, Bill La Vigne, Roy Damberg and Ted Juola.

Their competition during those first years included playing against other local teams which included Duluth Central, Virginia and Hibbing. Later, in the 1920s, the team played other teams such as: Duluth Denfeld, Fort Frances and Chisholm. On March 19, 1923, Eveleth beat St. Paul Mechanic Arts High School 9-2 on its home ice, for what was referred to back then as the state "mythical title." They repeated the feat two years later in a rematch at the Minneapolis Arena on March 14, 1925, this time narrowly beating Mechanic Arts 3-2. (Incidentally, there were four members of that 1925 team that later turned professional — Billy De Paul, Glee Jagunich, Oscar Almquist and Tony Prelesnik.)

Cliff Thompson, Don Clark and Bob Ridder (L to R) at the Hall of Fame

JOHN MARIUCCI

John Mariucci is the godfather of American amateur hockey and the patriarch of the sport in our state. In fact, what John did for the sport was immeasurable. With his passion for competing, teaching, and spreading the gospel about the sport he loved, Mariucci went on to become the country's most important figure in the development of amateur hockey. Here is the story of a true Minnesota legend.

John Mariucci was born the son of Italian immigrants on May 8, 1916, on the great Mesabi Iron Range in Eveleth — the birthplace of hockey in the United States. He grew up on Hayes Street, also referred to by locals as "Incubator Street" because it was said that there were so many nationalities living there, and every house had eight or nine kids inside. Many of the kids of the immigrants would play hockey to stay out of trouble. Some kids didn't even have skates, so they wore overshoes, while others used tree branches for sticks. John found his first pair of skates in a garbage can and, because he didn't have money to buy equipment, wrapped old magazines around his shins for pads.

Even though it was a mid-sized Minnesota Iron Range town, Eveleth was as sophisticated as New York City when it came to hockey. Eveleth even had a team, the "Reds" which played big-time pro hockey against cities such as Toronto, Philadelphia and Chicago. Eveleth kids would try to emulate the many Canadians who were imported to the city to play hockey as one of the forms of entertainment provided for the immigrant iron-ore miners. John learned the game from legendary hall of fame coach Cliff Thompson, whose tenure as the Eveleth High School hockey coach lasted nearly 40 years.

In 1936, Maroosh left the Range and headed south to the University of Minnesota. There, he starred as a defenseman for Larry Armstrong's Gopher hockey team and also played offensive and defensive end alongside of Butch Nash under legendary football coach Bernie Bierman. In 1940, led by Goalie Bud Wilkinson, the future football coaching legend at the University of Oklahoma, Mariucci captained the National AAU Championship team. (At the time that was the only championship available in college hockey.) After the season, Maroosh, who was named as an All-American, was offered the head coaching position at the U of M, but turned it down to play professionally.

After a brief stint with Providence in the American Hockey League, Maroosh joined the Chicago Blackhawks to finish out the 1940 season. At that time the NHL employed few Americans and not many college-bred players. (To put this into perspective, by 1968, only six Americans and five collegians had ever played in the NHL!) Johnny played there until 1942, when he was summoned to join the U.S. Coast Guard in New York. There, he played for the Coast Guard team in the Eastern Amateur League during the second world war. After turning down another offer to coach at the U of M, he returned to the Hawks for the 1945 season. Then, in 1947, Maroosh became the first American-developed player ever to captain an NHL team.

The rugged Maroosh was one of the biggest celebrities in Chicago during his playing days there. He became most famous among Windy City hockey fans for his brawls. One in particular, with Detroit's Black Jack Stewart, remains the NHL's longest ever — lasting nearly 20 minutes. In 1948, Maroosh left the Hawks. For his career in the NHL he scored 11 goals and 34 assists for 45 points over 223 games. He also played in two Stanley Cup playoffs. More importantly though, he led the team in penalty minutes, racking up more than 300 over his career. A goal-scorer he wasn't. This guy was a role-playing hatchet-man who protected and defended his teammates. That's why they loved and appreciated him.

"You know, when I was playing with New York I got to know the Bentley brothers, who played for years with John in Chicago," recalled Glen Sonmor, one of Mariucci's best friends. "Now John, as you know, was the ultimate warrior out on the ice. He knew his role and he loved it. He knew that he wasn't there to score 50 goals, he was there to play solid hockey and to protect his teammates. So, one time I asked those Bentley brothers about what it was like to play hockey with that big Dago, John Mariucci. They said that playing with John made hockey fun for them again. Before he got there (Chicago), other players used to intimidate them and make runs at them because they were the stars of the Blackhawks. Well, when John got there it took just one trip around the league for every team to learn not to even look funny at the Bentley brothers. They left them alone after that because anybody from that point on knew that if they tried anything with those guys, that John was coming to get them. And back then you didn't have any of the penalties or rules about coming off the bench to mix it up. I remember Max (Bentley) saying, 'Anybody who tried to intimidate us had to have some pretty big balls because as soon as they went after us they would have to turn around and get ready for big John, who would come flying off the bench in a hurry. And there wasn't any doubt as to why he was coming either because he left his stick and gloves back on the bench!' John used to love beating the crap out of guys and he was pretty darn good at it. Those Bentleys told me that after that no one would mess with them with the exception of one guy, Black Jack Stewart. They said that Black Jack would get bored out there sometimes and decide to make it interesting so he would take a shot at one of the Bentleys just so John would come after him. Those two used to love brawling with each other, and then they would go out and have beers together after the game. It was crazy, but that was the kind of guy John was, he would knock you down and then pick you back up."

"One time Maroosh was playing in a game against a Kansas City farm team," recalled Willard Ikola, a fellow Evelethian and friend of Maroosh. "A rookie gave Maroosh some stitches in that big honker he had with a cheap shot. Maroosh tried to run him down, but the kid, realizing who he had whacked, jumped right over the boards and ran up the stairs. Maroosh jumped up and followed him right outside. Sparks were flying from the stairs as Maroosh was yelling at him from behind. He chased him right out into the street in front of the arena, and then calmly walked back down the stairs to the ice. He was even talking to the ladies in the stands on his way back down. He went on the ice and finished his shift like nothing had happened. The next night Maroosh was still mad, but the front office wanted the kid who hit him to get some playing time, because he was going to get called up shortly. John agreed, but only if the kid came up to him and apologized in person. That night the kid came to John's room, terrified, and apologized. Maroosh just laughed it off, telling him to keep his damn stick down next time. Big John, the captain, took the kid under his wing after that, and helped him out. That's the kind of guy John Mariucci was."

Mariucci went on to play for St. Louis of the American League, St. Paul and Minneapolis of the U.S. League, and again with a Coast Guard team before hanging up his skates for good as an active player in 1951. He then turned to coaching, when he was named the head coach of Minneapolis Millers hockey team of the A.A.L.

After a year with the Millers, Maroosh finally elected to coach the Gophers, replacing former Blackhawk and Gopher, Doc Romnes. It was only a part-time job for him though, as he continued to also work as a salesman for the Falk Paper Company as well.

In his first season in Gold Country he was awarded Coach of the Year honors. It would be his first of many. Maroosh got Minnesotans excited about college hockey, and they responded by coming out in droves to see his Gophers. The U even had to add an upper tier of seats to the Williams Arena rink to accommodate them all.

Always a joker, Maroosh was always trying new things to keep the fans interested and was always on the lookout for new recruits. One time while watching the giant Bill Simonovich, from Gilbert, Minn., play with the varsity basketball team, John said: "Man, what a goalie he'd make! Give him a couple of mattresses and a pair of skis and nobody would ever score on him."

In a sport dominated by Canadians, Maroosh championed the Americans and in particular, Minnesotans. After watching an NCAA Final one time, he said: "It's assinine that the only two Americans on the ice for the NCAA championship game were the referees." Maroosh was a visionary and saw the potential growth of the sport.

"College could be a developmental program for our own country, for the Olympics and for the pros," he said. "College hockey is a state institution and should be represented by Minnesota boys. If they're not quite as good as some Canadians, we'll just have to work harder, that's all."

It became political for him as he battled to stop the importation of the older Canadians and give the American kids an equal playing field. In the late 1950s, the U's Athletic Director, Marsh Ryman, refused to play Denver's Canadian-filled teams. This ultimately led to the end of the WIHL and the creation of the WCHA in 1959.

"What I was against was the junior player who played in Canada until he was 21, then, if the pros didn't sign him, he would come to this country to play college hockey as a 22-year-old freshman against our 18-year-olds," said Mariucci. "It wasn't fair to our kids, who were finishing college at the same age Canadians were freshmen."

Although Maroosh never won the NCAA championship during his 14-year tenure at the U of M, he came pretty darn close in 1954 when his Gophers lost a 5-4 overtime heart-breaker to RPI with the best line ever to play college hockey: John Mayasich, Dick Dougherty and Gene Campbell, who, along with Ken Yackel, were all named to the All-American team that season.

The Noble Roman left the University in 1966 with a record of 207-142-15, including conference championships in 1953 and 1954, as well as three NCAA playoff appearances (including another Final Four appearance in 1961). Included in his tenure was an Italian homecoming of sorts, when he led the Americans to a silver medal in the 1956 Olympics in Cortina. There were 11 Minnesota natives on the team that stunned heavily favored Canada before falling to the Soviet Union in the gold medal game. Mariucci's successor at the U of M was Glen Sonmor, a former teammate with the Minneapolis Millers, and close friend.

In 1966, another chapter of Mariucci's storied life unfolded as he became chief scout and special assistant to Wren Blair, GM of the NHL's expansion North Stars. There, Maroosh applied his vast knowledge of recruiting, coaching, and scouting. In 1977 Mariucci coached the U.S. National team and a year later he rejoined the North Stars, this time as the Assistant G.M. under his former player, Lou Nanne. "One word of advice to all you coaches," said Maroosh. "Be good to your players — you never know which one might someday be your boss..."

John's accomplishments and honors are far too great to list here. Some of his more notable ones, however, include: Being inducted as a charter member of the U.S. Hockey Hall of Fame in his hometown of Eveleth; being inducted into the NHL Hockey Hall of Fame in Toronto; and receiving the NHL's coveted Lester Patrick Award for his contributions to U.S. hockey. He also made a difference by giving to others. In fact, he devoted much of his life to Brainerd's Camp Confidence, for the mentally-retarded, a cause he dearly loved.

On March 2, 1985, in an emotional ceremony to give thanks and immortalize the man forever, the U of M renamed the hockey half of Williams Arena as Mariucci Arena, in his honor. It was also declared as "John Mariucci Day" in Minnesota by Governor Perpich. During the ceremony, long-time friend Robert Ridder said: "During the 1980 Olympics, a U.S. Destroyer passed a Russian ship and signaled to it: 'U.S.A. 4, Russia 3.' Probably nobody on that boat ever heard of John Mariucci, but it wouldn't have been possible without John Mariucci." In 1987 Maroosh died at the age of 70 after a long bout with cancer. He had seven children and several grandchildren.

This gentleman brawler was a legend, on and off the ice. Although he was tough as nails, his wit, intelligence, and personality were one-of-a-kind. John was one of the toughest Italians who ever lived. His face has often been referred to as a "blocked punt," because it was so beat up. But what separated him from the goons was that he wouldn't just knock his opponents down, he'd pick them up and then make them laugh. Perhaps Herb Brooks said it best: "In all social causes to better an institution, there's always got to be a rallying force, a catalyst, a glue, and a magnet, and that's what John was, for American hockey. The rest of us just filled in after him."

Full of wit, he was described as a newspaperman's dream-come-true. From his famous brawls, which included once breaking thumb-wrestling champion Murray Warmath's thumb, Mariucci was a real character. Local reporters found themselves having a lot of dinners that turned into breakfasts while listening to his endless stories. The sports community was in awe of him, and he made journalists who hated the sport of hockey want to start covering it.

He was also the pioneer in the development of hockey in Minnesota. Because of that, his legacy will live on forever. Every kid that laces up his or her skates needs to give thanks to the man who started it all, John Mariucci. He started grassroots youth programs, put on coaching clinics, attended new arena openings in countless cities and towns across the state, helped former players find coaching positions, and even encouraged hockey moms to write to city councils to build new rinks and develop recreation programs.

Because of John Mariucci, hockey in Minnesota carries the same pedigree as basketball in Indiana or football in Texas. Described best by his friends and players as "father-like, magical, and even super-human," Maroosh was simply the greatest and will forever be missed.

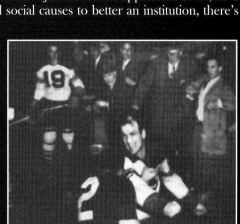

On December 4, 1946, Chicago's John Mariucci and Detroit's Black Jack Stewart fought toe-to-toe for nearly 20 minutes in the NHL's longest-ever brawl.

EVELETH JUNIOR COLLEGE

Eveleth Junior College was an institution in itself. So good was the team in fact, that in 1928, along with the University Club of Boston, Harvard University, University of Minnesota and Augsburg College, it was considered as a candidate by the United States Olympic Committee - under the chairmanship of General Douglas MacArthur, to represent the United States in the 1928 Winter Olympics in Amsterdam. However, due to a lack of financial backing, Eveleth Junior College respectfully declined the invitation to serve as the U.S. Olympic squad. (Ultimately, the U.S. was not represented at the 1928 Winter Games.)

In 1928-29, according to the college hockey ranking system of Princeton University's professor Theodore Tonnele, Eveleth Junior College was ranked as the No. 1 college team in the nation, followed by Yale, the University of Minnesota, and Clarkson, which was fourth. Eveleth J.C. was considered to be a powerhouse, and one of the reasons for its success was due, in large part, to its feeder system — the high school team, which was also coached by Cliff Thompson. Ironically, the toughest opponent that the J.C. faced that season was the Eveleth High School team, which they narrowly beat by the score of 4-3. That year was the best ever for the J.C., as they finished the season undefeated and went on to win college hockey's National Championship. Thompson coached the Eveleth JC team from 1928-40, recording an amazing record of 171-28-7.

National Ranking of Collegiate Hockey Teams, 1928-1929

BY THEODORE MILLS TONNELE (PRINCETON).

As the result of a number of years' study of the ranking of college athletic teams, the writer has concluded that a pragmatic formula may be devised for any sport, which, upon application to any group of teams, will result in a surprisingly sound ranking of them.

A formula worked out for, and applied to, the collegiate hockey teams throughout the country, gives the following ranking for the past season:

A TEAMS.

Ranking Order.	Team.	Index No.	Ranking Order.	Team.	Index No.
1.	Eveleth Junior Coll.	(19.00)	6.	Harvard	(10.38)
2.	Yale	(16.60)	7.	Marquette	(9.55)
3.	Minnesota	(16.08)	8.	Princeton	(9.50)
4.	Clarkson	(14.00)	9.	Wisconsin	(6.33)
5.	Dartmouth	(11.44)	10.	Michigan	(4.36)

B1 TEAMS.

Ranking Order.	Team.	Index No.	Ranking Order.	Team.	Index No.
11.	Boston Coll.	(4.00)	18.	Mass. Inst. Tech.	(.87)
11.	St. Mary's (Minn.).	(4.00)	19.	Cornell	(.63)
13.	California (Berkly.)	(3.50)	20.	Brown	(.33)
14.	Michigan Tech	(2.67)	20.	Colgate	(.33)
15.	Williams	(1.50)	22.	New Hampshire	(.05)
16.	Middlebury	(1.17)			
16.	St. Lawrence	(1.17)			

In 1926 an important event happened that forever would change the landscape of Eveleth hockey. That year Ade Johnson stepped down has the team's head coach and was replaced by Cliff Thompson. Thompson, a former Minneapolis Central and University of Minnesota player, who is considered even to this day as the most celebrated high school hockey coach in our state's history, also decided to take over the reigns as the coach of the Eveleth Junior College team as well.

Under Thompson's direction, Eveleth High School quickly gained a reputation as the team to beat in the state of Minnesota, and before long teams from the Twin Cities were lining up to take a crack at the boys from the Range. Eveleth held strong though, and answered most every challenge given to them. By 1929, the Golden Bears were riding an unbelievable winning streak, not having lost a game in more than three years against all of the Iron Range and Duluth schools. That year a metro high school all-star team of sorts, called the Cardinals, was assembled by former Minneapolis Miller great Nick Kahler. The Cards, who had won the Minneapolis Recreation title that year, was composed primarily of players from Minneapolis South and West High Schools. The Cards and Bears would do battle that year in front of a packed house at the Minneapolis Arena, with the all-star team edging Eveleth in a thriller by the narrow margin of 2-1. An idea of the caliber of talent on the ice that night was personified by the fact that six of the eleven Eveleth players and five of the eleven Minneapolis players would later play professional hockey.

Eveleth's Icy Reign of Terror

Eveleth continued to dominate hockey through the 1930s, and even through the years of the Great Depression. One of the reasons for this was due to the fact that people such as coach Thompson made sure that all of his kids had a good pair of skates under their feet as well as quality protective equipment around them. By the 1940s more and more schools were playing hockey, and it was inevitable that a state-wide tournament would come to fruition. So, in 1945, mainly through the efforts of hockey pioneer Gene Aldrich of St. Paul, that's just what happened when the Minnesota State High School League hosted the first-ever boys' state high school hockey tournament at the St. Paul Auditorium.

Thompson led his squad to that first tournament and showed the rest of Minnesota what the people on the Range had known for years -- Eveleth was awesome! Led by what many still consider today to be the greatest ever high school hockey line of Pat Finnegan, Wally Grant and Neil Celley, the Golden Bears breezed through the tourney and captured the state's first ever crown.

The Golden Bears shut-out Granite Falls 16-0 in their first quarter-final game, and in so doing set a rather unique record that still stands today: "LEAST STOPS BY A GOALTENDER" -- ONE, by Eveleth's Ron Drobnick," (On a shot from center ice nonetheless!) Eveleth rolled over St. Paul Washington 10-0 in the semifinal contest, and went on to edge a strong Thief River Falls team 4-3 for the title. Wally Grant, who would later star as a member of the infamous "G" line at the University of Michigan, tallied both the tying and go-ahead goals in that championship game.

That next season, in 1946, Eveleth narrowly missed a repeat title, finishing third, only to see one of their own native sons bring home the hardware instead. That's because former Eveleth goaltender Oscar Almquist, a former Golden Ram back in the 1920s, who went on to star at St. Mary's College and later for the St. Paul Saints, coached Roseau High School to its first title. Almquist, better known as the "Giant of the North," would go on to quite a prolific coaching tenure himself. Upon retiring in 1967, after 28 years behind the bench, Almquist led Roseau to 14 state tournaments en route to winning four state titles, while compiling an amazing record of 406-150-51.

Eveleth continued its domination of the event through 1956. During that 12-year span the Golden Bears won five championships, twice finished as runners-up and claimed three third place finishes. The team earned a berth in the first 12 state tournaments and rode two amazing winning streaks of 79 and 58 games. One era in particular was the greatest possibly in the history of high school sports. That was from 1948 to 1951, when the team posted a perfect 69-0 record over four consecutive undefeated seasons en route to winning four straight titles. Incidentally, Eveleth's unbelievable winning streak ended in 1952 when Iron Range rival Hibbing bested the Golden Bears, 4-3, in the title game.

Milt Brink

JOHN MAYASICH

John Mayasich has long been regarded as one of the finest amateur hockey players ever produced in the United States, and is without question the greatest player to ever lace em' up in the state of Minnesota.

Mayasich grew up playing hockey in Eveleth. "We got our start learning hockey on the ponds and outdoor rinks in the city," recalled Mayasich. "The older kids would pick sides and the younger kids would learn from them. It went on from generation to generation. When the ice melted, we played street hockey and broomball. We had a lot of fun and we learned a lot playing those sports as well."

After leading the Eveleth High School team to an amazing run of four consecutive undefeated state championship seasons from 1948-51, Mayasich headed to the University of Minnesota, where he would join up with another Eveleth hockey legend, Gopher coach John Mariucci. There, Mayasich led the Gophers to a couple of NCAA Final Fours, and took college hockey by storm. Before his career was over, the perennial All-American had tallied Gopher records of 298 career points and 144 goals. His totals worked out to an incredible 1.4 goals per game average, good for nearly three points per game. (To put it into perspective, Pat Micheletti, the next Gopher player on the career goal-scoring list, has 24 fewer goals despite playing in 51 more games. In other words, in his 162 games, Micheletti would have had to amass 435 points just to match Mayasich's per-game average. That's an additional 166 more than his career total!) Mayasich also holds the Minnesota records for most goals and most points in a single game. In his senior year, he had an incredible six-goal game against Winnipeg and also tallied eight points against Michigan that same season.

At the end of his playing career with the Gophers, Mayasich fulfilled his military obligations and then went on to play with eight U.S. Olympic and National Teams. He was also a member of the 1956 silver medal-winning U.S. Olympic hockey team in Cortina, Italy. The highlight of that tournament came against perennial power Canada, which had won seven of the eight Olympic gold medals since the Games had begun. There, John played an incredible game, scoring a hat trick, en route to defeating the mighty Canucks. The Americans played tough but wound up taking home a Silver medal for their efforts.

The most celebrated of his Olympic events, however, was the first "Miracle on Ice," the 1960 U.S. Olympic team, which won the gold in Squaw Valley, Calif. The U.S. team beat the mighty Russians for the first time that year, and, in the process, put hockey on the map.

"At the time we were thinking it would be a great accomplishment if we could win a bronze, we had no idea we would win a gold," said Mayasich. "Beating the Russians was amazing and very similar to the 1980 team victory as well. I think for both teams, playing at home, in America, was a big factor, because it's nice having the fans there to support you. This was probably one of the biggest thrills of my life."

This was the dawn of modern hockey in Minnesota, and Mayasich was rewriting the record books as he went along. He was a "velvety-smooth skater," with a keen, sixth sense into the psyche of the goalie's every move. He is credited as being the first college hockey player to develop the slap shot, a new weapon that instilled fear into an already perplexed group of goaltenders who tried to stop him. John was an artist with his stick and his stick-handling skills were legendary. On opponent's power-plays, he could kill penalties by toying with opposing defenses. He used to take the puck and simply weave around the rink without ever passing to a teammate until the penalty had been killed. With amazing ability like that, it's hard to believe that he was often criticized for passing too much.

"The camaraderie was the best, those friendships go back a long time," recalled Mayasich on his playing days at the U of M. "Playing with the players whom I had played against throughout my high school career was really exciting. We had great Gopher players like Dick Meredith, Dick Dougherty, Gene Campbell, Ken Yackel, Wendy Anderson and Stan Hubbard. I got to see the world through hockey, and the purity of the game is the bond that keeps these friendships together today. It was quite a time to be involved with the Gopher program as it was just taking off back then. It made me proud of the fact that I was there when all of this was happening. Now, to see what the program has grown into today, and to think that maybe, in a small way that I had something to do with it, is incredible. My time at the U of M was great."

Declining professional hockey opportunities in the then six-team NHL, Mayasich then devoted his remaining hockey career to the CHL's Green Bay Bobcats, where he served as the player/coach, on and off, from 1958-71. In 1969, he was named coach of the U.S. National team as well. After his hockey career John went into business with his old Gopher teammate Stan Hubbard, where he worked as an executive for KSTP Radio for many, many years.

Mayasich received numerous honors during his hockey days, including being the first Minnesotan to be voted into the National High School Athletic Hall of Fame. In addition, in 1976 he had a homecoming of sorts, when he was inducted into the U.S. Hockey Hall of Fame in his native Eveleth. And, in 1998 John received the coveted Lester Patrick Award, for his outstanding contributions to American hockey. Furthermore, in 1998 John became the first Gopher ever to have his number retired when his No. 8 was hung into the Mariucci Arena rafters forever.

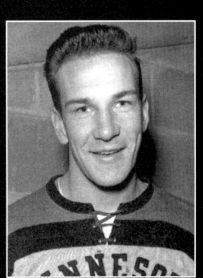

John Mayasich was the best hockey player ever to wear a sweater in the Gopher State, and is a real living legend. But as great an athlete as he was, so is his humility. Often in the limelight, he was always quick to share the credit and the glory with his teammates and coaches.

"I was blessed with the opportunity of playing with and against some great players," he said. "I was at the right place at the right time with the right people, and I made a contribution through a lot of hard work & effort."

"John Mayasich brought college hockey to a new plateau," said John Mariucci. "He was the Wayne Gretzky of his time, and if he were playing pro hockey today, he would simply be a bigger, stronger, back-checking Gretzky. The words to describe him haven't been invented. When I say he's the best, that's totally inadequate."

Those incredible Eveleth teams were led by so many outstanding young men, including the likes of John Matchefts and Willard Ikola. One man stands alone when it comes to "legendary status," however, and that distinction goes to John Mayasich, arguably the greatest player ever to lace up a pair of skates in Minnesota. Mayasich still holds 10 scoring records from the state high school hockey tournament, including most all-time points (46) and goals (36). The 1951 season was the one where Mayasich stole the show though, when he amassed 18 points in three games on 15 goals and three assists, including seven goals in a semifinal win over Minneapolis Southwest. Of course, Mayasich went on to become an All-American at the University of Minnesota, where he rewrote the Gopher record book, scoring 144 goals and 298 total points. He went on to compete on eight U.S. National or Olympic teams, and has earned the title of "the greatest American ever to play the game."

Some of the outstanding Eveleth players from that era included: Neil Celley, Wally Grant, Pat Finnegan, Clem Cossalter, John Matchefts, Willard Ikola, John Mayasich, Ron Castellano, Dan Voce, Dick Peterson, Ed Mrcronich, Andre Gambucci, Ron Martinson, Gene Klune, Bruce Shutte, Bob Kochevar, Ed Oswald, Dave Rodda, Mike Castellano and Dave Hendrickson.

Eveleth's Mother Lode...

The answer to why Eveleth is considered as the Hockey Capital of America can be traced back like a family tree. Young boys from this community branched out across the country and laid down roots for other hockey players to grow from. Gilbert Finnegan, former Eveleth postmaster and hockey historian stated that during one particular season during the 1930s Great Depression era, there were 147 Eveleth boys playing hockey on professional, college, semi-pro and senior open teams located throughout the United States.

It seemed that wherever hockey was being played in the country, Eveleth players were right in the mix of things. In many cities around the country, large companies that had their own hockey teams would stack their rosters entirely with Eveleth boys. Companies that wanted to secure a winning hockey team made sure to take care of the Eveleth boys by giving them good jobs in an attempt to secure their services. In turn, a pipeline of sorts was created back to Eveleth. Wanting to take care of their own, players soon insisted upon "package deals," which helped them get their friends and family the opportunity of a good job as well. Even during the Depression, Eveleth boys were finding good jobs around the country, and easing the job crunch and hard economic times back home on the Range. Hockey had gone from a game, to a meal ticket into greener pastures.

One such company was Hershey's Chocolate, in Pennsylvania, which had a team of all Eveleth players. Led by the Papike brothers, a team from San Diego won a string of Pacific Coast League titles throughout the 1930s with a squad composed almost entirely

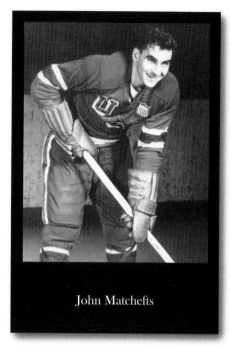

John Matchefts

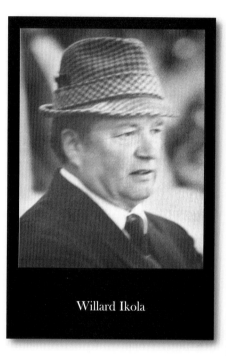

Willard Ikola

Doug Palazzari

of Eveleth players. In 1935 the National AAU tournament in Chicago featured 10 different teams from across the country. Nearly two-thirds of the players on those combined rosters were from Eveleth. The winning Chicago Baby Ruth team, coached by Eveleth's Connie Pleban, had nine Eveleth natives on its 13-man roster. That same Chicago Baby Ruth team went on to beat a very strong St. Cloud Teachers College, 2-0, in the National AAU Tournament. Incidentally, that St. Cloud team which posted a 45-7-0 record that year, was manned almost entirely by Eveleth players. By the late 1930s Vic Heyliger, the coach at the University of Michigan, had 13 kids from Eveleth on his team. And, the University of Illinois had at one time a complete roster of Eveleth boys. In addition, during the late 1930's and early 1940's countless Eveleth players migrated to the West Coast to play college hockey, where the allure of sunshine, a good job and good education awaited. As a result, some of the best college hockey in the country was played at USC, UCLA, Loyola, and Cal.

And of course, there were four Eveleth boys on the 1956 silver-medal winning Olympic team held in Cortina, Italy: John Mayasich, John Matchefts, and Willard Ikola, who was named the most valuable player in the Olympic competition. The coach of that squad was none other than John Mariucci.

By the mid-point of the century, Eveleth had become a household name in the world of hockey. Considered as the hub of the Missabe, Vermilion, and Cuyuna Iron Ranges — which at one time produced nearly 80 percent of the world's iron ore that in turn was used to make everything from automobiles, machines and skyscrapers — Eveleth's real "mother lode" was its exportation of top-notch players to the world of hockey. This community had embraced the sport of hockey like no other before or after, and was handsomely rewarded by the fact that it is today synonymous with the game. These Iron Rangers are passionate about sports, and not just about hockey. The sports scene in Eveleth was so intense even back in the 1920s, that they even imported a couple of refugees from the now infamous Chicago "Black Sox" team, who were banned from baseball for life for throwing the 1919 World Series, to play summer baseball on the town team. (Maybe "Shoeless" Joe Jackson himself learned to play hockey in Eveleth?)

As mentioned before, Eveleth was and still is an incredible melting pot of cultures, languages and nationalities, all brought together by the prosperity of mining. Those same mining companies used to put men of different nationality's together down in the mines on purpose, figuring that if they couldn't speak with one another because of the language barrier, that they would, in turn, work more. But in the end, all those immigrants fooled them, by learning bits and pieces of each other's languages and cultures. In the end, they celebrated their colorful diversity, while hockey gave them all a common bond in which to pull together for. Eveleth is to

American hockey what Detroit is to cars and Hollywood is to film making. Its story is one of the most unique and special in all of 20th century sports.

The U.S. Hockey Hall of Fame: Eveleth, MN...

Perhaps the most telling sign that Eveleth is indeed the hockey capital of America, is the fact that the US Hockey Hall of Fame is located there. "Why," you might ask, "is a national shrine of this significance dedicated to United States hockey, located in a town of merely 5,000 citizens?" The answer is simple. Eveleth was chosen for its unique long-standing history and incredible contribution to American hockey. And, perhaps most importantly, is the fact that no town of its size has ever produced more elite-level players in the history of the game.

There are several reasons as to why Eveleth is so hockey crazy. In the beginning, the superior Canadian players were imported down to Eveleth to play for the pro teams. In return they were given good paying jobs in the mines. This ultimately served as a wonderful form of entertainment for the miners and their families. Eventually, the game rubbed off on the kids in town who grew up wanting to emulate these new stars, and before they knew it, a whole generation of superstar hockey players was born.

There is a reason that the four major halls of fames are located in the small towns that they are. For instance, Abner Doubleday, the founder of baseball, has roots back to Cooperstown, NY, and that is why the Baseball Hall of Fame is located there. Jim Thorpe was from Canton, Ohio, and that surely played into why the Football Hall of Fame is located there as well. And, Dr. James Naysmith first played his newly created sport of basketball in Springfield, Mass., not coincidentally where the Basketball Hall of Fame resides today.

As for that "other" Hockey Hall of Fame that one is located in Toronto, Canada. There are but a handful of Americans enshrined into the National Hockey Hall of Fame, in Toronto. Perhaps that led to the decision in 1967 to form an exploratory committee into the idea of creating a U.S. Hockey Hall of Fame. The U.S. Hall of Fame was not created to compete with the Canadian Hall, rather it was built to celebrate the accomplishments of Americans in a game that up until recently was dominated by Canadians.

How the Hall began is an interesting story in itself. In 1967 that committee from the Eveleth Civic Association, known as the "Project H Committee," began an intensive historical search program to determine candidates (other American cities) that they felt were worthy of being host cities to the Hockey Hall of Fame. Their exten-

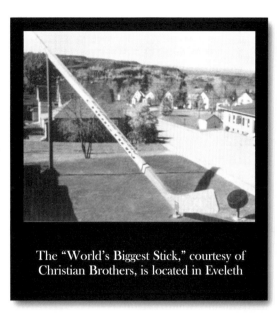

The "World's Biggest Stick," courtesy of Christian Brothers, is located in Eveleth

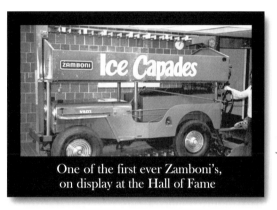

One of the first ever Zamboni's, on display at the Hall of Fame

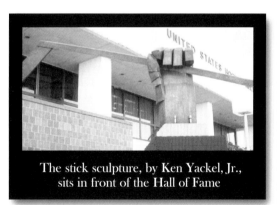

The stick sculpture, by Ken Yackel, Jr., sits in front of the Hall of Fame

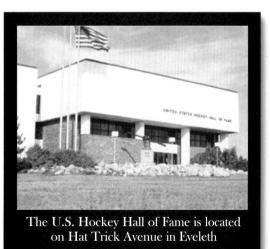

The U.S. Hockey Hall of Fame is located on Hat Trick Avenue in Eveleth

sive research showed that since the late 1800s, no other town had contributed as much to hockey's development; and no state had contributed more than Minnesota. So, on May 19, 1968, they requested the official endorsement from the Amateur Hockey Association of the United States (AHAUS) in Boston, Mass. AHAUS, in turn, gave its blessings to the project, and by 1973 the three-story U.S. Hockey Hall of Fame & Museum was completed along Hat Trick Avenue in Eveleth.

The non-profit corporation, U.S. Hockey Hall of Fame, Inc. was chartered in the state of Minnesota in 1968 and its first officers and directors included nine members from AHAUS: Robert Ridder, Walter Bush, Don Clark, J. Lawrence Cain, Edward Stanley, Charles Kunkle, Thayer Tutt, Cal Marvin, and Robert Fleming. From the Project H Committee, representing Eveleth, were Larry Doyle, Tony Nemanich and D. Kelly Campbell.

(Incredibly, nearly 10% of the Hall's inductees are from Eveleth. Those 12 individuals, who represent more than any other U.S. city, are: Sam LoPresti, Frank Brimsek, Mike Karakas, Oscar Almquist, John Mayasich, John Mariucci, John Matchefts, Willard Ikola, Connie Pleban, Wally Grant, Serge Gambucci and Doug Palazzari.)

By bringing the past to the present and into the future, the Hall serves as the focal point for preserving the history and heritage of American Hockey. To date, a total of 130 individuals have been enshrined in the U.S. Hockey Hall of Fame.

In 2007 USA Hockey, the National Governing Body for the sport of ice hockey in the United States and the Hall reached a cooperative agreement to work together as partners. The museum had fallen on hard economic times and needed a shot in the arm. With USA Hockey on board, that is exactly what they got. As a result, the Hall changed its name to the United States Hockey Hall of Fame Museum, Inc., and set out to work hand in hand with some of the top hockey minds in the world.

"This agreement will raise the national profile of the U.S. Hockey Hall of Fame for all parties involved," said Stan Hubbard, the Hall's outgoing president. "We're proud to have done our part to ensure the preservation and sharing of the rich history of hockey in the United States. With USA Hockey's extraordinary commitment to the U.S. Hockey Hall of Fame, we will have an unprecedented national footprint that this entity so richly deserves."

With that, Iron Rangers everywhere let out a collective sigh of relief that their beloved Hall would not be moved to the Xcel Center or even the Mall of America. It was staying put in Eveleth, where it belongs. Period.

United States Hockey Hall of Fame Inductees:

1973
Taffy Abel
Hobey Baker
Frank Brimsek
George Brown
Walter Brown
John Chase
Cully Dahlstrom
John Garrison
Doc Gibson
Moose Goheen
Malcolm Gordon
Eddie Jeremiah
Mike Karakas
Tom Lockhart
Myles Lane
Sam LoPresti
John Mariucci
George Owen
Ding Palmer
Doc Romnes
Cliff Thompson
Thayer Tutt
Ralph Winsor
Coddy Winters
Lyle Wright

1974
Bill Chadwick
Ray Chiasson
Vic Desjardins
Doug Everett
Vic Heylinger
Virgil Johnson
Snooks Kelley
Bill Moe
Fido Purpur

1975
Tony Conroy
Austie Harding
Stewart Iglehart
Joe Linder
Fred Moseley

1976
Bill Cleary
John Mayasich
Bob Ridder

1977
Earl Bartholome
Eddie Olson
Bill Riley

1978
Peter Bessone
Don Clark
Hub Nelson

1979
Bob Dill
Jack Riley

1980
Walter Bush
Nick Kahler

1981
Bob Cleary
Bill Jennings
Tommy Williams

1982
Cal Marvin
Bill Stewart

1983
Oscar Almquist
Jack McCartan

1984
William Christian
William Wirtz

1985
Bob Blake
Dick Rondeau
Hal Trumble

1986
Jack Garrity
Ken Yackel

1987
Jack Kirrane
Hugh "Muzz" Murray, Sr.

1988
Richard Desmond
Lawrence Ross

1989
Roger Christian
Robert Paradise

1990
Herb Brooks
Willard Ikola
Connie Pleban

1991
Robbie Ftorek
Robert Johnson
John Matchefts

1992
Amo Bessone
Len Ceglarski
James Fullerton

1993
Charles Schulz
John Kelley
David Langevin

1994
Joe Cavanagh
Wally Grant
Ned Harkness

1995
Henry Boucha
James Claypool
Ken Morrow

1996
Sergio Gambucci
Reed Larson
Craig Patrick

1997
William Nyrop
Timothy Sheehy
Charles Holt, Jr

1998
Lou Nanne
Mike Curran
Joe Mullen
Bruce Mather

1999
Gordy Roberts
Rod Langway
Sid Watson

2000
Neal Broten
Larry Pleau
Doug Palazzari

2001
Dave Christian
Paul Johnson
Mike Ramsey

2002
Mark Fusco
Scott Fusco
Joe Riley
Doug Woog

2003
John Cunniff
Dick Dougherty
Mark Howe
Pat LaFontaine
1980 U.S. Olympic Team

2004
Paul Coppo
Phil Housley
Mike Ilitch
Mark Johnson

2005
Keith Christiansen
Lane McDonald
Maurice Roberts
Murray Williamson

2006
Milton "Curly" Brink
Mike Milbury
Gary Gambucci

2007
Aaron Broten
Bobby Carpenter
John MacInnes
John Vanbiesbrouck

46

MAHA'S ROLE IN EARLY YOUTH HOCKEY IN MINNESOTA

The Duluth Glen Avon PeeWees, led by coach Bob Fryberger, won the 1951 national title in New York City, and even got the Key to the City from the Duluth Mayor.

The role of MAHA (Minnesota Amateur Hockey Association) in the state's growth of hockey has been immeasurable. Through the efforts of gentlemen such as Don Clark and Bob Ridder, the organization has been the backbone of not only Minnesota hockey, but in many ways hockey throughout the country. By 1973, at the modest registration fee of $2, there were some 2,000 teams enrolled in the state. Their mission became more focused over time: "To encourage and improve the standard of ice hockey in the Minnesota area; to conduct ice hockey tournaments and to select representative teams to participate in tournaments; to associate with other ice hockey associations; to do any and all acts necessary or desirable in the furtherance of the foregoing purposes; to buy, sell, lease and otherwise deal in all kinds of property, real, personal and mixed, for the purpose of creating further interest in amateur hockey."

The 1924 Olive Club Juniors (Hibbing)

In 1951, under the direction of MAHA Secretary-Treasurer Don Clark, the state's first-ever PeeWee tournament was held at the White Bear Lake Hippodrome. The statewide event, which included teams from Grand Forks, Wayzata, South St. Paul, East Grand Forks, Minneapolis, and St. Paul , was the first state youth tournament (under high school age) to be held in the United States. There, Duluth Glen Avon edged host White Bear Lake, 3-2, in the finals of the eight-team event before a crowd of some 700 fans. The Duluth team, led by coach Bob Fryberger and his three sons' line of Jerry, Bob and Dates, continued on to win the 1951 AHAUS National PeeWee Championship in New York's Madison Square Garden.

In addition to the Senior and PeeWee class tournaments, the next category to be formed was the Juvenile (today called Junior Gold), which featured players 18 years and under. The initial 1956 tournament was held in Duluth and was won by St. Paul Arlington, which defeated Mountain Iron in the finals of the four-team event. (MAHA's first state Midget tournament, held in Duluth in 1961, saw Duluth Lower Chester defeat Owatonna for the title. While the initial Junior B championship was staged at Polar Arena in North St. Paul in 1974.)

In 1960 Minnesota officially adopted the classes and nomenclature that the AHAUS, the national governing body, had decided to employ. The system, which had been borrowed from Canada, included Juniors, Juveniles, Midgets, Bantams, PeeWees, Squirts and Mites. By the 1970s girls hockey was also being organized.

Walter Bush and Bob Fleming, both of whom became involved in MAHA in the 1950s, would remain active in the sport on a national level as well. Bush has served as president of USA Hockey (AHAUS) since 1986, while Fleming has served as director, in addition to chairing the United States Olympic Ice Hockey Committee for many years. Peter Lindberg has been a USA Hockey vice president since 1988, and Bob Ridder served as team manager of the 1952 and 1956 U.S. Olympic teams. (In 1998 MAHA changed its name to Minnesota Hockey. An affiliate of USA Hockey, the organization is the governing body of amateur hockey in the state. In addition, in 1999 former NHL star and Eveleth native, Doug Palazzari was named as USA Hockey's Executive Director.)

Today, Minnesota Hockey is run by Mark Jorgenson, a top notch visionary who has made great strides in taking the organization to the next level and has certainly made us proud along the way.

U.S. National PeeWee Champs

1951	Duluth
1951	Duluth
1965	Duluth

U.S. National Bantam Champs

1951	Duluth
1952	Duluth
1953	Eveleth
1954	Eveleth
1958	Duluth
1970	Edina
1971	Edina
1972	Edina
1973	Mounds View
1974	Roseville

The 1973-74 Mounds View Bantams (led by future Gopher Steve Ulseth), finished with a 73-4-2 record and went on to beat Detroit for the National Championship

Duluth's Legendary Stauber Brothers...

NATIVE MINNESOTANS WHO HAVE PLAYED IN THE NHL

(Sources: Hockey Hall of Fame & hockeydatabase.com)

A
Rudy Ahlin
Andrew Alberts
Steve Alley
Earl Anderson
Russ Anderson
Mike Antonovich
Les Auge

B
David Backes
Bill Baker
Keith Ballard
Mike Baumgartner
Tim Bergland
Adam Berkhoel
Scott Bjugstad
Jason Blake
Brandon Bochenski
Brian Bonin
Henry Boucha
Joe Bretto
Frank Brimsek
Milt Brink
Aaron Broten
Neal Broten
Paul Broten
Bill Butters
Dustin Byfuglien

C
Jack Carlson
Steve Carlson
Ryan Carter
Jon Casey
Tom Chorske
Dave Christian
Steve Christoff
Ben Clymer
Bob Collyard
Mike Crowley
Mark Cullen
Matt Cullen
Jim Cunningham

D
Chris Dahlquist
Cully Dahlstrom
Brad DeFauw
Bob Dill
Joe Dziedzic

E
Bryan Erickson
Chad Erickson

F
Kelly Fairchild
Mike Farrell
Rusty Fitzgerald

G
Gary Gambucci
Ken Gernander
Tom Gilbert
Stan Gilbertson
Moose Goheen
Leroy Goldsworthy
Tom Gorence
Guy Gosselin
John Gruden

H
Al Hangsleben
Ben Hankinson
Casey Hankinson
Keith Hanson
Tim Harrer
Brett Hauer
Adam Hauser
Peter Hayek
Mark Heaslip
Bret Hedican
Matt Henderson
Darby Hendrickson
Sean Hill
Tom Hirsch
Phil Hoene
Paul Holmgren
Phil Housley

J
Don Jackson
Steve Janaszak
David Jensen
Steve Jensen
John Johannson
Craig Johnson
Erik Johnson
Jim Johnson
Mark Johnson
Virgil Johnson

K
Mike Karakas
Chris Kenady
Trent Klatt
Scott Kleinendorst
Matt Koalska
Jim Korn
Tom Kurvers

L
Bryce Lampman
Jamie Langenbrunner
Dave Langevin
Josh Langfeld
Reed Larson
Mike Lauen
Jordan Leopold
Pete LoPresti
Sam LoPresti

M
Chris Marinucci
John Mariucci
Paul Martin
Steve Martinson
Bob Mason
Chris McAlpine
Jack McCartan
Rob McClanahan
Jim McElmury
Bruce McIntosh
Mike McNeill
Joe Micheletti
Pat Micheletti
Corey Millen
Warren Miller
Joe Motzko
Rick Mrozik
Peter Mueller

N
Jeff Nielsen
Kirk Nielsen
Matt Niskanen
Craig Norwich
Bill Nyrop

O
Todd Okerlund
Mark Osiecki
Joel Otto

P
Aldo Palazzari
Doug Palazzari
Joe Papike
Bob Paradise
Zach Parise
Jeff Parker
Mark Parrish
Mark Pavelich
Tom Pederson
Mike Peluso
Toby Petersen
Lance Pitlick
Derek Plante
Shjon Podein
John Pohl

John Polich
Mike Polich
Tom Preissing
Chris Pryor

R
Mike Ramsey
Erik Rasmussen
Damian Rhodes
Todd Richards
Travis Richards
Jon Rohloff
Doc Romnes

S
Shaun Sabol
Scott Sandelin
Gary Sargent
Craig Sarner
Kurt Sauer
Butch Schaeffer
Clarence Schmidt
Neil Sheehy
Tim Sheehy
Steve Short
Randy Skarda
Dale Smedsmo
Wyatt Smith
Dave Snuggerud
Robb Stauber
Mark Stuart
Mike Stuart
Al Suomi

T
Jeff Taffe
John Taft
Dean Talafous
David Tanabe
Jeff Teal
Sean Toomey
Dan Trebil

W
Steve Wagner
Jim Warner
Jim Watt
Erik Westrum
Butch Williams
Tommy Williams
Mike Wong

Y
Ken Yackel
Tom Younghans

Z
Doug Zmolek

THE LESTER PATRICK TROPHY

The Lester Patrick Trophy is an award given annually for outstanding service to hockey in the United States. Eligible recipients are players, officials, coaches, executives and referees. The winner is selected by an award committee consisting of the President of the NHL, an NHL Governor, a representative of the New York Rangers, a member of the Hockey Hall of Fame Builder's section, a member of the Hockey Hall of Fame Player's section, a member of the U. S. Hockey Hall of Fame, a member of the NHL Broadcasters' Association, and a member of the Professional Hockey Writers' Association. Except the NHL President, each member is rotated annually. The Patrick Trophy was presented by the New York Rangers in 1966 to honor the late Lester Patrick — the long-time famed general manager and coach of the team.

Among the Minnesotans who have won the award include: Walter L. Bush Jr. (1973), Donald M. Clark (1975), John Mariucci (1977), The 1980 Gold Medal Winning U.S. Olympic Team (1980), Charles M. Schulz (1981), Bob Johnson (1988), Robert Ridder (1994) Neal Broten (1988), John Mayasich (1988),The 1998 Gold Medal Winning U.S. Women's Olympic Team (1999), Herb Brooks (2002), The 1960 Gold Medal Winning U.S. Olympic Team (2002), Reed Larson (2006), and Glen Sonmor (2006).

MINNESOTA'S ALL-TIME OLYMPIANS

Name	Olympic Team	Hometown	Name	Olympic Team	Hometown
Steve Alley	1976	Anoka	Jordan Leopold	2006	Minneapolis
Wendell Anderson	1956	St. Paul	Len Lilyholm	1968	Robbinsdale
Larry Bader	1972	Hopkins	Bob Lundeen	1976	Minneapolis
Bill Baker	1980	Grand Rapids	Bob Mason	1984	International Falls
Robert Baker	1948	Thief River Falls	John Matchefts	1956	Eveleth
Ruben Bjorkman	1952, 1948	Roseau	John Mayasich	1960, 1956	Eveleth
Scott Bjugstad	1984	New Brighton	Jack McCartan	1960	St. Paul
Jason Blake	2006	Moorhead	Rob McClanahan	1980	St. Paul
Alana Blahoski	1998	St. Paul	Thomas McCoy	1964	Minneapolis
Jeff Boeser	1976	Bloomington	James McElmury	1972	St. Paul
Robert Boeser	1948	Minneapolis	Bruce McIntosh	1972	Edina
Henry Boucha	1972	Warroad	Dan McKinnon	1956	Williams
David Brooks	1964	St. Paul	Richard Meredith	1960, 1956	Minneapolis
Herb Brooks	1968, 1964	St. Paul	Wayne Meredith	1964	Minneapolis
Neal Broten	1980	Roseau	Corey Millen	1988, 1984	Cloquet
Charles Brown	1972	Minneapolis	Jack Morrison	1968	Wayzata
Eugene Campbell	1956	Minneapolis	Lou Nanne	1968	Minneapolis
Keith Christensen	1972	International Falls	Ron Naslund	1972	Minneapolis
Bill Christian	1960	Warroad	John Noah	1952	Crookston
Dave Christian	1980	Warroad	Todd Okerlund	1988	Burnsville
Gordon Christian	1956	Warroad	Wally Olds	1972	Baudette
Roger Christian	1964, 1960	Warroad	Allan Opsahl	1948	Minneapolis
Steve Christoff	1980	Richfield	Arnold C. Oss, Jr.	1952	Minneapolis
Blaine Comstock	1976	Roseau	Joel Otto	1998	Elk River
Anthony Conroy	1920	St. Paul	Robert Owen	1960	St. Louis Park
Mike Curran	1972	International Falls	Robert Paradise	1968	St. Paul
Jack Dale	1968	St. Paul	Mark Parrish	2006	Bloomington
Natalie Darwitz	2002, 2006	Eagan	Mark Pavelich	1980	Eveleth
Dan Dilworth	1964	International Falls	Jack Petroske	1956	Hibbing
Dick Dougherty	1956	International Falls	Jenny Potter (Schmidgall)	1998, '02, '06	Eagan
Craig Falkman	1968	St. Paul	Mike Ramsey	1980	Minneapolis
J. Edward Fitzgerald	1920	St. Paul	William Reichart	1964	Rochester
Dates Fryberger	1964	Duluth	Travis Richards	1994	Crystal
Andre Gambucci	1952	Eveleth	Robert Rompre	1952	International Falls
Frank Goheen	1920	White Bear Lake	Donald Ross	1968, 1964	Roseau
Guy Gosselin	1992, 1988	Rochester	Gary Ross	1976	Roseau
Dan Griffin	1976	North St. Paul	Ed Sampson	1956	International Falls
Steve Griffith	1984	St. Paul	Gary Sampson	1984	International Falls
John Harrington	1984, 1980	Virginia	Frank Sanders	1972	North St. Paul
Rob Harris	1976	Roseau	Craig Sarner	1972	North St. Paul
Brett Hauer	1994	Richfield	Gary Schmalzbauer	1964	St. Paul
Bret Hedican	1992, 2006	N. St. Paul	Buzz Schneider	1980, 1976	Babbitt
Darby Hendrickson	1994	Richfield	James Sedin	1952	St. Paul
Sean Hill	1992	Duluth	Steve Sertich	1976	Virginia
Tom Hirsch	1984	Minneapolis	Tim Sheehy	1972	International Falls
Phil Housley	2002	South St. Paul	Dave Snuggerud	1988	Minnetonka
Jeff Hymanson	1976	Anoka	Larry Stordahl	1968	Roseau
Willard Ikola	1956	Eveleth	Eric Strobel	1980	Rochester
Chris Imes	1994	Birchdale	John Taft	1976	Minneapolis
Steve Janaszak	1980	White Bear Lake	Tim Thomas	1984	Richfield
David H. Hensen	1984	Crystal	Allan Van	1952	St. Paul
Paul Jensen	1976	Robbinsdale	Phil Verchota	1984, 1980	Duluth
Steve Jensen	1976	Plymouth	Cyril Weidenborner	1920	St. Paul
Jim Johannson	1992, 1988	Rochester	Krissy Wendell	2002, 2006	Brooklyn Park
Craig Johnson	1994	St. Paul	James Westby	1964	Minneapolis
Paul Johnson	1964, 1960	W. St. Paul	Thomas Williams	1960	Duluth
Phillip LaBatte	1936	Minneapolis	Kenneth James Yackel	1952	St. Paul
Jamie Langenbrunner	1998	Duluth	Thomas Yurkovich	1964	Eveleth

49

THE MINNESOTA NORTH STARS

Watching the Minnesota North Stars, er... sorry... Dallas Stars, win the Stanley Cup back in 1999 was particularly painful. I think back to how close the team came in 1981 and 1991 to winning it all, and just can't help but think that if it wasn't for that ?%@#!! Norm Green, maybe Lord Stanley's Cup would have been here, rather than in Texas. First of all, let's get the facts straight. Contrary to popular belief, the Stars did not leave town because the fans didn't support them. That was a crock. They became the Texas "Lone Stars" because the owner decided to pack up and move them there for personal reasons. The North Stars' attendance averaged more than 12,000 fans per game in their last decade in Minnesota, and were outdrawing the majority of NHL clubs around the league.

Since 1967 our Stars had done us proud at the old Met Center in Bloomington. But today, regretably, both are gone for good. Sure the Minnesota Wild's new digs at the Xcel Center are fantastic, but nothing was quite like tailgating with your pals at a Stars game. There were plenty of peaks and valleys with our Stars, but they were always the best show in town. So come on and take a trip down memory lane, and reminisce about one of Minnesota's greatest sports franchises, the North Stars.

By the mid-1960s, the Minneapolis Bruins and St. Paul Rangers were the only pro hockey teams in town. Both teams were minor league affiliates of the Boston Bruins and New York Rangers, respectively. Sure the Gopher Hockey team was competitive at that point, but there wasn't a professional hockey presence in town anywhere close to that of the big league's — the NHL. Now, during this period of time, pro sports was absolutely booming in Minnesota. The Twins and Vikings had both just arrived in 1961-62, and on top of that, the Gopher Football team was in its heyday, recently winning the National Championship and Rose Bowl during that same time period. Knowing this, one could understand why there would be some skepticism about the fact that in 1965, the NHL decided to expand from its original six, to 12 teams, and a group from Minnesota was making a run at getting one of those coveted franchises. Minnesotans didn't know if the community at large could support another professional team though. And on top of that, just where in the heck would they play? There was no arena during this time that could accommodate a new team.

The kingpin of that group leading the charge to seduce the NHL to Minnesota, was attorney, Walter Bush Jr. Bush, a former prep hockey star at Minneapolis' Breck School, played collegiately at Dartmouth, and also in the semi-pro ranks both as a player and coach. At the time, the former Olympic team manager was a part-owner of the Minneapolis Bruins, a minor league farm team of the NHL's Boston Bruins. Bush's co-owners included two other Minneapolis businessmen; television executive Gordon Ritz, and ex-Yale hockey captain and real-estate developer Robert McNulty. Now, with all of the competitive sports in town during that time, combined with the fact that the Minneapolis Bruins were forced to play in an antique arena, the group was finding it very difficult to sell their product to the public. So, they started a dialogue with Wes Adams, the Boston Bruins chairman of the board, about lobbying for one of the new NHL expansion franchises to be located in Minnesota. With 14 formal applications sent in from cities all across North America, the competition for one of the half dozen teams was fierce. The group knew that if they were going to have a shot at big-time hockey in Minnesota, they would have to come up with some big dough.

Cesare Maniago

Bush immediately seized the opportunity by putting together an eight-man investment group, comprised of two groups, each from both sides of the Mississippi. He figured that it was going to take a group effort to raise the dollars necessary, and didn't want to alienate the folks from St. Paul. From the Mill City side of town, investment banker Wheelock Whitney joined Bush, Ritz, and McNulty, while from St. Paul came television executive Bob Ridder, business executive John Ordway, lumber company executive John Driscoll, and trucking mogul Harry McNeely. (Later William Rasmussen would join the group.) Their similarities were eerie. Most all of them had played high school and college hockey, and all were graduates of Ivy League schools. They seemed well prepared for the challenge ahead of them.

Between them, the $2 million expansion fee was not going to be a problem. The group's biggest task, however, was to figure out just how they were going to convince the expansion committee that there was a suitable venue for their new team to play in. The NHL was demanding that the arena hold at least 12,500 seats, and unfortunately, the only options in the Twin Cities were the St. Paul Auditorium, with a capacity of 8,500, and the old Minneapolis Arena, which would seat only 5,000. They thought of every possible scenario on how to fit a square peg into the proverbial round hole but could not come up with a solution. They even explored the possibility of remodeling and expanding the Hippodrome at the state fairgrounds. The bottom line was that they did not want to pay for a new arena, which would cost millions of dollars. (This ultimately was the reason that the NBA's Minneapolis Lakers packed up and moved to Los Angeles only a few years earlier in 1960, because they too did not have an adequate facility to play in. They were even forced to move several NBA Championship Playoff games to alternate venues around the Twin Cities, because the Minneapolis Auditorium had been committed to host ice shows and sportsmen's conventions.)

For a while it looked like this was going to be a deal-breaker, and the group was going to be stuck on the outside looking in. Just when they thought things couldn't get worse, a second group of investors from St. Paul, led by businessman Henri Foussard, emerged out of nowhere with a bid of their own. Now, as if things weren't messed up enough, there were two groups from Minnesota who wanted a hockey franchise.

Trying to keep the calm, the two groups decided to get together before their meeting with the NHL's Board of Governors in New York to see if a compromise could be worked out. It couldn't, and stubbornly both groups made the trip to the Big Apple with the intention of presenting their bids. There, the two groups got together again and had it out with each other for better than two days straight, trying to work something out for the good of Minnesota. Finally, the two parties reached a compromise of sorts. Bush's group tentatively agreed that in addition to giving the St. Paul group a 10 percent ownership stake in the team, they would make a proposal to the committee for the renovation of the St. Paul Auditorium, knowing full well that a referendum would need to be passed back in Minnesota. The deal was shaky at best, and in the 13th hour the group changed their minds, deciding instead that they would either have to drop the whole thing altogether, or accept the fact that they were going to have to pony up the cash for a new arena.

In the end Bush's group decided to dig deep, and ultimately promised the Board a new arena, even though they had no idea where they were going to come up with the more than $7 million needed to build it. Not to mention the fact that they had neither architectural designs nor a chunk of property to put it on. With that, on Feb. 9, 1966, Bush's group was awarded one of the six new franchises, despite the fact that they were the smallest television market and had the smallest population of all of the applicants who were vying for a team. The NHL's expansion committee, knowing of the incredible popularity of high school and college hockey in Minnesota, was willing to gamble on the fact that a very strong fan base was already in place here. Now all the group needed to do was build their team a new home to play in.

(Knowing that there was no way in hell that Minnesota was ever going to get two franchises, then-NHL President Clarence Campbell, upon reviewing both Twin Cities bids, reportedly stated, "In my wildest dreams I could not visualize that a franchise would come out of the chaos surrounding the Minnesota bid." Lucky for us, it did!)

Bush's syndicate rushed home and, within a few months, arranged the financing for a new, state of the art hockey arena that was going to be built in the Twin Cities. But where? Now as you know, the sister cities of Minneapolis and St. Paul have not always seen eye to eye on competitive matters such as where to put a professional sports team. The bickering sisters would seemingly do anything to prevent the other from having territorial bragging rights, particularly over something as visible and full of testosterone as this. Such was the case with the Vikings and Twins only a few years before, who, in the end, wound up compromising their new homeland to a neutral "demilitarized- zone," very much like Switzerland. Yep, rather than building Metropolitan Stadium downtown, where the people and corporations were, they chose instead for a nice goat pasture, right in the middle of nowhere. The group, wanting to avoid further bickering and delays, figured that if they were going to get their arena built on time, would also build in the comfy confines of Bloomington. The local Stadium Commission agreed, and on Oct. 3, 1966, the ground was broken for the new, state-of-the-art Metropolitan Sports Center. The joke around town was that they would need to hire the construction crew that built the pyramids in order to get this impossible job done. Amazingly, in less than one year, Met Center was rushed to completion just in time for the beginning of the 1967-68 season under the direction of Bob McNulty. Upon its completion, NHL President Clarence Campbell called the 15,000+ seat ice palace, "the finest facility for viewing hockey that I have ever seen."

The NHL, which had been a six team league for 25 seasons with teams in New York, Boston, Detroit, Chicago, Toronto, and Montreal, now had franchises in Minnesota, St. Louis, Los Angeles, Philadelphia, Pittsburgh and Oakland. In addition, it was decided that the original six would make up the "Eastern Division," while the six new squads would make up the "West."

John Driscoll was named as chairman of the board, Bush became the team's president, and the other partners evolved into the team's board of directors. Now all they needed was a nickname. In 1966, some 1,200 hockey fans submitted their ideas for a new team name. Among the top creative choices included: Norsemen, Voyageurs, Blades, Mustangs, Muskies, Lumberjacks, Miners, Mallards, Pioneers, Polars, Marauders, Zips, Blades and Puckeroos.

Walter Bush

Tommy Williams

But the overwhelming winner was, of course, "Les Etoiles du Nord" — the North Stars.

The Bird is the Word
The team's first order of business was to hire a coach and general manager. There were numerous candidates considered, but in the end Bush decided to kill two birds with one stone by hiring Ontario native, Wren Blair, who had previously served as GM for his Minneapolis Bruins minor league team. Blair, or "the Bird" as he was affectionately known, had a long history of success while as a coach and GM of numerous professional, minor pro and junior clubs throughout Canada, as well as for the Boston Bruins, where he served as director of minor-league personnel. He also had a background in international hockey, having led the Whitby (Ontario) Dunlops, to the 1958 IHHF world championship. But what Blair was especially known for was his ability to scout young talent. His biggest find, none other than Bruin legend Bobby Orr. He had a very unorthodox style of coaching his players, seemingly getting every ounce of effort out of them, and ultimately everywhere he went he built winning teams. Known to have a rather large ego, the Bird simply could not stand to lose, and would tolerate nothing less from his players.

Blair's first job with the Stars would be to assemble a scouting staff in preparation of the NHL's upcoming expansion draft. Blair's first hire as his personal assistant was none other than John Mariucci, who was fresh off of coaching the U.S. National team. He then named Harold Cotton as his scouting director, followed by Ted O'Connor as chief scout. Blair's brother, Gerald, along with Leo Boivin, Bob Dill, and Murray Williamson were also named to the staff. Their job was to pound the proverbial underbelly of the hockey world for prospects. Blair even gave each scout a tape recorder, so that he could make immediate first hand observations right at rinkside.

Now, the NHL's expansion draft in 1966 was nothing like today's draft lottery. This was the first time that the league had done such a thing, and to say that there were some major flaws in the system would be an understatement. The way they had set it up was definitely in the favor of the original six clubs. The new teams were allowed to select players from the rosters of the established clubs, which were allowed to protect 11 skaters plus one goalie. Blair, a wheeler-dealer, loved the game of building from nothing, and found that he had to be very resourceful. He knew that if the Stars were going to be competitive, he would have to use every weapon at his disposal, including multi-player trades, dealing draft choices and buying unproven players from other clubs.

"Building an NHL team from the formula given us at expansion time was a real grind," said Blair in the book 'The Goldy Shuffle.' "It still is. It was like the neighborhood bully coming down the street and saying, 'Okay, let's choose up sides and play a game. I'm going to take the first 11 guys, now you can have one.' You know what the outcome of that game will be in any neighborhood in North America."

On June 6, 1967, the draft was held, and Blair went about the impossible task of selecting his team's 20 allotted nobodys and has-beens. So, with the first pick, Blair opted to draft a young goaltender from the New York Rangers by the name of Cesare Maniago, who was already known by the locals from his minor league playing stint with the Minneapolis Bruins of the CPHL. Among

TRAGEDY AT THE MET CENTER:
THE BILL MASTERTON STORY

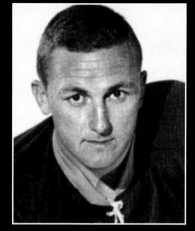

On January 13, 1968, midway through the North Star's first season, an event took place at the Met Center that forever changed the face of hockey around the world. Minnesota was playing Western Conference rival Oakland that night, when tragedy struck the sports world. Midway through the first period, Stars center Bill Masterton led a rush into the Seals offensive zone. As he got over the blue line, he back-handed a pass to his right wing, Wayne Connelly. Just then, Seals defensemen Larry Cahan and Ron Harris lined him up and nailed him with a hard, but clean body-check. Instantly, Masterton was flung over backwards, hitting his head on the ice. Now, during this era of pro hockey, he wasn't among the handful of players wearing a helmet. As a result, all of his 6-foot, 185 pound frame came crashing into the rock-hard ice surface, he was instantly knocked unconscious.

As the hushed crowd watched in horror, Masterton, who, by this time was bleeding profusely, was immediately taken from the ice on a stretcher and rushed to Edina's Fairview Hospital. For more than 30 hours doctors managed to keep him alive by use of a respirator, but regretably, he never regained consciousness. The massive brain injury was too severe, and consequently, early on the morning of January 15th, Masterton was pronounced dead at the age of 29. Left behind was his wife Carol, and their two children.

The tragedy touched every Minnesotan, and for the upstart North Star players - it was particularly tough. "The tragic death of Bill Masterton touched us all deeply in that first year, so deeply in fact that those of us who were on that club are reluctant to discuss it even yet," said general manager Wren Blair following that 1968 season. "However, let me say this: It was real heartbreak, and leading 20 young men back from that bitter experience, convincing them that life must go on, that the North Stars had a destiny, a cause and a goal was a challenge that I certainly had not counted on that first season. These were young people, most of whom had never faced a tragedy in their lives. Most of them were young enough that they had never lost a loved one, not their mother, father, sister or brother. No one that close. Yet suddenly, someone almost as close as you can get - a fellow teammate - was gone. Still the North Stars rallied and fought back with much of the leadership supplied by Carol Masterton, Bill's courageous young wife. To this day, Bill's memory is very special to the North Stars and Carol is one of our special favorites."

Bill "Bat" Masterton was born in Winnipeg on August 13th, 1938. He grew up playing hockey like most Canadian kids, one day dreaming of playing in the NHL. He first began to show signs of greatness while playing for the St. Boniface Canadiens in the Manitoba Junior Hockey League in 1956. In 1957 Bill was offered a hockey scholarship at Denver University. While there, he steadily improved his game. During his senior year at DU, he led the Pioneers to the NCAA championship, and was named as the MVP of the tournament. The All-American recipient graduated in 1961 with a bachelor of science degree in business, and then signed with the Montreal Canadiens organization - where he was assigned to their Hull-Ottawa farm club in the Eastern Professional Hockey League.

Masterton played in Hull-Ottawa for one season, and then was promoted to the Cleveland Barons of the AHL - where he finished sixth in the league scoring race with an impressive 82 points in 72 games. By 1963 Bill was tired of the minor league rat race. None of the other five NHL teams had shown an interest in drafting him, and rather than stay the course, he opted to give up his dream of playing in the NHL and retire from pro hockey. Instead he returned to Denver to pursue his master's degree in finance. "By that time I had gotten married," he said, "and there was this offer to work in contract administration for a big, established firm like Honeywell."

So, in 1964, Masterton moved to Minnesota, where he began working as an executive with the Honeywell Corporation. He also decided to keep playing hockey as well, first with the Rochester Mustangs in 1964-65, and then with the St. Paul Steers in 1965-66 - where he tallied 67 points in just 30 games. He went on to play on the U.S. National team in 1967 - scoring 39 points in only 21 games. Then something happened. The league expanded to 12 teams, and Bill got a call from North Stars GM, Wren Blair, inviting him to training camp for a tryout.

"I went to training camp knowing it wouldn't be a picnic, especially after being out of pro hockey for four seasons," said Masterton in June of 1967. "I had the opportunity to skate quite a bit last summer when I coached in a summer league, and I think that helped me quite a bit. I was in pretty good shape when I reported. I realize it's going to be tough, but if I get the opportunity to play, I'm confident that I can make it."

He did make it. He got to fulfill a lifelong dream by playing in the "show" for 38 glorious games, even scoring the team's first-ever goal. He scored just three more after that, and added eight assists for a mere 12 points during that 1967-68 season. On paper, Bill Masterton certainly wasn't a superstar. But, unfortunately, Bill Masterton is today a hockey legend. Sometimes legends have to make the ultimate sacrifice for a cause unbeknownst to them. And that is just what his legacy is all about. Bill Masterton woke up the hockey world, and forced it to take a hard look at protective headgear. As a result of Bill's untimely death, helmets are mandatory at all levels of the game today, including in the NHL. Masterton remains the only player in history to die from an injury suffered in an NHL game. And, thanks to the awareness that was brought about because of his tragedy, countless other deaths and head injuries have been averted.

Following the tragedy, the NHL governors in cooperation with the NHL Writers Association created the Bill Masterton Memorial trophy. The honor was originally given to the player who best exemplifies the qualities of sportsmanship and love of the game. In more recent years, however, the award has been given to players who have had to battle hardships due primarily to injury or illness, and have successfully returned to the game. While each team nominates one player for an overall winner, the nomination of a player in each city is a way of extending the value of the trophy and keeping Masterton's memory alive. A Bill Masterton Scholarship Fund, based in Bloomington, was also created in his memory. Montreal Canadien forward Claude Provost was the initial honoree, while other past winners include former North Star Al MacAdam, who won the award in 1980, as well as Pittsburgh's Mario Lemieux and Chicago's Tony Granato.

The North Stars, who in addition to creating an annual Bill Masterton Cup Award - which was given to the player voted most valuable by his teammates, also retired Masterton's no. 19 jersey forever into the rafters of the old Met Center in 1987.

the other skaters he chose that day included two diamonds in the rough from the Boston Bruins: Wayne Connelly and Bill Goldsworthy. Goldsworthy, of course, would emerge as the team's first superstar, carrying the franchise on his back for its first decade of existence.

The Stars were anxious to make an immediate impact in the league, and as a result, gambled away a lot of their future draft picks in order to obtain some immediate talent. Because the established clubs had been stockpiling talent in the minor leagues, they were able to pawn off their kids, who were green, as well as their veterans, who were too old, onto the expansion teams. Add to that the fact that the established clubs could bargain with the expansion teams with the lure of cash and future considerations in order to entice their counterparts to "pass over" their most coveted unprotected players. When it was all over though, Blair was optimistic to say the least about his new roster of players.

"Good Lord," said Blair to his scouting staff after the draft on the 20 players he had just obtained for the mere price of $100,000 each, "just look at this mess. This is supposed to be a major league hockey team. There are only four guys on this list who are major league players. Your job and mine is to unload the other 16 just as fast as we can, any way we can. I'll trade 10-for-one if I have to." Blair even wanted to stop taking players at one point in the draft, but NHL president Clarence Campbell told him that he had to take all 20.

The Stars' Maiden Voyage
The stage was now set. The anticipation for big-time hockey in Minnesota was immense, and season ticket sales soared even well before the team hit the ice. The team was forced to play their first four games on the road however, because the arena's new seats weren't quite finished being installed. On Oct. 11, 1967, the Stars played their first-ever contest against St. Louis. The Stars first-ever goal was scored by Bill Masterton, but the team wound up tying the Blues 2-2. On a side note, the first fight in franchise history also took place that night, between the Stars' Bill Plager and Blues defenseman, Bob Plager — who incidentally, was his big brother. Mom and Dad must've been so proud...

On October 21st, the Stars faced off against the Oakland Seals for their inaugural home opener. The packed Met Center crowd, which had seemingly waited a lifetime for the NHL to finally come to Minnesota, was delighted to see a young blonde-haired kid from Kitchener, Ontario, tally the team's first-ever goal in the new arena. His name was Bill Goldsworthy, but they would soon come to know him simply as "Goldy!" The Stars excited the crowd that night with a brand of hockey that Minnesotans had never known before, ultimately skating to a 3-1 win.

The Cinderella Stars
The team would play some solid hockey throughout its first few months of existence. Then, on January 13, 1968, tragedy struck the team when Bill Masterton was tragically killed during a game. The team moved on though, and pushed ahead with his memory weighing heavy on their hearts. With that the Stars played inspired hockey the rest of the way through their inaugural season. They finished the regular season with a modest record of 27 wins, 32 losses, and 15 ties — good for fourth in the Western Division, just four points out of first. Wayne Connelly led the team in scoring that first year with 35 goals and 21 assists for 56 points.

It was off to the playoffs for the rookie North Stars, who were matched up against all-star goalie Terry Sawchuk and the Los Angeles Kings. L.A. took the first two games of the best of seven series, only to see Minnesota rally back to even the series. The Kings went up 3-2, but the Stars came back one more time to tie it up at three games apiece. Stars forward Milan Marcetta won the sixth game with an overtime goal, and with the momentum on their side, the Stars went on to rout the Kings in Los Angeles, 9-4, in the deciding Game Seven. Minnesota, which scored a club record nine goals to win the rugged quarterfinal contest, would now face the Blues to determine who would play in the Stanley Cup finals.

Now, even though the Stars were hot, like any expansion team, they weren't yet exactly commanding a lot of respect around town. Such was the case for the second-round playoff series against St. Louis, when it was announced that five of the seven games had to be played in St. Louis because the Ice Capades had already booked the Met Center's ice for a show. Not even phased about losing their home ice advantage, the Stars marched ahead by winning two of the first three games against the Blues.

Game Four of the series was a grinder. Through the third period the Stars were up 3-0, only to see the Blues tally twice within a two minute span. Then with only 11 seconds to go in the game, Blues forward Jim Roberts scored his second goal of the game to send it to overtime. Then, just two minutes into the extra session, Gary Sabourin scored on a wrister to win it for the Blues. Excited to finally play in the Met Center, Minnesota got back on track the next night, only to lose another overtime heartbreaker. With their backs against the wall though, the guys in green came back in front of a packed house and crushed St. Louis, 5-1, in Game Six.

The Seventh and final game, which shifted back to the Gateway-Arch City, would go down as a classic. It would come down to which goaltender wanted it more, Cesare Maniago or St. Louis' Glenn Hall. The game was scoreless through the first two periods until Stars winger Walt McKechnie blasted a goal past Hall with only four minutes to go in the game. But, only seconds later the Blues would tie it up, forcing the teams to play yet another extra period. Just before the end of the game, Stars winger Wayne Connelly broke lose on a breakaway, only to get mugged by a Blues defender. As Connelly went down, the fans back home thought for sure that there would be a penalty shot issued, but it never came. The score was still 1-1 after the first overtime period, which meant double-overtime. Then, only three minutes into the second OT, the Blues' Ron Shock blasted a slapshot past Maniago for the game-winner. After nearly 83 minutes of great "old-time" hockey, it was a bitter pill for the Cinderella Stars to swallow. The Blues, who were absolutely spent by the end of this emotional and physical series, would then go on to get swept by Montreal in the finals.

The Stars had treated their fans to some great hockey, and even made some believers of themselves along the way. The team averaged nearly 12,000 fans per game that first year, not bad for a bunch of "misfits, unknowns and castoffs." The fans wanted to show their appreciation for the team's success that season, and decided to meet the club at the airport.

"We came home on Braniff Airlines, and they had to pull the plane away from the gate area because thousands of people had come out to welcome the team," said Al Shaver, the Stars play-by-play announcer. "Everyone was quite amazed by the recep-

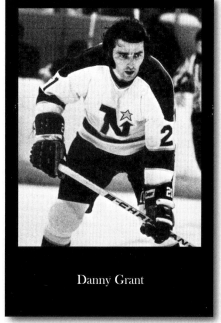

Danny Grant

tion because we didn't win the series."

"We were just thankful to have a job," said Bill Goldsworthy, who stood atop the playoff leaderboard with eight goals and seven assists. "We were a bunch of guys who just wanted to prove something and sell the game of hockey."

"It was just a phenomenal experience," said Lou Nanne, a Gopher All-American who joined the team after playing on the U.S. Olympic team. "To be able to have NHL hockey right in your own back yard and see it every week was something that I really was excited about. Playing was just a thrill for me and that the first season we had a pretty good year, making a great playoff run. For the first time, the Stars got some credibility after that playoff series with the Blues."

In the end, Blair had successfully taken a bunch of no-names well beyond their natural ability, and all the way to within one goal of going to the Stanley Cup finals. All in all it was a good start for the club which Blair had pieced together on a wing and a prayer. During that first year he wheeled and dealt like no other GM in the league in order to build his team. Some deals paid immediate dividends, such as the one that sent five players off his active roster for two Toronto minor leaguers — J.P. Parise and Milan Marcetta. (In that deal, all five players dealt were out of the league in only a few years, while Parise would emerge as an early star for the team.) Another involved dealing the very popular Billy Collins to get Jude Drouin, a lightning quick young center who would later finish as the runner-up in the 1971 Rookie-of-the-Year balloting. He also irked the local scribes when he swapped the big, fast, and very popular center, Danny O'Shea, for Chicago defenseman Doug Mohns.

"In that first year we played four games against each of the six original NHL clubs," said Blair. "Amazingly, we split with Boston and Detroit and went 1-1-2 with Chicago, Toronto and Montreal. Only New York eluded us completely. Unbelievable, yet we did it. How? By driving our players unmercifully, and in the process, driving ourselves unmercifully. The NHL was new in Minnesota, and we felt this had to be done to sell hockey here completely."

Over the next couple of years Blair would make countless more deals. He obtained Montreal goaltender Gump Worsley (a future Hall of Famer), and also defenseman Ted Harris, who would become the team captain and the club policeman. He followed those trades up by obtaining Barry Gibbs from the Bruins and Tom Reid from the Blackhawks. Each would go on to be big contributors for Minnesota in the years to come.

The Honeymoon Was Over Quickly...

The Stars knew it was going to be tough to top the heroics of their first season that next year. Although it was an exciting ride, it was particularly draining on Blair to serve as both GM as well as coach. It had been his intention all along to coach only until he could find the right guy to pass the reigns to. So, with the team sitting pretty in second place in the West, Blair named John Muckler as his new bench boss. Muckler, a minor league coach at the time, was about to receive a very rude awakening to the NHL. That's because the Stars suddenly went into a huge slump, plummeting to the divisional cellar. The fans were outraged, and as a result, Muckler became the scape-goat and got canned. (Incidentally, Muckler would go on to a long and illustrious NHL coaching career.) Blair returned to his perch behind the bench, and got the Stars fired up. They rallied late in the season, only to fall one game short of making a repeat trip to the playoffs. One of the highlights of the year was the performance of rookie Danny Grant, whose club-leading 34 goals and 31 assists earned him the Calder Trophy as the league's rookie-of-the-year. Other top performers included Ray Cullen, who tallied 63 points, and

Maniago, who posted a solid 3.30 goals-against average in net. In the end though, the team's pathetic 18-43-15 record was just not going to cut it.

Enter: The "Gumper"

After a thorough house-cleaning by Blair in the off-season, the Stars were ready to take on the world. Early in the 1969-70 season though, Blair was ordered to take some time off by his doctor. Charlie Burns, who had started the season as the team's second-line center, was named as the team's interim bench-coach. During Burns' tenure, the team went through a horrible 20-game non-winning streak that nearly set an NHL record. Burns, in an attempt to liven up the troops, decided to once again lace up his skates and serve as a player-coach. The team rallied behind their new skipper, had an amazing month of March, going 9-5-4, and wound up finishing third in the West. From there, however, they unfortunately were eliminated by their new nemesis, the Blues, four games to two in the playoffs. Incidentally, Goldy scored the two game-winners in the pair of home games that the Stars won.

One of the bright spots for the Stars that year was the addition of Montreal Canadien goalie, Gump Worsley. The "Gumper" was an instant fan favorite, partially because he was the last NHL goaltender to not wear a mask. The overweight, balding, often hilarious 40-something year-old Worsley, would prove to be a savior in getting the team out of their losing streak. Burns was at his wits end in the midst of the team's funk, and decided to call on the guy with the most experience to have some words of wisdom with the team.

"Charlie told me to go into the dressing room and say what I wanted to say," said Worsley in the 1972 book entitled: 'The Blazing North Stars.' "They hadn't won in so long that nobody wanted the puck. They'd come off the bench and sit there like wooden Indians. The first thing I did was talk to them. Next thing I knew they went up against Toronto and won, 8-0. I was on the bench and every time it got quiet I'd get up and start cheering and yelling. They had never had a guy like that before. When they were down a goal they'd get upset. I told them that in the NHL if you're down a goal you've got lots of time to get it back. All of a sudden we started to win. But what surprised me was that after only two practices they asked me to play." That March, Gump suited up in goal and beat Pittsburgh. Figuring the team was on a roll, Burns wanted to ride Worsley, and asked him to suit up between the pipes again that next night against the Rangers. Gump, no longer a spring chicken, hated playing back-to-back nights, but figured he'd do it for the team. The Stars played inspired hockey behind their new netminder, and thanks to a third period goal by Ray Cullen, Minnesota held on to win. "No doubt," said Worsley afterward, "it was one of the better games of my career."

Tommy Reid

Now, with the momentum on their side, the Stars faced off against the struggling Philadelphia Flyers for a shot at making the playoffs. With the Gumper in goal, North Star defenseman Barry Gibbs bounced a squibler past Flyer goalie Bernie Parent at 7:48 of the third period. Worsley held on to post a shut-out, and the North Stars won the game, 1-0. With the win, Philadelphia was eliminated, and Minnesota was in the post-season yet again.

"Sure, we were lucky," Gump added, "but that's hockey; it's a strange game. But the main thing is that we won and got into the playoffs."

In addition to the Gumper, the driving force behind the team's second half turn-around was the amazing line of "Goldy, Tommy, and J.P." J. P. Parise led all scoring with 72 points, while Duluth's Tommy Williams put in 67, Bill Goldsworthy tallied 65, and Danny Grant added 57 of his own to help the cause.

LORNE "GUMP" WORSLEY

Asked once in a post-game interview why he refused to wear a facemask, he replied: "What do you mean? I'm wearing one now..." Gump Worsley, then in his 40s, only played in Minnesota for four short seasons, but he is arguably the team's most popular goaltender of all time. Here is his wonderful story...

Lorne John Worsley was born May 14, 1929, in Montreal. He grew up in a tough end of town where his neighborhood buddies proclaimed that he looked like the then-popular roly-poly comic strip character "Andy Gump," and the nick-name stuck with him ever since. As a kid he loved hockey and tried to emulate his idol, Davey Kerr, the hero of the NY Rangers' 1940 Stanley Cup championship team.

While playing for a commercial league team in a Montreal suburb, Worsley got his first break after winning a try-out with a junior team called the Verdun Cyclones. In 1949, at the age of 20, he caught the eye of a Rangers scout who sent him an invitation to the Rangers training camp. After a few years in the minors, he finally got the call to come to Madison Square Garden and join the team in 1952. Gump would mind the nets in the Big Apple until 1963. The New York fans appreciated the pudgy goaltender's efforts, but his coach, the volatile Phil Watson, rode the Gumper hard about the size of his generous girth, and once accused him of having a "beer belly." To which the portly 5-foot-7, 200 pounder, calmly replied: "As always, Watson doesn't have the faintest idea what he's talking about... I never drink beer, only good Canadian whiskey!"

Working hard and playing hard, night after night Gump was bombarded with 40-50 shot onslaughts from the opposition. One time a reporter asked the goalie which team he thought gave him the most trouble. Worsley, quick to reply, exclaimed, "The Rangers!"

Then, on June 4, 1963, after nine years of live target practice with the Rangers, he was traded to the powerful Montreal Canadiens in a multi-player deal for goalie Jacques Plante. With a modest 204-271-101 record and a 3.10 goals against average, Worsley spent a total of 10 years on a Rangers team that failed to qualify for the playoffs five times and was eliminated in the opening round the other four. For Gump, who led the NHL in losses four times during his Rangers tenure, it was great news.

Though he spent much of the next two seasons up and down with Quebec of the AHL, Worsley got the call of his life on May 1st, 1965, when Habs coach Toe Blake notified him that he was going to start in Game Seven of the Stanley Cup finals against the Chicago Blackhawks. For the tubby 36-year-old second-stringer, it was an opportunity of a lifetime. Worsley, who was receiving pain injections for a previously injured thigh, wanted to play his best in front of his hometown fans. Although Montreal's ace center Jean Beliveau scored 14 seconds into the game, it was the Gumper who was the game's real hero, as he went on to blank the Hawks, 4-0.

The following season, both he and Charlie Hodge shared the Vezina Trophy as the league's top keeper, en route to helping the Canadiens win a second straight Stanley Cup. Worsley earned First Team All-Star honors following the 1967-68 season as he and Rogie Vachon shared the Vezina Trophy in the team's third consecutive Stanley Cup-winning season. The Gumper helped his team win a fourth Cup in 1969, but the pressure of playing goal for the mighty Canadiens finally got to him. Disenchanted with his poor treatment from management in Montreal, not to mention the increasing problems brought on by his fear of flying, Gump decided to hang em' up. "I'd had it," he said. "I didn't want to play anymore. I didn't want to fly anymore."

Worsley was a sort of enigma. Here was a man who thought absolutely nothing of standing in front of 100 mph slap-shots without even thinking twice about wearing a goalie mask, but try to get him in on an airplane and he would wimper like a puppy. It would be a mild understatement to say that the Gumper had an abiding distrust of air travel. His horrible fear of flying made him a complete wreck on team flights. The fear apparently dated back to his minor league days with the New York Rovers, when, on a return flight home from Milwaukee, one of the plane's engines caught fire and was forced to make an emergency landing. Although everyone survived unscathed, the Gumper was scarred for life. From that point on, every time he got on a flight he would sit on the aisle, clench the arm rests as tightly as possible, say a prayer, and hang on for dear life. "It's the one time I don't talk," he said, "I'm too scared to say anything!"

Another incident nearly forced him to give up the game for good. While on a Canadien's team flight, the plane hit some turbulence, causing the players to spill their meals all over themselves. Afterwards the captain calmly emerged from the cockpit and reassured his passengers that the airline was sorry about the incident and that it would pay for the dry-cleaning of their suits. At that point a freaked-out Gump stood up and screamed, "What about our shorts?"

That next year, Minnesota GM Wren Blair obtained the rights to negotiate with the 41-year-old goalie and convinced him to make a comeback. For Gump, who had suffered a nervous breakdown after his last season, it was another chance to play the game he loved. Playing with the enthusiasm of a rookie, Worsley, along with his new partner in crime Cesare Maniago, helped guide the Stars into the playoffs for three straight seasons. "Best move I ever made," said Gump. "We love Minnesota, and we love the team. Jack Gordon is a terrific coach. He tells Cesare and me, 'If you're having problems, don't come to me, go to each other.' So we watch each other for mistakes. We're roommates. We both know that one guy can't play for the bundle. Him and me admit it, just no way, eh?"

The Gumper gave Minnesota four solid seasons in net. And, incredibly, in his fourth and final year of 1974, after nearly a quarter-century of playing with his face as a back-stop, he finally decided to break down and put on a facemask. But it didn't come easily for the game's last goalie to go maskless. When asked why he would subject himself to constant cuts and stitches, he calmly replied rhetorically: "Would it have been fair not to give the fans the chance to see my beautiful face?" He took his share of licks over the years, too. Hundreds and hundreds of stitches, and dozens of concussions made the Gumper a huge fan favorite. "If Gump got hit in the face by a puck, it could only improve his looks," said Stars' scout John Mariucci. "If that's the case," Gump retorted "then you'd have to get hit in the face by a bus!"

Worsley finally played his 862nd NHL regular-season game on April 2, 1974, against Philadelphia. Conveniently, at the age of 45, the Gumper retired just about in time to start receiving his NHL pension checks. Worsley then moved into the Star's front office, where he became a team scout — a position he retained through the mid-1980s. Playing an amazing 25 professional seasons from 1949 to 1974, Gump finished his career with a 335-353-150 overall record and a 2.90 GA average in 862 games (a number surpassed only by Terry Sawchuk and Jacques Plante). In addition to his 43 regular season shut-outs, he also posted five shut-outs and a 2.82 GAA in 70 playoff games. Fittingly, he was elected to the Hockey Hall of Fame in 1980.

With his trademark crew-cut, and jovial pot-belly, the happy-go-lucky soul was not only one of the game's greatest and most durable players, he was also one of its most likable characters. A fun-loving man who claimed that his favorite post game meal was a beer and a cigarette, Gump once said of his profession: "If you want to be a good goaltender, it helps to be a little crazy. Not all goaltenders are nuts, only about 90 percent of them...". Sadly, the Gumper passed away in January of 2007, he was 77 years old.

Making History at the Forum

Wren Blair came back that following 1970-71 season, but came to the realization that he needed to hire a full-time coach — so he could focus on managing the front office. "I gotta get out of coaching," said Blair, "I love it, but it doesn't love me back."

Blair hired Jack Gordon to take over behind the bench that season. Gordon, who at the time was serving as general manager and coach of the American Hockey League's Cleveland Barons, was a former star with the New York Rangers. A four-time winner of the AHL championship in Cleveland, Gordon also served as the GM of the Rangers in the late 1960s. Gordon was a quiet man who was considered as a "player's coach." He emphasized teamwork, while his "laissez-faire" attitude allowed his players the freedom to train at their own pace. "Jackie would just tell me to be ready when the bell rings, and otherwise he doesn't care what I do," said the Gumper, who's sphelt figure was often the subject of criticism with his former Montreal coaches. "It's my own business, he figures."

The season got underway with a renewed sense of confidence that year, as the Stars came out with something to prove. They started out with seven wins, five losses and three ties over their first 15 games, and seemed to gel as a team as the season progressed. They finished out the season on a downer, however, losing four straight. But that was not going to deter this bunch, as they finished the season in fourth place with a 28-34-16 record and found themselves once again pitted against the heavily favored Blues in the playoffs. For the season, Jude Drouin led the team with 68 points, followed by Goldy, who tallied 65.

The Stars stole Game One of the quarterfinal series in St. Louis, only to lose Games Two and Three. They then rallied to win Games Four and Five by the tough scores of 2-1 and 4-3, respectively. Lou Nanne got the Game Five game-winner in St. Louis, and lit a fire under his teammates for Game Six, where they crushed the Blues at home, 5-2, in front of more than 15,000 screaming Minnesota puck-heads.

Now, it has been said that every young sports franchise requires a significant event (or series in this case) to earn the respect of its peers. For the underdog North Stars, that would happen on April 22, 1971, in a classic series against the flying Frenchmen from Montreal. The Canadiens, a fabled organization which had ruled the league for years, scoffed at the thought of one of the expansion teams winning a playoff game against them. After all, up to that point in league history, an expansion team had never beaten one of the "original six" established clubs in post-season play.

Gordon decided to start the Gumper in Game One at the Montreal Forum, hoping that he would play inspired hockey against the team that had released him the season before. Danny Grant put the Stars up 1-0 in the first, but Montreal's heavy artillery heated up after that to put the Canadiens ahead 4-1 by the end of two. The pressure was too much for Worsley, however, as the Habs rolled over the Stars, 7-2. "We had a real good 20 minutes," said defenseman Ted Harris. "The trouble is, the game was 60 minutes long."

It would now be up to the long and lanky Maniago for Minnesota, who prepared to make history in Game Two. "I have nothing against the job Worsley did in the opener," Gordon said, "but my plans were to alternate the two goalies from the beginning. You can't fault Worsley because our boys weren't in the game after the first period. We stopped checking, and we didn't play our positions. They just toyed with us."

By now, the Canadiens, who had beaten the Bruins in the opening round, had similar intentions for the kids from Minnesota. The Stars had other ideas that night though and came out smoking. They lit up the Canadiens and embarrassed them

Ted Harris

in front of their own standing-room-only crowd. Led by Danny Grant, who dished out three pivotal assists, along with Lou Nanne's third period game-winner, the Stars prevailed in the key semifinal game. Maniago stood on his head throughout the entire game, turning away shot after shot throughout the contest. It was a milestone for all of the expansion teams, in that one of their own had beaten a member of the exclusive "original six" fraternity.

"Scoring the game-winning goal in that game is still today one of the most memorable highlights of my playing career," said Lou Nanne several years later. "It really gave us a lot of confidence as a team, and got us a lot of respect and credibility around the league."

Back to Reality

Game Three switched back to Bloomington. By this time the art of tailgating had become a thing of legend at the Met Center, and rest assured, the suddenly optimistic crowd was primed and ready for our friends from north of the border. The Montreal players, still in a bit of shock over the outcome of Game Two, came prepared for the team that they had taken for granted. "None of us realized that the North Stars were that good," said Canadien's winger Pete Mahovlich.

The Canadiens, somewhat embarrassed over their lackadaisical performance in Game Two, came out flying and shell-shocked the Gumper, 6-3. In Game Four, both Murray Oliver and Danny Grant took advantage of power-play scoring opportunities, giving the Stars a 2-0 lead after the first period. Montreal scored two in the second, only to see Minnesota rally behind three third period goals from J. P. Parise, Ted Hampson and Oliver. The real hero though was Cesare Maniago, who turned away some three dozen blasts in the 5-2 Stars win. "We wanted to show the Canadiens we didn't want to be run out of the rink," Cesare said. "We'll have a few people talking now."

With the series now tied at two games apiece, it was anybody's game. Or so they thought. Montreal, thoroughly humiliated by this point, buried the Stars in Game Five in front of their home Forum fans. Maniago, starting for the injured Worsley, got thoroughly pasted, 6-1.

Red Light-Green Light-Go...

With their backs up against the wall, the Stars felt as if they had nothing to lose in Game Six, knowing that it was a "do or die" situation. On April 29, in Bloomington, the Stars dug in for one last shot at the mighty Habs. At 9:50 in the first, the crafty veteran winger Charlie Burns put the Stars up 1-0, giving the record Met Center crowd reason to believe. Montreal tied it up with less than four minutes to go, and then went ahead in the second on a Claude Larose garbage goal out front. Minnesota stayed calm though and played very physical against the more skilled Montreal club. Then, midway through the second, Jude Drouin beat the Canadien's All-Star keeper, Ken Dryden, with a top-shelf wrister to tie it up one more time. Maniago was solid, turning away shot after shot, until Rejean Houle beat him at 13:29 of the second to put the Canadiens up 3-2. The game went back and forth through the third period. Minnesota then pulled Maniago with just less than two minutes to go on the Met Center scoreboard. With six attackers, the Stars pressed for the equalizer. Dryden, a future hall of famer, played miraculously in the final seconds.

Just when everyone thought that the game was in the bag, Stars' center Ted Hampson flipped the puck over Dryden's leg pad and into the net. With no time remaining, the crowd went ballistic. As the team rushed the ice to mob Hampson, referee Bill Friday ruled that it was no goal. The green light had gone off prior to the goal being scored, and as a result the red one could not be illuminated. Time had expired on the game, and on the season for the tough-luck Stars. For the 15,422 fans in attendance, as well as the countless others throughout the Land of 10,000

Lakes, it was a dagger through the heart. Visibly shaken, the North Stars lined up at center ice for the traditional post-series hand-shaking ceremony, and under a scoreboard that read: "NORTH STARS ARE THE GREATEST ANYWHERE!", they wished their foes good luck in the Stanley Cup finals.

"The green light came on before the red one" said Jack Gordon. "I guess that's what counts. But I'm proud of these guys, they worked their guts off in this series."

"At that time, for a bunch of cast-off's like us to beat a dynasty like the Montreal Canadiens in a playoff game was quite a feat," added Goldsworthy.

Another Amazing Run

After four years of being in the league, Wren Blair had completely rewritten the team's opening day roster. Through trades over that time he had acquired several new faces, among them included: Danny Grant, Jude Drouin, J.P. Parise, Ted Harris, Tom Reid, Ted Hampson, Terry Caffery, Bob Nevin, Charlie Burns, Doug Mohns, Barry Gibbs, Gordon Labossiere, Dennis Hextall, Murray Oliver, and Gump Worsley. With all of this new talent, Coach Gordon became very good at sensing chemistry, and seemed to be able to put great lines together. In addition to the Goldy-Drouin-Grant line, he also scored big with the Lou Nanne-Dean Prentice-Murray Oliver tandem, which became one of the best in the west.

Emphasizing a strong defense, Gordon took his Stars to even greater heights in 1971-72, and made a late-season run at winning the division over rival Chicago. They would have to settle for second though, despite their impressive 37-29-12 record. Goldy led the way that year with 31 goals and 31 assists for a team-leading 62 points, while Murray Oliver and Jude Drouin each scored 56, and Lou Nanne added 49. Other key contributors in the team's success included Tom Reid, Dean Prentice, Danny Grant, Barry Gibbs, Doug Mohns, and Ted Harris. And, once again, Maniago was solid in net, posting a modest 2.65 goals against average. The fans came out in droves at Met Center that year, filling the arena to capacity for nearly every contest.

One of the highlights of the 1972 season happened in mid-season when the Met Center played host to the NHL's annual All-Star Game. The locals were entertained by some of the game's greatest, including Minnesota's very own Bill Goldsworthy, Ted Harris, Doug Mohns and Gump Worsley. And, although the East beat the West 3-2, the Minnesota fans thoroughly enjoyed the star-studded event.

Upon finishing second in the division, the Stars once again found themselves facing off against St. Louis in the playoffs. You know how there are just some teams that always, no matter what, just seem to have your number? Well, for the Stars, it was definitely the Blues. For whatever the reason, they owned Minnesota in the post-season. This time, however, the Blues were the underdogs — something that didn't sit real well with the Stars' coaches.

"St. Louis has been forced to fight all the way because they were battling for a playoff spot," said Jack Gordon about his team's chances against the undermanned Blues. "On the other hand, we've had our position clinched for some time and have been forced to push ourselves."

On April 5, 1972, before a record crowd of 15,482 at the Met, the North Stars hit the ice on yet another quest for Lord Stanley's Cup. Leading the charge for Minnesota was the ageless wonder, 42-year-old Lorne "Gump" Worsley. The Stars didn't disappoint either, jumping out to a 2-0 lead on goals by veterans Dean Prentice and Bob Nevin. Gump played huge, posting a 3-0 shut-out for the Stars. Incredibly, it was his ninth straight game against the Blues without a loss.

In Game Two, Minnesota took a quick 1-0 lead, only to see St. Louis come out swinging, literally. Only a few minutes into the game, Blues forward Garry Unger decided to mix it up with Minnesota's Barry Gibbs at center ice. The two scrapped for a bit, with the crowd clearly declaring Gibbs as the victor. "That's the way St. Louis plays," said Blair afterward. "They try to intimidate you right away. But I think this time they made a mistake. They gave us just what we needed. That fight and rough first period turned us on."

The Blues also got fired up, coming right at Maniago in second. They went up 2-1, and then again 3-2, only to see the Stars tie it up at 3-3 going into the third. Jude Drouin, after assisting on the two previous goals, put the Stars up one more time, 4-3, on a pretty shot past goalie Ernie Wakely. Blues forward Garry Unger then tallied to tie it, only to see Phil Roberto score to once again give the Blues the lead. Finally, with the seconds ticking away, 39-year-old left wing Dean Prentice pasted a shot into the top shelf of the St. Louis cage, sending the game into sudden death overtime.

Only 90 seconds into the extra session, that Stars' first line trio of Drouin, Goldsworthy, and Grant decided to get busy. With Jude skating the puck into the St. Louis zone, followed closely by Goldy and Danny, Drouin had a decision to make. Shoot or pass? He opted to shoot. His shot was tipped and flew right into Wakely's mask, where it promptly fell into the crease. Goldy, who just happened to be in the neighborhood, poked the puck through his five-hole for the game-winner. "I saw Bill," Drouin excitedly explained after the game, "and I heard him (call his name out). I was tempted to pass, but I had a good chance and he was in a perfect spot for a rebound. So I just let it go."

Despite the fact that the Stars were playing with grit, teamwork, good defense, decent forward backchecking, and solid goaltending, Gordon was nervous. They had been there before, and he knew with the series now in St. Louis that it could all change in an instant. Nearly 19,000 St. Louis fans greeted their team for Game Three, as Blues wingers Mike Murphy and Phil Roberto teamed up to make it one-nothing midway through the first. Roberto tallied again in the second on a long slapper, only to see Jude Drouin score in the third to make it close. The Stars pulled the Gumper with a minute to go, but could not capitalize. The Blues took the game, 2-1.

Game Four was full of drama as Drouin and Grant scored early to put the Stars up 2-0. Then, midway through the second, a controversial no-goal entered into the equation. Parise, on a sweet two-line pass from Tommy Reid, apparently beat the Blues goaltender, Jacques Caron, on a rebound stuff-in. Caron smothered the puck, but his momentum carried his body into the net for the conspicuous goal. But, the ref had already blown his whistle to signal a stoppage of play. Gordon went ballistic, pleading that the goal judge should've hit the lights. The play stood, and would prove to be controversial because just a few minutes later, Blues forward Kevin O'Shea scored to tie the game at 2-2. Then, with the teams mired in penalties, the Blues scored on a 4-3 power-play advantage to go up 3-2. The screened shot which ricocheted off of Maniago's leg pad, would prove to be the game-winner.

With the series tied 2-2, the North Stars returned to friendly confines of the Met. There, thanks to a Jude Drouin one-timer from Goldy late in the third, the Stars won the game 4-3. The series again shifted back to St. Louis for Game Six. After the Gumper let in a couple of quick ones, Goldy scored to bring the team to within one. Then something happened that scared the hell out of the Minnesota players. With seven minutes left to go in the first period, Blues winger Bob Plager came charging into the Stars' crease and crashed head-on into Worsley. The Gumper, unable to get out of the way,

J.P. Parise

smashed his head into the steel goalpost. Knocked out, the Stars could only think of one thing — Bill Masterton. Luckily though, the Gumper would come to, and skate off on his own power. Fortunately for Minnesota fans, the Gump, who didn't wear a helmet or facemask, had taken quite a few blows to the old melon in his day. "When that happens, said Gump after that game, "there's no place to hide. I don't remember anything after he hit me." Despite Parise's late third period goal, and a respectable replacement job in goal by Maniago, the Stars lost the game, 4-2.

So, with the series tied at three games apiece, it all came down to one last game. The Stars had earned home-ice advantage, and would need to capitalize on it right then and there if they wanted to advance to the semis. With that, on April 16, 1972, a nationally televised audience of nearly 10 million puck fans from across North America crowded around to watch a little bit of playoff hockey.

It was a classic rough-and-tumble affair that went back and forth for both squads. Blues goalie Jacques Caron owned the Stars for the first two periods, preserving his team's 1-0 lead. "I've never seen a goalie play better," J. P. Parise would say later. "We just couldn't beat him." Then, a few minutes into the third, Stars captain Ted Harris carried the biscuit over center ice and into the St. Louis zone. Faking a shot, he zipped a pass over to Charlie Burns, who was all alone in front of the net. Burns made them pay, flipping a backhander through Caron's five-hole to even it up at one apiece. Murray Oliver brought the 15,635 Stars fans to their feet on a last-second snap-shot with less than a minute to go, only to see Caron smother it in front of the net. The score remained 1-1 through regulation, and once again, it was sudden-death overtime.

For the first 10 minutes of OT it looked like the Stars were going to put the Blues away. Time after time Caron came up huge for St. Louis, as they missed several good scoring opportunities. Then, at 10:07 of the extra session, St. Louis' O'Shea brothers, Danny and Kevin, came in on Maniago. Danny dished to Kevin, who flipped a high wrister over Cesare's stick. The puck hit the cross bar, deflected straight back into the crease, off the back of the helpless goaltender's leg pad, and into the net. "For a moment," Maniago said, in the book 'The Blazing North Stars', "I must have been the only person in the building who knew it was in. There was a pause before the light went on, but the puck was too far back for me to reach it."

When it was all said and done, the crowd stood motionless, and in disbelief. The 1972 series, even by today's standards, is still considered to be one of the most exciting, "classic" confrontations in league history. "In a way, I'm proud," said Wren Blair. "I think we did something for expansion hockey in this series. It was a great game and a great series."

Beaten by the "Broad Street Bully's"
The Stars finished with a 37-30-11 record in 1972-73, good enough for third in the West. For their efforts, they earned themselves a first-round playoff date with the "Broad Street Bully's" of Philadelphia — the toughest dudes in the league. There, despite Dennis Hextall's two game-winning playoff goals, Philly beat Minnesota, four games to two. Hextall, acquired from California in a May 1971 trade, emerged as the teams' leading scorer with 30 goals and 52 assists that year. He was followed by Parise, who scored 75, and Drouin who added 73. Barry Gibbs and J.P. Parise made the All-Star team that year, while Cesare Maniago posted five bagels throughout the season as well.

The Suddenly Slumping Stars
The team took a nose-dive that next year. Wren Blair finally saw enough, replacing third-year coach Jack Gordon just 17 games into the season. He was replaced with Parker

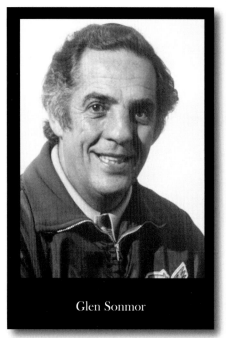

Glen Sonmor

MacDonald, who finished the year behind the bench. Despite another solid season from Hextall, who once again led the team in scoring, in addition to finishing third in the league with 62 assists, Minnesota finished the 1973-74 season with a disappointing 23-38-17 record — dead last in the West and out of the playoffs. One of the main reasons for the teams' lackluster play was due in large part to their lack of defense. Where the previous year's team had scored 254 goals and allowed just 230, the 74' squad tallied only 235 and gave up a whopping 275. On a bright note, Goldy and Hextall were named to the NHL's All-Star team.

Gordon returned as coach for the first half of the 1974-75 season, and in 38 games recorded a lousy 11-22-5 record. Charlie Burns, who came out of coaching retirement to see if he could do any better in the remaining 41 games, posted an equally pathetic 12-28-2 mark. Scoring only 221 goals while surrendering 341 was pretty easy math for anyone to see why this club was in the dumpster. Once again Hextall and Goldy carried the team on their backs, scoring 74 and 72 points each, respectively. The NHL, after expanding a few years earlier to several new cities, including: Vancouver, Calgary, Buffalo, Atlanta, New York (Islanders), Washington, Kansas City (who would move to Denver in '76), and Cleveland (who moved from Oakland/California in '76), decided to realign its divisions. The Stars managed to christen their newly created Smythe Division, by finishing in fourth place. Finding it all to be a bit too much, GM Wren Blair stepped down that year and was replaced by Jack Gordon. The Bird, one of Minnesota's most colorful characters, had been through it all, and would prove to be a vital cog in the evolution of the North Stars.

From Captain to Coach
The 1975-76 season saw former captain Ted Harris take over as the team's head coach. His first duty as the team's new skipper was to appoint Goldy to wear the "C" on the front of his green and gold sweater. The team's woes continued that year though, as the Stars' finished ahead of only the upstart Kansas City Scouts in the Smythe with a dreadful 20-53-7 record. The Stars started out the year losing a whopping 16 out of their first 20 games. They had virtually no chance after that. The team scored only 195 goals while yielding 303; 16 of them of the short-handed variety. One bright spot however, was the emergence of rookie Tim Young, whose 51 points led the team in scoring. Goldsworthy's 24 goals and 22 helpers helped the cause as well, earning him yet another trip to the All-Star game.

Buffaloed
An old friend said good-bye at the start of the 1976-77 season when longtime goaltender Cesare Maniago was dealt to Vancouver in exchange for fellow netminder Gary Smith. (The trade left Bill Goldsworthy as the only remaining "original" North Star from the 1967 expansion draft.) Smith split time that season in the nets with Eveleth native Pete Lopresti, who was the son of Chicago Blackhawk goaltending great, Sam Lopresti. The team had somewhat of a turnaround that year. Despite their porous defense which gave up 70 goals more than they scored, Minnesota finished second in the very weak Smythe Division with a 23-39-18 record. The team ended their four-year playoff drought by facing off against Buffalo in the first round of the playoffs. The Sabres extinguished any hopes that the Minnesota faithful had about making another run at the Cup that year though, as they swept the Stars in the best-of-three series, 4-2 and 7-1. Minnesota got another great year from Tim Young, who, in addition to leading the team in scoring with 95 points, was selected to his first All-Star team. Another bright spot that season included the addition of Swedish import Rolie

BILL GOLDSWORTHY

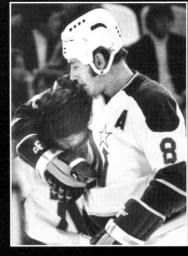

William Alfred Goldsworthy was born to Art and Manetta Goldsworthy on August 24, 1944 in the town of Kitchener, Ontario, located just northeast of Detroit. Art Goldsworthy was one of the city's best known athletes during the 1930s and early 40s, having made a name for himself as a star baseball pitcher. The Goldsworthys had two children, Ken, and his baby brother of five years, Bill. The two brothers, who shared a small bedroom with one bed, grew up playing together. One of the things that the two brothers looked forward to most was sitting down with their parents in front of the TV once a week to watch "Hockey Night in Canada."

At the age of six Bill laced up his first pair of skates. As a youngster, he displayed a lot of raw talent for the game. Within a year he was playing league hockey against the best kids in the city. Wanting to emulate his childhood hero, Detroit Red Wing's star right winger Gordy Howe, Goldy insisted upon playing on the right side.

Eventually, Bill was selected to play on a traveling Kitchener all-star team, which kept the mischievous youngster out of trouble. Playing on the team was a big commitment though, meaning he would have to carry his hockey bag for more than a mile to catch a bus each time the team played. Occasionally, if the road was icy enough, Goldy would simply skate to the rink.

Bill later starred as defensive safety on the high school football team. Having to practice football after school, walk home, eat, and then go to hockey practice at night, kept him in prime physical condition. Soon he was noticed by some of the local scouts. In addition to liking this skinny, temperamental blond kid's good speed and quick shot, they liked his unbridled spirit. Even back then, he was one tough S.O.B.

Goldy played his way through the Canadian amateur leagues, first with the Waterloo Siskins, and eventually for the Niagara Falls Flyers, a Junior A team in the Ontario Hockey Association that was affiliated with the Boston Bruins organization. By 1964, at the age of 20, Goldy was signed by the Bruins. However, although he was considered to be one of the organization's hottest prospects, he was only able to get called-up for three brief stints with the NHL team. It was a rough couple of up-and-down years for the six-foot, 190-pounder, who was unable to earn a regular spot on the strong Bruins roster.

He caught a break though, when on June 6, 1967, former Bruins scout turned North Stars GM, Wren Blair, selected him from Boston in the NHL's expansion draft. Wanting to make the most of his opportunity, the 23-year-old worked hard to make the club's opening-day line-up. He played in 68 games with the Stars in his first season, scoring a mediocre 14 goals and 19 assists. However, at the end of the regular season, Goldy caught fire in the playoffs and led all scorers with 8 goals and 15 total points. Figuring he could parlay that success into a break-through sophomore campaign, Goldy came back that next year with another mediocre 14-goal season. He would simply have to work harder.

Goldy came into camp in the best shape of his life that next year, and thanks to North Stars coach Jack Gordon putting him on the same line with center Jude Drouin and left wing Danny Grant, Goldsworthy scored 28 goals in 28 games in the second half of the season. One of the biggest reasons for his turnaround was due to the constant pushing and prodding by Blair. "I remember one day in our first year at Minnesota I told Goldy I would make a hockey player out of him if it killed us both," said Blair. "And right then I wasn't sure I was going to make it!"

Goldy continued to excel for the Stars, becoming the team's first superstar. One of the reasons why the fans seemed to love this kid so much was because of his now infamous post-scoring dance, affectionately called the "Goldy Shuffle." Yes, the "Shuffle" had taken Minnesota by storm by this point, and the fans couldn't get enough of it. You see, every time Goldy scored, he would immediately skate down the ice with one leg tucked up by his chest, and at the same time, holding his stick up in the air with his left arm, he would pump his right arm like he was trying to start a chain saw. Hard to describe but fun to watch, the little jig became a thing of beauty.

"I think I did the shuffle for the first time in my first year with the North Stars," he explained when asked about how it all began. "We were fighting for a playoff spot, and were playing Pittsburgh at home right near the end of the season. We needed a tie or a win. We tied 2-2, and I think I got both goals. I was so happy at the time that I did a little dance on the ice. Jeez, I got all kinds of letters from people who liked it. Then the press began to call it the 'Goldy Shuffle.' So now I do it whenever we're winning. When we're losing though, management doesn't like to see it too much."

Goldy was a strong veteran voice in the locker room and the players genuinely liked and respected him. One of his closest allies on the team was former linemate and Duluth native, Tommy Williams, whose guidance and friendship helped Goldy's career immensely. "You know, as far as I'm concerned Goldy is one of the best players in this whole league," said Tommy, who also started his career in Boston. "If he were with the Bruins now, he'd be a potential 50-goal scorer. I'm not kidding. Maybe more. Put him on Esposito's line for example. I'd say he'd score 50. He's that good."

Never one to shy away from a melee, Goldy endeared himself to the fans not only because he could find the back of the net, but also because he was willing to take a few stitches every now and then for the team. Always one who could be counted upon to dress for every game, his reckless, driving, thumping style of play made him a fan favorite for more than 11 seasons in Minnesota.

Goldy finally hung em' up in 1977, but not before becoming the first player on a post-1967 expansion team to score 200 goals and the first to score 250. In 1971, Goldy became the team's leading scorer (a mark he held for more than a decade), and his 48-goal season in 1973-74 was the club's best ever — until Dino Ciccarelli broke the mark eight years later. Known as a solid team player who could play at both ends of the ice, he was the first North Star ever to reach the 500-point plateau, totaling 267 goals and 239 assists for 506 career points over 670 games with the team. And, in addition to his five All-Star game appearances, he was also selected as a member of Team Canada's much celebrated "Summit Series" roster that defeated the Russians in 1972.

On February 15th, 1992, during a memorable ceremony in front of a sell-out crowd, Goldy's No. 8 was retired into the Met Center's rafters. Tragically, only two years later he was diagnosed with AIDS. On May 29th, 1996, at the young age of 51, Goldy tragically passed away.

LOU NANNE

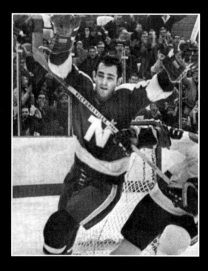

Lou Nanne is synonymous with the game of hockey in Minnesota. A native of Sault Ste. Marie, Ontario, Louie grew up playing Junior hockey with hall of famer's Phil and Tony Esposito. Originally wanting to go to college to be a dentist, Nanne emerged as a star defenseman on John Mariucci's Golden Gopher hockey teams from 1961-63. Nanne refers to Mariucci as his "second father," and is forever grateful to him for giving him the opportunity to play hockey in Gold Country.

Earning Gopher captain and All-American honors in his senior year, Nanne tallied a career-high 74 points, becoming the first defenseman to win a WCHA scoring title. For his efforts the newly naturalized American citizen was named as the league's MVP.

"I loved playing hockey at the University of Minnesota," said Nanne. "It was a real privilege. I had tremendous fun all the way through, and it was just a great experience. I really enjoyed the atmosphere, and it was something I will always cherish."

Upon graduating from the University, Nanne was drafted by NHL's Chicago Blackhawks. However, he got into a contract dispute with the team and ultimately refused to play for them, which led to a five year lay-off from pro hockey. While he sat out, he worked for Minneapolis businessman Harvey Mackay's envelope company and also coached the Gopher freshman hockey team for four years as well. During that time, he played on and off with the USHL's Rochester Mustangs, and also played international hockey for Team USA — even serving as the captain the 1968 Olympic hockey team in Grenoble, France. *(That's him in the photo in the middle with his old buddy, Herb Brooks, who is on the left.)*

When the NHL expanded to 12 teams in the late '60s, Chicago couldn't "freeze" him anymore because of the new reserve list, so Nanne became a free-agent. So, he decided to play for Minnesota's new expansion team, the North Stars. There, he quickly earned a reputation as being a solid team player and a real fan favorite. Polished at killing penalties, he developed into a fine checking forward who was often matched against the other teams' top lines. Nanne would

go on to play defense and winger for the North Stars through 1978, becoming the only player to play in all of the first 11 years of the team's existence. For his career, including the playoffs, he tallied 72 goals and 167 assists for 239 points with the Stars.

From there, he went on to serve as the team's general manager. And, one of the first things he did as the team's new GM, was to hire an assistant GM. Loyal to the bone, Louie hired his old college coach, John Mariucci, who was scouting for the team at the time.

"It was a lot of fun as a general manager, making very important day-to-day decisions, but there is not a better job in the world than actually playing the game on the ice. Whenever you can play something that you loved as a kid and then they pay you for it, well it doesn't get any better than that."

Of the players on the North Star's 1981 Stanley Cup team, only five were left from the team that Nanne took over in 1978. Bobby Smith was his first pick and Mike Modano would be his last. He quickly became known around the league as a wheeler and dealer of talent. He had clout with the other GM's around the league, and parlayed that into his favor. In 1979 he claimed Dave Semenko from Glen Sather's Edmonton Oilers in the expansion draft for the sole purpose of dealing him right back to Sather in a "gentleman's agreement" to leave Neal Broten available for them in that year's upcoming amateur draft. He would finish his amazing 24-year career with the Stars as the team president from 1988-1990.

Although Canadian by birth, Nanne became a well-known advocate of the Americanization of the NHL. He was one of the first to scout U.S. colleges for American talent and to take an active role in the support of player development programs, which also included Olympic and international competition.

Nanne was very involved in league politics too. In addition to helping lead the negotiations with the World Hockey Association that brought four new franchises into the league, he also served as chairman of the General Managers Committee. Furthermore, Nanne served as a member of the International Committee for USA Hockey and also served as Vice President of the NHL Players Association — as a member of the NHL Board of Governors, as a player, coach,

GM, and as president of the North Stars. In 1982, he also served as the chairman of the Central Hockey League's Board of Governors. (Nanne would also serve as the GM of Team USA for the Canada Cup tournaments in 1981, 1984 and 1987, as well as in the 1994 World Championships.)

A true friend to the game of hockey, Nanne has received numerous awards and honors over his illustrious career, including being named to the "50 Year WCHA All-Star team," and being awarded the prestigious Lester Patrick Award in 1980 for his outstanding service to hockey in the U.S. And, in 1998 he was also inducted into the US Hockey Hall of Fame.

Possibly the most recognized hockey figure in the state, Lou Nanne is extremely well liked and respected by his peers. He was a fixture with the North Stars from start to finish and is the authority on hockey in Minnesota today. His quick wit, colorful sense of humor and knowledge of the game have landed him several TV commentating jobs, including Stanley Cup playoffs and finals for "Hockey Night in Canada," CBS and NBC. But his favorite color-man gig is still covering the annual Minnesota State High School Hockey Tournament, something he has done now since 1964. Nanne currently works in the field of corporate finance and resides in the Twin Cities.

Eriksson, who made his North Stars debut by tallying 25 goals and 44 assists for 69 points that season.

The Merger with Cleveland

By the end of the 1977-78 campaign, things had hit rock-bottom for the Stars. They started out the nightmare season losing eight out of their first 10 games, only to follow up that streak by losing an amazing 16 out of their next 20. Ted Harris was canned as coach, and replaced with Andre Beaulieu. He would prove only to be a Band-Aid though, lasting for less than three months behind the bench before himself receiving the ax. The team finally gave the coaching position to winger Lou Nanne, who would serve as player-coach for the rest of that season. Finishing the season with a miserable 18-53-9 record, management knew something drastic had to be done quickly. Incidentally, Eriksson and Young were once more the lonely bright spots on the squad, leading the team scoring, while rookie defenseman Per-Olov Brasar also stepped up in his first season.

After six losing seasons things were looking bleak for Minnesota, which was mired in financial problems that put them in serious jeopardy of being sold off and relocated. You see, it was the height of professional hockey warfare throughout North America, as the upstart World Hockey Association was battling the NHL for the best players as well as for new turf. The ensuing chaos was wreaking havoc on the collective hockey world. The Stars ownership group, tired of losing their shirts, wanted to cut their losses and sell the club to new investors. Coincidentally, the struggling cash-strapped Cleveland franchise was also in the same boat, and as fate would have it, the two clubs decided to get together to further discuss the possibility of a potential merger.

The owners of the Cleveland Barons, brothers George and Gordon Gund, heirs to a billion dollar fortune, had also been suffering heavy monetary losses since they purchased the former Oakland/California Golden Seals and moved the fledgling club to Ohio in 1976. Knowing that they too had to take some drastic measures to avoid financial suicide, the Gunds were determined to make something happen. After approaching both the Washington Capitals and Vancouver Canucks, two other struggling small-market teams, about their interests in a merger, they decided to pull the trigger on a unifying deal with Minnesota. Here's how it all worked out. Ultimately, the Cleveland franchise folded, and all of the players who were under contract with the Barons became the property of the "new" Minnesota North Stars. As part of the transaction, the Gunds assumed ownership of the combined team from the nine Minnesota owners.

The league, anxious to "kill two birds with one stone," by taking its two worst franchises and putting them together, was eager to see the deal get done. Optimistic, the NHL figured that as long as the new team remained in Minnesota, where there was so much more interest in hockey than in Ohio, it would prove to be a win-win for both parties. Still, the merger was unprecedented in the history of modern sports, which gave the league reason to be concerned. At that time, only once had two pro sports teams merged within one league — and that brief union which came about during World War II between the Pittsburgh Steelers and Philadelphia Eagles, was only meant to be temporary.

While the Gunds took over as co-chairmen of the board for that upcoming 1978-79 season, John Karr was named as the team's new president, while the now-retired Lou Nanne was promoted to general manager. Harry Howell was named as the team's coach, but was replaced only a couple of months into the season by former Gophers and Saints coach, Glen Sonmor.

The merger injected some new life into the team's young roster. Nanne's task now was to begin melding the best possible team from a combination of the two rosters. The new team was allowed to protect 12 players from the original North Stars including: Tim Young, Glen Sharpley, Per-Olov Brasar, Bryan Maxwell and Pete LoPresti from the Stars; and from Cleveland the team acquired: Gilles Meloche, Dennis Maruk, Al MacAdam, Rick

BOBBY SMITH

One of Minnesota's favorite hockey stars of all time, Bobby Smith grew up like most kids in Canada playing hockey. He first starred in the major junior ranks for his home town Ottowa 67's in the Ontario Hockey Association. In 1978 he scored 69 goals and 123 assists for an amazing 192 regular season points and then tallied another 30 points in the playoffs. He topped the OHA in both assists and points and won the Canadian Major Junior Player of the Year award. From there, the North Stars selected the 20-year-old, 6-foot-4 phenom as the No. 1 overall player taken in that year's draft.

Smith established a torrid scoring pace in Minnesota in his first year, tallying 30 goals and 44 assists en route to winning the Calder Trophy as the NHL's top rookie. Smith instantly became a big fan favorite with the locals and led the North Stars in scoring four of his first five years with the club. His finest season with Minnesota came during the 1981-82 campaign when Smith achieved career highs in games played (80), goals (43), assists (71) and points (114).

In 1984, Smith was involved in one of the team's most talked-about trades ever, when he was dealt to the Montreal Canadiens for Keith Acton, Mark Napier, and a third-round pick. Smith played seven seasons north of the border, recording 70-plus points in five of those years. In 1986, he led the Canadiens to a Stanley Cup title by scoring the game-winning goal in a 4-3 win over the Calgary Flames.

In 1991, Smith, then a 33-year-old veteran, returned to his beloved Minnesota to lead the Stars back to the Stanley Cup Finals, this time against Badger Bob Johnson and the Pittsburgh Penguins. Smith's leadership and guidance on the ice and in the locker room was of great help to the younger players. He contributed eight goals and eight assists in the playoffs after a 46-point regular season, proving that he hadn't lost the edge that had always made him special in the minds of Stars fans.

For 15 seasons Bobby ruled the red line. He played in 1,077 games with the North Stars and Canadiens, scoring an amazing 1,036 points. And, after 13 playoff seasons and 184 games, Smith retired with 64 goals and 96 assists for 160 points, ranking him 12th on the NHL's all-time playoff point leaders list. He also played in four NHL All-Star Games in 1981, 1982, 1989 and 1990. In addition, from 1981-90, Smith served as vice president of the NHL Players' Association.

After retiring from hockey in 1993, Smith fulfilled a lifelong dream and went back to college at the U of M. He received his B.S. in Business and then went on to obtain an MBA at the Carlson School of Management. That experience would pay quick dividends, because, in 1996, he became the Phoenix Coyotes' first executive vice president of hockey operations. He would later take over as the team's General Manager.

Hampton, Mike Fidler and Greg Smith. All told, their were eight former Barons that made the North Star's opening day roster. Right winger Al MacAdam, who finished second in team scoring that season, and goaltender Gilles Meloche would prove to be the best of a bunch. In addition, and perhaps most significantly, because of the team's status as the league's worst franchise, the Stars retained the rights to the no. 1 overall pick in that year's upcoming amateur draft. With that pick, Minnesota selected a kid by the name of Bobby Smith. The talented young centerman would lead the Stars in scoring in his first season with 74 points, and for his efforts was awarded the Calder Trophy as the NHL's rookie of the year. Roland Eriksson was also named to that year's NHL All-Star team, as Minnesota, which had switched to the Adams Division in Cleveland's place, finished the season on an upswing, with an improved 28-40-12 record.

Philly Steak-Out

From April 7th, 1973 to April 7th, 1980, the North Stars won a grand total of zero playoff games, while during the same time frame they made seven different coaching changes. Needless to say, it had been a bumpy ride for the past several years for the franchise. That all changed though on April 8th, 1980, when the team beat Toronto, 6-3, to end their playoff win drought. The season was a steady improvement from the one the year before, and under the tutelage of their new coach, Glen Sonmor, the Stars prepared to embark on the new decade of the 1980's with a fresh sense of purpose.

The team had started its rebuilding plans, and had been invigorated by the merger with Cleveland. Led by the young talent on the "new-look" Stars, the team went from the Adams Division's basement to third that next year, with a 36-28-16 record. The season was filled with highlights along the way, including busting up the Philadelphia Flyer's unbelievable winning streak of 79'. Philly, which had broken the record for the longest undefeated streak of 29 games, previously held by Montreal, was at 35 consecutive non-loss games and counting when they were greeted by nearly 16,000 Met Center psychos on January 7, 1980. With the eyes of the entire sports world following their every move, the Stars made a little bit of history. Behind the chants of the fans screaming "Go home Flyers, Go home Flyers," Minnesota drilled the Flyers, 7-1, thus ending their glorious ride. By winning that game the Stars set a club record of their own, by playing 12 consecutive games without a loss at home.

The post-season would also yield a pair of series wins for the suddenly surging North Stars. First, the team went out and swept the Toronto Maple Leafs in the opening round of the playoffs. Next they pulled off a major upset by beating the defending Stanley Cup champion Montreal Canadiens, who were attempting to go for their fifth straight title. The series was one for the ages, with Minnesota winning Games One and Two, losing Three, Four, and Five, and then coming back to win Games Six and Seven. The finale came down to the wire, with Al MacAdam scoring on a third period wrister to put the Stars ahead, 3-2. Meloche held on in goal as Minnesota won the series in front of a stunned Montreal crowd. The Stars went on to face the Flyers in the semifinals, only to see Philadelphia exact a little bit of revenge. Still upset about having their streak broken in Minnesota, Philly eliminated the North Stars

Pete LoPresti

in five games to earn a trip to the finals.

The season ended on a positive note though, as the team gained a lot of confidence and a dramatic change of direction. MacAdam had a career year for the club, totaling 42 goals and 51 assists for a team-leading 93 points. The winger had earned himself quite a reputation around the league as a sharp-shooting sniper, scoring on nearly 25 percent of his shots. For his efforts he was awarded the league's Masterton Trophy, becoming the only player in team history to do so.

Gilles Meloche combined with journeyman goaltender Gary Edwards to shore up the team's defense, which for the first time since 1973, finally scored more goals (311) than it had allowed (253). In addition to MacAdam's great season, Steve Payne scored 85 points; Bobby Smith added 83; and Craig Hartsburg, who made his NHL debut on defense, produced 44-points. Hartsburg, Gilles Meloche, Payne, and former Bemidji State Beaver, Gary Sargent, all made the All-Star team that year as well.

The 1981 Cinderella Stars

The 1980-81 North Stars season will forever be remembered as one of the all-time greats in Minnesota sports history. It was our first taste of Stanley Cup finals' hockey, and it literally took the state by storm. A combination of youth and veteran experience played a big role in the Stars compiling a solid 35-28-17 record that season. Team leader Bobby Smith once again had a big year for the Stars, scoring 93 points on 29 goals and 64 assists. Other contributors included: Steve Payne, a 30-goal scorer; Craig Hartsburg, who escaped the sophomore jinx by scoring 43 points that year; Al MacAdam and Brad Maxwell. They were also joined by several newcomers that season who gave the team a greatly needed boost. Dino Ciccarelli, called up in February from Oklahoma City (Central Hockey League), became an instant fan favorite when he broke teammate Steve Christoff's record for the most goals by a rookie, with 14. Other newcomers included Brad Palmer, who, with his blistering slapshot, was a nice addition; and so was 19-year-old goaltender, Don Beaupre, who played fabulously between the pipes. Another youngster who really stepped up that year by adding some desperately needed skill and polish to the team's backline was former University of Minnesota-Duluth Bulldog star, Curt Giles. Giles, like Ciccarelli, was also called up the year before from Oklahoma City. The steady defenseman would go on to patrol the Met Center blue line for a total of 12 years.

Perhaps the biggest "future" star of the team, however, was someone who would get called up at the last second to join in on the post-season festivities. His name was Neal Broten, a Roseau native and former Gopher and Olympic gold-medalist, who brought more speed to an already quick roster. The Stars had even traded away center Glen Sharpley, thus freeing up Neal's lucky No. 7 jersey.

After breezing through the regular season, it was time for the Stars to finally get the proverbial playoff monkey off of their collective backs. Much to the approval of the Minnesota fans, the Stars opened the first round of playoffs on the road against rival Boston. Now, coming in to this best-of-five playoff series, the Stars were a collective 0-28-7 in Boston, having never won a game in the Boston Garden. There was clearly no loveloss between these two clubs, which earlier in

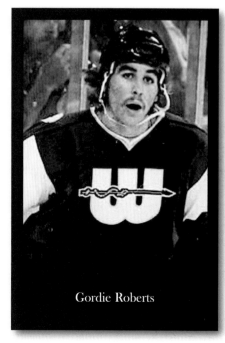

Gordie Roberts

the year had beaten the hell out of each other at Met Center for an NHL record 406 combined penalty minutes. The Stars went to Beantown expecting another blood bath. What they found however, was that Boston wanted to play some serious hockey, and with that, the fans were treated to a doozy of a series.

In Game One, with the score tied at 4-4 at the end of regulation, Steve Payne scored the game-winner at the 3:34 mark of overtime to give his squad a 1-0 lead in the series. Minnesota then followed it up with a 9-6 victory in Game Two. Things were looking up. The series shifted back to Bloomington for Game Three, and in what would play out to be a classic, the Stars, brimming with confidence, beat the Bruins by the score of 6-3 to sweep the series. "That had to be the biggest upset in Stars history," said legendary radio analyst Al Shaver after the game.

"Never had I seen the Met Center rocking like it was that night," added winger Steve Payne. "I remember sitting in the dressing room after the warm-ups and the building was literally rocking from the noise. People were so fired up. It was quite an experience."

Next up for Minnesota were the Adams Division champion Buffalo Sabres, who were sporting a gaudy .619 winning percentage. Steve Payne once again set the tone by scoring yet another overtime game-winner in Game One. The Stars didn't look back from that point on, winning both Games Two and Three, only to drop a Game Four double-overtime heart-breaker by the score of 5-4. They rolled on to win the series four games to one.

In the semis, the Stars found themselves pitted against another surprise team, the Calgary Flames. With Gilles Meloche and Donny Beaupre trading off in net, the Stars were proving to be a formidable force. Minnesota made a statement in the series opener by crushing the Flames, 4-1. Calgary came back to win Game Two on a late third period goal, only to see Minnesota win the next two games, 6-4 and 7-4. The Flames then rallied to win Game Five, 3-1, back in Calgary. But the Stars hung in there and behind Brad Palmer's game-winning wrister in the third period, took Game Six, 5-3. Protecting their home ice throughout the series, the Stars simply outplayed the Flames and ultimately won the series four games to two. With that, after several disappointing semifinal losses over the past decade and a half, the North Stars, for the first time in franchise history, had finally made it to the Stanley Cup finals.

"Getting the opportunity to play in the Stanley Cup finals was incredible," reminisced Bobby Smith years later. "I can still remember standing on the bench as the conference finals game against Calgary was winding down, and Brad Palmer had just scored an insurance goal for us. Just realizing that you had spent your whole life watching the Stanley Cup finals and now you were going to be playing in them was tremendously exciting."

The finals would prove to be a classic case of Cinderella vs. Goliath. Goliath, in this scenario, was the defending Stanley Cup champion New York Islanders, whose path to the finals went through Edmonton, and then Madison Square Garden, where they swept their cross-town rivals, the Rangers, in the semis. The Stars were now in uncharted territory as they geared up for the Isles, who were no strangers to the hoopla surrounding Lord Stanley's Cup. After all, the Islanders, who were used to the media circus, were the

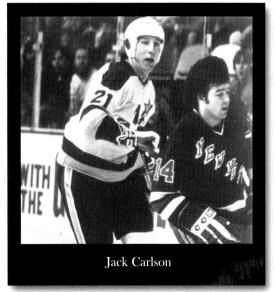
Jack Carlson

toast of the Big Apple. Minnesota, however, was a bit "star-struck" by it all — and it would show. The Isles were an intimidating bunch. Their roster was a regular who's who of hockey during that era, featuring legends such as Brian Trottier, Mike Bossy, Dennis Potvin and Butch Goring. Their leader, Billy Smith, a feisty goaltender who seemed to make a habit out of lodging his stick into his opponent's flesh whenever they came too close to his crease, was also playing outstanding in the net.

"So close you could taste it..."
Minnesota, primed on speed and enthusiasm, opened the best-of-seven series in New York City. There, in front of some 15,000 Long Island fans, the Stars prepared to make history. It wouldn't be easy. The Stars, visibly nervous and scruffy-looking (from not having shaved their playoff beards in several superstitious weeks), hit the ice with aspirations of winning professional hockey's most coveted prize. Things got off to a bumpy start for Minnesota though as New York jumped out to a quick 1-0 lead on a goal by Anders Kallur. The Stars then caught a break when Bob Bourne was assessed a major penalty for spearing. Unfortunately, however, the Islanders got a pair of short-handed goals from Kallur and Brian Trottier during the five-minute disadvantage, and the Stars were never able to regain their composure. A pair of third-period New York goals on only three shots secured an easy 6-3 Isles victory.

Game Two got off to a better start for Minnesota as Dino Ciccarelli scored a power-play goal to go ahead early. (Dino emerged as a star in the playoffs, scoring 14 goals and 21 points in 19 games, both NHL playoff records for a rookie.) Then, precisely one minute later, Bossy tied things up for New York, only to see both Potvin and Nystrom each score a goal to make it 3-1. But the Stars rallied and came back to tie it at three apiece in the second, on goals from Palmer and Payne. The defending champs got nervous, but their experience prevailed as Potvin, Ken Morrow, and Bossy each scored in an eight-minute stretch to mirror the result of the 6-3 series opening victory.

Game Three brought puck mania to the then so-called "hockey capital of the world," Bloomington, Minn. The Met Center was the site of many tailgate bashes as the adoring North Star fans welcomed home their heroes from the Big Apple. The Stars jumped out to a 3-1 lead after the first, and the crowd went crazy. But Goring tallied twice in the second as the Islanders took a 4-3 lead into the final period. Again, the Stars rebounded, tying the game at the 1:11 mark of the third, only to see the Islanders regain the lead less than a minute later. With New York up by one, Goring put the final dagger in the collective hearts of Minnesota fans, scoring again at the six-minute mark for the hat-trick to all but seal it up. The Isles added an empty-netter and came away with the 7-5 victory.

"We knew what to expect from their dominant guys, Potvin, Bossy, and Trottier," said Star's coach Glen Sonmor after Game Three. "But I don't think we were prepared for so much offense out of Goring."

Refusing to lie down and be swept by the Islanders, Minnesota played brilliantly in Game Four. Utility man, Gord Lane opened the scoring for the Isles to silence the crowd early in the opening frame. Then, midway through the period, with Minnesota on a power play, Brad Maxwell tallied on a blistering slapshot from the blue line. Or so he

Curt Giles

thought! Referee Andy Van Hellemond apparently never saw the shot, which was later seen on replay to rip right through the net. The crowd went nuts over the no-goal call, only to see Craig Harstburg's shot from the point seconds later beat Billy Smith. This time the red light was turned on and as a result, the crowd went berserk. With the score tied up at two apiece through two, Minnesota took the lead on Steve Payne's top-shelf slapper midway through the third. Bobby Smith then added an insurance goal late in the game to insure the 4-2 victory for the Stars. The 19-year-old phenom goaltender Donny Beaupre played huge in Game Four, turning away shot after shot against the mighty Islanders, who were held to fewer than five goals only three times in 18 post-season games. The Stars kept their cool during the game and it paid off. Of the four North Star goals scored in the game, two came on power plays and a third was scored three seconds after an Islander penalty had elapsed.

With the win, the Stars had lived to skate yet another day. The series once again shifted back to Uniondale, Long Island for Game Five. Unfortunately for the Stars, New York came flying out of the gates. And, once again it was Butch Goring who would do most of the damage. At 5:12 of the first period a North Star clearing pass deflected off referee Bryan Lewis and right onto the stick of Bob Bourne, who promptly fed the rushing Goring for the goal. Then, less than a half of a minute later, John Tonelli and Bob Nystrom dug the puck out from behind the Minnesota net and fed it to a wide open Wayne Merrick, who beat Beaupre to make it 2-0. That line was amazing. It was their 18th goal of the playoffs, all scored while at even strength against their adversaries' top lines. A few minutes later, Goring, who would capture the Conn Smythe Trophy as the playoff's MVP, scored again on a wrister, putting the game out of reach. Behind legendary coach Al Arbour, the Isles went on to win the game, 5-1, as well as the series. For New York, who had established themselves as one of the game's greatest hockey dynasties, the win would be the second in what would be a string of four-straight Stanley Cup titles.

The Stars had lost to one of the greatest teams of all time, and could still hang their hats high. New York went into the series with a game-plan. They were a stronger, more physical team which clutched, grabbed, hooked, and interfered with the younger, speedier Stars, thus neutralizing their superior skating attack. They also converted on five of 16 power play opportunities – allowing no shorthanded goals, compared to Minnesota, which could muster just six goals out of 33 power play chances.

The Stars' Cinderella fairy-tale escapade would prove to be a huge shot in the arm for Minnesota hockey though. The fans had fallen in love with their guys in green, and the future of the organization looked to be very bright indeed.

"Glen Sonmor was a great coach, and he just let us play the game," reminisced Broten of that magical season. "It all happened so fast, I had only played three games for the Stars' when we went to the Stanley Cup finals. I was so wet behind the ears, I didn't really know what was going on. Things happened so fast and the next thing I knew I was playing with guys like Bobby Smith, Steve Payne, Al MacAdam and Freddy Barrett. It was a great experience and I will always remember that first run at the Cup."

On the Rebound
Expectations were running high for the young Stars, who had gotten a whiff of Lord Stanley's coveted prize and wanted more. Because of league expansion and realignment, Minnesota started out the 1981-82 season by switching from the Adams Division to the Norris Division. Feeling that they had something to prove, the club went out and won the first divisional championship in the team's history,

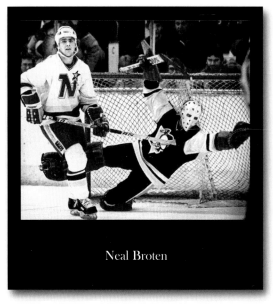
Neal Broten

finishing atop the Norris Division with a 37-23-20 record. Their 94-point campaign matched the then club record for wins in a season.

In the first round of the playoffs, the Stars found themselves pitted against their old foe's from the Windy City, the Chicago Blackhawks. The series opened on April 7th in front of 15,597 Met Center fans. The crowd was eagerly anticipating a return trip to the finals, and saw the lowly Hawks as merely a bump in the road. Boy were they wrong! Chicago stunned the Stars in Game One, when Hawk winger Greg Fox beat Gilles Meloche at 3:32 of the first overtime period to win the game, 3-2. Chicago's Denny Savard beat Don Beaupre for the game-winner in Game Two, as the Blackhawks beat Minnesota for the second straight night – this time by the score of 5-3. The series shifted back to the Chicago Stadium for Game Three, and there, in front of more than 20,000 fans, the Stars finally busted loose. Once Dino Ciccarelli's goal made it 2-1, the floodgates opened and the Stars pulverized Chicago, 7-1. But, the next night Hawks defenseman Al Secord put the final nail in the coffin for Minnesota, as the Hawks went on to beat the Stars, 5-2. With the win, Chicago had eliminated Minnesota from playoff competition. It was a disappointing loss, not to mention a major upset, for the young Stars.

There were some bright spots however. Bobby Smith had a break-out year, scoring 43 goals and 71 assists for an amazing 114 points. Ciccarelli also stepped up by scoring 106 points on 55 goals and 51 assists, while Neal Broten added 98 points on 38 goals and 60 helpers. Ciccarelli, Hartsburg, Meloche and Bobby Smith were all named to the 1982 All-Star squad.

The Curse of the Blackhawks
Minnesota helped itself during the offseason when they struck gold in the 1982 entry draft. Now, the amateur draft had long been considered as a crap-shoot by most of the NHL general managers who hated to leverage the future of their respective organizations on the shoulders of some unpolished 18-year-old kid fresh off the farm from Moose Jaw or Medicine Hat. With the second overall pick in the first-round of the draft, the Stars selected a young left winger from St. Catherine's, Ontario, by the name of Brian Bellows. Luckily for Minnesota fans, the Boston Bruins decided to go with defenseman Gord Kluzak with the first overall pick of the draft. Kluzak, plagued by injuries throughout his career, never panned out for the Bruins. But Bellows on the other hand, proved to be worth his weight in gold.

The Stars came out smoking for the 1982-83 season, losing only nine of their first 40 games. Then, on January 13th, 1983, longtime Stars coach Glen Sonmor stepped down as coach, and was replaced by his assistant, Murray Oliver. Oliver led the Stars to a second-place finish in the Norris Division with 40 wins and 96 overall points, both franchise records.

While Broten and Smith tied for the scoring lead with 77 points apiece, Stars rookie Brian Bellows finished with 65 points in 68 games. Beaupre and Meloche formed a solid tandem in goal, with Meloche posting a 20-13-11 record (3.57 GAA) and Beaupre compiling a 19-10-5 mark (3.58 GAA) during the regular season. The entire line of Broten-McCarthy-Ciccarelli was invited to play at the 1983 All-Star game, and they were also joined by Craig Hartsburg. (Another important event happened that year as well. Craig Hartsburg took over the captain's position from Tim Young, a title Hartsy would keep for more than seven years.)

Oliver led the Stars back to the playoffs that year, where they met the Toronto Maple Leafs in the first round. There, the Stars disposed of the Leafs three games to one. Bobby Smith scored both the game-winners for Games One and Two, with the latter being an overtime winner. They lost Game Three in Toronto, but came back to take Game Four, and the series, thanks to Dino Ciccarelli's overtime game-winner at 8:05 of the first extra session. Next up were their new arch-rivals from Chicago, the Norris Division champion Blackhawks. In a very physical and emotional series, the Hawks came out and took Games One and Two by the scores of 5-2 and 7-4. Minnesota came back to win Game Three at the Met, where Ciccarelli scored the early game-winner of a 5-1 blow-out. Thinking that the tide was turning, the Stars battled Chicago again that next night, only to see right winger Rich Preston beat Meloche at 10:34 of overtime to win the game and take a commanding three games to one lead in the series. Later, back at the Stadium, the Hawks took Game Five, 5-2, to win the series. For the Stars, it was yet again another disappointing early exit from the playoffs.

So-Long Bobby and Hello Gretzky

The Stars thought that they could once again help themselves during that offseason when they had the first overall pick in the NHL's entry draft. With the likes of Pat LaFontaine, Steve Yzerman and Tom Barrasso on the board, the Stars surprised everyone by drafting a New Jersey high schooler by the name of Brian Lawton. Touting their new rookie, the Stars prepared to bid for the Cup yet again.

At the beginning of the season, knowing they had to make some changes at the top, Minnesota hired long-time Canadian college coach Bill Mahoney to take over behind the bench. Then, in a shocker, just 10 games into the 1983-84 season, the Stars pulled off a blockbuster deal, trading Bobby Smith to the Montreal Canadiens in return for Keith Acton and Mark Napier.

"I was really very excited about going to the Canadiens," said Smith years later. "I realized that it would be an excellent opportunity and would lead to a very exciting time for me. I won a Stanley Cup in 1986 with them and without question, that is the biggest highlight of my career. On the other hand, it was very difficult to leave Minnesota. It was the place where I wanted to live. Although it was a very good move for my career, it was sad to leave."

Rather than lying down and pouting over the loss of Smith, the Stars rallied and actually played some inspired hockey. Under Mahoney the Stars once again regained the Norris Division crown by posting a 39-31-10 regular season record, their finest performance of the decade. Helping to fill the void created by Smith's absence was Neal Broten, who led the attack with 89 points. Brian Bellows, meanwhile, added 42 goals and 41 assists for a phenomenal sophomore campaign. Defenseman Brad Maxwell contributed not only 19 goals and 54 assists, but also 225 hard earned penalty minutes. Dino scored 38 goals and 33 assists, and newcomers Keith Acton and Mark Napier were also major contributors by scoring 55 and 41 points, respectively. The downside to it all was the fact that both Beaupre and Meloche were over the 4.00 goals-against mark, a tell-tale sign that the defense was soft.

The Stars were given a very tough test in the first round, facing off against their old nemesis from Chicago. But the Stars hung tough and ultimately prevailed. It wasn't easy though, as the Blackhawks stole Game One at the Met Center, 3-1 on Al Secord's slapper to put it away. Neal Broten scored the game-winner for the Stars in Game Two, in a heroic come-from-behind 6-5 thriller in front of a packed house in Bloomington. The Stars split the next two games in Chicago, winning Game Three, 4-1, only to lose Game Four, 4-3. But the series shifted back to Minnie for Game Five, and there the Stars prevailed, winning the contest by the score of 4-1 to win the series.

Jon Casey

Full of confidence from beating the Hawks, the Stars now prepared to take on the St. Louis Blues in round two. The inflatable "Dino the Dinosaur" dolls came out by the thousands at the Met Center on April 12th, when Ciccarelli scored the game-winner in a 2-1 nail-biter for the Stars. Doug Gilmour rained on their parade that next night though, beating Donny Beaupre at 16:16 of overtime to take Game Two. The Stars lost Game Three in St. Louis by the score of 3-1, only to come back and take Game Four by the score of 3-2 on Tommy McCarthy's game-winner in the third. With the series tied at two games apiece, the series returned to Minnesota for Game Five. There, Donny Beaupre blanked the Blues 6-0 for one of the biggest shut-outs of his career. In Game Six though, St. Louis returned the favor, this time shutting out Minnesota, 4-0, in front of their home crowd to once again even it back up at three each. Game Seven would prove to be a classic, with both teams beating each other up at both ends of the ice. But, with the score tied at 3-3 at the end of regulation, it all came down to one shot. And luckily for Minnesota, it was Steve Payne who made the difference. At 6:00 of the extra session, Payner knocked in a dribbler past Blues netminder Mike Liut to give the Stars the thrilling series victory.

The Minnesota fans were starting to sense another run at Lord Stanley's hardware, and now only Edmonton stood in the way. This is where the story gets really ugly, as the Stars were suddenly and maliciously beaten over their heads with a very stiff dose of reality. The Oilers, led by the "Great One" Wayne Gretzky, pummeled the Stars in the Campbell Conference finals. Led by Gretzky, Coffey, Messier, Linesman, Fuhr and Kurri, the powerhouse Oilers, which would go on to win the first of four Stanley Cups in five years that season, swept Minnesota in four straight games to win the series. For the Stars, it was a bitter pill to swallow. They had run up against yet another dynasty team that was not to be denied.

The Blackhawk Blues

Thoroughly distraught by their disappointing early final-four exit the year before, the Stars tried to do right by their fans in 1984-85. They opened the season with a miserable 3-8-2 record, and as a result, Glen Sonmor came down from the front office and returned to the bench to resume his coaching duties from Bill Mahoney. Glen didn't do much to help his cause though, as the Stars finished 18 games under .500, with a 25-43-12 record. The 62-point campaign was the team's worst finish in eight seasons.

Despite their dismal performance, however, the team managed to squeak into the playoffs. There, they faced the first-place Blues. While most were expecting a quick series, as in a quick exit for the Stars, it just so happened that it was the other way around. That's right, the Stars shocked everyone by coming out and sweeping the Blues in three straight. Keith Acton was the hero of the first round playoff match, scoring the game-winners for both of the first two games in St. Louis. A pair of nail-biters, the Stars won Game One, 3-2, and Game Two, 4-3. Tony McKegney got the third game-winner in Game Three, as Gilles Meloche posted a 2-0 shut-out to seal the fate of the Blues.

Thinking that they could make a run much like they had done in 1981, Minnesota was quickly brought back down to earth in Round Two by their old nemesis' from the second city — the Blackhawks. With the series opening in Chicago, Minnesota came out and steamrolled the Hawks in Game One by the score of 8-5. Chicago, none too pleased about being beat in their own house, came back the next night and manhandled the Stars, 6-2. They then proceeded to take Games Three and Four as well, on game-winners by Al Secord and Daryl Sutter. Game Five was back in Chicago, and Minnesota refused to roll over and play dead. In a bloody match, the Stars prevailed on Dennis

DINO CICCARELLI

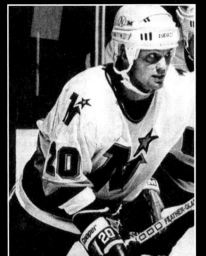

If Wayne Gretzky's "office" was the area just behind the net, then the "doorstep" area just to the side of the crease would have to be reserved for Dino Ciccarelli, who made his living redirecting and stuffing pucks past unsuspecting goalies from his favorite spot on the ice. He paid the price to camp out there though, and has the scars to prove it.

Dino Ciccarelli grew up in Sarnia, Ontario, and first emerged as a star on his London Knights junior team (OHA), where, at the age of 17, he won second team all-star honors in 1977-78 after a 142-point season. That next season though, Dino suffered a near career-ending knee injury that caused his draft stock to plummet. Consequently, he went unpicked in the NHL's amateur draft that year, and instead was signed as a free-agent by the North Stars. After spending a season with Oklahoma City, Dino battled back to make the Stars' roster in 1980-81, becoming an instant hit with the Met Center faithful. Ciccarelli set a rookie record by scoring 14 goals in the playoffs that year, helping to lead the team to the Stanley Cup finals. It wasn't long before the fans were bringing "Dino the Dinosaur" blow-up dolls to games, to cheer on their new hero. (Conversely, many of those dinosaurs were also maliciously pummelled and burned in the stands at such locales as Chicago and St. Louis when Ciccarelli came to town!)

Scoring 55 goals and cracking the Top 10 in league scoring with 106 points, Ciccarelli emerged as a superstar that next season. He scored 40 or more goals four times in the next eight years in Minnesota, twice going over the 100-point plateau. A five-time team goal-scoring leader, Dino's 332 goals rank second in franchise history behind only Brian Bellows' 342. In addition, he ranks third in total points with 651, and owns two of the team's three 50-goal seasons. On March 7, 1989, in what many Minnesota fans considered to be a very controversial trade, Dino was sent packing in a blockbuster deal to the Washington Capitals in exchange for Mike Gartner and Larry Murphy.

Dino went on to star for the Caps and also for the Detroit Red Wings, who he was later dealt to in 1992. Early in 1994, Dino banged home his 500th career goal, putting him a very elite fraternity. In 1996 Dino wound up in Tampa Bay, only to be dealt once again to the Florida Panthers two years later. There, on February 3, 1998, against his old mates from Detroit, he became just the ninth player in league history to score 600 career goals.

At 5-foot-10 and just 175 pounds, Ciccarelli was not big, quick or even flashy. An appropriate comparison might be that of the NBA's Dennis Rodman, in the sense that they both earned their bread and butter doing dirty work. Dino was a grinder. While Rodman prided himself on being a relentless rebounder, constantly getting hammered in the paint — Dino thrived at absorbing severe beatings at the hands of bigger, tougher, defensemen in order to hold his ground and pounce on rebounds and deflections in front of the net. Finally, in 1999, after 19 seasons in the NHL, Dino retired with 608 goals and 592 assists in 1,232 career games with five teams. A relentless "goalmouth garbage sniper," Ciccarelli went on to become one of the most prolific goal scorers in NHL history, making him a sure bet for the Hall of Fame.

"Pee Wee" Maruk's overtime goal just over a minute into the extra session.

To the melodic chants of "Secord Sucks!" — "Secord Sucks!", the Stars played strong, but came up short in Game Six. They lost yet another overtime thriller, this time by the score of 6-5, when Chicago winger Daryl Sutter scored his second game-winner of the series, at 15:41 of the first over-time. With the win, Chicago took the Conference finals, four games to two.

Brian Bellows, the sturdy, hard-working winger, led all scorers that year with 62 points, while Maruk finished second with 60. A trio of Minnesota goalies shared the netminding duties that year as well, as Donny Beaupre and Gilles Meloche were joined by Rollie Melanson, who appeared in some 20 contests for the Stars. Beaupre had the best goals against average of the bunch with a 3.69, while Meloche finished with a 3.80, and "Rollie the Goalie" came in with a respectable 4.10.

Enter the Mighty Casey
At the beginning of the 1985-86 season, North Stars GM Lou Nanne named ex-New York Islanders player and coach Lorne Henning as the teams' 13th head coach. Henning would quickly find out that the fans were starved for a winner here, and wanted one sooner than later. Knowing he was in the hot-seat, Lorne led his Stars to a respectable 38-33-9 record that year, good for second place in the Norris. In the first round of the playoffs, they met St. Louis, which was anxious to avenge its previous year's shocking upset at the hands of the Stars.

Brian Lawton

Despite Donny Beaupre's nearly 40 saves, the Stars lost Game One at the Met, 2-1. They rebounded in Game Two though, behind Dirk Graham's game-winner. Back in St. Louis, Bernie Federko scored the 4-3 game-winner for the Blues in Game Three. It was Graham playing hero yet one more time for the Stars in Game Four, as he once again got the game-winner in a 7-4 Stars equalizer. With the series tied at two games apiece, the contest came back to Minnesota. There, in front of 15,953 screaming fans, the North Stars got waxed, 6-3, to lose the series. "That was one of the toughest losses I've ever been a part of," said Donny Beaupre after the game.

Neal Broten had a career year, scoring 29 goals and 76 assists for a 105-point season — a first for an American-born player. Meanwhile, Ciccarelli scored 44 goals and 45 assists for 89 points, while Bellows added 31 goals and 48 assists for 79 points. The Stars also had a great season out of former Gopher, Scott Bjugstad, who scored 43 goals. While Beaupre played 52 games in goal that season, a newcomer, Jon Casey, a Grand Rapids native, made 26 appearances en route to posting a respectable 3.89 goals-against average. Incidentally, Casey replaced longtime North Stars keeper Gilles Meloche, who was traded to Edmonton (later Pittsburgh) for winger Paul Houck.

Some Lean Years
The 1986-87 and 1987-88 campaigns were not particularly good years if you were a Stars fan. Despite the fact that the team came within one point of the Norris Division crown in 1985-86, the North Stars missed the playoffs for the first

time in eight seasons in 1986-87. Glen Sonmor once again returned to the bench to serve as the interim coach, this time replacing Lorne Henning with only a month to go in the season. The team ended up with a dismal 30-40-10 record, good enough for only a fifth place finish in the Norris. Neal Broten, who lit it up the year before, was plagued by injuries that year, and despite the continued efforts of Ciccarelli and Bellows, the other players simply did not get the job done. An example of the scoring disparity was the fact that Ciccarelli, who scored 52 goals and added 51 assists for 103 points, finished the season more than 40 points ahead of his nearest teammate, Brian MacLellan. Kari Takko joined Donny Beaupre in goal that year, while Casey got some minutes under his belt in the minors.

On April 23, 1987, St. Paul's Herb Brooks became the 14th coach of the North Stars. Brooks, then 50 years old, had won 100 NHL games faster than any coach in the history of the league when he coached the New York Rangers during a 1981-85 stint on Broadway. "Herbie" was a Minnesota icon. A former Gopher coach who won three NCAA titles in the 1970s, he gained most of his notoriety as the coach of the legendary 1980 "Miracle on Ice" team that won the Olympic gold medal in Lake Placid. Despite being a brilliant tactician and true student of the European game, Brooks simply did not have the players to get the job done in only a year's time. Seemingly everybody was hurt that year. In fact, the team actually set a record for the most man-hours lost due to injuries. It was unbelievable. Despite Brooks' presence behind the bench, the team finished with a miserable 19-48-13 record, and once again missed the playoffs. Brooks left after only one season, knowing that the odds were stacked against him in a situation beyond his control. He was replaced by Pierre Page. Incidentally, Ciccarelli and Bellows led the way for the Stars that year, scoring 86 and 81 points respectively. Bellows was named to the All-Star team as well.

The Stars were indecisive and without direction at this point. Later that year, with the team clearly in a funk, Nanne resigned as the team's GM, opting to move upstairs to the front office. There, he replaced John Karr as the team's new president.

Herb Brooks Coached
the Stars in 1987

It's Ciccarelli for Gartner in a Blockbuster
Jack Ferreira, who took over as the team's new GM, decided to shake some things up from the top down. A major trade surprised the North Stars in 1988-89, and got them back on track. The blockbuster deal, which took place in March of 1989, sent fan-favorite Dino Ciccarelli packing to the Washington Capitals in exchange for all-star winger Mike Gartner. The trigger was pulled on the controversial deal after much deliberation from the Stars' front office. Nonetheless, the Stars responded by playing much better that season. Newcomer Dave Gagner, who was traded to Minnesota from the New York Rangers for Jari Gronstrand and Paul Boutilier back in October of 1987, was called up in 1988 and made a big impact in his first full season as well. He came out of nowhere to lead the club in scoring with 35 goals and 43 assists for 78 points. That year, the line of Neal Broten, Mike Gartner and Brian Bellows would prove to be one of the hottest trio's in the league.

Gagner, Gartner, Broten and Bellows, along with goaltender Jon Casey, who took over as the team's full-time starter that year, led the way for the Stars. Pierre Page's squad played much better than it had in years past and wound up finishing in third place in the Norris Division with an improved 27-37-16 record. Making a return trip to the playoffs, after a two-year drought, the Stars took on the Blues in round one. The Stars lost

both Games One and Two in St. Louis by the identical overtime scores of 4-3. Down but not out, the Stars tried in vain to win Game Three back in Bloomington. But, Blues winger, and former UMD Bulldog, Brett Hull got his second third-period game-winner of the series, beating Jon Casey on the top shelf, to lead St. Louis past the Stars, 5-3. Minnesota, refusing to be swept, came back behind Don Barber's third period game-winning slapshot to win Game Four, 5-4. The series then shifted back to St. Louis, where the Blues proceeded to crush the Stars, 6-1, thus ending their season. To add insult to injury, Gartner was held scoreless in the series. Afraid of losing him to free agency, the Stars traded Gartner to the Rangers for Ulf Dahlen the next season.

Enter Rookie Phenom Mike Modano
The North Stars finished fourth in the Norris with an improved 36-40-4 record in 1989-90. However, they were blessed by a talented young rookie phenom by the name of Mike Modano, who tallied 75 points on 29 goals and 46 assists en route to finishing second in the NHL's Calder Trophy voting that season. Team captain and resident enforcer Basil McRae kept pretty busy that year protecting his flock of young stars. Among them included: Brian Bellows, who racked up 55 goals and 44 assists for 99 points, Neal Broten, who's playmaking earned him 85 points, and Dave Gagner, who added 78 points.

The Stars back-doored it into the playoffs that season, where they once again found themselves facing Chicago. The Stars stole Game One in the Windy City thanks to a Brian Bellows goal late in the third which gave them a 2-1 victory. The Hawks rallied in Game Two, evening up the series on a Jeremy Roenick wrister that beat Jon Casey on the short side. Chicago returned the favor back in Bloomington, stealing Game Three, 2-1. Minnesota then tattoo'd the Blackhawks in Game Four, as Casey garnered a coveted 4-0 shut-out. With the series once again even, Game Five took place back at the old Chicago Stadium. There, in front of more than 18,000 fans, the Hawks beat up the Stars 5-1. Back at the Met the Stars rallied, and thanks to Larry Murphy's goal midway through the third, Minnesota won the game by the score of 5-3. Tied again at three games apiece, Chicago, behind a pair of goals from Jeremy Roenick, ended the Stars' season with a convincing 5-2 win at the Stadium.

BRIAN BELLOWS
After leading the Kitchener Rangers to the Memorial Cup championship, Brian Bellows was selected second overall by the North Stars in the 1982 Entry Draft. Bellows would go on to score 30 goals or more in eight of his 11 seasons in Minnesota, with his best season being in 1990, when he tallied 99 points. On August 31, 1992, Bellows was traded to the Montreal Canadiens for Russ Courtnall. During his 10-year tenure with the Stars, Bellows became the team's all-time leader with 342 goals and ranked second in both assists (380) and points (722). (Bellows would go on to star for Montreal, leading the team in scoring with 40 goals his first year, en route to winning a Stanley Cup. He would later play for Tampa Bay, Anaheim, and lastly with the Washington Capitals in 1999.)

"Do You Know the Way to San Jose?"

The 1990-91 season was without a doubt the craziest in the history of the franchise. An unbelievable turn of events took place that season, starting when the brothers Gund, faced with continuing financial losses in the Twin Cities, began exploring the possibility of moving the team to another city. Their main suitors were a group of financiers from Northern California. The group, located in San Jose, had a new arena and an interest in luring an NHL franchise to relocate there.

The NHL, which wasn't particularly interested in the concept of franchise relocation, saw a unique opportunity. What happened next was an unprecedented compromise that saved one franchise, and gave birth to another. Here's what went down. The league, sympathetic to the Gunds, decided to award them a new expansion franchise in San Jose. At the same time, the North Stars were to be spared from relocating, or worse, folding. As part of the arrangement, a new management/ownership group was to be set up in Minnesota. The Gunds, knowing that a new management team was going to come in and clean house, relocated many of the front-office personnel to San Jose to run the new "Sharks" franchise. Among them were GM Jack Ferreira, who would be eager to select many of the team's players in the upcoming dispersal draft.

As part of the "deal," the San Jose Sharks were allowed to select several key players from Minnesota at a dispersal draft which was held on May 30, 1991. There, as per prior agreement, San Jose claimed four players from the Stars' NHL roster and yet another 10 from their farm system. Among the big names claimed by the Sharks were enforcer Shane Churla and goaltender Brian Hayward. Now, because the Stars were taking such a hit from all of this, and basically getting raided by the Gunds' new team, the NHL decided to allow Minnesota to select several players from other NHL clubs during the 1991 Expansion Draft. There, they used the opportunity to claim several veteran players including Edmonton defenseman Charlie Huddy — who was later traded to L.A. for Todd Elik, and also Rangers centerman, Kelly Kisio — who was dealt back to San Jose in return for fan favorite, Shane Churla. Among the then lesser known minor leaguers who were also claimed included Stars' former No. 1 pick, Doug Zmolek, a Rochester native who would play for the Gophers.

Meanwhile, back in Minnie, a new ownership group had finally come together. It consisted of Howard Baldwin, a former managing partner with the Hartford Whalers, and his financial partner, Morris Belzberg. Now, here's where it gets confusing. Shortly after the transaction was completed with the Gunds, former Calgary Flames co-owner and mall developer extraordinaire, Norman Green, in a very shady deal, assumed control of the North Stars by buying out the Baldwin's ownership group, which then immediately became involved with the Pittsburgh Penguins ownership group. With that, Green would emerge as the team's sole owner. Green then came in and started firing the front office staff, including, Jack Ferreira and Pierre Page, who were replaced by former Philadelphia star Bobby Clarke, who was named as the team's new GM, and former Montreal hero Bob Gainey, who was named as the team's new coach.

One Last Shot at Lord Stanley's Cup

The 1990-91 season began ominously enough for Minnesota. To say that the fans were expecting big things from this team at the onset of the season would be quite an under-

Dave Gagner

statement. Afterall, only 5,730 fans showed up for the season opener. Things snowballed from there as the team managed only one win in its first nine games and got worse from there. The fans weren't coming out, the media was apathetic, and even free money giveaways from Norm himself couldn't get people off their butts and into the arena.

But, thanks to Stars new GM Bob Clarke, things were about to change. He bolstered the defense by trading offensive-minded defensemen, Larry Murphy, to Pittsburgh for defensive minded Jim Johnson and Chris Dahlquist — both Minnesota natives. In addition, he went out and got Calgary center Marc Bureau, who was a solid backchecking forward who could play tough defense. Other players began to step up as well, including Ulf Dahlen, who caught fire in the second half of the season by scoring 19 of his 21 goals in the last 42 games, including a hat trick against the Red Wings late in the year. Clarke's strategy of a strong defense was starting to take shape, and goaltender Jon Casey, who posted a 2.98 goals-against-average that season, was starting to play some good hockey.

Under the tutelage of first year coach, Bob Gainey, the Stars went 14-6-6 from late January until mid-March. With the team finally starting to heat up, the fans began to trickle in. The Stars finished the regular season with a very marginal record of 27-39-14, good only for fourth place in the Norris Division. Miraculously, a late-season slump almost dropped the Stars out of the playoff picture, but with a little luck and a few friendly bounces, they managed to squeak into the playoffs. They were led once again by the usual suspects. Dave Gagner, the team's lone All-Star that year, had 82 points, while Bellows posted 75. Broten added 69, Modano contributed 65, and Brian Propp, who had starred throughout the 1970s with Philadelphia, chipped in 73. And, Bobby Smith, who was reacquired from Montreal prior to the season, added a much needed veteran leadership presence to the young squad.

Hardly anyone gave the team much of a chance of doing anything in the postseason that year, and virtually no one thought that they would have a chance of being around playing hockey in May. It was a marginal season at best for a fourth-place team that had finished 12 games under .500. To put it into perspective, the Las Vegas odds going into the playoffs on the Stars winning the Stanley Cup were a staggering 25-1. But, the two Bobs, Gainey, who played on five Stanley Cup winners during his brilliant 16-year career with Montreal, and Clarke, who had a couple of his own from his playing days in Philadelphia, knew what it was going to take for their team to have any post-season success. By stressing a team approach to defense and controlling their own end, the Stars were primed and ready to go in the playoffs. Tired of being written off by the media as a fluke, sub-.500 team, coach Gainey put things into perspective before the opening face-off in Chicago. "The regular season is there to prepare teams for the playoffs. The teams you respect are the ones that are still playing in late May." And so began one of the most extraordinary playoff sagas in NHL annals.

First up for the Stars were the Norris Division champion Chicago Blackhawks, who, by virtue of their top regular-season record in the NHL that year, were the odds-on favorites to win it all. In Game One, the Stars had succumbed to the Hawks bullying tactics and found themselves not playing very disciplined hockey. They settled down however, and stuck to their game plan. The Stars

Mike Modano

took Game One, 4-3, on Brian Propp's goal just minutes into the first overtime session.

In Game Two, Chicago retaliated by beating up on the Stars, 5-2. Casey, who was replaced late in the game by back-up goaltender, Brian Hayward, was shell-shocked by Chicago's massive artillery. Minnesota wasn't focused and made poor decisions, even setting a team record for most penalty minutes in a playoff game. Game Three brought the series back to the Met Center, where the Minnesota fans could hardly contain themselves from going completely nuts. In the history of professional hockey in Minnesota, there is without question no bigger hated rival than Chicago. Dave Gagner carried the Stars on his back in the first period when he set an NHL record for the most points scored in a single period, tallying two goals and two assists. The Hawks played tough though, and in the end it was Jeremy Roenick's wrister late in the third over Casey's shoulder that gave Chicago a 6-5 victory.

Game Four was a different story though as Minnesota forced Chicago to play a slower, more defensive game. It worked as Mike Craig scored the second of two goals for the Stars, which was all Casey would need for the 3-1 win. With the series even, they headed back to the Second City for Game Five.

Gainey stressed playing physical without playing foolishly, and that turned out to be the difference in Game Five. The Hawks displayed their frustrations by taking a series of bad penalties. Minnesota, executing Gainey's strategy to perfection, was able to cash in on its opportunities, scoring five goals on power plays en route to a 6-0 shellacking. Casey stood on his head, and earned every bit of the coveted playoff shut-out. Game Six once again returned to Bloomington, where the humiliated Hawks found themselves fighting to stay alive. On April 14th, 1991, the Stars, behind Brian Bellows' fourth goal, and 12th overall point of the series, beat the Hawks, 3-1. Thanks to the spectacular goaltending of Jon Casey, who simply outplayed his rookie-of-the-year counterpart, Eddie Belfour, the Stars KO'd Chicago in six games. With the win, Minnesota had become the first team in 20 years to upset the top ranked team in the regular season in the first round of the playoffs.

Even though there were an amazing 487 total penalty minutes in the series, the Stars played with a high degree of discipline and were deadly on the power-play. "They [Chicago] were predicting a Stanley Cup and it was kind of like we were just in the way," said Stars left wing Basil McRae after the game. "That's what fired us up."

Feeling Blue

If the Stars thought that they could relax and coast through the playoffs, they were sorely mistaken. That's because the next opponent they would face was another old rival, the St. Louis Blues, which had finished the season with the second best record in the league. They were led by the dynamic duo of "Hull & Oates," better known as Brett Hull and Adam Oates, who had combined for over 240 points that season en route to finishing second and third, respectively, in league scoring.

St. Louis had 20 more victories and 37 more points than the Stars did that season, and they had no intention of suffering the same fate as their foes from Chicago either. Shane Churla was the unlikely hero of Game One, as the Stars beat St. Louis on the road to take a 1-0 series lead. The Blues came back in Game Two, as Adam Oates beat Casey twice in a 5-2 St. Louis win. Stew Gavin got the game-winner back at the Met for Game Three, as Minnesota beat the Blues, 5-1. Minnesota continued to roll in Game Four, pounding the Blues by the score of 8-4. Modano, Broten, Propp, Smith, Bellows and Gagner all got into the action for the Stars, who were playing inspired hockey. Game Five went back to St. Louis, where the Blues won a tight 4-2 battle.

Shane Churla

Then, back at the Met for Game Six, with the Stars leading 1-0 at 3:50 of the third period, Brian Bellows took a long pass and pushed it into the slot. There, the long armed Bobby Smith reached around a Blues defenseman and poked the puck through the crease. Old No. 18 then sturdied himself, gained control of the puck, and backhanded what would be the game-winner into the top right side of the net past goalie Vincent Riendeau. The Blues threatened with a few minutes left, but Casey held on as the Stars won the game, 3-2, as well as the series.

The Stars had played with the same discipline and style that had gotten them past Chicago. Perhaps the key to the Minnesota victory was their ability to shut down the Blues' deadly one-two punch of Hull and Oates. Gatean Duchesne and Stewart Gavin kept the two in check by serving as their constant shadows, ultimately holding the tandem to only a combined 13 shots on goal during the series. Another factor was the play of defenseman and resident tough-guy Mark Tinordi, whose aggressive style of play was effective at both ends of the ice. And, of course let's not forget about goalie Jon Casey, who was once again nothing short of phenomenal in the second-round matchup.

The Stars were suddenly red-hot, and the hockey world was starting to take notice. Said Blue's coach Brian Sutter after the game: "If anybody out there takes them for granted, they don't know what's going on."

The "Gretzky-less" Oilers

So, after beating the league's two best teams, the Stars were only four wins away from a Campbell Conference championship. It would not be easy though, because their next opponents were the defending Stanley Cup champion Edmonton Oilers. "The cliche's are all used up," said Stars owner Norm Green before the series. And that was exactly how the Stars players felt, knowing that they now had to go out and prove to everyone that they weren't just a fluke and really were for real.

Despite the fact that Gretzky had been dealt to the L.A. Kings that off-season, Edmonton was still a great team. Ignoring the five giant Stanley Cup banners that were hanging from the rafters of Edmonton's arena, combined with the fact that they hadn't won in Edmonton in more than 11 years, the Stars went out and kicked some butt in Game One. "Speed Kills," said Edmonton coach John Muckler after the game. He was referring, of course, to Minnesota's young horses, who out-hustled his bigger and stronger Oilers to a 3-1 victory. Led by Dave Gagner's second period game-winner, the Stars hung on behind an outstanding night in goal by Mr. Casey.

The Oilers rallied to crush the Stars in Game Two, however, winning by the score of 7-2. With the series now back in Minnesota, the Stars used their speed and skill to their advantage in Game Three. Bellows and Modano each scored breakaway goals, while Bobby Smith got the game-winner en route to a 7-3 Stars victory. "They play like we used to play," said a disgusted Oilers owner Peter Pocklington after the game.

Edmonton lost their composure and played ugly in Game Four, racking up 49 penalty minutes. The Stars capitalized on several of those five-on-four advantages, scoring two power-play goals. Mike Modano got the game-winner, with Broten dishing out a couple of helpers as well. Stars' keeper Jon Casey stopped 20 of 21 shots for a 5-1 Minnesota win. "There is another hero every night," said Stars winger Dave Gagner.

Game Five, back in Edmonton, was a much closer contest. With the game tied at two apiece early in the third period, Stars forward Stew Gavin dished a sweet pass to a breaking Bobby Smith, whose long reach was just enough to extend around Edmonton goalie Grant Fuhr's outstretched stick for what would prove to be the game-winner. The Stars went on to win the game by the final score of 3-2. Minnesota fans everywhere were beside themselves with excitement. In so doing, the North Stars had earned themselves a trip to the Stanley Cup Finals for just the second time in franchise history.

Once again it was hot goaltending that led the way. Casey, who really made a name for himself during the series, recorded an outstanding .991 save percentage. And, much like in the previous two series, Minnesota made the most of their opportunities by turning power-play advantages into goals. Amazingly, the team converted on four first-period power plays goals in the five-game series.

Next up for the "new Cinderella Stars" was a trip to the finals against the Pittsburgh Penguins and their feisty coach, "Badger" Bob Johnson, a Minneapolis native, who had played for John Mariucci's Golden Gophers back in the '50s.

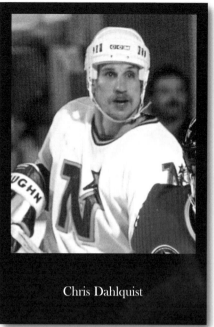

Chris Dahlquist

"Super Mario" and the Penguins

The North Stars, upon returning home from their trip to Edmonton, received a hero's welcome from the fans. Suddenly, they were front page news. "We're used to two reporters writing 'Stars Win' or 'Stars Lose', -- See Page 10C," said Brian Bellows sarcastically about the media horde covering the team during the finals.

Now the only thing standing in the way of Lord Stanley's Cup for the North Stars, was the Wales Conference champion Pittsburgh Penguins, which had just beaten the Boston Bruins in a seventh game overtime thriller. In addition to two-time MVP winner Mario Lemieux, the league's most explosive and dominant player, the Pen's featured a solid blend of young speedsters as well as several experienced veterans. While Kevin Stevens, Mark Recchi and Jaromir Jagr provided a balanced scoring punch, Stanley Cup veterans Paul Coffey, Bryan Trottier, and Joe Mullen added skill and character. Tom Barrasso, the team's goalie, was also playing excellent hockey at the time.

On paper this was a boring series featuring Minnesota, which finished the regular season with the sixth-worst record in the 21-team league, and Pittsburgh, a team which had made the playoffs only once in the previous eight years. The series had many subplots. Among them was the fact that it was the first time that two teams who had missed the playoffs the previous year had come back to make the finals. The Stars-Penguins series also marked the first time since the Red Wings and Blackhawks met back in 1934, that both finalists had never won a Stanley Cup. It was also the first finals meeting between two of the league's 1967 expansion teams.

Minnesota knew that if they wanted to win this thing, they would have to do two things. First, they would have to stay cool, force the Pen's to take stupid penalties, and capitalize on their power-play — which had registered 31 goals in the first three rounds of the playoffs. Secondly, and perhaps most importantly, they would have to try to contain both Mario Lemieux and Jaromir Jagr — two of the greatest players who would ever play the game.

The Stars opened the series in Pittsburgh, and thanks to a pair of Neal

The 1991 Stanley Cup runner-up North Stars

Broten goals, the Stars, much like they had done in their past three openers, took Game One, 5-4. Bobby Smith got the game-winner late in the third, as the Stars, who were visibly excited, tried to remain calm and focused on the task at hand.

The Penguins got revenge in Game Two, spanking the Stars 4-1. Bob Errey and Kevin Stevens put Pittsburgh ahead 2-0, only to see Mario Lemieux score one of the most incredible goals that has lived on forever in NHL highlight films. In one of the most dazzling solo efforts in recent memory, "Super Mario" skated in and waltzed around two Minnesota defensmen, deked left, then right, and then flipped the puck up and over a "used and abused" Jon Casey. As the Stars' defenders harmlessly watched Lemieux fly through the air and eventually land head-first onto the ice behind the net, the crowd went absolutely nuts. What made his graceful antics even more incredible was the fact that Lemieux, a six-foot-five, 230 pound centerman, is considered a giant by hockey standards.

The North Stars returned home from Pennsylvania to find that the state had gone hockey-mad. "I have been in seven Stanley Cup finals as a player and manager," said Stars' GM Bob Clarke on the hype surrounding the series. "There has never been anything like this. Never anything close."

The team was welcomed back to the Met by a standing-room-only crowd for Game Three. They also got a bit of good news during the pregame warm-up when they found out that while lacing up his skates in the locker room, Mario Lemieux had strained his back and would not be able to skate that night. With Lemieux out of the game, the Stars rolled. Dave Gagner beat Barasso late in the second on a nice wrister, only to see Bobby Smith get his second straight game-winner for Minnesota less than 30 seconds later. Jon Casey held the Pen's in check throughout the entire match as the Stars cruised 3-1 to take the series lead, two games to one. Was destiny in control of this "Cinderella" team? At this point it looked like Lord Stanley's cup was going to be hanging out at Lake Minnetonka for the summer, but there were still two games to be won.

Mario came back for Game Four, and just like that the Penguins were an entirely different team. Badger Bob had his boys play all-out from the opening face-off in this one, and they responded by scoring three quick goals in the first three minutes of the game. Pittsburgh got the Stars to take dumb penalties and took them right out of their game plan. Gagner kept it close for the Stars, but when former Islander Brian Trottier scored midway through the second to give the Penguins a commanding 4-1 lead, it didn't look good. Minnesota miraculously fought back on a Mike Modano power-play goal to get the team to within one goal by the end of the second, but couldn't capitalize on several good scoring chances to tie it up. Their best chance came on a missed doorstep one-timer by Neal Broten late in the period. An empty-netter by Phil Bourque late in the third iced the 5-3 series-tying win by the Pens. Much to the chagrin of Minnesota's checking line, who had so brilliantly shut down the likes of Jeremy Roenick, Brett Hull and Mark Messier in rounds one, two and three, they could simply not contain the game's premier player — Mario Lemieux.

The series moved back to the Steel City for Game Five, and unfortunately for the Stars, the Pens went straight for Minnesota's jugular. For the second straight game, Pittsburgh came out of the blocks quickly and the Stars were once again left to play catch up. By the time Penguin winger Mark Recchi scored his second goal of the game at the 13:41 mark of the first period, Pittsburgh had already jumped out to a 4-0 lead. Ron Francis added a goal in the third while Troy Loney added an insurance goal on a wild goal-mouth scramble late in the contest for the Penguins. Former North Star, Larry Murphy, also got into the action and finished with four assists as well. The Stars made it close late in the game on some nice plays by Broten, Gagner, Bellows and Smith, but ended up on the short side of the 6-4 contest.

With their backs against the wall, the Stars returned to the Met Center to try and even the series at three games apiece. What happened next, however, was one of the ugliest chapters in Minnesota hockey history. Anyone who was at the Game Six massacre, could probably attest that it was one of the most difficult things they have ever witnessed. It would be safe to say that after this fiasco, Jon Casey would need a large can of Solarcaine to help soothe all of the proverbial "goalie sunburn" on the back of his neck that was caused by all the red lights going off behind him.

Ulf Samuelsson started the barrage by scoring what would be the first of eight unanswered goals for the Penguins. Pittsburgh, who found the back of the net early and often, wrapped up the series in a 8-0 laugher. Team captain, Mario Lemieux, who scored four of his playoff-high 44 post-season points in the game, was named as the winner of the Conn Smythe MVP Trophy. And in the end, in front of the thousands of disappointed Minnesota fans, it was he who was presented Lord Stanley's Cup by then-NHL president John Zeigler. While the fans respectfully applauded the league's newest champions, many of the Stars' players could be seen consoling one another and even fighting back a few tears. It would prove to be the most lopsided Cup winning game in NHL history. For the Pen's, however, it would be the first of what would prove to be back-to-back Stanley Cup titles, as the team would go on to win it all again that next year as well.

The clock had struck midnight for the Cinderella Stars. But in the end, the underdogs had won the respect of the league and the loyalty of their fans, making believers out of countless hockey enthusiasts from around the country in the process. The Stars could hang their heads high.

One of the main factors for the Stars' success that year was due to the play of the team's goon squad: Basil McRae, Shane Churla and Mark Tinordi. During the playoffs, instead of beating the hell out of people, they played effective rough hockey while suckering their opponents into stupid penalties. Once it was five-on-four, Minnesota's power-play proved to be deadly. Although the trio combined for almost 200 penalty minutes (and countless stitches) throughout the playoffs, they chose their battles wisely and were there for every step of the way to protect their team's goal-scorers.

Brian Bellows and Dave Gagner led the way for the Stars in the playoffs, scoring 29 and 27 points, respectively. (The two also led the team in the regular season, with Gagner scoring 82 points and Bellows adding 75.) And, while Neal Broten and Mike Modano each added 22 & 20 points of their own, it was Bobby Smith's eight goals and eight assists in the playoffs (on top of a 46-

point regular season), that made the biggest difference for the team. While everyone had written off the 13-year veteran, who was supposed to be looking at his best hockey through his rear-view mirror, he proved that he had not lost his edge. His leadership and presence were immeasurable for the young Stars.

Player after player stepped it up during that series, making it truly a team effort. Mark the "Tin Man" Tinordi, once written off as a bruising goon, found himself skating on the team's coveted power-play line, where his defense was rock solid. And how about Jon Casey, who's 3.04 GAA over the playoffs established him as one of the league's big-time "money" keepers. He carried the team, often-times gambling and coming way out of the net to single-handedly bust up break-aways. Incidentally, following the series, he became the team's winningest goaltender in the post-season with 14 victories.

Credit should also be given to Stewart Gavin and Gaetan Duchesne, who fought in the trenches gallantly for the Stars. The two wingers were assigned the toughest jobs in the world during the playoff run — stopping each team's superstar. The two blue-collar wingers became the shadows of their targets, implementing a grinding brand of defensive that was crippling to a speedy winger who wanted to get free in center ice. Finishing the playoffs with an impressive +9 plus-minus ranking, Gavin and the Duke even held Brett Hull to a single shot on goal in Game One of the St. Louis series.

"I thought it was great for me to finish my career in Minnesota," said Bobby Smith. "I had played 12 years in the league at that point and was pretty excited about the opportunity to play for a team coached by Bob Gainey and managed by Bob Clarke. There was a huge interest in hockey in the Twin Cities at that point, and it was very exciting for the players. We had a lot of success that year and going back to the Stanley Cup finals was a real thrill for me."

Back to Reality

The euphoria of the team's amazing cup run soon wore off as the team finished in fourth place in the Norris Division in 1991-92, posting a very mediocre 32-42-6 record. They backed into the playoffs though, where they would face the Detroit Red Wings. Then just when everyone was about to write them off, a little bit of the magic came back as the Stars beat the Wings, 4-3 and 4-2, at the "Joe" (Joe Louis Arena) in Detroit. Back at the newly remodeled Met Center, they lost a close Game Three, only to come back and take Game Four. With Minnesota firmly in the driver's seat up three games to one, the fans started to get a little nostalgic. Playing inspired hockey, however, the Wings threw the Stars a pair of 3-0 and 1-0 shutouts in Games Five and Six. The series then shifted back to the Motor City for Game Seven, where Detroit prevailed over the worn-out Stars, 5-2.

After blowing a three games to one lead, things got pretty testy back at home. Owner Norman Green started to complain publicly that the team was losing money and started talking about the possibility of relocating the franchise elsewhere. The off-ice distractions drifted onto the ice and into the locker room as the team struggled to stay focused. Green had shaken up the front office as well. With GM Bobby Clarke departing to take over the expansion Florida Panthers, coach Bob Gainey was left to wear both hats. Under Gainey, and with relocation rumors running rampant, the Stars tried to keep it together, but it was going to be difficult.

One Final Ugly Chapter

Here is a rough chronology of what supposedly transpired during that very ugly and

Pittsburgh Penguins coach Badger Bob Johnson, a Minnesotan, holds the Stanley Cup after his Pen's beat the Stars in 1991.

painful final 1992-93 season: Let me first preface this nightmare by explaining that shortly after signing Mike Modano to a four-year $6.75 million contract (then the fifth highest salary in the NHL), Norm Green made it pretty clear to the world that the team was losing money, and could not make it here in Minnesota without some major concessions from the state as well as from the tax payers.

Green, a real-estate developer, apparently had high hopes for turning a remodeled Met Center into an extension of the newly constructed Mall of America. Complete with an enclosed skyway connection to the Mall, there were talks of developing the land around the Met Center for a Phase II expansion of the Mega Mall. When it became clear that this was not going to happen, all hell broke loose between the North Stars, the City of Bloomington, the State of Minnesota and the Metropolitan Sports Facilities Commission. Ultimately, Green, who had his eyes set on much greener real estate development pastures, knew that he wasn't going to make as much money by operating just the hockey team.

So, early in 1992, the team implied that unless the Metropolitan Sports Facilities Commission gave them an improved lease deal, the team would be forced to move. Among the places that the team threatened to go included: Anaheim, where a group of interested investors was apparently in place; St. Paul, to play in the old Civic Center; and Minneapolis, where a deal was in the works to play alongside of the Timberwolves at the relatively new Target Center.

By November of that year, on top of everything else, rumors circulated that Green's assistant was considering filing a sexual harassment lawsuit against him after his behavior forced her to quit back in August.

On January 30th, 1993, Green received bids from both the Target Center and Civic Center. On weighing the feasibility of moving the team from Bloomington, Green was quoted in the Star Tribune as saying: "I want to find out whether we can sell 10,000-12,000 tickets if we move downtown. I lost about $5 million last year and I'll lose more money this year. I am not going to lose any more money operating a hockey team."

As the suspense dragged on as to just what the hell Green was going to do with our Stars, Twin Cities celebrity author and envelope tycoon, Harvey Mackay, stepped up and offered to personally guarantee the sale of 1,000 season tickets if the team would stay in Minnesota and play at the Target Center. Green

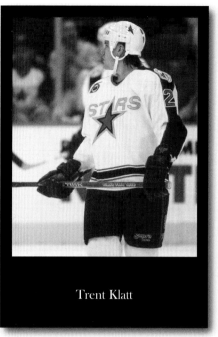

Trent Klatt

declined the offer, however, instead choosing to keep his options open. Ironically, later in February Green had the audacity to say that if indeed the Stars have to move out of the state, that it is because the fans did not buy enough season tickets.

On March 8th, upon returning from his Palm Springs mansion, Green called for a team meeting in which he criticized his skaters for their recent poor play. Two days later, after ruling out selling the team to local owners, an agreement was finalized to move the team to Texas, where they would become the "Dallas Stars."

Hearing the bad news, the team finished its last month of the season as lame ducks. On April 15th, tax day of all days, the North Stars played their final game against the Detroit Red Wings. Just before that last game, the Metropolitan Sports Facilities Commission, fearing that the fans were going to trash the joint in protest, placed an ad in the Star Tribune, entitled: "The Puck Stops Here; Please be Gentle..." which read in part: "We know that many people are disappointed that the team is leaving Minnesota. We agree it's unfortunate. But we want to remind everyone that the public, and not the hockey club, owns Met Center. And that we need to keep the building intact and in good repair for future uses."

Incidentally, the team's final game was actually played, and the Stars lost to Detroit, 5-3, finishing out their final season in Minnesota out of the playoffs with a record of 36-38-10. As the players took one last lap around the ice and saluted the fans who had stuck with them through thick and thin, the chants of "Norm Sucks!" "Norm Sucks!" echoed throughout the building. For the green and gold faithful, it was the saddest of times and a moment they will surely never forget.

(It is interesting to note that just 19 months later, the Metropolitan Sports Facilities Commission decided to demolish the Met Center, which was considered by many to be one of the NHL's best arenas. The recently renovated building had outstanding site-lines, plenty of parking and it sat next door to the largest tourist attraction in the Midwest, the MegaMall. How they couldn't make it work there simply boggles the mind. Regardless, the new owner of the land would be the Twin Cities International Airport, which wanted it for clearance issues regarding its new runway construction project. Incredibly, as of the year 2008, fully 15 years later, the parking lot and the land on which the Met Center once stood still sits vacant.)

With the Stars leaving town, many of the players chimed in on how they really felt about the country's biggest hockey state not having an NHL franchise.

"Minnesota is one of the top two or three best hockey areas in the U.S., with unbelievable support for high school, college and junior associations," said Dino Ciccarelli upon learning that the Stars were leaving Minnesota. "To not have an NHL team there doesn't make sense. With all that cold and snow, it was a great hockey atmosphere and I've got to believe they'll get a team, but it will be a team in trouble and you'll be starting from the bottom."

"It was like losing a relative," said Lou Nanne. "It was just a really disheartening experience for me."

"It was a very sad day for the NHL and certainly for hockey in the state of Minnesota," added Bobby Smith.

"It was tough for me to take," said Neal Broten. "A lot of people took it pretty rough, and it was a real big deal. I remember this strange feeling and thinking that this can't be happening to me. You didn't really think it was going to happen until it happened,

Blowing up the Met Center...

and then you're moving and driving down to Texas."

"It was tough for me, being from Minneapolis, and seeing that franchise leave even though it was really supported well by the public," said Jim Johnson. "And I mean that, because we averaged about 16,000 fans that year before the team moved. So, I had mixed emotions about moving to Dallas."

Fittingly, only a couple of years later, Green wound up selling the Dallas Stars. Then, in 1999, following Brett Hull's infamous Game Six "toe in the crease" game-winning goal, which beat the Buffalo Sabres, the "Greenless" Lone Stars went on to win the Stanley Cup Championship. Green would go back to the real estate businesss, leaving the sport of hockey to be run by hockey people. Minnesota would be teased a few years later, when the Winnipeg Jets nearly relocated to the Target Center, but a deal couldn't get done and the franchise relocated to Phoenix, where they became the Coyotes. Luckily, the NHL would decide to come back to the Gopher State a few years later and give us an expansion team of our own, the Minnesota Wild.

LEROY NEIMAN

Minnesota's very own LeRoy Neiman is one of America's premier artists. He is without question the most famous sports artist of the 21st century, and has painted nearly every famous American athlete over his career — including a lot of hockey players. His vivid colors and unique brush-strokes have made his works instantly recognizable.

LeRoy Neiman was born on June 8, 1921, in St. Paul, and grew up in the Frog Town neighborhood of the city. He loved sports and painting as a kid, and used to go ice fishing and sledding on White Bear Lake, as well as attend the St. Paul Winter Carnival. He got into hockey at an early age, and used to admire fellow St. Paulite, and Hall of Famer, Bobby Dill.

"I was always a goalie," Neiman would later recall. "I wasn't a good player and that's why I was a goalie. I played in Uniondale Playground in Frogtown, that was our domain and we used to play out there all day long. I also loved going to the Auditorium and watching the Saints play against the Millers, that was a great rivalry."

Neiman attended Washington High School in the late 1930s, until going into the Army. After his discharge from the service, in 1946, Neiman enrolled in courses in basic drawing techniques at the St. Paul Gallery and School of Art. There, he learned the principles of composition espoused by the French Impressionist Paul Cezanne, one of his early influences. Neiman later moved to Chicago and entered the School of the Art Institute of Chicago, where he would go on to become a teacher as well. He gained wide recognition early in his career as a contributing artist for Playboy, in the 1950s. From there, Neiman would go on to become one of the world's most recognized figures. He was the official artist at five Olympiads, and has become good friends with everyone from Mohammed Ali to Wayne Gretzky. It has been estimated that the more than 150,000 Neiman prints that have been purchased to date around the world "have an estimated market value exceeding $400 million."

Neiman & Wayne Gretzky

Today, Neiman lives in New York City and continues to do what he loves most, paint. He has written nearly a dozen books, given millions to charity and to museums, and shows no signs of slowing down. In 1995 he gave the School of the Arts at Columbia University a gift of $6 million to create the LeRoy Neiman Center for Print Studies. Among his recent works are paintings of Mark McGuire, Sammy Sosa and Joe DiMaggio. In addition, he has painted several hockey stars including Gretzky, Bobby Hull, Mario Lemieux, Stan Mikita, Glen Hall, and even his boyhood hero, Bobby Dill.

"Blue Hockey"
Depicting the 1980 Gold Medal Winning U.S. Olympic Team

"Great Gretzky"

73

THE MINNESOTA WILD

To the delight of countless Minnesota hockey fans, the NHL's expansion Wild finally hit the ice in the Fall of 2000. It was a long and arduous journey that finally came to fruition after many years of hard work and persistence. It had been a long hangover from that cold day back in 1993 when a jerk named Norm hijacked our North Stars to Texas, and Minnesota hockey fans everywhere were eager to get back into the mix.

It all started on June 25, 1997, when the NHL Board of Governors voted unanimously to award an expansion franchise to the state of Minnesota. Just hours later a celebration erupted in downtown St. Paul, where a parade of some two dozen Zambonis took to the streets. Shortly thereafter, a state-wide naming search was conducted with six finalists emerging: Blue Ox, Freeze, Northern Lights, Voyageurs, White Bears and Wild. The latter, of course, was chosen, and was officially unveiled at a naming party that November in front of a sell-out crowd at St. Paul's historic Aldrich Arena.

Team owner Bob Naegele, himself a high school and collegiate goaltender, later unveiled the plans for a new state-of-the-art arena which was to be located on the site of the St. Paul Civic Center. In June of 1998 the old Civic Center, complete with its classic see-thru dasher boards, met its fate with the wrecking ball. In its rubble, however, would emerge a thing of beauty — a brand spanking new $130 million state-of-the-art arena, named as the Xcel Energy Center. Complete with 74 luxury suites, and all the extras, this 18,600-seat "X" would truly mark the spot.

By now the team had begun assembling a front-office and hiring key members of its staff. Former NHL star Doug Risebrough was named as the team's first-ever GM and he would later hire the legendary Jacques Lemaire to serve as his head coach. Between them they had earned handfuls of Stanley Cup rings as members of the Montreal Canadiens. The pieces were starting to come together.

In June, the league held an Expansion Draft for its two new expansion teams, the Wild and Columbus Blue Jackets. There, the Wild selected several players who would make the roster, including: Goalie Jamie McLennan; Defensemen Filip Kuba, Curtis Leschyshyn and Sean O'Donnell; and Forwards Jim Dowd, Sergei Krivokrasov, Scott Pellerin, Stacy Roest and Cam Stewart. In addition, a couple of Gophers were added to the mix — Darby Hendrickson and Jeff Nielsen. Shortly thereafter, the 2000 NHL Entry Draft took place with the Wild selecting Winger Marian Gaborik from Slovakia with the No. 3 overall pick. Several other players were selected on that day as well, including Defenseman Nick Schultz, Winger Maxim Sushinsky and Defenseman Lubomir Sekeras, all of whom would pay dividends.

Risebrough wanted to assemble a team that would not only be a winner, but would also be entertaining and exciting for the fans. "We are going to build this team through the draft, waivers, free agency, by trades and through our farm system," he said. "It will be a real fun time, and also a real testing time for these guys who are going to have to come in here and perform. It is a honeymoon so to speak. History will be made as we go, and that is a very exciting

Bob Naegele

prospect."

In September of 2000 the Xcel Energy Center was completed for the Wild's inaugural NHL season. With the team wrapping up its training camp at Minneapolis' Parade Ice Garden, the opening day roster was starting to take shape. On September 19th the Wild played their first-ever preseason game, tying San Jose, 3-3, at the Rose Garden in Portland, Oregon. That next week the team finally returned home to play their first-ever preseason home game, beating the Mighty Ducks of Anaheim, 3-1.

The club, which was slotted to play in the newly realigned Northwest Division of the Western Conference, along with the Calgary Flames, Colorado Avalanche, Edmonton Oilers and Vancouver Canucks, opened the season on the road in Anaheim. There, Rookie Marian Gaborik scored the first-ever goal in Wild history, but the team wound up on the short side of a 3-1 game. Finally, on October 11, 2000, the Wild made their home debut vs. the Philadelphia Flyers at the "X." Fittingly, Richfield native Darby Hendrickson scored the first ever Wild goal at Xcel Energy Center and helped guide the team to an impressive 3-3 tie. The crowd went nuts. Hockey was back.

"It was a great pass and I was just in the right place in the right time," said Darby of that first goal. "But that was fun and very memorable. It was a huge thrill. At the time it didn't register. Trust me, at the time I was not thinking about making history and scoring the first ever goal at the X, but it happened and it was very special. We played Philly to a tie that night, which was a real positive, and it was the beginning of a great season that just got better and better. The entire atmosphere in the Twin Cities that night was incredible. Hockey was back and it was great to just be a part of it. It was truly awesome."

From there, the team just kept on rolling and the highlights followed. On October 22, Goalie Jamie McLennan recorded the first shut-out in team history, stopping 24 shots in a scoreless tie at home against Florida. A few weeks later the team notched its first-ever road victory by beating Calgary, 3-2, on Antti Laaksonen's thrilling overtime goal. On November 26th Laaksonen tallied the first-ever hat-trick in franchise history in a 4-2 home win against Vancouver. The team even got hot in January, extending its unbeaten streak to eight games at one point when Filip Kuba scored the team's first home overtime goal to defeat Detroit, 3-2. The sell-out crowds at the X were loving it.

The unequivocal highlight of the year, however, came on December 17, when the former North Stars, now the Dallas Stars, came to town. The atmosphere in the X was absolutely electric that night and the fans were looped. How would the Wild respond? They shined, spanking the Stars, 6-0, in front of an emotional record sell-out crowd. Minnesota natives Darby Hendrickson and Jeff Nielsen combined for three goals and an assist as the Wild scored a pair in each of the three periods to ice it. The Wild peppered Dallas Goalie Eddie Belfour all night while his former backup, Manny Fernandez, stopped all 24 shots he faced to earn the amazing shut-out victory.

"That was just unbelievable drama that night," recalled Hendrickson. "The fans were still chanting 'Norm Sucks!' from the old North Star days. I mean I grew up here and understood the entire saga, but most of the guys on the team had no clue about just how much the North Stars meant to this area. So, when we came out and crushed the Stars that night it was huge. The fans were so into it and I think I was even a fan that night. The atmosphere in there was unbelievable and everything just went our way. The fans really deserved that after all they had been through over the years."

"It's been great being back in Minnesota," added Grand Rapids native and former Gopher Jeff Nielsen. "I grew up watch-ing the North Stars and when they left for Dallas it was tough on everyone. I didn't think that pro hockey would ever come back after that, so to be a part of our state's new NHL team was really an honor. There was a lot of excitement in coming to a new fran-chise and to come together with 25 guys who came from different teams. I mean to be a part of the first ever Wild team was pretty special. The year started as kind of a struggle but as the season went on the team came together and played some great hockey. I think we have played beyond everyone's expectations and that just

A FEW WORDS WITH DOUG RISEBROUGH...

Doug Risebrough is a good hockey man and has the credentials to prove it. A hard-nosed centerman who was never afraid to back down to anybody, Risebrough tallied 185 goals and 286 assists for 471 points over his 13-year playing career. Most impor-tantly though, he is a proven winner. As a player he lost just 274 out of a total of 1,040 games. Over that span the Guelph, Ontario, native also won four consecutive Stanley Cups from 1976-79 as a member of the fabled Montreal Canadiens. He later appeared in two more Stanley Cup Finals as a member of the Calgary Flames in both 1986, as the team captain, and then again in 1989, as an assistant coach. From 1987 to 1995 he joined the front office and later became both the head coach and GM of the franchise. In 1995 he left the Flames to become the Vice President of Hockey Operations for the Edmonton Oilers, a position he held until joining the Wild in the Summer of 1999, when he was named as the team's first-ever Executive Vice President/General Manager. All in all, Risebrough has participated in the Stanley Cup Playoffs 26 of the 32 years that he has been in the league as a player, coach and exec-utive.

Risebrough has been the principle architect of the franchise and has instilled his vision for building a winning tra-dition here based on the values of team, preparation, honesty and passion. He has laid a foundation for future success through drafting and acquiring not necessarily the best players, but the right players — role players who will fit into his coaching staff's system of play. "Rizer," as he is affectionately known, has incorporated his philosophies of winning into the organization and that has paid big dividends. He is responsible for assembling a team that that will not only be a win-ner, but will also be entertaining and exciting for the fans. From the beginning, it was a journey.

"When it comes to building a new franchise it is a long process," he said early on in the process. "An expansion team is basically an acquisition of what people give you, and I want to make sure that we are solid from top to bottom. We are going to build this team through the draft, waivers, free agency, by trades and through our farm system. It will be a real fun time, and also a real testing time for these guys who are going to have to come in here and perform. Some of these players who we will be getting through the expansion draft are what I would describe as 'abused children' so to speak. You know, they have bounced around and nobody has really loved them. So for those guys, it will be an opportunity to come in, work hard, and finally get a chance to be loved."

Risebrough understood the building process, however, and also what it took to create a winning organization. "We want to make sure that we get players who have a passion to play the game, and will go out and play hard every night for the fans," he said. "I have found that a players' passion never gets tested when everything is going right, it gets tested in adverse conditions."

"One of the good things for an expansion player is that he is going to be coming into a new situation where he will have an opportunity to showcase his talent," he added. "These players are not joining a team, they are literally making and carving the team's new image. It can be a really fun time for a player. One of these guys is going to be the Wild's first-ever draft pick. Someone will score the first goal. Someone will get in the first fight. It is a honeymoon so to speak. History will be made as we go, and that is a very exciting prospect."

"I have been going to a bunch of high school and college games and can't believe the enthusiasm for hockey here," said Risebrough of the State of Hockey. "The fans are very educated and I would even say that I don't think there is a place in America where the collective watching of hockey is as high as it is in Minnesota. When you figure all the people watching hockey at the youth, high school, college, junior and professional levels, it is amazing to think about. In terms of attendance for all of those games, I don't know if there is a place in North America that can match that. As a result, we don't have to educate our fans about the game here the same way some of the other new expansion teams will have to — especially in the southern states, where hockey isn't as popular. So we feel like we have an advantage in the fact that our fans already appreciate and understand the game."

"I'm always open to improving our team," he said. "We are a very young and talented team, but we have to con-tinually try to get younger and work on developing our players. We can't just look for the quick fix because that won't work. The bottom line is that we want to get young players who ultimately start their careers here in Minnesota, so they become attached to the team and the area. We want the fans to identify with them, and mold their attitudes and work ethics from the get-go. This approach, in my opinion, is much better at this stage of the game than trying to mix and match a bunch of pieces together into your roster. We are flexible though, and are always willing to look for other players who can enhance our product."

"I just can't thank our fans enough," added Risebrough. "They are the best in the league, they really are. We are so lucky to be able to play in an area that supports hockey so passionately and has such educated fans. They have sold out the building every single game since day one, and that speaks volumes about just what type of hockey people there are in Minnesota. We can't thank them enough and we promise to work hard so that one day we can bring the Stanley Cup home to the State of Hockey."

goes to show you that if you get a bunch of guys playing hard every night that good things will happen. Nobody knew what to expect coming in to this season, what with it being the first year back for hockey, but it has been wonderful. As the season has gone on, the excitement has grown and we are playing really well as a team. We've had a lot of success in our own building, which has really helped, and there aren't a lot of big stars on the team — so everyone plays together and there is just a good chemistry. I think overall we have played beyond everyone's expectations, and that has been great."

"I think the biggest thing for us this year was to come in and establish an identity," he added. "You start a new franchise and you want the other teams to know what they're up against and to be concerned about your style of hockey when they play you, and I think we've done a great job with that. Teams know that they are going to have to play hard to beat us. We run a tight system and we can really frustrate our opponents with our defensive style of play if they don't stay with their game. I think that players around the league know that we have something special here, what with the knowledgeable fans and the new arena, and I just hope that we can keep building on that and have a lot of success in the future."

On March 28th the Wild established an NHL expansion team attendance record with their 39th consecutive sell-out against Phoenix. The team would ultimately finish the season with 41 consecutive regular season sellouts — good for an NHL expansion team record of 751,452 fans and an average of 18,329 per game. Throughout the year the fans got to know the players and the players got to know the fans. One player, however, stood out — rookie Marian Gaborik, who became the first Wild player to be named

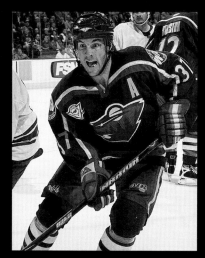

A FEW WORDS WITH WES WALZ...

"Being a member of the Wild means so much to me," said Walz. "I have been lucky enough to have been here since the very beginning and I certainly don't take that for granted. I will forever be grateful to the Wild organization for taking a chance on me and for giving me the opportunity to be a part of this family. I spent the first several years of my professional career up and down from the minors and then spent a few years over in Europe before getting the chance to prove myself here in Minnesota. They gave me a shot and I have worked hard to do my best in return. It was really a dream come true for me to tell you the truth. Had the league not expanded that year, I am not sure if I would have gotten a shot to make it in the NHL as an everyday player. So, I am very appreciative for the opportunity to be here and I won't ever take that for granted."

"The fans here, they are the best, they really are. There have been so many games where I have showed up either hurt or tired or whatever, just wondering how I was ever going to ever make it through the night. Then, to step out onto the ice in front of that packed house, it is like a shot of adrenaline. They are amazing. I have been here since day one and there has never not been a sell-out there, so that speaks volumes about what kind of fans we have here in Minnesota. They are so knowledgeable about the game too, way more so than most NHL cities, that is for sure. Most of them have either played the game or have had family members play it, so they truly 'get it.' The culture here is based around hockey and as a player you couldn't ask for anything more. So, I am very thankful to them for their support and for their encouragement over the years. They motivate me to be my best and I hope to be able to return the favor one day by helping to bring the Stanley Cup to Minnesota.

"Our home ice is a tough place to play for our opposition, no question. I talk to a lot of guys from other teams during and after the season and they tell me to a man that the Xcel Center is one of the top rinks in the league. The atmosphere in there which is created by the fans is so unique. The euphoria that they create night in and night out just travels right through the team. We as players take a lot of pride in playing well at home, for our fans, because they are the reason why we are even here.

"As for me personally, my family loves living here. We have been here for seven years now so, yes, we are officially Minnesotans. We have four kids who are all involved in different activities and we couldn't be happier here. Like most Minnesotans, our kids play hockey, so seemingly every spare moment of our lives involves going to games or practices. It can get pretty crazy. My wife and I grew up in Calgary, and it feels like home to me not only because of the weather, but because the people are so nice here too. They are so down to earth and have really made us feel welcome here. We live in Woodbury and love our neighbors, everybody is just super to us. We are really involved in our kids' school and our church, which have been great to us. We have dug some pretty deep roots here and have hung our hats here proudly.

"As for the state-of-the-state of hockey here, I would say it is fantastic. Hockey is such a part of the culture of life here. Everything revolves around it. Just seeing how many friends my son has made from playing in the Woodbury youth program, that is so neat. To see him and his buddies running around the Xcel Center during the state high school tournament, that just takes me back to when I was a little boy in Calgary. I remember the first time he asked me if he could skip school to go to the state tournament, because all of his friends were going to support Woodbury High School. I was like 'what do you mean everybody is going to the high school tournament? Get your butt back to class!' He was so bummed out, he was like one of just four kids who had to stay back and go to class that day. Once I realized what was going on I told him that he could go. How ironic, the one kid whose dad actually plays at the Xcel Center, couldn't go watch hockey over there. I felt terrible after that one. I just had no idea how big of a deal it is around here though. Even the NHL players who come to town can't believe that they sell out the Xcel Center for high school games. Even the girls tourney does real well, and that is just fantastic to see. I have a 10 year old girl who plays too and she just loves it as well. What a great tradition it is, and I couldn't be prouder to have that be a part of my community.

"You know, my father always told me that the best compliment anybody could ever pay you was to tell you that you were a hard worker. It didn't matter if you were a hockey player or a brick layer, it just mattered that you gave it your best and tried your hardest. That is how I have always tried to play the game. I am not the most talented guy in the world, but I come to work every day and gave it my all. Hopefully it will pay off down the road by being able to help bring a Stanley Cup to the fans of Minnesota, that would be about as good as it could get."

NHL Player of the Week, after scoring eight points in early March.

Finally, on April 8, 2001, the Wild completed their inaugural season by losing to Colorado, 4-2, at home. In the process, Wes Walz scored his seventh short-handed goal and ninth short-handed point of the season to set the individual expansion team record. Darby Hendrickson also scored his career-high 18th goal in this one as the Wild finished their inaugural debut with a solid record of 25-39-13-5, good for 68 points. The leading scorers for the Wild in its inaugural season were Andrew Brunette (69 points), Marian Gaborik (67 points) and Jim Dowd (43 points), while Goalies Dwayne Roloson and Manny Fernandez won 14 and 12 games, respectively, between the pipes as well. Lemaire's infamous "neutral zone trap" had worked its magic and the rest of the league stood up and took notice that these guys were not going to lie down for anybody. They were for real.

"I tend to look at our overall success in pieces, and the first piece was our fabulous new building," said Wild CEO Jac Sperling. "Our fans are truly blown away by the new arena, and as an organization that makes us very happy. From the design elements to the site-lines, it is really a fun place to watch a game. Secondly, the support of the fans and the community at large has been phenomenal. We have taken a real grass-roots approach to youth hockey and it has been great. Lastly, the team's performance on the ice has been just outstanding. Jacques (LeMaire) has been able to convince our players that they can win every night and our fans think that they can win every night as well. So, it has been an incredible story to watch. The fans have bonded to this team and they have fostered a great relationship. The fans know that Wild hockey is about hard work, old fashioned values, playing together as a team, and building for the long term. Overall, I think we're off to one hell of a start."

By all accounts that first season was a huge success. From top to bottom the organization embraced the "State of Hockey" and took them along for a real wild ride. The fans couldn't get

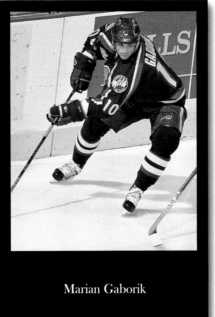

Marian Gaborik

enough of their new team and made an instant connection with the players. The players fed off of that and even threatened to make the playoffs at one point during that first season before slowing down at the end. It was also a rejuvenation of sorts for St. Paul, which also embraced the team by redeveloping Kellogg Boulevard and West Seventh Street, complete with new restaurants, bars and even a new children's museum.

"I think the success of this team can be traced back to a couple of places," explained Darby Hendrickson. "First, the leadership of Jacques LeMaire and his coaching staff has been outstanding. They picked a whole bunch of solid players who were hungry and that was nice to be around. Secondly, the ownership has just done everything right, from the marketing on down. And thirdly, the new building is just first-class and that has made it the place to be in Minnesota sports. We just have great fans here who really understand the game and want to get behind us. That entire situation is a great recipe for success. From there, the team has formed its own identity. I mean we were all disappointed on not making the playoffs, but we were a part of building something and that was special. Jacque's system is a good system for us and we play well in it. Plus, we have been very competitive and I think the fans really appreciate that. Give us some time, we will be there."

The 2001-02 season commenced on October 6th with a 0-0 tie against the San Jose Sharks, compliments of the team's new goaltender, Dwayne Roloson. The team got its first win the next night against the Kings, 4-3, on defenseman Willie Mitchell's game-winner. The team would ultimately go on a six-game unbeaten streak from there, eventually arriving back home on October 10th, where they beat the Bruins, 2-1, in their home opener. Stacy Roest was the hero in that one, scoring both goals, while Manny Fernandez turned away 35 of the 36 shots he faced in net.

One of the team's biggest wins came on November 2nd, when they beat the defending Stanley Cup Champions from

A FEW WORDS WITH NICK SCHULTZ...

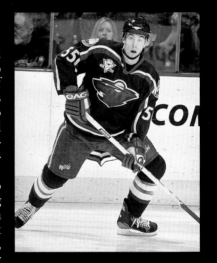

"Playing for the Wild is pretty special," said Schultz. "They are the team that drafted me and have brought me along for every step of the way. So, I feel very fortunate to be able to play for such an outstanding organization. Minnesota truly is the state of hockey and I couldn't be prouder to be a part of it. The fans here are so great. It is so much like Canada here because the fans really understand the game and are so into it. They know so much more about hockey than a lot of other places we play at, and as a player that makes it a lot of fun. It is pretty incredible to think that for every single game I have ever played at Xcel Center, it has been a sell-out. That kind of support is just awesome."

"It is hard to believe, but I have been a part of the team since it first came to be back in 2000. I remember being just an 18-year old kid with the team and trying to make my way. I will never forget my first trip on the team plane, I woke up from a nap and saw that everybody was laughing at me. I had no idea why until I realized that I had shaving cream glopped all over my head. It was tough being the youngest guy, but I got through it. It is crazy to think that I am a veteran now, even though I am only in my early 20s.

"I really enjoy living here too, it is a great place. I first lived in St. Paul when I was a rookie, and now I live in a condo over in the warehouse district of Minneapolis. I love Minnesota and really enjoy taking advantage of everything that there is to do here. My wife and I have a lot of fun here in the Twin Cities and especially like to the enjoy the outdoors. We go to shows, to the lakes and to various ball games — we just try to do a little bit of everything. It is pretty cool to live in a place where hockey is so huge. I grew up in Calgary, where hockey was everything, and this is definitely the most hockey savvy place I have ever been to in the U.S., that is for sure. I mean from our Wild games, to the Gophers and all of the other college games, to the high school tournament, and even to the Pond Hockey Championships — the people here really support their teams and that is great to see. There is such a love for the game here and I am really proud to be able to say that I am a small part in that."

A FEW WORDS WITH JACQUES LEMAIRE...

Jacques Lemaire grew up in LaSalle, Quebec, loving the game of hockey. As a player, Lemaire would rise up through the ranks and play his entire NHL career with the Montreal Canadiens from 1967-79. There, he was a member of eight Stanley Cup championship-winning teams, including four straight from 1976-79. Known for being a clutch player, the speedy centerman tallied the Stanley Cup-clinching goals in both the 1977 and 1979 Finals. Lemaire finished his illustrious playing career with 835 points (366 goals, 469 assists) in 853 regular season games, scoring 20 or more goals in each of his 12 seasons in the National Hockey League. Following his retirement, Lemaire began his coaching career in Switzerland, where he served as player/coach of the Sierre Club. He returned in 1981 to take over as the first head coach of the expansion Longueuil Chevaliers, of the Quebec Major Junior Hockey League, where he guided the team to the Finals in his first season.

From there, Lemaire began his NHL coaching career with his old team, the Canadiens. He took over the Habs midway through the 1983 season and guided them to the Wales Conference Finals. The next year, he coached Montreal to the Adams Division championship. Lemaire stepped aside as the head coach following the 1985 campaign, however, and spent the next eight years in the team's front office, playing a big role in both of Montreal's Stanley Cup titles in 1986 and 1993.

In 1993 Lemaire took over as the head coach of the New Jersey Devils. Over the next five seasons he would compile a record of 199-122-57 (.602), and guide the Devils to their first-ever Stanley Cup championship along the way, in 1994. For his efforts he was awarded the Jack Adams Trophy as the NHL's outstanding head coach. In 1998 Lemaire stepped down once again to serve as a consultant for his Canadiens. Then, in the Summer of 2000, Lemaire got back into the game when he was named as the first-ever head coach of the expansion Minnesota Wild. He has been here ever since, even winning another Coach of the Year Award in 2003 after leading his squad to the NHL's version of the Final Four.

Lemaire is the epitome of a player's coach, and is arguably the most respected man in the game today. With the Wild, he turned a little expansion team into the little-engine-that-could, making believers out of all the nay-sayers along the way. One of the most knowledgeable men in the game, Lemaire has proven that he can coach under any circumstances. Whether he is implementing his now infamous "neutral-zone trap," or trying to get a young player to get better, or even resurrecting a career of an older veteran, Lemaire is a teacher and a motivator. The 1984 Hall of Fame inductee is a winner in every sense of the word. Not only does he have his name on the Stanley Cup an incredible 11 times, as both a player and coach, but he also owns a career head coaching record of 456-353-124 in 13 NHL seasons. Further, Lemaire has taken 8 of the 13 teams he has coached to the post-season, and has a lifetime Stanley Cup playoff record of 58-48.

"We have been blessed to have had what has happened here in Minnesota," said Lemaire of the fan support his teams have received over the years. "These people lost their team, the North Stars, and they showed great patience in getting another one. The coaches, management and players just really appreciate the fans here because they are really, really good. The players know that the fans here support them and, to a certain point, will accept certain mistakes that they make. I know it will be tougher in the future because of the fact that we are ahead of our plan, but that just means we will have to work harder."

"Really, I don't think we have to do what we did (in 2003) as far as making it to the conference finals. Repeating that same performance year after year will be tough, and believe me, we are not there yet. We'll have some ups and downs along the way, and we will have to work very hard to keep this level of success. The fans have played a big part in that though, and I would like to thank them for their support. They are behind us and the players feel that. They don't feel the pressure of winning every night and that motivates our guys to play harder and to win for them. Win or lose, as long as they play hard, the fans can accept that. The fans realize too that we are a young team and are building for the future. We have a plan. We aren't there yet, but we will be in a few years."

"The whole experience has been just great for my wife and for me. We love it here and feel that it is very similar to Quebec with regards to the climate, the scenery and the lakes, and it just feels like home. As for being with the Wild, it has been wonderful. It is really more than I ever expected, no doubt. We had a plan and we are very much ahead of our plan now and that makes it a little tougher because now we aren't going to be drafting as low as we were supposed to. So, that makes it tougher for the next season to repeat and to improve on our success. But up to now we have done it and we are going to have to work even harder to get better. Our guys need to step it up. The older guys are being good leaders and the younger guys are following. Hopefully we will be able to continue that success in the years to come. Minnesota is just a great place and they take their hockey very seriously here. There is a lot of great hockey here, from the high schools to the Gophers, and that makes for some very knowledgeable fans."

Colorado, 4-2. More than 19,000 fans jammed into the X for this one as both Andrew Brunette and Jim Dowd each notched a goal and an assist in the win. Marian Gaborik made history the next week against Atlanta when he notched the franchise's second-ever hat trick en route to a 4-2 win over the Thrashers at the X.

Jacques Lemaire, coaching in his 600th career NHL game, beat his former team, the Montreal Canadiens, on January 8th by the final score of 4-2. Wes Walz scored three points, while linemate Antti Laaksonen added a goal and an assist in the emotional win. The team was up and down for the next several weeks, and then got hot in early March. The team posted back-to-back road victories for the first time in franchise history when it defeated the Dallas Stars, 5-3, in Big D. Marian Gaborik then registered

his second career hat trick two nights later in a 5-0 win over Columbus. Andrew Brunette set a franchise record with four assists in the win, while Dwayne Roloson turned away all 14 shots that came his way to earn the shut-out.

The team got its final win of the season against San Jose at the Xcel Center when they beat the Sharks, 3-1, thanks to Richard Park and Sergei Zholtok, who each tallied a goal and an assist in the victory. In the process, the team established a new franchise mark for wins in a season with 26. From there, the Wild ended the season with a solid 4-4 tie against rival Dallas. The men in red and green rallied from a 4-1 deficit on goals from Antti Laaksonen, Jim Dowd and Andrew Brunette to garner the point. Brunette, Gaborik, Benysek and Zholtok each registered multi-point games, while Dwayne Roloson came up with nine saves in relief of the injured Manny Fernandez to earn the tie. When it was all said and done the team finished the season with a very respectable 26-35-12-9 mark and a franchise-record 73 points.

The 2002-03 Wild established club records for wins and points, with 42 and 92, respectively. They would finish third in the Northwest Division and sixth overall in the Western Conference. The team also finished ranked first in the NHL in overtime wins and points with an impressive 8-1-10 mark, good for 26 points. Further, the team once again sold out all 41 home games at the X, as the fans kept coming in droves to see their squad in action. Minnesota made history right out of the gates by winning its first ever opening night game, beating Boston, 5-1, at the X. A few weeks later, Marian Gaborik made a little history of his own by nearly single-handidly beating Phoenix, 6-1, thanks to his franchise record six point performance against the Coyotoes. For his efforts, Gabby was named as the NHL Player of the Week, the first Wild player to earn such an honor. The speedy winger would later earn a roster spot at the NHL's All-Star Game as well, once again becoming the first Wild player to do so.

The team finished the month of October on a five game unbeaten streak by beating San Jose, 2-1, in overtime, on Sergei Zholtok's two goals. The thrilling game-winner came with just 9.1 seconds left in the extra session, causing the Xcel Center fans to erupt. There were many highlights that season, including back-to-back shut-outs by Manny Fernandez on Feb. 10th and 12th, both against Philadelphia. Fellow netminder Duane Roloson also got into the act, shutting out the league's top scoring team, the Vancouver Canucks, 3-0, on Feb. 25th, for his third blanking of the season. The team beat the New Jersey Devils for their first time ever, 3-2, in early March on Willie Mitchell's game-winner in the third period. Then, on March 23rd, the team made even more history when it beat Detroit, 4-0, to secure its first ever Stanley Cup playoff birth. From there, the team cruised into April, beating Columbus, 4-3, to secure a sixth seed in the Western Conference Playoffs. Gaborik, Filip Kuba, Pierre Marc Bouchard and Andrew Brunette all tallied two points apiece in the big win.

With that, the Wild headed west to face the Colorado Avalanche in the first round of the playoffs. The Avs had just won the Stanley Cup in 2001 and were the odds-on favorites to win it again this year. The Wild had other ideas, however, and opened the quarterfinals in Denver with a huge 4-2 win. The team jumped out to a 3-0 lead in the second period on goals from Kuba, Gaborik and Walz, and then held on behind Dwayne Roloson's 39 saves in net. The Avs rallied in the third, but Andrew Brunette iced it on a late unassisted goal. Colorado roared back to win Game Two the next night, 3-2, despite goals by Walz and Brunette. The series headed back to Minnesota for Game Three and the fans went nuts. It was the first time Minnesota had seen playoff hockey since the early '90s and the

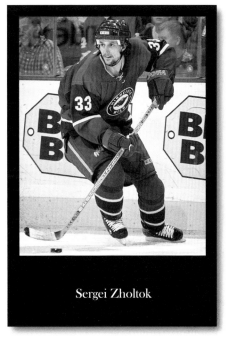

Sergei Zholtok

Willie Mitchell

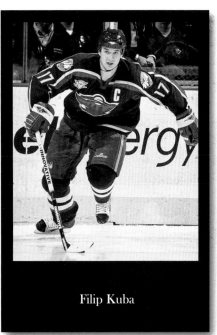

Filip Kuba

entire state of Minnesota had seemingy jumped on the bandwagon. Unfortunately, however, the team got blanked, 3-0, in front of a record crowd of 19,354 at the X. Avs Goalie Patrick Roy was the hero in this one, turning away all 18 shots he faced in net to post his NHL Playoff record 23rd shut-out. Game Four wasn't much better, as the Wild lost yet again, 3-1. Joe Sakic scored a pair of goals for Colorado, while Gaborik tallied the lone goal for Minnesota in the loss.

With a commanding 3-1 series advantage, the Avs were set to close out the Wild back home at the Pepsi Center in the Mile High City. Facing elimination, the Wild went with Manny Fernandez in net to shake things up. It worked. The team jumped out to 3-0 second period lead on goals by Willie Mitchell, Filip Kuba and Pascal Dupuis, and held on for a 3-2 victory to force a Game Six back in Minnesota. There, the Wild battled the Avs to a 2-2 tie on goals by Gaborik and Richard Park, to force overtime. Park would be the hero in this one when he notched the game-winning goal at 4:22 of the extra session. What ensued next was utter pandemonium in the X as the fans erupted.

Game Seven would be back in Denver and there, Minnesota would make even more history. The two teams battled to yet another 2-2 tie in regulation, forcing sudden death overtime. Peter Forsberg had put the Avs up 1-0 in the second period, only to see Dupuis answer on a power-play goal to even it up. Colorado went up 2-1 at 13:15 of the third on Sakik's series-leading sixth goal, but then saw the momentum swing the other away when Gaborik scored the equalizer just two minutes later. From there, the two teams went back and forth into the extra session. Finally, at the 3:25 mark of overtime, Andrew Brunette skated in and beat Patrick Roy on a fabulous deke in front of the net to score the biggest goal in franchise history. The stunned Colorado players couldn't believe their eyes, while the Cinderella Wild piled onto Manny Fernandez out on the ice in pure extacy. Minnesota had become just the eighth NHL team to come back from a 3-1 deficit to win a series.

Next up for the Wild were the Vancouver Canucks in the Western Conference Semifinals. The team opened the series on the road at GM Place and wound up losing a heart-breaker in Game One, 4-3, in overtime. Wes Walz scored twice in the loss, while Minnesota native Trent Klatt netted the game-winner in OT for the Canucks. The team rallied to take Game Two, however, 3-2, behind goals from Gaborik, Zholtok and Walz. Games Three and Four were back in Minnesota and both proved to be heart-breakers for the Wild faithful. Game Three saw Vancouver score three power-play goals to win 3-2, while Game Four saw the Wild lose by the same score in overtime. Gaborik scored both Minnesota goals in regulation, while Canucks forward Brent Sopel slipped the game-winner past Fernandez for Vancouver at the 15:52 mark of the extra session to give his team the big win.

A FEW WORDS WITH DARBY HENDRICKSON...

Darby Hendrickson grew up learning to love the game of hockey at Richfield's Fairwood Park. He went on to become a prep legend at Richfield High School, where he led his team to the state tourney in 1991. Hendrickson won the Mr. Hockey Award that same year and from there went on to play for the Gophers at the University of Minnesota. There, he would garner WCHA Rookie of the Year honors and take Gold Country by storm. He would go on to score 82 points in just 75 collegiate games before going on to play with the 1994 U.S. Olympic team, which competed in Norway. From there, he went on to play for 11 seasons in the NHL, first with Toronto, and then with the New York Islanders, Vancouver, Minnesota and finally with Colorado. In all, he would tally 65 goals and 64 assists for 129 career points in 518 games. He later spent a few seasons playing across the pond in Austria.

Hendrickson was acquired by the Wild in the expansion draft and was thrust into the role of home-town superstar. He dealt with the pressures of being home with the friends and family and handled it all in stride. He did suffer a bad eye injury at the end of the 2001 season and then missed several months of the 2002 season after breaking his wrist early in the pre-season. He recovered though and went on to play for four years with his hometown squad, even earning the coveted honor of wearing the captain's "C" as well.

"I knew that the expansion draft was coming up and that I wasn't going to be protected by Vancouver," said Hendrickson of getting the opportunity to come home to play in Minnesota. "I was optimistic at that point and hopeful that it was going to happen. Then, when I got the call I was sort of numb. I was so excited about coming back to play for my new home-town team and knew it was going to be a great opportunity for me in my career. Looking back I guess it was just meant to be and I am now really grateful that it all worked out the way it did."

"I grew up worshipping Neal Broten and wanting to play for the North Stars. Then, when they moved to Dallas, I was devastated. So, to be able to finally play pro hockey for my hometown team, that is about as good as it gets in this business. My time with the Wild was amazing, the fans were so good to me. I couldn't even begin to thank them enough for all of their support. Hey, I even got to make a little history by scoring the first ever goal at the Xcel Energy Center. I got a great pass from Maxium Suchinsky to set up one of many great memories I was fortunate to have there. That was a huge thrill and something I will never forget.

"Minnesota hockey fans are so amazing. They are so smart and so educated about the game and they really know what is going on both on and off the ice. I have also always felt that Minnesotans are pretty simple people who live by the golden rule of 'treat people the way you want to be treated,' and that is how I have always wanted to live my life as well. As a player I respected that so much and was so lucky to have played here at so many stops along my career. They were wonderful to me every step of the way, especially when I came home to play with the Wild, and I will never forget their generosity and kindness to me and my family. They are just first class fans and I could never begin to thank them enough for their support. I really appreciate it.

"Overall, I think the state of the game in Minnesota is great. To see so many guys who played either at the collegiate level or in the pros come back and get into coaching, that is just fantastic. They are passing on so much to the next generations of boys and girls here and that is really neat to see. As for the youth levels, I think we are strong and only getting stronger — for both the boys and the girls. The high school tournament is still very special, although it has lost a bit of its luster due to the fact that so many of the top kids are opting to play junior hockey nowadays instead. But, we are definitely doing something right. There is a lot of talent out there and the fact that we are getting kids onto the next level is a testament to the jobs our coaches are doing at the youth levels on up."

Down three games to one, the Wild were about to make even more history as the series headed back to the west coast. There, with Dwayne Roloson back in net, Minnesota staved off elimination thanks to five second-period goals by Cliff Ronning, Marian Gaborik, Jason Marshall, Andrew Brunette and Wes Walz, to win the game, 7-2. Game Six was back at the X and Minnesota won convincingly, 5-1. Rollie played solid between the pipes, while the Wild got a pair of goals from Andrew Brunette, and one each from Lubomir Sekeras, Darby Hendrickson and Antti Laaksonen to force a Game Seven back north of the border. There, Minnesota battled back from a 2-0 second period deficit on goals from Pascal Dupuis — a magical shot which he whacked out of mid-air and into the net, and Wes Walz, to even it up at 2-2 midway through the third period. Then, with just under six minutes to play, Darby Hendrickson beat netminder Dan Cloutier on a slap-shot for the game-winning goal to give the Wild its first-ever trip to the Western Conference Finals. Dupuis added an insurance goal late to ice it as the team went on to win

WILD FIRST ROUND DRAFT HISTORY

2000: Marian Gaborik (3rd overall)
2001: Mikko Koivu (6th overall)
2002: Pierre-Marc Bouchard (8th overall)
2003: Brent Burns (20th overall)
2004: A.J. Thelen (12th overall)
2005: Benoit Pouliot (4th overall)
2006: James Sheppard (9th overall)
2007: Colton Gillies (16th overall)

the game by the final score of 4-2, silencing the sell-out crowd at GM Place. With the win, the Wild became the first team in NHL history to come back from a 3-1 deficit twice in the same postseason, and also became only the second club ever to win two Game Sevens on the road in the same playoff year.

With their playoff beards in full bloom, the Wild then faced the Mighty Ducks of Anaheim in the 2003 Western Conference Finals. Game One, which was played at the Xcel Center, was brutal. The team got shut-out, 1-0, thanks to the brilliant netminding of Ducks goalie J.S. Giguere, who turned away all 39 shots he faced in goal. Game Two was even worse as Giguere simply dominated, shutting out the Wild yet again, this time by the final of 2-0. Incredibly, he did it for a third straight time in Game Three out in Anaheim at Arrowhead Pond, winning this one, 4-0. The Wild players were devasted. The NHL hadn't seen goaltending like this in decades. He was the hottest player in hockey and there was seemingly nothing Minnesota could do about it. They did manage to get a puck

"Being in Minnesota is great," said Boogaard. "I have really enjoyed my time with the Wild and am grateful for the opportunity that they have given me. I have a role to play on the team and I take great pride in that. It is my job to make sure that nobody takes liberties with any of my teammates, and if they do, then they will need to be held accountable for their actions. Being an enforcer in the NHL is all about respect. If you play the game the right way and don't play dirty, then you will be fine. I take a lot of pride in what I do and the fact that my teammates appreciate that means the world to me. I uphold the honor code out on the ice and that is something that is bigger than the game itself."

"As for living in the State of Hockey, it is fantastic. To see all of the fans come out and support us night in and night out is awesome. I can't thank them enough for all of their support and encouragement. They really do make a difference out there and that is why we have such a great home-ice advantage at the Xcel Center."

past him in Game Four, but it was too little too late as the Ducks went on to win the game, 2-1, on a pair of goals from Adam Oates to sweep the series. The magical ride was over. Andrew Brunette netted the Wild's lone goal of the series, while Manny Fernandez stopped 26 of 28 shots that came his way. Giguere, who fended off the late rally, posted a 4-0 mark in the series, turned aside 122-of-123 shots faced and recorded a 212:43 shut-out streak. The numbers were insane. It was a tough loss, but in no way did it overshadow the amazing season that the team put together. They would finish the year with a 42-29-10-1 overall mark, good for a franchise record 95 points. In addition, Jacques Lemaire was named NHL Coach of the Year, becoming just the fifth coach in league history to win Jack Adams Award twice.

"What an amazing ride that was," said Darby Hendrickson of the team's incredible season. "To come back and win those two series the way we did said a lot about our team and the make-up of our players. We just never quit and kept grinding it out. The fans were incredible too, they really were. They were so into it and really supported us. I thought we were going to go all the way but we just ran into the hottest goaltender in the game, at the time, and that was that. It was a really special time for all of us though and something I will certainly never forget. I just wish we could have brought the Stanley Cup home to the State of Hockey, that would have been the ultimate."

"What can you say, it was just an amazing story," added assistant coach Mike Ramsey of the team's post-season run. "I mean just for us to make the playoffs as early as we did and the way that we did was so amazing. The entire experience was very special and it was something that I will always remember. It was just special being a part of the original coaching staff right from the start. You could see all of the groundwork being laid for the foundation right from the get-go, and to see that all come to reality was very special. It is a real honor to be a part of this organization. Jacques (Lemaire) is a special person, and his outlook on the game is really outside of the box compared to other coaches. He has a passion for the game and the delivery of his message to the players is like nobody else's. His message has meaning and the players really respect him."

Dwayne Roloson

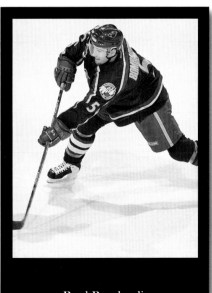

Brad Bombardir

The 2003-04 Wild hit the ice that next Fall with high expectations. They came out of the gates smoking, beating the Rangers in the home-opener, 5-3. Sergei Zholtok notched three points, while Andrew Brunette and Pierre-Marc Bouchard each chipped in with two points apeice as well. The team introduced its new third jersey that next week, an all red sweater with a circular team logo. (Incidentally, the boys would play tough in their new digs, going 6-4-3-1 in games that they wore them.) Among the highlights from this season were a three-game winning streak in late October and into November, which culminated with a 3-2 win over Washington at the X thanks to Andrew Brunette's game-winner in the third. One of the biggest come-from-behind wins of the season occurred on December 13th, at the X, when the Wild scored twice in the game's final five minutes to defeat the Buffalo Sabres, 3-2. Down 2-1 in the third period, Antti Laaksonen got the equalizer at the 15-minute mark, while Jim Dowd notched the game-winner with just 24 seconds to play in regulation.

The Wild made history on December 30th when they tied Edmonton, 2-2, in overtime. Willie Mitchell and Nick Schultz each scored their first goals of the season, while Manny Fernandez made 38 saves in net. In doing so, the franchise set a record by running its unbeaten streak to nine straight games. Another memorable moment came a few nights later when the team set a then-franchise record by scoring seven goals in a thrilling come-from-behind victory over Chicago at the Xcel Center. Eric Chouinard, Alexandre Daigle, Pascal Dupuis, Marian Gaborik, Richard Park and Nick Schultz all tallied two points apiece in the big win. February 2nd saw the Wild, behind Dwayne Roloson's 24-save shut-out, blank the Blues four to zip. In that game, Wes Walz tallied two goals, including the first-ever successful penalty shot at the X.

Later that week, the eyes of the hockey world shined upon Minnesota as the 54th annual NHL All-Star Game was held in St. Paul. Filip Kuba and Dwayne Roloson were named to the Western Conference All-Star Team, which ultimately lost to the East by the final score of 6-4. In the process, a new attendance record was set for a hockey game in Minnesota as 19,434 fans came out to take in the festivities. The State of Hockey rolled out the red carpet that week, including constructing an enormous ice palace across the street from the arena in conjunction with the St. Paul Winter Carnival.

The team played solid hockey in the second half of the season, including going on a six game unbeaten streak in early March. It was capped by a 5-2 win over Ottawa in which Marian Gaborik recorded his seventh career hat trick. Later that month the team exploded for a record eight goals in defeating Chicago, 8-2, at United Center. Pascal Dupuis tied a Wild record with four assists, while Richard Wallin added three points of his own in the win. A few nights later, on March 31st, the Wild got a trio of points each from Alexandre Daigle and Marc Chouinard en route to beating Colorado, 5-4, at the X. Chouinard tallied the game-winner just 53 seconds into overtime after the Avs had rallied back from a two-goal deficit in the third period to tie it up. The team finished the season strong behind Dwayne Roloson's 24-save shut-out against the Blues on April 4th. It was the club's third straight win, which gave them a final record of 30-29-20-3, good for 83 points and a fifth place finish in the Northwest Division of the Western Conference. It was the franchise's second consecutive winning season, but not good enough for post-season play.

Shortly after the season ended, labor negotiations for a new collective bargaining agreement between the players and the owners came to an impasse. Most hockey afficianados figured that the tussle would be resolved at some point that summer, but boy were they ever wrong. As things heated up, threats of a lock-out by the owners grew increasingly louder. Pre-season training camps were eventually cancelled, and before long players and fans alike started to get really nervous. By September things were looking bleak as rumors were running wild as to whether or not the players and owsners would come to their senses. On a bright note for Minnesota fans, however, in early September of 2004 the Xcel

Pascal Dupuis

Energy Center hosted four World Cup games which featured outstanding play from the United States, Canada, Russia and Slovakia.

Meanwhile, things finally boiled over on September 16th, when it was announced that a work stoppage had officially begun. As NHL arenas sat empty that season across North America, thousands upon thousands of workers who made their livlihoods either directly or indirectly from professional hockey, were forced to look elsewhere for employment. It started out ugly and it got even uglier as both sides dug in for the long haul. Finally, on February 16, 2005, NHL commissioner Gary Bettman made the painful announcement that hockey fans everywhere had been dreading, the 2004-05 NHL season had officially been canceled.

Eventualy, after several months of cooling off, the two sides got together again to negotiate how they could make the game not only better, but also more fiscally sound. With that, on July 22nd, the NHL Board of Governors ratified the terms of the CBA which had been set forth by the NHLPA, ending a 310-day work stoppage. In what the league referred to as "a new era of cooperation and partnership," the two sides shook hands and got ready to hit the ice for the 2005-06 season. What resulted in the aftermath of the lost season would actually be looked upon as great news by most hockey fans. The new rules would include getting rid of the red line, thus opening up the neutral zone for more passing and wide open play. Also included was the promise that the officials would cut down on all of the obstruction which had plagued the league for decades. No more hooking and holding or clutching and grabbing, which would free up guys like Marian Gaborik to do what he did best — score goals. In addition, the padding on the goaltenders would be reduced in size by more than 10%, which would also translate into more offense and more scoring. Lastly, a new rule would be implimented that would see games that ended in ties feature a shoot-out

A FEW WORDS WITH MANNY FERNANDEZ...

"It was great playing in Minnesota, it really was," said Fernandez. "I was very fortunate to have been able to come here early on and to be a part of such a first class organization. I really enjoyed my time here and loved the fans as well. With contracts and salary caps, you just never know when the business side of hockey will enter into the mix. I was fortunate to have been able to be with the franchise for as long as I was though and really enjoyed my time there. As for leaving Minnesota, I am sad to leave but happy for new opportunities. I wish Niklas (Backstrom) all the best. He is a great guy and I'm sure he will continue to do well. There are no hard feelings. It is just business and you have to move on. I would love to be remembered as a guy who just worked hard and was a good teammate. I tried my best to give the team a positive image and really enjoyed my time here."

"As for playing for my Uncle Jacques (Lemaire), it had its positives and its negatives. He was one of nine kids, so there were a lot of cousins and aunts and uncles growing up in my family. I knew about him, obviously, as a kid because he was a pretty famous guy up in Montreal, where I grew up. We really only saw his family once every few years, at a family Christmas party, though. So, it wasn't like we were super close when I was a kid. As for our relationship with the Wild, we kept it pretty business-like. That was probably for the best. There wasn't any nepotism or anything like that. I earned my way onto the team and never got any special treatment just because the coach was my uncle. There was always a little weight on my shoulders regarding that, but I just tried to make the best of it. Any time you go into business with a family member it can be tough, so we stayed away from each other to be honest. We never socialized or anything like that during all the time I was in Minnesota, never, it just wasn't like that."

"Living in Minnesota for all these years was great though. Hockey is so big here and that is pretty neat to see. You know, I played hockey in Texas before I came here and I guess I would equate hockey to Minnesota as football is down there. People just love the sport here and have a real passion for the game. That is just great to see. Growing up in Canada I think it was the same way, but to see it here in the States is pretty neat. As for the fans, all I can say is thank you for all your support. They were always there for me and I really appreciated that. There were a lot of great memories along the way, I just wish we could have won a few Stanley Cups for them."

A FEW WORDS WITH MIKE RAMSEY...

Mike Ramsey was born in Minneapolis and went on to star on the Minneapolis Roosevelt High School hockey team. From there, Ramsey wore the Maroon and Gold at the University of Minnesota, where he helped lead the Golden Gophers to the 1979 NCAA National Championship. Ramsey then went on to become the youngest player, at just 18, to play for the fabled 1980 "Miracle on Ice" Olympic team which won the gold medal in Lake Placid, NY.

From there, Ramsey joined the NHL's Buffalo Sabres, which had drafted him with their No. 1 pick the year before. Ramsey would go on to play for 14 years in Buffalo before being traded to Pittsburgh in 1993. That next year, however, the sturdy defenseman was dealt to the Detroit Red Wings, where, after playing in the Stanley Cup Finals, he would ultimately retire in 1996. In all, Ramsey would play in the NHL for 18 seasons, where he tallied 79 goals and 266 assists for 345 points in 1,070 career games . He also played in four NHL All-Star Games (1982, 1983, 1985 and 1986) and racked up 1,012 penalty minutes along the way.

In 1997 Ramsey became an assistant coach with the Sabres. He would remain in Buffalo for three seasons before coming home in 2000 to take over an assistant with the expansion Wild. Considered to be among the brightest young coaching minds in the game today, Ramsey has had a lot to do with the team's success. As a former blue-liner, he works with the team's defensemen — a hallmark the Wild have been known for since day one.

"As a player I thought like a coach," said Ramsey. "I saw the game like a coach and I always saw myself becoming a coach one day. By no means, however, did that mean I was ready to be a coach yet. I am still learning the ropes. So, as an assistant, my relationship is much different with the players than it is with the head coach. In Jacque's (Lemaire) system, the players know that they can come and talk to any of us anytime. I think the assistants act as a sort of buffer, however, to filter out a lot of stuff before it gets to the top. Sometimes players just feel more comfortable coming to me for certain things and I really enjoy that. My relationship with the players is great because since I played so long in the National Hockey League, I feel like I truly understand what they are thinking and feeling out on the ice. Once you establish that credibility with your players, then you can talk to them much more openly and honestly to help them deal with certain situations."

"To be a great coach you have to have a lot of great qualities," he continued. "You've got to know how to motivate players, baby-sit players, know the X's and O's, be able to communicate, teach, handle the press and do about a million other things. So it is tough. But overall you need the right mix of personalities in the room to create good chemistry. That goes all the way back to your management and your scouts, and which types of players they are bringing into the locker room. From star players to 'plumbers,' it all comes down to how the coach can mold them into his style — because how he deals with them affects how well they will react both on and off the ice."

"I am very simple in my approach," he said. "I just try to be a good listener, be realistic, be honest, work hard and try to learn as much as possible. I remember after I won that gold medal in the 1980 Olympics, I just sat back and thought 'wow, everybody should be able to feel what this feels like, it was just awesome.' I think that is why I am coaching. Obviously I get paid to coach, which is a great way to make a living, but when you win, you get that great feeling. It is a different kind of feeling winning as a player versus now as a coach, but it is still the best thing in the world. It is such a feeling of accomplishment and it's a real high that is very fulfilling. If you could bottle that and sell it, you would be a billionaire."

"Overall, I appreciate the fact that so many people have followed my career, that is just amazing to me," added Ramsey. "From the Gophers to the Olympics to Buffalo to Pittsburgh to Detroit and finally back to Minnesota, it has been a great ride. I just really appreciate their support and would want to thank everyone who has been there for me. It is a real honor to be thought of that way and I am very lucky."

at the end of the game. The purists would hate it, but the majority of the fans would love it. Most importantly, however, was the fact that there would now be a salary cap which featured not only a roof, for the big spenders, but also a floor, for the cheapskate franchises who didn't want to spend any cash. The players agreed to take much less money both in the short term as well as in the long term, which was key to the deal. The league would now have "cost certainty," which was essential for the long term growth of the game. In the end it would turn out to be a painful short term pill to swallow for the long term good of the game.

The Wild hit the ice in 2005-06 with several new faces, including that of All-Star winger Brian Rolston, who would wind up leading the team in scoring with 34 goals and 45 assists for 79 points. Hockey officially returned to Xcel Energy Center on October 5th as the Wild kept their all-time home-opener unbeaten streak alive with a 6-3 victory over Calgary. All three Wild centermen: Pierre-Marc Bouchard, Todd White and Marc Chouinard, scored three points apiece in this one, with Chouinard tallying his first career hat trick. Dwayne Roloson got his first shutout of the year that next week against Vancouver, blanking the Canucks, 6-0, behind right winger Matt Foy's first two goals of his

NHL career. The Boogieman, Derek Boogaard, the team's beloved enforcer, notched his first ever NHL goal the following week in a 6-1 victory over San Jose at the X. The crowd ate it up and showed him plenty of love and appreciation for all of the dirty work he does in protecting his teammates.

With an impressive 4-2-1 record in late October, the team was looking good. Among the highlights of the first half of the season included the team's first ever shoot-out game. It came on October 27th in a 2-1 loss to Columbus despite Dwayne Roloson's amazing 52-save performance. Pierre-Marc Bouchard tabbed the lone Wild goal in regulation while Todd White got his name in the record book for scoring the team's first ever shoot-out goal. The team would earn its first shoot-out win that next week in a 4-3 victory over Anaheim on Randy Robitaille's eventual game-winner in the extra session. The team later broke a four-game losing streak on December 5th in Pittsburgh by exploding for five unanswered goals against the Penguins. Leading the charge for the Wild were Alexandre Daigle, Brian Rolston, Andrei Zyuzin and Marian Gaborik, who each tallied a pair of points, while Manny Fernandez stopped all 22 shots that came his way in net to earn the shut-out. Another emotional win came on the 17th when the team beat the

A FEW WORDS WITH BRIAN ROLSTON...

"It's been such a pleasure playing for the Wild, I just can't say enough good things about Minnesota and the great people here," said Rolston, who was acquired by the Wild in 2004. "The fans here are unbelievable. To have the opportunity to play here in front of so many great fans has been a real thrill for me. Their enthusiasm and love for the game is unlike anything I have ever seen before. It is unparalleled to anywhere I have ever played, it really is."

"What I would like to say to the Wild fans, first and foremost, is just thank you for all your support. It is such a special feeling to wear a Wild jersey and to be a part of the new tradition that has been started here. To play in front of all of those fans night in and night out is so much fun. They are so smart about hockey and they really do give us a home-ice advantage out there. They are up on their feet, cheering for us, and are so supportive of us, regardless of how we are playing. As players, we truly want to do our best for them, they bring that out of us. The fans are so enthusiastic and that just motivates me to do my best every night. I want to please them by playing my best and do whatever I can do to help the team win. Playing at the Xcel Center is almost like playing in a college atmosphere, it is just that exciting. The building is such a great place to play and the fans are the reason for that. Every single game is memorable in there because the fans are just so into it. I mean I still get goose bumps when I come out onto the ice for the pre-game warm-ups.

"The ownership really gets it here too. What a first class group of individuals. They've embraced the whole community and have done such a great job of getting everybody involved. You just can't say enough good things about how they run this organization. They really connect with the fans and as a result the fans are there for us night in and night out. You know, there is kind of a feeling among players in the league with regards to coming to Minnesota to play for the Wild. It has been said that it is one of the toughest places to get players to come to, and then, conversely, it is one of the toughest places to get them to leave from once they are here. So, that speaks volumes about what kind of a place Minnesota is and about how much the players enjoy playing and living here. Once they get here they realize just what a fabulous place this is. You really can't beat it.

"I grew up in Detroit and spent most of my adult life living and playing on the east coast, but I can honestly say that this is the strongest hockey community in the country. Everybody understands the game here; so many people play the game at various levels; and the fans are so into it. That is why hockey is such a part of the fabric of life here. The kids start so young and they are lucky in that there are so many great youth coaches and volunteers to help them along and show them how to play the right way. The people really support hockey at all levels, both boys and girls, and that is so neat to see. The hockey community is so special and they feel like a big family. It doesn't matter where you are from, everybody is sort of living that same lifestyle, which has hockey at the center of it. Anybody who has kids who play hockey can certainly relate to what I am talking about. We all share that love of the game.

"My wife and I love living in Minnesota too, what a great place to raise a family. My son plays mites in the Stillwater district and we are just having a ball watching him learn the game. The community really embraces hockey so much here and that is so refreshing to see. I mean the head coach of the Stillwater High School team is my old teammate, Phil Housley, one of the greatest American players of all time. How neat would that be if my son someday played for him? That's the kind of stuff that really makes living here so special. Overall, I am proud to be a member of the Wild. I am proud to have made a statement as a player and to have had successes both as an individual and as a member of the team. It is such an honor to wear the red and green jersey and to say that I represent the State of Hockey. I just want to bring the Stanley Cup to Minnesota so badly, that is my main goal and my ultimate dream. The fans here deserve that so much and I will do everything in my power to make that happen some day. That would just mean so much to me."

Montreal Canadiens, 4-3, in overtime thanks to Kurtis Foster's game-winner at the 3:13 mark of the extra session. For LeMaire and Risebrough, who won several Stanley Cups with the Canadiens back in the '70s, the victory was oh so sweet.

It would be a December to remember for the team, which went 8-7-1 that month behind Brian Rolston and Manny Fernandez. Rolston tallied 21 points in December, good for NHL Offensive Player of the Month honorable mention accolades. Fernandez, meanwhile, went 7-2-1 with a 2.09 goals-against-average and a .925 save percentage — good for NHL Defensive Player of the Month honorable mention accolades. The team played inspired hockey over this stretch, capping the month by sweeping Edmonton, 4-1 and 4-2, before knocking off Vancouver on New Years Eve, 4-3, at the X.

The team kicked off the new year by beating Detroit, 4-2, at Joe Louis Arena, behind Brian Rolston's game-winner which gave the club its fifth win in six games. The team went cold in early January, however, but was able to snap a three-game losing streak by beating Toronto, 5-3, thanks to a pair of Marc Chouinard goals. The team got hot from there and went on a franchise record five-game winning streak, beating Chicago twice, as well as Phoenix and Nashville. Following a three-game losing streak, the team got back on track in early February by winning three straight over San Jose, Phoenix and L.A. Against the

Sharks, the Wild got a thrilling shoot-out victory thanks to Marian Gaborik's game-tying goal in the third, followed by Brian Rolston's game-winner in the shoot-out. Meanwhile, Wes Walz and Marian Gaborik each tallied twice in the win over Phoenix, while Gaborik, Rolston and Pascal Dupuis each recorded three points in the win over the Kings.

Things got ugly from there though as the team lost seven of its next nine games throughout February and into March. One of the reasons for the up and down play was due to the fact that several Wild players would be tired from playing in the 2006 Olympics in Turin, Italy. Three players did medal, however, including: Daniel Tjarnqvist, who won a gold with Sweden; Mikko Koivu, who won a silver with Finland; and Filip Kuba, who won a bronze with the Czech Republic. Brian Rolston and Marian Gaborik also competed with Team U.S.A. and Slovakia, respectively. It would be an up and down finish for the team as it rounded out the season. Among the highlights down the stretch were a 3-1 victory over the Flames in which Marian Gaborik scored two goals, including his franchise-record 31st of the season.

The team then went on to post a trio of shoot-out victories. The first came on March 31st over Vancouver, 2-1, on Mikko Koivu's dazzling game-winner. The second occurred on April 4th, in a 5-4 win over the Blues. In that game, rookie goalkeeper Josh Harding made 22 saves and stopped two of the three shots he faced in the shoot-out to become the first goalie in NHL history to win his first game in a shoot-out. Stephane Veilleux, Mattias Weinhandl, Marc Chouinard and Wes Walz all scored in regulation, while Brian Rolston got the game-winner in the shoot-out. The third win came against Edmonton a few nights later as Rolston was once again the hero, scoring the 2-1 game-winner in the shoot-out. Rolston's signature shoot-out slap-shot from just inside the dots was quickly becoming the most feared shot in the NHL. Harding was in net due to the fact that team decided to trade longtime goalie Dwayne Roloson to Edmonton midway through the year in exchange for a first round draft pick. It was sad to see Rollie go, but necessary in order for the team to bring in some new pieces of the puzzle.

The team got hot down the stretch run, beating Colorado, 5-2, and Chicago, 2-0. Marian Gaborik notched four points, including his first hat trick of the season, against the Avs; while Manny Fernandez made 40 saves in goal for his 30th win of the year. Josh Harding then got his first career shut-out in just his second NHL start, behind goals from Stephane Veilleux and Pierre-Marc Bouchard. The team then lost its final two contests of the year on the road to Nashville and Dallas to finish the season with a 38-36-8 record, good for 84 points — second best in franchise history. Despite that fact, the team missed the post-season yet again, leaving the fans begging for more. But, with more than 200 consecutive sell-outs at the X, they showed no signs of losing interest in their beloved Wild.

The 2006-07 season was all about change, from top to bottom. The ownership group opened up its collective wallet that pre-season and brought in a host of new talent in an attempt to get the team back into the play-offs. In June the team made headlines by sending one of their first-round draft picks, which had come from Edmonton via the Roloson deal, along with prospect Patrick O'Sullivan, to the Los Angeles Kings in exchange for All-Star winger Pavol Demitra. Demitra would fit in nicely with his fellow countryman from Slovakia, Marian Gaborik. In addition, just a few weeks later the team signed several top free agents, including defensemen Keith Carney and Kim Johnsson, as well as winger Mark Parrish, a Bloomington native who skated at St. Cloud State University.

The team continued its fantastic home-opener winning streak for the seventh straight season, beating Colorado, 3-2, on Todd White's game-winner at the 3:57 mark of overtime. The win would be the first of six straight, and nine out of ten, catapulting the team into first place in the division. Of those first six wins, two came in overtime with another two coming in shoot-outs, proving that the newly acquired players were gelling with their new teammates and could be counted on in clutch time. Petteri Nummelin got the game-winner in the first shoot-out, a 2-1 win over Vancouver; while Mikko Koivu netted the other shoot-out game-winner in the 3-

Pierre Marc Bouchard

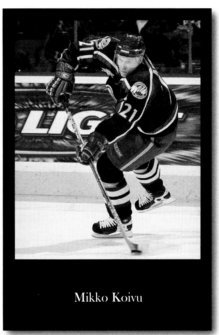

Mikko Koivu

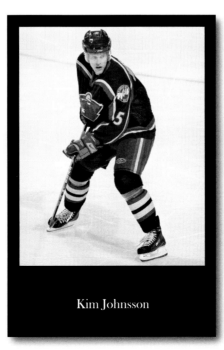

Kim Johnsson

2 win over Washington; and Marian Gaborik notched the final game-winner in the 2-1 overtime win over Los Angeles.

In November the team went into a slump, going just 4-9 along the way. The team's 11-game home winning streak came to an end on November 4th during a 4-3 loss to Nashville. Among the highlights over this stretch included Todd White's 3-2 shoot-out game-winner over Los Angeles on the 11th. The team also made history on the 16th, rallying back from a three goal deficit to beat Nashville, 7-6, on Brian Rolston's shoot-out game-winner. Niklas Backstrom got his first NHL shut-out victory that next week in a 4-0 drubbing of Phoenix, stopping all 28 shots that came his way. The team got hot again in early December, winning three in a row in dramatic fashion. The first was a 3-2 shoot-out victory over Chicago, compliments of Pierre Marc Bouchard's game-winner; the second was a 3-2 shoot-out win over Calgary, on Mikko Koivu's game-winner; and the third was an overtime win over the Blackhawks, courtesy of Mark Parrish's hat trick game-winner.

The rest of December was rough though, as the team won just four of its next 10 games. One of the pre-Christmas highlights, however, came on December 23rd, when Pierre Marc Bouchard netted the overtime game-winner just 45 seconds into the extra session en route to leading his Wild past the Red Wings, 3-2. Further, Wes Walz also netted an overtime game-winner that next week in a 4-3 win over Columbus. The team then closed the books on the year 2006 with its league-leading 16th home win over Anaheim on New Year's Eve behind a pair of points each from Rolston and Bouchard.

After opening the new year with a 5-1 win over Atlanta, on Bouchard's four-point performance, the team went on a slide and lost three straight. They recovered though, and won three in a row on the road against Vancouver, Edmonton and Chicago behind Gaborik's five goal outburst and Demitra's shoot-out game-winner over the Blackhawks. The rest of January was back and forth, but the team got red hot in February, winning nine of 12 over that stretch. The team was playing inspired hockey and was positioning itself for a post-season appearance, something that was long overdue in the State of Hockey. Among the highlights this month included a 1-0 victory over Phoenix compliments of Gaborik's game-winner and Niklas Backstrom's second shut-out on 29 saves. Pavol Demitra also extended his points streak to eight games in a 4-1 win over Nashville; and Mikko Koivu netted yet another shoot-out game-winner in a 2-1 victory over Dallas at home on the 20th.

March rolled in with a 5-0 blanking of Edmonton behind goaltender Josh Harding's first ever shut-out. From there, things got interesting. After losing a pair to Vancouver and San Jose, the team caught fire, winning its next nine straight games. The streak started with a 2-1 win over Boston thanks to Bouchard's game-winner; a 5-1 win over Buffalo on Dominic Moore's two goals; a 3-2 overtime win over Colorado on Brent Burns' game-winner; a 3-2 overtime win over Vancouver on yet another Brent Burns' game-winner; a 2-1 win over Edmonton on Gaborik's game-winner; a 4-2 win over Calgary on Stephane Veilleux's game-winner; a 3-2 victory over Phoenix courtesy of a pair of two-point performances from Gaborik and Demitra; a 5-1 win over St. Louis thanks to a trio of points each from Gaborik and Bouchard; and a 4-1 win over L.A. behind Josh Harding's 32-save performance. They nearly made it a perfect 10 in a row, but lost a shoot-out heart-breaker to Calgary, despite Backstrom's 24-save shut-out through regulation.

After losing their next two to Calgary and Colorado, the team finished up the regular season in style, beating Edmonton twice and St. Louis once for a final tally of 48 wins, 26 losses and eight ties, good for a franchise record 104 points. The stretch run was exciting, as each win had playoff implications with regards to where the team was going to wind up being seeded. As it turned out, the team would open up the playoffs on April 11th on the road at Anaheim, against the league's best team. The Ducks were tough and had incorporated a philosophy of physical play and intimidation, as evidenced by the fact that the team had six times as many fighting majors as did the Wild. It was going to be a battle in more ways than one.

Game One of the Stanley Cup playoff quarterfinal series got underway with the Wild jumping out to a 1-0 lead at 14:51 of the second period on Pavol Demitra's 15-foot slapper that beat goalie Ilya Bryzgalov, who had started in place of Jean-Sebastien Giguere. Teemu Selanne then tied it up about four minutes later though to make it 1-1. It remained that way into the third period, until Anaheim's Dustin Penner scored with 5:20 remaining to lift the Ducks to a 2-1 victory. Penner poked the puck in after Wild defenseman Kim Johnsson crashed into goalie Niklas Backstrom, sending him sprawling back into his net. The puck had been sitting in the crease until Penner took a couple of whacks at it and forced it in. Backstrom, who made 32 saves in the game, thought the controversial goal should have been disallowed, as did most of the Minnesota fans back home watching on TV.

Game Two was also a tight one as

the Ducks won 3-2 and went up two games to none in the best-of-seven games series. The Ducks jumped out to a 1-0 lead midway through the first period on defenseman Francois Beauchemin's power play goal that found Backstrom's five hole from the blue line. The Wild answered at the 3:33 mark of the second on a Marian Gaborik goal from Pavol Demitra and Kurtis Foster to make it 1-1. Beauchemin got his second power play goal of the game about 15 minutes later though, making the Wild pay for their untimely penalties. The killer came just two minutes later, when the Wild, themselves on the man-advantage, got burned by Ducks winger, Ryan Getzlaf, who beat defenseman Martin Skoula to score a shorthanded goal and make it 3-1. Mikko Koivu pulled the Wild to within one on a goal from the top of the crease with just 4:56 remaining, but it was too little too late as the Ducks hung on to take a commanding 2-0 lead in the series.

The series returned to St. Paul for Game Three and the fans were stoked. Ironically, it was the first postseason game at Xcel Energy Center in nearly four years, the last being on May 12, 2003, when Ducks goalie Jean-Sebastien Giguere shut-out Minnesota, 2-0, in Game Two of the Western Conference finals. The teams played it pretty close to the vest throughout the first period until Anaheim made it 1-0 on Andy McDonald's power play goal with just under four minutes to go.

Keith Carney

After a scoreless second period, Ducks All-Star defenseman Rob Niedermayer made it 2-0 midway through the third. Minnesota finally got on the board with just 38 seconds to go in the game when Petteri Nummelin got the puck past Bryzgalov on a late power play goal, but that was as far as the team could get, losing by the final of 2-1. Losing their third one-goal game in a row was dejecting to say the least, but the Wild players hung tough and regrouped for Game Four that next night.

Game Four was tight early. The game was physical and the Wild knew that if they were going to have a chance to win that they were going to have to penetrate past the Duck's stifling defense. After a scoreless first period, the Ducks jumped out to a 1-0 lead early in the second on a Chris Pronger power play goal. The Wild hung tough though and rallied back. Jacques Lemaire's decision to put his top three scorers: Brian Rolston, Marian Gaborik and Pavol Demitra, on one line paid off as the team was finally able to move the puck against the league's top defensive team. Pierre-Marc Bouchard tied it up at the 18:03 mark of the second on a Derek Boogaard assist and the fans went nuts. Then, just three minutes into the third period, the tide turned for good when Marian Gaborik finally scored a rare power-play goal to give the Wild a 2-1 lead. Brian Rolston then made it 3-1 about six minutes later when he grabbed a loose puck along the boards and beat Bryzgalov on a beautiful give-and-go from Pavol Demitra. A Mark Parrish tally just over a minute later then nearly sent the fans into a frenzy.

"I tell you what, the last home game we had against Anaheim was unbelievable," said Brian Rolston. "I have never heard it as loud as it was in there that night. It was just amazing. You have to sort of pinch yourself in situations like that when you look up and see all of those people cheering for you."

The game wasn't without its share of controversy though, and things got physical from there. After Parrish's goal, Anaheim forward Corey Perry charged Wild defenseman Brent Burns, who decked Perry with three straight overhand rights. The bad blood continued to flow in the final minutes when Kent Huskins and Shawn Thornton went after Wild forward Adam Hall. Then, during the melee, Anaheim's agitator, Brad May, raced in and sucker-punched Wild defenseman Kim Johnsson from behind, sending him to the ice in a heap. The attack, which drew a match penalty and a game misconduct for May, was one of the filthiest ever witnessed at the Xcel Center. May's cheap-shot on Johnsson, not known as a fighter, infuriated the Wild players – especially enforcer Derek Boogaard, who promised revenge. "It shows that a guy like Brad May has no respect, so he deserves no respect from anybody," said Boogaard, "and that's how he's going to get treated." The Boogie-man stalked the Ducks bench looking for a fight in retaliation, but got no takers. So, he would have to wait until Game Five, back in Anaheim.

Game Five started out with a bang, literally, as both teams got into a scrap during the pre-game warm-ups. The Minnesota players were upset over Brad May's shot on Kim Johnsson, and felt that his three-game suspension by the league was not long enough to justify the crime he had committed. Johnsson was out indefinitely and they wanted justice. It started when Boogie skated into the Duck's end of the ice looking for a dance partner. Duck's enforcer George Parros came out to challenge him and the two started to exchange words with a little bit of extra curricular shoving. With no officials on the ice at this point, many feared an all-out riot, but cooler heads prevailed and the teams went back to business. Then, a little while later, Ducks All-Star Teemu Selanne got struck in the face with an errant shot during the pre-skate warm-up, requiring several stitches above his left eye. Anaheim alleged that a Wild player did it intentionally, but nobody admitted to doing it or saw it. It was a mystery.

Eventually the game got going, however, with the Ducks jumping out to a quick 1-0

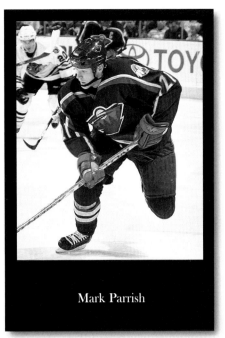

Mark Parrish

Nicklas Backstrom

Sean Hill

(The Duluth native joined the team for the 2007-08 season)

lead on Chris Pronger's wicked slap-shot that hit the top-right corner of the net just a minute into the game. Anaheim was inspired by the return of All-Star goalie Jean-Sebastien Giguere, who had been out due to a family related issue regarding a problem with his newborn son's vision. Giguere, one of the top goaltenders in the league, would give his teammates a huge emotional life and prove to be the difference maker in this one. The Wild answered back late in the second period on a shorthanded goal from Marian Gaborik to make it 1-1, but Ryan Getzlaf scored less than a minute later on a power play goal to put his squad back on top for good. The Ducks were too tough down the stretch and wound up winning the game, 4-1, after a pair of third period goals from Corey Perry and Travis Moen, which was an empty-netter. They would win the series and eventually go on to win the Stanley Cup, proving that they were indeed the best team in hockey.

In the end, the Ducks were too tough defensively and made the Wild pay dearly for their mistakes. The Wild couldn't capitalize on their opportunities either, finishing the series just 2-of-27 on power plays. All in all though, it was a great season. The team continued its amazing streak of sell-outs and had clearly taken a big step forward. Leading the charge that year for the team were Brian Rolston and Pavol Demitra, who led the team in scoring with 64 points each, while Marian Gaborik and Pierre Marc Bouchard finished with 57 points apiece as well.

The team's goaltending duo of Manny Fernandez and Nicklas Backstrom were the best in the business, literally, as evidenced by the fact that they would recieve the coveted William M. Jennings Award, which recognized the NHL's top goaltending tandem with the fewest goals scored against them. Ironically, this would prove to be a blessing as well as a curse for the team. You see, having two top goalies in the new era of salary caps and "cost-certainty," the Wild had a tough decision to make. Figuring that Backstrom, a 29-year-old rookie from Finland, who was the NHL's stingiest goalie during the regular season, had a lot more upside, they decided to trade Fernandez that off-season. It was a tough decision, but the team felt that if they could only have the dollars to spend on one of the two keepers, then the most upside was with Backstrom. As a result, Fernandez was dealt to Boston in late June in exchange for winger Petr Kalus. It would mark the end of an era for the team's first goalie who had joined the club at its original inception back in 2000.

The future looks very bright indeed, however, for our beloved Wild. With so many outstanding players and so many outstanding front office executives steering the ship, it is only a matter of time before Stanley finds his way to the "State of Hockey." And yes, even all these years later, it is still safe to assume that "Norm Still Sucks!"

	PLAYER	Pos.	GP	G	A	PTS	+/-	PIM
1.	Marian Gaborik	RW	408	164	167	331	+34	236
2.	Wes Walz	C	427	81	97	178	+18	266
3.	Andrew Brunette	RW	245	54	110	164	-11	60
4.	Pierre-Marc Bouchard	C	273	48	110	158	+10	82
5.	Brian Rolston	C	160	65	78	143	+20	96
6.	Pascal Dupuis	LW	334	67	74	141	-5	162
7.	Filip Kuba	D	357	33	99	132	-19	236
8.	Jim Dowd	C	283	32	89	121	-15	203
9.	Antti Laaksonen	LW	323	55	63	118	-8	92
10.	Sergei Zholtok	C	210	48	62	110	-5	65
11.	Todd White	C	138	32	52	84	+7	42
12.	Alexandre Daigle	RW	124	25	54	79	-10	26
13.	Mikko Koivu	C	146	26	49	75	-3	98
14.	Richard Park	RW	217	37	37	74	-4	54
15.	Lubomir Sekeras	D	209	17	52	69	-27	120
16.	Pavol Demitra	C	71	25	39	64	0	28
17.	Nick Schultz	D	367	17	45	62	+25	138
18.	Darby Hendrickson	C	182	29	31	60	-31	100
19.	Willie Mitchell	D	288	9	48	57	28	333
20.	Andrei Zyuzin	D	188	19	36	55	-15	132
21.	Marc Chouinard	C	119	25	26	51	+5	51
22.	Kurtis Foster	D	115	13	38	51	-6	112
23.	Stephane Veilleux	LW	203	19	30	49	-16	153
24.	Stacy Roest	RW	134	17	31	48	0	28
25.	Cliff Ronning	C	80	17	31	48	-6	24
26.	Brent Burns	D	185	12	35	47	-1	70
27.	Aaron Gavey	C	146	16	25	41	-29	90
28.	Randy Robitaille	C	67	12	28	40	-5	54
29.	Mark Parrish	RW	76	19	20	39	+9	18
30.	Scott Pellerin	LW	58	11	28	39	+6	45
31.	Brad Bombardir	D	212	3	33	36	-7	93
32.	Sergei Krivokrasov	RW	63	8	16	24	-2	37
33.	Branko Radivojevic	LW	82	11	13	24	-9	21
34.	Matt Johnson	LW	227	15	7	22	-23	698
35.	Kim Johnsson	D	76	3	19	22	-4	64
36.	Jason Marshall	RW	137	7	15	22	-5	235
37.	Martin Skoula	D	98	1	20	21	+9	46
38.	Petteri Nummelin	D	51	3	17	20	-15	22
39.	Daniel Tjarnqvist	D	60	3	15	18	-11	32
40.	Jason Wiemer	C	62	7	11	18	-6	106
41.	Keith Carney	D	80	4	13	17	+22	58
42.	Sean O'Donnell	D	63	4	12	16	-2	128
43.	Ladislav Benysek	D	159	3	12	15	-26	74
44.	Kyle Wanvig	RW	64	5	9	14	-10	87
45.	Cam Stewart	LW	54	4	9	13	-3	18
46.	Andy Sutton	D	79	5	8	13	-15	166
47.	Alex Henry	D	134	2	9	11	0	179
48.	Jeff Nielsen	RW	59	3	8	11	-16	4
49.	Jeremy Stevenson	LW	35	5	6	11	+5	71
50.	Maxim Sushinsky	RW	30	7	4	11	-7	29

WILD ALL-TIME ACCOLADES & AWARDS

JACK ADAMS TROPHY
(The NHL coach adjudged to have contributed the most to his team's success.)
Jacques Lemaire (2003)

FRANK J. SELKE TROPHY
(The NHL forward who demonstrates the most skill in the defensive component of the game.)
Wes Walz (2003 – finalist)

WILLIAM M. JENNINGS AWARD
(The NHL goaltender(s) having played a minimum of 25 games for the team with the fewest goals scored against it.)
Niklas Backstrom and Manny Fernandez (2007)

MBNA ROGER CROZIER SAVING GRACE AWARD
(The goaltender having played a minimum of 25 games with the NHL's best save percentage)
Dwayne Roloson (2004)
Niklas Backstrom (2007)

NHL ALL-STARS
Marian Gaborik (2003)
Filip Kuba (2004)
Dwayne Roloson (2004)
Brian Rolston (2007)

NHL ALL-STAR AWARDS
Marian Gaborik (2003 – Fastest Skater)
Marian Gaborik (2003 – Second Star)

NHL YOUNG-STARS
Marian Gaborik (2002)
Nick Schultz (2003)
Pierre-Marc Bouchard (2004)

OLYMPIANS
Marian Gaborik; Slovakia, (2006)
Mikko Koivu; Finland, (2006 – silver)
Filip Kuba; Czech Republic, (2006 – bronze)
Brian Rolston; USA, (2006)
Daniel Tjarnqvist; Sweden, (2006 – gold)

NHL THREE STARS OF THE WEEK / PLAYERS OF THE WEEK
Marian Gaborik (week of March 4, 2002)
Marian Gaborik (week of October 21, 2002)
Dwayne Roloson (week of December 15, 2003)
Manny Fernandez (week of December 26, 2005)
Niklas Backstrom (First Star – week of February 19, 2007)

YEAR BY YEAR RESULTS

SEASON	RECORD	PTS	DIV/CONF RANK	ATTENDANCE	FINISH
2000-01	25-39-18	68	5th/14th	751,472	Out of Playoffs
2001-02	26-35-21	73	5th/12th	756,596	Out of Playoffs
2002-03	42-29-11	95	3rd/6th	758,536	Western Conference Finals
2003-04	30-29-23	83	5th/10th	759,776	Out of Playoffs
2004-05	*NHL Season Cancelled Due to Lock-Out*				
2005-06	38-36-8	84	5th/11th	761,614	Out of Playoffs
2006-07	48-26-8	104	2nd/7th	760,280	Western Conference Quarterfinals

YEAR BY YEAR OFFENSIVE LEADERS

SEASON	GOALS LEADER	ASSISTS LEADER	POINTS LEADER	PIM LEADER
2000-01	M. Gaborik, W. Walz & D. Hendrickson, 18	L. Sekeras, 23	M. Gaborik, 36	M. Johnson, 137
2001-02	M. Gaborik, 30	A. Brunette, 48	A. Brunette, 69	M. Johnson, 183
2002-03	M. Gaborik, 30	M. Gaborik, 35	M. Gaborik, 65	M. Johnson, 201
2003-04	A. Daigle, 20	A. Daigle, 31	A. Daigle, 51	M. Johnson, 177
2004-05	*NHL Season Cancelled Due to Lock-Out*			
2005-06	M. Gaborik, 38	B. Rolston, 45	B. Rolston, 79	D. Boogaard, 158
2006-07	B. Rolston, 31	P. Demitra, 39	P. Demitra, B. Rolston, 64	D. Boogaard, 120

Source: Wild Media Guides

GAMES
1. Wes Walz 427
2. Marian Gaborik 408
3. Nick Schultz 367
4. Filip Kuba 357
5. Pascal Dupuis 334
6. Antti Laaksonen 323
7. Willie Mitchell 288
8. Jim Dowd 283
9. Pierre-Marc Bouchard 273
10. Andrew Brunette 245

GOALS
1. Marian Gaborik 164
2. Wes Walz 81
3. Pascal Dupuis 67
4. Brian Rolston 65
5. Antti Laaksonen 55
6. Andrew Brunette 54
7. Sergei Zholtok 48
   Pierre-Marc Bouchard 48
9. Richard Park 37
10. Filip Kuba 33

ASSISTS
1. Marian Gaborik 167
2. Pierre-Marc Bouchard 110
   Andrew Brunette 110
4. Filip Kuba 99
5. Wes Walz 97
6. Jim Dowd 89
7. Brian Rolston 78
8. Pascal Dupuis 74
9. Antti Laaksonen 63
10. Sergei Zholtok 62

POINTS
1. Marian Gaborik 331
2. Wes Walz 178
3. Andrew Brunette 164
4. Pierre-Marc Bouchard 158
5. Brian Rolston 143
6. Pascal Dupuis 141
7. Filip Kuba 132
8. Jim Dowd 121
9. Antti Laaksonen 118
10. Sergei Zholtok 110

PLUS/MINUS
1. Marian Gaborik +34
2. Willie Mitchell +28
3. Nick Schultz +25
4. Keith Carney +22
5. Brian Rolston +20
6. Wes Walz +18
7. Pierre-Marc Bouchard +10
8. Martin Skoula +9
   Mark Parrish +9
10. Todd White +7

PENALTY MINUTES
1. Matt Johnson 698
2. Willie Mitchell 333
3. Derek Boogaard 278
4. Brad Brown 267
5. Wes Walz 266
6. Sylvain Blouin 251
7. Marian Gaborik 236
8. Jason Marshall 235
9. Jim Dowd 203
10. Alex Henry 179

POWER-PLAY GOALS
1. Marian Gaborik 46
2. Brian Rolston 28
3. Andrew Brunette 26
4. Pierre-Marc Bouchard 19
5. Pascal Dupuis 18
6. Sergei Zholtok 16
7. Filip Kuba 14
8. Mikko Koivu 12
9. Todd White 11
10. Two Players Tied 10

POWER-PLAY ASSISTS
1. Marian Gaborik 68
2. Pierre-Marc Bouchard 54
   Andrew Brunette 49
4. Filip Kuba 38
   Brian Rolston 38
6. Jim Dowd 36
7. Kurtis Foster 25
8. Alexandre Daigle 22
   Sergei Zholtok 22
10. Lubomir Sekeras 21

POWER-PLAY POINTS
1. Marian Gaborik 114
2. Andrew Brunette 75
3. Pierre-Marc Bouchard 73
4. Brian Rolston 66
5. Filip Kuba 52
6. Jim Dowd 46
7. Sergei Zholtok 38
8. Pascal Dupuis 36
9. Kurtis Foster 31
10. Two Players Tied

SHORTHANDED GOALS
1. Wes Walz 14
2. Brian Rolston 6
   Antti Laaksonen 5
4. Marian Gaborik 4
   Pascal Dupuis 4
   Stacy Roest 4
   Filip Kuba 4
8. Marc Chouinard 3
   Darby Hendrickson 3
   Richard Park 3

SHORT-HANDED ASSISTS
1. Wes Walz 7
2. Antti Laaksonen 5
3. Pascal Dupuis 4
4. Andrei Zyuzin 3
   Filip Kuba 3
   Willie Mitchell 3
   Darby Hendrickson 3
8. Eight Players Tied 2

SHORT-HANDED POINTS
1. Wes Walz 21
2. Antti Laaksonen 10
3. Pascal Dupuis 8
4. Brian Rolston 7
   Filip Kuba 7
6. Darby Hendrickson 6
   Marian Gaborik 6
8. Willie Mitchell 4
   Stacy Roest 4
   Richard Park 4

WILD GOALTENDER CAREER STATS

GOALTENDER	GP	MINS	GAA	W	L	OT	SO	GA	SV	SV%
Manny Fernandez	260	14,902	2.47	113	102	8	12	614	6,488	.914
Dwayne Roloson	167	9,659	2.28	62	71	27	15	367	4,181	.919
Niklas Backstrom	41	2,227	1.97	23	8	6	5	73	955	.929
Jamie McLennan	38	2,230	2.64	5	23	9	2	98	934	.905
Josh Harding	10	546	1.65	5	3	1	2	15	242	.942

GAME-WINNING GOALS
1. Marian Gaborik 33
2. Wes Walz 15
3. Brian Rolston 13
4. Filip Kuba 9
5. Pascal Dupuis 7
   Antti Laaksonen 7
   Andrew Brunette 7
   Sergei Zholtok 7
   Pierre-Marc Bouchard 7
10. Richard Park 6

OVERTIME GOALS
1. Wes Walz 2
   Brent Burns 2
   Antti Laaksonen 2
   Richard Park 2
4. 13 Players Tied 1

SHOTS ON GOAL
1. Marian Gaborik 1,348
2. Pascal Dupuis 729
3. Wes Walz 638
4. Brian Rolston 598
5. Filip Kuba 554
6. Antti Laaksonen 439
7. Sergei Zholtok 414
8. Richard Park 406
9. Pierre-Marc Bouchard 404
10. Jim Dowd 322

MULTI-POINT GAMES
1. Marian Gaborik 87
2. Brian Rolston 36
3. Andrew Brunette 35
4. Wes Walz 33
5. Pierre-Marc Bouchard 30
6. Pascal Dupuis 22
7. Jim Dowd 21
8. Pavol Demitra 20
   Sergei Zholtok 20
9. Four Players Tied 17

TIME ON ICE/TOTAL
1. Filip Kuba 8,537:53
2. Marian Gaborik 7,142:26
3. Nick Schultz 6,905:04
4. Wes Walz 6,872:51
5. Willie Mitchell 6,209:35
6. Pascal Dupuis 5,375:54
7. Antti Laaksonen 5,228:19
8. Brad Bombardir 4,443:20
9. Lubomir Sekeras 4,390:05
10. Jim Dowd 4,283:26

TIME ON ICE/GAME
1. Filip Kuba 23:55
2. Kim Johnsson 23:33
3. Sean O'Donnell 23:00
4. Willie Mitchell 21:34
5. Lubomir Sekeras 21:00
6. Brad Bombardir 20:58
7. Brian Rolston 20:48
8. Pavol Demitra 20:39
9. Andrei Zyuzin 20:22
10. Martin Skoula 20:20

FACEOFF WIN %
1. Stacy Roest 56.2
2. Marc Chouinard 53.1
3. Jim Dowd 50.3
4. Mikko Koivu 49.6
5. Todd White 49.1
6. Pavol Demitra 47.8
7. Wes Walz 47.3
8. Cliff Ronning 47.0
9. Darby Hendrickson 46.8
10. Brian Rolston 46.0

89

THE FIGHTING SAINTS

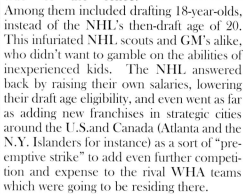

Maybe it was because they played during the North Stars' bleakest era. Or maybe it was because Glen Sonmor was somehow able to magically bring together a mix of pint-sized speedy, goal scorers, with a bunch of outcast prospects and goons who played with a reckless abandon. For whatever the reason, the Saints were one of the most colorful teams in Minnesota hockey history. And, although they only lasted for five years in downtown St. Paul, they managed to build a loyal grass-roots fan base that was second to none throughout the Twin Cities. Whether it was playing hard on the ice, or partying hard off of it, the fans fell in love with these guys and simply couldn't get enough of them. Here is their story:

The upstart World Hockey Association was conceived on September 13th, 1971, by two young California attorneys, Gary Davidson and Dennis Murphy, who had previously been involved with starting the now defunct American Basketball Association. Their vision was to create a rival major pro hockey league that would compete directly against the powerful NHL, something that hadn't happened in more than 50 years.

The league then recruited potential investors throughout the U.S. and Canada who were interested in purchasing franchises. A year later the WHA set up shop with 12 teams in two divisions, including: the New England Whalers, Cleveland Crusaders, New York Raiders, Quebec Nordiques, Ottawa Nationals and Philadelphia Blazers (all of the Eastern Division), as well as the Minnesota Fighting Saints, Winnipeg Jets, Chicago Cougars, Houston Aeros, Edmonton Oilers and Los Angeles Sharks (all of the Western Division).

On February 12, 1972, the WHA held its first draft. The owners of the new league, wanting quick returns on their $7 million franchise fee investments, went right after the NHL by attacking their deep rosters and farm teams. They knew that if they lured away a few big-name stars, to give themselves some instant credibility, and combined them with a bunch of other lesser-known younger players, they would have a decent product to sell to the fans. They began by paying existing NHL players more money to jump ship, and also did their best to sign away junior prospects, minor leaguers, and Europeans who were looking for opportunities to get more ice time.

At first, the NHL laughed at the new league, thinking it would dissolve much like the others that had come and gone through the years. But when the WHA's Winnipeg Jets signed Chicago Blackhawks superstar Bobby Hull to a multi-million dollar contract, the NHL quickly took notice. The NHL soon realized that these guys were for real, and knew that they had to do something to protect their interests. As a result, the NHL dug deep into its financial reserves and tried to tie-up a lot of its players' contracts, to prevent them from straying to the renegade league. The WHA then responded with a

Virginia's Legendary
Carlson Brothers:
Jack, Jeff and Steve (L-R)

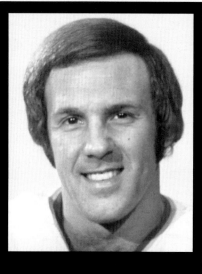

Gary Gambucci played for the
Gophers, Saints and North Stars

Mike "Shaky" Walton

variety of political ploys to attract players to their side of the fence. Among them included drafting 18-year-olds, instead of the NHL's then-draft age of 20. This infuriated NHL scouts and GM's alike, who didn't want to gamble on the abilities of inexperienced kids. The NHL answered back by raising their own salaries, lowering their draft age eligibility, and even went as far as adding new franchises in strategic cities around the U.S.and Canada (Atlanta and the N.Y. Islanders for instance) as a sort of "pre-emptive strike" to add even further competition and expense to the rival WHA teams which were going to be residing there.

The WHA also knew that they had to differentiate themselves from the other guys to win over the fans. One of the things that they did was to allow their players to use big banana curves on their hockey stick blades. While the NHL allowed just a 1/2 inch curve, the WHA allowed for a whopping 1 1/4 inches for its players to lift the puck into the arena's rafters. Another thing that they did was to use a different colored puck. Much like the old ABA used red, white and blue basketballs to separate themselves from the NBA, the WHA also wanted its own identity from the NHL. So, instead of using traditional black pucks, they decided to try a flaming red puck. But, because the paint quickly peeled off of it, they went to a color called "superpuck-blue." And, even though these proved to be soft and often bounced erratically on the ice, they became the instant trademark signature of a very different league.

Now, the genesis of the Minnesota Fighting Saints is an interesting one. When the new league was formed, they immediately considered Minnesota as one of its prime candidates to house a franchise. By the early 1970s the North Stars were struggling, and had been playing to half empty crowds at the Met Center. Several Twin Cities businessmen with ties to local hockey, including Lou Kaplan, Frank Marzitelli and Len Vannelli, realized that there was an opportunity for another team to come to town and give the North Stars a run for their money. They got together and successfully lobbied the city of St. Paul to transform the newly constructed Civic Center into the Saints' new home arena. The group was awarded a franchise in August of 1971, and immediately started to put together the pieces of their new organization.

Their first appointment was then Gopher hockey coach, Glen Sonmor, who was hired to serve as the team's first coach and GM. Next, they prepared for their team's inaugural draft. Now, the way it all worked back then, was that each team picked four "preferred players" to put on their wishlist so that the owners could determine which teams wanted which players. One of those players that the Saints picked was former

Warroad High School star, Henry Boucha. But, Boucha, fresh off of playing on the 1972 silver-medal winning U.S. Olympic team in Japan, opted instead to sign with the NHL's Detroit Red Wings. The first player they did manage to sign, however, was former Olympic goalie and International Falls native, Mike Curran. Their first NHLer was former North Star Wayne Connelly — then of the Vancouver Canucks. Other players from that inaugural draft included North Stars' legend Bill Goldsworthy, Montreal Canadiens forward Peter Mahovlich and Vancouver winger Dale Tallon. In addition, they brought in a bunch of local Minnesota boys, including Mike Antonovich, Keith "Huffer" Christiansen, Craig Falkman, Jack McCartan, Len Lillyholm, Dick Paradise and Bill Klatt.

It was a veritable gold mine for players, who, for the first time in their careers, now had a choice of where they could play. But some thought that it was too much too soon, and that ultimately these inexperienced players would dilute the game's talent pool to a lower level. One thing was for sure, the games were going to be rough, with plenty of fights and big hits to entertain the fans.

"From my Olympic team alone, there were eight players, some of average ability, who were offered lucrative contracts," said 1972 Olympic coach and former Gopher All-American Murray Williamson. "They were jumping quickly. Our goaltender, Mike Curran, left a $12,000 teaching job in Green Bay for a $35,000 contract with the Fighting Saints. Frank Sanders, Wally Olds, Jim McElmury, Dick McGlynn, Kevin Ahearn, Tim Sheehy, Craig Sarner, Bruce McIntosh, Tom Mellor and Henry Boucha, all fresh from the Olympic team, were looking at offers from both leagues. Perhaps one or two were ready for major pro hockey at that time."

Sonmor drafted a roster chock full of potential stars, unproven wannabe's, has-been's, maybe's, and in keeping with traditional Sonmor values — a bunch of tough guys who could really mix it up. All of whom were delighted to be playing pro hockey in the Twin Cities. They opened their training camp in Duluth that first year, and prepared for battle in the Western Division.

Wayne Connelly scored the first-ever Saints goal at the 13:04 mark of the first period in a 4-3 loss to the Winnipeg Jets on October, 13, 1972. They got their first-ever win against the Chicago Cougars on October 13th, when Mike Antonovich got the 3-2 game-winner late in the third. The Saints had their ups and downs that first year and went on to finish the season with a 38-37-3 record, good for just fifth place in the six-team division. The Saints provided some dramatics at the end of the year though, when they managed to squeeze into the playoffs by beating a tough Edmonton Oilers team in a sudden-death overtime thriller. And, although they lost in the first round of the playoffs to Winnipeg, four games to one, they had laid the foundation for a solid team. The fans came out to see them, and they proved that the Twin Cities could indeed support two pro

Warroad's Henry Boucha played with the Saints in 1976

Bill Butters played with the Gophers, Stars and Saints

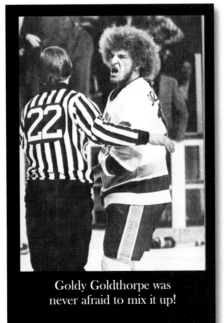
Goldy Goldthorpe was never afraid to mix it up!

hockey franchises.

One of the bright spots on the team that first season was the play of Wayne Connelly, who led the Saints in scoring with 40 goals and 30 assists for 70 points. But, the Saints scored only 250 points in 78 games that year, which ranked 11th among the 12 WHA teams. That was reason enough for Sonmor to make some changes. He needed to bring in some heavy artillery, and that's just what he did for the 1973-74 season.

After combing the countryside with new coaches Harry Neale and Jack McCartan, looking for new talent, Sonmor added seven new faces to the team that next year, including the likes of Mike "Shaky" Walton, Murray Heatley and Steve Cardwell, as well as goalie John Garrett. The new blood would pay big dividends for Sonmor's Saints, scoring a combined 132 goals and 195 assists. That new blood, plus a solid nucleus of veterans, helped to propel the Saints to a much improved 44-32-2 record, good for the second best record in the WHA and a trip to the playoffs.

There, the team went on to beat Edmonton four games to one in the first round of the playoffs, and then went on to face the Houston Aeros in the second round. The Aeros were led by none other than Gordie Howe, who had come out of his two-year retirement that year to join his two teen-aged sons, Mark and Marty, to form the famed "Howe-Line." Gordie, now in his 40s, still managed to score 100 points that season. The Aeros proved to be too much for the young Saints and went on to beat them, four games to two, in the best-of-seven series.

Although they lost that disappointing series to Houston, it was still a much improved year overall for the Saints. Walton, a former 50-goal scorer with the Boston Bruins, proved to be the team's best acquisition. By season's end the speedy winger had tallied 57 goals and 117 points, both tops in the league. At one point during the season, he went on a tear, scoring in a league record 16 straight games — including a stretch where he tallied 11 goals over three consecutive nights against Los Angeles, New England and Winnipeg.

Gord Gallant proved to be another major contributor. After coming to Minnesota from Cleveland, the tough defender, who played on a line with Mike Walton and Jim Johnson, wound up leading the league in penalty minutes with 223. Wayne Connelly also played big for the Saints, scoring 42 goals and 53 assists for 95 points. One of the biggest highlights from that season included George Morrison's amazing 43-second pure hat trick in a game against Vancouver. The offense was so good that it even set a league mark with 332 goals.

Another trademark of Sonmor's teams was tough defense, and that year's squad was no exception as John Arbour, Rick Smith, Mike McMahon, Terry Ball, Dick Paradise, Bob Boyd and Ron Busniuk patrolled the blue line with authority. In addition, the goaltending was solid. While Mike Curran and Jack McCartan shared the netminding duties during the first season, John Garrett was added to the mix in 1974. Both Curran and Garret played great all year. In addition, Sonmor moved over to serve as the GM that next year, leaving Harry Neale as the team's coach for year two. The team would start off well that next season with the new players coming together and gelling. At one point midway through the season, Curran reeled off a fabulous record of 13-1-1, while Garrett posted eight consecutive wins at the end of the season and into the playoffs.

Most importantly though for the Saints that year, was the fact that the fans came out in droves to support them. Averaging better than 6,500 for the season, the Saints averaged more than 9,000 during the playoffs against Houston. So popular was the team that during one playoff game, some 17,211 Saints fans piled into the Civic Center to root them on. Not only was it a WHA attendance record, at the time it was also the largest crowd ever to watch a hockey game in Minnesota. Another high-light from that 1974 season occurred that winter at the Civic Center, when the WHA's All-Star Game was played before a sell-out crowd. There, in front of his home fans, Saints winger Mike Walton earned the game's MVP award.

Ever the perfectionist, that next year Sonmor was at it again, tinkering with his line-up card to the extent of bringing in yet another dozen players to enhance his club's roster. Among them included: for-wards Fran Huck, Gary Gambucci, Don Tannahill and Danny O'Shea, two-way defenseman Ron Busniuk, as well as tough guy's Bill "Goldy" Goldthorpe and Curt Brackenbury. Perhaps his most interesting signings that year, however, were the brother's trio of Jack, Jeff and Steve Carlson, as well as Dave Hanson — who were then play-ing for the Johnstown Jets of the NAHL. Now, for those of you who don't quite remem-ber, Jeff, Steve and Dave made up the original "Hanson Brothers" from the classic movie "Slapshot." They would truly put the "fight-ing" in Fighting Saints. Jack was supposed to be in the movie, but got called up to play with Edmonton, leaing Dave Hanson to take his place on the set.

Former Gopher Bill Butters was also brought in, adding another solid defensive presence to the team. The Saints would play well that year and finish their 1974-75 cam-paign with a very respectable 42-33-3 record. From there, they went on to first beat New England in the first round of the playoffs. The highlight of that series came on April 11, when a 32-minute melee broke out early in the sec-ond period. Fans who sat through the almost four hour game (setting eight WHA records for penalty minutes) were blown away when Jack Carlson pounded on Whaler's tough guy Nick Fotiu, who was considered the undisput-ed champion of the league at the time. The

PAUL HOLMGREN

Former St. Paul Harding High School and Gopher star Paul Holmgren played with the WHA's Fighting Saints and North Stars before joining the Philadelphia Flyers. He is also one of the few Americans to have ever coached in the NHL, having led both the Philadelphia Flyers and the Hartford Whalers during the late 1980s and early '90s. One of the toughest men ever to lace em' up, Holmgren played more than 10 years in the NHL. He is currently the GM of the Flyers.

NATIVE MINNESOTAN SAINTS

Mike Antonovich	Calumet
Bill Butters	St. Paul
Henry Boucha	Warroad
Jack Carlson	Virginia
Jeff Carlson	Virginia
Steve Carlson	Virginia
Mike Curran	Int. Falls
Craig Falkman	St. Paul
Gary Gambucci	Eveleth
Paul Holmgren	St. Paul
Billy Klatt	Minneapolis
Len Lillyholm	Minneapolis
Jack McCartan	St. Paul
Dick Paradise	St. Paul
Frank Sanders	St. Paul
Craig Sarner	St. Paul
Pat Westrum	Minneapolis

Mike Antonovich

brawl swung the momen-tum for the Saints as they advanced on to the next round of the playoffs. There, unfortunately, they wound up losing a seven-game heart-break-er to the Quebec Nordiques to end the season. It would be the closest the club would ever get to sipping from the league's champi-onship trophy, the Avco Cup.

Several star players joined the Saints in 1975-76, including former Gopher Paul Holmgren, Hall of Famer Dave Keon, John McKenzie and even Henry Boucha. The team's future appeared to be as bright as ever that year, but unfortunate-ly, and unexpectedly, the economics of the game finally caught up to the club. Poor attendance and rising salaries all con-tributed to the fact that in February of 1976, after playing only 59 of 81 scheduled games, the ownership group was forced to file bankruptcy and terminate the team. A stunned Saints faithful was left in a state of shock. The team had a 30-25-4 record going up to that point that season, and was really caught off guard when the news was announced.

The pity-party was short lived though. That's because just a few months later, (WHA) Cleveland Crusader's owner, Nick Mileti, who also owned the Cleveland Indians and Cavaliers, of MLB and the NBA, decided to move his struggling WHA franchise to downtown St. Paul, where it would be transformed into the "New" Fighting Saints. The new team would replace the team's old blue and gold sweaters with scarlet, white, and gold sweaters — giving the franchise a new make-over. Mileti then installed Robert Brown as the team's new pres-ident and also rehired Glen Sonmor as his coach and GM. To get the fans back, Sonmor immediately brought back some of the old Saints favorites, including Dave Keon and Mike Antonovich. With that, the second incarna-tion of the Saints had officially begun.

Having moved over to the Eastern Division, the Saints started out the first half of the year on a good note by posting a respectable 19-18-5 record. But, in January of 1977, after just 42 games, the team announced that it was folding, leaving all of its players as homeless free agents. Yes, the Saints had been killed yet again, this time due to slumping ticket sales — or so they would say. For whatever reason, it was a sad ending to an otherwise wonderful story. (Ironically, the Crusaders were the first of two Cleveland hockey teams that would ulti-mately move to Minnesota, as the Cleveland Barons made the trek north just a year later to merge with the fledgling North Stars.)

The WHA lasted just two more sea-sons after that, ultimately following the Saints into early retirement in 1979. While the

Mike Curran

Pat Westrum

WHA had won many of the battles along the way, in the end it had appeared that the NHL won the war. Before going away for good, however, the WHA had some "conditions" that had to be met before they signed a final settlement treaty. Now, much like the American Football League and the American Basketball Association before them, the WHA also wanted to become a successful "second" league that was every bit as good as its big brother predecessor. And, ultimately, much like the AFL merged with the NFL, and several ABA franchises merged with the NBA; in the end a victory of sorts was declared for the WHA, as four of its franchises were merged into the NHL: the Hartford Whalers (now the Carolina Hurricanes), Quebec Nordiques (now the Colorado Avalanche), Winnipeg Jets (now the Phoenix Coyotes), and the Edmonton Oilers — who were led by a young kid by the name of Wayne Gretzky.

When it was all said and done, there were 32 teams that played in 24 cities during the WHA's tumultuous seven-year tenure, with New England, Winnipeg, Houston and Quebec each taking turns holding the championship Avco Cup. The WHA proved itself in the end, by showing that a rival league could produce top-level players and break the "anti-trust" mentality of its bully big brother. It became a safe-haven for many Hall of Famers who wanted to extend their careers, as well as a showcase for countless European players who wanted an opportunity to showcase their talents and get a job in North America. In the end, many of the kids who were given a chance to prove themselves as teen-agers in the WHA, went on to become the stars of the NHL in the 1980s. Perhaps, and most importantly though, was the fact that the WHA became a portal of sorts for American hockey players everywhere who wanted to advance their careers as professionals. As a result, the WHA proved to be a sanctuary for American talent in the Canadian-dominated NHL, which also translated into countless more opportunities for Minnesota kids to play pro hockey. The WHA changed the rules of the game forever, and in the process, brought a lot of joy to countless hockey fans everywhere. The Saints will forever be remembered as a wonderful side-bar in our rich hockey history. As they saying went, "The Fighting Saints...", boy were they ever.

THE MINNESOTA MOOSE

Early in 1994, Minnesota rejoined the long-running International Hockey League (the Millers and Saints played in the IHL back in the early 1960s), when the expansion Minnesota Moose, led by businessmen Kevin MacLean and Roger Sturgeon, hit the ice at the Civic Center. The group named Coleraine native Frank Serratore as their coach and director of hockey operations, while Glen Sonmor was named director of player development. The team, which competed in the Midwest Division of the Western Conference (along with Atlanta, Houston, Kansas City and Milwaukee), featured Dave Snuggerud and John Young as its first two stars.

The team got off to a shaky start, losing its first regular season game on the road to Denver by the final of 4-1. Blair Atcheynum notched the team's first-ever goal in the loss. The Moose rebounded a few nights later, when, on October 16, 1994, thanks to Stephane Morin's game-winning goal, they notched their first win in a 6-1 victory at Chicago. After losing their home-opener to Milwaukee, they finally got their first home-win on November 15th, when they beat the Chicago Wolves, 4-3. The team was a big hit with the fans, who immediately started to buy up all of the Minnesota Moose paraphernalia they could get their hands on. Within a short period of time, the team's logo became so hot that it led all of minor league hockey in merchandise sales.

With the North Stars gone to Dallas, the community was eager to rally behind a new club. Soon their games were being carried on MSC-TV, and near-capacity crowds were showing up at the arena to support their new team. The club was up and down throughout that first year, but one of its first highlights came on January 18th, 1995, when winger Stephane Morin garnered three assists for the Western squad in the IHL's annual All Star Game. After winning their final home game against Las Vegas, the Moose, led by the league's leading scorer, Stephane Morin, finished their inaugural 1994-95 season with a 34-35-12 record. With their fourth-place record in the division, the team clinched a spot in the Turner Cup playoffs. There, the Moose were swept by the eventual champion Denver Grizzlies, despite losing a heart-breaking Game Three at the Target Center by the final of 4-2.

That next season the team signed a working agreement with the Winnipeg Jets to become an affiliate "minor league" team. And, after finishing the 1995-96 season in the divisional cellar, with a 30-45-7 record, and out of the playoffs, Winnipeg soon became the team's permanent address. That's because following that season the team decided to move to Winnipeg, where they became the Winnipeg Moose. It was widely speculated at the time that there was going to be a "swap" of sorts, with the NHL's Winnipeg Jets coming to Minnesota, and the Moose going there. But, in the final hour the whole thing was botched, and the Jets wound up going to Phoenix instead, to become the Coyotes. Meanwhile, Minnesota would be left with no pro team until the Wild would arrive in 2000.

In addition to Snuggerud, some of the other players with a Minnesota connection over the team's two year stint here included: Scott Bell, John Brill, Dave Christian, Parris Duffus, Tod Hartje, Chris Imes, Reed Larson, Kris Miller, Larry Olimb, Mark Osiecki, Frank Pietrangelo, Gordie Roberts and Brett Strot.

Frank Serratore would go on to coach at the Air Force Academy following his stint with the Moose

THE MINNESOTA GOPHERS

While it appears that Johns Hopkins University of Baltimore may have been the first college in the United States to "officially" play the sport of ice hockey, back on December 26, 1894, that honor can certainly be disputed with the University of Minnesota. You see, the Gophers had "officially" begun playing the sport just a month later, in January of 1895, but the game had been played on campus "unofficially" for several years prior.

The first University of Minnesota team, unsanctioned by the college, was organized by Dr. H. A. Parkyn, a quarterback on the Gopher football team, who had learned the game in Toronto. Parkyn coached the U of M team, comprised mainly of kids who were experienced ice polo players. These games would serve as a warm-up for an upcoming contest against one of Canada's best teams of that era, the Winnipeg Victorias. A big reason why the Gophers were able to schedule a game with the Manitoba team was because at that time, there was no railroad connection between Eastern and Western Canada. So, the Victorias, who had to ride the rails through the Twin Cities on their way out to play Ontario and Quebec, decided to schedule a tune-up match along the way. On February 18, 1895, the Gophers beat the Victoria's by the score of 11-3. The game was played at Minneapolis' Athletic Park, which was located at Sixth Street and First Avenue North (the present sight of the Butler Square Building, next to the Target Center). The park was also the home of the professional Minneapolis Millers Baseball Club, before they moved to Nicollet Park.

This article describing the gala event appeared in the Minnesota Ariel on February 16, 1895: *"The University of Minnesota hockey team will play a game for the championship of Minneapolis against the Minneapolis Hockey Club at their rink, at the corner of Fourth Avenue and Eleventh Street South. The game is preparatory to the game to be played Monday afternoon by Winnipeg and the University of Minnesota. Winnipeg is champion of the world. *(Incidentally, this statement was incorrect: Winnipeg did not win the Stanley Cup until the following year, in 1896.) Winnipeg has returned from a rough trip through eastern Canada and was defeated without too much trouble: Montreal, Toronto, Victoria, Ottawa, Quebec, and the Limestones. The University started practice two or three weeks ago and played against a Minneapolis team, being defeated 4-1. A week and one half ago they defeated the same team, 6-4. Tonight they play the tie off for the championship. Dr. H.A. Parkyn has been coaching the boys every afternoon. He has a couple of stars in Willis Walker and Russel. Walker plays point and Russel coverpoint, with Van Campen in goal. Parkyn and Albert are center forwards. Dr. Parkyn's long experience with the Victoria team of Toronto, one of the best, makes him a fine player. Thompsen and Head, the other two forwards, are old ice polo players and skate fast and pass well. Van Campen, quarterback on last year's football team, plays goal well. Many tickets have been sold for tonight's and also Monday's game. Tickets are 25¢, ladies come free. The excitement of these games is intense, and surpasses that at a football game."*

Three days later, on February 19, 1895, this article ran in the St. Paul

The old barn

Pioneer Press: *"The first international hockey game between Winnipeg and the University of Minnesota was played yesterday, and won by the visitors, 11-3. The day was perfect and 300 spectators occupied the grandstand; co-eds of the University being well represented. Features of the game was the team play of the Canadians, and individual play of Parkyn, Walker, and Head for the University. Hockey promises to become as popular a sport at the University as football, baseball, and rowing."*

From those humble beginnings, the University of Minnesota's fabled hockey program got its start. The game continued to grow in the coming years, with more and more kids wanting to get involved. The first attempt to organize varsity ice hockey on the U of M campus took place in November of 1900, when a committee composed of George Northrop, Paul Joslyn, and A.R. Gibbons was appointed to draw up a constitution for the club and look into other problems concerning playing the game at the school. A committee conferred with the Athletic Board and decided not to flood Northrop Field, and instead to play at Como Lake in St. Paul. No scheduled games were played during the 1900-1901 season, and it was not until late in 1903 that the U of M played any games on a formal basis. Only two contests were played that season, both resulting in wins for the Gophers. Minneapolis Central High School was defeated, 4-0, and the St. Paul Virginias, 4-3. Team members were: John S. Abbott, Frank Teasdale, Gordon Wood, Fred Elston, Frank Cutter, R.S. Blitz, W.A. Ross, Arthur Toplin and captain Thayer Bros.

The 1903 season proved to be the last for ice hockey on a formal varsity-sport basis at the U of M until 1920, nearly two decades later. In 1910 unsuccessful efforts were made to revive the sport and even to persuade several other midwestern universities to form a Big Ten Conference for hockey.

In January of 1914, the school's Board of Control finally voted to outfit a hockey team. The next year a series of unofficial "pick-up" games were played against Minneapolis and St. Paul high schools, St. Thomas College, and even some of the school's fraternity teams. Many of the games were played outdoors at Northrop Field with the finals and playoffs often being played at the indoor "Hippodrome" on the state fairgrounds in St. Paul. This continued for the next several years with more and more intramural teams becoming involved, including women's hockey teams as well — many of which were coached by the frat boys.

Under the direction of St. Paul's Beaupre Eldridge, a student at the time, the Gophers finally became an official varsity sport just after WWI, in 1920. One of the team's biggest games that year came against St. Thomas (then considered as the state's collegiate champions), which they beat by the final of 3-1 in a game played at St. Paul's Coliseum Rink (which was located on Lexington Avenue near University Avenue). While the team beat Hamline that year as well, most of its games were canceled due to warm weather. Many of the other large university's around the midwest were also organizing teams by this point, making it possible for the Gophers to travel to other schools for more competition.

The 1921-22 team, under new

The 1933 Gopher National AAU Champs

coach I.D. MacDonald and captain Chet Bros, defeated Wisconsin, Luther Seminary, Hamline and Michigan Mines, while losing only to Hamline and Michigan Mines (twice), en route to an overall record of 7-3. The next year, Emil Iverson, an exhibition skater and skating instructor from Denmark, took over as the Gophers' new skipper and led the team to a 10-1-1 record. That next year, behind captain Frank Pond and goalie Fred Schade, Iverson led the team to an impressive 13-1-0 record, and in so doing, the Gophers were declared as the National Champions. One of their biggest rivals that year was Marquette University, which was incidentally coached by Iverson's brother, Kay.

In 1925 the Gophers moved into the newly constructed Minneapolis Arena, complete with artificial ice, where they brought the "U" no less than a share of top national honors for six consecutive seasons. From 1923-1929, Iverson's teams compiled a tremendous record of 75-10-11, with Chuck McCabe, Joe Brown and John Peterson each earning All-American honors. Iverson left the program in 1930 (he would later coach the NHL's Chicago Blackhawks), the same year his 11-2-1 club shared the national title with Yale. Among the Gophers' competition during the 1920s included: Michigan Mines, Michigan, Marquette, Notre Dame, Hibbing, Eveleth Junior College, North Dakota, North Dakota Aggies, St. Thomas, Hamline, Luther Seminary, Ramsey Technical School, Manitoba, Dallas A.C. and Tulsa A.C.

A large number of Gopher players during the '20s came from Minneapolis, with a few from St. Paul, Duluth and the Iron Range mixed in. Among the stars of this era included: Chuck McCabe, Joe Brown, Osborne Billings, Frank Pond, John H. Peterson, Cliff Thompson, Ed Owen, W.B. Eldredge, Chet, Ken and Ben Bros, Don Bagley, Reuben Gustafson, Fred Schade, Walt Youngbauer, Vic Mann, Ed Olson, Phil Scott, Jack and Bill Conway, Lloyd Russ, Herb Bartholdi, Leland Watson and H.J. Kuhlman.

Former team captain Frank Pond took over the program in 1930. The Two Harbors native iced very strong nationally ranked teams during his five-year tenure, ultimately finishing in 1935 with an impressive 46-21-4 record. The 1932 team, led by future Gopher athletic director Marsh Ryman, became the first Minnesota team to play a team from the East Coast, when they lost to a formidable Harvard team, 7-6 in Boston. As a result, the Gophers would finish ranked No. 2 in the country (according to the Tonelle system of rating), to those same Crimson. The Maroon and Gold were led that year by a group of kids from Eveleth (Alex MacInnes, Andy Toth, Ben Constantine and John Suomi), a pair from Duluth (Gordon Schaeffer and George Todd), and the rest from Minneapolis (Howie Gibbs, Laurie Parker, Bucky Johnson, Phil La Batte, George Clausen, Harold Carlsen, Fred Gould and John Scanlon). The next year the Gophers, behind the "Pony Line" of Russ-Gray-Munns, pummeled Wisconsin, 14-1, at the Hippodrome. La Batte was later selected as a member of the 1936 U.S. Olympic team.

Former St. Paul Saints coach Larry Armstrong became the team's third coach when he took over the program in 1935. One of his first highlights came in 1937, when the Gophers, behind All-American goalie Bud Wilkinson, defeated the University of Manitoba for the first time in 11 seasons. The 1938-39 sextet finished second in the National AAU finals with a modest 15-6 record. They won their first two games, swamping the

Clyde Russ, Russell Gray & Bill Munns

Philadelphia Arrows, 10-1, edging the St. Nicholas Club, 3-2, and then losing in the finals to Cleveland Legion, 4-3. Had there been a 1940 U.S. Olympic team, several members of the Gopher roster would undoubtedly have been selected. That next year would be a special one for Gopher boosters, as the team posted an undefeated 18-0 record en route to winning the National Amateur Athletic Union of the U.S. (AAU) title. (At the time, that was considered the country's national championship since there was no NCAA tournament back then.) Before rolling over the New England All Stars (Amesbury), 9-4, and Connecticut's Brock Hall, 9-1, in playoffs, the Gophers took care of Michigan, Michigan Tech, Illinois, London (Ontario) and Yale. Led by John Mariucci, Babe Paulson, Frank St. Vincent, Hayden Pickering, Jim Magnus, Ken Cramp, Fred Junger, Dave Lampton, Al Eggleton, Norb Robertson and goalie Marty Falk, the team outscored their opponents 138 to just 25.

During the war years the Gophers schedule was curtailed as many colleges did not ice teams and the government discouraged travel. Minnesota scheduled a few college contests against Dartmouth, Michigan and Illinois, but the bulk of their schedule was against local amateur clubs such as Honeywell, Fort Snelling, Berman's and Wold Chamberlain. In addition, the team played against Canadian Junior teams from Winnipeg, Fort William and Port Arthur. Among the leading players during the war period were Bob Graiziger, Paul Wild, Bill Klatt, Bill Galligan, Bob Carley, Allan Van, Al Opsahl, Dick Kelley, Mac Thayer, Jack Behrendt, Pat Ryan, Don Nolander, Bob Arnold and Burton Joseph.

By the season of 1946-47, Armstrong's last, the Gophers had a nucleus of a strong team. Minnesota-bred players such as Bill Hodgins, Roland DePaul, Bob Harris, Jim Alley, Ken Austin, Al Opsahl, Dennis Rolle, Jerry Lindegard, Cal Englestad, Bill Klatt, Jerry Remole, Dick Roberts and Tom Karakas, were welcome additions to the club. Harris, Roberts, Austin, Alley, Lindegard and Englestad were among the first players form northwestern Minnesota to play for the Gophers. They were natives of such small communities as Warroad, Roseau and Hallock. Injuries and ineligibility dogged the team, but they managed to finish the 1946-47 campaign with a respectable 12-5-3 record. Armstrong held the Gopher coaching spot for 12 seasons, finishing with a 125-55-11 overall record.

White Bear Lake's Elwyn "Doc" Romnes, a St. Thomas grad and former Chicago Blackhawk star, took over for the 1947-48 season. One of the highlights of Romnes' tenure happened on February 17, 1950, when the Gophers defeated the Michigan State Spartans, 12-1, before a crowd of 3,734 in the inaugural game in the "new" Williams Arena. The facility, which had been constructed in 1928, was retrofitted with a wall that divided the arena into two ends — one end for basketball and the other for ice hockey. Finally, after playing like nomads for their first 31 years at places such as the St. Paul Auditorium, the Minneapolis Arena, and the Fairgrounds Hippodrome, the Gophers finally had a home of their own.

Romnes' best season came in 1951, when the Gophers started out slow but came back to win their last nine games to finish with a 14-12 record. The team's senior line of Rube Bjorkman, Gordon Watters and Cal Englestad led the offense, while Jim Sedin, Frank Larson and Tom Wegleitner were the team's leading

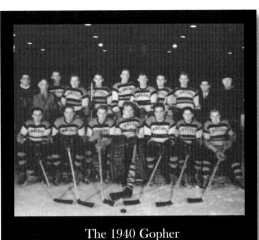

The 1940 Gopher
National AAU Championship Team

defensemen. The next year was the beginning of one of Minnesota's most glorious, the John Mayasich era. The kid from Eveleth, who would go on to become the greatest ever to wear the Maroon and Gold, was joined by a cast of all-stars that year including Dick Dougherty, Gene Campbell, Dick Meredith, Ken Yackel, Gordy Watters, Larry Ross and Jim Mattson, as well as the Duluth line of Bodin-Strom-Nyhus. Together they would finish the season with a 13-13 record, good enough for fifth in the newly formed Midwest Collegiate Hockey League. (The league, which was the first forerunner of the WCHA, included: Colorado College, Denver, Michigan, Michigan State, Michigan Tech, Minnesota and North Dakota.) In addition, Rube Bjorkman, Ken Yackel and Jim Sedin were members of the Silver Medal winning 1952 U.S. Olympic team.

In 1952-53 the Gopher program was blessed when one of its own came home to take over as the program's new head coach, Eveleth's John Mariucci, a former Gopher football and hockey star in the 1930s. Romnes, who finished with a modest 52-59 overall record with the team, would turn over the reins to Mariucci in order to pursue interests outside of hockey. Mariucci would go on to lead that 1953 squad to a 22-5-0 record and an WIHL conference title in his first season behind the bench. Soon record crowds were pouring into Williams Arena to see these kids. (In 1954 Minnesota led the nation in college attendance by attracting some 103,000 fans for 18 home games, compared to North Dakota, which was second with 54,000, and Michigan which had only 39,000.) From there, the Gophers just kept on going, all the way to the NCAA college hockey final four in Colorado Springs. In the first game the Gophers beat a tough Rennselaer Polytechnic Institute (RPI) team by the final score of 3-2, only to lose in the finals to rival Michigan, 7-3, in the title game to finish as the No. 2 team in the country.

Although Maroosh would never win the NCAA championship during his 14-year tenure at the U of M, he would come pretty darn close that next season with, arguably, the best line ever to play college hockey. When the 1953-54 collegiate hockey season started, the U of M was on a mission to avenge their NCAA Finals loss to Michigan and win it all that season. Despite losing their first two games that season, the Gophers got back on track and lost only one of their next dozen contests. After splitting with Michigan, Minnesota then swept Michigan State twice, Michigan Tech, North Dakota, and Denver, only to get beat twice by Michigan at season's end. The Gophers finished the year with a 24-6-1 record, the best in the nation, and won their second straight WIHL Conference crown.

Hockey fans were anticipating a rematch in the NCAA Finals in Colorado Springs between Minnesota and Michigan, but the Maroon and Gold had to first get by Boston College in the semifinals. Minnesota went on to pummel an out-manned BC club, 14-1, behind an amazing effort from the best

Lou Nanne

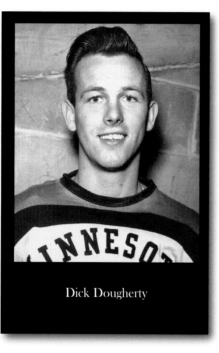

Dick Dougherty

Larry Ross

line in college hockey: John Mayasich scored three goals and added four assists, Dick Dougherty scored four goals and added two assists, while Gene Campbell added three goals and two assists. Then, to the Gophers' disappointment, they found out that the Michigan Wolverines had been knocked off by unheralded Rennselaer Polytechnic Institute (RPI) in the semifinals.

Minnesota was clearly favored to win it all (by five goals) in most spreads. The game with RPI got underway with the Gophers falling behind early. Down 3-0 in the second period, however, the Gophers rallied behind a Kenny Yackel blast, followed by a Dougherty one-timer from Campbell that made it 3-2. Then, after peppering the Engineer goalie, Mayasich put in a back-hander to even it up at three-apiece in the third. Four minutes later Mayasich set up Dougherty on a pretty "five-hole" goal to finally take the lead. But, at 16:10, the men from Troy, N.Y., evened things up to send the game into overtime.

Then, at 1:54 of the extra session, following a mix-up out in front of the net, RPI's Gordie Peterson grabbed a loose puck on the doorstep and promptly drilled it past Mattson to win the game by the final of 5-4. It was a huge upset. It was also a devastating blow to Mariucci, who wanted so badly to win the big one for Minnesota. After the game, the players huddled around their coach to shield him from the press and their cameras. It was the first and only time Minnesota hockey players would ever see this giant of a man shed a tear. Despite the loss, Yackel, Mattson, Dougherty, and Mayasich were each named to the All-American team.

"It's a loss that sticks with me still today," said Mayasich on the loss to R.P.I.. "To lose in overtime was bitter. It's not the ones you won that you remember, it's the ones you lost. To me, that was probably my biggest individual disappointment in all my years of hockey."

In 1956 Mariucci coached the U.S. Olympic team to a silver medal in Cortina, Italy, with several members of his team including: John Mayasich, Dick Meredith, Gene Campbell, Dick Dougherty, Wendell Anderson and Jack Petrosky.

In 1958 Mariucci flexed his muscles about an issue that was very important to him, the lack of Americans who were playing college hockey at that time. During this era of college hockey, there were no restrictions regarding the eligibility and recruiting of older, more experienced Canadian junior players. While Mariucci's rosters were made up predominantly of Minnesota kids, other schools in the league had recruited line-ups full of the top Canadian juniors who couldn't foresee making it in the six-team NHL, and thought it would be better to go to college rather than bounce around in the minors until they got called up. (Michigan even had a kid on its roster who had played briefly for the Toronto Maple Leafs!) This all came to an impasse during a series at Colorado College, when Minnesota got waxed by several teams who were comprised mostly of these players.

Mariucci took his frustrations out on whomever he felt was the main perpetrator, Denver coach Murray Armstrong, in what would evolve into one of the most bitter feuds in college hockey history. Other teams agreed and one by one, each team began to withdraw from the WIHL, ultimately forcing the league to fold in protest. The teams all cooled down and came back together a year later, this time as the WCHA, but with an understanding that things were going to be different. As a result, the NCAA tournament, which had always been held at the Broadmoor World Arena in Colorado Springs, was relocated to Minneapolis that next year — where Denver beat North Dakota, 6-2, in the championship game. It would be quite a few years before Mariucci would be comfortable playing Denver, however. When he was finally forced to do so a few years later at the NCAA tournament in 1961, he had Lou Nanne, a naturalized American citizen from Canada, hold up a sign in front of the press that read, "We fry Canadian bacon!"

Mariucci would coach at his alma mater until 1966, when he decided to take a position with the newly formed Minnesota North Stars of the NHL. He was replaced by longtime friend Glen Sonmor, a former teammate of his with the minor league Minneapolis Millers. Mariucci had amassed a 215-148-18 record during his tenure, capturing league titles in 1953 and 1954, while placing second in 1961 and 1966, and third in 1955, '64 and '65. Their best showing, following the upset loss to RIP in 1954, came in 1961, when they finished in third place at the NCAA Tournament. After losing to the hosts from Denver, 6-1, in the opener, they battled back to beat RPI, 4-3, to get some revenge and finish No. 3.

John Mayasich was the star of this era, not only leading the Gophers in scoring for four consecutive seasons (1952, '53, '54 and '55), but also the entire league as well. Upon graduating, Mayasich would be joined by Dick Meredith and goalie Jack McCartan as members of the 1960 gold medal winning U.S. Olympic team, while Herb Brooks, Dave Brooks, Gary Schmalzbauer and Jim Westby all played on the 1964 U.S. Olympic squad as well. During Mariucci's tenure, the following players were selected to the All-American team: John Mayasich (1953, '54, '55), Jim Mattson (1954), Ken Yackel (1954), Dick Dougherty (1954), Jack McCartan (1957, '58), Dick Burg (1958), Mike Pearson (1958), Murray Williamson (1959), Lou Nanne (1963), Craig Falkman (1964) and Doug Woog (1965).

Other highlights from this era included the success of former Gophers Herb Brooks, Larry Johnson, Ken Yackel, Murray Williamson, Bob Johnson, Lou Nanne and Doug Woog, all of whom continued on to brilliant coaching and managing careers after their playing days. In addition, Eveleth and St. Paul Johnson High Schools made quite an impression on the Gopher landscape during this era. Along with Herb Brooks, Johnson pro-

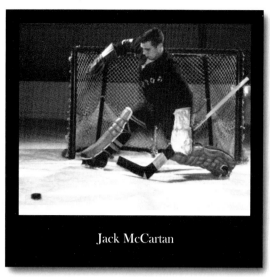
Jack McCartan

"Badger Bob" Johnson, Ken Yackel and Dick Meredith

Jim Mattson

duced nearly all of two famous lines: the "Buzz-Saw Line" of David Brooks, Len Lilyholm and Gary Schmalzbauer (Lilyholm was from Robbinsdale), and the Mike Crupi, Greg Hughes and Rob Shattuck trio. It is also interesting to note that in the four-year period of 1961-64, three of the scoring leaders, namely Norman, Constantine and Nystrom, were Eveleth products.

Meanwhile, Glen Sonmor, who at one time had been Mariucci's freshman coach, became the Gophers seventh mentor in 1966. With an overall record of 21-12, the Gophers captured the 1969-70 WCHA title that season, edging out Denver and Michigan Tech. Goalie Murray McLachlan and the pint-sized Mike Antonovich, from Greenway of Coleraine, led the way for the Maroon and Gold. In the finals of the WCHA playoffs, however, Michigan Tech snuck past the Gophers, 6-5, to dash any hopes that they had of going to the NCAA Tournament. In 1971 the Gophers, saddled with a losing regular season of 11-16-2, advanced to the NCAA finals at Syracuse before losing to Boston University, 4-2. In the semifinal game Minnesota edged Harvard, 6-5, in one of the most exciting over-time games in team history.

Frank Sanders, Mike Antonovich, Dennis Erickson, John Matschke, Wally Olds, Craig Sarner, Doug Peltier and Dean Blais were among the players who took a leading role in the surprising finish of the 1971 team. From the Sonmor era, Wally Olds (1970), Gary Gambucci (1968) and Murray McLachlan (1970) were chosen to the All-American team. In addition, Bill Klatt led the WCHA in scoring in 1968 with 23 goals and 20 assists in 31 games. Players from this era who played or coached for the U.S. during the Olympics included: Herb Brooks, Jack Dale, Craig Falkman, Len Lilyholm, Gary Gambucci, Tom McCoy, Lou Nanne, Larry Stordahl and Murray Williamson (in 1968); and Wally Olds, Bruce McIntosh, Frank Sanders, Craig Sarner, and Murray Williamson (in 1972).

Sonmor left the program early in the 1971-72 season to take over as the head coach of the upstart Minnesota Fighting Saints of the World Hockey Association. He was replaced by interim coach Ken Yackel, himself a former Gopher three-sport star in the 1950's. Sonmor posted a 79-82-6 record in his five-plus seasons with the team, and became a big-time fan favorite on campus.

Yackel was replaced at the beginning of that next season by another former Gopher, Herb Brooks. Brooks, who grew up in the hockey-happy East Side of St. Paul, came from a hockey conscious family. His father had been a well known amateur player in the 1920's and his brother, David, played for the Gophers in the early 1960s and also on the 1964 U.S. Olympic team. Brooks, who spent the better part of the 1960s playing on nearly every U.S. Olympic and National team, had recently coached at the junior level, as well as with the Gophers — as the program's freshman mentor under Sonmor.

Brooks took over the program, which had finished sixth in the WCHA the season before, and quickly turned things around. After a season of hard work and steady improvement, the team made history in 1973-74, when Brooks led them to their first ever NCAA hockey championship.

After starting 0-4-1, the Gophers put together a nine-game winning streak that included series sweeps of North Dakota, Michigan State, and St. Louis. Minnesota went on to win all but two of it's final 16 home games at Williams Arena. They finished with a 14-9-5 conference record, good for second place in the WCHA, behind Michigan Tech.

The Gophers went on to beat two tough Michigan and Denver teams in the WCHA playoffs, and suddenly they found themselves on their way to Boston, where they would face the top-ranked, hometown Terriers of Boston University in the NCAA final-four. The Cinderella Gophers felt right at home in the Boston Garden, as they proceeded to knock off BU in a nail-biter, 5-4, thanks to Mike Polich's shorthanded goal at 19:47 of the third period. In the finals, they then faced off against their old WCHA nemesis, Michigan Tech, for the title.

The Gophers went back and forth with the Huskies throughout the first period, until John Sheridan scored late to give the Maroon and Gold a one-goal lead. John Perpich then beat the Tech goaltender to make the score two-zip in the second. The Huskies came back though, scoring at 3:24 of the same period, to get within one. It remained that way until the third, when John Harris and then Pat Phippen both scored 12 minutes apart to put the Gophers up for good. The Huskies added another one with less than a minute to go, but it was too little, too late. With an impressive 39 shots-on-goal, the Gophers held on to win the title, 4-2. Brooks had hit the jackpot, and Minnesota had its first NCAA hockey crown.

Brooks had led the Gophers to a 22-12-6 overall record, becoming the first team in 25 years to win the title with a team comprised exclusively of American players. And, he did it with only two years' worth of talent that he had recruited. For his efforts, Brooks was named as the WCHA Coach of the Year. Team captain Brad Shelstad was chosen as the tournament's MVP, while Les Auge and Mike Polich were named to the All-Tournament team. Centers Mike Polich and John Harris led the team in scoring. (While Polich would go on to a successful career in the NHL, Harris would find success in another career path altogether and emerge as a star on the links, where he won the 1993 U.S. Amateur Golf Championship, became a perennial member of golf's Walker Cup team, and even went on to play on the PGA's Champions Tour at the age of 50.)

Moving from last place in the WCHA to first could not have been accomplished without unique leaders. "My first year, our two captains, Billy Butters and Jimmy Gambucci, were tremendous leaders who just did a great job of getting the program returned to a good, solid footing," said

Former Minnesota Governor
Wendell Anderson

Former Gopher Dean Blais hoists
the McNaughton Cup as the
Coach of the UND Fighting Sioux

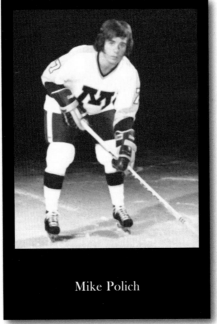

Mike Polich

Brooks. "It was tremendously gratifying getting the school's first championship coming from where we did. The players weren't in awe of anything, and they were extremely strong mentally, plus they could really compete. They played well on the road, they played against the odds and overcame a lot that season. That first title was very special to me."

After beating Harvard, 6-4, behind Warren Miller's hat trick, Michigan Tech got their revenge against Minnesota that next year, beating the Gophers, 6-1, in the NCAA Finals, which were held in St. Louis. Miller and defenseman Reed Larson were picked for the All-Tournament team. Herbie's boys rallied back in 1976 though, winning the WCHA with a 24-8-0 mark. The Gophers then opened the post-season by playing a classic against Michigan State in East Lansing. In that game the Gophers downed the Spartans, 7-6, in triple overtime behind goalie Jeff Tscherne's NCAA record 72 saves. From there, they advanced on to the NCAA Tournament in Denver, where they downed Boston University, 4-2, in the semifinals. Next up were the Huskies from Michigan Tech. This one started out ugly. Down 3-0, early, the Gophers rallied behind goals from Vannelli, Micheletti, Baker, Gorence, Phippen and Miller to win the title, 6-4. It was a thrilling end to an amazing season.

Minnesota's Tom Vannelli, who led the team in scoring that year with 69 points, was named as the tournament's MVP. After the big win Gopher forward Pat Phippen had this to say to the naysayers: "They called us shabby, they called us inconsistent, now they call us NCAA champions."

Three years later, in 1979, Brooks led his team back to the promised land yet again. The final series of that season featured a tough North Dakota team coming to town in what would prove to be a WCHA championship showdown. The Gophers took the opener, 5-2, but the Sioux rallied to take the title, in one of the best series ever witnessed at Williams Arena. In the playoffs, the Gophers went on to sweep both Michigan Tech and UM-Duluth at home. They then knocked off Bowling Green, winners of the CCHA, earning a trip to Detroit to compete in yet another NCAA tournament.

In the first game of the Final Four, led by Eric Strobel's hat trick, Minnesota held on to beat New Hampshire 4-3. It was now on to the finals, where the Gophers would meet their neighbors from North Dakota for all the marbles. Minnesota got out to an early lead on goals by Steve Christoff, John Meredith, and captain Bill Baker, to make it 3-1 after the first. The Sioux rallied in the second, narrowing the gap to 3-2. Then early in the final period, Neal Broten, the freshman sensation from Roseau, scored on a fabulous, sliding chip-shot in what would prove to be the game winner. UND added another goal late, but the incredible goaltending of Gopher senior netminder Steve Janaszak proved to be the difference as the Gophers held on to win, 4-3, and the right to be again called national champs.

GLEN SONMOR

One of the most colorful and popular figures in Minnesota sports history, Glen Sonmor is legend in the world of hockey. The Moose Jaw, Saskatchewan, native rose up through the ranks of the OHA, WCHJL and USHL to play three seasons in the AHL before making his NHL debut with the New York Rangers in 1953. Sonmor's professional hockey career started in 1949 with the Minneapolis Millers and ended with an eye injury in 1955 while playing for the Cleveland Barons. His old teammate with the Millers, John Mariucci, then made him his freshman coach with the Gophers and got him enrolled in classes at the U of M.

From there, Sonmor got into coaching. After a brief stint in the AHL, he spent the next six years teaching and coaching high school hockey in Hamilton, Ontario. Then, after coaching at Ohio State for one season, Sonmor accepted an invitation to become the head coach of the Gophers in 1969. He would waste little time in making a name for himself in Gold Country, leading the team to its first WCHA title in 16 years that season, earning WCHA Coach of the Year honors along the way. Sonmor led the Gophers to the national championship game the following season, where they were edged by Boston University, 4-2.

Sonmor would leave the team in 1971 with a career 78-80-6 record to take over as the head coach of the St. Paul Saints in the upstart World Hockey Association. He would later go on to take over as the head coach of the NHL's Minnesota North Stars in 1978, in what would be the first of three different stints with the team from 1978-87. He would lead the club to its first Stanley Cup appearance against the New York Islanders in 1981 as well.

Among his many honors, in 2001, Sonmor was named as one of the 50 most significant players and coaches in the history of Gopher hockey. In October of 2006, he was awarded the NHL's Lester Patrick Trophy for his outstanding service to U.S. hockey. Then, in 2007, the University bestowed him an honorary letter for his service to the school's hockey program. That same year he was inducted into the school's "M" Club Hall of Fame. Sonmor would go on to serve as a radio analyst for Gopher hockey games as well as a scout for the NHL's Minnesota Wild.

"I was so appreciative of John Mariucci," recalled Sonmor of his old friend. " He helped me get started in this business, he got me to go to school and get my degree, and he took me under his wing. We were teammates on the old Minneapolis Millers back in 1949 and he was just the best. I will never forget what he told me after that season, he said 'Glen, I have played pro hockey now for 10 years and nearly every one of my teammates was Canadian. You are the first one I have met who actually graduated from high school, so you are going to college, period!' So, he took me down to the University of Minnesota and got me enrolled. I was just a kid, but I listened and started going to summer school. Then, that changed my life later on when I lost my eye in 1955. I will never forget lying in a hospital in Pittsburgh scared to death. My wife and I had just had our first baby four days earlier and she was still in the hospital back in Cleveland. I didn't know what I was going to do. I knew that my playing career was over and was terrified. Just then, John Mariucci called me and said, 'hey kid, don't you worry about a thing, I have arranged for you to come to Minnesota where you can finish your degree and be my freshman coach for the Gophers.' Wow, it was like God had spoken to me."

"Then to come back to the University, that was just such a great time. John really almost adopted me because he was just so good to me and my family. A few years later when John left to go to the North Stars, he was the one who got me the head coaching job with the Gophers. I had been at Ohio State coaching and getting my masters degree, but was elated to come back to Minnesota. I have been here ever since. And do you know what? I graduated with high distinction, which is something I am very proud of. John went to all that work to get me in and I wasn't going to let him down. So I studied hard and worked my tail off. John and I were friends for so long and he was really a father figure to me as well as my best friend. I say even to this day that every kid in Minnesota who plays college hockey anywhere in this country should say a little prayer to John Mariucci, and thank him for all the work he did."

With 35 saves, Janaszak, fittingly, was voted as the tournament's MVP. Three other Gophers also made the all-tournament team, including freshman defenseman Mike Ramsey and forwards Steve Christoff and Eric Strobel. Additional honors would cascade down to a couple of other future Gopher legends as well. Bill Baker, who scored a then-single season record of 54 points by a defenseman, was selected as an All-American, and Broten was named WCHA Rookie-of-the-Year. Meanwhile, Steve Christoff and Don Micheletti led the team in scoring with 36 goals each. As a team, the Gophers rewrote the record books that season, scoring an amazing 239 goals in 44 games, while also recording the most wins in a season with 32.

"We were playing against a tremendous North Dakota team," recalled Brooks. "I think they had 13 guys who turned pro that next year. Broten scored a dramatic goal, sliding on his stomach and hitting a chip-shot over the goalie. It was incredible. I remember speaking at a Blue Line Club meeting the year before and saying that we were going to win it

Reed Larson

all that next season. It leaked out in the press and went across the country, putting a lot of pressure on our team. I kind of wish I wouldn't have said it now. But I just felt real strong about that team. I put a lot of pressure on those kids and I really raised the bar. But, because of their mental toughness and talent, we won the championship."

"I remember playing at the old Olympia Arena in Detroit," added Broten. "Just being in there and thinking about Gordie Howe and all those old Red Wings teams that had played there was really neat. North Dakota was our biggest rival back then, and beating them in the finals was a great win for us. That year was great and I have a lot of great memories of my teammates from that season, it was pretty special."

Brad Buetow, who had played under Brooks and was his assistant coach, took over the head coaching duties at Minnesota on an interim basis for the 1979-80 season when Brooks was named as the head coach of the U.S. Olympic team. There would be a total of nine Gophers who would be joining him in Lake Placid, NY, as well: (Neal Broten,

Bill Baker, Steve Janaszak, Eric Strobel, Phil Verchota, Mike Ramsey, Buzz Schneider, Rob McClanahan and Steve Christoff). The team, of course, would go on to shock the world by winning the gold medal. For the record, Les Auge, Mike Polich, Tim Harrer, Neal Broten and Steve Ulseth were all named as All-American selections during the Brooks era.

Buetow, a former three-sport Gopher athlete from Mounds View, took over as the team's new head coach in 1980 when Brooks opted to pursue a professional coaching career in the NHL. Despite losing a boat-load of players to the NHL that year (following the Olympics), the Gophers finished with an overall record of 26-15-0, good for second place in the league standings. The team was led by Tim Harrer, who won the WCHA scoring crown and set a school record of 45 goals on the season. Steve Ulseth, Peter Hayek, Bob Bergloff, David H. Jensen, Mike Knoke, and goalies Jim Jetland and Paul Butters, were among those who helped fill in nicely for the dearly departed. In addition, Neal Broten returned from the Olympics to reunite his old Roseau High School line consisting of his brother, Aaron, and best pal, Butsy Erickson. The trio would form the best line in college hockey that year.

With an overall finish of 31-12, Buetow led the 1980-81 team to the WCHA title, finishing ahead of Michigan Tech and Wisconsin by six points. The Gophers then went on to defeat Colorado College and UMD in the WCHA playoffs. From there, they beat Colgate by 9-4 and 5-4 scores in the NCAA Playoffs for a ticket back to the NCAA final four — which was being held up in Duluth. Minnesota beat up on Michigan Tech in the opener, 7-2, but were upset in the finals by "Badger" Bob Johnson's Wisconsin team, 6-3, in the title game. It was a bitter end to an otherwise fantastic season. In the end, despite Steve Ulseth capturing the WCHA scoring title, and Aaron Broten leading the nation in scoring with 106 total points, Neal Broten was awarded the innaugural Hobey Baker Memorial Award as college hockey's top player.

In 1982-83 Minnesota won its second league crown in three years with an overall record of 33-12-1. In the league playoffs the Maroon and Gold defeated UMD but lost to Wisconsin in the WCHA finals. Minnesota, behind Scott Bjugstad and Corey Millen, then went on to beat New Hampshire by the scores of 9-7 and 6-2, in the playoffs, to advance to the NCAA final four in Grand Forks. There, the Gophers lost to Harvard, 5-3, in the opener and then to Providence, 4-3, in the consolation contest to round out the season.

While UMD dominated league play for the next several years, the Gophers continued to play well, advancing to two more NCAA tournaments. Brad Buetow left the Gopher program following the 1985 season, however, with a 171-75-8 record. During his reign, Tim Harrer (1980), Neal Broten (1981), Steve Ulseth (1981) and Pat Micheletti (1985) all garnered All-American honors. Another significant event happened in 1985, when, in an emotional ceremony, the hockey half of Williams Arena was renamed as Mariucci Arena in honor of

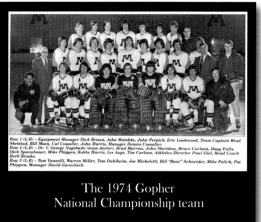

The 1974 Gopher
National Championship team

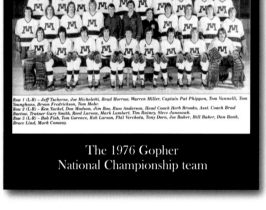

The 1976 Gopher
National Championship team

The 1979 Gopher
National Championship team

the "Godfather of Minnesota Hockey," John Mariucci. (Sadly, Maroosh would pass away just two years later.)

Former Gopher All-American and South St. Paul prep star Doug Woog took over as the team's new head coach in 1985. Woog, who had previously coached the St. Paul Vulcans and the Minnesota Junior Stars of the USHL to league and national titles, wasted little time in making a name for himself in Gold Country. The "Wooger" led the Gophers to a new school record of 35 wins and to a spot in the NCAA final four that first year. There, in Providence, the team played great but ultimately lost to Michigan State, 4-3, in the semifinals. They came back to beat Denver, 6-4, to take third though, behind Corey Millen and Pat Micheletti, who led the Gophers in scoring that year, and John Blue, who led all WCHA goalies with a 3.08 GAA.

In his second season, Woog posted a 34-14-1 record and led the team back to the NCAA's final four, this time in Detroit. There, the Gophers took third place yet again by beating Harvard, 6-3, in the consolation game after losing in the first round to Michigan State, 5-3.

After losing Corey Millen, Dave Snuggerud, Tom Chorske, Todd Okerlund and John Blue to the 1988 U.S. Olympic team, Duluth Denfeld goalie Robb Stauber led the Gophers to the 1988 WCHA crown, and yet another trip back to the final four, that year in Lake Placid, NY. Following wins over Michigan State, 4-2 and 4-3, in the playoffs, the Gophers wound up losing to St. Lawrence and then Maine in the semifinals to finish fourth.

Things looked promising for the team at the start of the 1988-89 season. Dave Snuggerud and Tom Chorske had returned from the Olympics and would lead the team in scoring; the soon-to-be-named Hobey Baker Award winner, Robb Stauber, was in goal; and returning leadership could be found in such players as: Randy Skarda, Todd Richards, Lance Pitlick, Luke Johnson, Jason Miller, Ken Gernander, Dean Williamson, Peter and Ben Hankinson, Larry Olimb, Sean Fabian, Grant Bischoff, Jon Anderson and David Espe. In addition, there were two highly regarded freshmen in Tom Pederson and Travis Richards, who would both contribute that season.

The Gophers opened the season by winning 12 of their first 14 games, including sweeps over Wisconsin, Denver, North Dakota and Colorado College. The team was awesome that year, losing back-to-back games only once. They went on to win the WCHA crown by a seven-point margin over Michigan Tech, making it back-to-back McNaughton Cups for the first time in the history of Gopher hockey. With an impressive 34-11-3 overall record (26-6-2 in conference play), they then went on to meet Colorado College in the first round of the WCHA Playoffs. There, they swept the Tigers, 5-4 and 7-1, only to lose to Denver and Wisconsin at the WCHA's version of the Final Four, which was held at St. Paul's Civic Center.

Down but not out, Minnesota then swept the Badgers in the ensuing NCAA playoffs, also at the Civic Center, by a pair of matching 4-2 scores. This now set up a rematch with their old

NEAL BROTEN

Born on November 29, 1959, Neal Broten is one of Minnesota's most sacred hockey cows. To understand Neal, you have to go back to his hometown just south of the Canadian border, Roseau — a tiny town of some 3,000 souls, yet it has three hockey arenas. Roseau has sent a team to the State High School Hockey Tournament an unprecedented 30 times, more than any other team, en route to winning a record seven championships along the way.

The tiny community has one of the richest hockey traditions of anywhere in the country, thanks to the three Broten brothers — Neal, Aaron and Paul. They all played for the Roseau Rams, the Gophers, the Stars (in both Minnesota and in Dallas), and for U.S. National Teams.

For the brothers Broten, it started at sun-up, when their parents would awaken before 6:00 a.m. on frigid winter mornings and drive their kids to hockey practice. "When he was a peewee, he was scoring five, six, seven goals a game," said Gary Hokanson, Broten's coach at Roseau. "You could see then that he was going to be something special. He was a little guy who could handle the stick and put it in the net like nothing I'd ever seen."

Neal starred for the Roseau High School Rams alongside his brother Aaron, and best pal Butsy Erickson. They took the Rams to State several times, but could never bag the big one. In 1978, shortly after leading his Rams to a tough semifinal loss to Edina in the state tournament, Neal, considered to be the best prep hockey player in the nation, made it official — he would become a Golden Gopher. Some were skeptical as to how the small-town kid would do in big-time college hockey under the demanding U of M coach, Herb Brooks. But it only took Neal less than one season to establish himself as one of the Gopher's greatest players of all time. In 1979, as a freshman, Broten easily exceeded everyone's expectations when he broke John Mayasich's 25-year-old school assist record by dishing out 50 helpers to his teammates. In the process, the WCHA's Rookie of the Year winner helped to lead the Gophers to an NCAA title. In fact, he netted the game-winning goal in the title game.

The next chapter of Neal's life story proved to be the one that may well have linked his name to the sport of hockey forever. That off-season, Neal was selected to be a member of the much-celebrated 1980 U.S. Olympic team that shocked the world in Lake Placid, NY. Neal would play center on the storied squad, finishing as the team's fourth-leading scorer. Named as one of Sports Illustrated's "Athlete's of the Year," Neal would gain instant celebrity status after the Winter Games.

From there, Neal could've easily turned pro, having been drafted in the second round by the North Stars. Instead, he returned to the U of M to be reunited with his two former line-mates from Roseau, his brother Aaron, and Butsy Erickson, who had recently transferred to the "U" from Cornell. There, new Gopher coach Brad Buetow quickly assembled the three to make up one of the most feared scoring lines in all of college hockey. The trio led the Gophers to the NCAA Championship game for the second time in three years, ultimately losing to Wisconsin, 6-3, in the 1981 finals. Neal went on to earn All-American honors that year and was also honored as the first-ever recipient of the Hobey Baker Memorial Award, which recognized the nation's top collegiate player. Over his incredible career at Minnesota, Broten scored 72 goals 106 assists for 178 points in only 76 games.

That season marked the end of Broten's collegiate career. But for Minnesota hockey fans it would only be the beginning. Neal left the "U" just in time to join the Cinderella North Stars as they were heading into the Stanley Cup playoffs. The Stars had even traded center Glen Sharpley, freeing up Neal's lucky No. 7 jersey for him. The Stars made it all they way to the finals that year, before losing to the New York Islanders in five games. He would then go on to finish as the runner up to Winnipeg's Dale Hawerchuk in the NHL's Rookie of the Year balloting in 1981-82.

One of the biggest highlights of his career happened in March of 1990, on a weekend when Roseau High School won the state high school hockey tournament. The Stars hosted "Broten Brothers Day," during a game against the New York Rangers at the Met. Neal and Aaron were both playing for the Stars at that time, and baby brother Paul was in town playing for the Rangers. "It was great supporting the Rams, the town, and to see them win the championship like that was incredible, said Neal."

He led the Stars back to their only other Stanley Cup finals appearance in 1991, where, after scoring nine goals and adding 13 assists in 23 playoff games, Minnesota wound up losing to the Pittsburgh Penguins. Later that summer, a contract dispute forced Broten to hold-out, and ultimately start the season with Team Preussen in the German League. The Minnesota fans freaked-out at the possibility that Neal would not return to Minnesota and demanded that he get signed. Their cries were heard, as his return to the line-up was met with a standing ovation from his loyal fans.

For 13 seasons Broten dazzled the Minnesota faithful as a member of the North Stars. His stats are remarkable. A four-time All-Star, Broten led the Stars in scoring from 1982-86 with 405 points, and was an 80-plus point producer four times in the decade. He also became the first U.S.-born player ever to score 100 points in a season when he tallied 105 in 1986.

When the North Stars moved to Dallas, Broten played two seasons in Texas before being traded to the New Jersey Devils during the 1994-95 season. Ironically, he was dealt for fellow Northern Minnesotan, Corey Millen, of Cloquet. There, Broten became the final piece in the Devil's Stanley Cup puzzle. He ignited New Jersey's offense by scoring seven goals, including four game-winners, while dishing out 12 assists during their playoff run to become one of the first Gopher players ever to have his name inscribed on Lord Stanley's Cup.

"I can remember sitting there in the locker room with him after they won it," said Neal's father Newell. "He looked at me and said, 'Dad, can you believe it after all these years?'"

Neal competed in his 17th and final NHL season in 1996-97, back with the Dallas Stars. At the time of his retirement, Broten held many franchise records, including: most assists (634), most games (1,099), most points (923 — 289 goals + 634 assists), most NHL seasons (16), most assists in a season (76), and most points by a rookie (98). He was also ranked second all-time in points by an American with 923, and had played in the most games as an American with 1,099.

Among his many honors and accolades, Broten was awarded the Lester Patrick award in 1998 for outstanding service to hockey in the U.S. That same year, Broten, along with fellow Gopher John Mayasich, were selected to the All-Time USA Hockey Team by the members of USA Hockey as a component of the organization's 60th anniversary celebration. In addition, on February 7th, 1998, Broten's No. 7 jersey was retired by the Dallas Stars in a special ceremony before a game against the Chicago Blackhawks at Reunion Arena, recognizing his outstanding 16 years with the franchise — 13 of them in Minnesota. Further, in 2000 Broten was inducted into the U.S. Hockey Hall of Fame.

Neal Broten is without a doubt Minnesota hockey's most beloved all-time player, and possibly the most humble as well.

adversaries from the East – Maine, in the NCAA Final Four. Revenge was sweet for the Maroon and Gold, as they crushed the Black Bears, 7-4, behind Jon Anderson's hat trick.

So, the stage was set. The Gophers, on their home-ice, would now face Harvard for all the marbles in the NCAA Finals. Minnesota jumped out to a 1-0 lead when Jon Anderson went downstairs, stick-side, off a sweet Benny Hankinson pass at 6:24 in the first. Harvard's Ted Donato and Lane MacDonald then each scored in the second to pull ahead by one. Bloomington's Jason Miller evened it up at two apiece when he scored off a Lance Pitlick rebound. In the third both teams exchanged power-plays until Ted Donato tallied again to put the Crimson back on top. But, like so many times before that season, the Gophers came back. This time on a Pete Hankinson wrister to make it three apiece. The buzzer sounded and with that, both teams headed to overtime.

Now, just as the fourth period got underway, Randy Skarda skated down the ice, made a move and took a slapper at Harvard Goalie Chuckie Hughes. All you could hear was a loud dull plunk. That could've only meant one thing: Skarda hit the pipe. Then, at 4:16 of sudden-death, Harvard's Ed Krayer got a gift. After goalie Robb Stauber stopped a shot that took him out of position, Krayer picked up the rebound and slid a back-hander under his sprawled out pads. It was a dagger sent right into the collective hearts of Gopher fans everywhere.

Stauber, who stood on his head the entire game, stopping 24 shots and earning every bit of his Hobey Baker award from the year before, sat motionless on the ice in utter disbelief. As the nearly 16,000 Minnesota fans sat in silence, shock set in as they pondered just how close they had come to winning it all. Many in the large crowd thought that the 4-3 decision might have been the best college hockey game that they had ever viewed.

"I don't like to think about it," said Stauber, who led the WCHA in goaltending that year, and incidentally, has never watched the video of the game. "I remember the shot, and I reached for the rebound but missed it. There were so many things in that game I would've done differently. Sometimes in big pressure games you tend to be more reserved and play more conservatively than you'd like to. But, that was a great year, and we had nothing to be ashamed of that season at all."

Randy Skarda had come within one inch of getting that 900-pound gorilla off Doug Woog's back on that fabled day in April. "It was probably the most crushing defeat of my life," said Skarda. "Kenny Gernander set me up, and I hit the inside of the pipe. Afterwards I couldn't leave my house for two weeks, I was devastated."

As for the Wooger, the thought of coming that close was something he will never forget. "We had the advantage of being at home in St. Paul that year, and the disadvantage of not getting to bed the night before until 3:00am because of all

Aaron Broten

Bill Baker

From 1982-86 Pat Micheletti tallied 120 goals, which remains second all-time behind only John Mayasich.

the fans," said Woog. "I remember Hankinson scoring late and tying it up for us as we came back, and I can still see Randy Skarda making a rush on their goalie and the sound of the puck hitting the pipe. That one pipe changed the history of Gopher hockey forever. There is always something that puts humility into the pot, and that's the one you gotta answer every week: 'When will we win the big one?' "

By 1990 the Gophers had won 17 WCHA/WIHL Championships since the league's inception back in 1951 and Woog would add to that number considerably during his tenure. Minnesota had also made 14 appearances in the NCAA Final Four by now, tying them for the all-time lead with Boston University. In Woog's first five years behind the bench, he achieved the highest winning percentage of any collegiate coach in the country at .715%. In addition to winning back-to-back WCHA league titles in 1987-88 and 1988-89, his teams had also made it to the NCAA Final Four in four of the last five years as well.

With that, Minnesota entered the 1990-91 season with a nice mix of veterans and talented newcomers, including 15 returning lettermen. Among them were goalies Tom Newman (19-13-2, 3.84 GAA) and Jeff Stolp (5-1-0, 4.75 GAA), both solid netminders. A gaping hole had been left by those who had graduated and moved on, however, including the team's top two scorers in captain Peter Hankinson and Scott Bloom, who tallied 66 and 52 points, respectively. The other key players absent from this season's line-up were Jon Anderson, Dean Williamson, Brett Strot and Lance Pitlick – who would go on to have a very successful career in the NHL.

Replacing all of that firepower would not be easy. Filling in would be an outstanding trio of forwards, headlined by captain Ben Hankinson and alternate captains Ken Gernander and Grant Bischoff. Others expected to provide scoring punch that season were Jason Miller, Trent Klatt, Cory Laylin, Joe Dziedzic, Jeff Nielson, Andy Mills and Craig Johnson. The blue line corps included the likes of Travis Richards, Doug Zmolek, Tom Pederson, Larry Olimb and Luke Johnson, as well as newcomer Chris McAlpine.

"We need to find roles for some of our veterans," said Woog. "If they are going to score goals, they will be on the power play. If not, then maybe we will put them on the penalty-killing unit. Either way, I feel it is important to find a role for them so they can feel involved in the game."

Minnesota started the season on fire, not losing a single game in its first 12 WCHA contests. The team finally came back to earth on November 30th when they lost to UND up in Grand Forks, but remained ranked at the top of the national polls at the midway mark of the season with an impressive 14-1-3 record. The second half of the season was up and down, producing some big wins as well as some humbling defeats. A big turning point came when two of the team's top scorers, Trent Klatt and Craig Johnson, left to compete for Team USA in the World Junior Championships in Canada.

The Gophers played solid into the New Year, sweeping both Denver and then St. Cloud State, which had joined the WCHA after competing for a few seasons as a Division One independent. Minnesota hung in there and looked good entering the home stretch after beating defending national champion Wisconsin by the scores of 5-3 and 8-1. From there, the Minnesota-Duluth Bulldogs played spoiler by beating the Gophers on their home ice in the first game of a weekend series and then gained an overtime tie in Game Two. Northern Michigan then took three of four points that next weekend in a pair of overtime thrillers to really throw a monkey wrench into their plans.

Minnesota rebounded with a pair of sweeps over both North Dakota and Michigan Tech at home, and kept it going into the WCHA tourney, where, after sweeping Michigan Tech and then beating Wisconsin, they came up short against the eventual national champions from Northern Michigan in the championship game, 4-2.

The Gophs went on to sweep Providence in the first round of the NCAA tourney and then headed east, to Orono, Maine, where they faced the Black Bears for the right to advance to the NCAA Championship Tournament. Motivating the Maroon and Gold was the fact that if they beat the Bears, they would get home to play the NCAA Finals in their own backyard at the St. Paul Civic Center. Eager to avenge their NCAA Finals overtime loss to Harvard just two years earlier at the Civic Center, there was plenty of incentive for the Gophers to play hard. Maine wasn't about to roll over though and promptly handed them their first shut-out of the season, 4-0, in Game One. They then followed that up with a 5-3 nail-biter the next night to end Minnesota's season on a sour note.

The team finished with an impressive 30-10-5 overall record along with a second place WCHA finish, marking the seventh straight year that they had finished no lower than second in the league. Larry Olimb led the squad in scoring with 19 goals and 38 assists in just 45 games, while Grant Bischoff and Trent Klatt added 47 and 44 points of their own, respectively. With regards to post-season honors and accolades that season, Larry Olimb was named as a second-team All-WCHA selection. In addition, Chris McAlpine and Craig Johnson were named to the WCHA All-Rookie Team.

Minnesota knew that they had their work cut out for them right out of the gates in 1991-92. In fact, the team had one of its toughest schedules ever that season, playing 15 games against opponents which had qualified for the NCAA Tournament the year before. The Gophers started out their campaign pretty rough, going 4-5 through their first nine games before finally getting back on track against Wisconsin. The Gophers won a 5-4 nail-biter in the opener at Mariucci Arena on

Steve Christoff

Dave Snuggerud

Paul Broten

Trent Klatt's game-winner, and then completed the sweep with a 4-1 win behind Jeff Stolp's 26 saves in front of nearly 16,000 fans in the "Border Battle" game at the Met Center.

"That Wisconsin series really got us going," said Head Coach Doug Woog. "After that, we played consistently strong hockey for the remainder of the season."

From there, Minnesota got hot and rattled off sweeps over Alaska-Anchorage and North Dakota to end the month of November. In all, they won 19 of their next 21 games, including a league-high 11-game win streak that ended at the hands of the Badgers in Madison. Over the next three months the Gophers climbed to the top of the national polls and finished the season fully 12 points ahead of their nearest competitor. In all, there were 11 weekend sweeps for the Gophers and an impressive 30 wins in the final 36 games. The team capped off the season by winning the WCHA's MacNaughton Cup at home on February 22, with a 7-3 win over Denver, in front of 7,503 ecstatic fans. It was the program's ninth title and the third in the seven-year tenure of Coach Woog.

Minnesota then went on to win two out of three games from the Fighting Sioux in the first round of the WCHA Playoffs, followed by a 5-1 win over Colorado College in the WCHA Final Four at the St. Paul Civic Center. They then lost a 4-2 heartbreaker to Northern Michigan in the Final Four. From there, the team headed to the "Joe," where they got thumped, 8-3, by the eventual national champions from Lake Superior State in the NCAA Quarterfinals at Joe Louis Arena in Detroit to end their season.

For the record, senior goaltender Jeff Stolp, who finished with a 26-9 record and a 2.91 GAA, led the WCHA in almost every category and was the backbone of the team's league-leading defense which held its opponents' to a stingy 2.75 goals per game. The defensemen were led by All-American Doug Zmolek, a No. 1 draft choice of the North Stars whose rights were later obtained by the San Jose Sharks. Joining him on the blue line were Travis Richards, Sean Fabian, Eric Means and Chris McAlpine.

The offensive charge was led by Hobey Baker finalist Larry Olimb. The Warroad native led all scorers that season with 80 points, becoming just the seventh Gopher to score 200 career points to date. He also set the program's career assist mark with 159 as well. Forward Trent Klatt notched 30 goals and 36 assists, while Craig Johnson tallied 58 points of his own. In addition, Richfield's Darby Hendrickson garnered WCHA Freshman of the Year honors as a result of his 55 point season.

The defending WCHA champion Golden Gophers came into the 1992-93 season knowing that they were going to have to rebuild and reload with the next wave of talent. Coach Woog was optimistic heading into the season.

"Our team has suffered some tremendous losses in the past year due to graduation

HERB BROOKS

Born in St. Paul on August 5, 1937, Herb Brooks grew up in a modest duplex at the corner of Payne and Ivy, the son of a plumber who found himself selling insurance after the Great Depression. Herb's family loved hockey. His father was a well known amateur hockey player in the 1920s, while his kid brother, David, would go on to play for the Gophers in the early 1960s and also on the 1964 U.S. Olympic team as well. As a boy growing up on St. Paul's tough East Side, a training ground for many future Minnesota hockey stars, Herb was a typical hockey playing rink-rat. He would go on to star at St. Paul Johnson High School from 1952-55. As a senior, the speedy forward led Johnson to a 26-1-2 record en route to winning the state championship. Here is how it all went down:

The 1955 Minnesota State High School Hockey Tournament started out innocently enough, until the third quarterfinal game rolled around. That game, between Minneapolis South and Thief River Falls, would prove to be one of the most famous of all-time. That's because it lasted an incredible 11 overtimes, the longest game ever to be played in tourney history. The game roared back and forth all night. Well, after nine overtimes, and no end in sight, the officials decided to start the evening game between St. Paul Johnson and Roseau at 11:30 pm. The two games then rotated back and forth in between periods. Finally at 1:50 of the 11th extra session, South's Jim Westby scored the game-winner to end the unbelievable marathon.

Incidentally, and completely overshadowed, was Ken Fanger's first period goal which would prove to be all that Johnson would need to hang on for a 1-0 win over Roseau in their quarterfinal game. Then, in the semifinals, Brooks put his Johnson squad up 1-0 midway through the first, while Stu Anderson and Roger Wigen each tallied in the third to give the Governors a 3-1 win, and a ticket to the title game. There, Johnson and their Mill City rivals from Southwest faced off for all the marbles in front of a packed St. Paul Auditorium crowd. The hero of the game would prove to be none other than Herbie, who got the Governors on the board at 2:32 of the first period. His teammate, Stu Anderson, then tallied less than seven minutes later, only to see Brooks score his second goal of the game just a minute and a half after that. It would prove to be the final nail in the coffin as Coach Rube Gustafson's Governors cruised to a 3-1 victory.

"Winning the state championship was great, but my most memorable moment is not from the title game but the game we had to follow," said Herbie of the 11-overtime quarterfinal thriller. "We had to wait and wait in the dressing room; we'd take our skates off, put them on, shuffle our feet, this and that. It was hard to wait, and it was after one in the morning when our game was finally over, but we won and went on to win the championship. Winning the state championship, that represented your neighborhood. I would have to say that it was my biggest thrill ever. It was special."

An outstanding athlete, Herb earned three varsity letters as a first baseman on the Johnson baseball team as well. Before long, the colleges were calling.

"I had an interview with the Air Force Academy, because I really wanted to be a fighter pilot," said Brooks. "Unfortunately, because I was slightly color blind, I washed out of the Academy. I also had a scholarship at the University of Michigan, but my dad encouraged me to walk on at the University of Minnesota and try to play for John Mariucci, so that was the route I took."

At Minnesota, Brooks became known for his blinding speed. "He was one of the fastest, if not the fastest, player in college hockey in that era," Mariucci would later recall. Brooks would learn a lot from "Maroosh," saying that he had more to do with shaping his ideas in hockey than any other individual.

"At first I was scared to death of him," recalled Herbie. "I was fresh out of high school. I remember in practices my first year he used to call me Pete. For the longest time he never knew my name, and I was terrified of him."

"He was like a father to me, we were very close. He wasn't long on words, and didn't want to be everybody's buddy like some coaches try to be. John was an entirely different guy as a coach. You took care of yourself under John. He never called you to take care of you, or told you to go to class. His psychology of coaching was to take care of yourself, or get the hell out. You grew up pretty fast under John. He was a throwback, and was an entirely different coach than you'd see today. He was such a great guy. I remember the day they renamed the arena in his name. It was his happiest day, and such a memorable moment for him.

"I patterned several aspects of my coaching after John. He was a pioneer and faced immense competition as a coach. When the '80 Olympic team won the gold, John said it was one more piece to the puzzle for American hockey. I shared those hopes, dreams and aspirations with him, and was proud of the fact that there were 12 of us from Minnesota on that team."

"In all social causes to better an institution, there's always got to be a rallying force, a catalyst, a glue, and a magnet, and that's what John was, for American hockey," Herbie would later say in a Star Tribune article. "The rest of us just filled in after him."

Brooks wore a Golden Gopher sweater from 1957-59, scoring 45 points over his three-year career. He graduated from the U of M in 1961 with a B.A. in Psychology — a degree he would put to use in more ways than one over the ensuing years.

Dreams Can Come True

The next phase of Brooks' life involved his lifelong dream, the Olympics. After graduating, he began to build a successful career in the insurance business, but never fully got away from the game that continued to dominate his life. He would play off and on with some local semipro teams, including the St. Paul Steers and Rochester Mustangs over the next year, and then tried out for the 1960 U.S. Olympic team which was set to play at the Winter Games in Squaw Valley, Calif. He played well, eluding every cut except the final one, when he was literally the last player to be released from the team's final roster. He was devastated.

Herb then sat at home with his father, Herb Sr., and watched his former teammates, some of the same kids with whom he used to play hockey with out on the frozen ponds in St. Paul, bring home the gold. Herb was torn. On one hand he was genuinely happy for his old pals. On the other hand he was jealous as hell, because they were living out his dream. At that very moment Herb's father looked over at him and said: "Looks like Coach Riley cut the right guy..." It was right then and there, on February 27, 1960, that Herbie knew his destiny. He was going to make the 1964 U.S. Olympic team, and one day, he was going to coach an Olympic team. Period.

From there, Brooks worked like a dog and went on to spend the next decade playing on nearly every U.S. Olympic and National team. In fact, from 1961-70, he played on two Olympic teams and five National teams — more than any player in the history of United States hockey — even captaining several of those teams along the way. More importantly, he would become a student of the game, learning about coaching from the world's best.

"To me the Olympics are not about 'Dream Teams,' they're more about dreamers," said Herb. "They're not about medals, but the pursuit of medals. The Olympics are not about being No. 1, they're about sacrificing and trying to be No. 1. That's why the Olympics will always be special to me."

Finding His True Calling

Herbie went into coaching after that, becoming an assistant under Coach Glen Sonmor at the U of M. At the same time, he pioneered Junior Hockey in the state as the first coach of the Minnesota Junior Stars in the Minnesota/Ontario Junior-A League. In 1970, Herb was considered for the head coaching job at the University of Wisconsin, a job which ultimately went to fellow Minnesotan Bob Johnson. How scary to think that if that had happened it might have been "Badger-Herbie" instead of "Badger Bob!" Luckily for us, however, that next year Sonmor left to become the coach of the WHA's Fighting Saints and the following season Brooks was named as the Gophers' new head coach. The youngest college hockey coach in the country, Brooks would inherit a program that had just finished in last place. The challenge of turning it all around was just what Herb was looking for.

The chant "Her-bee! — Her-bee!" would become an all too familiar sound at the "Old Barn" throughout the tenure of the man who would become Minnesota's greatest hockey coach. Brooks instilled a new brand of pride and tradition that next season, starting with his newly designed jerseys which proudly featured the Minnesota "M" on the front. Brooks promised he would bring, "exciting, dynamic people into the program," and he kept his word. In only seven years, he would build a dynasty at Minnesota. More importantly, he did it all with Minnesota kids.

With his extensive knowledge and experience in European hockey, Herb became an advocate of the Russian style of play and in particular, the coaching style of Anatoli Tarasov. He would instill this philosophy in motivating his own players. From 1972-79, Brooks was simply dominant. With his no-nonsense style, he went on to win the first three NCAA National Championships in Gopher Hockey history: 1973, 1976 and 1979. While at the University of Minnesota, Brooks won 175 games, lost 100, and tied 20 for a .636 winning percentage. Brooks also guided five All-Americans: Les Auge, Mike Polich, Tim Harrer, Neal Broten and Steve Ulseth, while 23 of his protégés went on to play in the NHL as well.

"We went to the finals four of my seven years there, and we made a great run of it," said Brooks. "I think I put a lot of pressure on the players, and I had a lot of expectations of them. I didn't give them an 'out,' and I think I was always able to find the kids who were really competitive. The common denominator of all the guys who played throughout my seven years was that they were really competitive, very hungry, very focused, and mentally tough — to go along with whatever talent they had. I think that really carried us."

Do You Believe in Miracles?...Yes!

The next chapter of Brooks' life was the one that would make him a household name, the legendary "Miracle on Ice." Sure, he had built the University of Minnesota hockey program into a dynasty, but for Herbie, coaching the Gophers was just another rung on the ladder. You see, for Herbie, coaching the Olympics had always been what it was all about. That was his dream, to coach the U.S. squad at the Olympics. Now, his dream was about to become a reality. He was about to make history.

"The Olympians, the amazing athletes like Jesse Owens, they are the ones who have always captivated me," said Brooks. "The Olympics are a world sporting spectacle on an international stage. It is national pride with so much wonderful history. I grew up with that history, so to me the Olympics transcend the game itself."

After coaching the 1979 U.S. National team at the World Games in Moscow, Herbie was then named as the coach of the fabled 1980 U.S. Olympic team.

"Having played international hockey for so many years, it gives me an awfully warm feeling to be selected as head coach for the 1980 Olympics," said Brooks of his new job. "I'm extremely honored and humbled. To be picked when there are so many outstanding amateur hockey coaches in the nation, well, let's just say it's something I never really expected to happen."

The Americans, who, since the inception of the Winter Games, had won one gold medal (1960), four silver medals (1924, 1952, 1956 & 1972), and one bronze (1936), were eager to bring home some hardware on their native soil. Having finished fourth during the previous Olympics, in 1976, at Innsbruck, Austria, under coach Bob Johnson, the U.S. knew it would never have a better opportunity than the one they had in front of them right then in Lake Placid, N.Y.

Brooks now had the responsibility of selecting the 20 players to fill out his roster. He didn't want to take any chances, so he went with who he knew and who he could trust — local boys. He researched countless candidates, made thousands of phone calls, and tried to find out which players he could count on when the game was on the line.

"When he had to pick the 1980 Olympic team, I remember Herbie calling the high schools of the potential Olympians to find out their records on grades, if they got into trouble, did drugs, and what kind of people they were," recalled Herb's brother Dave. "When I asked him why the hell he was doing that, he said that he wanted to know what kind of player he was going to have when it came down to the last two minutes of a game. He said he wanted to know which kids he should have on the ice come clutch time."

When it was all said and done, fully 12 Minnesotans had made the final cut. In addition, nine were players that Brooks had coached as Gophers: Roseau's Neal Broten, Grand Rapids' Bill Baker, White Bear Lake's Steve Janaszak, Rochester's Eric Strobel, Duluth's Phil Verchota, Minneapolis' Mike Ramsey, Babbitt's Buzz Schneider, St. Paul's Robb McClanahan and Richfield's Steve Christoff. The three other Minnesotans were: Warroad's Dave Christian, who played at North Dakota, and Virginia's John Harrington and Eveleth's Mark Pavelich — both of whom played at Minnesota-Duluth. In addition, Mark Johnson, who was born in Minneapolis but raised in Wisconsin, also made the team.

From there, Herbie worked the kids relentlessly, taking them on a world-wide tour to test them both mentally and physically. In early September, the team began as challenging an exhibition schedule as had ever been organized for an American

Olympic squad. Beginning with an initial European tour, the team played a 61-game pre-Olympic schedule against foreign, college and professional teams, ultimately finishing with a 42-16-3 record. It was during this time together that the players were introduced to Brooks' new offensive game-plan, called the "weave." Brooks felt that if his club was going to compete against Europeans, then they had better learn how to play like Europeans.

Brooks' free-flowing, criss-crossing offensive style allowed his players to be creative. It was a loose style which allowed for a lot of improvisation, or "sophisticated pond hockey," as Herbie would call it. It was an amalgam of the North American style with the European game, and it worked. Brooks pushed the kids relentlessly. He watched their diet, had them do dry-land training in soccer fields to work on their footwork and flexibility, and trained them like they had never been trained. He challenged them, prodded them, screamed at them and drove them beyond what they thought they could achieve. They were in shape too, as he worked them to death in his legendary practices. He wanted to make sure that they were ready to go in the third period of a big game. He was their motivator, their teacher, their psychologist and their father — all wrapped up into one. And, he was their worst nightmare too. He was tough as hell on them, never cutting them any slack.

Entering the XIIIth Winter Olympic Games, the team was a decided underdog, an evaluation that seemed to be confirmed by a 10-3 defeat at the hands of the mighty Soviets in the final exhibition game in New York City's Madison Square Garden. Though seeded seventh in the 12-nation pool, the Americans felt that they had something to prove. The Yanks took on Sweden in the opening game, as Bill Baker scored with 27 seconds remaining in the third period to give the U.S. a 2-2 tie. The goal acted as a catalyst for the young Americans, who then upset Czechoslovakia, and the amazing Stastny brothers, 7-3, thanks to goals from Pavelich, Schneider, Verchota and McClanahan.

After beating both Norway and Romania, now only West Germany (the team that knocked them out of the bronze medal in 1976), stood in the way of getting into the medal round. Down 2-0 in the first, the Minnesota boys came through big as McClanahan and Broten each tallied to tie it up. McClanahan then scored again on another breakaway in the third, while Phil Verchota lit the lamp late to give the U.S. a 4-2 win over the West Germans. This gave the Americans a round robin record of 4-0-1, and a date with the Soviets — which were led by Vladislav Tretiak, the world's premier goaltender. The Soviets, who had outscored their opponents, 51-11, through their first five games, were just another of a long line of dynasty teams which had won the last four Olympic golds, and five of the last six. In fact, the only team to beat them since 1956 was the U.S. squad, 20 years earlier in 1960 — the team that Herbie had been cut from.

Going for Gold

Herbie now had his boys right where he wanted them. He knew that the Soviets were ripe for defeat. Sure, they were technically superior to any team in the world. They were fast, strong and better in nearly every way. Every way but one, they lacked heart — something Brooks was banking on. He knew that they were overconfident and knew that the time was right to go for it. And that is just what he did. The game had all the hype imaginable, with political and social implications written all over it. Amidst the backdrop of the Iranian hostage crisis, the Soviet invasion of Afghanistan, the realization that the U.S. economy was in disarray with interest rates and inflation soaring — not to mention the fact that President Carter had already announced an American boycott of the Summer Olympics in Moscow, the team hit the ice. Talk about pressure.

With that, the "Iron Range" line of Pavelich, Harrington and Schneider got the Americans on the board. Down 1-0 early in the first, Pavelich fed Schneider for a nice slap shot which found the top corner. The Russians answered back three minutes later, only to see Mark Johnson tie it up with just seconds to go in the period on a nice open ice steal and break-away. When they returned to the ice following the intermission, the U.S. team was shocked to see that Soviet coach Victor Tikhanov had angrily replaced Tretiak in goal with back-up goaltender Vladimir Myshkin. While it would appear that the great bear was wounded, the Soviets came back to take the lead, having now out-shot the Yanks 30-10 through two periods. Johnson then got his second of the game at 8:39 of the third to tie it at 3-3, setting up the heroics for the Iron Rangers.

Midway through the third, Schneider dumped the puck into the Russian zone and Harrington dug it out to his old UMD wingmate Mark Pavelich. Pavelich then floated a perfect pass to the top of the circle, where team captain Mike Eruzione fired home "the shot heard 'round the world." The team erupted. The final 10 minutes of the game were probably the longest in U.S. hockey history, but the Americans somehow held on behind goalie Jim Craig's brilliant netminding down the stretch. Then, as the crowd counted down the final seconds, famed television announcer Al Michaels shouted *"Do you believe in miracles,...Yes!"* Our boys had done it. And with that, the Americans had made it into the gold medal game.

After the players were through celebrating on the ice, Herbie, ever the psychologist, quickly put them back in their place in the locker room. He screamed at them not to get too cocky, and that they were just lucky, and hadn't won anything yet. The next day at practice, Brooks put the team through a grueling work-out, constantly reinforcing to his men that he was not their friend, and they had proved nothing up to that point. This was all part of his ingenious master plan, to get the players to despise him, and force them to rally amongst themselves to become stronger.

In the gold medal game the U.S. would face Finland, a team which had beaten the Czechs in the other semifinal. The players would respond to Brooks' famous words: *"You were born to be a player. You were meant to be here. This moment is yours."* Despite being down early in the second period, Steve Christoff got the Americans on the board at 4:39 with a nice wrister down low. The Finns hung tough, however, and went into the third period up 2-1. After an emotional speech between the intermission from Brooks, reminding his players ever so eloquently that they would regret this moment for the rest of their collective lives if they let it slip away, the U.S. came out inspired. The team had come from behind in nearly every one of its games, a true hallmark of greatness. The constant reminder of Herbie saying *"Play your game... Play your game,"* was comforting to the players, who knew that they were on the verge of making history.

The hero this time would prove to be Phil Verchota, who took a Dave Christian pass in the left circle and found the back of the net at the 2:25 mark. With that, the Americans started to smell blood and immediately went for the jugular. Just three minutes later, Robbie McClanahan went five-hole with a Mark Johnson pass to give the U.S. a 3-2 lead. Johnson then saved the day by adding a short-handed backhand goal just minutes later to give the U.S. a two-goal cushion. From there, Jim Craig just hung on for the final few minutes of the game as Al Michaels this time screamed: *"This impossible dream, comes true!"*

It was suddenly utter pandemonium in Lake Placid, as the players threw their sticks into the crowd and formed a human hog pile at center ice to the chants of *"USA! – USA!"* Herbie, meanwhile, thrust his arm into the air in a brief moment of uncharacteristic jubilation and satisfaction, only to then sneak out the back door, leaving the players to celebrate their achievement amongst themselves.

Afterward, many of the players were visibly moved by what they had done, as evidenced during the singing of the National Anthem, where the entire team gathered on the top podium to sing the Star-Spangled Banner.

While Mark Johnson, son of ex-Gopher, "Badger Bob" Johnson, led the team in scoring, the Iron Range Line of Schneider-Pavelich-Harrington led the team's four lines in scoring with 17 goals and 20 assists. Brilliant goaltending by Jim Craig, who played all seven contests, was a big factor in the victory, as was the stellar play of defensemen Dave Christian, Ken Morrow, Mike Ramsey, Neal Broten and Bill Baker.

The event will forever remain etched in our memories as one of the greatest sporting events of all-time. Looking back, the icy miracle was achieved by enormous ambition, coupled with great passing, checking, speed, and sound puck-control. Brooks refused to play the typical clutch-and-grab, dump-and-chase style of hockey that was so prevalent in North American hockey. Shrewdly, he had beaten the Europeans and Russians at their own game.

"I didn't want the team throwing the puck away for no reason," he said. "That's stupid. It's the same as punting on first down. The style I wanted combined the determined checking of the North American game and the best features (speed and stick handling) of the European game."

A Lasting Legacy

A grateful nation, saddened by what was happening in the world, hailed the team as heroes. A visit to the White House followed, as well as appearances in cities across the land. Before long the player's faces were featured on magazine and newspapers everywhere, as well as on the cover of the Wheaties box. Awards, honors, speaking engagements and a whole lot of hoopla would follow. In the heart of the Cold War, beating the mighty Soviets was something bigger than they could've ever imagined. The country went crazy with a newly found sense of national pride, all thanks to Herbie's incredible achievement. Sports Illustrated went on to name the team, collectively, as *"Sportsmen of the Year;"* Life Magazine declared it as the *"Sports Achievement of the Decade;"* and ABC Sports announcer, Jim McCay, went on to call the spectacle, *"The greatest upset in the history of sports."*

"They were really mentally tough and goal-oriented," said Brooks. "They came from all different walks of life, many having competed against one another, but they came together and grew to be a real close team. I pushed this team really hard, I mean I really pushed them! But they had the ability to answer the bell. Our style of play was probably different than anything in North America. We adopted more of a hybrid style of play — a bit of the Canadian school and a little bit of the European school. The players took to it like ducks to water, and they really had a lot of fun playing it. We were a fast, creative team that played extremely disciplined without the puck. Throughout the Olympics, they had a great resiliency about them. I mean they came from behind six or seven times to win. They just kept on moving and working and digging. I think we were as good a conditioned team as there was in the world, outside of maybe the Soviet Union. We got hot and lucky at the right times, and it was just an incredible experience for all of us."

After the Olympics, all of the players went their separate ways. Many went on to play professional hockey, while others went into business and began their careers elsewhere. They would not all be reunited again, however, until 2002, when the team was brought together in an emotional gala to collectively light the Olympic caldron at the Winter Games at Salt Lake City. Looking back, the event was extremely significant for the growth of American hockey. The historic win brought hockey to the front-page of newspapers everywhere, and forever opened the door to the NHL for American-born players from below the 49th parallel. The impact of the event was far reaching, and is still being felt today. Since that milestone game back in 1980, hockey in the U.S. has grown significantly at both the professional and amateur levels. The fact that we now have hockey in Arizona, North Carolina, Florida, California and Texas can all be traced back, in part, to the icy miracle. The event would later be named as the "Sporting Event of the 20th Century," not bad for a kid from Payne Avenue in St. Paul.

From the Big Apple to St. Cloud to the Met to Jersey to Pittsburgh, the Adventure Continued...

After coaching in Davos, Switzerland, that next year, where he rested and reevaluated his future, Herb's coaching success continued in the National Hockey League with the New York Rangers. Herbie took the Big Apple by storm, even being named as the NHL Coach of the Year in 1982, his rookie season. Brooks would guide the Rangers for four seasons, leading his team to the playoffs each year and earning 100 victories faster than any other Ranger coach before him. In all, Brooks would coach the Rangers to a .532 winning percentage and twice he led the team into the second round of the playoffs, losing both times to rival New York Islanders teams which went on to win Stanley Cups.

In the pros, Herbie did things which were truly revolutionary at the time. He had off-season training back when off season training consisted of golf and fishing. He brought in his old buddy from Minnesota, Jack Blatherwick, to teach his players about exercise physiology, and it worked. He even monitored his players' body fat and insisted that they eat right, and even chew sugar free gum. Then, he instilled a European style of hockey into the rough and tumble, clutch and grab, dump and chase North American game which had been commonplace for decades. People thought he was crazy, but when his "Smurfs" beat Philly's mighty Broad Street Bullies by skating around them, no one was laughing. Herb truly changed the game. (Many of his players were small and quick, earning the nickname "Smurfs," in reference to the little blue cartoon characters.)

Herb's Broadway stint with the Rangers lasted until 1985. He had just gotten tired of dealing with temperamental and arrogant millionaire players who didn't show him the same respect that he had been accustomed to, and wanted out. It was drastically different from coaching amateur kids in college and in the Olympics. He was also frustrated with the team's lack of personnel moves. In college, if he needed a quick centerman, he would recruit one. Here, it was more difficult to get the agents as well as the team's management to make a deal for what he wanted. Couple that with the fact that his dad had died during training camp that year, and that he was just tired of living in hotel rooms away from his family, and the writing was on the wall.

When Herb came home, he took some time off to recharge his batteries. Shortly thereafter, however, he got the coaching itch. So, in an amazing move, Brooks accepted the head coaching position at St. Cloud State University in 1986. He would be revered as the school's savior, leading the Huskies to a third place finish in the national small-college tournament, and more importantly, getting the program elevated to NCAA Division I status. He stayed for only a year, but really got the Huskies' program turned around. He did it as a personal favor to his mentor, John Mariucci, to help build the base of the pyramid and get more opportunities for more Minnesota kids. And, with his political clout, he was even able to lobby the legislature to help fund a new arena for the school, the National Sports Center.

"St. Cloud was a very positive experience for me, and John was very influential in that endeavor as well," said Herb. "We felt that there were more kids in Minnesota than opportunities for them. He encouraged me to go up there for a year, get the program from Division III to Division I, raise money for the new rinks, and get them going in the right direction. Then I left. John was very much a visionary, and had a lot to do with my decision in going up there."

The next stop in Brooks' hockey resume was Bloomington, to coach the NHL's Minnesota North Stars. It was another homecoming of sorts, as Herb took over the reigns from Lorne Henning and became the first Minnesota native to coach the team. The season, however, didn't go well for Brooks. Lou Nanne had just resigned as the teams' general manager and newcomer Jack Ferreira had just come in. Unable to overcome an enormous number of injuries, the Stars finished in the Norris Division cellar that year. So, citing philosophical differences with management, Brooks resigned after the season. It was a bad deal all the way around.

Brooks then took some well deserved time away from coaching for a few years after that to embark on a successful business career which included motivational speaking, TV analysis, NHL scouting and occasional coaching. Then, in 1991, he got back into the action when he took over the New Jersey Devils minor league team in Utica, NY, and was later promoted to be the head coach of the NHL team in 1992. There, he guided the Devils for one season, compiling a record of 40-37-7 along the way.

It is interesting to note that Herb lobbied to coach the 1992 U.S. Olympic team at that time. He proposed the development of a full-time U.S. National team, made up of non-NHL players which would stay together through the 1994 Olympics in Lillehammer as well. But USA Hockey officials were only willing to hire him for the 1992 Winter Games, so Herb, very principled, walked away.

After scouting and working in the private sector, Brooks got the coaching bug yet again a few years later, when he agreed to guide the French Olympic team at the 1998 Winter Games in Nagano, Japan, – even upsetting Team USA, 3-1, in the World Championships just prior to the tournament. Herbie just loved to coach and loved new challenges.

Following that, Brooks became a full-time scout with the NHL's Pittsburgh Penguins, ultimately taking over as the teams' head coach in 1999. Herb really didn't want to take over as the Penguins' head coach, but did it out of loyalty to his good friend Craig Patrick, who was the team's general manager. Brooks seized the moment behind the bench, demanding speed, hard work, excitement and fun from his players. He was determined to make things happen, and happen they did, as his club rallied back from a lousy start to end up with a respectable 29-23-5 finish and a first-round playoff series win.

Herbie then came full circle again in 2002 when he guided the U.S. Olympic team to a dramatic silver medal at the Winter Games in Salt Lake City. There, Herbie was a kid in a candy store, guiding America's best professional players in a venue so near and dear to his heart. Once again, Herbie had made America proud. A 6-0 opening round win over Finland sparked America's interest and set an early tone for Team USA. Later, after beating Russia, 3-2, in the semifinals, it all came down to the wire in the gold medal game against Canada. There, the U.S. hung tough through two periods, but came up short in the third, losing 5-2. It wouldn't have been a miracle this time around, but Herb certainly brought some magic back to the game and to the fans of American hockey. Just his mere presence behind the bench brought back so many wonderful memories of that special time in Lake Placid some 22 years earlier. The players this time around weren't college kids either, they were "dream-teamers," who all grew up watching the "Miracle on Ice." The resepect that they showed to Brooks was incredible.

The New York Rangers came calling again in 2003, but Herbie had had enough, even turning down a multimillion-dollar multi-year offer. He was serving as the director of player development for the Penguins at the time and did not want to get back into the rat race. He was enjoying life and enjoying the fruits of his labor. He had five grandchildren now and was having a ball. Sure, it was tempting for him, as he went back and forth over many sleepless nights debating whether or not he wanted to get back into the New York City sports scene or not. But in the end, he chose his family. When it was all said and done, Brooks' career NHL coaching record with the Penguins, North Stars, Devils and Rangers added up to a respectable 219-221-66.

A True Legend with a Truly Amazing Legacy

Tragically, on the afternoon of August 11, 2003, Herb was killed in a one car accident just north of Minneapolis on Interstate 35 near Forest Lake. Ironically, he was returning home from the U.S. Hockey Hall of Fame Golf Tournament in Biwabik Minn., where he was once again doing his part to promote the growth of American hockey. He was just 66 years old. Herb's funeral was a venerable who's who of the hockey world, with several thousand dignitaries, politicians, family members, friends, coaches and fans alike, all coming out to pay their respect to one of the true patriarchs of the game. Honorary pall bearers carrying hockey sticks saluted Herbie as he left the St. Paul Cathedral while a formation of World War II planes flew overhead in his honor. The funeral mass began with a lone bagpiper playing "Amazing Grace," and ended with the singing of "The Battle Hymn of the Republic." In typical Herbie fashion, the Mass was a wonderful mix of the rich and famous alongside the blue-collar and poor. Former Gopher Billy Butters and former Olympian Mike Eruzione each spoke beautifully in his honor as well. Then, in a lighter moment, fellow St. Paulite Reverend Malone spoke of Herbie's East Side roots.

"I have a message for the East Siders here," he said, "and this is coming from someone who grew up three doors down from the old (rival) Harding High School. Consider just some of the accomplishments of Herb Brooks, as hockey player at the University of Minnesota and for two Olympic teams, coach of three Gopher national champion teams, coach of U.S. Olympic hockey teams that won the 1980 gold medal and 2002 silver and as a professional coach. Incredible. But for a moment, imagine if he had lived on the right side of the East Side and gone to Harding, not Johnson. It boggles the imagination!" The church erupted with laughter and smiles. Even Herbie would've cracked a smile at that one.

Throughout his career Herb earned great recognition, both individually and for his country. Among his many honors and accolades, he was inducted into the Hockey Hall of Fame, U.S. Hockey Hall of Fame, the International Ice Hockey Hall of Fame, the University of Minnesota and the State of Minnesota Halls of Fames, while also receiving the coveted Lester Patrick Award for his contributions to American hockey.

As a public speaker, Herb was one of the very best, frequently being asked to speak to the executives of Fortune 500 companies from coast-to-coast. There, he would speak about team building, leadership, perseverance and commitment. He would also talk about dreams, because Herbie was a dreamer. He encouraged those in attendance to believe in their dreams and follow their passions. When he was done, oftentimes those in attendance would rise up in unison and applaud, pausing only long enough to wipe away their tears. After listening to him speak, many felt that they too could beat the mighty Soviets. That was Herbie.

One of our nation's most charismatic and innovative coaches, Herb Brooks was a true American hero and a real Minnesota treasure. Whether he was competing in the business world, on the ice, or even on the diamond of a world championship fast-pitch softball team, he took the same no-nonsense attitude and intensity to whatever he did, and that's why he was so successful. His legacy will live on forever in the youth of America as they continue to enjoy the fruits of his hard work. In the world of coaching, no one was larger than Herb Brooks. He was simply the best of the absolute best, and is dearly missed.

As it has been said so many times, Herb never forgot where he came from. Whether he was enjoying a burger and talking hockey at Serlin's Cafe, or having a cold one with his high school pals at Yarusso's, Brooks stayed true to his colorful working-class neighborhood roots. On St. Paul's East Side, Herbie was royalty, but if you asked him, he would just say that he was a "Joe Six Pack" from Payne Avenue.

His legacy also lives on in the Disney movie *"Miracle,"* which starred Kurt Russell as Herbie, and has educated a whole new generation of kids about the man who lived by the adage that *"the name on the front of the jersey was always more important than the one on the back."* In addition, a statue of Herbie was erected in St. Paul's Rice Park across from the one of famed author F. Scott Fitzgerald. Ironically, it was Fitzgerald who wrote the now infamous line: *"Show me a hero and I will show you a tragedy."* How fitting. Gone from this earth, Herbie has earned his place in sports immortality.

CHARLES SCHULZ

Charles Schulz was born in Minneapolis on November 26, 1922, and grew up in St. Paul loving hockey. As a kid he loved going to St. Paul Saints and Minneapolis Millers games, and even had a rink in his family's backyard. After graduating from St. Paul Central High School, Schulz went on to attend art school in Minneapolis. There, he created a comic strip about the adventures of a group of pre-schoolers (including a kid named Charlie Brown) called "Li'l Folks," which appeared in the St. Paul Pioneer Press in 1947.

United Features Syndicate bought the strip in 1950 and renamed it "Peanuts" because 'Li'l Folks" sounded too much like "Li'l Abner." Seven newspapers carried the original "Peanuts" cartoon strip on October 2, 1950, and the numbers have grown ever since.

He later moved on to California, where he became one of the world's most famous cartoonists. The multiple Emmy winner's cartoons are still read by several hundred million people in nearly 75 countries, who speak more than two dozen different languages. *(Charlie Brown is Carolius Niger and Snoopy is Snupius in the Latin version.)* He has been one of the Top 10 highest-paid entertainers in the U.S., and built an empire surrounding that lovable pooch, Snoopy.

Through it all his love of hockey only grew. Schulz even started a senior hockey tournament at his arena (which he purchased) in the early 1970s called the "Snoopy Open" which grew into one of the world's largest senior hockey competitions. Charles even used to play a mean left wing in the "over-70" bracket.

Among his many honors and accolades, in 1981 Schulz received the Lester Patrick Award for his outstanding service to American hockey, and in 1993 he was inducted into the U.S. Hockey Hall of Fame. Sadly, Schulz passed away in 2000 at the age of 78.

Today, the Minnesota Cartoonists League meets in his honor at O'Gara's piano bar in St. Paul under an original portrait of Snoopy that was drawn and signed by Charles himself. The reason they meet there is because that building was, from 1942 to 1952, Charles Schulz's father's barbershop. *"Good Grief!"*

and professional signings," said Woog. "The first big question is who will replace Jeff Stolp, the top goalie in the WCHA last year; Larry Olimb, a Hobey Baker Finalist and arguably one of the top playmakers in the country; Trent Klatt one of the top scoring forwards in the country; and three veteran defensemen, including All-American Doug Zmolek. Throw in the versatile Cory Laylin and you have seven players who were veterans of the WCHA and four who were legitimate stars. You just don't replace those kinds of losses overnight.

"Last year we scored over five goals per game in the WCHA and that obviously played a big part in our success. The loss of Olimb, Klatt and Laylin up front will reduce our firepower initially, but those spots will be filled by our up-and coming veterans. We feel that we have a nucleus of very fine group of forwards returning, with Craig Johnson (19-39=58), Darby Hendrickson (25-30=55), Steve Magnusson (9-24=33), Jeff Nielsen (15-15=30), Justin McHugh (14-9=23), Scott Bell (15-7=22), Joe Dziedzic (9-10=19) and John Brill (8-9=17) all back. We look at it as more of a reloading year, because we feel the returning players, along with the talented newcomers could give us an even more explosive attack."

Behind goalies Tom Newman and Jeff Callinan, the Gophers opened the season with a split at home with North Dakota, followed by a split at Colorado College. The latter game of that series, a 6-7 loss, wound up being the first of four consecutive overtime games for the Gophers, of which they tied the next three against Northern Michigan and Wisconsin. They managed to take three points from Denver, then swept Michigan Tech and St. Cloud State before heading into the Christmas break. It was a tough January, however, with one of the top highlights coming at Duluth on January 9th, where freshman phenom Brian Bonin got the game-winner in a thrilling 6-5 overtime victory.

The team showed tremendous resolve though and regrouped from their mid-season slump by winning 12 of their last 14 games. Down the stretch they even swept hated North Dakota, 6-4, and 5-4 in overtime, in the first round of the WCHA Playoffs. After beating Wisconsin in the WCHA Final Four, thanks to Jeff Nielsen's overtime game-winner, they dug deep and came up with a 5-3 victory over Northern Michigan for the WCHA Tournament title. From there, they wound up beating Clarkson in the NCAA Quarterfinals in Worcester, Mass., only to get beat the next night by Maine, 6-2, to end their season.

The Maroon and Gold finished with a 22-12-8 overall record that year, good for second place in the WCHA with a 16-9-7 mark. More importantly though, they battled back into the post-season picture by garnering the program's ninth consecutive NCAA Tournament appearance.

Leading the charge offensively was junior center Craig Johnson, who tallied 22 goals and 24 assists en route to earning All-WCHA Honorable Mention honors. Junior forward Jeff Nielsen followed Johnson with 21 goals and 20 assists, while All-WCHA Second Team defenseman Travis Richards was third in scoring with 12 goals and 26 assists. (Nielsen also took home the coveted WCHA Student-Athlete of the Year Award that year as well.) Richards finished his illustrious career in Gold Country as the school's second all-time leading scorer in both goals and assists for a defensemen, behind only his older brother Todd, who tallied 128 from 1985-89.

In addition, Senior Goalie Tom

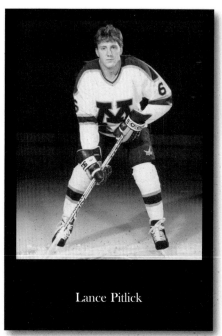

Lance Pitlick

Newman started out slow but came on strong, finishing the season with a WCHA-leading 3.12 GAA and a 14-4-2 record. Another great senior campaign was had by versatile winger John Brill, who finished with 12 goals and 13 assists, and meant a great deal to the team's overall chemistry. Freshman center Brian Bonin also contributed right away with 10 goals and 18 assists en route to earning All-WCHA Rookie Team honors.

Big changes hit Gold Country in 1993 and none was bigger than the brand spanking new Mariucci Arena, which was built across the street from the old one. While many fans were sad to be leaving behind one of college hockey's greatest old shrines, most were excited to be moving into what was considered to be the premier college hockey facility in the country. The new arena opened on August 21st with the Alumni Legends Game, followed two months later by the regular season home-opener against St. Cloud State, where Brian Bonin's two goals and an assist gave the Gophers a 4-4 tie against the Huskies.

The 1993-94 Gophers were young but had a lot of promising young talent. Gone were Craig Johnson and Darby Hendrickson to the U.S. Olympic Team, as were Travis Richards, John Brill and Tom Newman to graduation. Add in the season ending back injury to Scott Bell and it was readily apparent that there were going to be some holes to fill. Leading the charge, however, was pre-season All-American defenseman Chris McAlpine, who was known not only for his toughness in the defensive zone, but also for his knock-out punch scoring ability inside the opponents' blue line. Up front, the Gophers also had their second leading scorer back from a year ago in All-American candidate Jeff Nielsen, as well as Joe Dziedzic, Jed Fiebelkorn, Justin McHugh, Tony Bianchi, Steve Magnusson, Brian Bonin, Brandon Steege, Andy Brink and Bobby Dustin. In goal this year were a pair of talented underclassmen in Junior Jeff Callinan and sophomore Jeff Moen.

"This team is kind of an unknown because of the turn-over in players," said Woog. "But if we get the kind of solid defensive play that we had a year ago and the goaltenders are solid, then we won't give up a lot of goals. On offense, we need our veteran forwards to lead the way, names like Nielsen, Dziedzic, Fiebelkorn, McHugh and Bonin have to appear in the scoring summary every night or we will struggle. I think if the veterans do their part, the younger players will fill in the gaps and we'll really add some excitement to our offense."

The 1993-94 schedule was brutal, as the team played seven of its first eight regular season games on the road. The young Gophers started 0-5-1, the second-worst start in program history, but then rattled off a 6-2-2 record heading into the new year. The Gophers then posted a 14-4-1 second-half record in the conference, finishing just a half game away from winning the WCHA title. They then rattled off four straight WCHA playoff wins over Denver (twice), followed by Michigan Tech and St. Cloud State, to notch their second straight WCHA Tournament Championship. Nick Checco scored a pair of goals in the title game, including the game-winner, while Jeff Moen made 25 saves en route to the big win.

The Gophers were now NCAA bound and headed to East Lansing, Mich., to face Lowell. There, Goalie Jeff Callinan, who had rattled off 12 victories in his last 15 starts, was huge. Behind Nick Checco's third period equalizer goal, and Jeff Nielsen's dramat-

Robb Stauber

ic game-winner in double overtime, Minnesota advanced back to the NCAA Final Four — which was being held at the St. Paul Civic Center.

With the bad memories of the 1989 NCAA Finals overtime loss to Harvard still fresh in their minds, the Gophers hit the ice against Boston University with high hopes that March 31st. Callinan came up with 29 saves that evening, but wound up on the wrong side of a 4-1 loss. The more than 16,000 fans in attendance were crushed, yet again.

The team finished the season with a 25-13-4 record though, recording one of the most remarkable turn-arounds in NCAA hockey history along the way. While All-WCHA co-captains Jeff Nielsen and Chris McAlpine led the way individually, with 45 and 30 points, respectively, this was clearly a team effort. All-WCHA honorable mention honoree Brian Bonin tallied 44 points; Justin McHugh finished third on the team with 36 points; Tony Bianchi came out of nowhere to score eight goals and a team-high 27 assists; Eric Means tallied 16 points while playing great defense; and Joe Dziedzic scored nearly a point a game in a frustrating season that saw him miss 26 of 44 games with two separate fractures of his right arm. The 1993-94 season will go down as a memorable one as this group of over-achievers battled back from a lot of adversity and thanks to a dramatic late-season rush, wound up back in the Final Four for the fifth time in the last nine years.

"We certainly started off on a rocky note," said Woog of the season. "But our players never got down on themselves and they picked each other up. The team battled and clawed its way into the Final Four and that's what the Minnesota tradition of 'Pride on Ice' is all about."

With 18 returning letter winners and the highest-rated recruiting class in more than a decade coming in, the state of the state of Gopher hockey looked very bright indeed heading into the 1994-95 campaign. Jeff Callinan and Jeff Moen both had solid seasons between the pipes in 1993-94, and were joined that season by sophomore Steve DeBus — giving the team a trio of quality netminders. Among the frosh who were expected to contribute right out of the gates were Casey Hankinson, the youngest brother of former Gophers Peter and Ben, and the highly touted Mike Crowley, who earned "Mr. Hockey" honors after leading Bloomington Jefferson to its third consecutive state high school hockey title. Add to that the fact that Scott Bell was returning after missing an entire year due to a back injury, and there were high hopes in Gold Country this year.

Minnesota sprinted out to a 6-0 start on its way to the No. 1 ranking in college hockey by sweeping their perennial intra-state rivals from Minnesota-Duluth, followed by the cheese-heads from Wisconsin and then the Huskies from St. Cloud State. From there things got a bit dicey, as the team would earn just one point in splits with UND and Michigan Tech at home. After beating Michigan State and Michigan to capture the College Hockey Showcase over the Thanksgiving weekend at the Civic Center, the Maroon and Gold struggled through December and January. First place Colorado College had jumped up to the top of the pack and everybody else was chasing them in the standings. The Gophers' once potent power play was on the fritz and the team needed to regroup.

In February the team came back to

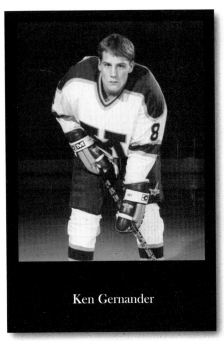

Ken Gernander

life, taking three of four points from Tech and then sweeping Duluth and Denver on back-to-back weekends, thanks in large part to the efforts of Bonin and Bell, who were lighting the lamp early and often. Then, after garnering a pair of ties with North Dakota, the team swept St. Cloud State and Duluth yet again, to head into the WCHA Playoffs. In the Duluth Series, Casey Hankinson scored the overtime game-winner in Game One, while Crowley tallied the third period game-winner in Game Two. At the WCHA Playoffs the Gophers came out swinging and upended the Fighting Sioux thanks to more Hankinson heroics, with this game-winner coming in the third period. After losing to CC, 5-4 in overtime, Minnesota rallied back to beat Denver, 5-4, on Bell's overtime winner at 17:14 of the extra session. Things were looking up.

Woog's crew had come on down the stretch and found themselves back in the NCAA Tournament for the 11th straight year, and 10th under Woog. The team opened up the quarterfinals at the Dane County Coliseum in Madison by blanking RPI, 3-0, thanks to a pair of Nick Checco goals and a perfect 22 for 22 saves by Goalie Jeff Callinan. From there, Minnesota beat CC, 5-2, behind a pair of Dave Larson goals, to advance on to the NCAA championships for the second year in a row. Making it even more special was the fact that the victory was Woog's 300th as the Gopher's head coach.

Eager to finally bring home the hardware, the team headed east to the Providence Civic Center, where they faced off against Boston University in the Final Four. Despite first period goals by Crowley and Jesse Bertogliat, the team allowed four unanswered goals in the third period to wind up on the wrong end of a 7-3 contest to end their season on a big downer.

When it was all said and done, Minnesota ended the year with a solid 25-14-5 record, finishing third in the WCHA standings, the WCHA Final Five, and the NCAA tournament. Incredibly, Woog had now led his teams to the NCAA tournament in each of his 10 years behind the Gopher bench, reaching the Final Four six of those times.

As for individual accolades, it was all about Center Brian Bonin, who finished with 63 points (32 goals, 31 assists) to lead the team in scoring. For his efforts, he was selected as a first-team All-American, was named one of 10 finalists for the Hobey Baker Award, won the WCHA Player of the Year award, and was the WCHA scoring champion. Other top players included Junior Dan Trebil who not only led all WCHA defensemen in scoring with 43 points (10 goals, 33 assists), but was also named to the Academic all-Big Ten team. Joining him on that elite squad was Justin McHugh, who, along with scoring 40 points, was also named as the WCHA Student-Athlete of the Year.

In addition, Goaltender Jeff Callinan finished as the WCHA goaltending champion, posting the lowest goals-against average in the league at 2.73. Callinan earned all-WCHA honorable mention honors and placed himself among the leaders in career and single-season goaltending records at Minnesota. As for the freshman, Minnesota placed two members on the All-Rookie squad. In fact, Mike Crowley was named as the WCHA's Freshman of the Year for his 38 point (11 goals, 27 assists) performance. Joining him was Center Ryan Kraft, who recorded 46 points (13 goals, 33 assists) to finish second on the team in scoring.

Minnesota hit the ice in 1995-96 with

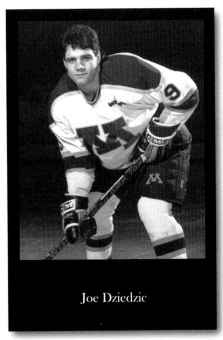

Joe Dziedzic

DOUG WOOG

Doug Woog grew up playing hockey on St. Paul's south side. Before graduating in 1962 from South St. Paul High School, he earned all-state hockey honors for an amazing three consecutive years. He also starred in football and was a good student to boot. From there, Doug fulfilled a life-long dream by accepting a scholarship to play for the U of M and learn the game from one of the all-time great coaches, John Mariucci.

Woog went on to a fabulous career in Gold Country, earning All-American honors his junior season after leading the team in scoring. He was named as captain for his senior season en route to leading the team to a 16-12-0 record, and a second place finish in the WCHA. For his efforts he was named the team's MVP. From 1964-1966 the speedy center scored 48 goals and 53 assists for 101 career points. Doug graduated with honors from the U of M in 1967.

From there, he went on to play for the 1967 U.S. National Team and was a candidate for the 1968 U.S. Olympic team. It was then off to the real world for the Wooger though as he began teaching geography while coaching football and hockey at Hopkins West Junior High School. In the fall of 1968, he took a job at his high school alma mater, where he became the head soccer coach as well as an assistant on both the hockey and baseball teams. While coaching at South St. Paul, his soccer program won six conference titles and twice finished as runner-ups at the state championship.

From 1971 through 1977 he branched out to coach the St. Paul Vulcans and the Minnesota Junior Stars, which he led to two U.S. Junior National titles. From there, he would go on to coach as an assistant with Team USA on the international level. Then, in 1985, Woog got his big break when he was named as the new head coach at the University of Minnesota. There, he would guide the Golden Gophers to seven league championships (four regular season and three post-season) over his illustrious 14-year career. During his tenure in Gold Country the Gophers were among the nation's very best, garnering WCHA Final Four/Five and NCAA appearances in 12 of 14 seasons, posting seven 30-win seasons, and appearing in six NCAA Final Fours. In 1999 Woog resigned as the team's head coach to take an assistant athletic director position at the school. He would leave as the progeam's all-time winningest coach with a gaudy 389-187-40 record (.664).

Among his many honors and accolades, in 2002 he was inducted into the U.S. Hockey Hall of Fame in Eveleth. Today, in addition to his work in corporate sales with the University of Minnesota, Woog is a television analyst for Gopher Hockey games. He also runs his own summer hockey camp in Breezy Point as well.

"It was a life-long dream come true for me to be able to play for the Gophers," said Woog. "The fact that we had scholarships was just a means to an end. Back then there weren't that many opportunities for us after college as far as hockey was concerned, with only six NHL teams and all. So, we played for the love of the game and were happy to get to school to be able to make a living. Yeah, being a Gopher was pretty special."

yet another outstanding crop of freshman, including the 1995 recipient of the state's "Mr. Hockey" award, Erik Rasmussen from St. Louis Park, as well as Bloomington's Mike Anderson, Warroad's Wyatt Smith and Anoka's Reggie Berg.

The Gophers struggled out of the gates, going 1-2-1 over their first four games on the road at Michigan Tech and eventual WCHA champion Colorado College. The friendly confines of Mariucci Arena were a welcome sight as the team took out their frustrations on Alaska-Anchorage by outscoring the Seawolves, 13-3, en route to a weekend sweep. Kraft, Crowley, Berg and Bonin tallied eight of the goals in the shellacking. This was just the beginning of one of the greatest stretch runs in Gopher hockey history as the team took off from there. After sweeping St. Cloud State, the Gophers split with Denver. From there, the team went up 35W and did what no other team in WCHA history had ever done before, pull off a shutout road sweep at Duluth. The pucks kept bouncing Minnesota's way after that as the team ended the month by claiming the College Hockey Showcase title in Milwaukee with wins over both Michigan and Michigan State.

While November was utterly fantastic for the Maroon and Gold, December and January proved to be even better as the team went 13-0-1 over the next two months. After sweeping North Dakota at home, the team took three of four points on the trip to Alaska-Anchorage — always a tough task to pull off with the long travel time and lack of sleep. Reggie Berg tallied a hat trick and Jeff Moen stopped all 20 pucks he faced in the

second game, a 5-0 shut-out. The team said good bye to 1995 with its first Mariucci Classic title in four seasons by beating Harvard and Bowling Green, thanks to outstanding goaltending from both Moen and DeBus, who let in just four goals between them during the tourney.

The new year was good to the Gophers as they enjoyed their first unbeaten and untied January in school history. With sweeps over Denver, UMD, Wisconsin, and Northern Michigan, the team found itself riding a school record 19-game unbeaten streak into February. The wheels came off shortly after that, however, as the team won just two of their next eight games. In fact, in between sweeps by North Dakota and Wisconsin, the team managed a couple of really tough splits with first place Colorado College and then St. Cloud State. Incidentally, the first game of the home-and-home with St. Cloud State saw the team pummell the huskies, 8-3, behind Rasmussen's hat trick and a pair of goals from Brian Bonin — his 200th career point as a Gopher.

Jeff Nielsen

In March the team got it figured out. After sweeping Alaska-Anchorage in the first-round of the WCHA Playoffs, Minnesota ended Wisconsin's season at the WCHA Final Five thanks to Berg and Bonins' third period goals, followed by Nick Checco's overtime game-winner. From there, the team beat Michigan Tech in the title game to clinch their 12th consecutive bid to the NCAA Tournament.

In the opener the Gophers beat Providence, 5-1, behind a pair of Wyatt Smith goals to set up a rematch with Michigan in the quarterfinals. There, ironically, for the third consecutive time in as many years, the eventual national champion would knock out the Gophers and send them packing. This time it was the Wolverines as they rallied late in the game to come up with a pair of third period goals to win, 4-3, in East Lansing, Mich. Casey Hankinson tied it up at three apiece with five minutes to go, but DeBus got beat just a few minutes later to seal the deal. It was a bitter loss to cap an otherwise fantastic year.

The honors and accolades that season started and stopped with Center Brian Bonin (81 points) and Defenseman Mike Crowley (63 points), who were both named as Hobey Baker Finalists. Both players were also named as first team All-Americans, marking the first time since 1981 (Neal Broten and Steve Ulseth) that two Gophers were honored as such in the same season. Bonin, who became just the fifth player in league history to win back-to-back league scoring titles, also took home both the WCHA regular-season and tournament MVP honors. Crowley, meanwhile, broke the single-season points record with his four-assist effort in the WCHA Final Five championship game against Michigan Tech, giving him 46 helpers on the year — three better than previous record-holder Todd Richards, who set the record back in 1987.

In addition, senior defenseman and co-captain Dan Trebil (46 points) was named as a second team All-American as well as a second-team Academic All-American. For his efforts, he was given the prestigious WCHA Student-Athlete of the Year Award. Trebil also became just the second blue-liner in Gopher history to tally 100 or more assists in his career. Other Gophers honored by the WCHA included goaltender Steve DeBus and freshman Erik Rasmussen, who were named to the All-WCHA first team and All-Rookie team, respectively.

On a side note, Minnesota's "Pride on Ice" was the subject of national media attention when it was featured on ESPN's "NCAA Today" show that year, highlighting the unique fact that every player on the roster was home grown from Minnesota.

The 1996-97 Season opened with a bang. The festivities celebrating the 75th anniversary of Gopher hockey kicked off by honoring all of their past All-Americans in a weekend series against three-time defending WCHA champion Colorado College. Erik Rasmussen's pair of goals led the Gophers to a 4-2 victory in the opener, but the team came up a goal short the next night, 2-1, to split the series with the Tigers. From there, Minnesota split a pair of series with both Duluth and Wisconsin, but rebounded in November by sweeping North Dakota, Michigan Tech and Northern Michigan to catapult to the top of the WCHA standings. In the second game with North Dakota, Casey Hankinson scored four goals and added a pair of assists as Minnesota crushed the eventual national champions, 10-6. Then, against Michigan Tech, Freshman Goalie Erik Day made history when he debuted with back-to-back shut-outs, becoming the first Gopher netminder in school history to accomplish the feat in his first two collegiate starts.

Minnesota then lost the opener against Michigan at the College Hockey Showcase in Detroit, but rallied back behind Wyatt Smith's third period goal to beat Michigan State, 4-3, for third place. From there, the Gophs came up with an impressive 4-1 win at SCSU, highlighted by senior Dan Hendrickson's four assist effort, but lost the

Larry Olimb

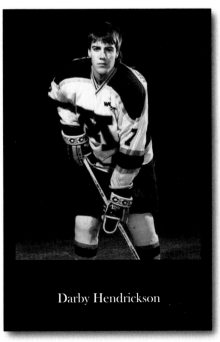

Darby Hendrickson

back end of the series in overtime, 4-3, despite a pair of Rico Pagel goals. The team rounded out the year by winning the Mariucci Classic with wins over Boston College, 4-2, and Miami University, 7-4.

January opened with the team garnering a tough road sweep over Alaska-Anchorage behind junior Ryan Kraft's hat trick in the Saturday game, giving him WCHA Player of the Week honors. Minnesota then split with Denver, winning the opener, 3-2, on Nick Checco's thrilling overtime goal at 1:35 of the extra session. After splitting with St. Cloud State in a tough home-and-home series, the Gophers rebounded to sweep Michigan Tech, outscoring the Huskies by a 13-6 margin. Freshman Ben Clymer had a goal and an assist in the opener and then notched his first career hat-trick in the Saturday game.

Things got ugly when the Gophers then headed up to Grand Forks though, as the Sioux swept the Maroon and Gold to open up a three-point lead in the WCHA standings. Determined, Minnesota rebounded to sweep Northern Michigan, 4-3 and 2-1, on Billy Kohn's game-winner in Game One and Ryan Kraft's two goals in Game Two. UMD crushed the Gophers that next weekend in the opener, 8-4, only to get hammered by Minnesota the next night, 7-1, behind Duluth East grad Dave Spehar's two goals and Ryan Kraft's four assists. Minnesota then captured three out of four points on the road against Colorado College, followed by a sweep of rival Wisconsin at home thanks in large part to the efforts of Kraft, who tallied five goals in the series. For their efforts, the team finished as co-WCHA champs with a record of 21-10-1 in league action.

After sweeping Alaska-Anchorage in a first round WCHA playoff series at Mariucci Arena, Brian LaFleur scored a pair and then Mike Crowley clinched it in overtime to lift the Gophers to a dramatic come-from-behind, 5-4, win over St. Cloud State at the WCHA Final Five in St. Paul. The next night, however, North Dakota eked out an overtime win of their own over the Gophers, winning 4-3, despite goals from Hendrickson, Spehar and Checco. With the Broadmoor Trophy in hand, UND got the higher seed and forced the Gophers to travel to Grand Rapids, Mich., to face Michigan State. There, they dominated the Spartans, 6-3, behind Casey Hankinson's two goals and two assists.

With that, the Gophers now found themselves in hostile territory, facing rival Michigan for the second consecutive season in an NCAA quarterfinal showdown. The defending NCAA champs didn't disappoint either, jumping out to a 4-0 lead and beating Minnesota convincingly, 7-4, despite a pair of unassisted goals from Erik Rasmussen. The team finished with a very respectable 28-13-1 overall record, but simply could not get the 900 pound gorilla otherwise known as Michigan off of their backs.

When the smoke had finally cleared, Mike Crowley, who scored 56 points that season, was named as the WCHA Player of the Year, a Hobey Baker Finalist, and earned first-team All-American honors for the second year in a row — just the third player ever to do so in back-to-back seasons. In addition, Goalie Steve DeBus, a Rochester native, was named to his second straight All-WCHA first team. DeBus led the league in wins (18) and was among the top four netminders in the league in goals-against average (3.081) saves (705), shut-out periods (32) and minutes played (1,675). The other top scorers from that season included Ryan Kraft, who tallied

46 points; Casey Hankinson, who added 41 points; and Dave Spehar and Reggie Berg, who each notched 37 points apiece.

The Gopher's 1997-98 campaign was all about splits early on, and ultimately ended in frustration as the team wound up bowing out in the first round of the WCHA playoffs. Minnesota began the year by splitting the season-opening series with Hockey East power Maine at Mariucci Arena, 1-6 and 3-2. From there, they headed to Duluth, where Junior Center Wyatt Smith scored four goals in the weekend series split against the Dogs. The team then earned splits with both North Dakota and Wisconsin, in four tight games that were each decided by a goal. Erik Westrum and freshman Aaron Miskovich each tallied two goals in the 6-5 win over the defending national champs from North Dakota in the Friday game, while Reggie Berg's two goals capped a great comeback in the 4-2 Friday win at Wisconsin.

To say that November and December were tough on the Maroon and Gold would be an understatement to say the least. The Gophers embarked on a rough nine-game losing streak which included sweeps at the hands of Alaska-Anchorage, Colorado College, and both games of the College Hockey Showcase against Michigan and Michigan State. The only silver lining was the fact that six of the seven losses during that stretch were by only one goal. Following a pair of losses to St. Cloud State, Minnesota finally got a "W" with a 6-3 win over Brown at the Mariucci Classic, thanks to Wyatt Smith's four points and Dave Spehar's two goals. They lost to Northeastern that next night, but rebounded to sweep Mankato State the next weekend, 6-2 and 4-3, in their first ever meeting. Wyatt Smith scored six points in the series while Dylan Mills added three of his own.

January would prove to be much better for the Gophers. After a home split with Denver, they went on to sweep the UMD Bulldogs behind hometown hero Dave Spehar's four goals in the series. In addition, Defenseman Brett Abrahamson notched the game-winner on Saturday, earning him WCHA Defensive Player of the Week honors in the process. The team closed out the month on a downer, getting swept up in Houghton, Mich., by Michigan Tech. One bright spot, however, was the play of Junior Forward Mike Anderson, who notched six goals and four assists while scoring a point in seven of the eight games during the month.

From there, the team got it together by sweeping Wisconsin, 4-1 and 7-0. The Gophers snapped the Badger's 13-game unbeaten streak in Game One thanks to a pair of Ryan Kraft goals. Then, in Game two, Wyatt Smith scored a hat trick; Ryan Kraft scored four points; Stuart Senden scored a pair of his own, and Steve DeBus stood on his lips by turning aside all 34 shots that came his way in front of nearly 15,000 fans at the Target Center.

Minnesota then lost to UND, 4-2, in Game One of the next series, and then blew a 3-0 third period lead to the defending NCAA champions in the finale. The team headed to

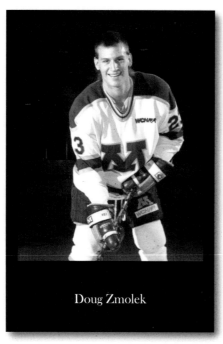

Doug Zmolek

Eric Westrum

Brian Bonin

Alaska-Anchorage that following weekend and won Game One, 3-0, behind Steve DeBus' 14 saves, and Wyatt Smith's two goals. Kraft, Sendin, Spehar and Berg all tallied in the 4-2 Saturday win to complete the sweep.

Despite Wyatt Smith's five goals against CC that next weekend, which resulted in him earning WCHA Offensive Player of the Week honors, Minnesota got swept by the Tigers, 4-3 and 9-6. Minnesota rallied to sweep St. Cloud State that next week though, 6-2 and 5-3, behind Reggie Berg's hat trick in Game One and Casey Hankinson's game-winner late in the third in Game Two.

Hoping to make a splash in the post-season, Minnesota got trounced by UMD, 7-3, in the first round of the WCHA playoffs, but came back behind DeBus' 5-0 shutout at the DECC in Game Two. The third and final game, however, saw UMD score four unanswered goals in the third period to send the game to overtime. There, Duluth's Mike Peluso scored the 5-4 heart-breaking game-winner, giving the Dogs a 2-1 series win. With that, an otherwise marginal season by Gopher standards was over, courtesy of an ugly first-round exit.

The Gophers ended the season with a 17-22-0 overall record and a 12-16-0 mark in conference action. Despite the team's average season, they did manage to set the NCAA Attendance Record with a total home attendance of 201,126 for 20 home dates. In fact, Minnesota became the first school in NCAA hockey history to average over 10,000 per game in a single season with 10,056.

Among the honors and accolades that year, Reggie Berg was named to the all-WCHA second team. Berg finished with 39 points, good for a share of the WCHA scoring crown. In addition, Wyatt Smith was named to the All-WCHA third team after leading the Gophers in overall points with 47, and tying for the WCHA lead with 17 tallies in league games.

Coming off of one of the worst seasons in recent memory, the Gophers were anxious to get the ship turned in the right direction in 1998-99. Among the positives heading in: the league's scoring co-champion in Reggie Berg, and the league leader in goals in all games in Wyatt Smith were back. Add to the mix several proven veterans in Dave Spehar, Mike Anderson, Nate Miller, Bill Kohn, Mike Lyons, Ryan Trebil, Dylan Mills, Aaron Miskovich and Erik Westrum. Then, toss in freshman sensation Johnny Pohl of Red Wing, the Minnesota's all-time state high school scoring leader, and things looked promising. But, the team lost Ben Clymer that summer when he opted to pursue a pro career, as well as goalie Steve DeBus, to graduation. Freshman Adam Hauser was going to be thrown to the wolves and nobody knew how well the kid was going to do. Despite all of the speculation, Coach Woog learned a lot from the year before and was optimistic.

"In some ways, we all probably benefited from last season," said Woog. "We all learned that you can't take things for granted, and that you've always got to work hard. There were many times when I was pleased with the effort I was seeing last season, but everything from the injuries to the bad bounces just made every mistake we committed magnified more than normal. I'm really looking forward to getting this season going more than any other in recent memory. This team has some very talented, hard working players who I feel can be good examples to some of our younger players. If we can get some answers in the nets and on the blue line, this has the potential to be a good team."

Minnesota opened the year on a positive note, beating St. Lawrence and Ohio State before taking three out of four points from UMD at home. Aaron Miskovich scored a pair of goals in the 3-1 win against Duluth. Hauser then proved he was the real deal when he blanked St. Cloud State in Game Five, turning away all 26 shots he faced that night. The Gophers then lost the back end of the series at the National Hockey Center in St. Cloud the next night, as the Huskies scored with just 16 seconds to go for a 6-5 win. From there, Minnesota pulled off a pair of 3-2 victories to earn a hard fought sweep over the Wisconsin Badgers at the new Kohl Center in Madison. Erik Westrum and Dave Spehar each tallied a pair of goals in both games to play spoiler.

Things got tough from there, however, as back-to-back series' against Colorado College and North Dakota yielded just one point for the Gophers — a 4-4 tie against the Sioux. One bright spot though was the outstanding play of freshman defenseman Jordan Leopold, from Robbinsdale, who went on to score five goals in the next five games.

The Gophers earned a split up at Alaska-Anchorage before returning home for the College Hockey Showcase. A 3-2 loss to Michigan was followed with a 2-1 win over Michigan State, thanks to Wyatt Smith's third period power-play game-winner from Dave Spehar. From there, Minnesota stumbled with rare losses to both Princeton and Ohio State at the Mariucci Classic. The new year kicked off with an embarrassing 8-4 loss to Boston College, followed by a 3-3 tie, which saw the Gophers rally to score a pair of third period goals from Anderson and Pagel to secure a point in the standings. They tied Denver by that same score the following weekend, only to get blanked, 5-0, in Game Two.

A pair of ties to Minnesota State-Mankato were then followed up with a pair of crushing defeats at the hands of the top ranked Fighting Sioux, 5-4 and 6-5. The Gophers ended the month on a positive note though, returning home for a pair of 4-2 wins over Michigan Tech thanks to sophomore Matt Leimbek's two goals and three assists, which earned him WCHA Offensive Player of the Week honors. Minnesota's ensuing trip to Colorado College saw the team score just two goals in what turned out to be a pair of blow-out losses.

After earning just a split with Alaska Anchorage at home, Minnesota posted a pair

Dave Spehar

Jeff Taffe

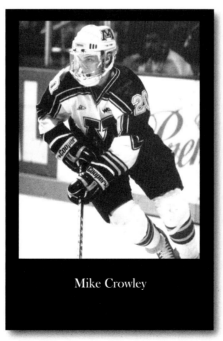

Mike Crowley

of ties against St. Cloud State, 4-4 and 2-2. The highlight of February came in a road sweep of UMD at the DECC in Duluth. There, the Gophers put on an offensive show, taking the opener, 10-7, on Wyatt Smith's hat trick. They then took Game two, 4-1, on Reggie Berg's four-goal masterpiece. Next up was Wisconsin, where, despite a pair of goals from sophomore Erik Westrum, the Badgers took Game One, 6-4. Minnesota earned a 2-2 tie in the finale, however, thanks to goals from Berg and Leopold. Hauser played big in that game too, kicking away 33 of 35 shots.

Hauser kept it going the next series as well, blanking Alaska-Anchorage, 4-0, in Game One and then 1-0 in Game Two. Rico Pagel had the game-winner in the second game as Minnesota headed into the WCHA Final Five at the Target Center with some solid momentum behind them. There, Minnesota got a pair of goals each from Berg and Spehar to open the post-season with a 5-3 win over St. Cloud State. The team's bid for an invitation to the Big Dance, the NCAA Championships, then died the following evening when top-ranked North Dakota skated past the Gophers, 6-2, thus ending Minnesota's season. To make matters worse, the team lost the third-place game to Colorado College the following afternoon, 7-4, putting an exclamation point on an otherwise mediocre season.

The Golden Gophers ended the season with a 15-19-9 overall record and a mark of 10-12-6 in WCHA regular season action. Leading the way for the Maroon and Gold was senior forward Reggie Berg, who, in addition to becoming the 23rd member of the Gopher's 150-Point Club, led the team in total scoring with 20 goals and 28 assists for 48 points. Senior forward Wyatt Smith was named to the all-WCHA third team after leading the team with 23 goals, ultimately finishing his career with 129 points in 152 career games. In addition, freshman Jordan Leopold, who led all Gopher rookies in scoring with seven goals and 16 assists on the season, was also named to the all-WCHA third team as well as the league's all-rookie team.

That off-season, big changes hit the program hard as Doug Woog stepped down as the team's head coach. In his 14 seasons behind the Gopher bench, Woog posted an outstanding 390-187-40 record, good for a .665 winning percentage. He would also go down in the books as the program's all-time winningest coach. Woog didn't go far though, as he was named as an assistant Athletic Director with U of M's Athletics Dept. working with fundraising and corporate sales.

Woog's replacement was another Minnesota boy, Don Lucia, a Grand Rapids native who played college hockey at Notre Dame. Lucia's resume was solid. A former head coach at Alaska-Fairbanks, Lucia came to the Gophers via Colorado College, where he had guided the program from 1993-99. There, he led his teams to a pair of Frozen Fours in 1996 and 1997 and was a two-time WCHA Coach of the Year as well.

Expectations were high under the new coach, but he came in ready to make his mark.

"I am really looking forward to getting things going this season and getting back on the ice," said Lucia. "I told the guys when I took the job that I was not going to look at any tape of them over the last year and make any judgments, positive or negative, about their performances based on that alone. Everyone starts this year with a clean slate, and is going to have to prove himself once practice starts in the Fall. I like the attitude and comments I've heard from the players as I have come in contact with them this summer. Most of all, I'm just excited about the opportunity to be coaching back in my home state, and to be a part of a tradition like Golden Gopher hockey."

The new coach was also optimistic about the talent he inherited on his new roster for the 1999-2000 season.

"We have some nice depth and talent at each position," he said. "I've seen more of the veteran guys than some of the others, but I like the reports I've heard on the younger players. Obviously, we'll need some more goal scoring production out of guys like Spehar, Westrum, and Miskovich to help offset the loss of (Reggie) Berg and (Wyatt) Smith. And as an opposing coach, I always respected the work ethic and effort of guys like Westrum and Miller. Last year seemed to be kind of a break-out type season individually for Westrum, and he definitely possesses the type of make-up to be one of the best in the league this season. I know players like Pagel, Leimbek, and Senden have been on the shelf for quite a few games over the last few years, and hopefully our luck will change in that department this season so we can all see what these players can do given a full season without interruption."

The new-look Gophers hit the ice under Coach Lucia on October 16th, 1999, on the road at Maine. There, despite four goals from Erik Westrum, the Gophers got swept by the Black Bears, 5-3 and 5-4, to start the season on a real downer. Minnesota came back that next weekend, however, to gain a hard earned 2-2 tie at home against North Dakota, thanks to goals by Leopold and Spehar, not to mention a career-high 44 saves from sophomore goalie Adam Hauser. They came up short that next night though, dropping Game Two, 3-2. The team's lone victory of the month came that next weekend against top-ranked Boston College, where they got an overtime goal from senior captain Nate Miller for a 6-5 win. (Incidentally, those three teams: Maine, North Dakota and Boston College, would all advance to the NCAA Frozen Four that year.)

Coach Lucia had a homecoming of sorts when he faced his old squad from Colorado College that next week. After dropping the first game, Minnesota broke a 10-game losing streak to the Tigers as Nate Miller notched both Gopher goals in a 2-1 win. A trip to Wisconsin the following weekend resulted in two bitter losses to the hated Badgers, with both contests being decided on the final shots of the game. Incidentally, Erik

Peter Hankinson

Ben Hankinson

Casey Hankinson

Westrum tallied his first career hat trick in the second game, a 5-4 loss. The Gophs rebounded and got their first sweep of the season against Minnesota-Duluth, beating the Bulldogs 5-3 and 4-0. Sophomore forward Johnny Pohl had a hand in four of the five goals in Game One, as the team capitalized on six power-play goals that weekend. The team then rounded out November with a solid 6-1 win over Michigan on the road.

December began with a series split with the Seawolves up at Alaska. From there, the team managed just one conference point out of a home-and-home confrontation with St. Cloud State. Game Two was particularly frustrating as the team squandered a two goal lead with less than five minutes to play in the game. By now the team was sporting a 6-10-2 record heading into the Mariucci Classic. There, the Gophers pulled it together and posted convincing wins over Harvard, 5-2, and Northern Michigan, 6-2, to lay claim to the tourney title. Fully nine different Gophers scored goals in the two games while Adam Hauser stopped 40 of 42 shots in the Northern Michigan win.

Into January the Gophers came out swinging, sweeping Denver, 7-6 in overtime, and then 7-3. Johnny Pohl made his presence felt in the series as he assisted on four goals in the overtime victory and then netted his first career hat-trick in Game Two against the Pioneers. They kept it going that next weekend too, earning a hard-fought split with the eventual national champions from North Dakota. Goalie Adam Hauser was outstanding in goal, outplaying UND first-team All-American Karl Goehring by stopping 67 of 70 shots on the weekend. Mankato was next and thanks to Pohl's two goals, the Gophers took the opener, 3-2. But, the second game was a heart-breaker as the Mavericks rallied for a 6-5 overtime win to even the series at one apiece.

February began with a sweep on the road by the Minnesota-Duluth Bulldogs. Junior forward Stuart Senden notched the 3-2 game-winner in Game One, while Nate Miller's two-goals paced the Gophers in the 4-1 sweeper victory. Minnesota pummeled Colorado College, 6-2, in the opener of the following weekend series behind Aaron Miskovich's four point night, only to see the Tigers answer back with a 5-1 decision of their own on the following evening. The Gophers then swept Michigan Tech on the road, 9-2 and 4-2, thanks to Dave Spehar's first career hat trick. Also getting in on the action were freshman Jeff Taffe, who had four assists, and Dan Welch, who scored a pair of goals as well.

Minnesota got some bad news that next week when it was learned goalie Adam Hauser would be sidelined for two weeks with mononucleosis. Walk-on freshman goalie Erik Young filled in admirably against the visiting Badgers, stopping 57 of 65 shots, but still came up short as Wisconsin prevailed, 4-2 and 5-4. The slide continued from there as St. Cloud State swept the Gophers in a home-and-home to end the regular season on a sour note. As a result, the Gophers had to play the first round of the WCHA playoffs on the road at Colorado College. There, the team came up huge behind a now healthy Adam Hauser, sweeping the Tigers, 4-2 and 3-2, to catapult into the WCHA Final Five quarterfinals against Mankato at the Target Center.

Against the Mavericks the Gophers got a pair of goals from Erik Westrum and rallied to win, 6-4, setting up a highly anticipated fifth meeting against top-ranked Wisconsin. Would Minnesota rise to the challenge? Nope. They got goals from Westrum, Pohl and Leopold, but came up on the wrong end of a 5-3 contest. Down but not out, they tried to rally in the third-place game against St. Cloud State, which in essence was an NCAA tournament game to the players. There, Minnesota got a pair of goals from Nate Miller, but could not rally back from a 3-1 first period deficit and lost, 6-4. With that, the season was over.

The team, which played by far the toughest schedule of any program in the nation, finished with a respectable 20-19-2 overall record, good for 13-13-2 in the WCHA. Sophomore Johnny Pohl led the team in scoring that season with 18 goals and 41 assists for 59 points. Erik Westrum was second with 53 points, while Nate Miller finished third with 35.

The Gophers opened the 2000-01 season with Coach Lucia taking on his alma mater, Notre Dame, in the Hall of Fame Game at the Xcel Energy Center in St. Paul. Highlighting the 7-3 victory was freshman Matt Koalska netting his first career goal on his very first shift. The Gophers then traveled north for a first-ever meeting against Bemidji State, and thanks to Erik Westrum's career-high five point effort, Minnesota won easily, 9-3. From there, the Gophers swept Duluth and then took three of four points against Alaska Anchorage.

The festivities continued into November as the team swept previously unbeaten Wisconsin at Mariucci Arena behind Adam Hauser's shut-out in the series-opening 4-0 win. With that, the team found itself with a gaudy 7-0-1 record and ranked No. 1 in the nation. Minnesota then traveled to North Dakota, where they got a little humble pie, taking just one point from the Sioux with a 7-5 loss and 5-5 tie. They rebounded to sweep the Huskies of St. Cloud State as Hauser registered his second shut-out of the season with a 2-0 victory in Game One. Game Two was much closer, winning 4-3 on goals from Pohl, Anthony, Westrum and Taffe. Their No. 1 ranking was lost that next week, however, when the Gophs dropped a pair of home games in the College Hockey Showcase to Michigan State, 3-2, and Michigan, 4-1.

The slump continued into December with the Maroon and Gold

Chris McAlpine

Erik Rasmussen

Troy Riddle

getting swept on the road at Denver. Scoring just one goal in the series, the team had now managed to score just four goals in four games — the fewest in program history in nearly a half century. Minnesota rebounded with a convincing 11-2 victory over Quinnipiac, however, thanks to Stuart Senden's first career hat-trick. Following a three-week holiday break, the team returned well rested and rejuvenated, winning the Mariucci Classic by upending Union and Lake Superior State.

The new year was ushered in with a sweep at Alaska-Anchorage, behind Johnny Pohl's five-point weekend. From there, the team split with top-ranked UND, taking the second game by scoring five unanswered goals in a 5-1 victory. Another split ensued at Wisconsin as the Badgers won the opener, 4-2, only to see Minnesota come back behind Grant Potulny's first career hat-trick and win 8-2. Into February the team kept rolling with sweeps of Michigan Tech and at Mankato. Erik Westrum posted a six-point weekend against the Mavericks and as a result was named as the WCHA Player of the Week. The next week things got even better as the Gophers swept Colorado College. Goalie Adam Hauser picked up his third WCHA Player of the Week honor after holding the Tigers to just a pair of goals in the series.

With that, the red hot Gophers headed up 35W to face Duluth. They were not welcomed with open arms, however, as they got upset by the last place Bulldogs, 5-4, in overtime. They came back the next night behind goals from Koalska, Leopold, Westrum and Taffe, though, to win 4-0. Despite plenty of power-plays from the more than 100 penalty minutes, Hauser was able to hang on for his third shut-out of the year.

March rolled in with Minnesota needing a sweep over St. Cloud State in its regular-season finale to claim a share of the MacNaughton Cup. What they got, however, were a pair of ugly 5-2 and 6-1 losses. The Gophers wound up finishing third in the conference, their first top-three finish in four seasons. As such, they hosted Michigan Tech in a first-round WCHA Playoff series, beating the Huskies, 7-2 and 3-1, to advance on to the WCHA's Final Five. Nick Anthony and Stuart Senden each tallied a pair of goals in the series. Next up was St Cloud State, which proceeded to beat the Gophers like a drum, 3-0. The Gophers then lost to CC, 5-4, in the third-place game.

Despite the two setbacks in the Final Five, the Gophers still got invited back to the NCAA Tournament. Incredibly, it was their first trip in four years. There, they faced Maine in the opener out in Worcester, Mass. The two teams needed overtime to settle this one, and in the end it was not pretty for the Gophers. Pohl and Potulny scored in the first and second periods, respectively, to make it 2-2. Potulny then notched his second goal of the game, which was followed by Westrum's go ahead goal in the third to make it 4-3. Maine hung in there though and wound up scoring a power-play goal on penalty by Paul Martin with less than a minute to play. Then, with their goaltender pulled for an extra attacker, the Black Bears miraculously got the equalizer with just three seconds to play to send it to overtime. There, the game roared back and forth with both teams getting several quality scoring chances. Finally, at 13:04 of the extra session, Maine's Robert Liscak beat Hauser to give his team the horrifying 5-4 victory. Season over.

Minnesota posted a much improved 27-13-2 overall record and 18-8-2 mark in the WCHA that year — good for third place. The Gophers also served notice that they were back among college hockey's elite. Erik Westrum led the team in scoring with 26 goals and 35 assists for 61 points. Junior defenseman Jordan Leopold was second with 49 points. For his efforts he was honored as a first-team All-American and was named as a Hobey Baker Finalist as well. In addition, freshman Grant Potulny paced the nation with 16 power-play goals, while Johnny Pohl finished second with 13. Grant Potulny, Troy Riddle and Paul Martin all earned All-WCHA Rookie Team honors to boot.

Minnesota opened the 2001-02 season against North Dakota in the Hall of Fame Game as UND christened its brand new Engelstad Arena in Grand Forks. The Gophers spoiled the party though as they rallied from a 5-3 deficit and came up with four unanswered third-period goals. The momentum carried over after that as the team went on to destroy Bemidji State and Colgate at home by the insane margin of 31-3. Johnny Pohl tallied four goals against the Beavers, while Goalies Adam Hauser and freshman Justin Johnson each notched back-to-back shut-outs against the Raiders. Riddle, Anthony, Martin, Pohl, Tallackson, Erickson, Leopold, Ballard and Martin all had multiple points in that series as well.

Minnesota opened their WCHA schedule at Michigan Tech over the first weekend in November and managed to rally for a win and a tie against the Huskies. Six unanswered goals were the big story in the opener, while Jordan Leopold's power-play equalizer with 1:09 to play in the game was the difference in the 5-5 Game Two. Back at home the Gophs swept both Mankato and Duluth to improve their record to an impressive 10-0-1. Jeff Taffe then tallied his first career hat-trick in a 5-2 win over Michigan at the College Hockey Showcase. Two days later against Michigan State the Gophers rallied from a third period deficit on goals from Potulny, Wendell, and Tallackson to salvage a 4-4 tie. The undefeated Gophers finally got their first loss on November 30th at home against St. Cloud State, 3-2.

The team began the month of December with a rematch against St. Cloud, this time rallying back from a 2-0 lead on goals from Barry Tallackson and Jordan Leopold to salvage a 2-2 tie. The next week Adam Hauser stopped 30 of 31 shots in a 2-1 opening win against Denver, but the team got upended, 4-3, in the second game. Minnesota went on to win the Mariucci Classic after Christmas break, beating Ferris State, 3-2, in the opener, followed by a 6-1 shellacking of Providence in the championship game thanks to Johnny Pohl's two goals and two assists.

January was all about the second game of the weekend series as the team went 0-3-1 in the openers, but rebounded to go 4-0-0 in the rematches. UND was next on the docket for the Gophs as they saw the Sioux

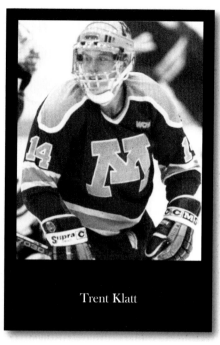

Trent Klatt

Wyatt Smith

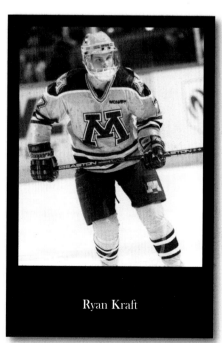

Ryan Kraft

rally back from a 3-0 third period deficit to take the opener, 4-3. Then, in the rematch game the following night, All-American Jordan Leopold became the school's all-time leader in goals by a defenseman when he netted a pair of lamp-lighters in the third period to rally his squad back for a 2-1 victory. Against the Badgers in Madison, Wisconsin pounded Minnesota, 8-3, in Game One, only to see the Gophers take Game Two, 6-2, behind Adam Hauser's 34 saves. The following week was tough as the Maroon and Gold allowed Anchorage to score with one second remaining in the game to steal a point and a 3-3 tie. The team rallied in Game Two, however, behind a pair of Jeff Taffe goals to earn a 5-2 win. The month came to a close with a rematch against then-No. 1 Denver. The Pioneers took the opener, 3-1, only to see the Gophers erupt for a 6-1 rout in Game Two behind Keith Ballard's two goals and Pohl's goal and two assists.

The team got back on track in February despite its opening 5-2 loss at UMD. After rebounding to take the revenge game, 2-1, to earn a split, the Gophers swept UND in Grand Forks. Jon Waibel's Game Two game-winner with 10 seconds left was the highlight of the series as the team rallied from a 3-1 deficit for a 4-3 win. After a tough 6-5 loss at home against Colorado College the next week, the team came back to earn the split by defeating the Tigers, 7-3. From there, Minnesota beat rival Wisconsin, 6-3, at Mariucci Arena in Game One, and then completed the 4-3 sweep the next night courtesy of Jordan Leopold's overtime goal at 2:01 of the extra session.

March was magical as the team went 6-1 into the post-season with a lot of momentum behind them. They closed out the regular season with a St. Cloud sweep, winning the opener, 5-4, and then the rematch, 3-1, behind Adam Hauser's 25 saves on Senior Night at Mariucci Arena. The team kept rolling into the WCHA Playoffs, where Johnny Pohl's four points led Minnesota past rival North Dakota in Game One at Mariucci, 7-2. Game Two was a thriller and was ultimately decided on Keith Ballard's game-winner in overtime with less than two minutes to play in the extra session.

That next week the Gophers took on St. Cloud State in the Final Five at the Xcel Energy Center. Leopold, Riddle, Taffe and Koalska all lit the lamp in this one as the team cruised to a 4-1 win. Lady luck ran out on our boys in the championship game against Denver, however, as Pioneer goaltender Wade Dubielewicz stopped 38 shots to lead his team in a 5-2 win. Minnesota earned an NCAA Tournament bye though and came out refreshed against Colorado College in the West Regional in Ann Arbor, Mich. There, Minnesota rallied with goals from Grant Potulny, Nick Angell and Jeff Taffe, and then sat back and relaxed after Johnny Pohl's short-handed break-away goal in the third to seal the 4-2 win. With that, the team had earned themselves a trip to the Frozen Four, which, ironically, was right back in St. Paul at the Xcel Energy Center.

Finally, the Gophers were back in the final four of college hockey. Sure, they were no strangers to the pinnacle of March Madness, but it had been nearly a quarter century since they had won it all. Things were looking good for the Gophs though. After all, the NCAA's Frozen Four was being held at the posh "X" in St. Paul, right in their very own backyard. West Seventh Street was overflowing with Maroon and Gold that afternoon as a record crowd of 19,234 showed up to watch the team do battle in the opening semifinal round against the University of Michigan.

The Gophers drew first blood in this one when Jeff Taffe, who was forechecking in to the offensive zone, deflected a clearing attempt towards the net. There, Grant Potulny grabbed the deflection and, while on his knees, flipped it past Michigan goaltender Josh Blackburn to make it 1-0 midway through the first period.

Minnesota then made it 2-0 at the 4:33 mark of the second period when Potulny netted his second tally of the evening — this one coming on the power play. Potulny redirected a Jordan Leopold slapper from the point to beat Blackburn through the five-hole on that one as All-American Johnny Pohl gathered his second assist of the evening. Hauser played tough through this point and particularly stood on his head with just over 30 seconds to go in the second when he made a leaping glove save across the crease to stop Jed Ortmeyer's scoring attempt.

The third period was eerily similar to the previous two in that the Gophers wound up tallying an early goal. This time it was junior Jeff Taffe, scoring his team-best 34th of the season on a thrilling break-away just over a minute into it. Taffe took a sweet pass from his Hastings High School teammate, Dan Welch, to burn up the ice and deposit the biscuit between Blackburn's legs on a backhander. It was now 3-0 and things were looking good.

But, as in all good stories, this one would have its share of drama as well. The Wolverines were not about to lie down and proceeded to roar back midway through the third, finally scoring at the 13:55 mark on a shorthanded goal by J.J. Swistak that beat Hauser through the five hole. Then, with just under a minute and a half to go in the game, Michigan, playing with six skaters and their goalie pulled, made it 3-2 when Ortmeyer beat Hauser on that very same five-hole with a tough angled wrister from the goal line.

The drama was thick at this point as the Gophers tried to hang on for their dear lives to stop the Wolverines in the games' final moments. Hauser, who stopped 25 of 27 shots that night, came up huge in the last minute and when the buzzer finally blew, the Maroon and Gold suddenly found themselves back in their first national championship game since 1989.

"Losing to Denver in the Final Five probably made our playoffs to tell you the truth, because that humbled us and we needed that," said Jordan Leopold. "We were not

Ben Clymer

Keith Ballard

Nate Miller

focused going into that and that forced us to get back to the basics and not get too overconfident. We then got a first round bye, and that was huge. From there, we faced a very good Colorado College team in the opener, and wound up coming out on top. Then, to come home to St. Paul was awesome. It was really magic in that Final Four opener with Michigan. We felt confident going in, but didn't actually play our best game at all. We did enough to win though and that was all that mattered."

The Finals would go down as one of the greatest ever as Minnesota took the ice that next night against the University of Maine. The Gophers opened the scoring at 7:18 of the first period on the power-play when a streaking Keith Ballard slammed home a beautiful one-timer courtesy of Troy Riddle that beat Maine Goalie Matt Yeats through the five-hole.

The Black Bears rallied to tie it up at the 4:47 mark of the second period, however, when Michael Schutte tallied on a power-play goal that saw Adam Hauser get screened big-time out front. The Gophs jumped back on top less than a minute later though on an awesome wrister by Johnny Pohl which beat Yeats top-shelf glove side. And, with that timely 27th goal, his 77th point of the season, Pohl was able to clinch the national point-scoring race, pulling ahead of New Hampshire's Darren Haydar.

Maine tied it up early in the third as Schutte tallied his second goal of the game, this one coming on a one-timer from the point which beat Hauser low to the glove side. With everything tied up at two apiece, the action was fierce. Things stayed that way for another 14 minutes too, until Maine's Robert Liscak banked a floater off of Hauser's leg pad from behind the net with under five minutes to go to give the Black Bears their first lead of the game. The fans at the X were crushed.

Minnesota, which had played conservatively throughout the third period, now rallied fiercely in the game's final moments. Maine hung in there though and it appeared to be all but over. Shortly after a time-out, Coach Lucia pulled Hauser with 58 seconds remaining in the game and put an extra attacker out on the ice. Then, in one of the greatest goals in Gopher history, Matt Koalska tied it up with 54 seconds on the clock to knot the game at three apiece and send the home crowd into hysterics. Johnny Pohl, who won the face-off in the Maine zone, dropped the bouncing puck back to Troy Riddle. Riddle then deflected it over to Koalska in the high slot, where he pounded home a low liner between Yeats' legs to light the lamp.

So, it was now off to overtime, where the collective breath of every Minnesota hockey fan was being held. The other two times that the Gophers had lost NCAA championship overtime games were back in 1954, when John Mariucci's club was upset by RPI, and then again in 1989, when Wooger's club was beaten by Harvard at the Civic Center in St. Paul. This one, however, was not going to have the same outcome.

In the extra session the two teams battled mercilessly up and down the ice for near-ly 17 agonizing minutes. The fans were beside themselves as the tension mounted with every face-off. Then, at the 16:58 mark of overtime, history was made when North Dakota native Grant Potulny, the Maroon and Gold's lone non-Minnesotan, ended it all. Here's how it went down: Maine, play-ing on the short side of a controversial power-play for tripping, was trying to ice the puck out of their own end. A face-off in the Black Bear's end wound up going right to Jordan Leopold at the point. Leo then shot the puck into traffic in front of the net with the rebound bouncing to Pohl. Pohl then slid it to Potulny, who slapped the puck under Yeats' pads for the thrill of a lifetime. Minnesota had won the game, 4-3. Utter bedlam ensued in the arena as well as throughout the Land of 10,000 Lakes.

Absolute insanity erupted not only in the streets of St. Paul, but throughout the "State of Hockey," as the fans rejoiced. A friendly riot even took place back in Dinkytown just for good measure. That 23-year-old monkey was now off their backs and the Gophers were NCAA champions for the fourth time in team history. The players, coaches and staff all stormed the ice and cel-ebrated amidst a sea of sticks, gloves and hel-mets which now littered the rink. Minnesota was finally back on top of the hockey world.

"That was one of the most exciting games I have ever been a part of and it will go down as a classic," said Leopold, who fin-ished with 48 points that season — tops in the nation among defenseman. "It was just an amazing moment for everybody who has been involved in Gopher Hockey and it is certainly something that I will never forget. All the emotion that came out on the ice fol-lowing that incredible ending was indescrib-able. To be out there with my teammates and friends was so special. It was really a day I will always look back on and cherish forev-er."

When it was all said and done, Jordan Leopold and Johnny Pohl were named as first team All-Americans. In addi-tion, Leo, a two-time WCHA Defensive Player of the Year, was given the ultimate prize in college hockey, the Hobey Baker Memorial Award. Other Gophers getting in on the action included sophomore defense-man Paul Martin, who was named to the All-WCHA second-team, while junior Jeff Taffe was a third-team honoree. Keith Ballard was named to the WCHA's All-Rookie Team as well. Furthermore, Potulny, Pohl and Adam Hauser, who stopped 42 shots in the title game and 69 of 74 shots in the tourney, were named to the Frozen Four All-Tournament Team. Incidentally, with the win, Adam Hauser become the WCHA's all-time leader in wins with 83.

The defending National Champion Golden Gophers opened their 2002-03 cam-paign right back at the Xcel Energy Center, where they pummeled Ohio State in the Hall of Fame Game, 7-2. Keith Ballard had four points in the game but the bad news came afterwards when it was determined that jun-

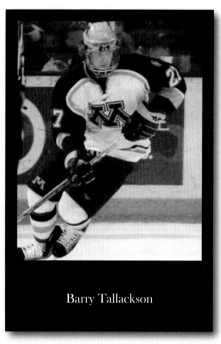
Barry Tallackson

Adam Hauser

Matt Koalska

ior captain Grant Potulny got injured and would be on the shelf for several months. From there, the team headed east to play New Hampshire in a battle between No. 1 and No. 3 in the country. The Gophers managed to capture just one point against the Wildcats, as they tied 5-5 in Game One behind a pair of goals each from Riddle and Martin, but then lost the rematch, 3-1. October came to a close on the road at Michigan Tech, where fresh-men Thomas Vanek and Gino Guyer scored two goals apiece in a 5-4 win. Minnesota had to settle for a 3-3 tie in Game two, however, when Goalie Justin Johnson let in the Husky equalizer with just a few minutes to go in the game.

The month of November was chris-tened in style as the Gophers raised their 2002 NCAA Championship banner just prior to their game with Alabama-Huntsville, and then proceeded to pound the Chargers, 12-1, behind hat tricks from Troy Riddle, Jon Waibel and Thomas Vanek. After taking the follow-up game, 4-2, the team hit the road to play Minnesota State, Mankato. There, the Gophers watched the Mavericks score three unanswered third period goals in a span of just over seven minutes for a shocking 3-2 win. Troy Riddle, who was still suffering from a separated shoulder, contributed two goals and two assists in the 7-4 revenge victory the next night. Things got scary the next weekend as CC came to town and spanked the Gophers, 7-3, in the opener and then salvaged a 2-2 tie in Game Two to take three of four points in the series. The home-stand continued with a 4-2 win over Michigan Tech in Game One, followed by a dramatic 2-1 come-from-behind win in Game Two, which featured third peri-od goals from Paul Martin and Dan Welch. The month came to a close at the College Hockey Showcase, where Vanek posted a hat-trick in a 5-5 tie versus Michigan State. The team then dropped its next game against Michigan by the final score of 3-1.

The first half of the season came to a close on a positive note when Minnesota swept rival Wisconsin. Goalie Travis Weber posted 31 saves in securing his first career shut-out in 3-0 Game One, while Matt DeMarchi was the hero of Game Two when he got the game-winner late in the third to seal a 3-2 victory. Following a three-week holiday hiatus, the team resumed play by winning its fourth straight Dodge Holiday Classic title. After a big 7-3 win over Yale, the team beat Boston College in the title game thanks to Troy Riddle's overtime goal at 2:30 of the extra session to secure the 2-1 victory.

The new year was up and down for the Gophers as they got off to a rocky start by earning just one point in a home-and-home series with St. Cloud State. The team's woes continued that next weekend as they suffered a 4-2 home loss to North Dakota in the open-er but then rebounded behind Matt Koalska's four assists to take Game Two, 6-3. The Gophers were down 3-2 in this one but rallied back with four third-period goals to seal the deal. Following a bye week, the Gophers host-ed Minnesota State, Mankato, and wound up with a couple of 2-2 and 4-4 ties. The next week they hit the road for Anchorage, where Troy Riddle scored two goals and Travis Weber recorded his second shut-out of the season, blanking the Seawolves with 18 saves in a 4-0 Game One win. The team then completed the sweep with a 4-1 win in Game Two as Justin Johnson stopped 20 of 21 shots and Thomas Vanek added two goals and an assist.

Top-ranked Colorado College was next on the schedule and the Tigers came out swinging in Game One, pouncing on the Gophers, 6-2. The next night was much different though as the Maroon and Gold rallied in the third period to win 3-2 behind goals from Thomas Vanek and Jake Fleming to earn a hard-fought split. Minnesota pounded on Wisconsin that next weekend at Mariucci Arena, outscoring the cheese heads, 13-3, in a two-game sweep. Highlighting the festivities were Koalska and Tallackson, who each netted a pair in Game Two. They kept rolling the next week up in Duluth, where Vanek's two goals in the third period helped seal a 5-4 Game One victory. Game Two was a heartbreaker though as UMD's Jon Francisco tied the game with 11 seconds to go on the clock and then scored the game-winner just a minute into overtime to secure a 5-4 Bulldog win. Denver was next for the Gophers and they came to town ready to roll, jumping out to a quick 3-0 lead at Mariucci Arena. Minnesota hung in there though and got a pair of goals late from Grant Potulny to secure a 3-3 tie. The exact same scenario happened the next night too, but this time the three goal deficit was not only matched, but surpassed when Minnesota scored four goals in a span of 3:54 against All-American Goalie Wade Dubielewicz, en route to a huge 8-5 win.

The Gophers closed out their regular season at St. Cloud State with a 5-3 win over the Huskies in Game One, followed by a 1-1 tie thanks to Troy Riddle's second period tally from Koalska and Martin. With those three points, the team finished tied for second-place in the WCHA. From there, Grant Potulny put the Gophers on his back as the team opened the post-season at home with a pair of wins over Michigan Tech. Potulny scored three goals in the 3-1 and 5-2 victories, giving his squad a ticket to the WCHA Final Five in St. Paul. There, the eventual tournament MVP came up huge again, this time notching the game-tying goal late in the third period against the Mavericks. Vanek then took over down the stretch, scoring the overtime game-winner at 3:57 of the extra session. In the finals against top-ranked Colorado College it was all Potulny yet again as he this time scored two goals and added an assist in the first six minutes of the game en route to leading his team to a 4-2 victory, and its first Broadmoor Trophy since 1996.

With that, the Gophers earned the top seed in the NCAA West Regional at Mariucci Arena. There, the Gophers took care of business, pounding on Mercyhurst in the first round, 9-2, on Potulny's three goals and Guyer's five assists. The next day CCHA Champion Ferris State came to town and thanks to Vanek's two goals, Minnesota hung

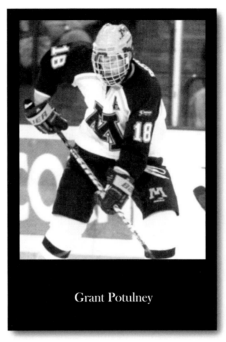

Grant Potulney

Jordan Leopold

Johnny Pohl

on to beat the Bulldogs, 7-4, and advance on to the Frozen Four for the second straight year. Determined to make it a repeat, the Gophers wound up meeting their old foes, the Michigan Wolverines, in the national semifinals in Buffalo, N.Y. Michigan came out firing on all cylinders in this one, outshooting Minnesota, 15-5, in the first period. Travis Weber played big though, allowing just one goal during that frame, and kept his squad in it. Minnesota roared back in the second, out-shooting the Wolverines, 15-6, but found themselves down 2-0 late in the period. Troy Riddle finally got Minnesota on the board at 17:45, on a couple of sweet passes from Vanek and Koalska. They rolled from there as Guyer took a centering pass from Tallackson and buried it at 1:35 of the third to tie it up at two apiece. Both teams played well down the stretch and the game ultimately went into overtime. There, Vanek proved to be the hero yet again as he scored on an unassisted goal at 8:55 of the extra session to complete the comeback and send his club back to the NCAA championship game.

The title tilt had the Gophers facing off against New Hampshire, a team which had beaten them earlier in the season. Minnesota came out fired up in this one and controlled the puck for most of the game. DeMarchi got the Gophers on the board first at 10:58, only to see the Wildcats even it up on a power-play with just 19 seconds to play in the first period. The Gophers had plenty of chances in the second but could not find the back of the net. Luckily for Minnesota fans, neither could New Hampshire, as Weber played solid between the pipes. Then, at 8:14 of the third frame, Vanek lit the lamp for his 31st tally of the year on a gorgeous set up by Koalska and Riddle to give his club a 2-1 lead. From there, the boys smelled blood and went for the kill. Jon Waibel scored on a nice centering pass from Vanek just three minutes later, and Tallackson put the final nail in the coffin when he scored a pair of goals down the stretch to give the Golden Gophers their second NCAA title in as many years. Travis Weber turned away 26 of 27 shots in net as the Gophers cruised to a 5-1 victory and back-to-back championships. Again, the team went crazy with a huge yard sale at center ice, celebrating every second of their magical moment.

When it was all said and done, Minnesota had become the first team in more than 30 years to repeat as NCAA Champions, when Boston University last accomplished the feat back in 1972. It was the school's fifth NCAA Championship, with the other three coming in 1974, 1976 and 1979 under legendary coach Herbie Brooks. As for individual accolades, Thomas Vanek became just the fourth freshman since 1948 to be named Most Outstanding Player of the NCAA Frozen Four. Joining Vanek on the All-Tournament Team were Matt DeMarchi, Paul Martin and Travis Weber. In addition, junior defenseman Paul Martin, who finished with a career-high 39 points, was named as a second-team All-American. Martin, Vanek, who led the team with 62 points, and Keith

Ballard, who tallied 41 points of his own, were all named to the All-WCHA second-team as well. Troy Riddle, who wound up finishing second on the team in scoring with 51 points, was selected to the third-team. Riddle, along with Harrington and Vanek were also named to the league's all-rookie team, with Vanek being named as the WCHA Rookie of the Year to boot.

As back-to-back national champions, the Gophers knew that they were going to be marked men in 2003-04. And, with the return of all but three regulars from the previous year's title team, including Potulny, Riddle, Koalska, Tallackson and Vanek — who was drafted fifth over-all by the NHL's Buffalo Sabres that Summer, the Gophers were gunning to become just the second team to ever win three NCAA Championships in a row. Gone were blue-liners Paul Martin and Matt DeMarchi, as well as goaltender Travis Weber, but they reloaded with prized recruits, Ryan Potulny and Danny Irmen — both North Dakota natives. It was not going to be easy, that was for sure. Coach Lucia was optimistic but very realistic about his team's chances.

"Our sights are set on becoming the best team that we can possibly be when the end of the year rolls around," said Lucia. "Our goal is to get to the NCAA Tournament and then take our swings at it like every other team. That's what we've done in the past and I don't think it will be any different this season. We're not going to change our routine or our thought process on what we're trying to do. We're going to worry about us and be the best hockey team this group is capable of becoming. Every time you lose some pieces of the puzzle, you have to start over. Just because we won it last year doesn't guarantee us anything this year."

The Gophers opened the season as the consensus No. 1 team in the nation. That apparently did not impress Maine in the least, however, as the Black Bears shut-out the two-time defending champs in the opener, 4-0, snapping a 91-game streak of games without being shut-out. They rebounded in a big way in their second game though by coming from behind, 3-0, to score seven unanswered goals and beat Nebraska-Omaha, 7-3. From there, things got ugly as the Gophers returned home only to get swept by rival Duluth 4-3, in overtime, and then 4-2. Aside from the raising of the 2003 NCAA Championship banner and the ceremony which honored the late Herb Brooks, it was a total disaster. To add insult to injury, defenseman Keith Ballard suffered a knee injury which resulted in him missing seven games. By no coincidence the team went 1-5-1 over that same stretch which included a split with Denver and a sweep by North Dakota. Their lone win came on October 31st, when they beat Denver, 6-2, behind Grant Potulny's two goals and Matt Koalska's goal and two assists.

November was pretty rough for the Maroon and Gold. Following the debacle at Grand Forks, Minnesota headed to Madison, where they managed just one point in the standings against rival Wisconsin. To make

Thomas Vanek

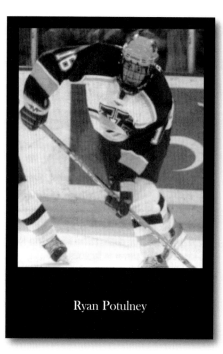

Ryan Potulney

Danny Irmen

matters worse, the Badgers rallied from two-goal deficits each night to tie, 3-3, and win, 4-3. Maybe that was the breaking point for the Gophers because from there on out they were a changed team with a whole new attitude. Minnesota went on to sweep Michigan Tech, 6-2 and 3-0, as freshmen Danny Irmen and Jake Taylor notched goals and rookie goaltender Kellen Briggs posted his first career shut-out. Next up was the College Hockey Showcase, where Minnesota posted 52 shots on goal and cruised to a 5-1 win over Michigan State on their home ice in East Lansing. The Gophers then won the title the next night by rallying from a 2-1 deficit on a short-handed goal by Troy Riddle, followed by a pair of even-strength tallies from Andy Sertich and Barry Tallackson to bring home the hardware for the first time in eight years.

The Gophers had a solid December by going 3-1 and getting back on track. Kellen Briggs posted his second shut-out of the year in a 4-0 opening series win at Alaska Anchorage. Game Two was another story though as UAA rallied back in the third period to win, 6-4. The team then returned home where they proceeded to capture their fifth straight Dodge Holiday Classic title with a pair of big wins. The first was a 9-0 blow-out over Princeton, and the second was a rematch of the 2003 NCAA Championship game against New Hampshire. And, just like the last time the two teams met, the Gophers came out on top. With two points each from Matt Koalska, Keith Ballard and Chris Harrington, the Gophers beat UNH, 4-2. With that, Minnesota was above the .500 mark for the first time on the season.

The Maroon and Gold opened the new year in style by going on a six-game unbeaten streak. Chris Harrington, Keith Ballard and Troy Riddle each had four-point weekends to lead the U to a pair of 5-5 ties against Boston University. From there, the team swept Colorado College, 2-1 and 3-0, followed by Minnesota State, where they outscored the Mavericks by the whopping margin of 16-3. Vanek had a seven-point weekend, while Briggs earned both wins, including a shut-out to set a new Minnesota rookie-record with four blankings on the year. Next up was No. 1 ranked North Dakota at home. The Gophers went up 2-1 in the opener, only to see the Sioux rally back behind three third period goals to win, 4-2. Game Two then saw the Gophers break the team's 14-game unbeaten streak thanks to goals from Danny Irmen and Matt Koalska, which made it 2-1. Riding the wave of momentum the Gophers rolled over Wisconsin that next weekend, sweeping the Badgers 4-2 and 3-2. Ballard was the difference in the series, earning Player of the Week honors after having a hand in three of the team's seven goals.

The Gophers came back to Earth in February, going 4-4-0. They opened the month on a strong note, sweeping Bemidji State, 2-1 and 5-1, as Keith Ballard, Troy Riddle and Brett MacKinnon each had three-point weekends for the Maroon and Gold. From there, things got ugly as the Duluth Bulldogs crushed the Gophers at the DECC,

6-1 and 4-1, to extend the nation's-longest unbeaten streak to 12 games. The season sweep was UMD's first-ever over the Gophers and it couldn't have come at a worse time. Gino Guyer and Danny Irmen both had three-point outings en route to a sweep over Alaska Anchorage that next week. With the good came the bad though, as Minnesota followed its winning sweep with a losing one on the road that next week at Denver, getting spanked, 6-2 and 6-3. Goalie Kellen Briggs struggled and was ultimately relieved in favor of Justin Johnson on both nights.

Things got turned around in a big way in March, however, as the team went 7-1-0 during the month. With WCHA play-off implications on the line, the Gophers, behind four point outings each from Thomas Vanek and Barry Tallackson, went out and swept St. Cloud State, 7-4 and 4-2, to clinch a tie for fourth place with Denver. With that, Minnesota opened the WCHA Playoffs against St. Cloud State — for the second meeting in as many weeks. And, just like the week before, the Golden Gophers swept the Huskies, 6-1 and 7-3, to move their record to 20-0-0 all-time in first-round playoff games at home. Troy Riddle had an amazing nine point weekend, while Ryan Potulny added six of his own. They would now advance to their sixth straight WCHA Final Five tournament.

Minnesota then went on to successfully defend its Final Five title by downing third-ranked UMD, 7-4, and top-ranked North Dakota, 5-4, to claim yet another Broadmoor Trophy. Minnesota had 12 different players score at least one point against UMD with Danny Irmen leading the attack by scoring two goals. Duluth led 3-1 in the first period, but the Gophers rallied back to advance to the finals. There, the Gophers got goals from Irmen, Waibel, Vanek and Riddle to make it 4-4 midway through the third. The game roared back and forth and featured no less than two lead changes and four ties. Then, at the 13:58 mark of the final frame, Grant Potulny scored to give Minnesota a thrilling 5-4 victory. Kellen Briggs, who turned away 35 shots that night, was named as the tournament's MVP.

With that, Minnesota earned a No. 1 seed for the NCAA Midwest Regional in Grand Rapids, Mich., where they proceeded to defeat Notre Dame, 5-2, in a great come from behind showing. Matt Koalska, who finished with a goal and an assist, got things started for the Gophers by scoring off a nice pass from Vanek just 24 seconds into the second period, slicing Notre Dame's lead to 2-1. After Danny Irmen deflected in a shot by Chris Harrington midway through the period to make it 2-2, Vanek took over. Minnesota out-shot Notre Dame 21-7 in the second period, and an Irish turn-over allowed the awesome Austrian to grab the puck and put it in the back of the net for what would prove to be the game-winning goal at 16:34. Vanek scored again midway through the third, while Riddle added an empty netter for good measure.

Next up for the Gophers were their longtime nemesis', Minnesota-Duluth. The Dogs came out smoking in this one and held a two goal lead into the third period. Grant Potulny finally got Minnesota on the scoreboard at 5:25 of the final frame when he tallied on a short-handed goal from Guyer and Tallackson. Duluth was too tough down the stretch though and wound up winning the game, 3-1, behind Goalie Isaac Reichmuth's 22 saves, to end the Gopher's chances of an NCAA Championship three-peat. UMD wound up beating Minnesota in five of six meetings that season and made it count when it matter most, moving on to their first Frozen Four appearance

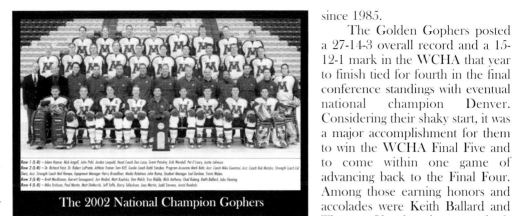
The 2002 National Champion Gophers

since 1985.

The Golden Gophers posted a 27-14-3 overall record and a 15-12-1 mark in the WCHA that year to finish tied for fourth in the final conference standings with eventual national champion Denver. Considering their shaky start, it was a major accomplishment for them to win the WCHA Final Five and to come within one game of advancing back to the Final Four. Among those earning honors and accolades were Keith Ballard and Thomas Vanek, who were both named to 2003-04 All-WCHA Team. Ballard, who tallied 36 points that season, earned first team honors, while Vanek, who led the team with 26 goals and 25 assists for 51 points, was named to the second team. In addition, Ballard was also one of 10 finalists for the 2004 Hobey Baker Memorial Award, presented to the best Division I college hockey player in the nation. Incidentally, Troy Riddle finished third on the team in scoring with 49 points, while Matt Koalska came in fourth with 39 of his own.

Minnesota started out their 2004-05 campaign on a high note, downing the defending NCAA champs from Denver in the Hall of Fame Game at St. Paul's Xcel Center. Grant Potulny was the hero in this one, tallying a hat trick right out of the gates to lead the Gophers past the Pioneers, 5-2. The team headed north to Alaska that next week, where Potulny lit the lamp yet again and Goalie Kellen Briggs turned away all 17 shots he faced to blank Massachusetts, 1-0, at the Nye Frontier Classic tournament. After losing to Alaska-Anchorage in the tourney finals, the team returned to the Lower 48, where they faced off against rival North Dakota up in Grand Forks. There, the Gophers lost to UND in Game One, 4-2, but came back in a big way the next night behind Briggs' second shut-out of the season to crush the Sioux, 6-0. Leading the charge yet again was Potulny, who had a pair of goals and an assist in the big win. Minnesota kept it going that next week too, beating up on Minnesota State, 9-2, back at Mariucci Arena. Eight different Gophers found the back of the net in this one while Mike Howe scored his first two of the year. The next night was much more interesting, however, as the Gophers rallied behind Kris Chucko's overtime game-winner at 1:48 of the extra session to make it 3-2 and take the series.

The Gophers opened the month of November with a series sweep over Wisconsin, 3-2 and 4-2. Gino Guyer and Danny Irmen each notched third period goals to secure the come-from-behind win in Game One, while each had two points apiece in Game Two as well. From there, the Gophers hit the road to take on Denver. Potulny had a pair of goals in the opener as the team fended off a four-goal barrage in the third period to hang on to a 5-4 win. Denver then took the night-cap, 5-2, to earn the split. Back at home that next weekend it was all about Potulny yet again as his two goals paced the Maroon and Gold past Michigan, 5-1. Then, the following night, Kellen Briggs stopped all 23 shots he faced as the Gophers blanked Michigan State, 5-0. After getting swept that next week by CC out in Colorado, the Gophs returned home to face St. Cloud State in a home-and-home series. Game One was a thriller up in the Granite City as Jake Flemming got the overtime game-winner at 2:21 of the extra session to give his squad a 2-1 victory. Irmen, Potulny, Sertich and Guyer each then scored that next night back home to secure the 4-2 sweep. The annual Dodge Holiday Classic was next up on the docket as the Gophers pounded on Merrimack, 6-2, and then rolled past Northern Michigan, 4-1,

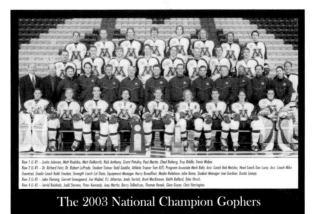
The 2003 National Champion Gophers

behind a pair of Tyler Hirsch goals to secure the title.

Minnesota ushered in the new year by beating Boston University, 2-1, thanks to goals by Guyer and Irmen in Game One. The roles were reversed that next night, however, as BU beat the Gophers by that same 2-1 margin. The next weekend was tough as the team got swept by CC, which included a heart-breaking 3-2 overtime loss in the opener. The Maroon and Gold got back on track from there though, taking both games from Minnesota State that following week, 9-6 and 2-1. Danny Irmen notched a hat-trick in Game One, while Kris Chucko got both goals for the Gophers in Game Two. Following a tough home sweep at the hands of Michigan Tech that next weekend, the Gophers could only manage a split with UMD on the last series of the month.

February was ushered in with yet another split, this one with rival Wisconsin in Madison. After dropping the opener, 3-1, the team rebounded to take Game Two, 5-3, on goals by Irmen, Hirsch, Potulny, Tallackson and Sertich. Then, the team managed to earn just one point at home against Alaska-Anchorage that following weekend. After dropping the opener, 3-2, they wound up with a 5-5 overtime tie which saw them squander a 5-4 lead with just over a minute to go in the game. Minnesota went on to win the front-end of the home-and-home with St. Cloud State that next weekend behind a pair of Alex Goligoski goals, which resulted in a 5-4 victory. After dropping the revenge match, 4-1, the team went on to sweep Michigan tech on the road. Hirsch, Irmen, Stevens and Sertich each tallied in the 4-2 Game One win, while Game Two was all about Goalie Justin Johnson, who stopped all 26 shots he faced that night to earn the tough 5-0 shut-out.

Minnesota kept it going that next week, sweeping Minnesota State, 7-2 and 5-3, in the first round of the WCHA Playoffs. Tallackson and Irmen each had a pair in the opener, while Johnson stopped 25 of 28 shots in Game Two. The team hit the wall after that though, getting shut-out by Colorado College in the semifinal game, 3-0, and then dropping the third place game as well, 4-2, to North Dakota. As luck would have it, the Gophers got an invite to play in the NCAA West Regional Final that next weekend, which was being held at Mariucci Arena. There, with their home crowd behind them, the Maroon and Gold beat Maine, 1-0, on Evan Kaufmann's overtime game-winner at 1:46 of the extra session. The Gophers, who out-shot the Black Bears 38-25, were unable to capitalize on nine power-play opportunities during the game, but hung in there thanks to some outstanding goaltending from Kellen Briggs, who turned aside all 25 shots he faced that night.

From there, the team went on to upset Cornell that next night, 2-1, in yet another overtime, to advance back to the

Phil Kessel

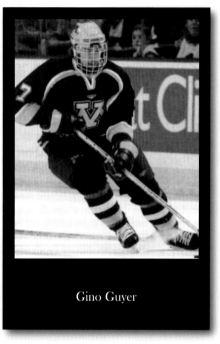

Gino Guyer

Blake Wheeler

Frozen Four. The Big Red got on the board first in this one when Mitch Carefoot beat Briggs on a short-handed three-on-one midway through the second period. But the Gophers quickly responded with Andy Sertich tying the score just over a minute later on a backhander from Smaagaard out front. After a scoreless third period, "Mr. March," Barry Tallackson, took over in overtime, as he took a pass out of the corner from Mike Howe and beat Cornell Goaltender David McKee, five-hole, on his own rebound. Tallackson was then mobbed by his teammates, just a few feet from where Evan Kaufmann was the center of attention the night before. With that, Tallackson and fellow seniors Garrett Smaagaard, Jake Fleming, Jerrid Reinholz, Justin Johnson and Judd Stevens were going to their third Frozen Four in four years.

With the hopes of making it three NCAA titles in four years, the Gophers headed to Columbus, Ohio, where they faced off against hated North Dakota in an all-WCHA NCAA Frozen Four semifinal. (Denver and Colorado College were the other two teams and Denver would ultimately win its second straight title.) Expectations were high going in, but this one was all UND as the Sioux led from start to finish and came away with a big 4-2 win. Erik Fabian, a fourth-line winger from Roseau, scored two early goals while Travis Zajac added two third-period scores of his own to put the Sioux up 4-0 in the third. Goaltender Jordan Parise, from Faribault, stopped 26 shots and was almost unbeatable in net, making a number of acrobatic saves and frustrating the Gophers all night. He faltered briefly in the third period when Mike Howe and Guyer each scored power-play goals just 90 seconds apart to make it interesting, but he hung on down the stretch to come up with the win and end Minnesota's season.

Kellen Briggs and Ryan Potulny were named to the All-WCHA team that year, while defenseman Alex Goligoski earned All-WCHA Rookie honors. Tyler Hirsch led the team in scoring with 44 points, with Irmen and Potulny adding 43 and 41, respectively.

The Gophers hit the ice that Fall for the 2005-06 season with a tough 4-3 overtime loss to Alaska Fairbanks at Mariucci Arena, and then rallied to a 3-3 tie that next night on Andy Sertich's third period equalizer. The team came back to sweep Minnesota State the following weekend at home, beating the Mavericks, 5-2 and 4-3. The highlight of Game One was freshman sensation Phil Kessel scoring his first goal ever on a penalty shot. The team hit the road from there, getting a split against St. Cloud on the road. Then, after earning just one point up in Duluth, the Gophers returned home and promptly swept Alaska Anchorage by final scores of 9-0 and 4-3. Kessel tallied four points in the opener, while the line of Ben Gordon, Phil Kessel and Mike Howe combined for six points in Game Two.

From there, Minnesota went back on the road, where they tied Denver in Game One, 3-3, and then beat the Pioneers in Game Two, 4-3, behind a pair of Kris Chucko goals. They then beat Michigan, 6-3, followed by a 2-2 overtime tie against Michigan State. Following a rough home sweep by hated Wisconsin, the

Gophers went on an amazing roll, losing just once in their next 20 games. The streak started with a sweep over the Sioux up in Grand Forks. Danny Irmen and Ryan Potulny, both North Dakotans, each tallied a goal in both games to lead the charge. The team continued its winning ways through December, winning the Dodge Holiday Classic at Mariucci. On January 13th the team headed back up to UND, where they once again beat the Sioux, 6-1, in Game One, behind Danny Irmen's four points and Mike Vannelli's three. The team took it on the chin the next night, however, despite a 43-shot barrage.

The streak continued into January and February with sweeps over Colorado College and Wisconsin. Against CC, the Gophers were led by a pair of Andy Sertich goals in Game One, while Phil Kessel tabbed the game-winner in the 3-2 Game Two victory. Against the Badgers, the Gophers jumped out to a 5-1 lead on Danny Irmen's hat-trick and then held on behind goalie Kellen Briggs to win, 5-4. Potulny, Gordon and Kessel each tallied the next night to then secure a 3-1 win as well. The next weekend the team headed to Michigan Tech, where they won easily in Game One, 7-4, thanks to a trio of points each from Ryan Potulny and Mike Vannelli. Game Two was much tighter, however, as the team could only manage a 2-2 tie. Back at home on Feb. 17th, the team edged past Denver, 3-2, in the opener behind Potulny's two goals; and then rolled over the Pioneers in Game Two, 5-1, thanks to a pair of Irmen tallies.

After sweeping Alaska Anchorage up north of the border, the team blanked UM-Duluth, 7-0 and 2-0, behind a pair of Jeff Frazee shut-outs. The team was presented with the MacNaughton Cup following the win in Game One, signifying the program's 11th such WCHA title. Ryan Stoa and Evan Kaufmann each scored twice in the big win. Ryan Potulny was the hero of Game Two, meanwhile, scoring both Gopher goals in the 2-0 victory. Next up was Alaska Anchorage in the first round of the WCHA Playoffs at Mariucci Arena. There, Potulny continued to make a case for himself regarding the Hobey Baker Award by recording his third hat-trick of the season en route to leading the Gophers to a 7-4 win. Meanwhile, Phil Kessel, Blake Wheeler and Ryan Stoa each tallied twice in the 6-2 victory the next night to complete the sweep.

The team then hit the skids big time, losing a heart-breaker to St. Cloud State in overtime, 8-7, in the WCHA Final Five. This one went back and forth all night and came down to the wire. Once again Ryan Potulny carried the squad on his back, scoring an amazing four goals in this one, including the equalizer at the 17:59 mark of the third to send it into overtime. Following the team's crushing loss, they went on to get blanked by Wisconsin that next night, 4-0. They still wound up getting an NCAA bid, however, drawing tiny Holy Cross in a game that would be played up in Grand Forks. There, the Gophers made history by choking like they had never done before. After a scoreless first

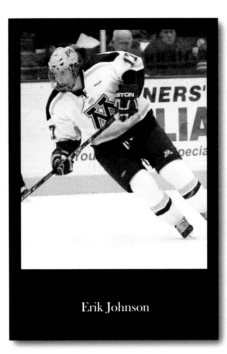

Erik Johnson

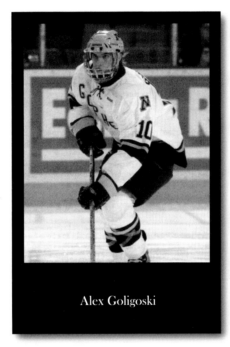

Alex Goligoski

Kyle Okposo

period, Mike Howe and Phil Kessel each tallied in the second to make it 2-2. Alex Goligoski gave the Gophers the lead early in the third, only to see Holy Cross tie it up just five minutes later. Minnesota goalie Kellen Briggs played tough through the third and the two teams wound up going in to overtime. Then, just 53 seconds into the extra session, winger Tyler McGregor scored for Holy Cross to give his program, arguably, the biggest upset in NCAA hockey history. It was indeed Holy Cross' "Miracle on Ice." The Gophers stood stunned and devastated as the UND crowd went nuts for their David vs. Goliath. With that, the season was over.

Incidentally, Ryan Potulny, who would lead the team in scoring with 63 points, would earn All-WCHA and All-American honors after the season — narrowly missing out on the Hobey Baker Award balloting as well.

Following the team's biggest collapse in program history, the 2006-07 Gophers hit the ice that October without the services of their star freshman, Phil Kessel, who signed with the Boston Bruins that off-season after being chosen as the team's No. 1 pick in the draft. The Gophers re-loaded with some new talent though and kicked off their season by losing to Maine, 3-1, in the U.S. Hockey Hall of Fame Game at the Xcel Energy Center. From there, however, the team went on a tear, going unbeaten in their next 22 games. The streak started with sweeps over Wayne State and Ohio State, followed by a 2-0 Game One shut-out over Colorado College, courtesy of goalie Kellen Briggs, and an 8-1 pasting of CC in Game Two, compliments of newcomer Kyle Okposo's hat trick. By now it was November and with that the team headed north to face UM-Duluth. There, the Gophers got past the Dogs in a couple of nail-biters, 3-2 and 3-2, with Tyler Hirsch tallying the overtime game-winner in Game Two.

The following weekend the team battled St. Cloud State to a pair of overtime ties, 5-5 and 3-3. The team then rallied to get a pair of third period goals in the second game up in the Granite City, courtesy of Jay Barriball and Mike Vannelli. Minnesota continued to roll the next weekend, beating Wisconsin, 2-1 and 3-1, at Mariucci Arena. Barriball got the third period game-winner in Game One, while the Gophers rallied behind a trio of third period goals from Ryan Stoa, Tony Lucia and Blake Wheeler to take Game Two. After beating Michigan and Michigan State, the team tied Minnesota State in Mankato, 5-5, before beating the Mavs back in Minneapolis for Game Two, 2-1, on goals from Wheeler and Okposo. The streak continued through December as the team rolled over Michigan Tech, Alabama Huntsville, Ferris State and Minnesota State, before finally losing on the road to Wisconsin, 2-1. The team did rally to earn the split, however, behind Jim O'Brien's lone goal and Jeff Frazee's 30-save shut-out in Game Two.

The squad would finally hit a rough patch in late January back at home, splitting with Denver and then getting swept by the hated Sioux. They rallied to sweep Alaska

DON LUCIA

Don Lucia grew up in Grand Rapids and went on to graduate from Grand Rapids High School in 1977. There, he led his team to a pair of State High School hockey titles in 1975 and 1976, as well as a pair of third-place finishes in 1974 and 1977. The sturdy defenseman not only earned all-state honors in hockey his senior year, but also on the gridiron as a linebacker on the football team as well. From there, Lucia, who was later drafted by the NHL's Philadelphia Flyers, went on to play hockey at the University of Notre Dame. Lucia would emerge as the team captain with the Fighting Irish, graduating in 1981.

Lucia then got into coaching, with his first job coming at the University of Alaska-Fairbanks, where he served as an assistant from 1981-85. In 1985 he moved over to the University of Alaska Anchorage, where he served as an assistant for two seasons before returning to Fairbanks for his first head coaching position. Lucia served as the coach at Fairbanks for six years, posting four winning seasons and an overall record of 113-87-10, before leaving the Nanooks in 1993 to take over as the head coach at Colorado College.

At CC Lucia took over the reins of the program that had not experienced a winning season in the previous 13 campaigns. Lucia proceeded to guide the Tigers to a record of 23-11-5 and the WCHA regular-season title in his rookie season — the program's first in 37 years, and was named as college hockey's Coach of the Year. Lucia didn't stop there though, guiding the Tigers to an unprecedented three straight outright regular-season league titles in his first three years behind the bench. Colorado College won a school-record 33 games in 1996, and made it all the way to the NCAA championship game. For his efforts, Lucia was named WCHA Coach of the Year that same season, and added a second league coach of the year trophy at the conclusion of the 1997 season as well, when he led his Tigers back to the NCAA Frozen Four semifinals. In all, Lucia would spend six seasons in Colorado Springs, racking up a gaudy 166-68-18 record along the way.

On April 9, 1999, the University of Minnesota announced that Lucia would become the 13th head coach in Golden Gopher Hockey history. Nearly three years to the day later, Lucia raised the NCAA Championship Trophy above his head at the Xcel Energy Center in St. Paul. Led by Hobey Baker Award winner Jordan Leopold, and All American Johnny Pohl, the Gophers hung on to beat Maine in one of the greatest Finals in history that year. Amazingly, he would do it again that next year too, making it back-to-back national championships as the Gophers this time beat New Hampshire in the Finals of the Frozen Four in Buffalo, New York.

With nearly 500 career wins as a Division One head coach, Lucia is among the top five winningest active coaches in college hockey. Just one of six coaches in NCAA history to lead two different teams to the Frozen Four, Lucia has established himself as one of the premier collegiate coaches in the nation. Don and his wife Joyce live in Plymouth and have four children: Alison, Jessica, Mario and Tony — who currently plays for his old man on the Gophers.

"The people here have been so great to me and my family, and we really appreciate that," said Lucia. "This is my fourth coaching job and while they have all been great, it is particularly special to be back in Minnesota and having success. The fans here are so smart and so enthusiastic and that makes our jobs so much easier as coaches. It is so sweet to see that the whole state embraces our hockey program, even though there are four other division one schools here as well. That just does not happen anywhere else and I am very lucky to have that kind of support. It is special."

Anchorage and Colorado College, only to get swept in a tough home-and-home against St. Cloud State. Then, after splitting a series with Michigan Tech, the team got hot as it entered the WCHA Playoffs. After defeating Alaska Anchorage in a best-of-three series, Minnesota beat Wisconsin in the opening round of the WCHA Final Five at the Xcel Center thanks to a Blake Wheeler hattrick. They then rallied to beat North Dakota in the Finals, 3-2, in overtime, compliments of Wheeler, who got the game-winner at the 3:25 mark of the extra session.

Minnesota then hit the road for the opening round of the NCAA Tournament, playing Air Force in the West Regional in Denver. There, the Gophers got a trio of third period goals from Ryan Stoa, Jim O'Brien and Mike Carman to rally past the Falcons, 4-3. The team now had to get past UND for the right to go to St. Louis, home of that year's Frozen Four. This one would come down to the wire as Mike Carman put the Maroon and Gold up 1-0 early in the first period. The Sioux rallied to make it 1-1 just a few minutes later, with both teams playing tough defense. After a scoreless second period, the Sioux went up 2-1 early in the third. Jay Barriball then got the equalizer on a power-play goal from Mike Vannelli and Alex Goligoski midway through the third to make it 2-2. From there, it headed to overtime, where UND's Chris Porter beat Jeff Frazee at the 9:43 mark of the extra session to end the season.

Minnesota regrouped in 2007-08 after losing several of their top guys to the NHL, including Alex Goligoski, Jim O'Brien and Erik Johnson — the first Minnesotan ever to be selected first overall in the NHL draft (by St. Louis). They will regroup like they always do though, and play tough under coach Lucia as they head into the future.

GOPHER FIRST TEAM ALL-AMERICANS

Year	Name, Position	Year	Name, Position
1940	John Mariucci, Defense	1975	Les Auge, Defense
1940	Harold Paulsen, Forward	1975	Mike Polich, Center
1951	Gordon Watters, Center	1979	Bill Baker, Defense
1952	Larry Ross, Goalie	1980	Tim Harrer, Wing
1954	Ken Yackel, Sr., Defense	1981	Neal Broten, Center
1954	Jim Mattson, Goalie	1981	Steve Ulseth, Wing
1954	Dick Dougherty, Wing	1985	Pat Micheletti, Wing
1954	John Mayasich, Center	1988	Robb Stauber, Goalie
1955	John Mayasich, Center	1995	Brian Bonin, Center
1958	Jack McCartan, Goalie	1996	Brian Bonin, Center
1958	Dick Burg, Wing	1996	Mike Crowley, Defense
1959	Murray Williamson, Wing	1997	Mike Crowley, Defense
1963	Lou Nanne, Defense	2001	Jordan Leopold, Defense
1964	Craig Falkman, Wing	2002	Jordan Leopold, Defense
1965	Doug Woog, Center	2002	Johnny Pohl, Center
1968	Gary Gambucci, Center	2004	Keith Ballard, Defense
1970	Murray McLachlan, Goalie	2006	Ryan Potulny, Center
1970	Wally Olds, Defense	2007	Alex Goligoski, Defense

THE HOBEY BAKER AWARD: A MINNESOTA TRADITION

Each April the nation's best collegiate hockey player receives the Hobey Baker Memorial Award, college hockey's equivalent to the Heisman Trophy. The recipient is the player who best exemplifies the qualities that Hobey Baker himself demonstrated as an athlete at Princeton University in the early 1900s. Baker was considered to be the ultimate sportsman who despised foul play — picking up only two penalties in his entire college hockey career. With his speed and superior stick handling, Baker opened up the game of hockey and set new standards for the way the game was played. A true gentleman, his habit of insisting upon visiting each opponent's locker room after every game to shake their hands became a model for today's players. A hero, Baker gave his life as an American pilot in W.W.I.

In 1981 Bloomington's Decathlon Club founded the Hobey Baker Memorial Award. The trophy, sculpted by Bill Mack of Bloomington, Minn., is 40 pounds of bronze and clear acrylic, and represents art and athletics at their best. The model for the "Hobey" is Steve Christoff, who starred at Richfield (Minn.) High School, the University of Minnesota, with the 1980 U.S. Olympic hockey team and in the NHL with the Minnesota North Stars. The balloting for the award is voted on by the nearly 50 NCAA D-I coaches who are asked to pick the top three players in their league as well as the top three in the nation. (There used to be a Division II award as well.) The nation's top hockey coaches, players, media and fans from around the country, as well as the finalists themselves, fly in to the Twin Cities to attend the annual gala event.

In 1991, the senior members of the Hobey Baker Memorial Awards Committee determined that a Foundation should be formed to ensure the continued protection and growth of this prestigious award. The Foundation's primary mission is to ensure the long-term stewardship, success and expansion of the Hobey Baker brand. Results of the Foundation's efforts to improve the award include the "Hobey Hat Trick," whereby the top three candidates are announced prior to the announcement of the winner at the NCAA Frozen Four Hockey Tournament. Other programs that have been added in years past include the "High School Character Award," which are presented to high school hockey players showing exemplary character and sportsmanship; and the Legends of College Hockey Award, which annually honors one of the all-time great contributors to the game of college hockey.

MINNESOTA'S HOBEY FINALISTS:

Year	Player	Hometown
1981	*Neal Broten, Minnesota	Roseau, MN
	Steve Ulseth, Minnesota	Roseville, MN
	Steve Carroll, Mankato State (D-II)	Edina, MN
	Mark Hentges, St. Thomas (D-II)	New Hope, MN
1982	Bryan Erickson, Minnesota	Roseau, MN
1983	Bryan Erickson, Minnesota	Roseau, MN
	Scott Bjugstad, Minnesota	New Brighton, MN
	Kurt Kleinendorst, Providence	Grand Rapids, MN
	Tom Kern, Mankato State (D-II)	
1984	*Tom Kurvers, UMD	Bloomington, MN
	Jon Casey, UND	Grand Rapids, MN
	Joel Otto, Bemidji State (D-II)	Elk River, MN
1985	*Bill Watson, UMD	Powerview, Man.
	Pat Micheletti, Minnesota	Hibbing, MN
1986	Scott Sandelin, UND	Hibbing, MN
	Brett Hull, UMD	West Vancouver, B.C.
	Norm MacIver, UMD	Thunder Bay, Ont.
1988	*Robb Stauber, Minnesota	Duluth, MN
	Paul Ranheim, Wisconsin	Edina, MN
	Ken Hilgert, Mankato State (D-II)	
1989	Robb Stauber, Minnesota	Duluth, MN
1992	Larry Olimb, Minnesota	Warroad, MN
1993	Derek Plante, UMD	Cloquet, MN
1993	Fred Knipscheer, St. Cloud State	Fort Wayne, IN
1994	*Chris Marinucci, UMD	Grand Rapids, MN
1994	Kelly Hultgren, St. Cloud State	Bloomington, MN
1995	Brian Bonin, Minnesota	White Bear Lake, MN
	Chris Imes, Maine	Birchdale, MN
1996	*Brian Bonin, Minnesota	White Bear Lake, MN
	Mike Crowley, Minnesota	Bloomington, MN
1997	Mike Crowley, Minnesota	Bloomington, MN
	Jason Blake, UND	Moorhead, MN
1999	Jason Blake, UND	Moorhead, MN
2001	*Jordan Leopold, Minnesota	Golden Valley, MN
2002	Mark Hartigan, St. Cloud State	Fort St. John, BC
2003	Ben Eaves, Boston College	Minneapolis, MN
2004	*Junior Lessard, UMD	St-Joseph-de-Beauce, PQ
2004	Keith Ballard, Minnesota	Baudette, MN
2004	Brandon Bochenski, UND	Blaine, MN
2004	Zach Parise, UND	Minneapolis, MN
2005	Patrick Eaves, Boston College	Faribault, MN
2006	Ryan Potulny, Minnesota	Grand Forks, ND
2006	*Marty Sertich, Colorado College	Roseville, MN
2007	Bobby Goepfert, St. Cloud State	Kings Park, NY

Denotes the Hobey Baker Winner

ALL-TIME HOBEY RECIPIENTS:

Year	Player	School
2007	Ryan Duncan	University of North Dakota
2006	Matt Carle	Denver University
2005	Marty Sertich	Colorado College
2004	Junior Lessard	University of Minn-Duluth
2003	Peter Sejna	Colorado College
2002	Jordan Leopold	University of Minnesota
2001	Ryan Miller	Michigan State
2000	Mike Mottau	Boston College
1999	Jason Krog	New Hampshire
1998	Chris Drury	Boston University
1997	Brendan Morrison	University of Michigan
1996	Brian Bonin	University of Minnesota
1995	Brian Holzinger	Bowling Green University
1994	Chris Marinucci	University of Minn-Duluth
1993	Paul Kariya	University of Maine
1992	Scott Pellerin	University of Maine
1991	David Emma	Boston College
1990	Kip Miller	Michigan State University
1989	Lane MacDonald	Harvard University
1988	Robb Stauber	University of Minnesota
1987	Tony Hrkac	University of North Dakota
1986	Scott Fusco	Harvard University
1985	Bill Watson	University of Minn-Duluth
1984	Tom Kurvers	University of Minn-Duluth
1983	Mark Fusco	Harvard University
1982	George McPhee	Bowling Green University
1981	Neal Broten	University of Minnesota

LEGENDS OF COLLEGE HOCKEY:

1981	John Kelly	1995	John Mayasich
1982	Vic Heyliger	1996	Len Ceglarski
1983	John Mariucci	1997	Lou Lamoriello
1984	Murray Armstrong	1998	Ned Harkness
1985	Herb Gallagher	1999	Glen Sonmor
1986	Amo Bessone	1999	John MacInnes
1987	Murray Murdoch	2000	Bob Johnson
1988	Fido Purpur	2001	Bob Peters
1989	Jim Fullerton	2002	Sid Watson
1990	Al Renfrew	2003	Lefty Smith
1991	Jack Riley	2004	Ron Mason
1992	Connie Pleban	2005	Murray Williamson
1993	Bill Cleary	2006	Cooney Weiland
1994	Jack Kelley	2007	Ed Saugestad

MINNESOTA'S HOBEY WINNERS

Neal Broten (U of Minn.)
1981

Robb Stauber (U of Minn.)
1988

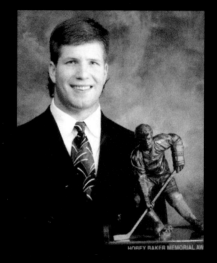

Brian Bonin (U of Minn.)
1996

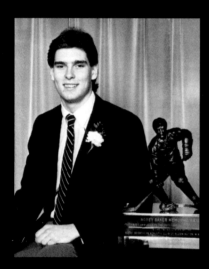

Tom Kurvers (UM-Duluth)
1984

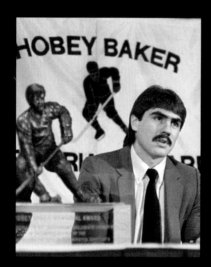

Bill Watson (UM-Duluth)
1985

Chris Marinucci (UM-Duluth)
1994

Jordan Leopold (U of Minn.)
2001

Junior Lessard (UM-Duluth)
2004

Marty Sertich (Colorado College)
2006

THE UM-DULUTH BULLDOGS

The University of Minnesota Duluth Bulldogs have established a hockey tradition that is second to none in Minnesota. For many, hockey is a religion in northeastern Minnesota, and the Dogs have gained a tremendously loyal following. The history of this school, which dates back to 1895, when it was founded as the Duluth Normal School, takes us back to when ice polo was just evolving into ice hockey along the shores of Lake Superior.

Hockey first began in Duluth as an outgrowth of the game of ice polo in the 1890's. By 1893, the Glen Avon Curling Club Rink was in full swing, with ice polo teams from Duluth battling squads from the Twin Cities on the 126' x 80' ice surface. By 1900 adult hockey teams in Duluth and Superior were playing teams from Two Harbors, Eveleth and from Upper Michigan's Copper Country. The first strong Duluth hockey team was probably Northern Hardware, a men's senior team that, after earning the 1908 Minnesota title, defeated Cleveland and Detroit for the national championship. By 1913 interest in the game peaked in the port city when the new Duluth Curling Club Arena was built on the corner of 13th Avenue East and London Road, complete with a large ice surface and seating for 2,000 fans.

The Duluth Hornets emerged in 1920 to play in the United States Amateur Hockey Association with such teams as Eveleth, St. Paul, Minneapolis, Cleveland, Chicago, Winnipeg and Pittsburgh. To accommodate the large crowds, the Duluth Amphitheater, with seating for more than 4,000 fans, was built, becoming one of the first buildings in the state to feature artificial ice. With so much hockey going on, it only seemed natural that the high school and college games would emerge. Cliff Thompson's Eveleth Junior College team already had their own little dynasty going 60 miles up the road by this time. Duluth's college hockey team would soon join in the fun.

On December 10th, 1930, Duluth State Teachers' College, which had been converted a few years earlier from a two-year normal school to a four-year teachers college, announced that intercollegiate ice hockey would be added to the institution's varsity sports program. The Bulldogs first hit the ice on January 13th, 1931, at the Amphitheater against Duluth Central High School. The team's first coach was Frank Kovach, who also helped start the school's football and basketball programs that same year as well. That first roster included the likes of Gary Bartness, Cliff Heidman, Woody Wanvick, Cliff Johnson, Lawrence Rudberg, Benny Knutila, Merrill Boreen, Walt Thygeson, Herman Jappe, Gordy Pomroy, Henry Antoskiewicz and A. Caldwell.

The Dogs were blanked by the young Trojans that opening night by the final score of 3-0. The goalie on that first Bulldog team was Duluth native Gary Bartness.

"Actually, losing to the high school team was not that great a disgrace, although we might have taken it harder if we had known to what heights the college's hockey teams would one day rise," said Bartness.

Huffer Christiansen takes the ceremonial opening face-off at the Duluth Arena...

Connie Pleban

Eveleth's Connie Pleban, in addition to his international successes as both a player and manger of several U.S. National teams, coached at UMD during the 1950s. There, he led UMD's transition from small to major-college status, and in four years there, his teams never lost a game in the MIAC.

"Central had had teams for a number of years and playing college teams was not exactly new to them. The only other high school team in the Duluth area was Duluth Cathedral, so the Trojans had to schedule high school and junior college teams from the Iron Range."

The Bulldogs wound up losing their only other two games of the season in their inaugural campaign, the other two coming at the hands of mighty Eveleth Junior College, 8-2 in Eveleth, but only 4-2 later at home in the "Amp."

"I like to think the latter score reflects our progress during our abbreviated season, added Bartness. "Losing by only two to a team as strong as Eveleth was an achievement."

Bartness had a lot of fond memories about that first season, including the late arrival of the team's equipment. "By the time we put on our brand new green-and-gold uniforms, the season was almost over," he joked. He also remembered scrimmaging against many other teams that year, including a tough bunch called the "Amphitheater Rink Rats." The Rats were the maintenance guys who swept the ice between periods of the games played by the Duluth Hornets at the Amp, and in return they got all the free ice time they wanted. Among those players included Rip Williams, the Godfather of Duluth hockey.

The next season the Dogs sported a 2-5-0 record, winning their first game in a 3-2 decision over Two Harbors High School. But, following that 1931 season, the college dropped the sport for what would amount to 14 years, until finally reinstating it for the 1946-47 season. (One of the players who played at the school during this "unofficial" period was Hall of Fame goalie Sam Lopresti, from Eveleth, who played on a club team from 1936-38, after spending a season between the pipes at St. Cloud Teachers' College in 1935.)

The Depression and War were consuming most people's spare time in the 1930s, but hockey managed to survive. While the semi-pro Duluth Hornets packed up and moved to Wichita in 1933, several senior leagues popped up throughout the area. Under long-time Duluth hockey booster Rip Williams, Duluth joined the International Amateur League (along with Eveleth, Virginia, Port Arthur and Fort William), which later evolved into the Duluth Industrial League, which was composed of the Coolerators, Butlers, Coast Guard and Clyde Club. During that stretch of the mid-1930s, the thing to do in Duluth was to go and watch the Duluth Zephyrs at the Amp. The "Zephs" won the IAHL title in 1936, and proved to be the big show in town during the Great Depression era.

In 1939, an event took place which set back hockey's development in Duluth. One night, during a Fireman-Policeman benefit game in front of some 4,000 fans, the roof of the Amphitheater caved in. Although no one was injured, the growth of hockey suffered until 1953, when artificial ice was installed in the Curling Club Arena.

On June 10, 1946, hockey made its triumphant return to the school, where the Bulldogs, playing an independent schedule, posted a respectable 11-6-1 record under coach Joe Oven. In 1949 two major things happened to the school. First, Duluth State Teachers' College was evolved into a coordinate campus of the University of Minnesota; and secondly, the new University of Minnesota Duluth Bulldogs joined the Minnesota Intercollegiate Athletic Conference (MIAC), where they could now compete regularly against other colleges from around the state including: Augsburg, St. Mary's, Macalester, St. Thomas, St. John's, Hamline, Carleton, Gustavus and Concordia. On February 24th of that year, Bulldog goalie Norm Thompson shut out Carleton College, 3-0, to close out the year with a 7-0-0 overall record in what would prove to be the school's only unbeaten and untied season in history.

In 1955 Connie Pleban, a veteran of international coaching, took over as the team's skipper. He would prove to be instrumental in leading the school's transition from small-college to major-college in status. (Among other things, Pleban also successfully lobbied NCAA rule-makers to expand body checking from half to full ice — a major change for the game at the time.)

The team would dominate the MIAC, while at the same time play competitively against many of the country's largest university teams. In 1957 UMD beat Michigan Tech by the score of 5-3 for its first triumph over an NCAA Division I institution. Another highlight from this era happened on February 18th, 1959, when junior center Orest Wojcichowsky tallied 10 points (four goals and six assists) en route to beating Concordia College 16-0, in what would stand as a Minnesota-Duluth (pre-NCAA Division I) single-game record. A lowlight happened that next season, however, when UMD's star center John McCormick, from Fort William, lost his eye after being hit in he face by a puck during a game at the Curling Club.

In four years, Pleban's UMD teams never lost a game in the MIAC. Pleban left in 1959 and was replaced by Ralph Romano, a former goaltender at Duluth Central. Romano kept up the winning tradition, adding on to Pleban's winning streak until finally getting to 56 straight wins over MIAC opponents. Duluth was so good, it really wasn't fair, often times winning games by margins of 10 to 20-plus goals. Teams would try anything to slow these guys down, even letting the grass grow up through the ice in an attempt to gain equal ground. Finally, in 1961, after winning nine consecutive MIAC titles, the Dogs left the conference to play an independent schedule against big-time Division I Schools. (Some of the teams that the Dogs played in addition to the MIAC schools throughout the 1940s and 1950s included: Eveleth Junior College, Duluth Junior College, Virginia Junior College, Hibbing Junior College, West End Civic Club, Eveleth Rangers, St. Cloud State, Bemidji State, Taconite, Warroad Lakers, Fort Francis, UND, Michigan Tech, Regina Pats, Minneapolis Bungalows and Minneapolis Millers.)

Glenn "Chico" Resch

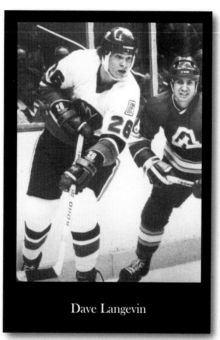

Dave Langevin

Brett Hull

In hopes of landing in the prestigious Western Collegiate Hockey Association (which included: Minnesota, North Dakota, Colorado College, Denver, Michigan, Michigan State and Michigan Tech), the Dogs began playing a rigorous schedule against much stiffer competition. One of those games came on December 19th, 1964, when UMD senior goaltender Bill Halbrehder made an amazing NCAA record 77 saves in his team's 6-5 overtime loss to the University of Michigan in Ann Arbor. After paying their dues for a few years, the Dogs were finally admitted into the WCHA in 1965 — where they have remained a formidable force ever since.

With the move came word that the city of Duluth was going to finalize the plans for a new state-of-the-art facility which was to be built along the city's Canal Park waterfront, called the Duluth Arena. After starting out 0-14, the Dogs finally got a win that first year when they beat North Dakota in Grand Forks, 3-2 in overtime. Although the Dogs finished last in the WCHA their first campaign, they did manage to get a huge win that next season. On November 19th, 1966, the hated Gophers came to town to baptize UMD's new icy palace, which would later become known as the Duluth Entertainment and Convention Center, or DECC for short. The star of the UMD team was a kid from International Falls by the name of Keith "Huffer" Christiansen, who played the Gophers that night like a fiddle, scoring six points in an 8-1 drubbing before a sell-out crowd of 5,700. Huffer went on to earn All-American as well as conference MVP honors that year, in addition to leading the WCHA in scoring with 46 points in just 23 games. And, on top of that, his two wingmates, Pat Francisco and Bruce McLeod, finished second and third in WCHA scoring as well. (McLeod, would later go on to become UMD's athletic director.)

Terry Shercliffe took over as the Dog's new coach in 1970, replacing Bill Selman, who had been behind the bench since 1968. One of the highlights of his coaching tenure came that next season on December 17th, 1971, when UMD tattooed the Gophers, 15-3, in Minneapolis. More than a dozen new single-game records were shattered that night as All-American centers Walt Ledingham and Pat Boutette each tallied hat tricks to lead the scoring onslaught for the Dogs — which struck for nine goals in the second period alone. Another highlight came on January 13th, 1973, when the Dogs rallied from a 6-2 deficit with just over five minutes remaining in regulation to edge Michigan Tech, 7-6, in overtime at the Duluth Arena for one of the school's greatest all-time comeback wins. Led by Pat Boutette's natural hat trick in a span of 2:37 in the third, the Dogs won the game on rookie right winger Tom Milani's overtime game-winner at 3:02 of the extra session.

Gus Hendrickson took over behind the bench for UMD in 1975. One of his first highlights came on October 24th of that year, when, in his first collegiate game, freshman right winger John Harrington took an Ernie

UM-DULUTH ALL-AMERICANS

Pat Boutette (C)
1972-73

Ron Busniuk (C/D)
1969-70

Keith Christiansen (C)
1966-67

Matt Christensen (C)
1985-86*

Chad Erickson (G)
1989-90

Mike DeAngelis (D)
1987-88*

Beau Geisler (D)
2003-04*

Curt Giles (D)
1977-78, 1978-79

Brett Hauer (D)
1992-93

Bob Hill (D)
1965-66

Murray Keogan (C)
1969-70

Rick Kosti (G)
1983-84*, 1984-85

Tom Kurvers (D)
1983-84

Bob Lakso (LW)
1983-84*

Walt Ledingham (LW)
1970-71, 1971-72

Junior Lessard (RW)
2003-04

Norm Maciver (D)
1983-84*, 1984-85, 1985-86

Chris Marinucci (LW)
1993-94

Mark Pavelich (C)
1978-79

Derek Plante (C)
1992-93

Bill Watson (RW)
1983-84, 1984-85

*second team selection

131

Powell centering pass and flipped it past goal-tender Blane Comstock at the 4:04 mark of overtime to give the Dogs a thrilling 4-3 win over the U.S. Olympic Team.

The Bulldogs continued to grow as a team and to command the respect of its WCHA rivals. In 1979, for the first time, the team won a two-game, total-goal WCHA quarterfinal playoff series against the Denver Pioneers at the Duluth Arena to advance to the second round of the league's post-season tournament. All-Americans Curt Giles and Mark Pavelich helped guide the Dogs that year to their third place finish in the final WCHA standings.

In 1980 UMD was blessed to have a couple of Olympians on its roster: Mark Pavelich and John Harrington, who would go on to star on the "Miracle on Ice" team that won gold in Lake Placid, and also Curt Giles, who would go on to play for his native Canada in 1992. Another significant event happened that year when Dan Lempe graduated as the team's all-time career points leader, finishing with 79 goals and 149 assists for 222 points.

In 1982 a new coach took over for the Dogs by the name of Mike Sertich. The Virginia native was himself a former defense-man for the Dogs back in the late 1960's. "Sertie" didn't take long to make his mark with the team either, leading them to their first-ever NCAA playoff appearance that next year. And, although they lost to Providence College, the Dogs had become a force in college hockey. They came back that next season with something to prove.

In 1984, the Dogs finished with an impressive 29-12-2 overall record, the best in school history, while going 19-5-2 in the WCHA, good enough to win their first-ever conference title in their 20 years in the league. Led by All-Americans Tom Kurvers and Bill Watson, UMD came as close as a team can possibly come to winning a national champi-onship, in what many say was the greatest game ever played in college hockey.

Sertich's Dogs, fresh off their first-ever showing in the NCAA playoffs against Providence the year before, started out their magical season by receiving a lesson in humil-ity by getting spanked by the U.S. Olympic team, 12-0. Winger John Harrington of Virginia, and goaltender Bob Mason of International Falls were both former Bulldogs who played on that 1984 squad. Another highlight that season came in December, when the Dogs split a two-game exhibition series with the Junior Red Army team in Leningrad and in Moscow to become the first American collegiate ice hockey team to tour the Soviet Union.

UMD settled down after that and kicked off the WCHA season by sweeping Colorado College. From there, the Bulldogs won eight of nine and finished the regular sea-son losing only four of their final 16 games. They swept Wisconsin at the season's end to win their first McNaughton Cup, signifying the conference title.

Forced to host a "home" series at Williams Arena in Minneapolis due to a scheduling conflict with the Duluth Arena,

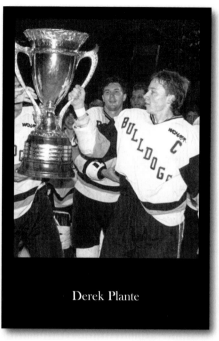
Derek Plante

Shjon Podein

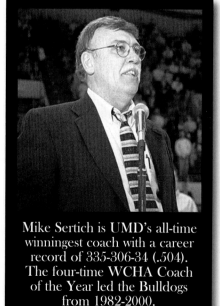
Mike Sertich is UMD's all-time winningest coach with a career record of 335-306-34 (.504). The four-time WCHA Coach of the Year led the Bulldogs from 1982-2000.

the Dogs slaughtered North Dakota, 8-1 and 12-6, before near-capacity crowds in the WCHA championship series to advance to the NCAA quarterfinals at home against Clarkson College. They split with Clarkson, and earned themselves a trip to Lake Placid for the right to take on North Dakota again, this time in the Final Four. There, in an over-time thriller, the Dogs beat the rejuvenated Fighting Sioux, 2-1.

Their opponents in the championship game were the champions of the CCHA, Bowling Green, who had knocked off Michigan State in the semifinals. It was a tale of two teams and two different playing styles. Bowling Green, whose line-up was dominated by Canadians, had only four Americans on the squad. Duluth on the other hand, com-prised mostly of home-grown Minnesotans, had only four Canadians. The sell-out crowd of nearly 8,000 people had no idea that they were about to be a part of intercollegiate hockey history when the opening puck dropped.

For the first time in two games, UMD fell behind as Bowling Green defenseman Garry Galley crashed into Bulldog goalie Rick Kosti, and went top-shelf on a back-hander at 5:58 of the first. The Dogs came back, as they had done so often that season, when Aurora's Bob Lakso stole the puck in the Bowling Green zone and slipped a pass to Chisholm's Mark Baron, who flipped the bis-cuit under the crossbar to tie it at one apiece.

Then, after being stymied on their first three power-play attempts, Hoyt Lakes' Matt Christensen directed a face-off to the left point, where Bill Watson proceeded to tip in a Tom Kurvers blast to go up by one. In the third, Lakso spurted between two Falcon defensemen and fired a low wrister to beat goaltender Gary Kruzich on the short side. Things were now looking pretty good for the Bulldogs as they went up 3-1. It didn't last long though, as Falcon forward Jamie Wansbrough, pressured by Bulldog defense-man Jim Johnson, went five-hole on Kosti to make it a 3-2 game. UMD then answered right back at the 11:55 mark when International Falls' Tom Herzig tallied on a hard wrister.

As it went back and forth throughout the third period, Bowling Green scored once again at 12:42. Kosti stopped a blue line blast by Falcon defenseman Mike Pikul, but got caught up in traffic in front of the net as he tried to recover. Forward Peter Wilson put in the garbage goal to make it 4-3, still in favor of Duluth. Then with just 1:37 to go in the game, Bowling Green tied it up on a fluke goal. With their goalie pulled, the Falcons dumped a long, off-target shot into the zone from beyond the red line that many people felt was off-side. Oddly, the puck bounced off the end boards and past Kosti, who had stepped behind the net to control a puck which would never arrive. The puck hit a crack in the dasher board, deflected to the net, hit the left post and stopped in the crease. With Kosti way out of position, John Samanski, who had sprinted down the slot, tapped in a "freebie" to tie it up.

"I've never seen it happen, but I've heard of it happening," said the goaltender on the tough-luck bounce. "However, it never happened to me. It happened so fast that I didn't know what to do. I felt helpless."

From there, the two teams went to overtime. In fact, it would go an incredible four overtimes! Save after save, both goalies battled to stay alive. In the blur of the over-times, Kruzich and Kosti, both freshmen goalies, played out of their heads. Kruzich stopped three UMD break-aways while Kosti stopped 19 shots in the final 37 minutes. Time stood still. It was unbelievable. Both teams were visibly fatigued and seemed to be skating only on adrenaline.

Finally, at 7:11 of the fourth over-time it ended. And with it broke the collective hearts of UMD hockey fans forever. Falcon forward Dan Kane sped into the Bulldog end from the neutral zone and, from the high slot, threaded a pass to Gino Cavallini, who broke in all alone on Kosti. Cavallini took the puck from left to right, and put a back-hander in to make college hockey history.

Kosti, who tied a tournament record with 55 saves, really had no chance on the game-winning goal. Kane made the perfect pass, and Cavallini made the perfect shot. That was it. As soon as the puck hit the back of the net, Kosti skated straight to his bench, where he was met by his teary-eyed team-mates, who sat motionless in disbelief.

The Bulldogs and Falcons had skated for 97 minutes and 11 seconds at Olympic Arena, in a game that took nearly four hours, while taking part in the (then) longest and most memorable game in college hockey history. The historic arena in Lake Placid that housed the famed "Miracle on Ice" Olympic team four years earlier, had now played host to the "Marathon on Ice."

"The thing I remember most about the overtimes was being really tired and gasping for air during the whistles," said team captain Tom Kurvers. "I think we only played four defensemen for most of the game. After a while, you didn't take any chances. You just played your position and tried not to make a mistake. The whole overtime was confusing. I hardly remember any of it. I was hugely disappointed at the loss, but it was an incredible game."

"Just to be going into overtime was a huge letdown, and we didn't feel that we had to be there," said Bill Watson. "It's one thing to score late to get into overtime, and it's another thing to squander the lead to get into overtime. The excitement level was incredible. The overtimes went on and on and on, and it just became a situation of survival and mind over matter as to just how much you wanted to win. It was tough playing on the much bigger Olympic ice surface too. It was probably my toughest loss ever as a hockey player."

UMD turned the corner that night in the world of college hockey. No longer were they just the second-best team in Minnesota. Bulldog hockey had arrived big-time. In an ironic twist, UMD returned to the Final Four

In his seven winters behind the Bulldog bench, Coach Scott Sandelin has compiled an overall record of 109-143-31 and taken UMD to three of the past five WCHA Final Five Tournaments.

UMD's OLYMPIANS

Keith Christiansen, USA (1972)
Mark Pavelich, USA (1980)
John Harrington, USA (1980, 84)
Bob Mason, USA (1984)
Guy Gosselin, USA (1988, 92)
Brett Hauer, USA (1994)
Mike DeAngelis, Italy (1992, 94)
Curt Giles, Canada (1992)
Chris Lindberg, Canada (1992)
Brett Hull (1998, 2002)

UMDs HOBEY WINNERS

Tom Kurvers	1984
Bill Watson	1985
Brett Hull	1986
Norm MacIver	1986
Derek Plante	1993
Chris Marinucci	1994
Junior Lessard	2004

Isaac Reichmuth

again the following year. This time, led by a young freshman named Brett Hull, they lost a triple-overtime heart-breaker, 6-5, to RPI in Detroit. They rebounded to finish third in the nation by winning the consolation game, 7-6, over Boston College, in, of course, over-time. For his team's efforts, third-year head coach Mike Sertich was selected as the WCHA's Coach of the Year for an unprecedented third season in a row.

Another major milestone came for Hull that following season, when, on March 1st, in the Bulldogs' WCHA quarterfinal series with Northern Michigan at the Duluth Arena, he beat goalie Chris Jiannaris at the 15:38 mark of the third period for his 50th goal of the year (and fourth of the night) to eclipse the previous Bulldog single-season mark of 49 goals set only the year before by Bill Watson.

The Dogs roared into the 90's through some up and down seasons. In 1993 the team rebounded to win its third WCHA title by blanking visiting St. Cloud State University 4-0, on junior winger Chris Marinucci's two goals. The team then went on to sweep Alaska Anchorage in the first round of the WCHA playoffs at the DECC, thus finishing the year with a 17-1-0 home record and a .944 winning percentage, the best single-season mark in school history. After beating Brown, the team ultimately lost to Lake Superior State, 4-3, in the NCAA's Western Region finals. But, as a small consolation, the Dogs did manage to clean up at the annual WCHA Awards Banquet. Senior center Derek Plante was named as the league's MVP, and fellow All-WCHA first team defenseman Brett Hauer was named the Student-Athlete of the Year — a Bulldog first. Sertich rounded out the evening by bringing home his fourth Coach of the Year trophy, becoming only the second conference coach ever to do so.

One of the biggest moments in Bulldog history happened on March 15th, 1998, when the team, left for dead and down 4-0 with less than 14 minutes remaining in regulation, rallied back to beat the Gophers 5-4 in the third and deciding game of their best-of-three WCHA playoff series at the DECC. Five different Dogs scored in the historic victory, including senior Mike Peluso, who got the game-winner at 10:49 of sudden death. After the game, in a classic display of emotion, Sertich flew down the ice and slid into his team's net on his back.

After a couple of rough seasons in 1999 and 2000, Sertich stepped down as the head coach of the Dogs. He was replaced by Scott Sandelin, a Hibbing native who played collegiately at North Dakota before going on to play professionally for seven seasons, including stints in the NHL with Montreal, Philadelphia and Minnesota. Sandelin paid his dues with the Dogs and went through a couple of rough seasons before turning the corner.

Among the early highlights of his coaching tenure included a 6-4 victory over Minnesota State University-Mankato in 2003 to capture third place honors at the WCHA Final Five tournament at St. Paul's Excel

Energy Center. The Bulldogs ended the year as one of college hockey's hottest teams, going unbeaten in 12 of their final 16 games. One of the stars of that team was center Tim Stapleton, who led the team in scoring, becoming only the third freshman ever (and the first in more than a quarter century), to do so.

In 2003-04 the Bulldogs definitely made their presence felt in the WCHA, finishing second in the conference and advancing all the way to the NCAA Frozen Four in Boston. The team got hot in February, going unbeaten in 15 straight games. During that stretch the team swept Bowling Green, Denver, Colorado College (twice), Michigan Tech, Minnesota and then got a win and a tie against Minnesota State Mankato. In the second series sweep over CC, on February 21st,

The DECC is one of the most picturesque hockey arena's in the country...

Junior left wing Marco Peluso tallied his first collegiate hat trick, all of which came on the power play to equal a UMD single-game record.

The Dogs would go on to beat Mankato in the WCHA Final Five Playoffs, only to lose to the rival Gophers in the title game. They had beaten Minnesota in four straight that season but couldn't get the fifth win in the end. The team would get another crack at them, however, in the NCAA Midwest Regionals in Grand Rapids, MI. After beating Michigan State, 5-0, in the opener, UMD faced off against Minnesota on March 28th with a ticket to the Frozen Four on the line. It would be the first NCAA playoff meeting ever between the two archrivals.

UMD's ALL-TIME LEADING SCORERS

	PLAYER (YEARS)	GP	G	A	TP	PPG
1.	Dan Lempe (1976-80)	146	79	143	*222	1.52
2.	Derek Plante (1989-93)	138	96	123	219	1.58
	Matt Christensen (1982-86)	168	76	143	219	1.31
4.	Bill Watson (1982-85)	108	89	121	210	*1.94
5.	Gregg Moore (1979-83)	148	99	107	206	1.39
6.	Scott Carlston (1978-82)	147	87	116	203	1.38
7.	Tom Milani (1972-76)	146	*100	98	198	1.36
8.	Keith Christiansen (1963-67)	102	75	121	196	1.92
9.	Tom Kurvers (1980-84)	164	43	149	192	1.17
10.	Norm Maciver (1982-86)	165	39	*152	191	1.16
11.	Bill Oleksuk (1978-82)	156	90	100	190	1.22
12.	Chris Marinucci (1990-94)	151	77	96	173	1.14
13.	Dan Fishback (1979-83)	154	63	109	172	1.12
14.	Curt Giles (1975-79)	143	36	135	171	1.20
15.	Skeeter Moore (1983-87)	149	60	105	165	1.11
16.	Mike Peluso (1994-98)	153	80	83	163	1.07
17.	Monty Jones (1973-77)	141	70	83	153	1.09
18.	Tim Stapleton (2002-2006)	162	63	89	152	0.93
19.	Mike Newton (1972-76)	144	67	81	148	1.03
20.	Bob Lakso (1980-84)	150	69	76	145	0.94
21.	Brett Hull (1984-86)	90	84	60	144	1.60
22.	Mark Pavelich (1976-79)	110	57	85	142	1.29
	Junior Lessard (2000-04)	160	74	68	142	0.89
24.	Rusty Fitzgerald (1991-95)	147	60	81	141	0.96
25.	John Harrington (1975-79)	134	65	73	138	1.03
26.	Walt Ledingham (1969-72)	95	66	68	134	1.41
27.	Pat Francisco (1963-67)	105	69	64	133	1.27
	Brad Federenko (1992-97)	152	67	66	133	0.88
29.	Pat Boutette (1970-73)	101	53	78	131	1.30
	Tom Herzig (1981-85)	161	57	74	131	0.81
31.	Keith Hendrickson (1975-80)	150	35	94	129	0.86
	Lyman Haakstad (1970-74)	140	59	70	129	0.92
33.	Jeff Scissons (1996-00)	153	52	76	128	0.84
34.	Evan Schwabe (2001-05)	160	51	75	126	0.79
35.	John Rothstein (1975-79)	143	56	69	125	0.87
36.	Glenn Kulyk (1976-80)	136	44	75	119	0.88
	Mark Odnokon (1982-86)	164	39	80	119	0.73
38.	Merv Kiryluik (1970-74)	128	37	80	117	0.91
39.	Brian Johnson (1983-87)	158	36	76	112	0.71
40.	Doug Torrel (1988-92)	156	54	57	111	0.71
	Colin Anderson (1996-00)	140	44	67	111	0.79
42.	Mike Tok (1962-65)	98	61	47	108	1.10
43.	Dave Langevin (1972-76)	142	35	72	107	0.75
44.	Joe Rybar (1994-98)	149	38	67	105	0.70
45.	Jon Francisco (1999-03)	154	42	62	104	0.67
46.	Cam Fryer (1969-72)	94	40	62	102	1.09
	Ken Dzikowski (1994-98)	150	36	66	102	0.68
48.	Tom Nelson (1998-02)	138	33	68	101	0.73
49.	Mike Krensing (1979-83)	144	41	59	100	0.69
50.	Sean Toomey (1983-87)	144	58	40	98	0.69
	Beau Geisler (2000-04)	157	19	79	98	0.62

*UMD (as an NCAA Division I member) record
Note: Statistics are included only from post-NCAA era (1961-62 to present)

Minnesota, the two-time defending national champions, was the favorite heading into the game, but junior goaltender Isaac Reichmuth thought otherwise as he turned aside 22 of 23 shots en route to leading his team to an impressive 3-1 victory. Three different Bulldogs tallied goals in the big win, UMD's fifth in six tries against the Gophers that season, while Reichmuth was tabbed the tournament's Most Valuable Player.

With that, the Dogs were headed back to the Frozen Four, a place they had not been to in nearly two decades. On April 8th, the Dogs hit the ice against the University of Denver in the semifinals. UMD jumped out to an early 3-1 lead behind a pair of Junior Lessard goals and felt good about their chances heading into the third period. After all, they had not lost a game that they were leading while heading into the third period in over a year. Their streak would sadly end that night, however, as Denver rallied in the final frame, scoring four answered goals in the final 18 minutes of play to beat the Dogs, 5-3. It was a heartbreaking end to an otherwise fantastic season.

When it was all said and done, the Dogs finished the season with a stellar 28-13-4 record. Senior right winger Junior Lessard, who led the league in both scoring and goals, was named as not only the WCHA's Player of the Year, but also as a first team All-American. Further, he was named as the national Player of the Year by both insidecollege hockey.com and USCHO.com. And, if that wasn't enough, he also took home college hockey's highest honor, the Hobey Baker Memorial Award, becoming just the fourth Bulldog in history ever to do so. Lessard, the first Quebec native to ever lace up a pair of skates at UMD, paced the country in scoring with 63 points; in goals, with 32; and in power play tallies, with 14.

In addition, Scott Sandelin was named as the WCHA Coach of the Year after guiding his squad to its highest league finish (second place) in 11 years. Sandelin would also win the Spencer Penrose Award as the NCAA Division I Coach of the Year as well, joining Mike Sertich (1983-84) as the only two Bulldog skippers to ever take home that coveted piece of hardware.

That next year the Dogs hit the ice running, going 5-0-1 to open the season. As such, on October 25, 2004, UMD found itself ranked No. 1 in the college hockey polls for the first time in 15 seasons. The team, which was projected to take the WCHA title in the pre-season coaches poll, struggled from there on out though and wound up finishing the season with a mod-

Mason Raymond & Matt Niskanen

Beau Geisler

Trent Palm

est 15-17-6 record, good for just sixth place in the conference. The team had finished the season strong, with wins over Denver, Bemidji and Wisconsin, but then got swept by rival North Dakota in the WCHA playoffs to end the year on a sour note.

The Dogs posted an 11-25-4 mark in 2005-06, and then went 13-21-5 in 2006-07, good for a only pair of ninth place conference finishes. One of the highlights of this era, however, came on February 3, 2006, when Brett Hull returned to the DECC to have his No. 29 jersey retired between periods of a game between the Bulldogs and Wisconsin. Hull, who still owns a number of UMD scoring records, retired from the NHL earlier that year as its third all-time leading scorer behind only Wayne Gretzky and Gordie Howe. With the honor, Hull joined Keith "Huffer" Christiansen as the only other Bulldog to have his number forever enshrined into the rafters of the DECC.

Things are on the upswing for 2007-08. Senior Matt McKnight was chosen as the team captain that season and, in the process, became the first Bulldog to fill that role in back-to-back seasons since Curt Giles, a two-time All-American defenseman in both 1978 and 1979. Only five other players besides Giles: Gord McDonald (1973-74 and 1974-75), Owen Rogers (1964-65 and 1965-66), Bill Lenardon (1961-62 and 1962-63), Harvey Flaman (1956-57 and 1957-58) and Wally Heikkinen (1949-50, 1951-52 and 1952-53), have been entrusted with team captain responsibilities for more than one season in the 64-year history of the UMD hockey program. McKnight entered his senior season ranked first among current Bulldogs in career scoring (53 points) and games played (99). Meanwhile, Junior left wing Andrew Carroll, who was a co-captain with McKnight in 2006-07, and defenseman Travis Gawryletz, one of just four seniors on the 2007-08 Bulldog roster, were named as the alternate team captains as well.

Since their first game back in 1931, the University of Minnesota Duluth has established a rich hockey tradition that is second to none throughout the ranks of college hockey. The program, which started from humble beginnings, has grown into a consistent NCAA power. The program is first rate and with the luxury of being the "only show in town," enjoys the support of the entire community. Much like the Nebraska football program has the total support of its community, the Dogs too have the run of the joint and show no signs of slowing down. Let's just hope that the program can get its new arena plans into production, it would be a great community asset.

Hull & Huffer:
The only two retired jerseys
in Bulldog Hockey history...

THE ST. CLOUD STATE HUSKIES

Founded in 1896 as a teacher's college, by 1899 the school had a hockey team that was competing against several area teams in the region. The school's first ever game was against the mighty St. Paul Hockey Club. And, although St. Paul easily won the game, 6-0, at the Virginia Rink in St. Paul before a crowd of some 400 fans, it put the city on the map as one of the state's hot-spots for the growth of the game.

The game continued to grow in the area, and by the 1930s, St. Cloud Teachers' College was one of the state's biggest hockey powers. The school's first official team hit the ice in 1931, and under the tutelage of head coach Ralph Theisen, the squad posted an impressive 8-1-7 record. Ludwig Andolsek took over that next year and found the key to his team's success to be a couple hundred miles to the northeast, in hockey-crazy Eveleth. From 1933 through 1935, St. Cloud Teacher's College, manned almost entirely by Eveleth players, posted an astonishing 42-4-1 record. In 1935 the 25-2-0 Huskies finished second in the National AAU Tournament (which was the considered as the national championship), in the Windy City, losing 2-0 to the Chicago Baby Ruth's, which coincidentally was composed entirely of Eveleth players. The stars of that era also included a pair of Hall of Fame goaltenders: Frankie "Mr. Zero" Brimsek, and Sam LoPresti, both from Eveleth. (Both would go on to play between the pipes in the then six-team NHL — Brimsek with Boston, and LoPresti with Chicago.) Others top players included: Roland Vandell at right defense, Walter DePaul at left defense, Ray Gasperlin at right wing, Bernard Bjork at center and Cletus Winter at left wing.

St. Cloud continued to dominate against the local small colleges and produce top players throughout the 1930s and '40s, rising to a prominence which provided college hockey with a tremendous boost. "No institution did more for collegiate hockey in the '30's and '40's than St. Cloud," said John Mariucci, also an Eveleth native who would have come to play for St. Cloud had it not been for the whopping $100 scholarship that the Gophers offered him to come there instead. "The Vandell brothers, Bjork, Gasperlin, Gambucci, Strand and DePaul all ended up at St. Cloud State and were instrumental in helping the hockey program. Gambucci (later) started the high school hockey program in Grand Forks and Robert DePaul was the coach at International Falls."

George Lynch guided the Huskies from 1938 to 1942, posting a modest 20-15-2 record. The school then shut down its hockey program from 1942-46, due to WWII. In 1946 former star player Roland Vandell took over behind the bench, and over the next five years led the Huskies to an impressive 39-19-2 record against such schools as the University of Manitoba, Minnesota

Duluth, North Dakota, Michigan Tech, Bemidji State, St. Thomas, St. Olaf, St. John's, Concordia, Macalester, Hamline, Carlton, Gustavus and St. Mary's. The star of that era was Eveleth's Sergio Gambucci, a two-time team captain who twice led the team in scoring. The Huskies, after posting a 12-4 record, won the 1948 St. Paul Winter Carnival Championship after beating St. Thomas, St. John's and St. Olaf. The title was symbolic of the college hockey championship of Minnesota at time. One of the school's other big wins of that era happened on February 20, 1949, when they beat Bemidji State by the final score of 13-0.

After five different coaches in five years, Jack Wink finally took over as the team's new skipper in 1956. Wink would lead the Huskies to a 68-69-2 record over a 12-year span until 1968, when he was replaced by Charles Basch. During that time St. Cloud played tough against several newcomers, including the University of Colorado, Lake Superior State and Augsburg. Basch came in and got the program focused on playing bigger and better schools, eventually joining the NAIA with several other local colleges, while later gaining Division II status. Ultimately, Basch would guide the Huskies to a 181-193-7 record from 1968-1984. During that period, the team played several new teams including: the Air Force Academy, Alaska Anchorage, Illinois-Chicago, Chicago State, Iowa State, St. Scholastica and several Wisconsin State schools. Basch posted a winning season every year he served as the team's coach, while his best stretch was from 1979-84, when he posted an outstanding 127-75-60 record against a lot of bigger Division I and II schools.

The 1970's produced five all-Americans in Ronald Gordon (1970), Paul Oberstar (1971), John Fitzsimmons (1973), Pat Sullivan (1974, '75), and Dave Reichel (1978, '79). Reichel (who would go on to star as a member of the U.S. Bandy Team), led the Huskies in scoring from 1977-79, finishing his career with an impressive 138 points. Meanwhile, Fitzsimmons, who led his teams in scoring in 1971 and 1973, finished with 103 points.

In 1980, long-time coach Charlie Basch led the Huskies into the Northern Collegiate Hockey Association (NCHA), the inaugural season of the league. It was the school's first step in getting to what they felt was a realistic level, NCAA Division I. Some of the stars of that era included TV news anchor Jeff Passolt, who would finish his illustrious career in the Granite City with 67 goals and 69 assists for 136 career points from 1977-81. In addition, goalie Rory Eidsness and defenseman Dan Pratt were both named as All-Americans in 1981-82.

Upon his retirement from coaching in 1984, Basch was replaced by former Gopher John Perpich, who also

The 1899 Huskies

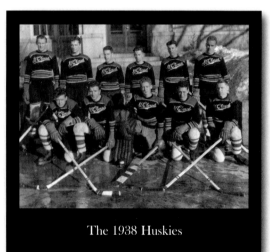

The 1938 Huskies

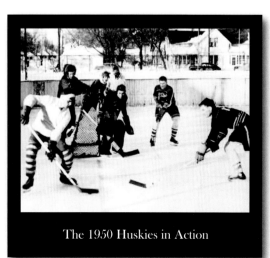

The 1950 Huskies in Action

played the game professionally for the St. Paul Fighting Saints in the late 1970s. Although Perpich would only stay for two seasons in St. Cloud, he led the Huskies to back-to-back winning seasons and renewed interest in Husky hockey. During his tenure, Perpich posted a 30-24-4 record, highlighted by his 1985 second-place finish in the NCHA. The following season, after leading the NCHA on six different occasions before darkhorse Mankato State and perennial power Bemidji State took over, the Huskies recorded a 16-11-2 overall record and finished fifth in the league. The Hibbing native left the Huskies in 1986 to become the head coach at Ferris State, a Division I school in Michigan.

After Perpich left, the school really got serious about getting to the next level. What they needed was someone to come in who had a lot of credibility and clout. Someone with enough star power to get legislation passed to finally move the program to the Division I level. Their prayers were answered in 1986, when former Gopher, Olympic and NHL coach Herb Brooks agreed to come to St. Cloud and take over as the team's 15th ever coach. "It was a wonderful opportunity for a Division I school and would provide more opportunities for kids," said Brooks. "There are more kids in Minnesota than there are places to play."

With the big news, a whole new wave of excitement erupted onto the St. Cloud community. The first step in implementing their long range plan for turning the program into a Division I Hockey power from its current Division II status, required lobbying for a new arena. Design plans soon got underway for an heir apparent to Municipal Ice Arena, the "National Hockey Center," complete with two Olympic-sized sheets of ice and seating for more than 6,000 fans.

In Brooks' first and only season as head coach at SCSU, the Husky hockey team broke or tied 45 school records on the way to posting a 25-10-1 record and a third place finish at the NCAA Division II Hockey Championships. Playing to capacity crowds, Herbie worked his magic, gaining grass-roots level support and starting a massive recruiting initiative to get the state's best blue-chip players to come there. The Huskies went 17-4-1 on their home ice, finished first in the NCHA with a 13-6-1 record, and won the conference's post-season tournament. He had instilled a new winning attitude and the players responded big time.

"Herb breathes winning," said Burnsville senior forward Herm Finnegan, "I think we were afraid to lose."

The Huskies were seeded first in the Western Division and went on to defeat Salem State in the first round of the NCHA Division II Championships. The series win over Salem State then sent the Huskies to the Final Four, which was being held in Plattsburgh, N.Y. There, the Huskies played tough but came up just short. While they dropped their opening game to Oswego State, 5-2, they did rally to defeat conference rival Bemidji State, 6-4, in the consolation game to finish third in the nation. One of the stars of

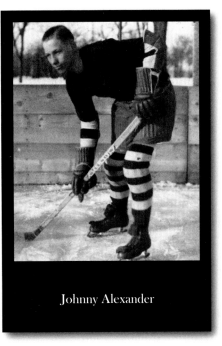

Johnny Alexander

Dale Carmichael

Bill Fritsinger

that team was two-time All-American selection Mike Brodzinski, who tallied 146 career points with the team. Brodzinski, from Blaine, had 18 goals and 29 assists for 47 points to lead the team in scoring that season.

"We had a commitment from the president," said Brooks, who was inspired to take the position on some advice from his former coach and mentor, John Mariucci. "He encouraged me to go up there for at least a year and put something back into the game. It was more for philosophical reasons that I went there, and that year went fast for me. Basically, that was one of the most enjoyable years I ever spent in hockey; it was fun."

In late May of 1987, after an arduous battle with the state legislature, the school's arena proposal was approved under Governor Rudy Perpich's Olympic and Amateur Sports Initiative, which included building various sports facilities around the state. While the construction of the National Hockey Center was underway, the Huskies decided to take a leap of faith and join the ranks of the nation's best NCAA Division I teams. They would be classified as a Division I-Independent, and then petition to join the WCHA. Brooks, who left the school to take over as the North Stars new head coach after a year in St. Cloud, passed the torch to his top assistant, former University of Wisconsin-River Falls and Bethel College hockey coach Craig Dahl. Dahl now began the long journey of getting his team prepared for the rigors of D-I hockey.

The Huskies got a little "baptism by fire" in their first game that next year, when they got waxed by the Gophers, 6-0, in Eveleth for the annual Hall of Fame game. It wasn't easy at first, but Dahl led the Huskies to a modest 11-25-1 overall record in his first season. His Huskies showed a big improvement at the end though, when they won five of their last eight games, including an impressive 4-3 upset win over third-ranked Lake Superior State on the final night of the season.

The Huskies opened the 1988-89 season by beating Division I mainstay Notre Dame by the final score of 4-3, giving the program a much needed shot of confidence. Dahl's club went on to win three of their first five games and began to peak the interests of recruits from all around the state. Another big event happened early that season as well, when, on December 16, 1989, the Huskies christened the National Hockey Center by beating Northern Michigan, 5-4, in front of some 4,000 fans. The team beat several established Division I teams that year as well, including: Notre Dame, Alaska-Fairbanks, Clarkson, Air Force, Dartmouth, Brown and Alaska-Anchorage, to finish with an impressive 19-16-2 record. For their efforts, the team received an invitation to the first round of the NCAA Division I playoffs in Sault Ste. Marie, Mich., for a best-of-three series against Lake Superior State. There, the Huskies ended their season with a pair of toughly contested 6-3 and 4-2 losses. Winger Lenny Eseau led the team in scoring with 39 points.

The Huskies kicked off the 1989-90 season with a 5-4 and 4-2 sweep of former

Mark Parrish

Bret Hedican

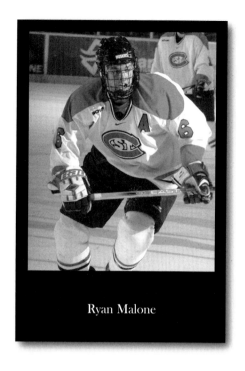

Ryan Malone

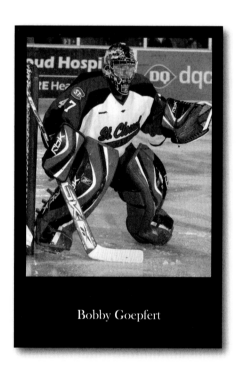

Bobby Goepfert

Brandon Sampair

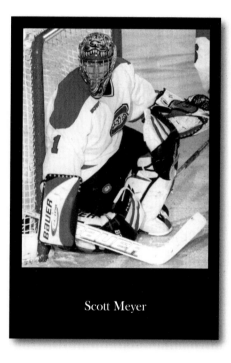

Scott Meyer

Taj Melson

Jeff Saterdalen

Mike Brodzinski

Tyler Arnason

Fred Knipscheer

Grant Sjerven

Mark Hartigan

Brian Leitza

Joe Motzko

Tim Hanus

Matt Cullen

Nate DiCasmirro

139

NCAA Champion Northern Michigan. Dahl's boys went on to garner a 17-19-2 record that year, which included big wins over Denver, Wisconsin, Michigan Tech, Air Force, Bowling Green, and a tie with UMD. Not only were new recruits taking notice, but so were other college coaches. At the end of the season, the Huskies were ranked second in the NCAA Division I Independent Coaches Poll behind only Alaska-Anchorage. Bloomington's Jeff Saterdalen led the team in scoring that season with 24 goals and 33 assists for 57 points.

In the fall of 1990, the Huskies' wish finally came true – they were accepted into the prestigious Western Collegiate Hockey Association. In their first-ever WCHA game, the Huskies tied the Gophers in a 3-3 over-time thriller in front of a record home crowd of 7,051 screaming fans. The Huskies played a great rookie campaign in the conference that year, ultimately finishing fifth in the league with a 12-16-4 record. The season came to a climax when they took North Dakota to three games in the first round of the conference playoffs. After opening the series with a 4-2 win, the Sioux tied it up by beating St. Cloud, 10-2. Then, in the third and final game, the Huskies blew a 4-0 lead by giving up seven unanswered goals to lose the game. While

KMSP-TV Ch. 9 News anchor Jeff Passolt was a star winger (and bruis-er...) for the Huskies from 1977-81.

winger Brian Cook had 50 points for the team to lead all scorers, junior defenseman Bret Hedican of North St. Paul was St. Cloud's first All-WCHA First Team selection.

Hedican opted to leave the Huskies the following season to play for the 1992 U.S. Olympic Hockey team in Albertville, France. Then, upon returning from the Olympics, Hedican decided to join the St. Louis Blues. (He would go on to become a star in the NHL, where he has been playing ever since. One of the highlights of his career came in 2006, when his Carolina Hurricanes won the Stanley Cup.) The Huskies posted a 14-21-2 record in their second season as a member of the WCHA. While freshman winger Sandy Gasseau was named to the WCHA All-Rookie team, seniors Jeff Saterdalen and Tim Hanus completed their careers with 179 and 172 career points, respectively, to become the top all-time scorers in Husky Hockey history.

While St. Cloud State's program con-tinued to grow and gain respect throughout the annals of college hockey, they quickly learned that there was going to be no free lunch in the tough WCHA. In 1992-93 the team posted a 15-8-3 record, good only for seventh place in the conference. Centerman Fred Knipscheer, who led the team with 34 goals and 26 assists for 60 points, was named to the 1993 All

HUSKY HEAD COACH CRAIG DAHL

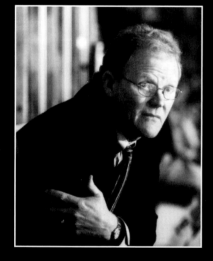

A native of Albert Lea, Craig Dahl turned down a chance to play hockey at Dartmouth and instead accepted a scholarship as a football quarterback under Murray Warmath at the University of Minnesota in 1971. But, when Cal Stoll took over for Warmath in 1972, Dahl's Gopher gridiron career came to a screeching halt. Dahl then decided to transfer to Pacific Lutheran University in Tacoma, Wash., where he played both football and also defense for the Burien Flyers Junior hockey team in Seattle. Upon graduating with a degree in physical education and social sciences in 1976, Dahl found a job teaching and coaching football and track at Winona State and later in Billings, Montana.

One of his buddies there, who went on to coach football at Bethel College in St. Paul, later recommended him for his school's open hockey coaching position. Eager to learn the art of college hockey coaching, Dahl sought the advice of several Minnesota hock-ey coaching legends, including: Ed Saugestad, Brad Buetow, Gino Gasparini, Don Roberts and Chuck Grillo. Grillo signed him for a summer hockey camp, where Dahl did as much listening and learning as he did instructing. In 1980 Dahl began his collegiate coaching career at Bethel. There, he produced a modest 61-75 overall record, led the Royals to a MIAC championship in 1982, a NAIA consolation title in 1984, and was named as the MIAC Coach of the Year in 1985. That same year he left Bethel to take over for the University of Wisconsin-River Falls, where his Falcons knocked off St. Cloud for the final spot in the Northern Collegiate Hockey Association playoffs.

It was at Bethel though, where Dahl caught another break. Herb Brooks, who was leaving the country to coach in Switzerland right after the 1980 Olympics, was looking for someone to house-sit his home near Bethel. He had heard that Bethel had a new hockey coach, so he called Dahl to see if he was interested. The result was a beautiful friendship that would later pay big dividends for the young Dahl. In 1986, Brooks accepted the SCSU coaching position, and as fate would have it, his top assis-tant (and predecessor in waiting) would be Dahl. Dahl, of course, took over the head coaching position in 1987, and after a cou-ple of seasons of playing Division I hockey as an independent, led his team into the WCHA in 1990.

One of the hardest things for Dahl to overcome, was the fact that because state dollars were ultimately used to fund the pro-gram's new arena, many critics expected Dahl to "do the right thing" by recruiting only Minnesota kids – like the Gophers did at the time. So, when Dahl recruited some top-notch Canadian kids, some people got bent out of shape.

"Unfairly, I think, we took some heat," Dahl said. "It was said that this program was supposed to be a program for Minnesota kids. In my mind, it will be."

And he did that through the years, by giving countless Minnesota kids scholarships and opportunities to advance their hock-ey careers at the university. In all, Dahl coached the Huskies from 1987-2005, posting a 338-309-52 (.521) career record. The winningest coach in school history, Dahl led his Huskies to five NCAA post-season appearances. In addition ,the 1998 WCHA Coach of the Year brought home his first Broadmoor Trophy in 2001 with a WCHA Final Five win over North Dakota. The respected coach finaly stepped down in 2005 on his own terms to pursue a career in the world of finance.

"We have just great, great fans here and they have been super supportive of us through the years," said Dahl. "So, thanks to all of them, we couldn't do it without you. Husky hockey is a big source of community pride for these people and I am just proud to be a part of that. Win or lose, it is a big night out on the town up here and that is just a great thing. You know, it is like the Barry White song, 'I just can't get enough of your love baby!' That is how I feel about our fans up here, I just love them."

American squad — the team's first as a Division I school.

Incidentally, on March 5, 1994, the main ice sheet inside of the National Hockey Center was officially named as the Brendan J. McDonald Ice Rink. McDonald, who served as the school's president from 1982-92, was a strong advocate for the school's move to Division I.

Defenseman Kelly Hultrgren's 37 points led the way for the Dogs in 1994, as the team once again cracked the 20-win plateau. The biggest highlight of the year came during the post-season, where after defeating UMD in the first round of the WCHA playoffs at home, the Huskies went on to beat the University of Wisconsin, 3-2, in overtime in the semifinals at the Bradley Center in Milwaukee. After goals from Dave Paradise and Tony Gruba in the second, Dave Holum got the game-winner at 1:04 of the extra session to give the Huskies their first-ever birth in the WCHA Championship Game. There, it would be another overtime contest that would determine the winner, and unfortunately for SCSU, it was the Gopher's Nick Checco who beat Husky goalie Grant Sjerven at 1:47 of the sudden death session to give the U of M the win. Dave Paradise and Gino Santerre each scored for St. Cloud in the loss. While SCSU ended their season with a 21-13-4 overall record, they proved to be lethal at home, losing just once at the National Hockey Center.

In the 1994-95 season, the Huskies posted a 17-20-1 overall record en route to finishing fifth in the WCHA with a 15-16-1 conference mark. After winning seven of their last 11 games, SCSU earned home ice for the WCHA playoffs, but ultimately lost to the University of North Dakota in two games. Center Brett Lievers' 48 points were tops for the Dogs in 1994, while freshman goaltender Brian Leitza was named to the WCHA All-Rookie team.

After finishing in the WCHA basement in 1995-96 with a 10-18-4 record, Craig Dahl's Huskies rallied to make their second appearance in the WCHA Final Five by upsetting the No. 3 ranked Denver Pioneers in the first round of the playoffs. The Huskies won Game One, 3-1, lost the second match 6-4, and then came back behind Brian Leitza's 4-0 shut-out to win the final game. From there, SCSU went on to face Michigan Tech in the WCHA Final Five, ultimately losing to the Huskies, 4-3, in overtime. Sacha Molin opened the scoring for the Huskies at 4:45 of the first, followed by a sweet power-play goal that was set up by two great passes from Mark Parrish and Taj Melson to Matt Cullen with just under four minutes to go in the sec-

Herb Brooks

ond. Geisbauer added the third tally at 7:21 of the third, but it was too little too late as Michigan Tech went on to beat SCSU, 4-3. Freshman sensation Matt Cullen, who would go on to star in the NHL, was named to the WCHA All-Rookie Team.

The 1996-97 season was the best ever for the Huskies, who finished not only with an impressive 23-13-4 overall record, but also an 18-10-4 conference mark as well — good or third place in the WCHA. The team then advanced on to the WCHA Final Five for the second consecutive year, where, on March 14th, they lost to the Gophers, 5-4, in an overtime thriller at the Civic Center in St. Paul. Matt Noga, Sacha Molin, Jason Goulet and Matt Cullen all scored for the Dogs in what was arguably one of the most crushing defeats in school history. Gopher All-American Mike Crowley would notch the game-winner at 9:37 of sudden-death to end the game. After the season, two of Husky hockey's greatest players, Matt Cullen and Mark Parrish, left school early to join the NHL — Cullen for the Anaheim Mighty Ducks and Parrish for the Florida Panthers. Both still star in the league to this day, Cullen with Carolina and Parrish with the Wild.

In 1998 the Huskies posted their second consecutive 20-win season, finishing third in the WCHA with a 22-16-2 record. For their efforts the squad earned a trip to their third straight WCHA Final Five, where they this time decided to make some noise. On March 19th, in Milwaukee, the Dogs played a wild one against UMD. While Jason Goulet opened the scoring for St. Cloud at 12:05 in the first, Duluth would rally back to take a 3-1 lead. Matt Noga and Mark Parrish tied it up at 3-3 in the third, however, and sent the game to overtime. Then, at the 3:40 mark of the extra session, Husky winger Matt Bailey beat Duluth goalie Gino Gasparini to give his team a thrilling 4-3 victory.

Up next for SCSU that next night were the mighty Sioux from North Dakota. After falling behind 3-0 through the second, the Huskies rallied behind goals from George Awada, Jason Stewart and Ryan Frisch, but ultimately came up on the losing end of a 4-3 heart-breaker. The next night the Dogs then got pounded by Colorado College, 6-1, to end their season. For his efforts, SCSU head coach Craig Dahl was named as the WCHA Coach of the Year. Meanwhile, sophomore phenom Josh DeWolf decided to leave school early at the end of the year and signed with the NHL's New Jersey Devils.

In 1999 the Huskies finished the season with a respectable 16-18-5 record. Some of the highlights of the season included series

ST. CLOUD STATE ALL-AMERICANS

Name	Pos.	Year	Hometown
Ronald Gordon	G	1970	Minneapolis
Paul Oberstar	F	1971	Hibbing
John Fitzsimmons	F	1973	Roseville
Pat Sullivan	F	1974, 75	Crookston
Dave Reichel	F	1978, 79	Hopkins
Rory Eidsness	G	1982	Fargo, ND
Dan Pratt	D	1982	Minneapolis
Mike Brodzinski	F	1986, 87	Blaine
Fred Knipscheer*	F	1993	Fort Wayne, IN
Mark Parrish*	F	1997	Bloomington
Mike Pudlick*	D	2000	Blaine
Scott Meyer*	G	2001	White Bear Lake
Mark Hartigan*	F	2002	Fort St. John, BC
Bobby Goepfert*	G	2006	Kings Park, NY

*Division I

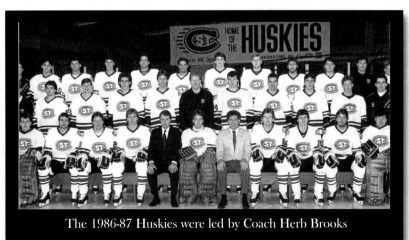

The 1986-87 Huskies were led by Coach Herb Brooks

sweeps of UMD, Mankato, Nebraska-Omaha and Wisconsin. Perhaps the biggest win of the year, however, came on October 24th, when they beat the Gophers, 6-5, in front of a jam-packed "dog pound." The Huskies' Ritchie Larson opened the scoring in that game at 9:24, when he beat Gopher netminder Willie Marvin. Just four minutes later winger Brian Gaffaney made it 2-0, only to see the Gophers tie it up just five minutes after that on goals from Wyatt Smith and Dave Spehar. At 7:21 of the second, Mike Pudlick scored a power-play goal, and then, just five minutes later, Brandon Sampair found the back of the net to give the dogs a two-goal advantage. The Gophers rallied, but Pudlick's second tally of the night made it 5-3. The Gophers continued to press, as both Reggie Berg and Nate Miller beat Husky keeper Dean Weasler to tie it up at five-apiece with only 46 seconds to go. Craig Dahl's boys then came through huge when George Awada and Tyler Arnason set up Jason Goulet with just 16 seconds to go in the game to give the team a thrilling 6-5 victory over their Gopher rivals.

Then, after a pair of huge 5-2 and 3-2 wins over Wisconsin, in Madison on March 13th and 14th, the Dogs found themselves pitted against the Gophers in the WCHA playoffs. There, despite a pair of goals from George Awada and another from Matt Bailey, SCSU wound up on the losing side of a 5-3 game to end their season. Matt Noga led the team with 33 points that year, followed by Tyler Arnason's 31 and George Awada's 30. In addition, senior captain Kyle McLaughlin was named as the 1999 WCHA Student Athlete of the Year, while Tyler Arneson was named to the WCHA's All-Rookie team.

The 1999-2000 Huskies wound up finishing the year with an impressive 16-9-3 overall record, good for a third place finish in the WCHA. The team finished up the season on a high note, sweeping the rival Gophers in a home-and-home series, 5-0 and 4-3, in overtime. From there, the team advanced onto the WCHA playoffs, where they beat UMD in a best of three series. Then, after beating North Dakota, 7-3, the Huskies wound up losing to those same Fighting Sioux in the WCHA Final Five semifinals by the same 7-3 score. Lee Brooks, Joe Motzko and Matt Bailey all tallied for SCSU, but it was not to be that night. They hung tough though and rallied to beat Minnesota in the third place game. The team jumped out to a 3-1 first period lead on goals from Brian Gaffney, Mike Pudlick and Mark Hartigan. Mark Parrish added one of his own in the second, while George Awada and Matt Bailey eached tallied in the third to seal the deal.

With that, the team advanced on to play Boston

ST. CLOUD STATE CAREER POINTS LEADERS

1.	179 - Jeff Saterdalen (78g 101a)	1989-92
2.	172 - Tim Hanus (73g 99a)	1989-92
3.	165 - Mark Hartigan (86g 79a)	2000-02
4.	142 - Joe Motzko (52g 90a)	2000-03
5.	140 - Ryan Malone (56g 84a)	2000-03
6.	136 - Tyler Arnason (61g 75a)	1999-01
	136 - Nate DiCasmirro (51g 85a)	1999-02
8.	129 - Brandon Sampair (49g 80a)	1998-01
9.	124 - Brett Lievers (53g 71a)	1991-92,94-95
	124 - Brian Cook (48g 76a)	1988-91
11.	122 - Dave Paradise (66g 56a)	1994-97
12.	119 - Chris Scheid (73g 46a)	1988-91
13.	113 - Jon Cullen (44g 69a)	2000-03
14.	112 - Matt Hendricks (54g 58a)	2001-04
15.	111 - Fred Knipscheer (58g 53a)	1991-93
	111 - Tony Gruba (40g 71a)	1991-94
17.	107 - Kelly Hultgren (28g 79a)	1992-95
18.	102 - Sacha Molin (47g 55a)	1996-98
	102 - Andrew Gordon (51g 51a)	2005-07
20.	100 - Joe Jensen (45g 55a)	2003-06
21.	93 - Peter Szabo (23g 70a)	2002-05
22.	91 - Bill Lund (27g 64a)	1993-95
23.	90 - Matt Noga (33g 57a)	1997-00
24.	89 - Mike Doyle (40g 49a)	2002-05
25.	88 - Jason Goulet (46g 42a)	1996-99
26.	86 - Matt Cullen (27g 59a)	1996-97
	86 - Eric Johnson (27g 59a)	1992-95
	86 - Justin Fletcher (26g 60a)	2004-07
29.	85 - Vic Brodt (30g 55a)	1988-90
	85 - Taj Melson (26g 59a)	1993-96

The 2001 WCHA Final Five Champs

University in the 2000 NCAA Eastern Regional in Albany, NY. There, BU went up 3-0 in the first period and never looked back. The Huskies got a pair of goals in the second from Mike Pudlick and Ryan Malone, as well as a late third period tally from Lee Brooks, but it was too little too late as BU cruised to a 5-3 victory.

The Huskies came back strong in 2000-01, posting an overall record of 31-9-1. The team played outstanding hockey all season long, posting winning streaks of 10 and nine games between December and February. After sweeping Alaska Anchorage in the opening round of the WCHA play-offs, the Huskies spanked the Gophers, 3-0, in the opening round of the Final Five at the St. Paul Civic Center. The Huskies got goals from Chris Purslow, Nate DiCasmirro and Tyler Arnason, while goalie Scott Meyer turned away all 23 shots he faced in net to earn the coveted shut-out. St. Cloud State then went on to defeat North Dakota in the Finals, 6-5, in overtime. Tyler Arnason scored a hat trick and Derek Eastman added a pair of goals, including the game-winner at the 11:33 mark of the extra session, to give the Huskies their first ever Final Five title. The Sioux tallied four third period goals to send it into overtime in this one, but Meyer hung on down the stretch.

With that, the team headed to Grand Rapids, Mich., where they would face the University of Michigan in the opening round of the NCAA Western Regionals. The Wolverines jumped out to a quick 2-0 lead in this one, only to see Brandon Sampair make it 2-1 midway through the second period. Michigan got it to 3-1, when the Huskies rallied behind a goal from Mark Hartigan to make it 3-2. Michigan scored again in the third to make it 4-2, but SCSU answered at the 14:52 mark on a power-play goal by Keith Anderson from Joe Motzko and Jon Cullen to make it a one goal game with just over five minutes to go. The Huskies pressed, pulling Meyer in the final minute of the game, but couldn't get the equalizer as the Wolverines won the game, 4-3. It was a sad ending to an otherwise fantastic season.

The 2001-02 squad opened the season by winning its first 10 games of the year. They continued to play outstanding hockey throughout the entire season, and ultimately wound up beating UMD in the opening round of the WCHA playoffs, 5-4 (OT) and 6-3. Things went south from there though as the team lost to the Gophers, 4-1, in the WCHA Final Five semifinals. Ryan Malone got the lone Husky goal in the loss. They then lost the third place game the next night to Colorado College, 2-1, despite Colin Peters' early goal that put the team up 1-0 in the first period. Despite the two tough losses, the team still got an invitation to play in the

NCAA tournament. They drew a bad seeding, however, and wound up heading to Ann Arbor, Mich., where they would face the University of Michigan on their home ice at Yost Arena in the opening round of the Western Regionals. The Wolverines went up on the Huskies, 3-1, in the first and then hung on to win the game, 4-2. Jeff Finger scored in the first period and Jon Cullen tallied a power-pay goal in the third, but it wasn't enough as the team ended the season yet again on a sour note.

The Huskies, despite finishing with a modest 17-16-5 record, made it back to the NCAA post-season in 2002-03. Despite losing to UMD in the WCHA playoffs, the team still got an invite to play New Hampshire in the NCAA Northeastern Regionals in Worcester, Mass. There, Ryan Malone got SCSU on the board in the first period on a nice goal from Matt Hendricks and Joe Motzko. New Hampshire played tough though and went up 3-1 in the second period before Jeff Finger made it 3-2 at the 7:08 mark of the second session. New Hampshire added another goal in the third though and that is how the game would end, with the Huskies coming out on the losing end of a 5-2 contest.

The 2003-04 Huskies finished sixth in the WCHA with an 18-16-4 record. The season ended poorly, however, with the team losing its final seven games, four of them coming at the hands of the hated Gophers in the regular season finale and then in the WCHA playoffs. The next season wasn't much better either as the team finished the year with a 14-23-3 record, good for just ninth place in the conference. The club rounded out the year by getting swept by Colorado College in the WCHA playoffs.

With the loss, rumors started to swirl. Sure enough, that off-season, long-time coach Craig Dahl decided to step down. Coach Dahl was ready to try his hand at something else and pased the torch with grace. His replacement would be former Husky Bob Motzko, who played for the Huskies from 1984-86 and later served as an assistant alongside Dahl to Herb Brooks back in 1986-87. It would be a tremendous homecoming of sorts for Motzko, who had been serving as an assistant coach to Don Lucia at the University of Minnesota since 2001.

Motzko would jump right in to his new role behind the Husky bench in 2005-06 and hit the ground running. He would guide his new team to a very respectable 22-16-4 record in his freshman campaign, and then make some noise in the post-season that year as well. After beating nationally ranked Colorado College in a best-of-three series to open the WCHA playoffs, Motzko's Huskies then beat UMD in the Final Five quarterfinals, 5-1, thanks to a pair of goals from Billy Hengen. Nate Dey, Brock Hooton and Andrew Gordon would each tally a goal as well, while goalie Bobby Goepfert stopped 36 of the 37 shots that came his way.

Next up were the Gophers, in what many would consider to be the most exciting Final Five semifinal in WCHA history. The Huskies went back and forth in this one at the Xcel Center in St. Paul and ultimately won it in overtime, 8-7, behind Matt Hartman's thrilling game-winner at the 9:14 mark of the extra session. The Huskies were up 6-5 in the second and then fought off a Minnesota rally in the third. Gopher All-American Ryan Potulny got the equalizer with just 15 seconds to go, but the Huskies hung in there during overtime and came away victorious. SCSU got a pair of goals each from Hartman and Brock Hooton, and then one apiece from

Husky Head Coach Bob Motzko

Justin Fletcher, Andrew Gordon, Casey Borer and T.J. McElroy. The game would go down as one of the all-time classics.

Needing to win the Final Five championship in order to have any hopes of advancing onto the NCAA playoffs, the team hit the ice that next night against North Dakota. Things looked good early on as the Huskies went up 1-0 on Konrad Reeder's power-play goal early in the first period. UND rallied though, and wound up scoring five unanswered goals before Brock Hooten could make it 5-2 late in the second period. Billy Hengen made it 5-3 early in the third, but that was as close as the Huskies could get. The Fighting Sioux, behind goalie Jordan Parise, hung on from there and won the game by the final score of 5-3.

For his efforts, Motzko was named as the WCHA Coach of the Year, marking just the second time ever that a SCSU skipper would win the coveted award. In addition to being named as a finalist for the AHCA's Spencer Penrose Coach of the Year Award, Motzko was also named as Inside College Hockey's top collegiate coach. The Austin native had officially arrived and was determined to get his Huskies over the hump and into some future Frozen Fours.

The 2006-07 Huskies came together under Motzko in his second season in the Granite City, finishing with a 22-11-7 overall record, good for second place in the WCHA standings. The team got on a hot streak from November into February where they lost just two games out of 20, emerging as the hottest team in college hockey.

The team went through a rough patch down the stretch run, but got a big boost in the WCHA playoffs when they beat UMD in a pair of 3-2 overtime thrillers. Nate Dey and Andreas Nodl each got the game-winners, while goalie Bobby Goepfert came up with an amazing 67 saves in Game Two. From there, the team faced off against North Dakota, where, despite a couple of goals from Nodl and Andrew Gordan, the Huskies wound up on the wrong end of a 6-2 hockey game.

Andreas Nodl, Ryan Lasch and John Swanson each scored for SCSU in the consolation game versus Wisconsin, but it wasn't enough as the Badgers edged out the Huskies, 4-3, in overtime. The Huskies were up 3-1 in this one, only to see the Badgers rally to score three unanswered goals late in the game to take it. From there, the team headed to Rochester, NY, to play in the opening round of the NCAA Eastern Regional playoffs against the University of Maine. Justin Fletcher put the Huskies

Matt Cullen & Bret Hedican
with the Stanley Cup in 2006...

up 1-0 at the 3:39 mark of the first period to give the team a 1-0 lead. The two teams battled from there, but Maine proved to be too much down the stretch as they got four unanswered goals past Goepfert to win the game by the final score of 4-1.

The Huskies have consistently been one of the top collegiate hockey programs in the country and seem poised for even much bigger and better things in the future. There are scores of Husky alums playing in the National Hockey Leauge as of late and that speaks volumes about the calibre of the people running the program. One thing is for certain, the fans of St. Cloud definately owe a debt of gratitude to Herb Brooks, who took over the program in 1986 after coaching the New York Rangers. Brooks lobbied the legislature to get the new arena built and was instrumental in elevating the program from Division II status to Division I. He only stayed for a year, but it was arguably the most significant year in the program's rich history.

THE MINNESOTA STATE MAVERICKS

On January 16th, 1970, Maverick winger Jim Lang scored a goal that would signal the beginning of a pilgrimage of sorts. The goal, just one of two in an otherwise meaningless 8-2 drubbing from the hands of St. Cloud State, would prove to be much more significant than just the first ever in MSU men's varsity ice hockey history. It was the first step of a 30-year long journey that eventually led this Division III school into a Division I contender that began the new millennium as members of the prestigious Western Collegiate Hockey Association.

In 1868 the Mankato Normal School first opened its doors in the picturesque river valley town of Mankato, with its primary role being to train teachers for work in rural schools throughout southern Minnesota. In 1921 the school became Mankato State Teachers' College and was authorized by the State to offer a four-year curriculum. With enrollment at the school averaging some 700 students through the 1930s and 40's, a surge in the late 1950s strained the capacity of the tiny campus. So, a new campus on the hilltop overlooking the city was planned, and with it came a growing reputation for academic and athletic excellence.

By 1969 Mankato State's first varsity ice hockey program began playing an independent small college schedule. Leading the program was St. Louis Park native Don Brose, who joined the Mankato State coaching staff in 1965 as a baseball assistant. On January 24th, 1970, Dave Kramer's hat-trick (the first in school history) led the Mavs to their first-ever win, a 5-2 upset over UW-Stout. The Mavs went 5-8-1 during their inaugural season, which also included wins over St. Olaf, St. Cloud State and Rochester Junior College. While freshman winger Bill Techar was named as the team's captain and MVP, defenseman John McNamara would go on to earn small-college All-American honors.

Mankato exploded out of the gates in their second season, winning their first six games en route to an impressive 15-2-1 record. On February 5th, 1971, Greg Jagaros scored the 100th goal in school history at 15:47 of the third period, the final goal in an 8-0 pummeling of Iowa State. The Mavs went on to crush the Cyclones, 13-4, the next night as well.

The Mavs continued to flourish over the next couple of seasons. In 1975 the program got a much needed boost when it gained university status, and with it came an opportunity for the school to compete in post-season play. On March 3, 1975, in their first-ever Western Intercollegiate Hockey Association (WIHA) post-season appearance, the Mavs beat Illinois-Chicago, 7-3, behind two third-period goals by Steve Forliti. They went on to beat Hamline, 5-2, that next year for their second WIHA Championship, and then finished second in 1977 after first losing to St. Cloud State, 5-4, in the finals.

In 1978, after first losing to Lake Forest, 5-2, in the WIHA Finals, MSU went on to earn a third-place finish at the NCAA Division II National Championships. The Mavs lost to Merrimack in the opener, 6-1, but then rallied to beat Elmira (NY), 5-3, in their first-ever NCAA appearance. Maverick goalie Dave Pilot made 33 saves, while Marc Peckham scored an empty-netter

Mike Weinkauf

with only a few seconds to go to secure their third place finish. Mankato went on to earn a second-place finish the following year after first beating Salem State, 5-3, but then fell to Lowell in the finals, 6-4. One of the highlights of that season came on November 16th, when forward John Passolt's five points led MSU to an 8-3 victory over Hamline for the team's 150th win.

The 1979-80 season was filled with highlights for the Mavs. On December 7th, during a 13-2 rout of UW-Eau Claire, Mankato center Paul Mattson scored a school-record six goals, while his linemate, Steve Forliti, set records for assists, with seven, and points, with nine. MSU rolled that season, first over St. Scholastica, 14-6, in the Western Regional finals, and then past Lowell by the finals, 8-1, to reach the NCAA Division II Championship game. There, behind All-American goalie Steve Carroll's 42 saves, the Mavs beat Elmira, 5-2, to win their first national title. It was a spectacular end to a spectacular 30-9-1 season for the team.

That year the team decided to join the newly formed Northern Collegiate Hockey Association (NCHA), which was created by the dissolving of the WIHA. The D-II & D-III conference included Mankato State, Bemidji State, St. Cloud State, UW-Eau Claire, UW River Falls and UW Superior. MSU would gain another third-place finish at the NCAAs the following year by beating Concordia, 9-7, after first falling to Lowell in a heart-breaking 8-7 overtime thriller the night before. They lost to Merrimac in the 1982 NCAA D-II quarterfinals, only to do the same in 1983 against Rochester Institute Tech. After that season, one of the greatest players ever to wear the purple and gold hung em' up. Tom Kern, the 1983 NCHA Player of the Year, graduated as the Maverick's all-time leading scorer with 129 goals and 110 assists for 239 points from 1979-1983.

The NCAA decided to dissolve the Division II post-season tournament following the 1983-84 season, and as a result, MSU decided to switch to Division III competition for the next seven years. And, although they missed the post-season in 1984, the Mavs rebounded in 1985 to win the NCHA title and got back to into the tourney. After beating Gustavus in the Western finals, they lost a tough fought series against Bemidji State in the NCAA quarterfinals.

In 1986 Mankato won their second NCHA title and went on to finish fourth at the 1986 NCAA Division II-III Tournament, after losing a pair of games to Plattsburgh State and Rochester Institute Tech. But, something exciting happened along the way. Thanks to a couple of Dan Horn goals, the Mavs got coach Don Brose his 300th career victory, a 6-5 win over St. Thomas in the first game of their NCAA quarterfinal series.

After a couple of dismal seasons in the late 1980s, the Mavs made a return trip to the NCAA Division III Tournament in 1991. The season kicked off on a mixed note. While Dan Brettschneider scored the 3,500th goal in team history, the Mavs opened their season with a 5-2 loss at Alaska-Anchorage. They went on to post a very modest 23-7-6 record that year though, en route to winning their third NCHA title. MSU

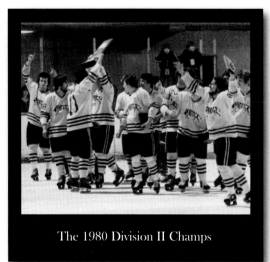
The 1980 Division II Champs

MAVERICKS HEAD COACH DON BROSE

Born and raised in St. Louis Park, Don Brose graduated from Concordia College in Moorhead in 1962, where he earned 12 varsity letters in hockey, baseball and football. Brose then went on to earn his master's degree in physical education from the University of Maryland in 1964, while coaching freshman baseball for the Terps as well. Brose later returned to Minnesota and assumed the football and baseball coaching duties at Heron Lake High School before joining the Minnesota State Mankato coaching staff in 1965. Brose, who was serving at the time as a baseball assistant to Jean McCarthy, was asked to start Mankato's hockey program in 1969. He agreed, and the rest they say, is hockey history.

From 1969-2000 Brose accumulated a 536-335-79 record with the Mavericks and posted winning records in 26 of his 30 years at the helm. In addition, nearly three dozen of his best players went on to earn All-American honors, with countless others going on to play in the professional ranks. Brose's Mavericks made it to the NCAA national tourney on 11 different occasions, with the pinnacle coming in 1980, when they won an NCAA Division II national title. In addition, the 1979 and 1991 squads finished as the national runners up, the 1978 and 1981 teams took third, while the 1986 club placed fourth. For his efforts, Brose was named as the American Hockey Coaches Association Coach of the Year in 1980 and the Northern Collegiate Hockey Association Coach of the Year in 1987.

Brose was also very active in the promotion of hockey. He was a member and chairman of the NCAA Ice Hockey Committee; was selected to the coaching staff of the national Midget Camp (1981, 1982 and 1985) in Colorado Springs; and was a member of the coaching staff of the 1992 US Olympic Trials. Brose was also selected to a four-year term on the Board of Governors of the AHCA and was the AHCA's president from 1992-94. In addition, Brose served as the president of the WIHA and was also the chairman of the NCAA rules committee for seven years. A true student of the game, Brose even spent the 1984 season studying and learning European hockey techniques in Sweden, and also studied in Russia for a short time in 1976 as well.

With a rock-solid work ethic and a firm commitment to his kids, Brose, a tenacious taskmaster, was the driving force behind getting the Mankato program to where it is today. "This is a dream come true," he would say of finally getting his program elevated to Division One status. "The progress has been long, but amazing. It is hard to believe we started as a club team with no indoor or outdoor hockey rink in Mankato. Thanks to the tremendous support of the Mankato community and leadership from several individuals, MSU and Mankato can be very proud of the new heights reached by MSU Hockey."

Minnesota State hockey and Don Brose have become synonymous with one another. Starting from scratch back in the late 1960s, Brose built Mankato hockey from nothing into one of the nation's top small-college programs through a lot of hard work and dedication. Now, they are a force in D-I as well. His teams earned a "lunch bucket" reputation for their spirit and desire, both direct reflections of their tireless leader. WIth 536 career wins, Don Brose is truly a Minnesota hockey institution.

rallied in the post-season to first beat Gustavus in the D-III quarterfinals, 4-4 and 7-2, to then advance on to the NCAA D-III Final Four held in Elmira, NY. There, after beating the hosts from Elmira, 7-2, MSU lost a tough 6-2 contest to UW-Stevens Point, to finish in second place in the nation.

After that season, the school announced its intentions to elevate their program to NCAA Division I status, a move that would prove to be full of conflict and political debate. What started the ball rolling was the fact that in 1992, NCAA legislation deemed that the Mavericks, along with several other of the better, larger, Division II affiliated schools, could not compete at the Division III level. Forced to make an affiliation decision, the Mavs chose to go D-I. They knew though, that in order to play at that level, they would need to get out of Four Seasons Arena and into a new, bigger facility. In October, a $25 million bond referendum was presented to the people of Mankato to build a new arena, complete with an Olympic sized sheet of ice, which was to be called the Mankato Civic Center. Many of the locals opposed the measure because it included the addition of .5 percent sales tax to cover bonding costs. But, thanks to high turn-out in student precincts, the referendum was passed. With the approval by the community of a bond referendum, former MSU president Margaret Preska announced that the program would join the NCAA Division I ranks for the 1992-93 season. That announcement would later be rescinded in the fall, however, when the school's board denied the program's attempt to make the switch. Mired in controversy, the Mavs began playing as a Division II "Independent" squad for the 1992-93 season, while construction began on the new Mankato Civic Center.

Despite losing in the 1993 NCAA Quarterfinals, Dan Brettschneider's two-goal effort in a 4-2 win over UW-Superior enabled Coach Brose to become just the 14th coach in NCAA

history to record 400 career wins. The Mavs finished the '93 season with a 12-17-5 record, followed by a 11-15-1 record in 1994.

On February 3rd, 1995, Chris Hvinden christened the newly completed Mankato Civic Center with a goal at 1:58 of the first period. In addition, forward Ryan Rintoul's goal at 6:55 of the third, which began a late four-goal rally in MSU's 6-3 win over Alabama-Huntsville, was also the 4,000th goal in school history. The 1995-96 year ended with the Mavericks holding an overall record of 16-12-4 in their final season as a NCAA Division II Independent.

In December of that same year, after years of lobbying from the private sector, including a group of business leaders which later formed the team's Blue Line Club, the Board of Minnesota State Colleges and Universities finally approved MSU's bid to become an NCAA Division I member. In January of 1996 the NCAA made if official when they too approved their status as Division I.

"I think it's great," said former 1980 All-American goaltender Steve Carroll. "I feel happy for coach Brose and the program, especially with what they've gone through the past few years. He's really persevered to bring a first class hockey program to MSU."

On October 11th, 1996, the Mavs, now an independent member of NCAA Division I, hit the ice against Ferris State, in Michigan. Despite Todd George's power-play goal at 6:28 of the second for the team's first-ever D-I goal, MSU wound up on the losing end of a tough 4-3 overtime contest. They rallied back that next night though, this time beating the Bulldogs, 5-4, behind Andy Fermoyle's goal just 55 seconds into overtime for their first D-I win. And, thanks to a pair of Aaron Fox goals in front of a packed Civic Center crowd, the Mavs got their first home win on November 2nd in a 5-3 victory, also over Ferris State.

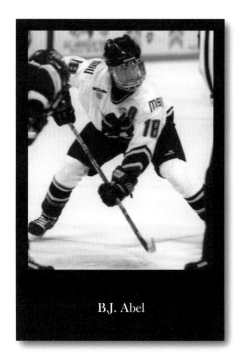

B.J. Abel

David Backes

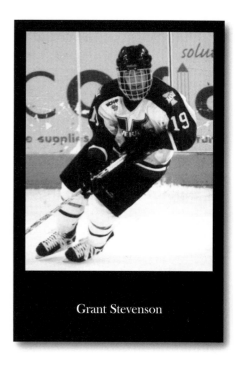

Grant Stevenson

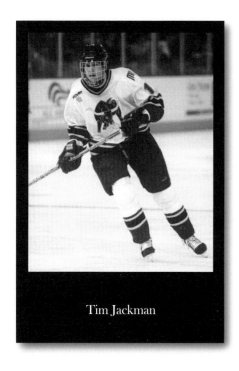

Tim Jackman

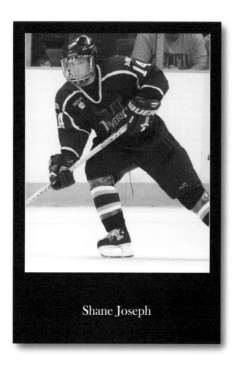

Shane Joseph

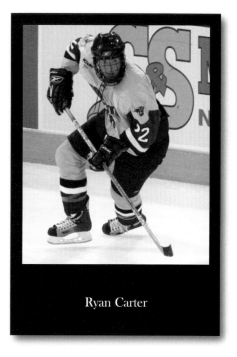

Ryan Carter

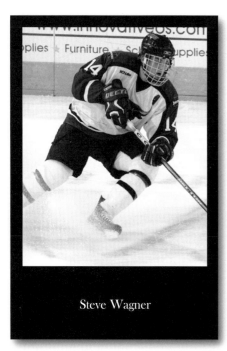

Steve Wagner

Ryan Carter Hoists Stanley

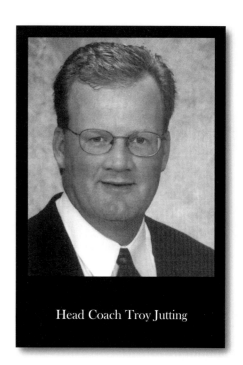

Head Coach Troy Jutting

That was just the beginning, as the Mavericks played against several big-time teams that "transition" year including: Michigan Tech, Notre Dame, Air Force, Ferris State and Army, to finish with an impressive 17-14-3 record. After 27 years of D-II and D-III hockey, the boys from Mankato had officially arrived. But they wanted to get to the next level, and that meant only one thing joining the Western Collegiate Hockey Association. So, that summer the team petitioned the WCHA for admission, and received notice that they would be allowed to participate in the league's 1998 post-season tournament as the 10th ranked team.

"When we were having success in the late 1970's and early 1980's, when we were one of the top Division II-III teams in the country, I felt we could be competitive with the Division I teams," said Coach Brose. "Then when St. Cloud State made the move to Division I and started having success, both in the win column and at the gate, I felt maybe it was something we should be looking at."

With its first completely Division I schedule in place, MSU, behind goalie Des Christopher's 36 saves, opened the 1997-98 season by handing the Bulldogs a 2-1 loss in Duluth. The Mavs went on to record wins that year against Denver, Air Force, Alaska Anchorage, Nebraska-Omaha and Ferris State, as well as ties against St. Cloud, Michigan Tech and Union. In addition, they played the Gophers to a tough 4-3 loss, letting the hockey world take notice that they were indeed for real. On March 14th, 1998, the Mavericks concluded their 15-17-6 season after a heart-breaking 5-4 loss to the top-ranked Fighting Sioux from North Dakota in WCHA first-round playoff action. So impressive was their showing, however, that after that season, Brose was named as one of 10 finalists for the Spencer Penrose Award as the NCAA Division I Coach of the Year.

On May 1st, 1998, MSU's prayers were answered when the WCHA announced that their application for membership had been accepted and that the team would begin playing a full conference schedule in 1999-2000. The event marked the Association's first expansion since the addition of the University of Alaska Anchorage as a league member back in 1993-94.

In issuing a joint statement on behalf of the WCHA, league commissioner Bruce McLeod and chair of the association, Norm Chervany (Faculty Representative from the University of Minnesota) said, "We are delighted to welcome Mankato State University into the Western Collegiate Hockey Association family. Mankato State is a quality academic institution with an outstanding athletic and Division I ice hockey program and an impressive commitment to the student-athlete."

To celebrate the team's accomplishment, University officials decided to give the Mavs a new identity. On September 18th, 1998, Mankato State University officially changed its name to "Minnesota State University." (The last time the program did

Pat Carroll

Darren Blue

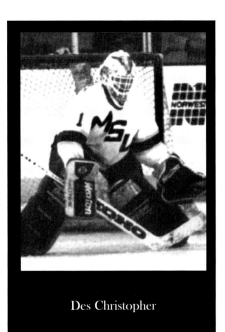

Des Christopher

something drastic was back in 1977, when Mankato State changed its nickname from the "Indians" to the "Mavericks," due to sensitivity issues regarding Native Americans.)

"This is a significant step forward for our University," said MSU president Richard R. Rush. "The new name will help us better accomplish our mission as one of the premier higher education institutions in this state and region. Our goal is to make this University the other great public University in Minnesota. This name change, coupled with our outstanding programs, is the next step toward accomplishing that goal."

The Mavs opened the 1998-99 season by winning their first five games. Ultimately finishing with a tremendous 18-16-5 overall record, the Mavs ended their last ever season as a D-I Independent by knocking off the No. 1 nationally ranked Fighting Sioux in the WCHA playoff series opener, only to lose the three-game series. An overtime goal from junior defenseman Andy Fermoyle led the Mavericks to the historic 3-2 win over UND, while freshman goaltender Eric Pateman stopped 44 of 46 Sioux shots that came his way. Meanwhile, winger Aaron Fox led the Mavs in scoring in 1998 with 22 goals and 25 assists for 47 points. One of the highlights that year happened on October 26th, in an 11-3 victory over Canisius, when head coach Don Brose entered college hockey's pantheon by earning his 500th career win. In so doing, he became only the 13th coach in U.S. college hockey history to reach the coveted 500-win plateau.

The 1999-2000 Mavs finished the season with an improved record of 21-14-4. They would go on to beat Alaska Anchorage in the first round of the WCHA playoffs, only to lose to Minnesota, 6-4, in the Final Five. Among the highlights from that season included a game on January 22, when sophomore goalie Eric Pateman shut-out top-ranked Wisconsin in a big 3-0 victory at home. Another big win came just a week later at Mariucci Arena, when the Mavs beat the Gophers for the first time in program history. Andy Fermoyle got the thrilling overtime game-winner at the 2:01 mark of the extra session as MSU beat Minnesota by the final score of 6-5. Another memorable moment occured on Feb. 26, when a school record and standing-room-only crowd of 5,144 fans packed into the Civic Center to watch the Mavs play No. 2 ranked North Dakota to a tough 1-1 tie.

Following the season, long-time head coach Don Brose decided to step down as the team's bench boss. He was thrilled to get his program to this level and was ready to pass the torch. Brose would finish his illustrious career in Mankato with a 536-327-72 all-time record, good for a then-seventh place ranking on the NCAA's all-time career coaching wins list. He would be replaced by his longtime assistant coach, Troy Jutting, a Richfield native who played for the Mavs from 1982-86. A 10-year assistant with the program, Jutting appointed Eric Means, a former University of Minnesota defenseman, who had also been with the club for several years, to serve as his top assistant. It would mark a new day in Mankato hockey history as Jutting and his staff would take over a program just in its infancy, ready to make its mark on the college hockey scene.

Jutting's Mavs hit the ice in 2000-01 with a pair of tough series sweeps on the road, losing to Colorado College and then Wisconsin. The team rebounded that next week though behind goalie Todd Kelzenberg and got their new coach his first win, a 6-2 thrashing of North Dakota on their home ice at the Midwest Wireless Civic Center. The team got hot at mid-season, winning six straight and then sweeping UMD at home, followed by Denver on the road. They would wind up losing to Colorado College in the WCHA playoffs, however, by the final scores of 3-0 and 7-3, to end the season with a 19-18-1 overall record.

The 2001-02 Mavs would play stretches of solid hockey, mixed in with some rough patches. The team ultimately finished the season with a 16-20-2 record, rounding out the year with a tough 7-3 loss to the Wisconsin Badgers in the first round of the WCHA playoffs. Forward Tim Jackman, the program's first ever player to be drafted, left the program in the Summer of 2002 to sign with the NHL's Columbus Blue Jackets.

Minnesota State turned the corner that next year, finishing with an impressive 20-11-10 record en route to making their first-ever NCAA post-season appearance. The team finished the season strong, with sweeps over Duluth, North Dakota and Colorado College. In fact, in February, the team went on an amazing 17-game unbeaten streak, tops in the nation. From there, they went on to beat Wisconsin in the first round of the WCHA playoffs, 2-1 and 6-5 in double overtime. It was a huge victory for Jutting and his Mavs. The team then lost a tough 3-2 overtime heartbreaker to Minnesota in the WCHA Final Five, and then lost again to UMD, 6-4, in the consolation game. Regardless, the team had earned a ticket to the NCAA playoffs, where they would face Cornell in the Eastern Regionals. There, the Mavs came up short, losing a tough 5-2 contest to end their otherwise outstanding season on a sour note. For his efforts, Coach Jutting was named as the WCHA's Coach of the Year. In addition, forwards Shane Joseph and Grant Stevenson were named as First Team All-WCHA selections and All-Americans — the first ever to do so for the upstart D-I program.

The team struggled big time in 2003-04, finishing with a 10-24-5 overall record, with just six WCHA victories. Among the highlights that year, however, was an 8-7 home win over the eventual National Champs from Denver University. The Mavs, behind Shane Joseph's hat-trick, rallied from a 7-1 deficit to beat the Pioneers in stunning fashion. Another bright spot came in the WCHA playoffs, when the Mavs beat UMD in overtime, 4-3, in the best-of-three series opener. The Bulldogs came back to win the series though and in so doing, put an end to a pretty disappointing season.

The 2004-05 campaign was slightly better as the team finished up with a 13-19-6 overall mark. The team did show signs of life early on, sweeping Bemidji State, Alaska Anchorage,

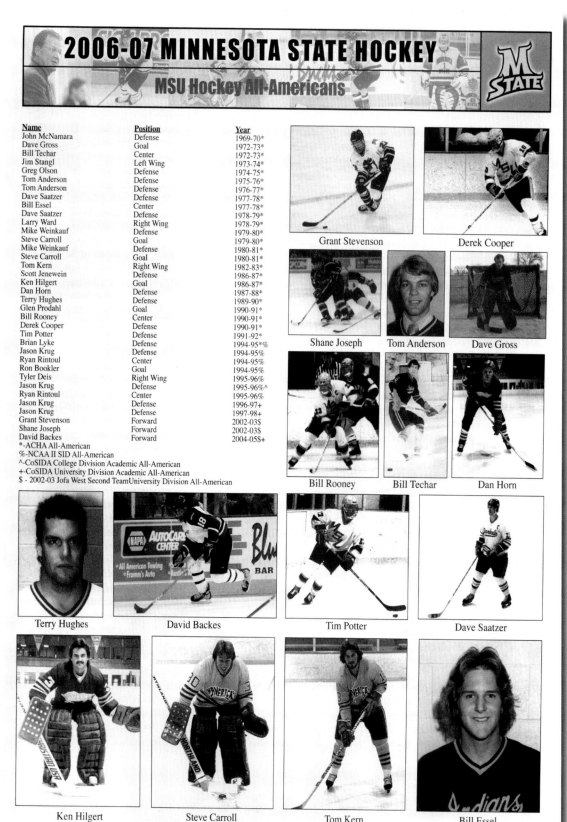

2006-07 MINNESOTA STATE HOCKEY

MSU Hockey All-Americans

Name	Position	Year
John McNamara	Defense	1969-70*
Dave Gross	Goal	1972-73*
Bill Techar	Center	1972-73*
Jim Stangl	Left Wing	1973-74*
Greg Olson	Defense	1974-75*
Tom Anderson	Defense	1975-76*
Tom Anderson	Defense	1976-77*
Dave Saatzer	Defense	1977-78*
Bill Essel	Center	1977-78*
Dave Saatzer	Defense	1978-79*
Larry Ward	Right Wing	1978-79*
Mike Weinkauf	Defense	1979-80*
Steve Carroll	Goal	1979-80*
Mike Weinkauf	Defense	1980-81*
Steve Carroll	Goal	1980-81*
Tom Kern	Right Wing	1982-83*
Scott Jenewein	Defense	1986-87*
Ken Hilgert	Goal	1986-87*
Dan Horn	Defense	1987-88*
Terry Hughes	Defense	1989-90*
Glen Prodahl	Goal	1990-91*
Bill Rooney	Center	1990-91*
Derek Cooper	Defense	1990-91*
Tim Potter	Defense	1991-92*
Brian Lyke	Defense	1994-95*%
Jason Krug	Defense	1994-95%
Ryan Rintoul	Center	1994-95%
Ron Bookler	Goal	1994-95%
Tyler Deis	Right Wing	1995-96%
Jason Krug	Defense	1995-96%^
Ryan Rintoul	Center	1995-96%
Jason Krug	Defense	1996-97+
Jason Krug	Defense	1997-98+
Grant Stevenson	Forward	2002-03$
Shane Joseph	Forward	2002-03$
David Backes	Forward	2004-05$+

*-ACHA All-American
%-NCAA II SID All-American
^-CoSIDA College Division Academic All-American
+-CoSIDA University Division Academic All-American
$ - 2002-03 Jofa West Second TeamUniversity Division All-American

Grant Stevenson   Derek Cooper

Shane Joseph   Tom Anderson   Dave Gross

Bill Rooney   Bill Techar   Dan Horn

Terry Hughes   David Backes   Tim Potter   Dave Saatzer

Ken Hilgert   Steve Carroll   Tom Kern   Bill Essel

and then got a win and a tie over Alabama Huntsville, but they went up and down from there. Mixed in between was a nice 4-3 overtime win over Wisconsin, as well as a 4-3 win over North Dakota up in Grand Forks. The team was then swept by rival Minnesota in the first round of the WCHA playoffs by the scores of 7-2 and 5-3, to end the season.

The Mavs finished the 2005-06 season with an improved 17-18-4 overall mark, including 12 wins in the very tough WCHA. The team got off to an awful start that year, losing its first seven games before beating Alaska Anchorage, 5-1, up north of the border. The team got hot in December though and went on a tear, losing just three games over the next six weeks. After getting swept on the road in North Dakota, the Mavs rallied to sweep Duluth, 5-4 and 7-1, as they headed down the home stretch. Perhaps the highlight of the year came in mid-February, when MSU swept both St. Cloud State and Wisconsin at home. The series with the Huskies was particularly exciting as the team was able to win both games in overtime. From there, the Mavs kept rolling, beating UND, 3-2 in overtime, in Game One of the three game series. The Sioux took over from there though, and came back to win Games Two and Three, 4-1 and 5-3, to end Mankato's season. David Backes would lead the team in scoring for the second straight season, finishing the year with 42 points.

Incidentally, another highlight that season occurred on December 22, 2005, when, for the first time ever, two former Mavs — Grant Stevenson and Tim Jackman, faced off against each other in a National Hockey League game between San Jose and Phoenix. It was yet another indicator as to just how far this program had come in such a short period of time.

The 2006-07 Mavs got off to another slow start, winning just two of their first 10 games. One of the early highlights on the season came on December 1st, when the team rallied from a 5-3 deficit on goals from Jon Kalinski and Joel Hanson, who tallied with under a minute to go in the game to salvage a 5-5 tie with the Gophers at Mariucci Arena. Another big win came on February 3rd, when the Mavs beat Michigan Tech, 2-1 in overtime, on Geoff Irwin's game-winner at the 3:35 mark of the extra session. The team was up and down all year but then finished out the regular season with a sweep over Colorado College. They took Game One, 3-2, behind Mick Berge's third period game-winner, and then won Game Two, 6-4, thanks to goals from Kael Mouillierat, Joel Hanson, James Gaulrapp, Joel Hanson, Travis Morin and Trevor Bruess. Meanwhile, goaltenders Chris Clark and Dan Tormey combined for 22 saves in the win. The team couldn't keep the momentum going though, and wound up losing in the first round of the WCHA playoffs to North Dakota, 5-2 and 2-1, to end the season. Travis Morin and Steve Wagner led the Mavs in scoring that season with 39 and 29 points, respectively.

Following the season, Minnesota State junior forward Jon Kalinski was selected by Philadelphia in the sixth round in the 2007 National Hockey League Entry Draft. Kalinski totaled 17 goals and 10 assists for 27 points in 37 games in 2006-07, to rank fourth on MSU's scoring charts. His 17 goals tied with Travis Morin for the team lead and he tied for second in the nation and led the Mavericks with four short-handed goals as well. The Lacorey, Alta., native had two overtime game-winning goals during the course of the season too: in the 3-2 win over Notre Dame on Oct. 14th, and in the 3-2 victory over Nebraska-Omaha on Jan. 16th. The kid was clutch,

no doubt about it.

As for the future of the Mavs? It looks very bright indeed. Coach Jutting is recognized as one of the top young college coaches in the nation. What he has been able to do with the program in such a short amount of time is simply outstanding. Sure, he has gone through the rebuilding phase that all programs go through, but with several strong recruiting classes in the bank, there is no doubt that Jutting and his staff will be poised for much bigger and better days ahead.

MSU Hockey 1979-80 - NCAA Division II first place

MSU Hockey 1978-79 - NCAA Division II second place

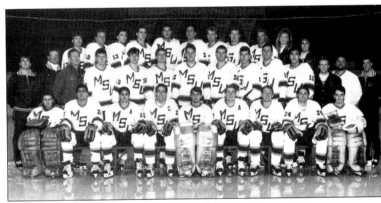
MSU Hockey 1990-91 - NCAA Division III second place

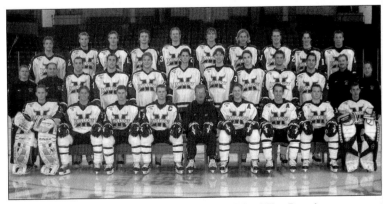
MSU Hockey 2002-03 - NCAA Division I First Round

THE BEMIDJI STATE BEAVERS

Bemidji State began as a Normal School in 1919 and soon became one of the leading teachers' colleges in the region. By the 1930s and '40s the school was bustling with students from across Minnesota, the Dakota's and even Canada.

In 1947 John S. Glas, the school's then vice president of finance, approved a $100 budget to ice the school's first 15-man Beaver hockey squad. The money went for hockey sticks, some old football jerseys and a set of goalie pads. Under coach Jack Aldrich, the team's first "intercollegiate contest" took place on January 26th, 1947, against Itasca Junior College. Official records indicate that Ken Johnson scored the first goal in Bemidji State history, while Ledge Burhans got the first assist. Meanwhile, the first ever game played at the Bemidji Sports Arena was against the Grand Rapids Raiders. There, the senior team squashed the Beavers, 12-1, as goalie Ed Johnson got a rude welcome to the world of college hockey.

Eric Hughes took over as the team's coach in 1948. The Beavers finished with 9-6-0 record in their second season, finally getting their first win on February 1st, 1948, when they beat International Falls, 6-2. John Whiting also recorded the school's first hat-trick in the win. After playing to an 8-7-0 record in 1949, something tragic happened in the Bemidji Sports Arena. The facility, which was not originally intended to house a hockey rink, and was plagued by problems from the beginning — ranging from poor sight lines to poor seating, not to mention its undersized ice surface, collapsed. It happened on January 4th, 1949, at 2:20 PM, during an open skating session, when the roof fell in due to structural failure. Several children, who were skating directly under the caved in section, miraculously escaped the falling beams and timbers. As a result, the team ultimately had to abandon the facility, and for nine years the team's lack of a rink forced the school to cease its hockey program.

Some of the school's opponents during the late 1940s included North Dakota State, UMD, St. Cloud State, Augsburg, Rainy River Legion, Fort Frances Aces, Bemidji Independents, Detroit Lakes Rangers, Grand Forks Legion, Crookston City, Thief River Falls VFW, Itasca JC, Concordia and Ontario.

The team would persevere through the slushy confines of a semi-frozen Lake Bemidji on an informal basis until Dr. Vic Weber could revitalize the Beaver's hockey program in 1959, following the nine-year layoff. That year hockey was reintroduced on campus, first at the 17th Street Rink near the high school for a couple of games, and then at the College Rink located on 19th Street. Some 200 fans came out to celebrate the return of Beaver hockey on February 13th, 1960, as BSU lost to St. Cloud State, 4-2, on their new outdoor rink.

Bemidji State's 13 National Titles:

NAIA	1968, 1969, 1970, 1971, 1973, 1979, 1980
NCAA D-II	1984, 1993, 1994, 1995, 1997
NCAA D-III	1986

Bemidji vs. St. Cloud: Back in the Day...

In 1949 the thin ice got the best of Bemidji's ice-resurfacer...

The program grew and prospered through the early 1960s, as the Beavers finished the 1960-61 season with a 6-4 record. They went on to win eight games in 1962 and 1964, followed by 10 in 1965 and an impressive 12 in 1966. Some of the stars of this era included Ron "Red" Aase, Paul LaFond, Vic Chaput, Jim Thomson, Marv Sanderson, Jerry O'Neil, John Hopkins and Rich Budge. Then, in 1966 the program got great news. Then-University of North Dakota head coach Bob Peters decided to leave the NCAA Division I hockey program he was currently coaching in lieu of a small college program in its early stages of existence, Bemidji State.

"I knew a new arena was going up," said Peters. "All we needed was a foundation to build on. Every time a new arena goes up, there is another hockey base to build on."

While Peters led the Beavers to a 13-5-1 record in his first season, it was his second that helped put Bemidji hockey on the map. After closing out their last game ever at the College Rink on February 4th, 1967, with an 8-1 thrashing of UW-Superior, the Beavers opened the 1967-68 campaign by christening their newly constructed arena, the BSU Fieldhouse — a state-of-the-art facility that rivaled most Division I arenas. The Beavers also joined a new four-team league that year as well, called the International Collegiate Hockey Association (ICHA), that included St. Cloud State, UW-Superior, and Lakehead of Thunder Bay, Ontario.

The first win at the Fieldhouse came on November 28th, when the Beavers beat Fort Frances, 4-3. They kept rolling from there, ultimately going on to post a 16-8-0 record en route to their first ever NAIA national tournament crown (small college hockey's championship), defeating Boston State, 11-0, in the semifinal and Lake Superior State, 5-4 in overtime, in the finals to win the title. Terry Bergstrom got the game-winner at 3:57 of the extra session for the Beavers, while Len Kleisinger came up with 18 saves in goal. Terry Burns and Ric Anderson captained the team while Bryan Grand, the tournament's MVP, along with Burns, Barry Dillon, Jim McElmury and Terry Bergstrom all garnered NAIA All-Tournament honors. For the Beavers, the title was the school's first national championship in any sport.

BSU finished the 1968-69 season with a sensational 23-2-0 record. After beating Lakehead, 8-0, to win the ICHA Championship, the Beavers once again joined three of the other 23 NAIA intercollegiate hockey teams in Sault Ste. Marie, Mich., for the second annual NAIA Championships. In the semifinal games, Bemidji State wiped out Salem State, 14-2, while Lake Superior State moved past Gustavus, 6-2, to set up a rematch between two programs which were slowly emerging as small college hockey powers. There, the Beavers rolled over Lake Superior State, 6-2, to win the title. Blane Comstock, Austin Wallestad, Terry Burns, and NHL draft picks Charlie Brown and Jim McElmury earned All-Tournament honors, while Bryan Grand was named as its MVP.

The good times just kept on rolling for Peters and his boys from Bemidji that next year. After finishing with a 24-3-0 record and their second ICHA Championship, the Beavers went on to skate past Gustavus Adolphus, 5-2, to meet their new rivals from Lake Superior State for the third straight year in the NAIA title game. The Lakers, who crushed Alaska Methodist, 22-3, in their semifinal game, were anxious to exact a little revenge. But, like both times before, the Beavers hung on to win on the Laker's home ice in Sault Ste. Marie, Michigan, 7-4. Blane Comstock earned MVP honors, while Bryan Grand, Jim McElmury, Charlie Brown and Dennis Lemieux were named to the All-Tournament Team.

By 1971, the word dynasty was being associated with Bemidji State. The Northern Minnesota juggernaut made it four in a row in 1970-71, as they once again finished with a 20-7-1 record, and yet another ICHA title. After cruising to a 12-1 semifinal win over Augsburg, the Beavers found themselves pitted against Lakehead University, which had slipped past Gustavus, 6-5, to reach the title game. The finals, which were being held that year at the recently dedicated John S. Glas Fieldhouse in Bemidji, gave the locals a chance to watch small college hockey's best two teams duke it out. The Beavers made quick work of Lakehead though, winning the game easily 6-2 to win their fourth straight NAIA title. Bruce Falk, Dennis Lemieux, Blane Comstock, Charlie Brown and Jim McElmury earned All-Tournament honors for the Beavers.

The 1971-72 season was a reality check for Bemidji State, which finished the season with a very modest 13-12-1 record. After losing the final two games of the year to Lake Superior State, the season was over for the Beavers. But, on the bright side, defensemen Jim McElmury and Charlie Brown both

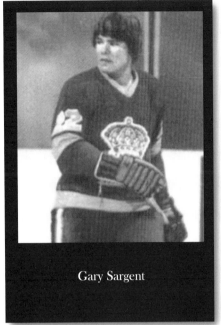

Gary Sargent

went on to play on the 1972 silver medal winning U.S. Olympic hockey team that competed at the Winter Games in Sapporo, Japan.

The Beavers rallied back in 1973 to finish with a 23-6-1 record and another ICHA Championship. Then, in the playoffs, the Beavers upended Boston State, 8-1, and Gustavus, 6-3, to reach the NAIA finals against Lakehead, which had beaten Augsburg and Lake Superior State to get there as well. Playing in Lakehead's backyard, Thunder Bay, Ontario, Bemidji forward Mark Eagles got both the game-tying and game-winning goals in a 3-2 overtime thriller, as BSU took its fifth NAIA national title.

The Beavers won the ICHA title in 1974 with a 20-10-1 record, but wound up finishing as the NAIA runner-up's after being ousted by Lake Superior State in the finals, 4-1. In 1975 the school achieved university status — which was about the only good news for the slumping 13-15-0 Beavers, as they failed to make the playoffs. They came back to win their sixth ICHA Championship in 1976 though. After first beating Stout, the Beavers lost in the playoffs to UW-Superior to wind up in the consolation round. There, BSU got beat, 4-3, by Gustavus to finish fourth in the NAIA national championships. They won their seventh ICHA crown in 1977. After first losing to St. Scholastica, the Beavers rallied to beat Augsburg, 5-2, to finish third in the 1977 NAIA national championships.

In 1978 Bemidji State finished strong with a 25-5-1 record and their unprecedented eighth ICHA title. After pounding St. Francis (Maine), 16-2, and St. Thomas, 7-1, the Beavers lost a 4-3 heart-breaker to Augsburg in the NAIA finals. The 1979 squad was finally able to bring the hardware back to Bemidji, however, in what would prove to be an exciting round of playoff hockey. After pummeling St. Francis, 17-1, and then UW-River Falls, 7-5, the 27-2-0 Beavers went on to capture the school's sixth NAIA crown with a 5-1 victory over Concordia-Moorhead. Rod Heisler was named MVP, while Mike Gibbons, Pat Kinney and John Murphy each earned All-Tournament honors.

BEMIDJI STATE UNIVERSITY
1967 - 1968
NAIA NATIONAL CHAMPIONS

Front row (L to R): Blane Comstock, Richard Anderson, Terry Burns; ass. coach Lorne Humphreys, head coach RH "Bob" Peters, Buzz Oslon, Phil Dupas, Len Kliesinger. 2nd row (L to R): Doug Swenson, Dick Erikson, Austin Wallestad, Laurie Gires, Jim McElmury, George Ganyo, Dennis Schroeier, Terry Bergstrom, George Maniser, Gord Payne. 3rd row (L to R): Bruce Falk, Bryan Guard, Ken Anderson, Barry Dillon, Dennis Sauter, Tim Gerber, Bill Weller, Not Pictured: Jim Aumphtrey.

JOEL OTTO

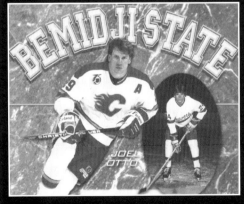

Born on October 29, 1961, in St. Cloud, Joel Otto grew up playing hockey just outside the Twin Cities in Elk River. A 1984 graduate of Bemidji State University, the three-time All-American led the Beavers to their first NCAA D-II National Championship in 1984, en route to becoming only the second team in NCAA history to record a perfect season at 31-0. For his efforts, Otto was awarded college hockey's most prestigious honor, the Hobey Baker Memorial Award (NCAA D-II). Otto would finish his illustrious career at Bemidji State with 204 points.

Drafted by the Calgary Flames in 1984, Otto would go on to play for 14 seasons in the NHL, recording 195 goals and 313 assists for 508 career points. One of the highlights of his career came in 1989, when he got his name engraved on Lord Stanley's Cup as a member of the Calgary Flames. His game-winning goal in Game Seven of the Smythe Division finals that year proved to be a defining moment in his storied career. "You think of all the things that went your way during the season and in the playoffs to win it, and it's really incredible," said Otto. "This is one of the hardest won trophies in sports."

A veteran of several U.S. Olympic and National teams, Otto played for Team USA at the Canada Cup in 1987 and was co-captain of the team that reached the finals of the 1991 event. In addition to serving as captain of the 1996 U.S. team that beat Canada in the World Cup, Otto also played for Team USA at the 1998 Olympics in Nagano, Japan.

Blessed with size and great hands, Otto was one of the best all-around centermen in the game. His tough and physical play-making skills earned him a host of NHL accolades, including nominations for the Bill Masterton Memorial Award, given for dedication and sportsmanship, and the Frank J. Selke Trophy, awarded to the game's best defensive forward.

It was more of the same in 1980 as the Beavers won their seventh and final NAIA national title with a 4-3 victory over the University of Michigan-Dearborn. Brian Carlton got the game-winner at 18:29 for BSU, on assists from Irwin Frizzell and Gary Krawchuck. After finishing with a 24-8-0 record, the Beavers beat St. Olaf, 5-2, and then UW-Superior, 8-3, to reach the title game. Jim Scanlan, Irwin Frizzel, Gary Krawchuck and Dale Baldwin were named to the All-Tournament team.

In the summer of 1980 the NCAA Division II-III Northern Collegiate Hockey Association (NCHA) was created from a combination of college teams belonging to the now-defunct International College Hockey Association and the Western Intercollegiate Hockey Association. It's six charter members would include: Bemidji State, Mankato State, St. Cloud State, UW-Eau Claire, UW-River Falls and UW-Superior.

The Beavers finished third in 1981 when, after losing to UW-Superior, 6-4, they rallied to hammer Michigan-Dearborn, 11-2, in the consolation game. Although the Beavers won back-to-back NCHA titles in 1982 and 1983, they finished as NAIA runner-ups in both years as well. After beating Hamline, 6-2, and

BOB PETERS

Bob Peters is not only the winningest coach in the history of Minnesota college hockey, he is also the second winningest coach in the history of all college hockey. That's right, only one coach, Ron Mason of Michigan State, has won more games than Peters. Synonymous with hockey in Minnesota, Peters, who built a 35-year dynasty at Bemidji State, which remains unparalleled in the world of collegiate athletics, has become a coaching legend in the Land of 10,000 Lakes.

A native of Fort Frances, Ontario, Peters went on to star as a goalie at Fort Frances Collegiate High School. A 1960 graduate of the University of North Dakota, Peters spent his college days playing goaltender for the Fighting Sioux. (His son Steve later followed his old man to play between the pipes at UND as well in the late 1980s.) Upon graduating, Peters coached on the high school level for one season before rejoining the UND staff as an assistant coach. In 1964, Peters was named as UND's head coach and during his initial campaign his team won the WCHA championship and finished third at the NCAA Championships. For his efforts, Peters earned WCHA Coach of the Year honors. Peters would coach for a total of two years in North Dakota, finishing his reign at UND with a 42-20-1 mark.

In 1966 Peters decided to leave the NCAA Division I school in lieu of a small college program in its early stages of existence — Bemidji State University. Within two seasons Peters had led BSU to its first NAIA national championship and set the foundation for what would become one of the most dominant programs in college hockey. In all, there would be 27 post-season playoff appearances, 15 conference championships, and 13 national championships over the next 35 years under his tutelage. By the time he hung it up in 2001, he had amassed 744 victories as a head coach, 702 coming at Bemidji State alone — making him the first coach to win 700 or more games at a single school.

In addition, he still holds national collegiate records for most wins in an unbeaten season (31-0-0 in 1983-84) and the longest unbeaten streak (43 games from Nov. 8, 1983 to Jan. 1, 1985). Peters also owns the distinction of being the only collegiate head coach to have teams reach the final four in each division of national collegiate hockey championships: NCAA-I, NCAA-II, NCAA-III and NAIA. During his tenure, Bemidji State produced more than 80 All-Americans, eight U.S. National Team Players, five Olympians, four NHL players and a host of minor professional players in the U.S. and Europe. Most importantly to Peters, however, is the growing list of Beaver alumni who have gone on to work in the hockey ranks as high school and college coaches, officials and administrators.

Ever the task-master, Peters was a student of the game. His routine behind the bench often included writing notes on his opponents' shooting tendencies, studying the mannerisms of his opposing goalies, and constantly making sure that his boys were skating hard.

"When you play a Bob Peters team, you better be ready to skate," said longtime Augsburg Coach Ed Saugestad. "You won't see many teams that go harder for 60 minutes than the Beavers."

A recipient of more than a dozen Coach of the Year awards, Peters was later honored by having the College Hockey America (CHA) regular-season championship trophy, called the "Peters Cup," named in his honor. Peters also served on championship committees for the NAIA and NCAA for over 20 years, and in 2001 was named as a Hobey Baker Legend of Hockey.

After successfully transitioning his club to the Division One level, Peters finally stepped down as the head coach at BSU in 2001. Although he is now retired from coaching, Peters still remains heavily involved in the sport he so dearly loves. His latest challenge is overseeing the continued growth of the upstart College Hockey America conference, having been named as the league's commissioner in the Spring of 2001. In addition, Peters also continues to volunteer and provide administrative assistance to the BSU athletic department. His longtime Bemidji International Hockey Camp is no more, and he is finally getting to spend more time with his wife, kids and grandkids in Bemidji. Hey, if it weren't for Paul Bunyan, this guy would most definitely be Bemidji's biggest legend!

"I am most proud of the fact that we built a program that provided opportunities for so many, many players," said Peters. "So many kids went on to play professionally and so many others got the opportunity to play here and get an outstanding education in the process. We created a great hockey culture here and that is something I am very proud of. We also really worked hard on producing high school hockey coaches and a lot of great teachers and coaches came out of here as a result. You know, longtime coaches like myself, we laid it on the line and 'done our darndest.' I am proud of that. When your players come back and think that they were lucky to play for you, then that makes it all worth while."

"As for the fans, I am so grateful to them. I am also so grateful to my players and what they did for us — not for me, but for the team and for the university. We didn't have scholarship money in my time, and our boys had to buy their own skates until we turned Division One. I am so appreciative of that. We had such a high caliber of players in our program and the fans really appreciated that too.

"With regards to my legacy, I cared about the game and I cared about people. For me, my players always came first. I am just so grateful that I had the opportunity to have the best job in the world. I am so appreciative of the people who came before me, and the tradition and history that came before me, and I am very proud to be able to give back."

UW-River Falls, 7-0, the Beavers lost to Augsburg, 8-3, in the 1982 finals. Then, after beating Gustavus, 6-3, and then Babson, 3-1, the Beavers once again lost to Augsburg, this time by the final score of 6-3. (Incidentally, coach Peters took a leave for the 1983 season, and was replaced by former player-turned interim coach, Mike Gibbons, who led the team to an impressive 30-6-1 record.)

Coach Peters returned in 1984 to lead his team to its first NCAA Division II national title in style by posting college hockey's first unbeaten record of 31-0. Led by future NHL star Joel Otto, the Beavers defeated Alaska Fairbanks, 9-6 and 4-2, in a two-game total-goal series format, and then went on to defeat Merrimack, 6-3 and 8-1, for the title. That game featured the largest crowd ever to see a game in the Fieldhouse as 2,773 Beaver fanatics jammed in to see the festivities. Joel Otto, Drey Bradley, Eric Gager, Galen Nagle and Dave Jerome would all earn All-Tournament honors. Otto, a three-time All-American, also went on to be named as the 1984 NCAA D-II Hobey Baker winner as the nation's top player.

On January 1st, 1985, the Beavers finally lost to Augsburg, 9-2, bringing an end to an incredible NCAA record unbeaten streak of 43 straight games. After losing to the Rochester Institute of Technology (RIT) in the 1985 finals, 5-1, the Beavers came back in 1985-86 to finish the season with a 25-9-1 record. On February 1st, 1985, something happened at the Fieldhouse that hadn't happened in nearly four seasons. The Beavers finally lost a home game, 5-4, to St. Cloud in overtime. That's right, since December 16th, 1981, BSU had won 55 consecutive games at home. Bemidji State then captured its only NCAA Division III national title with a championship game victory over Plattsburgh State, 8-5, at the John S. Glas Fieldhouse. After beating Elmira in a best-of-three format, 4-2, 3-5 & 3-0, BSU earned a dramatic 5-4 overtime victory in the semifinals over RIT, scoring a last second goal to force the extra session. Mike Alexander, Bucky Lescarbeau, Todd Lescarbeau and Jim Martin each earned All-Tournament honors. (Apple Valley's Mike Alexander, a two-time All-American in 1985 and 1986, remains as Bemidji State's all-time leading scorer with 252 points.)

In 1987, after winning seven straight NCHA titles, the 22-12-1 Beavers wound up finishing fourth in the NAIA finals after losing to St. Cloud, 6-4, in the consolation game. The 1988 squad fared no better, this time losing to UW-River Falls, 6-4 and 5-3, to once again place fourth in the nation. And, believe it or not, the 1989 team did the same thing by finishing fourth after getting stomped by Stevens Point, 11-0 and 6-3. It would be safe to say that New York was not Bemidji's "kind of town," seeing as all three of their disappointing fourth place finishes took place there, in Plattsburgh, Elmira and Rochester, respectively.

The 1990 team finished out of the playoffs altogether, while the 1991 squad rebounded to win the school's eighth NCHA championship with a 21-6-3 record. After a disappointing 1991-92 season, the 1992-93 BSU team looked to be the beginning of the next Beaver hockey dynasty. Finishing with a 24-7-1 record, the Beavers first beat UW-River Falls and then UW-Stevens Point, en route to welcoming the NCAA Division II championship back with a title series victory over Mercyhurst, 10-6 and 5-0, at the Fieldhouse. (The NCAA had discontinued the Division II event from 1985 to 1992.)

In 1994 BSU won its 11th national title after shocking Alabama-Huntsville on its home ice with a comeback victory in the first meeting between the schools. The Chargers, which entered the series ranked No. 1 in the NCAA's poll, took the first game, 5-3, but the Beavers battled back to take Game Two by a 2-1 count, followed by a 3-2 sudden death victory in the mini-game to secure the title. In that exciting overtime match, Bemidji winger Jason Mack took a Kris Bjornson pass at 15:48 and beat Charger goalie Derrek

COACH PETERS' LEGENDARY LIST OF "26 RULES"

1. Never retaliate after receiving a big hit or a cheap shot!
2. Never go off-sides on a 3-on-2 or a 2-on-1.
3. Never carry the puck into your own end except on a power play.
4. Never throw blind passes from behind the opponent's net.
5. Never pass diagonally across the ice in your own zone unless you are 100% certain.
6. Backchecker backchecking between the blue lines on a defensive 3-on-3 should pick up and check the weak side lane unless he has an offensive angle on the puck carrier.
7. Second man go all the way for a rebound.
8. When the defense has the puck at the opponent's blue line, look four places before shooting.
9. Forward in front of opponent's net must face the puck and lean on the stick.
10. Puck carrier skating over center with no one to pass to and no skating room must dump the puck
11. No forward must ever turn his back to the puck at any time.
12. Never check or board an opponent from behind.
13. No player is allowed to position himself more than two zones away from the puck.
14. Never allow our team to be out-numbered in the defensive zone.
15. Delayed penalty on opposition – sixth attacker tactics.
16. Be aware of the clock near the conclusion of a power-play!
17. Backchecking 2-on-2 or 1-on-1, even on a power-play, pick up an open man trailer, or come in behind the defense.
18. Two men in forechecking responsibilities of the third man.
19. Never clear the puck from behind the dots in our zone when you are in a crowd or on your backhand unless 100% sure.
20. Nearest forward to a 1-on-1 boards scrum must support the puck.
21. Don't "dick" with the puck at either blue line... be deliberate!
22. The second forward must always go to the net of offensive attempts and opportunities.
23. Our defensemen must be mobile enough not to get beat 1-on-1, they must have good enough hands to make the quick simple effective break-out pass, and be tough enough to control the corners and the front of the net.
24. Blocking shots: 6 to 8 blocked shots per game will translate into one goal for and one goal against, resulting in two goals.
25. What it takes to be a Beaver hockey player: Hockey is a contact sport, very fast, and very competitive. Games are won with people who have the competitive patience and determination to attack the puck and be there first. People who have these characteristics will play on the winning side 95% of the time, or to put it another way, players who quit or arrive late will play on the winning side 5% of the time. We want players who compete and players who dominate the six pits (the four corners and the fronts of the nets). These are the people who will wear our sweater proudly and will get ice time. These are also the people who will experience success and excel at this level!
26. Here are some other points of emphasis to take note of:
A. Win defensive zone face-offs.
B. Block out on face-offs won, get to coverage if lost, and know where you go on all face-offs.
C. Use wall or glass to bank pucks.
D. Chip pucks two zones ahead if possible.
E. Always try and be on forehand to make a play. You will always be a threat and the opposition will honor your forehand by playing more soft.
F. If you are in a situation where trouble may occur in offensive zone, cycle behind the net or in the corner to get good position.
G. Always finish checks so people are eliminated to get involved in play and to maintain a physical presence.
H. Create a defensive presence so nobody wants to come in front of our net. Make people pay the price!
I. If the puck is at point, go grab a man and get your sticks up. Remember rebound management.
J. Never lose one-on-one battles; be competitive and tenacious.

BEMIDJI STATE ALL-AMERICANS

1968
#4 Terry
Bergstrom

1968
#9 Terry
Burns

1968
#12 Barry
Dillon

1968-69-70
#10 Bryan
Grand

1968-69-70-71
#20 Jim
McElmury

1969
#14 Austin
Wallestad

1970
#16 Glen
Beckett

1970-71
#4 Charlie
Brown

1970-71
#1 Blane
Comstock

1971
#15 Bruce
Falk

1971
#8 Denny
Lemieux

1973
#5 Gary
Sargent

1973-74
#30 Chuck
Scanlon

1973-74-75-76
#17 Mark
Eagles

1977-78
#30 Jack
Korner

1977, 1979
#11 John
Murphy

1978-79
#16 Rod
Heisler

1978-79
#5 Mike
Gibbons

1980
#24 Dale
Baldwin

1981
#5 Tony
Montebello

1981
#18 John
Hansen

1981-82
#1 Jim
Scanlan

1982
#12 Brian
Hartman

1982
#22 Joe
Knudson

1982-83-84
#24 Joel
Otto

1983-84
#21 Drey
Bradley

1983-84-85
#1 Mark
Liska

1984
#27 Scott
Monsrud

1985
#5 Dennis
Gibbons

1985
#19 Eric
Gager

1985-86
#22 Mike
Alexander

1986-87
#11 Greg
Biskup

1987-88
#21 Ian
Resch

1987
#29 Todd
Lescarbeau

1988-89
#1 Steve
O'Shea

1989
#8 Dan
Richards

154

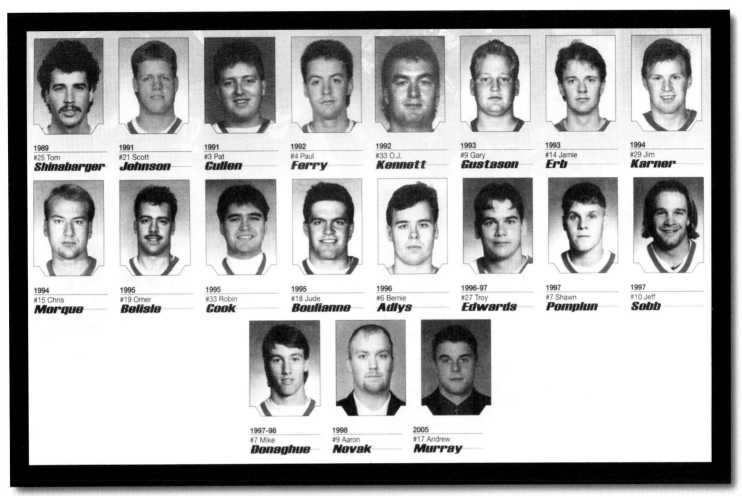

1989 #25 Tom **Shinabarger**	1991 #21 Scott **Johnson**	1991 #3 Pat **Cullen**	1992 #4 Paul **Ferry**	1992 #33 O.J. **Kennett**	1993 #9 Gary **Gustason**	1993 #14 Jamie **Erb**	1994 #29 Jim **Karner**
1994 #15 Chris **Morque**	1995 #19 Omer **Belisle**	1995 #33 Robin **Cook**	1995 #18 Jude **Boulianne**	1996 #6 Bernie **Adlys**	1996-97 #27 Troy **Edwards**	1997 #7 Shawn **Pomplun**	1997 #10 Jeff **Sobb**

1997-98 #7 Mike **Donaghue** — 1998 #9 Aaron **Novak** — 2005 #17 Andrew **Murray**

Puppa on a nice wrister to seal the deal.

The Beavers took to the road for their 12th national championship in 1995, edging Mercyhurst, 5-4, in Game Two of the title series after a 6-2 win the previous night in Erie, Pa. The Lakers entered the championship with a perfect home record of 13-0-0 and a 23-1-2 record overall, but BSU rallied to take the title on the Lakers' home ice. Bemidji center Eric Fulton's hat-trick late in the third period gave the Beavers the dramatic win.

After losing to Alabama-Huntsville to finish second in 1996, the Beavers came back for revenge in 1997 by winning their 13th and final Division II championship over those same Chargers from Alabama. Meeting for the fourth time in the title series, the Beavers edged the rival Chargers, 3-2, in the first game, and then came out to win the second, 4-2, thanks to a pair of goals from winger Josh Klingfus in the second and third periods. The packed Fieldhouse in Bemidji saw some great hockey, as the Beavers went on to win their fourth D-II title of the 1990's.

Bemidji State and Alabama-Huntsville met yet again that next year in the 1998 finals, this time on the Chargers' home ice in Huntsville. The boys from 'Bama got even this time, winning both games, 6-2

Beaver Olympians:

Charlie Brown	1972
Jim McElmury	1972
Blane Comstock	1976
Gary Ross	1976
Joel Otto	1984, 98

and 5-2 to bring the D-II title back down to Dixie. Then, in an effort to get ready for their big jump to Division I hockey, the Beavers played an independent schedule against NCAA I, II and III teams for the 1998-99 season, ultimately finishing with a 17-13-0 record in their 18th and final year in the NCHA.

On May 26th, 1998, Bemidji State University announced, that its men's ice hockey program would be joining the National Collegiate Athletic Association (NCAA) Division I ranks. The decision was made following a 60-day campaign to raise funds needed to support the move.

"This is a landmark day in Bemidji State hockey history," said Bob Peters. "This is a natural evolution for our program. Our tradition has endured and prospered since 1947, and this is the dawn of a new era."

"By recommendation of the Division I Exploratory Committee, we have decided to go forward with our commitment to moving the Bemidji State University men's ice hockey program to Division I," said BSU president Dr. Jim Bensen. "Based on the results of our fundraising efforts and the response from the community and our alumni, we have every confidence that Bemidji State will have the necessary support to fund a quality Division I men's

Rob Sirianni

Matt Climie

TOM SERRATORE

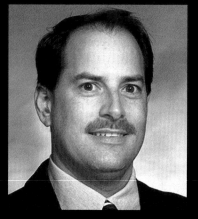

Tom Serratore grew up in Coleraine and went on to play college hockey at Western Michigan University from 1977-79, before earning his degree in physical education from Bemidji State University in 1982. Serratore lettered four years in hockey at the two schools, playing goalie. At BSU, Serratore played in a couple of NCAA D-III national hockey tournaments for the Beavers, including the 1986 squad which won the national championship. Serratore went on to play two years with the St. Paul Vulcans in the USHL before playing professionally with the Nashville South Stars in the CHL in 1982.

Serratore then got into coaching, and went on to coach in the USA Hockey Developmental Program until 1985. From there, Serratore took over as an assistant at the University of North Dakota from 1987-89. After that, Serratore got into junior hockey coaching, and coached both the USHL's Rochester Mustangs, whom he led to a national championship, and later the Austin Mavericks, posting a 247-103-6 record along the way. In addition, Serratore also coached at the high school level, first as an assistant at Brainerd High School and later at Henry Sibley High School, where he served as the head coach in 1991. In 1993, Serratore was named as the associate head coach at St. Cloud State University, where, under coach Craig Dahl, he led recruiting efforts and was instrumental in helping the program reach national prominence.

In 1998 Serratore went back to Bemidji State to serve as an assistant under legendary coach, Bob Peters. There, he would play a big part in the transition to Division I hockey and also was involved in building College Hockey America, the nation's newest Division I hockey conference. Then, in 2000, Serratore got his big break when Peters decided to finally step down after becoming the second winningest college hockey coach in history. In the six seasons years since Serratore has been behind the Beaver bench, he has led his teams to a pair of CHA regular season and tournament titles, as well as a pair of NCAA post-season appearances. In all, he has posted a modest 73-72-22 record with the team.

Incidentally, Tom and his brother Frank, head coach at Air Force, had the distinction of being one of just two sets of family members who coached against each other in the same conference in any sport. (Bobby Bowden, the head football coach at Florida State and his son Tommy, the head coach at Clemson, were the others.)

ice hockey program."

With that, BSU began playing its its first full Division I schedule in the fall of 1999, joining the University of Minnesota, the University of Minnesota-Duluth, St. Cloud State University and Minnesota State University, Mankato, as the fifth Minnesota school with an NCAA Division I ice hockey program. The Beavers would not play in the WCHA with the aforementioned teams however. They instead played in the newly formed College Hockey America Conference, a seven-team Division I league that began play in 1999. The seven founding institutions and charter members include: Bemidji State, Alabama-Huntsville, Air Force, Army, Findlay (Ohio), Niagara (NY) and Wayne State (Mich.).

The 1999-2000 Beavers opened the season with a sweep over Army at home, 5-2 and 3-0. Things got a lot tougher from there though as the team won just one of its next 12 games. They got back on track in mid-December, sweeping Princeton at home, only to lose the next two series' against Minnesota State and UMD. Coach Peters' Beavers got hot in Mid-January, however, sweeping Air Force and Findlay, and then splitting with Alabama-Huntsville before sweeping Wayne State. It was by far the team's best run of the year. From there, they wound up losing a tough series against No. 2 ranked North Dakota up in Grand Forks and then lost to Alabama-Huntsville in the CHA playoffs. They did come back to beat Air Force in the consolation though, 5-4 in overtime, to end the season on a positive note. In all, the team finished with a 8-8-1 conference record, good for third place in the CHA.

The next season was a rough one for Beaver fans as the team struggled right out of the gates, losing its first 10 games. In fact, the

The Beavers celebrate yet another title...

Andrew Murray

team would win just four games all year. One of the biggest highlights, however, came on Feb. 9, 2001, when coach Peters led his Beavers to a 6-2 win over Niagara. In so doing, he surpassed the 700 wins plateau, becoming the first college hockey coach in history to lead one school to 700 victories. It would be the coaches' last hurrah though as he would step down after the season to become the school's athletics director. He would be replaced by Tom Serratore, a former 1987 Beaver team captain from Coleraine, who had been serving as an assistant coach under Coach Peters for the past three seasons. Prior to that, he had served as an assistant at St. Cloud State, where he became known for his recruiting ability. Serratore would waste little time in making a name for himself as the Beaver's new bench boss. He had helped Peters oversee the transition to Division One and had been groomed by one of the game's greatest all-time coaches.

The 2001-02 Beavers were a dramatically improved team, finishing the season with a 12-18-5 overall record, good for second place in the conference. They opened the season with a dramatic 7-6 win over Minnesota State and then cruised from there. From Jan. 26 through Feb. 9, the team tied a school record by putting together a five-game unbeaten streak. The team enjoyed a 21-day run tied atop the CHA standings and wound up earning a first round bye in the conference playoffs. Under Serratore's tutelage, right wing Marty Goulet was named to the All-CHA first team, while center Riley Riddell earned CHA Rookie of the Year honors to boot. Riddell, along with goalie Grady Hunt, earned All-CHA second team honors as well. For his efforts in turning the program around, Serratorre was named as a finalist for the Spencer Penrose Award, given annually to college hockey's top coach.

Serratorre kept the momentum going that next season, guiding his Beavers all the way to the CHA championship game. The team, which rode a seven-game winning streak coming into the title game, lost a tough 3-2 decision to Wayne State to finish in second place. The squad played tough all year though, even setting an NCAA single-season record for playing in 15 overtime contests. In fact, the school set a record by opening the season with five straight overtime games. In all, the team won eight of those matches and tied four, giving them a 14-14-8 overall record on the year. Among the highlights incuded a 3-2 overtime win over UMD in early December, as well as a heart-breaking 4-3 loss to No. 2 ranked UND up in Grand Forks later that month.

In 2003-04 BSU finally turned the corner, winning their first ever CHA crown with an impressive 20-13-3 overall record — fully five points ahead of their closest competitor. The team also captured the R.H. "Bob" Peters Cup, awarded to the CHA regular season champions. In addition, Serratorre was named as the College Hockey America Coach of the Year. The Beavers led the league in scoring and scoring defense and finished with the second best power-play percentage in league history. Despite the team's fantastic season, a 4-3 overtime loss to Niagara in the conference playoff title game ended the team's hopes of advancing on to the NCAA tournament. Junior forward Brendan Cook and senior defenseman Bruce Methven were named to the All-CHA First Team, while junior forward Riley Riddell, senior defenseman Anders Olsson and senior goaltender Grady Hunt were all named to the second team. Further, freshman winger Luke Erickson was named as the CHA Rookie of the Year.

The 2004-05 Beavers finished the season with their best record to date, a 23-13-1 masterpiece, which included the program's first ever trip to the NCAA playoffs. The team then made it back-to-back Peters Cups, winning the conference title for the second straight year. After sweeping Air Force and then beating Alabama-Huntsville to take the conference crown, the team headed east to play in the NCAA's Northeast Regional Semifinals in Amherst, Mass. There, they played tough, taking the No. 1 ranked Denver Pioneers to overtime before finally losing by the final score of 4-3. It was a sad ending to an otherwise fantastic season. Bemidji had certainly made Minnesota proud. For the record, senior captain Andrew Murray was named as both the CHA Player of the Year as well as the CHA Student-Athlete of the Year. Senior defenseman Peter Jonsson joined Murray on the All-CHA First Team, while senior wing Brendan Cook earned second team honors. For his efforts, Serratorre was again named as a finalist for the college hockey coach of the year award.

The 2005-06 season started out fantastic and ended on a downer. The team roared out of the gates to open the season with an 8-2 record, sweeping both UMD and

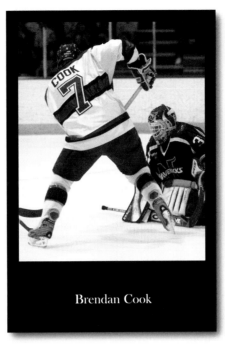

Brendan Cook

Luke Erickson

Marty Goulet

Minnesota State. In the process, the team garnered its first ever national recognition, charging into the top 15 of the USA Today/USA Hockey poll. The team was up and down from there though, ultimately rallying to sweep Alabama-Huntsville at the end of the season to salvage a tie for second in the CHA regular season standings. From there, the Beavers went on to beat Alabama-Huntsville yet again, this time in a 4-3 overtime thriller, in the conference tournament semifinals. Jean-Guy Gervais netted the game-winner in overtime, his second goal of the game. BSU then went on to beat Niagara in the tournament championship game to earn their second straight title as well as the CHA's first ever repeat visitor to the NCAA Tournament. The Beavers had rallied from a three-goal deficit to win behind goals from Luke Erickson, Tyler Scofield and Rob Sirianni.

At the NCAA's Midwest Regional in Green Bay, Wis., things did not go well. There, for the second consecutive season, the Beavers lost in the opening round to the eventual NCAA national champion. Like Denver the year before, this time they lost to the University of Wisconsin, 4-0. The shut-out loss was a bitter pill to swallow for the team as they looked to build on the experience in the future.

Overall though, it was a great season. The team finished with a 20-14-3 overall record, and lost an amazing nine one-goal games along the way. Who knows, a few bounces here or there might have meant a more favorable seeding come tournament time, but that was just the way things went for the Beavers that season. Luke Erickson led the team with 35 points, while Ryan Miller and Rob Sirianni each added 29 as well. Further, Erickson and defenseman Luke Martens were each named to the All-CHA First Team. In addition to that, fully 16 BSU skaters were recognized for their academic achievements. Under Serratorre's watch, no less than 69 student-athletes have been named to the Academic All-CHA team, 14 more than any other program.

The 2006-07 Beavers finished the season with a modest 14-14-5 record, good for second place in the College Hockey America Conference at 9-6-5. The team got hot in December, winning nine of ten, but cooled off down the stretch. One of the highlights during that time was a dramatic overtime win over rival UMD in which the team rallied to win on four unanswered goals. Blaine Jarvis had two of them, including the game-winner at 2:56 of the extra session.

The Beavers rounded out the season with a tough 7-5 loss to Robert Morris in the CHA tournament semifinals, unable to earn yet another NCAA post-season invitation. Luke Erickson and Travis Winter netted a pair of goals each in the loss. In addition, goaltender Matt Climie and forward Travis Winter were named as All-CHA First-Teamers.

Under Serratore, this program is destined for greatness and continues to make Minnesota proud every step of the way.

DIVISION III COLLEGE HOCKEY

THE MINNESOTA INTERCOLLEGIATE ATHLETIC CONFERENCE (MIAC)

In the early 1900's the organization and control of hockey was for the most part student-centered. Issues such as eligibility restrictions, scheduling procedures, awarding championships, and the establishment of consistent rules and regulations were sporadic at best. As a result, conferences and associations began to appear in an attempt to formalize athletic competition.

One such organization was the Tri-State Conference, which was made up of colleges from both Minnesota and the Dakotas. In 1919, after a heated debate between the two factions regarding rule changes and eligibility, the Minnesota contingent broke away and formed their own conference called the Minnesota Intercollegiate Athletic Conference. The MIAC's first charter members included: Carleton College, Gustavus Adolphus College, Hamline University, Macalester College, St. John's University, St. Olaf College and the University of St. Thomas. (Concordia College-Moorhead joined the conference in 1921, Augsburg College in 1924 and St. Mary's University in 1926. Bethel College later joined in 1977.) The University of Minnesota Duluth, which had joined in the 1950s, made the jump to Division I in 1962. In addition, both Macalester and Carleton would both later drop their hockey programs.

Recognized as one of the toughest and most prestigious NCAA Division III intercollegiate athletic conferences in the country, today, the MIAC sponsors championships in 23 sports; 12 for men and 11 for women. And, because its members are all private undergraduate colleges, none of them can offer athletic scholarships to its student athletes. So it really is about the kids, and hockey.

AUGSBURG

Augsburg Auggies

Founded in 1872, Augsburg University is one of Minnesota hockey's pioneer institutions. The program first got going "officially" in the early 1920s, but had "unofficially" been playing for many years prior.

By the late 1920s the school was pounding schools from around the area, and in 1927, the undefeated Auggies won their first MIAC title. The leaders of that team were none other than the "original" Hanson brothers: Oscar, Emil, Julius, Joe and Lewis. That's right, not to be confused with the three Virginia, Minn., Hanson Brothers, from the 1977 hit movie "Slapshot," the Augsburg Hanson's were some of the first hockey superstars Minnesota would know. Other members of the team included Gordon Schaeffer, George "Red" Malsed, Wallace Swanson, Willard Falk and Chuck Warren.

The next year, former Minneapolis Millers star - turned team owner, Nick Kahler, a future hall of famer, was selected to coach the Augsburg College team, which had recently been picked by the Amateur Athletic Union (AAU) Ice Hockey Committee to represent the United States in the 1928 Olympics, in St. Moritz, Switzerland. The fame of that Augsburg team and its five Hanson brothers made them a top candidate for selection by the AAU, which also approached Harvard, University Club of Boston, and Eveleth Junior College regarding participation in the games. (Either due to lack of funds or absence from school for such a long period of time, all of the clubs but Augsburg passed on the chance.) Kahler helped to formulate the necessary plans, and even led a fund-raising effort to help with the team's expenses as they prepared for the big event. But, after much internal wrangling with the United States Olympic Committee, General Douglas MacArthur, who served as the committee's chairman, came out and termed the Auggies "not representative of American hockey," and vetoed them as their choice. As a result, no U.S. team was sent to the Olympics that year and a dark cloud loomed over amateur hockey in America.

For the boys from Augsburg, the news was devastating. They had been deprived of their greatest opportunity for international fame, and the community was very upset as well. Undeterred, the Hansons and the Auggies went on to dominate small-college hockey throughout the late 1920s and early 30's, both in the MIAC as well as against other local senior teams. Upon graduation, Oscar went on to enjoy an amazing professional career with the St. Paul Saints, Minneapolis Millers and Chicago Blackhawks. In addition, Oscar won three AHA scoring titles in the 1930s, highlighted by his 1939 season with the Millers, where he scored 89 points in just 48 games to set a long standing season scoring record for all of professional hockey. Emil, like his brother, would also go on to play for the Millers, Saints and later the Detroit Red Wings.

After a brief lay-off during the War years, the program resumed in the late 1940s. One of the team's stars during the 1950s era was a kid by the name of Ed Saugestad, who also served as a hard-nosed tackle on the Augsburg football team. In 1958 Saugestad was asked to take over as a playing coach. He agreed, and the rest, as they say, is history. Later taking a teaching position as well, Saugestad led the Auggies through some dark years in the MIAC, but slowly but surely got better and better over time. By 1971 the Auggies were one of the strongest small college teams in the country and went on to beat Gustavus, 8-6, to finish third in the NAIA finals (small college's national championship).

In 1973 Augsburg lost to Boston State, 4-3, to finish sixth in the NAIA championships. That next year the program got a huge boost when Augsburg Arena, complete with two rinks, was built on campus. "People get excited about a rink on campus," said Saugestad. "But it can be an educational tool as well. It gave us visibility at the very least. You go to Southdale and find a kid with a hockey jacket and he knows where Augsburg Arena is."

Although they came close on countless occasions (including posting undefeated regular seasons in the MIAC in both 1973 and 1975), the Auggies finally won a MIAC championship in 1977, nearly 20 years after Saugestad first took over behind the bench. "I think we finished in second 10 of 12 years," added Saugestad.

With their new rink, coupled with the addition of a huge new centerman by the name of Stan Blom, the Auggies repeated

The 1928 Augsburg team was led by the five legendary Hanson Brothers: Oscar, Emil, Julius, Joe and Lewis.

as MIAC champs in 1978. But they didn't stop there. After beating Ferris State, 6-4, in the quarters, and UW-River Falls 10-2 in the semis, Augsburg went on to beat Bemidji State, 4-3, to win the NAIA National Championship.

In 1979 Augsburg won its third straight MIAC title, and went on to lose to Concordia, 5-3, in the NAIA championship quarterfinals. The same thing happened in 1980, only this time they lost in the quarters to Michigan-Deerborn, 6-3. The following season, 1981, would prove to be a break-out year for the Auggies.

Led by star winger John Evans, who had spent a season in Austin playing in the USHL, the Auggies, after winning yet another MIAC title, advanced on to the NAIA playoffs. There, after beating UW-River Falls, 9-2, and then Michigan Deerborn, 7-4, in the semifinals, Augsburg beat UW-Superior, 8-3, to win their second NAIA title. Once again the Auggies were the best small college team in the land.

After posting an all-time MIAC best 16-0 record (which included averaging nearly eight goals per game), the Auggies made it six MIAC's in a row in 1982. Then, after beating UW-Eau Claire, 7-6, and Michigan Deerborn, 5-4, in the playoffs, Augsburg found themselves back in the NAIA title game. There,

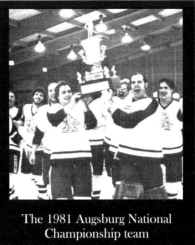

The 1981 Augsburg National Championship team

the Auggies went on to beat Bemidji State, 6-3 to finish as back-to-back national champs. The Augsburg program was now a dynasty, and the pride of Minnesota hockey.

Although the Auggies continued to play well in the conference as well as throughout the ranks of Division III, that would be the last MIAC title for the team through the millennium. Aside from advancing to the NCAA D-III Final Four in 1984, the Auggies had a relatively quiet stretch until the mid-1990s.

But, for coach Saugestad, whose achievements included garnering three national championships, seven MIAC titles and 15 runner-up finishes over his storied career, the best was yet to come. That's because in 1996 he won his 500th career game, joining an elite fraternity of just 12 other college hockey coaches to have done so. After 37 years behind the Augsburg bench, the legendary coach retired from the game after that season with a final record of 503-354-21. The six-time MIAC Coach of the Year was later honored by the league when it named its playoff championship trophy as the Ed Saugestad Cup.

"At Division III, you are always a teacher first and a coach second," said Saugestad. "What I have always tried to do is teach my players that sports, like life, is made of decisions.

ED SAUGESTAD

Ed Saugestad grew up in Minneapolis and graduated from South High School in 1955. From there, Saugestad went on to play hockey at Augsburg, where he also served as a hard-nosed tackle on the Auggie football team. In 1958 Saugestad was asked to take over as a playing coach. After graduating with a double minor in physical education and biology in 1959, Saugestad went to attend graduate school at the University of Minnesota, where he got his master's degree. Saugestad then came back to his alma mater in 1964 to teach biology and coach hockey. He would also serve as an assistant under Edor Nelson on the Auggie football team — a position he would hold for 25 years. (Saugestad would later serve as the school's athletic director from 1981-87 as well.)

Saugestad would lead the hockey Auggies through some dark years in the MIAC, but slowly but surely they got better and better over time. By the early '70s the Auggies were one of the strongest small college teams in the country, and would go on to win six MIAC titles in a row from 1977-82. Mixed in was a third place finish at the 1971 NAIA finals — small college's national championship; as well as NAIA National Championships in 1978, 1981 and 1982. During this stretch, the Auggies were a dynasty in small college hockey. In addition, the team would go on to advance on to the NCAA D-III Final Four in 1984 as well.

"Winning the national championship for the first time back in 1978 over Bemidji, that was very, very special," said Saugestad. "I will never forget when (Gustavus Coach) Don Roberts came over to the bench afterwards and said, 'We did it, the MIAC finally won it!'."

But, for coach Saugestad, whose achievements included garnering three national championships, seven MIAC titles, nine appearances in the NAIA national tournament, one appearance in the NCAA Division III national tournament, and 15 runner-up finishes over his storied career, the best was yet to come. That's because in 1996 Saugestad won his 500th career game, joining an elite fraternity of just 12 other college hockey coaches to have ever done so. After 37 years behind the Augsburg bench, and 24 All-Americans later, the coach retired from the game after that season with a final record of 503-354-21. At the time, his 503 wins ranked him fifth all-time in NCAA Hockey history.

Among Saugestad's many honors and accolades, he earned three NAIA Coach of the Year awards, six MIAC Coach of the Year awards, and the governor of Minnesota even declared an official "Ed Saugestad Day" on February 17, 1996. In 1998, the MIAC even christened the playoff championship traveling trophy as the "Ed Saugestad Trophy" in his honor. Fittingly the first team to win the Saugestad Cup was Augsburg, that same year. Further, in 2002, Saugestad was honored for his contributions to the growth of amateur hockey in the United States with the American Hockey Coaches Association's John MacInnes Award, which recognizes coaches who have achieved exceptional success with athletes on and off the ice. A brilliant tactician and teacher, Ed Saugestad is synonymous with Augsburg hockey and will forever be known as a true Minnesota hockey coaching legend.

"Our fans, they were great," said Saugestad. "They were just absolutely great. A large part of your success is the support you get from around you. Everybody was so enthusiastic at our games and we just appreciated all the support we got from our fans, students, parents and community. When you have great fan support the players feed off of that, and then the fans feed back off of the players reacting to their enthusiasm, and it just snowballs from there."

"I really enjoyed the practices and just being with the guys," he added. "When you retire that is what you miss the most and I bet every coach would say that. That was the fun part of it. I mean how many people get to spend their careers staying in college and never having to go to work? I was lucky. Hockey was all consuming, but I just tried to have fun with it and help as many kids as I could along the way."

Decisions come from reactions. Now my system of playing hockey may not have changed much in thirty-some years, but the options have. That's what you teach a player. Use your options."

Mike Schwartz, a 1983 Augsburg grad, took over as the team's new coach. A former scout with the NHL's San Jose Sharks who also coached in Italy, Schwartz had spent the past four years as a high-school head coach and physical education teacher. Schwartz would have some pretty big shoes to fill, replacing a guy who had just won over 500 career games, but was up for the challenge. In fact, in only his second year behind the Auggie bench, he led the team to a fourth place finish at the NCAA Division III National Championships. For his efforts, he was named as the MIAC Coach of the year.

In addition to claiming their first MIAC regular-season championship since 1982, the Auggies also won their first-ever MIAC playoff title. After sweeping UW-River Falls in the NCAA quarterfinals, 3-2 and 4-3, the Auggies qualified for their second-ever trip to the NCAA Final Four (the last trip came in 1984). There, however, the Auggies lost their national semifinal game, 5-2, to the eventual national champions from Middlebury (VT). They then lost, 9-5, to host Plattsburgh State (NY) in the third-place game. Schwartz would guide Augsburg until 2002, racking up an impressive 82 wins over his six-year tenure with the program.

The Auggies would go through their share of ups and downs over the ensuing years, finishing as high as third in the MIAC in 2000, 2002, 2003 and then again in 2007. There were plenty of highlights along the way, however, including the play of Jaro Cesky, who earned MIAC Player of the Year honors and was named to the AHCA Division III All-American West First Team in the 2002-03 season.

Then, in April of 2006, former Auggie assistant Chris Brown was named as the new head coach of the team. Brown had previously served as the head coach at Marian College (Fond du Lac, Wis.) from 2000-04 and then at Hamline University for the 2004-05 season. Brown played collegiate hockey at the University of Wisconsin-River Falls, where he served as a captain on the Falcons' 1993-94 NCAA Division III National Championship team.

One of the stars of Brown's new team was Aaron Johnson, who played three seasons at Augsburg after transferring from Division I Michigan Tech. Johnson, who earned All-MIAC honors all three seasons he played for the Auggies, was named MIAC Player of the Year in 2006-07, and earned AHCA Division III All-American West First Team honors in both 2005-06 and 2006-07, becoming just the fourth Auggie to earn multiple All-American honors in the program's history. Johnson finished his career with 126 points (38 goals, 88 assists), and was one

Augsburg's Critter Nagurski

Augsburg's Jara Cesky

of only two Division III players to appear in the 2007 NCAA Pontiac Frozen Four Skills Challenge, held at the NCAA Division I men's hockey Frozen Four in St. Louis, Mo.

Another star of late who played for the Auggies was International Falls native Critter Nagurski, the grandson of Gopher and Chicago Bears football legend Bronko Nagurski. Critter earned All-MIAC honors during all four years he played with the Auggies (honorable mention his freshman year, first-team his sophomore, junior and senior years), and finished his career with 60 career goals and 58 assists for 118 points in 98 games.

BETHEL

Bethel College, in Arden Hills, began its four-year Christian liberal arts instruction in 1947, but can trace its roots all the way back to Bethel Seminary, with was founded in 1871.

Bethel's formal program began in 1979-80, when Craig Dahl, who would go on to serve as the head coach at St. Cloud State, took over as the team's first coach. From 1980-85, Dahl led the Royals to a modest 61-75 overall record. The highlight came in 1982, when he guided the Royals to their first MIAC regular season title. The star of that team was NAIA All-American winger Dave Johnson, who led the squad with 48 points.

In 1984 Dahl led Bethel to the NAIA National Tournament consolation title, and was named as the MIAC Coach of the Year in 1985. That same year he left Bethel to take over for the University of Wisconsin-River Falls, before eventually going to St. Cloud State. The stars of that era were Division III All-Americans John Abrahamson and Doug Voss. Abrahamson scored 148 points from 1983-86 to become Bethel's all-time leading scorer, while Voss finished his Royal career with more than 1,017 saves in the nets.

Steve Larson took over for Dahl in 1985-86 and led the team to a second place finish in the MIAC in his first year with an 11-5-0 conference record. Over the next seven years Larson guided the Royals to a 36-80-7 record. Peter Aus took over as the next Royals skipper in 1992-93. Aus, who has dedicated much of his life to traveling throughout the United States and Canada working with Christian Athlete Hockey Camps as a power skating specialist, would lead the team until 2007. Aus, a former Murray High School and then St. Olaf hockey stand-out, has more than three decades of high school coaching experience at both Litchfield and Willmar. (In addition, his brother, Whitey, was the longtime coach at St. Olaf until retiring at the end of the 1997 season.)

In the mid-1990s, Bethel began playing its home games at Mariucci Arena on the U of M campus. In 1996 former Gopher Coach Bill Butters, a former Gopher, North Stars and Fighting Saints star during the 1970s, joined the coaching staff. The school showed immediate improvement under Butters, and in 1997, his son, Ben, earned All-American honors. The Royals skated to a 11-13-1 record in 1998-99, while finishing with a modest 8-7-1 record in the MIAC.

Among the stars of the modern era include Kevin Adam, who played for the Royals from 1996-00 and whose 181 points are tops in school history. In addi-

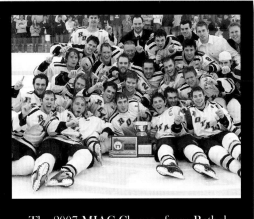
The 2007 MIAC Champs from Bethel

Bethel's Jeff Balvin

Bethel's Neal Carlson

tion, a trio of players who laced em' up from 1998-02, all rank in the top-10 in total scoring. They include: Chad Anderson, who tallied 111 career points; Corey McKinnon, who scored 109 ; and Brenton Balvin who chipped in with 83.

The Royals went through their share of ups and downs over the ensuing years but then got hot in 2005, when they finished with a 17-8-0 record, good for third place in the MIAC. They slipped to fourth in 2006, but then put it all together in 2007 when they posted an 18-10-1 record and won their first ever conference crown. Winger Nick Miller paced the squad with 29 points, while Aaron Damjanovich played solid between the pipes en route to leading the squad to the promised land.

From there, the team went on to beat out a solid River Falls team, 2-1, on Benoit Duhamel's third period game-winner in the first round of the playoffs. The team then wound up losing a tough one to St. Norbert in the NCAA Division III Quarterfinals, 4-1, however, to end their otherwise fantastic season on a sour note. One of the reasons for the team's success that year could be attributed to the fact that their program got a new sheet of ice at the SuperRink in Blaine, right next to the new Herb Brooks training facility. The new digs brought the fans out in droves and the players responded big-time.

Following the season it was announced that after 13 successful seasons as head men's hockey coach, Peter Aus had decided to retire and would be replaced by longtime assistant coach Joel Johnson. During his tenure at Bethel, Aus developed the program into one of the top in the conference, posting the most wins of any hockey coach in team history with a career record of 120-191-13. A two-time MIAC Coach of the Year, he was most recently inducted into the Minnesota Hockey Coaches Association (MHCA) Hall of Fame for 30 years of success in the high school and junior high ranks before coming to Bethel.

Johnson, meanwhile, was a three-sport Bethel captain in soccer, hockey, and baseball, and had previously served as the head assistant coach for the University of Minnesota women's hockey team for six seasons before coming to Bethel. While there, he helped guide the Lady Gophers to numerous National Tournament appearances and to two National Championships in 2003-04 and 2004-05. His experience will certainly pay big dividends for the program down the road.

CONCORDIA

Concordia College was founded in 1891 as a mostly Norwegian Lutheran school. The first hockey team in the history of Concordia College took the ice in 1928 under the direction of player/coach Rene Wambach. The Cobbers' first win came against Moorhead State Teachers' College, by the final of 9-1. The team went on to post two more wins that first year, over North Dakota State, 6-5, and Moorhead High School, 20-5. The team played for several years, until finally quitting the program on a formal basis until 1946. Hockey returned to campus that year under the tutelage of Bob Bain, who led the Cobbers to a 2-3 record.

By the 1950s the Cobbers were playing against both MIAC schools as well as in the Fargo Senior League. In 1974 the Cobbers made it all the way to the NAIA playoffs, ultimately losing to (now D-I power) Lake Superior State by the final of 7-1. Led by NAIA All-American Dan Travica, of Greenway, who set a Cobber single-season record that year for scoring by a defenseman, with 32 points, the Cobbers posted a 16-6-1 record in 1975, and earned another invitation to the NAIA National Tournament.

Defenseman Gary Samson, a Hibbing native, earned his second NAIA All-American nomination in 1977, the same year he received the MIAC award as the league's MVP. Samson led the Cobbers to a 13-10-1 overall record that year, as the Cobbers gave up their bid in the NAIA by losing 8-5 and 5-2 to Gustavus in final season action.

Under the guidance of coach Al Rice and his star wingers, Jeff Frider of Hibbing and John Villalta of International Falls, the Cobbers had an outstanding season in 1979. Concordia made it back to the postseason this time by beating Augsburg, 5-3, in the quarterfinals, followed by St. Scholastica, 6-3, in the semifinals to reach the NAIA championship game. There, they lost to the tough Bemidji State Beavers, 5-1, to finish as the nation's runner-up.

They made it back in 1980, this time losing to UW-River Falls, 5-4, in the quarterfinals in St. Paul. Then, in 1981 the Cobbers skated to their first ever MIAC title. Later that next year Steve Baumgartner, a senior center from Regina, Saskatchewan, became the first Cobber ever to be invited to play in the senior all-star game (for Division I players), which was held at the Met Center in Bloomington. Baumgartner even tallied in the final minute to put the West ahead of the East, 5-4. (In addition, Coach Al Rice was selected by the American Hockey Coaches Association to coach the West all-star team.) Baumgartner would go on to become a four-time All-MIAC performer for the Cobbers from 1978-82, and was named MVP in the MIAC as a senior. Following the 1982 season, he signed as a free agent with the NHL's New York Rangers.

Then, in 1987, Baumgartner took over as the team's new head coach. He would waste little time in making a name for himself, leading his Cobbers to their second ever MIAC championship with 12 wins in 16 conference games. Highlighted by a huge overtime win over rival St. Thomas, the Cobbers went on to challenge longtime foe Bemidji State in the first round of the

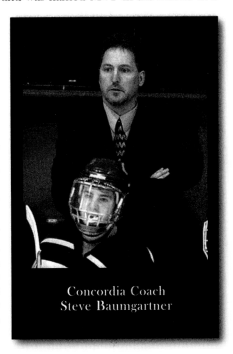

Concordia Coach
Steve Baumgartner

NCAA Division III playoffs, but lost in a two-game sweep. Moorhead's Mark Rice was named to the All-American team while also finishing as the league MVP that year. In addition, Thief River Falls native Brian Johnston earned All-MIAC honors that year as well.

Through the 90's the Cobbers were competitive in the MIAC. In 1994 All-American Marc Terris helped a talented Cobber team finish tied with Augsburg for fourth in the league, and in 1999 the Cobbers finished with a respectable 14-12-3 record, good for third place in the regular season standings. The team's good fortunes continued from there as they finished as the conference runners-up in both 2000 and 2001.

Coach Baumgartner, now in his 22nd year behind the Cobber bench, was named as the MIAC Coach of the Year for the third time in 1999-00 after leading the Cobbers to the NCAA quarterfinals. During his tenure as head coach, Concordia has made the playoffs on seven different occasions. Baumgartner is the second all-time winningest coach in men's hockey history at Concordia, having amassed over 200 career wins. In addition, he currently ranks third in the MIAC in total victories among active coaches.

The 2007 Cobbers struggled, finishing just 3-13 in the conference, but had plenty of reason to be optimistic heading into the future. Senior Mark Buchholz and sophomore Alec Holen earned MIAC post-season honors that year, with Buchholz being named to the MIAC All-Conference Team and Holen receiving honorable mention honors as well.

GUSTAVUS

Founded in 1862 by Swedish immigrants, Gustavus Adolphus College bears the name of the famous 15th century Swedish monarch, Gustav II Adolph, better known as the "Warrior King." Fittingly, today's Gustavus Adolphus College boasts one of the premier Division III hockey program's in the nation.

The Gusties hockey program was originally founded back in 1928 by a group of seven students, including Gustavus Hall of Famer Charles Frawley, who starred as a defenseman. In addition to playing the other MIAC schools, the Gusties took on local senior teams from towns throughout the Minnesota Valley area. Bill Young and John Holcomb, both Hall of Famer's, were members of the first "recognized" team, which played in 1937. Holcomb, already an accomplished goalie from the Shattuck School, had an offer to play for the Gophers but came to St. Peter instead to play both football and hockey for coach George Myrum. In addition to providing all of the protective pads for the team, he is likely to be remembered as the person who first legitimized hockey at Gustavus. While Thief River Falls native Robert Hansen served as captain of the '41 team, the 1949 team, which played indoors on Myrum Memorial Fieldhouse's natural ice surface, was the first Gustavus squad to produce a winning record with six wins and five losses. In addition, Dwight Holcomb, who starred during this era, went on to serve as the team's coach in 1951.

The program got a big boost in 1964, when the school decided to formally recognize the sport on a varsity basis. They needed someone to take over as the team's new coach, and decided to ask former Gustavus football star, Don Roberts. Roberts, despite knowing very little about hockey at the time, jumped in

DON ROBERTS

Don Roberts grew up in Appleton, Minn., and went on to graduate from Appleton High School in 1952, where he starred in football, basketball, track and baseball. From there, Roberts would go on to play football, basketball and baseball at Gustavus, graduating in 1956. Roberts lettered in his first two years in basketball and also won a letter in baseball as a sophomore. It was football that was his forte though. He lettered four years on the gridiron under Coach Hollingsworth, playing on three championship teams and earning all-MIAC honors as a fullback and defensive lineman his senior season.

Then, as a platoon leader in the Marine Corps, Roberts went on to coach baseball and football at Camp Pendleton. Two years later he came back to Gustavus to teach physical education and coach baseball (1960-64), football (1961-65) and even wrestling for a short stint. In 1964 Roberts was asked to take over the hockey program, and by 1966, despite not knowing a thing about hockey, he had produced a conference champion. That, is the sign of a great coach.

Over the next four decades Roberts' hockey teams would go on to win 13 MIAC titles, including eight straight starting in '65, and he only missed post-season play on three occasions. The first coach to ever win 500 games, Roberts also led the Golden Gusties to three national championship finals as well.

Don Roberts took a hockey program in its infancy and turned it into a dynasty. For his efforts he was named conference coach-of-the-year on eight different occasions and was also named as both the NAIA and American Hockey Coaches Association Coach of the Year in 1975. In 1993, he received the AHCA's John MacInnes Award for his lifetime commitment to the sport of hockey. More recently he was honored with the creation of the Don Roberts Trophy, which is now awarded annually to the MIAC Conference Champion. In addition to developing 28 All-Americans and 66 All-Conference players, Roberts led the Gusties to a fifth place ranking on the all-time Division III win list as well.

Because he knew so little about hockey in the beginning, Roberts truly became a student of the game. He read whatever he could and talked to whoever would listen. He even traveled with his teams to Europe every few years to play clubs over there, and to see how they did things across the pond. In all, Roberts would coach the Gusties for a total of 40 years and finished with a career record of 532-278-25. When it was all said and done, he had very quietly become the winningest hockey coach in NCAA Division III hockey history. The ultimate tribute, however, came in 1998 when the school renamed Lund Arena as Don Roberts Arena in his honor.

Don and his wife had four children, including two who followed their old man in playing football for the Gusties. Upon his retirement from the game in 1997, Don reflected:

"The winning and the losing, that's something we all do as coaches," he said. "Starting the youth hockey program in St. Peter and building the indoor rink at Gustavus are among the most rewarding things I've done. I'll always remember the great friendships I've made and all the traveling I've done because of hockey."

MIAC HOCKEY TITLES WON OR SHARED (1922 - 2007)

SCHOOL	NO.	LAST WON	YEARS WON
St. Thomas	27	2006	1923, 1934, 1938, 1940-42, 1947, 1949, 1951-53, 1974, 1983, 1985-86, 1989, 1990-95, 1998-02, 2006
Gustavus Adolphus	13	1993	1966-73, 1975-77, 1984, 1993
Macalester %	12	1963	1923, 1930-33, 1936-37, 1939, 1950-51, 1962-63
UM-Duluth+	9	1961	1953-61
Augsburg	8	1998	1928, 1977-82, 1998
St. John's	7	2005	1935, 1950, 1996-97, 2003-05
St. Mary's	4	1988	1929, 1964-65, 1988
Hamline	3	1948	1923, 1932, 1948
Concordia	2	1987	1981, 1987
St. Olaf	2	1939	1938-39
Bethel	1	2007	2007

+ No longer a member of the MIAC
% No longer offer varsity hockey (play as a club team)

head first and started recruiting. After playing a solid first season, Roberts led the team to its first MIAC title in 1965-66.

One of Roberts' first players, Chuck Linnerooth (who would go on to become the first hockey player inducted into the NAIA Hall of Fame), reminisced about those first few years, "Don didn't know a thing about hockey," joked Linnerooth. "Sometimes, during a game the ref would blow the whistle for icing or off-side and Don would turn to us and ask, 'What was that whistle for?'" Don picked up the game quickly, though, and wound up leading his Gusties to an amazing 10 MIAC championships from 1966 through 1977 (including a record eight straight titles from 1966-73).

In 1971 the team welcomed one of the most intense and aggressive players in Gustavus hockey history, Jim Miller, who brought his massive shot and bone-crushing checking skills to St. Peter from Rainy River Junior College. Miller tallied 39 goals in 39 games in his two-year playing career and ranks third in school history in career points per game at 1.82 (39 goals and 33 assists for 72 points). A two-time all-conference and All-America selection, Miller, who would later turn pro, led the Gusties to two MIAC titles and two NAIA National Tournament appearances, finishing fourth in 1971 and second in 1972.

After losing to (now D-I power) Lake Superior State, 11-3, to finish fourth in the NAIA tournament in 1973, followed by a 6-5 victory of St. Thomas to finish third in 1974, Roberts led his Gusties back to a second place finish at the NAIA National Championships in 1975. In 1976 the Gusties annihilated Portland-Gorham, (Maine) 22-1, in the quarterfinals, only to lose to St. Scholastica, 6-5, in an overtime thriller in 1976. In 1977 the team finished third in the nation after beating Augsburg, 5-2, in the quarterfinals.

In 1982 the Gusties placed third at the NCAA Division III Championships, and went on that next season to make the quarterfinals of the 1983 Division II championships in Lowell, Mass. All in all, the Gusties played in virtually every NAIA tournament from 1968-82, in

addition to several D-II & D-III tourney's throughout the late 1980s. Gustavus regained the MIAC title in 1984, and then again in 1993. Since then the Gusties have been a formidable force in the world of Division III hockey.

In 1997, after 33 years behind the Gustavus bench, Don Roberts retired as the winningest D-III coach in the history of hockey with a record of 532-278-25. In fact, when he retired he was also the third winningest coach all-time, for all divisions of hockey, behind only Bemidji's Bob Peters and Michigan State's Ron Mason. Not bad for a guy who never even played hockey before! In fact, he had to learn the rules from his players and from reading instructional books.

After serving as an assistant coach for 16 years, Larry Moore, who played for Roberts from 1973 through 1976 and earned All-America honors as a goalie in 1976, became the Gusties' new head coach in 1997. The Gusties compiled a mark of 13-12-2 in Moore's first season, while posting a modest 13-11-1 record in 1999.

After finishing in the MIAC cellar in 2001, the Gusties roared back in 2002 to take second place in the conference. Leading the charge were Jerod Klava, Dan Melde and Joe Ulwelling, who each garnered all-conference honors that season. It was a huge boost for the program and the man who deserved much of the credit for the turn-around was new coach Brett Petersen, who was named MIAC Coach of the Year for his efforts. Petersen, a Roseville native who took over the program in 2000, started his coaching career with the St. Paul Vulcans of the United States Hockey League and later served as an assistant coach at St. Cloud State University for six years before taking over at Gustavus.

Under the tutelage of Petersen, the team just kept rolling, finishing in fourth place in 2003 and third in 2004, before falling back to the middle of the pack in 2005. A trio of Gusties earned All-MIAC honors in 2003-04, including Tom Awaijane, Keith Detlefson and Joe Ulwelling, while Jon Keseley and Mike Hosfield took home the hardware in 2004-05. Two other stars

MIAC TITLES WON OR SHARED (1922-2007)

School	No.	Last Title
University of St. Thomas	27	2006
Gustavus Adolphus College	13	1993
*Macalester College	12	1963
+UM-Duluth	9	1961
Augsburg College	8	1998
St. John's University	7	2005
St. Mary's University	4	1988
Hamline University	3	1948
Concordia (Moorhead) College	2	1987
St. Olaf College	2	1939
Bethel	1	2007

+ No longer a member of the MIAC
* No longer a varsity sport (played as a club team)*

from this era who rank among the top scorers in program history include Joe Ulwelling, who tallied 102 points for the Gusties from 2001-05, and Keith Detlefsen, who scored 101 points from 2002-06. The 2006-07 Gusties finished with a 11-13-2 overall record, good for fifth in the MIAC. Leading the way that season were Jon Keseley and Eric Bigham, who each recieved all conference accolades as well.

HAMLINE

In 1854 a pioneering group of Methodists founded Minnesota's first university. The school began playing hockey as a varsity sport in 1920, when the Pipers played several games against both the University of Minnesota and also St. Thomas. In 1922 Hamline split a two game series with the Gophers, winning 2-1 and losing, 3-2.

The Pipers went on to become one of the better teams in the MIAC through the 1920s, 30s' and 40s, as their only three MIAC titles came in 1923, 1932 and 1948. That 1948 title team, which was led by Arnie Bauer and George Karn (now a famous artist and painter), was the last to bring home a conference title.

John Neihart coached the team from the 1950s and into the 1970s, producing many solid players and competitive teams. In 1982 the Pipers had a resurgence, making it all the way to the NAIA national playoffs, which were held in Superior, Wis., that year. And, although they lost to the Bemidji State Beavers in the quarterfinals, 6-2, it was a significant achievement for the program to advance that far into the postseason.

Tim Cornwell was the coach for nearly a decade from the early 1980s into the '90s, and was replaced by Kurt Stahura, who won a National Championship as a member of the Wisconsin Badgers in 1990. Pat Cullen took over late in 1999 and guided the Pipers alongside his top assistant, Gordy Genz, a St. Paul native and 1950s Hamline hockey star. Genz's leadership and coaching experience would prove invaluable for the young Pipers. Genz, who retired from high school coaching and teaching after a 35-year Minnesota head hockey coaching career at both Warroad High School (1959-62) and Roseville's Alexander Ramsey High School and Roseville Area High School (1962-1994), is a member of the Minnesota Hockey Coaches Hall of Fame.

In addition to winning more than 500 high school games, Genz has coached six conference championships and seven Minnesota State Tournament teams. His Alexander Ramsey teams were Region Champions in 1963 and 1965, and the 1973 team was runner-up to Hibbing in the Minnesota State High School Hockey Championship. In 1995, he was the recipient of the Minnesota High School Coaches Association "George Haun Award" for outstanding service and leadership to the game. Furthermore, Genz was selected by USA Hockey and the U.S. Olympic Committee to be an assistant coach to Brad Buetow and the West hockey team at the 1983 National Sports Festival. The West team won the gold medal and many of its members were selected to the 1984 Olympic team, including Roseville's Steve Griffith.

"It's always nice to come back to your alma mater," said Genz. "Hamline has always had such a long tradition of hockey excellence, and I am just proud to be a small part of it."

The team went through its share of ups and downs over the ensuing years, unable to crack the MIAC's top five in the final rankings. Chris Brown took over as the head coach in 2004 but only stayed for one season before moving on to lead Augsburg. His replacement was Scott Bell, a former two-time captain with the Golden Gophers back in the late '80s. Bell was determined to turn the program around and set the bar much higher for his Pipers.

"Our minimum goal for the season is to make the MIAC playoffs and give ourselves a chance to compete for a championship," Bell said. "I don't know if it's possible or not, but you should set your goals high. Anybody with any kind of competitive spirit always goes into a game thinking they're going to win."

Bell, who had served for two seasons (2001-03) as general manager and head coach of the Rockford Ice Hogs in the United Hockey League, was the youngest head coach in all of professional hockey at just 30. Since taking over, he has instilled a new winning attitude into the Piper hockey program and is determined to get the team back on top of the MIAC. The Pipers made a three-game improvement in the win column from 2005-06 to 2006-07, and finished that season with a record of 7-18, and 3-13 in the MIAC. The team is young and Bell is optimistic about the future.

Sophomores Dustin Fulton and Joe Long each were named All-MIAC first team, while freshman Cory Krogen earned MIAC All-Rookie honors as well. Fulton, a two-time first-teamer, led the Pipers with 34 points on 13 goals and 21 assists in '07. Long, meanwhile, ranked third in overall team scoring with 23 points on 13 goals and 10 assists.

Hamline's Joe Long

MACALESTER

Founded in 1874, Macalester College has long been one of Minnesota's premier higher learning institutions. The school began its hockey program during the early 1920s, when it was formally recognized on an official basis. The Scots proved to be one of the best teams through the 1930s, winning outright MIAC titles in 1930, '31, '33, '36 and '37, and then shared the honors in 1932 with Hamline, and again in 1939 with St. Olaf.

Macalester continued to field several outstanding teams throughout the early 1950s and early 60s as well, winning additional MIAC crowns in 1950, 1951, 1962 and 1963. Then, in 1973, after finishing in the MIAC cellar with a 1-13-0 record, Macalester decided to end its hockey program due to lack of interest and suitable facilities.

ST. JOHN'S

Founded in 1857, St. John's University has a long tradition of hockey success. Hockey at the school first began informally on Lake Sagatagan around 1910. Then, in 1925, Friar Damian Baker organized the school's first

Hamline's Dustin Fulton

intramural program. In preparation of the new game, the administration had the carpentry shop construct some ice scrapers, to clear away the snow, and also some ankle high goals were built out of two-by-fours as well.

In 1929 one of the better intramural squads began playing regularly against the St. Cloud Lions, a senior team. Then, in 1932, Simon Ryan, a football player who had played on the Minneapolis West High School hockey team, proposed that St. John's should sponsor a hockey team. Friar Damian agreed to be the team's new coach, and soon the Johnnies were playing against several of the MIAC schools. Led by future Minnesota Senator Eugene McCarthy, St. John's beat St. Cloud Normal School, 4-1, in their first official game.

After going 0-6 in 1933, the school rebounded behind the Maus brothers from St. Cloud, Eddie and Dick. Eddie went on to become one of the most prolific scorers in St. John's history. By 1935 the school had won its first MIAC hockey championship. Led by Maus, McCarthy and goalie Bill Dreher (who allowed only three goals that entire season against conference teams), the Jays went 4-0 in conference play that year. In addition, the roster included five natives from St. Cloud: Leonard Werner, Willard Nierengarten, Robert Kyle and the Maus brothers.

In 1942, because coach Vernon McGee had enlisted in the Army, Eugene McCarthy, now a teacher at the college,

ST. JOHN'S ALL-AMERICANS

1977-78 - Bob Hanson - G (NAIA)
1978-79 - Bob Hanson - G (NAIA)
         Dick Gunderson - D (AHCA)
1981-82 - Pat Conlin - F (NAIA)
1986-87 - Andy Clark - D (AHCA second team)
1997-98 - Tryg Sarsland - D (AHCA first team)
         Matt Erredge - F (AHCA second team)
1998-99 - Matt Erredge - F (AHCA second team)
2001-02 - Mike Possin - F (AHCA first team)
2002-03 - Rick Gregory - G (AHCA second team)
         Ryan Langenbrunner - F (AHCA second team)
2003-04 - Scott Bjorklund - F (AHCA first team)
         Darryl Smoleroff - D (AHCA first team)
         Adam Hanna - G (AHCA second team)
         Adam Holmgren - D (AHCA second team)
         Kevin Willey - F (AHCA second team)
2004-05 - Adam Hanna - G (AHCA first team)
         Darryl Smoleroff - D (AHCA first team)
         Scott Bjorklund - F (AHCA second team)
2005-06 - Adam Hanna - G (AHCA first team)
         Scott Bjorklund - F (AHCA second team)
         Darryl Smoleroff - D (AHCA second team)

became the team's new coach. He lasted just a season though, as all intercollegiate competition was suspended in the MIAC during the war years of 1943-46. The 1947 team put together a seven-game winning streak, then won the St. Paul Winter Carnival championship by defeating Eveleth and St. Cloud. Later, the team defeated a couple of local semi-pro outfits out of the States Dominian League from Crookston and Grand Forks.

The 1950 Johnnies finished their best season in years with an 8-2-1 record to win their second MIAC title. In addition, the team won its second St. Paul Winter Carnival title in four years. A few of the leaders of that team included goalie Ted Joyce, Lou Cotroneo, Fred Schultz and Frank Macioch. In 1952 Bob Boeser took over as the team's new coach. A graduate of De La Salle High School in Minneapolis, Boeser was selected by the Olympic Committee to represent the U.S. as a member of the 1948 Olympic team. After the Games, he traveled with amateur teams in England, France and Eastern European countries before settling down at the University of Minnesota, from which he transferred to St. John's in 1951.

In 1955 legendary football coach John Gagliardi was appointed as the new coach of the hockey team. By his own admission "Gags" was clearly underqualified for the post. When asked why he had been selected as the new skipper, he replied, "I had an uncle in Chicago who once went to a Blackhawks game!"

JOHN HARRINGTON

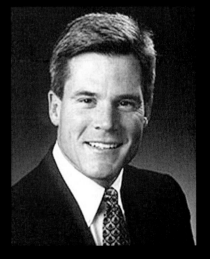

John Harrington grew up on the Iron Range and played high school hockey at Virginia under longtime Coach Dave Hendrickson. From there, Harrington went on to star for the University of Minnesota-Duluth Bulldogs from 1975-79. That next year Harrington gained fame as a member of the fabled 1980 U.S. Olympic hockey team which captured the gold medal at the Winter Games in Lake Placid, NY. Harrington played hockey in Lugano, Switzerland for one season in 1981, before returning home as a member of the U.S. National Hockey Team in the 1981, 1982 and 1983 World Hockey Championships. He then completed his international playing career as a member of the 1984 U.S. Olympic Hockey team, which competed in Sarajevo, Yugoslavia.

From there, Harrington came home to serve as an assistant coach at Apple Valley High School from 1981-84. His big coaching break came that next year when he became an assistant coach at the University of Denver, where he would serve from 1984-90. In 1990 he came home to serve as an assistant at St. Cloud State University under Coach Craig Dahl. Then, in 1993, Harrington became the head hockey coach and assistant soccer coach at St. John's University, where he has been ever since. In 1996, Harrington guided SJU to its first MIAC regular season title since 1950, its second trip to the MIAC playoff finals and its first-ever bid to the NCAA Division III tournament. In 1997 the Johnnies repeated as MIAC regular season and playoff champions and proceeded to advance to the NCAA Division III hockey Final Four, bringing home the third-place trophy to boot.

Harrington ended his 14th season as head coach at Saint John's University in 2006-07. In all, Harrington has guided the Johnnies to a 228-130-29 (.627) record during his tenure with the program. The winningest hockey coach in school history, Harrington has led the Johnnies to five MIAC regular season titles, the MIAC playoffs 12 times and the NCAA tournament five times, including 2003 and 2005. Harrington's 14 years at SJU is the longest tenure of any hockey coach in school history.

Among Harrington's many coaching accolades, he is a four-time MIAC Coach-of-the-Year. In addition, he is a member of the U.S. Hockey Hall of Fame, and also received the Lester Patrick Award in 1980 for outstanding service to hockey in the U.S. He is also a charter member of the U.S. Olympic Hall of Fame, a 1990 inductee into the Minnesota Olympic Hall of Fame and a 2001 inductee into the Minnesota-Duluth Athletic Hall of Fame. Harrington also served as the president of the American College Hockey Coaches Association during the 1999-2000 season.

John and his wife Mary presently reside in St. Cloud and have three children. Incidentally, his son Chris played for the Golden Gopher hockey team from 2002-06 and currently plays professionally in the AHL with the Toronto Marlies.

Gagliardi led St. John's to a fourth place conference finish that year, highlighted by a 5-4 victory over the powerful Duluth Bulldogs. Gagliardi (who would go on to become the all-time winningest coach in the history of all divisions of college football), led the hockey Johnnies until 1960, finishing with a modest 69-46-1 record.

In 1966, led by all-conference winger Jim Trachsel and Wally Blaylock, the Johnnies stunned the University of Wisconsin Badgers, whose coach had scheduled St. John's to pad his schedule in anticipation of an easy win. That next year the Johnnies, who were now playing indoors at the new St. Cloud Municipal Ice Arena, finished 12-5-1, good for second in the conference. A highlight of the season came in the first Minnesota Small College Hockey Tournament, when St. John's got by Gustavus and St. Mary's, only to lose to a Canadian-loaded Bemidji team in the finals.

In 1976, Stacy Christensen, a product of Minneapolis West High, finished as the school's (then) all-time scoring leader with 66 goals and 76 assists for 142 points, thereby supplanting Mike Musty's 111 points registered in 1968. For his efforts, he was awarded All-American honors. Two years later, SJU goalie Bob Hanson was awarded back-to-back NAIA All-American honors as well. The Johnnies featured two more All-Americans a few years later: Dick Gunderson, who finished with 102 career points from 1976-79, and Pat Conlin, who tallied 112 points from 1979-82. In addition, centerman Rick Larson scored 113 points of his own during this same era.

Finally getting a facility worthy of its program, the Johnnies began playing in the newly constructed state-of-the-art National Hockey Center in nearby St. Cloud in 1989. The team went through its share of ups and downs through the 1980s under coaches Jerry Haugen, Denny Hartman and Todd Delveaux, who led the team until 1993. Among the highlights of this era was the play of Craig Herr and Steve Persian. Herr scored 80 goals and 77 assists for 157 career points from 1988-92, the most in school history, while Persian tallied 65 goals and 79 assists for 144 career points from 1984-88, the second most in school history.

In 1993 the Johnnie hockey program caught a huge break when former Olympic star John Harrington agreed to take over as the team's new head coach. Harrington, a former prep star at Virginia High School, went on to star for the UM-Duluth Bulldogs from 1975-1979 before gaining fame as a member of the fabled 1980 gold medal winning U.S. Olympic hockey team.

Harrington came out of the gates and won a pair of MIAC Coach-of-the-Year awards in

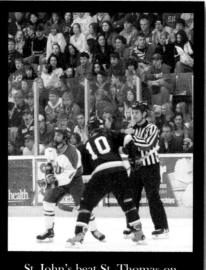
The Johnnies MIAC Three-Peat (2003-05)

St. John's beat St. Thomas on Feb. 12, 2005, in front of a record crowd in Collegeville.

both 1993-94 and 1995-96, by posting 14 and 17-win seasons respectively. In 1995-96, Harrington directed St. John's to its first MIAC regular season title since 1950, its second trip to the MIAC playoff finals and its first-ever bid to the NCAA Division III tournament. In 1996-97, the Johnnies repeated as MIAC regular season and playoff champions and entered the NCAA D-III tournament as the No. 1 seed in the West Region. From there, the Johnnies proceeded to advance to the NCAA D-III hockey Final Four, where they lost in the semifinals but rallied to win the consolation game and were able to bring home the third-place trophy. At the time it was the highest finish ever for a MIAC hockey team in the NCAA tournament.

The Johnnies posted a modest 13-12-2 record in 1998-99, good for second in the conference. Then, after finishing in third place in both 1999-00 and 2000-01, followed by a fourth place finish in 2001-02, the team won the MIAC title in 2002-03 with an impressive 20-7-1 overall record.

That was just the beginning of the Johnnie dynasty run, however, as the team went on to win the next two championships as well, in 2003-04 and 2004-05, to make it a hat-trick. (The highlight of the 2003 finale came in the MIAC title game against rival St. Thomas, when Brady Lundblad tallied the game-winner at the 5:00 mark of overtime to give the Johnnies a thrilling 4-3 victory.) They came close in 2005-06, coming in just behind St. Thomas, and then fell back to the middle of the pack in 2006-07 as the team started to rebuild.

Among the All-MIAC selections of the new millennium include: Steve Aldrich and Chad Helmer (1999-00); Chad Helmer and John Konrad (2000-01); Mike Possin, Chad Schmidt and Rick Talbot (2001-02); Scott Bjorklund, Rick Gregory, Adam Holmgren, Ryan Langenbrunner and Darryl Smoleroff (2002-03); Scott Bjorklund, Adam Hanna, Adam Holmgren, Ryan Langenbrunner, Chad Schmidt, Darryl Smoleroff and Kevin Willey (2003-04); Scott Bjorklund, Aaron Getchell, Adam Hanna, Adam Holmgren, Ryan Langenbrunner, and Darryl Smoleroff (2004-05); Scott Bjorklund, Adam Hanna, Darryl Smoleroff and Blake Williams (2005-06); & Justin Wild (2006-07).

Harrington is a proven winner and fits perfectly into the unbelievable winning tradition that St. John's has carved out for itself over the past century. It is just a matter of time before he brings home a national championship to the fans of St. John's, the same way coach Gagliardi has done time and again for the Johnnie fans on the Collegeville gridiron.

The Johnnies' Adam Hanna

Legendary football coach John Gagliardi also coached the St. John's hockey team for a while...

ST. MARY'S

Founded in 1912, St. Mary's College of Winona has had a glorious hockey history. Then known as the Redmen (now nicknamed the Cardinals), St. Mary's hit the ice "officially" in 1928. Led by several natives of Eveleth, including goalie Oscar Almquist, (who would go on to become a legend as the coach of Roseau high school), Tony, Ed and Louis Prelesnik, and Matt Lahti, as well as Chick and Chester Eldridge of St. Paul, the Redmen won their first MIAC title in 1929. Almquist, Prelesnik and Lahti would all go on to earn All-American honors that year as well.

Quickly becoming a force to be reckoned with in college hockey, the team competed against a broad array of local and national schools, including St. Thomas, Macalester, Eveleth Junior College, Fort Snelling, Michigan Tech, North Dakota and Waterloo (Iowa). In addition, the Redmen traveled throughout the Midwest and to the East Coast on several occasions to play teams such as Harvard, Yale, Princeton, Providence Athletic Club, Crescent Athletic Club of New York City and Chicago. (They even beat Crescent AC in Madison Square Garden back in 1932, 3-2, on Tony Prelesnik's game-winning goal.) Big Ten schools such as Minnesota, Michigan and Wisconsin would not play St. Mary's though, because the school allowed freshmen to play — something that was frowned upon by most institutions, which red-shirted their frosh. On Sundays, many of the St. Mary's players would suit up with the local senior team — the Winona Owls, to battle other teams from neighboring Faribault, Owatonna, Rochester, North Mankato and even South St. Paul, to name a few.

Because of the fact that the team didn't have indoor facilities, and that they were always facing the disadvantages of playing on outdoor ice in southern Minnesota, in 1933 St. Mary's decided to drop the sport, after just five seasons. (During mild winters, they sometimes had a 4-6 weeks less ice-time than did the kids of northern Minnesota.)

Hockey was eventually revived on the St. Mary's campus during the late 1950s though. The conditions were suspect to say the least, as the kids played on an old outdoor rink called affectionately the "Rink on the Hill." One time the snow knocked out the power transformers and the players had to finish their game by having both team buses shine their lights on the ice from both ends of the rink. There wasn't even a warming house to get dressed in, just an outdoor barracks of sorts that was near the rink. The team struggled through a few sub-par seasons, until the

early 1960s, when something happened that turned the program around for good. That's when a big, strong barrel-chested forward defenseman from Shawinigan, Quebec, by the name of Andre Beaulieu came to town.

Beaulieu was a legend back in Quebec. At just 15, he won the scoring title in the Quebec Junior A League, and just a few years later he was already playing for Muskegon of the International Hockey League. He didn't want to play pro hockey though (Montreal had his draft rights), but instead wanted to pursue a life as a teacher and coach. So, Beaulieu worked with his high school counselor to find a college in the States that would be a good fit for him. One of those schools was St. Mary's.

"I was looking for a place to go to college," said Beaulieu. "I wanted to learn English badly. I knew I didn't want to end up working in a foundry in my hometown the rest of my life."

Because he had played in the IHL, he was ineligible to play NCAA D-I hockey. But, St. Mary's, a member of the NAIA at the time, had no such restrictions. Head coach Max Molock worked out the details and got Andre a student work-study job, appropriately enough, building a new rink on campus. Starting from scratch, Beaulieu and his buddies took that summer and built St. Mary's their new outdoor rink — goals and all.

St. Mary's hit the ice in their new rink in 1961 with Beaulieu leading the way. As both player and assistant coach, he scored an amazing 41 points in just 16 games that season. That next season Bob Paradise, a star defenseman from Cretin High School who would later star in the NHL, joined the team. This combo proved to be lethal for St. Mary's, which went on to win back-to-back MIAC title in 1964 and 1965. (In those days, with Duluth out of the league to play D-I, Macalester and St. Thomas were the teams to beat.) Thousands of St. Mary's fans would brave the freezing temperatures at the outdoor rink to see the team and its new stars tear up the ice.

Beaulieu went on to score 62, 63, and 68 points respectively over his next three years, finishing with an unbelievable 134 goals and 99 assists for 233 points in just 63 games — tops all-time in the MIAC. (That's an average of 3.7 points per game on an outdoor rink!) Beaulieu once even scored nine goals in a 9-0 win over Augsburg. He finally got some national attention by being featured in Sports Illustrated's "Faces in the Crowd," after scoring 13 goals in a pair of weekend games against St. Olaf and Carleton. (Beaulieu, who later became a pro scout and even briefly coached the North Stars in 1978, went on to become a math teacher and head hockey and tennis coach at Stillwater High School, but his legend lives on in Winona.)

In 1972 another star came to town by the name of Tom Younghans. He only stayed for two seasons

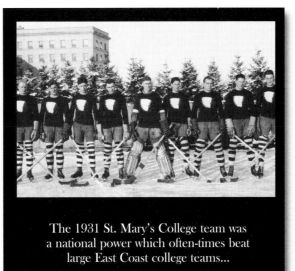

The 1931 St. Mary's College team was a national power which often-times beat large East Coast college teams...

OSCAR ALMQUIST

Oscar Almquist starred as a goalie on Eveleth's high school team from 1923-27. Then, after a two-year stint with Virginia of the Arrowhead Amateur League, he went on to play between the pipes at St. Mary's College, where he earned All-American honors in 1932 & '33. Almquist then began his professional career, first with the Eveleth Rangers, followed by three seasons with the St. Paul Saints. Then, after coaching for a year at tiny Williams High School in 1937, Almquist moved to Roseau, where he began coaching, and also playing for the amateur Cloverleafs. In 1941 the "Big O" became the team's head coach, a position he would hold until 1967. During this period Roseau High School became a perennial power, winning state titles in 1946, 1958, 1959 and 1961. The Rams appeared in the state tourney 14 times, and finished as runner-ups on four occasions as well. Before retiring to become the school's athletic director and principal, the "Giant of the North" had posted an amazing record of 404-148-21, including a 49-game winning streak from 1957 through 1959.

though, before going on to star for the University of Minnesota and then in the NHL with the North Stars. A few years later Don Olson took over as the team's new coach. He would finally get them a new facility and has been steering the ship of a very successful program ever since.

Olson led the Cardinals to the 1981 NAIA Championships, but were knocked off in the quarterfinals by Bemidji State, 5-1. The Cards then made it to the NCAA Division III National Tournament in 1989, but lost to Bemidji State again, 5-4 and 7-2, in the best-of-three games. Their last trip came in 1994, when the St. Mary's team advanced to the NCAA Division II National Tournament in Huntsville, Ala., only to lose to UW-River Falls in the quarterfinals.

One of the stars of the early '90s was Chris Valicevic. A three-time All-Minnesota Intercollegiate Athletic Conference selection, and the MIAC's Player of the Year his senior season, the sturdy defenseman scored 27 goals and added 80 assists for 107 points in his three-year Saint Mary's career. Valicevic would go on to play professionally in the East Coast Hockey League, with the Greensboro Generals and the Louisiana IceGators. Incredibly, in 2003, he would be named to the ECHL's 15th Anniversary All-Time Team. The league's MVP in 1998-99, Valicevic was a four-time ECHL Defenseman of the Year, a five-time first team All-ECHLer and a seven-time ECHL All-Star.

The Cardinals would eventually move to the SMU Ice Arena, a new structure that was built where the old rink (which had a bubble roof installed in 1983) stood for years. The team was consistent through the late 1990s, and posted a modest 11-10-4 overall record in 1998-99, good for fourth in the MIAC.

The team finished with at 9-14-2 overall record in 1999-2000 and was led by Kevin Mackey, who was named to the All-MIAC First Team following the season. After a pair of sixth place finishes in 2000-01 and 2001-02, the 2002-03 Cardinals finished up at 11-13-1, good for the eighth spot in the MIAC. The team was led by juniors Al Schumacher and Sam Phillips, who were both named as First-Team All-MIAC selections. Schumacher scored a team-leading seven goals and added four assists for 11

St. Mary's' Andre Bealieu

points, while Schumacher tallied 18 goals and added seven assists for a team-leading 25 points in 25 games.

The Cards had their best season as of late in 2003-04, when they finished in fourth place in the conference with a 13-11-2 record and made it into the MIAC playoffs. The team, which appeared in its first MIAC playoff game since the 1996-97 season, landed three players on the All-MIAC First-Team as well, including senior Lenny Hofmann, junior Chad Damerow and sophomore Marcus Reszka.

The Cards went 10-14-1 in 2004-05, good for sixth in the conference. They were led by Chad Damerow, who paced the team with 18 points. For his efforts, he was named as an All-MIAC First-Teamer for the second straight season. The 2005-06 Cards went 8-8 in conference play and again came in at the No. 6 spot. The team then posted a 7-17-1 record in 2006-07, good for just seventh place in the MIAC, and out of the playoffs. Anthony Bohn led the team in scoring that season with 27 points, while Adam Gill added 22. For his efforts, Gill, along with goalie Dan Smith, were named to the All-MIAC First Team.

ST. OLAF

Founded in 1874 as a co-ed, residential, four-year private liberal arts college, St. Olaf's hockey program first began in 1926, when the team started playing against local college and senior teams in the area. The school began MIAC competition shortly thereafter and soon developed several good rivalries with Shattuck, Augsburg, Macalester and St. Thomas. The team was one of the best in the state through the 1930s, and went on to win what would prove to be the school's only two MIAC titles in 1938 and 1939.

After the War years, the program went through its share of highs and lows, ultimately leaving the MIAC in 1950 to play in the Midwest Conference. The team, under the tutelage of coach Tom Porter, himself a 1951 St. Olaf star, twice tied for the

DON OLSON

Don Olson grew up in Duluth and went on to play hockey at Denfeld High School, graduating in 1967. From there, Don headed east to play hockey at Harvard. After graduating in 1971, Olson returned to Minnesota to take some time off. Instead, he wound up coaching a peewee team in West Duluth, and before long he found himself serving as an assistant at Duluth Cathedral High School. One year later he became their head coach. He would remain at Cathedral for four years before going on to take over as the head hockey coach at St. Mary's in 1976. He would be taking over a hockey program which didn't even have an arena, but he was up to the challenge.

The nearest arena was 50 miles away in Rochester, which made it tough to recruit. But Olson hung in there and more than 300 wins later, he is still going strong. Olson eventually got his arena built, and with it so too came the kids and the victories. In 1982 he would take over as the school's athletic director, a position he would hold until 1999, when he gave it up to focus solely on coaching hockey. In addition, Olson also coached cross country and golf over the years at St. Mary's as well.

Entering his 30th season at SMU, Olson currently boasts a 368-385-39 career record and has had a lot of post-season success too. In 1981 he led the Cardinals to an NAIA National Tournament appearance and for his efforts was named as the NAIA Men's Hockey Coach of the Year. In 1988 Olson coached the Cardinals to the MIAC regular-season hockey title, and in 1989 and 1995 he guided them to MIAC post-season hockey titles as well. In all, Olson has guided the Cardinals to the MIAC playoffs 13 times. Further, Olson-led teams have also made two NCAA Division III post-season appearances as well.

Among Olson's many coaching accolades and honors, he was named as the MIAC Coach of the Year three times: 1980, 1988 and 1995. In addition, in 1988 and 1989 he was named as the Division III West Region Men's Hockey Coach of the Year. He is also a member of the SMU Sports Hall of Fame.

Midwest Conference championship in 1961 and 1966 and then won it outright in both 1969 and 1970. One of the best era's of Ole Hockey came in the late 1950s and early '60s, when standouts such as Jerry Roce, Duane Swenson, Whitey Aus and Harold Vinnes were all starring for the squad.

By 1971, after 12 years behind the Ole bench, Porter had posted an impressive 70-27-1 record. The Oles played at various rinks on campus until the late 1970s, something that hurt the team's productivity. During one stretch in 1974, coach Porter's Oles had to delay the start of their season due to a fire at the school's home rink at the Shattuck School in Faribault.

St. Olaf returned to the MIAC in 1975. That next year, 1976, Whitey Aus took over as the team's new skipper. It would be a position he would hold for 20 seasons in Northfield. Aus had been coaching for the past 15 seasons prior at Roseville High School. Over his two-decade tenure on The Hill, Aus would win MIAC and NAIA Coach of the Year honors, as well as become the school's all-time winningest coach.

One of the highlights of the program came in the early 1980s, when the Oles made a couple of runs at the NAIA National playoffs. In 1980 the team got beat by Bemidji State, 5-2, in the opening round, and then lost to Michigan-Deerborn in the 1981 quarters. They rallied back to beat UW-River Falls after that, only to lose to St. Thomas in the consolation finals. They made it again in 1983 and '84, losing to UW-River Falls and Bemidji, respectively. Some of the stars of the '80s included: Chuck Abrahamson, a goalie from Roosevelt; Steve Nelson, an All-American from White Bear Lake; Guy Considine, who remains as the Oles' all-time leading scorer with 161 total points; and Edina's Craig Ranheim, who tallied a record 70 goals in 1983.

Up and down throughout the 1980s and '90s, the Oles played solid, fundamental hockey under Aus. Some of the team's stars during the '90s include: All-American Brent Eilefson, who remains second all-time in scoring with 150 career points; John Klaers, who is third with 137; and Adam Rice, an All-American from Cottage Grove.

In 1997, 500 games later, Aus retired both from coaching, as well as from teaching at St. Olaf. With 192 wins he would go out as the program's all-time winningest coach and remains a legend at the school to this day. One of his top assistants that last year was former Ole winger Tod Dungan, himself a former prep legend at the Marshall School in Duluth. (Incidentally,

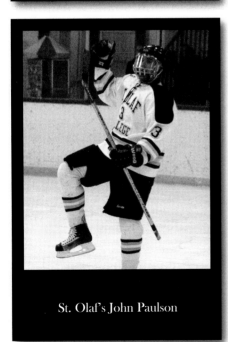

St. Olaf Coach
Sean Goldsworthy

St. Olaf's John Paulson

Aus' brother, Peter, has coached for more than 30 years at both the high school level, with Litchfield and Willmar, and later at Bethel College as well.)

Throughout the program's rich history, the Oles have competed both as independents as well as in the NAIA. Today, however, the team competes entirely in the MIAC, which is an NCAA Division III affiliate. In 1997, Sean Goldsworthy, the son of former North Stars legend Bill Goldsworthy, took over as the coach of the program. Goldy starred for the Oles back in the early '90s and even led the MIAC in scoring in '94, earning All-MIAC honors along the way. Now in his 10th season as the Ole's head coach, and 100 wins later, he continues to work on building the program's rich hockey tradition.

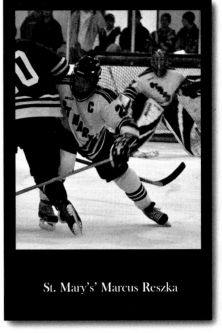

St. Mary's' Marcus Reszka

The team struggled throughout the early years of the new millennium, finishing in the middle of the conference pack from 1999-2003. The team turned the corner in 2003-04, however, finishing in fifth place in the MIAC with an 11-12-4 overall record and advanced on to the conference semifinals. Then, in 2005-06, St. Olaf captured its first NCAA tournament berth in school history with their 5-1 win over the University of St. Thomas in the MIAC Championship. The Oles were back!

The team played well in 2006-07, finishing in fourth place in the MIAC with an overall record of 11-14-2 and advanced on to the conference semifinals. Dylan Mueller led the squad with 21 points, while Jeff Budish added 17 as well.

ST. THOMAS

Founded in 1885, in what was once a farmers field, the University of St. Thomas originally began as St. Thomas Aquinas Seminary. From those original 62 students, the school has evolved into Minnesota's largest independent university with more than 11,000 students. With a rich hockey tradition that goes back to the turn of the century, St. Thomas has been a small college hockey power in Minnesota for nearly 100 years.

The St. Thomas College hockey program began in 1899, when the students from the school began playing against some of the local high school, college and senior teams. Among the school's first opponents throughout the early 1900s included the Mic Macs, Virginias, Victorias and Chinooks, as well as Mechanic Arts and St. Paul Central High Schools, and Luther College.

In 1915, St. Thomas College played a series of games against a team representing the University of Minnesota. However, the team was not recognized by the U of M Athletic Board at that time and the games played were classed as only "pick-up" contests. The Tommies also played several games during this era against some of the better U of M fraternity teams. The matches were often played on outdoor ice at Northrop Field with the finals and playoffs often being played at the indoor "Hippodrome" ice arena at the State Fairgrounds in St. Paul.

By 1921, the Tommies, which were considered in hockey circles as the Minnesota State Champions, played the "now-varsity" Gophers to a tough 2-1 loss at the Coliseum Rink on Lexington Avenue near University Avenue in St. Paul. Head coach Harold Dudley led the Tommies to a 6-1 record that year, as the team went on to defeat Hamline and St. Mary's that season as well. The next year St. Thomas helped to create the newly formed Minnesota Intercollegiate Athletic Conference, which would include several teams during that era, including Augsburg, Hamline, St. Mary's, Gustavus, Macalester, St. Olaf, St. John's, Bethel and Concordia.

The team won its first MIAC title in 1923, under then-head coach Joe Brandy. It would be the first of many for the Tommies. A couple of the team's toughest losses that year came at the hands of the Gophers and also Eveleth Junior College — both of whom were top-10 nationally ranked powers. By the mid-1920s St. Thomas was by far the strongest of Minnesota's small colleges, winning several more conference championship throughout the latter half of the decade.

Some of the stars during this era included White Bear Lake's Dick Conway and Hall of Fame winger Doc Romnes, also of White Bear Lake. In 1926 Romnes led the Tommies past nationally ranked Michigan Tech, 8-1, up at Calumet in the Upper Penninsula, and 8-0 in a return contest in St. Paul. Upon graduating from St. Thomas, Romnes would go on to star for the NHL's Chicago Blackhawks, where he led the team to the 1938 Stanley Cup Championship. In 1936, as one of only a handful of Americans playing in the NHL, Romnes was awarded the NHL's coveted Lady Bing Trophy for outstanding sportsmanship, an award Wayne Gretzky would later win.

St. Thomas went on to win MIAC titles in 1934 and again in 1939, '40, '41 and '42. They played many of their games during this era at the State Fair Coliseum, which was originally known as the Hippodrome. It's been said that its 260-foot ice surface was like skating on a lake! The school's biggest rivalry would emerge around this time, with St. John's, as the two power-house

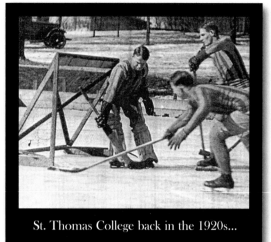

St. Thomas College back in the 1920s...

programs would continue to do battle against one another for many decades to come. The War years put a damper on hockey, but by the late 1940s, under head coach Bill Funk, the Tommies were back ·in action, winning MIAC titles in 1947, '49, '51, '52, and '53. During the early 1950s the team was playing many of its games on the corner of Selby Avenue and Finn Avenue, on some flooded tennis courts. One of the biggest games of this era came against future WCHA power Colorado College, which beat the Tommies in a pair of 1954 contests.

In 1953 Duluth came into the league and dominated it until the early 1960s, when they finally left to go Division I. The Tommies, which were now playing their home games at St. Paul Academy, played competitively throughout this period under head coach Gus Schwartz, but didn't win a title until 1974, when Jeff Boeser, who tallied 201 points from 1971-75, led the way. That year the Tommies made it all the way to the NAIA Championships (small college hockey's championship), which were held in Bemidji. There, the Tommies lost to Gustavus in the Final Four to finish fourth in the nation.

In 1976 the Tommies played Hamline at the Fairgrounds Coliseum, beating the Pipers, 7-4. The Coliseum would serve as the home of St. Thomas hockey for the next quarter century. In 1977 the school went co-ed, giving young men from around the state all the more reason to come to the school. In 1978 St. Thomas made it back to the NAIA Championships, this time held in St. Paul. There, the Tommies beat Gustavus, 6-5, in overtime to advance to the championship round, where, after losing to Bemidji State in the semis, they beat UW-River Falls, 7-6, to finish third in the nation. A couple of the stars from this era include Jeff Keys, who scored 186 points from 1973-77,

TERRY SKRYPEK

Terry Skrypek grew up in the Midway area of St. Paul and went to graduate from Cretin High School in 1966 as a multi-sport star. From there, Skrypek played hockey at St. Mary's in Winona, graduating in 1970. Skrypek then went directly from the St. Mary's campus to work at Hill-Murray High School, where he served as the school's head hockey coach for 17 years. During that time he recorded an amazing 325-42-2 record (.883) and led his team to 12 berths in the state high school hockey tournament. His Pioneer teams were state champions in 1983 and state runners-up three other years.

Skrypek, who also coached football and baseball, won a state baseball title in 1976 as well. Among his many high school accolades, Skrypek was named as the Minnesota State Coaches' Association Coach of the Year in 1983. In 1987 Skrypek left Hill Murray to take over as the head hockey coach at St. Thomas. He would end his illustrious high school coaching career as one of the state's all-time best.

That next year Skrypek led the Toms to the MIAC title and was named conference Coach of the Year. It would be the first of many. Now entering his 21st season behind the Tommy bench, Skrypek has established himself as one of the top collegiate coaches in the country. During his tenure at STU, Skrypek has posted a 374-168-37 (.680) record, including a stellar 246-55-19 (.801) record in the rugged MIAC. His 374 victories rank him among the top 70 on the all-time, all-division hockey coaching chart (30th among active head coaches). Skrypek ranks in the top 10 among active D-III coaches in wins and winning percentage.

Skrypek's first 20 Tommie teams have won 12 conference championships and have never finished worse than third place in the MIAC standings. His teams have advanced to the conference playoffs all 20 years, made the finals 19 times, and won the 2004 and 2005 post-season crowns on the road as a No. 2 seed. In addition, Skrypek's teams have reached the NCAA playoffs nine times and are the only conference team to reach a national championship game. Further, Skrypek has coached 22 All-Americans in 20 seasons, including 2000 Division III Player of the Year Steve Aronson. He's also coached seven MIAC Player of the Year recipients. Incredibly, Skrypek, the 2005 National Coach of the Year, will coach his 700th college game in February of 2008.

Skrypek has never had a losing record in his 45 years of organized hockey as a prep and college player, a 17-year high school coach at Hill-Murray, and in his first 20 seasons with the Tommies. Among his many honors and accolades, Skrypek is a member of the Athletic Hall of Fames at both St. Thomas and at his alma mater, St. Mary's, where he was a stand-out hockey player. Terry and his wife Valerie have raised four children — all Tommie graduates. Their son Bryan was an All-MIAC defenseman and four-year starter for the Tommy hockey team as well.

and Mark Hentges, who scored an amazing 226 points from 1977-81. (Hentges' 83-points in just 28 games in 1979 remains No. 1 all-time in the record books for points scored in a season.)

In 1980 and 1981 the Tommies advanced to the NAIA Tournament, but were knocked off by UW-Superior both times. In 1981, after losing to UW-Superior, 7-6, the Toms then rallied to defeat St. Mary's, 6-4, and St. Olaf, 12-3, to take the consolation title. They picked up where they left off in 1983, winning three MIAC titles (and a runner-up in '84) through 1986, when former Hill Murray High School coach Terry Skrypek took over from then head coach Terry Abram, who led the team from 1982-87. In 1985 the Toms made it to the NCAA D-III tourney but lost to Rochester Institute of Technology (NY), 5-3 and 5-2, in the quarters. One of the stars of this era was Hopkins native Bo Snuggerud, who scored 121 points from 1983-85.

In 1986 the Tommies made it back to the D-III Tournament, but lost this time to Mankato State in a best-of-three games series, 6-5, 1-6 and 2-0, at Augsburg Arena. They made it back in 1988, only to lose this time to Bemidji State, 5-1 and 3-1. In 1989, in his second season at the St. Thomas helm, Skrypek led the Toms to yet another MIAC title, and for his efforts was named as the conference's Coach of the Year. In 1990 the College of St. Thomas became the University of St. Thomas, but it was still business as usual for the hockey Tommies. UST won the MIAC crown again in 1990, and achieved a No. 5 national ranking as well as a berth in the NCAA Final Eight.

By 1992 Skrypek had made it four MIAC titles in a row and again took his team into the NCAA quarterfinals. Again selected as the MIAC Coach of the Year, the St. Paul native's squad had to pull off a couple of 3-2 and 3-1 victories over his alma-mater, St. Mary's, during the final weekend of the 1993 regular season for his fifth consecutive MIAC title. The Toms made it six straight MIAC titles under Skrypek in 1993-94, and made it back to the NCAA quarterfinals, where they this time lost to eventual NCAA runner-up UW-Superior. The 1994-95 Toms extended the MIAC title streak to seven but lost in the conference tourney finals. The Toms took third in 1996 and second in 1997, before winning the MIAC title again in '98. They made it two in a row in 1999, behind star winger Steve Aronson, only to lose to UW-Superior in the NCAA playoffs.

The team would go on an amazing run over the next four years, winning four straight MIAC titles from 1999 to 2002. The 2000 Tommies made it all the way to the NCAA D-III Final Four, where they lost to Norwich in the finals, 2-1. The team won the title that next year though, with a 15-9-3 overall record. Leading the charge was forward Tony Lawrence, who led the team in scoring with 46 points. In 2002 the Toms won the MIAC tournament in grand fashion, beating Gustavus, 3-2, on Eric Wenkus' game-winner, to earn their third NCAA berth in four seasons. There, however, they ultimately lost to Superior in the playoffs, 2-1.

The Toms would go on to finish in second place for three straight years, from 2002-03 to 2004-05, before winning it all again in 2005-06. In 2003 the team made big news when it moved out of St. Paul's historic State Fairgrounds Coliseum, the arena they had called home for the past 25 seasons. They would be moving into the newly christened 1,000-seat Saint Thomas Arena in

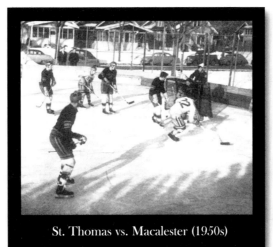

St. Thomas vs. Macalester (1950s)

Mendota Heights.

In 2003 the Toms beat Augsburg in the MIAC tourney semifinals, 7-6, thanks to Dustan Lick's goal at 14:54 of sudden-death overtime. They would then go on to lose to St. John's in the title game, 4-3, in yet another overtime thriller. That next season the team got revenge over their rival Johnnies, however, beating SJU in the MIAC Playoff Finals, 4-3, in overtime. Dan Krmpotich got the game-winner just 31 seconds into the extra session to end the Johnnies' 16-game winning streak. It also ended a two-year, five-game losing streak to the Johnnies. Goalie Zach Sikich made 34 saves in net while Dustan Lick scored two goals and Brandon Wilcox had a goal and three assists. With the win, the team advanced on to the NCAA Division III playoffs for the fourth time in six seasons. There, however, the Toms lost to River Falls in the playoffs, 3-2, in overtime.

The 2004-05 Tommies beat St. John's in the MIAC Playoff finals, 2-1, and then beat the Johnnies again in the NCAA Playoffs, 4-1. From there, they went on to beat St. Norbert (Wis.), 3-2, to advance on to the NCAA D-III Final Four. There, they beat Trinity (Ct.), 4-1, in the semifinals, but got swept by Middlebury, 5-0, in the Finals to finish as the 2004-05 national runner-ups. For his efforts, Coach Skrypek was named Division III National Coach of the Year. His injury-plagued Toms pulled off three upset road wins in an eight-day stretch over teams ranked in the top five nationally.

In 2005-06, the Toms beat Bethel in the MIAC Playoff Semifinals, 5-4, in overtime, on Matt Kaiser's goal just 2:31 into sudden-death to stun fourth-seeded Bethel. From there, the Toms lost to St. Olaf in the MIAC Playoff Finals, 5-1, to end their season. The 2006-07 Tommies, meanwhile, went on a 10-game winning streak in late January through early March, to advance on to the MIAC Playoffs. There, the conference runner-ups beat Augsburg in the semifinals, 3-1, but then lost to Bethel in the Finals, 5-3. Leading the way was junior forward Nick Pernula, who earned All-America honors after finishing with 25 goals and 22 assists for 47 points in just 27 games. Joining Pernula on the All-Conference First Team that season were Nick Harris, Kevin Rollwagen and Ryan Van Bockel.

Overall, St. Thomas is the Division III leader in all-time victories and just one of two institutions in the nation to have surpassed 900 total wins. The Tommies are now 971-567-62 in the 84-year history of their program. In all, St. Thomas has made 12 NCAA playoff appearances, including five in the last nine seasons. The Tommies have also earned 31 All-American honors since 1970. In addition, UST is the lone MIAC team to reach the NCAA D-III title game, when they did so on two occasions, in 2000 and in 2005.

The Toms have been dominant in the post-season as well. In fact, they have advanced to the MIAC post-season playoffs in all 22 years that the format has been in existence, and reached the finals 20 times. In all, the Tommies have posted 25 consecutive winning seasons. They have won 29 conference championships, including 13 in the last 19 seasons, and have placed first or second in the MIAC 43 times, including 23 of the last 25 seasons. Coach Skrypek has even helped St. Thomas hockey maintain its No. 1 rankig in all-time wins among 68 Division III programs. The numbers are simply amazing.

St. Thomas' Steve Aronson was named as the NCAA D-III Player of the Year in 2000 after scoring 91 points in just 33 games. The MIAC's all-time leading scorer, with 244 points, Aronson went on to sign the first ever player contract in 2000 with the NHL's Minnesota Wild.

MINNESOTA'S OTHER D-III & JUNIOR COLLEGE PROGRAMS

UM-CROOKSTON

In addition to Minnesota's five D-I hockey schools, and the nine D-III MIAC schools, there are two other D-III college hockey programs in the Land of 10,000 Lakes: UM-Crookston and St. Scholastica. While Crookston competes in the Northern Sun Intercollegiate Conference (NSIC), the school's Golden Eagle Hockey team competes in the Midwest Collegiate Hockey Association (MCHA). Prior to that, the school played in the junior college ranks against teams in the Minnesota Junior College Athletics Association (MJCAA).

In 1973, Crookston, under head coach Dale Stinar, and behind their star player, Jim Clauson, won the state junior college championship and then placed second in the nation in Lake Placid, NY, at the National Junior College Hockey Tournament (NJCAA). One of the program's top stars in the early '90s was Crookston native Jeff Perreault, who earned NJCAA First-Team All-American honors in 1990 after leading the nation in scoring with 32 goals and 46 assists for a total of 78 points. In 1993 and 1994 the Golden Eagles won back-to-back NJCAA titles, going undefeated in '94. With Head Coach Scott Oliver at the helm, the team went on to defeat Erie Community College of New York, Hibbing Community College, and NDSU Bottineau for their second crown, outscoring their opponents 36-5 along the way. Nathan Pitt, Bill Trew, Jeff Malawski and Ken Essay all garnered All-American honors for their efforts that season.

As members of the MCHA, the team has played outstanding hockey. In fact, Crookston won back-to-back MCHA Championships in 2002-03 and 2003-04. Leading the way were wingers Brock Amundson and Ed Turcotte, as well as goalie Erik Kraska, who all played a big part in rewriting the record books during their tenures as Golden Eagles.

ST. SCHOLASTICA

The College of St. Scholastica, located in Duluth, plays in the Northern Collegiate Hockey Association (NCHA) with UW-River Falls, St. Norbert, UW-Stout, UW-Superior, UW-Stevens Point, UW-Eau Claire, Lake Forest. Minnesota State Mankato, St. Cloud State and Bemidji State all used to be members of the conference back in the '80s, but left when they made the leap to D-I status. Due to the fact that they are the only Minnesota team in the league, the Saints play most of the MIAC schools during the season as well. St. Scholastica, which joined the league in 1983, began its hockey program back in 1972 under the tutelage of head coach Del Genereau. The team went 19-5-2 that initial campaign, and then went on to win NAIA National Championships in both 1975 and 1977. Andy Speak, the program's all-time leading scorer, and Scott Robideaux, the program's all-time leading scoring defenseman, both played a big role in those teams' success. Today the Saints are led by third year head coach Mark Wick, a Hermantown native and 1985 graduate of St. Scholastica, who has made great strides towards once again making the Saints a small college hockey power. As of late, the team is paced by Joey Martini and Mark Menzies, who have both earned All-NCHA honors for their hard work and dedication to the team.

RAINY RIVER COMMUNITY COLLEGE & THE EVOLUTION OF JUNIOR COLLEGE HOCKEY IN MINNESOTA

It is interesting to note that there have been many other D-II and D-III schools over the years, such as Winona State, Macalester and Carleton, which have dropped varsity hockey at the NCAA level and made it a club sport instead. There was also a thriving junior hockey circuit in Minnesota back in the day as well. The JUCOs sent numerous young men into the ranks of Division I, II and III, MIAC and NCHA schools over the years and proved to be an outstanding venue for kids on the bubble between high school and a four-year college. In addition to teams such as Crookston, which played in the Minnesota Junior College Athletics Association, there were others who played in the Minnesota Community College Conference (MCCC), such as Rainy River Community College.

RRCC was a junior college power for nearly four decades. In 1967 legendary International Falls High hockey coach Larry Ross started the RRCC hockey program from the ground level while also coaching the Broncos high school team. Two years later, George Schlieff took over behind the bench and led his team to the 1971 state title. He was also instrumental in hosting the first ever National Junior College Athletic Association National Tournament in 1972 as well. That same year, the Voyageurs finished second in state, regional and national play.

In the early years of Voyageur hockey, the team played several big-time schools, including: the Gophers, Badgers, UMD, St. Cloud State, UND, Michigan Tech, and the Air Force Academy. By the early-1970s, the conference was made up of Rainy River, Itasca, Hibbing, Crookston, Northland, Mesabi, and Lakewood. In 1976, Anoka-Ramsey entered into the picture, and in early 80's, Rochester, Brainerd, Fergus Falls, and Vermilion also joined the circuit.

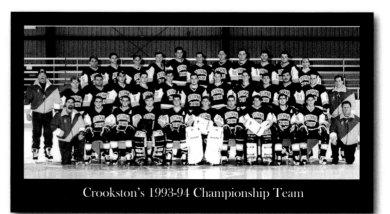

Crookston's 1993-94 Championship Team

Crookston's Jim Clauson

Crookston's Jeff Malawski

Crookston's Brett Shelanski

In 1976, coach John Sirotiak led the Voyageurs to the state finals, only to lose to the Hibbing Cardinals, which would win their third title in a row. Former Voyageur Terry Thompson took over in the fall of that year and led the Voyageurs to the National Title in his first season. The Voyageurs were 21-3-1 and won the Triple Crown: State, Region XIII, and the National Championship. Rainy River beat Mesabi, 7-3, to win the State Championship, then went on to beat Canton ATC, 5-2, for the national crown.

The 1977-78 season brought together the most prolific forward line combination in school history. Thompson put sophomore All-American Dave Olson with freshmen Kevin Gordon and Chuck Green. This combination provided the Voyageur fans with 197 points in just 20 games. Kevin Gordon finished his Rainy River career with 105 goals and 87 assists for 192 points in 45 games (a 4.26 points per game average), while receiving All-American honors after his second season as well. The Voyageurs then finished second in the 1978 MCCC State Tournament as Mesabi revenged the loss in the 1977 state final.

In 1979-80 Thompson earned his second Triple Crown in four years. Rainy River was led by the All-American duo of Barry Woods and Steve Readmen, as well as Mike Auran, Bill Mason, and goaltenders, Tim Port and Mark Pelowski, who were all instrumental in the State and National run. A fourth place conference finish put the Voyageurs against Hibbing in the first round

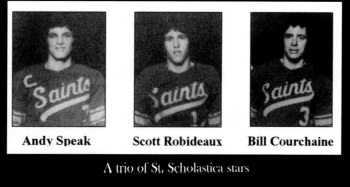

Andy Speak   **Scott Robideaux**   **Bill Courchaine**

A trio of St. Scholastica stars

of the Minnesota Community College Conference (MCCC) State Tournament. The upset minded Voyageurs beat Hibbing and then beat Mesabi, 5-4, for the State Title. Rainy River traveled to Eveleth for the 1980 NJCAA National Tournament and beat powerhouse Canton, 6-5 in overtime. They then lost a three-goal lead in the second period and lost 8-7 to the College of DuPage in the championship game.

Thompson finished his coaching career at Rainy River in 1985 as the school's all-time winningest coach with a career record of 158-60-1. Former UMD Bulldog Bill Mason was called upon to fulfill the coaching opening, but the league had dwindled. Meanwhile, nearby Hibbing Community College had won a pair of NJCAA National Championships in 1984 and 1985, showing the rest of the hockey world just what Iron Range hockey was all about.

By the late 1980's, the conference included only Rainy River CC, Itasca CC, Hibbing CC and UM-Crookston. Mason would coach the Voyageurs for five seasons before turning over the duties to another former Voyageur, Scoff Riley, in 1990. In 1994, the Voyageurs were upset in the first round of the State Tournament by Hibbing and missed their chance at earning a birth in the 1994 National Tournament. Chad Shikowsky led the team in scoring and was named to the All-American team. That same year Dan Huntley took over as the team's new skipper.

Crookston dropped out of the conference following the

DEL GENEREAU

Del Genereau is a Duluth hockey icon. Genereau served as the head hockey coach at Duluth Cathedral High School for eight years and built the program into a prep powerhouse. As head coach at Cathedral, he produced a 139-38-5 record and won an impressive four consecutive Minnesota State Catholic High School Hockey League championships in the late 1960s. Genereau was appointed head coach at St. Scholastica in 1972, and after his inaugural season, the Saints joined Bemidji State in the ICHA for the 1974 season. St. Scholastica emerged as ICHA champs in 1976 and went on to win the NAIA national championship. The Saints then went on to win their second NAIA national championship in 1977 as well. From 1972-77 Genereau posted a career record of 72-36-3 at St. Scholastica, building the program into a small college power.

1994 hockey season as the school evolved into a four-year institution. Bottineau joined what would become a new conference, called the Western Junior College Hockey League, which included Rainy River, Itasca and Hibbing. In 1995 the Voyageurs, seeded third, needed two overtimes to beat Itasca, 4-3. The Voyageurs then faced conference champion Bottineau for the right to advance to the National Tournament in Lake Placid, N.Y. The Voyageurs lost a nail biter, 6-4, but responded the next day by beating Hibbing, 4-3, to finish as the Region XIII runner-up. Goaltender Pat Fermoyle made 73 spectacular saves to earn the victory over Hibbing, while Chad Mitchell was named to the All-American team.

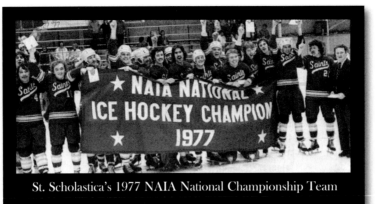
St. Scholastica's 1977 NAIA National Championship Team

tations for the program. Todd Sether, Barrett Olson, and Jon Cooper were named to the All-American team.

In the 1997 Region tournament, Rainy River lost a heart breaker to Bottineau 2-1, and in 1998 the Voyageurs lost to the Lumberjacks, 6-0, for the second year in a row in the Region title game. In 1999 Rainy River ripped off 13 straight victories to win the conference championship for the first time since 1980, and would sweep through the Region XIII playoffs. In round one of the 1999 NJCAA National Tournament (which was hosted by the Voyageurs), RRCC beat Erie CC 4-3 on a Lee Jenke breakaway goal with five minutes left in regulation. In round two, RRCC beat MSU-Bottineau for the fifth time with a 6-4 victory. Round three would bring national power SUNY-Canton, and the Voyageurs would fight from behind to win, 6-3, and gain their second National Title in school history.

On the 20th anniversary of Rainy River's first National Championship, the Voyageurs would return to the National Tournament. Once again the Voyageurs were the third seed in the Region XIII tournament and would have to dig deep to outlast Bottineau. The Voyageurs pulled off the 4-3 upset though, on Derek Bilben's goal with 1:08 left in the third period. The next night, Rainy River would face conference champion Itasca for a shot at the National

St. Scholastica's Joey Martini

St. Scholastica's Tyler Johnson

Sadly, due to budget constraints, the two year college hockey programs in Minnesota started to become extinct around the turn of the new millennium. The NJCAA offers just a handful of hockey programs now, including: Hibbing Community College and Mesabi Range CTC, which is located in Eveleth/Virginia. The Mesabi Range Norse Stars, which began play in 2006-07, is a non-varsity club hockey team that falls under the jurisdiction of the D-III American Collegiate Hockey Association (ACHA).

Tournament. For the second year in a row, there would be a double overtime game against Itasca. There, goaltender Todd Sether played spectacularly and Ross Gruye scored the game-winner to send the Voyageurs packing for Lake Placid. Rainy River lost all three games in the National Tournament but raised expec-

MINNESOTA'S JUNIOR & COMMUNITY COLLEGES

While there was once a flourishing Junior College or Community College circuit in Minnesota, which played in the Little Ten Conference, today their are just a handful of two-year school's which even offer hockey as a sport.

Some of the Junior College and Community College programs through the years in Minnesota have included:

1. Itasca Community College (Grand Rapids)
2. Hibbing Junior College
3. Rainy River Community College (International Falls)
4. Eveleth Junior College
5. Anoka Ramsey Community College
6. Fergus Falls Community College
7. Century Community College (White Bear Lake) *[NE Metro Tech & Lakewood CC Combined]*
8. Northland Community College (Thief River Falls)
9. Central Lakes Community College (Brainerd)
10. Mesabi Community College (Virginia)
11. Vermillion Community College (Ely)
12. Rochester Community College
13. Duluth Junior College
14. University of Minnesota-Crookston

JUNIOR HOCKEY IN MINNESOTA

Junior hockey has played a vital role in the development of hockey in America, and the genesis of how this division of 17-20-year-olds came to be makes for an interesting story. Although junior hockey had been highly successful in Canada since the turn of the century, it was a relatively new thing for Minnesotans back in the mid to late-1960s.

In the early 1960s it was becoming readily apparent that kids who weren't quite good enough to get college scholarships out of high school were dropping out of hockey altogether because they had no organized place to play competitively. With that, a group of Minnesota hockey boosters started a summer-league program for post-high schoolers and college freshman, to give some of these kids an opportunity to improve their skills and get noticed by some of the local colleges. In 1965, a group led by Ron Woodey, Larry Hendrickson, Jim Steichens, Harry Sundberg and others, took a team of Minnesota junior all-star players from the Junior Olympic Hockey Association summer league to Colorado Springs to play in the National Junior Championships. The team, called "Duff's Bar" (the only sponsor they could get), went on to surprise a few people by winning the national title over a highly touted team from Detroit.

Suddenly enlightened, that next year Walter Bush, Jr., Win Stephens, Jr., Bob Somers, Ron Woodey, Harry Brown, Red Kairies, Harvey McNair, Harry Sundberg, Ken Austin and several other local hockey boosters, organized the first junior hockey league in Minnesota, called the Minnesota-Ontario Hockey League. The circuit, which initially played throughout the Twin Cities and Ontario consisted of just four teams: the Win Stephens Buick Juniors, which were first coached by Larry Hendrickson, the Minneapolis Bruins (which were later led by the Carlson brothers — of the movie "Slapshot" infamy), and two teams from Thunder Bay — the Vulcans and Flyers. (A team from Fort Frances also played briefly.)

The league, which evolved into the Canadian-American or Can/Am League, progressed over the next couple of years with solid results. It was giving post-high schoolers more experience and also getting more scouts to check out the Minnesota hockey scene as well. (It would be safe to say that Rodney Dangerfield's famous line of *"I went to a boxing match and a hockey game broke out..."* was very applicable during the first couple of years of the league.) It was rough, and the fans loved it. One of the early fan-favorites was one of the toughest hombres ever to hit the ice, Goldy Goldthorpe (as in Ogie Ogelthorpe from "Slapshot), who starred for the Thunder Bay Vulcans. He led the team to a couple of early titles and

The 1971 Minnesota Junior Stars, coached by Herb Brooks.

The USHL's Clark Cup & Anderson Cup

later played for Glen Sonmor's Fighting Saints.

Now, after a couple of seasons, the Win Stephens team evolved into the Minnesota (Bloomington) Junior Stars. Herb Brooks coached the team for part of the 1971-72 season, and when he took over the Gopher coaching position from Glen Sonmor later that year, he handed the coaching reigns over to future Gopher coach, Doug Woog. Woog then led the Junior Stars to the national championship that year. The Junior Stars went on to win the Can/Am title in 1973, and then proceeded to gain a berth in the Centennial Cup, an annual tournament held to determine the best Canadian Tier II juvenile team. There, after advancing to the semifinals, the Stars wound up losing a tough seven-game series to the Pembroke Lumber Kings.

Going back to the Fall of 1972, Walter Bush (an owner with the North Stars), and Murray Williamson (the coach of the 1972 silver medal-winning U.S. Olympic team in Sapporo, Japan, who was also with the North Stars at the time), decided to explore the idea of starting a new circuit that would rival Canada's most prestigious Tier II leagues, complete with 60-game schedules and eventual international competition. It was an ambitious goal, but they felt that the timing was right.

Now, there were a number of factors in their decision to start this new league. First of all, this was a very tumultuous time in not only American hockey, but also in politics, as the Vietnam War was winding down. With the termination of the draft, an influx of 18-year-old men soon became readily available to play hockey after high school. Among the other factors fueling their decision included the fact that by 1972, professional hockey was exploding across North America. While the upstart World Hockey Association (WHA) was rapidly expanding into new markets, the NHL, in an effort to protect their interests, was counteracting by aggressively expanding themselves. Both rival leagues began bidding wars for players, and anyone with a heartbeat and a slapshot was seemingly getting a try-out to play somewhere. The WHA rolled out 14 new pro teams, and the NHL had recently expanded from six to 16. So, in less than five years, from 1967-72, pro hockey went from six franchises to 30, creating the biggest demand for hockey talent in modern history. It was a boom era for fringe players, probably unparalleled in any other pro sport's history. Suddenly there were some 400 professional job openings available, and teams needed personnel fast. Not only did they need players at the top levels, but they also needed to fill in their suddenly depleted minor-league systems as well.

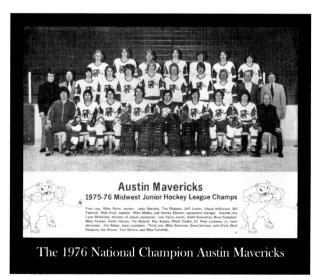

Austin Mavericks
1975-76 Midwest Junior Hockey League Champs

The 1976 National Champion Austin Mavericks

PHIL HOUSLEY

Arguably the greatest offensive defenseman in National Hockey League history, Phil Housley is one of America's best ever. After scoring 65 points in just 22 games at South St. Paul High School, Housley played for the St. Paul Vulcans in 1981 before going on to make the leap straight to the "show" at just 18 years of age. Selected as the sixth overall pick of the first round by the Buffalo Sabres at the 1982 National Hockey League Entry Draft, Housley quickly made a name for himself at the professional level and went on to become one of the league's sturdiest blue-liners.

While Housley began his career with Buffalo, where he compiled 558 points in 608 games with the Sabres, he would go on to play for eight different teams in his illustrious 21-year NHL career, including the Buffalo Sabres, Winnipeg Jets, St. Louis Blues, Calgary Flames, New Jersey Devils, Washington Capitals, Chicago Blackhawks and Toronto Maple Leafs. At the time of his retirement in 2003 he was ranked fourth in all-time goals scored by a defenseman with 338 and fifth in assists by a defenseman with 894. In addition, after 1,495 regular-season games played, then the most by any American, Housley ranked as the top scoring U.S.-born player, with 1,232 points (338 goals and 894 assists).

Housley has also left his mark as an amateur player as well, serving on seven U.S. National Teams (1982, 1986, 1989, 1996, 2000, 2001 and 2003), as well as a member of the 2002 silver medal-winning U.S. Olympic Team that competed in Salt Lake City. There, Housley recorded five points in six games, and registered the game-winning goal in the semifinal round of the 3-2 victory over Russia. Among his numerous honors, in 2000 Housley was presented with USA Hockey's Bob Johnson Award for excellence in international competition. In addition, the former NHL All-Star's jersey was also the first ever to be retired into the rafters at South St. Paul High School, when he was honored at a ceremony in 2004. Further, in 2004 he was inducted into the U.S. Hockey Hall of Fame.

As for what he is doing now that he is retired? When he is not golfing, he is giving back to the sport by serving as the head coach of the Stillwater (Minn.) High School hockey team. Presently, Phil and his wife, Karin, reside in Lakeland, Minn., with their four children.

The Canadian dominated NHL, feeling the pressure big-time, began looking to the U.S. for hockey talent, something they never would have dreamed of doing before. The NHL Board of Governors, led by then commissioner Clarence Campbell, who had been contributing financially to the Canadian junior systems for years, figured it would be a good opportunity to start developing a junior hockey feeder system in the U.S. similar to the one they had created north of the border. So, after some lengthy negotiations, they agreed to help subsidize the new league financially.

Couple in the fact that American colleges, which were overflowing with Canadian players, were begging for experienced American talent, and that our state's high school hockey program was producing top-level players who wanted to take their game to the next level, but had few opportunities, and it all started to make some sense. With that, Bush and Williamson knew that they would be doing a tremendous service for not only American hockey, but for Minnesota hockey — which was something that was near and dear to both of them.

In February of 1973, the new Midwest Junior Hockey League (MJHL), via merging with several of the now-defunct Can/Am teams, opened for business with six franchises. They included: Bloomington, St. Cloud, St. Paul, Fargo-Moorhead, Chicago and Thunder Bay. (Here's where it gets confusing. Over the ensuing months, the Thunder Bay Vulcans and Flyers both merged into one team, called the Hurricanes. The Minnesota Junior Stars franchise was sold to a new group in St. Paul that included Somers, Woodey and Sundberg, where they renamed their new club as the St. Paul Vulcans. And finally, a new group, led by Walter Bush and Murray Williamson took the "old" Minnesota Junior Stars name and created a new team called the "Bloomington Junior Stars," and set up shop at the Met Center.)

As the league started to come together, next came the issue of recruiting top-level players and coaches who could ultimately give the league the

appearance of being Tier II in status by Canadian standards. As it turned out, that would be the easy part. Ken Austin of Owatonna agreed to become the league's first president; St. Mary's star Andre Beaulieu left Hill-Murray High School to coach the Bloomington Junior Stars; Bob Gernander left Coleraine High School to guide the Fargo Sugar Kings; former Blackhawks star Ken Wharram took over the Chicago Nordiques; and Rich Blanche (and later Frank Zywiec) left his assistant coaching job at Denver University to head up the St. Cloud Saints franchise. With that kind of coaching talent, it wasn't long before some of the state's top players joined on. Numerous future NHL stars, including: Reed Larson, Gary Sargent, Paul Holmgren, Steve Short and Dave Geving all jumped on board as well.

The league got off to a good start that year, the competition was fierce, and the fans began to come see what it was all about. Pretty soon scouts from most WHA and NHL teams were frequenting the action, and in no time, college recruiters were bypassing the long trek to Canada to check out the new league.

It wasn't without its share of controversy though. Opposition to junior hockey immediately surfaced from existing high school, senior and small colleges teams. High school coaches suddenly found themselves fighting for their collective lives. They knew that they were stuck with the fact that they could only schedule 20-game seasons, while the MJHL could offer their top players three-times as much game experience — against much tougher competition. They were forecasting that eventually the state's top high school players would simply skip their junior and senior year's to play juniors. On the other hand, college coaches such as Herb Brooks at the U of M, were basking in their own private minor-league feeder systems. No longer did they have to gamble on a scholarship with a young, unproven player, when they could now send him to the juniors for a year to get a little "seasoning," and then reevaluate his progress a year later. (Incidentally, Brooks would have some 15 former

Doug Woog coached the Junior Stars and St. Paul Vulcans during the early 1970s before taking over as the coach of the Gophers.

Vulcans alone on his three NCAA titles teams in the 1970s.)

Williamson, a veteran of U.S. international play, desperately wanted to get AHAUS involved at that point, to create a world junior team. After a little politicking, the league sent an all-star team of sorts (which became the U.S. National Junior Team), to Russia, to take part in an international junior tournament. The league figured that it would not only be great experience for its top players, but it would also serve as a good recruiting and publicity tool for themselves. Once there, after being stranded for five days without their equipment in Leningrad, the U.S. team hit the ice against national junior teams from Sweden, Russia, Finland and Canada. And, although they lost all four games, they did rally back to beat the Czechs to finish fifth in the six-team tournament.

Later that season, a two-game series was arranged with one of Canada's premier junior teams, the Peterborough Pete's, from the prestigious Ontario Hockey Association. Virtually every scout in North America flew to Minneapolis to watch the super-hyped match, as the U.S. National Junior team beat the Pete's by the final score of 2-1. The win only solidified what Minnesotans had known all along, this league and these kids were for real.

The Thunder Bay Hurricanes tied the Junior Stars for the lead league that inaugural 1973-74 season, only to see the Vulcans defeat the Junior Stars, 5-4, in the post-season championship. By all accounts that first season was a success. One barometer for just how good the league fared that year came during the 1974 amateur draft, when fully 21 players from the league were selected by either the NHL or WHA. In addition, some 26

Kevin Hartzell played for the St. Paul Vulcans in 1977-78 and then, after playing for the Gophers, served as the team's head coach from 1983-89. He currently serves as the head coach of the USHL's Sioux Falls Stampede, where he has won a pair of Anderson Cups over the past seven seasons.

MJHL players were offered D-I college scholarships that first year — 22 in the WCHA alone.

Another significant event happened in February of 1974, when the Vulcans became the first American Junior team to beat a Canadian Tier I team, the Westminster Bruins, who, as winners of the Memorial Cup, were Canada's top Tier I Junior A team. The game, which was played in Bismarck, ND, saw the Vulcans beat the Bruins, 4-2, despite the fact that the Bruins had seven players who would get drafted and go into the NHL following that season, including N.Y. Ranger's future All-Star Ron Greschner.

Then, a major road-block hit the league. After that first year, a competing junior league operator in Chicago blew the whistle to the NCAA on the "suddenly successful" amateur league, for accepting money from the NHL. Now, at the time, the NCAA had strict standards regarding subsidies and sponsorship from professional organizations. As a result, on August 28th, 1974, the NCAA ruled that the MJHL was professional in status. The news was potentially deadly for the league, and its players who suddenly got very nervous about the possibility of losing their college eligibility. After a short legal battle, however, the ruling was reversed and the league resumed as business-as-usual. But, unfortunately, some collateral damage had been done. The league's image had been tarnished, and the NHL, which was mired in financial problems of its own, decided that it could no longer help out financially.

Chicago dropped out after that season, while a new franchise, the Austin Mavericks, which was headed by Leon Abbott, was added. Following that next season, after suffering heavy finan-

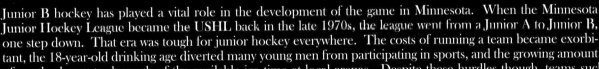

MINNESOTA'S JUNIOR B's

Junior B hockey has played a vital role in the development of the game in Minnesota. When the Minnesota Junior Hockey League became the USHL back in the late 1970s, the league went from a Junior A to Junior B, one step down. That era was tough for junior hockey everywhere. The costs of running a team became exorbitant, the 18-year-old drinking age diverted many young men from participating in sports, and the growing amount of youth players took much of the available ice time at local arenas. Despite these hurdles though, teams such as the St. Croix Stallions, North Suburban Junior Hawks and Tri-Metro Junior Whalers were able to remain intact. Coaches Dave Sanden of the Whalers and Dick Jenkins of the Junior Hawks were two of the key people who worked hard to keep the league operating for the countless young men who weren't yet seasoned enough to get a good look from a college or Junior A scout.

By the late '80s, two more teams were added to the MJHL, the West Suburban Junior Kodiaks and the Northland Voyageurs from Duluth. (The Northland's team is named so because they played their home games in Cloquet, Coleraine, Silver Bay, Eveleth, Two Harbors, Duluth and Superior. The team was coached by Butch Williams, the son of Rip Williams, who was very influential in promoting junior hockey throughout Minnesota. In addition, there was even a Rip Williams Challenge Cup, a junior tournament in Duluth, which was created in his honor.) In 1989 the Tri-Metro Whalers won the 1988-89 International Junior Championships, a first for a Minnesota Junior B squad. That next year the Northlands Voyageurs won the National Junior B championship by beating the Amherst (NY) Knights, 6-3, in Royal Oak, Mich. The Whalers added another title in 1992 as well.

By the mid-1990s the South Suburban Steers, East Metro Lakers, North Metro Owls, Junior Kodiaks, Minnesota Ice Hawks and the Shattuck St. Mary's Sabres comprised the MJHL. During that era, the Kodiaks brought home the hardware on three different occasions: 1993, '95 and '97. That same year, 1997, the Lakers made it to the Junior B National Tournament in Toledo, OH., and in 1998, the Lakers won the league championship before going on to finish second at the Junior B National Tournament in Simi Valley, CA. In 1999 the Iron Range Yellow Jackets (out of Coleraine), were added to the circuit. That same year the East Metro Lakers beat the St. Paul Steers, 8-1, to win the MJHL title. The Lakers then went on to win the Minnesota Junior B League's double-elimination KSTP Cup Tournament, which was held at the newly constructed Blaine Super Rink.

In June of 2007, USA Hockey announced that the Minnesota Junior Hockey League had been officially certified as a Tier III Junior A league. The league, which was established in 1973, is affiliated with USA Hockey. Considered to be one of the premier Junior B developmental leagues in North America, the nine-team MJHL now boasts six clubs in Minnesota (Granite City Lumberjacks, Minnesota Flying Aces, Minnesota Ice Hawks, Minnesota Owls, St. Paul Lakers, Twin Cities Northern Lights); two from Wisconsin (Hudson Crusaders, Wisconsin Mustangs); and one in Missouri (St. Louis Lightning). Teams in the MJHL play a 48-game regular season schedule and can play up to 57 games, including the playoffs and at the National Tournament. MJHL alums have advanced to D-I, II and III college programs, Canadian and U.S. Jr. A, and European and U.S. pro minor leagues.

cial losses, Fargo and St. Cloud both dropped out. But the league pressed on and continued to get kids into the next levels. The Vulcans repeated in 1975, as Doug Woog's team dominated. (Some of the top players in the mid to late 1970s included: Paul Holmgren, Butsy Erickson, Pat Phippen, Steve Ulseth, Jim Boo, John Sheridan, Craig Hamner, Paul Klasinski, Mitch Horsch, Tommy Gorence, Mark Wenda, Russ Welch, Jim Cunningham, Bob Graiziger, David Hanson, Kevin Hartzell and Frank Serratore.)

After a last place finish in their inaugural season, Austin, led by Ray Kurpis, won it all in 1976, beating the Vulcans, 5-3, to win the U.S. Junior A title. The Mavs' coaching reigns were handed from Leon Abbott (who became St. Lawrence University's head coach) to Lou Vairo, a native New Yorker who would go on to later coach the 1984 U.S. Olympic team.

In 1977 the Vulcans won the MJHL title, and were awarded the Anderson Cup. That year, five Vulcans went on to play for Michigan State, while several others earned D-I scholarships as well. Coach Doug Woog left after that season to take over the South St. Paul High School team, and was replaced by former Vulcan, Kevin Hartzell.

"Those were the days," recalled the Wooger. "It was a great time for hockey in Minnesota and really a wild ride. I can remember all the ups and downs we went through to get that whole thing going, it was exciting to be a part of it all."

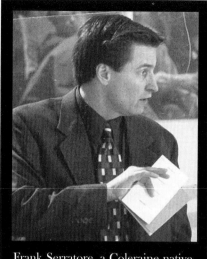

Frank Serratore, a Coleraine native, played and coached in the USHL before going to become the head coach of the Air Force Academy.

By now, the league was struggling financially. The teams, which made money not only from the NHL (which was drying up), but also by getting kick-backs from pro teams that signed the MJHL players, were hurting. This, in itself was a driving factor in the type of players that the league was producing. Because the pro leagues at that time wanted big, tough kids who could not only play physical, but also fight, those types of players began to be the ones who got drafted. As a result, the toughest guys on the team were actually the most valuable, because they were generating income for the clubs. In a sense, the goons were dictating the style of play in those days, and that proved to be very controversial.

Desperate, the league had to do something drastic to stay alive. That's when the United States Hockey League (USHL) came calling. The USHL had been a men's senior league up until that point, with several teams having played in Minnesota during the 1960s and '70s, including the Minneapolis Rebels, Minnesota Nationals, St. Paul Steers, Duluth Port Stars and Rochester Mustangs. Once the backbone for U.S. National team development, they too were having financial troubles, and proposed a merger. They agreed, and a year later the MJHL became the "junior" USHL.

The 1977 USHL featured six teams: the Bloomington Junior Stars (which finished first with a 51-20-29 record), Austin Mavericks, St. Paul Vulcans, Sioux-City Musketeers, Waterloo Blackhawks and Green-Bay Bobcats. In 1978 the Austin Mavericks won another Junior title, and that same year the Anoka Nordiques were added to the league. By 1979 the league had officially gone 100 percent juniors, as there had been some cross-over for the past two seasons between the junior and semi-senior teams. The league started out well and proved to be a very exciting brand of hockey in the state.

Jason Blake played with the Waterloo Blackhawks from 1993-94

The circuit would feature seven teams in two divisions. The North Division included the Hennepin Nordiques, Bloomington Jr. Stars, Green Bay Bobcats and St. Paul Vulcans; while the South included the Austin Mavericks, Sioux City Musketeers and Waterloo Black Hawks. Meanwhile, the Des Moines Buccaneers entered the league in 1980 and the Hennepin Nordiques moved to Waterloo and become the Black Hawks.

In 1982, Vulcans star Phil Housley was drafted by the Buffalo Sabres as the No. 6 overall pick of the first round. That same year the St. Paul Vulcans were sold to Stanley Hubbard, owner of Hubbard Broadcasting (KSTP-TV). Hubbard's sons had played on the team, and he knew the importance of having a strong junior program in the state. He even bought the team a new airplane, so that they would have a competitive advantage.

Under Hubbard, the team now had the resources to travel abroad. In December of 1984 the Vulcans became the first team (other than a U.S. National team) to play in Czechoslovakia. There, on live Czech TV, the Vulcans won the Liberation Cup, the championship trophy awarded to the winner of a 16-team holiday tournament in Brno, Czechoslovakia. That next year the team became the first American team, amateur or pro, to play in Hungary, where, in front of some 10,000 fans, they lost to the Hungarian National team. (Some of the Vulcan's top players of this era included future NHL stars Shaun Sabol and Jim Johnson.)

Green Bay would later drop out and be replaced with North Iowa, while Madison and Thunder Bay joined the league in 1984. That same year Bloomington changed its name to the Minneapolis Stars, only to fold just a year later. In 1985 the Rochester Mustangs, a perennial senior league power since the 1950s, with one of the richest traditions in Minnesota hockey history, merged with the Austin Mavericks to join the league. The team played its first season in Austin, winning the title that year behind their star defenseman, Ken Martell. The Mustangs then moved to Rochester in 1986, where, under former Bemidji State All-American goalie Frank Serratore, they soon became a power in the league. In their first six years in Rochester, the "new" Mustangs won three National Junior A titles. In 1987 the Mustangs swept the USHL's Anderson (season champion) and Clark (playoff champion) Cups, and the AHAUS National Junior A Championships. Incredibly, 14 players moved into Division I college hockey from that team. Among them was Rochester native, Shjon Podein, who attended UM-Duluth before going on to star with Philadelphia, Colorado and St. Louis in the NHL.

Serratore left after that season to take over as an assistant at UND. "The team has now come to reflect Rochester, a pretty glamorous place to play junior hockey," said Serratore when the franchise shifted to Rochester in 1986. "The franchise, in my opinion, one of the five best Tier II programs in North America, has become a great thing for hockey and for southern Minnesota."

In 1988, led by Hutchinson's Mark Bahr, who would go on to play for the Gophers, the Mustangs won their second National Junior A title by beating Detroit Compuware. The coach of that team was Kevin Constantine, a former all-state goalie from International Falls during the late 1970s, who would go on to become the head coach of the NHL's San Jose Sharks and Pittsburgh Penguins.

Serratore returned to the USHL in 1989, this time as the new head coach of the fledgling Omaha Lancers. The Lancers, which were miserable in 1987, did a complete 180 under Serratore, who led them to the USHL regular season and playoff championship in 1990. The worst-to-first Cinderella season earned Serratore the league's GM and Sportsman of the Year awards. (Serratore, who finished with a 247-103-6 record in the USHL, went on to become the coach at Denver University, followed by the IHL's Minnesota Moose, and finally at the Air Force Academy, where he remains today.)

In 1990, led by two-time USHL All-Star Jay Ness, the Mustangs won their third National Junior Championship in four years, by once again beating Detroit Compuware, 4-2, in Madison, Wis. Not to be outdone, the St. Paul Vulcans then proceeded to win yet another National Junior Championship in 1991 as well. The USHL went through its share of ups and downs in the '90s, but overall the league has been very successful. Expansion teams were added over the years, including: the Des Moines Buccaneers, Dubuque Fighting Saints, Green Bay Gamblers,

Kevin Constantine, an International Falls native, led the Rochester Mustangs to the 1988 USHL title before going on to coach in the NHL.

Lincoln Stars, North Iowa Huskies, Omaha Lancers, Rochester Mustangs, Thunder Bay Flyers and the Fargo-Moorhead Bears (later the Ice Sharks) in 1996. In addition, the Sioux Falls Stampede and Cedar Rapids Rough Riders have joined the league as well. That same year the St. Paul Vulcans changed their name to the Twin Cities Vulcans. Sadly, just three years later the team announced that it was moving to Kearney, Neb., and would be renamed as the Tri-City Storm, thus ending their storied history in Minnesota. That same year Fargo-Moorhead moved to Bensenville, IL and became the Chicago Steel. Many more teams would come and go over the years, but when Rochester closed up the front doors in 2002, it would be the end of the league's long association in Minnesota.

The USHL, which is governed by USA Hockey, has positioned itself to be the No. 1 Junior A hockey league in the country. The league continues to operate throughout the Midwest and remains the only Tier I junior league in America. It is one of the prime feeder programs for the country's top Division I colleges, not to mention the international, Olympic, professional and small college ranks. The junior programs have also helped to level the playing field, by proving that more and better playing

MURRAY WILLIAMSON

Murray Williamson was born in Winnipeg and grew up playing in the minor hockey systems in Manitoba. As a 15-year-old he was recruited into the sponsorship system of the Montreal Canadiens, where he competed for three seasons. In 1952, as an 18-year-old, he coached a neighborhood team to the Manitoba Bantam A title. Williamson left the St. Boniface Canadian junior system in 1954 to come to Minnesota. There, he attended Eveleth Junior College, where he also played for the Eveleth Rangers in the Thunder Bay Sr. League.

In 1955 Williamson came to the University of Minnesota to play for John Mariucci, ultimately earning All-American honors with the Gophers in 1959. After graduating with a bachelor's degree in business administration, Williamson went on to play semi-pro hockey in the Ontario Hockey Association Senior League. Then, in 1962, Williamson became the player/coach of the USHL's St. Paul Steers, and that next year assumed ownership of the team. Under his tutelage, the Steers became such a power in the league that by 1965 the team was converted into the U.S. National team. It would be the beginning of a very long and illustrious coaching career for Williamson, who, over the years would go on to coach more than 200 international senior matches as well as five National and two Olympic teams.

Williamson, who was now a naturalized U.S. citizen, then coached the U.S. National Hockey Team in the World Championships in Vienna in 1967. That next year Williamson became the youngest man to ever coach a U.S. Olympic Hockey team, leading Team USA to the 1968 Winter Games in Grenoble, France. Over the next two years Williamson would guide the U.S. National Teams at the World Championships in both Bern, Geneva, and Bucharest, Hungary. Then, in 1972, Williamson made history when he led the U.S. Olympic Hockey Team to the Silver medal in Sapporo, Japan. With a roster that included the likes of Mark Howe, Robby Ftorek, Huffer Christianson, Lefty Curran and Henry Boucha, the team came from nowhere to shock the hockey world.

In 1974 Williamson organized America's first International World Junior team, a club which would go on to participate in the World Junior Invitational Tournament in Leningrad. Three years earlier Williamson had become the first North American coach ever to visit inside the Russian Army Training Camp in Moscow, at the invitation of Anatol Tarasov, the famous Soviet hockey coach. A true student of the game, Williamson learned a great deal from the Russians and applied that knowledge to his own players back home in Minnesota.

Williamson's overall record included more than 130 victories against some of the best competition, home and abroad, and his longevity as a coach of Olympic and National teams ranks second only to the late Walter Brown, former owner of the Boston Bruins. Williamson, who later coached a Swiss team in Geneva, would also go on to start one of the most successful and well respected summer training camps for youth hockey players in the world, Bemidji International Hockey Camp, which, with legendary Bemidji State Coach Bob Peters, he ran from 1967-2000. Literally, tens of thousands of kids made the trek to Bemidji to learn the game of hockey up in the great northwoods and it has long been recognized as the first hockey camp in the world.

After coaching, Murray went on to become a very successful businessman. Presently, he has a lot of investment property in the real estate business and owns several hotels and restaurants throughout the country as well. Murray and his wife reside in the Twin Cities and have two sons who also coach hockey, Kevin and Dean, who played for the Gophers — just like the old man. When it comes to International hockey, as well as junior hockey, Murray Williamson is without a doubt, a coaching legend, and someone who should be thanked for all that he did to promote the game for Americans as well as for Minnesotans. Williamson, a 2006 enshrinee into the U.S. Hockey Hall of Fame, has truly made a difference in the world of hockey.

Dave Peterson, a Minneapolis native, guided several U.S. National Junior Teams in International competition before taking over as the head coach of the both the 1988 & 1992 U. S. Olympic Teams.

Cloquet's Jamie Langenbrunner opted to play in the Canadien Major Juniors with the Ontario Hockey League's Peterborough Pete's back in 1993-94 before going on to star in the NHL.

opportunities for American kids was better than legislating and restricting against the Canadian game.

Today the state of junior hockey in Minnesota is a mixed bag. From what started with very humble beginnings in the '60s, has grown into an essential and vital component of American hockey today. While some of the USHL franchises are extremely popular and lucrative in places such as Omaha, where they are the only show in town, Minnesota is faced with a much more competitive hockey environment. The fans are more knowledgeable about the game here, and have a wide variety of hockey choices with which they can spend their time and money. The successful clubs have found new and innovative ways to provide their fans with a fresh and exciting means of sports entertainment. Nonetheless, the junior level is growing and giving more 17-20-year-old Minnesota kids new opportunities to play college and pro hockey every year.

For the coaches who work with these kids on a daily basis, the job is tough. With annual team turn-overs sometimes approaching 60-70 percent, for team's to be competitive year after year is an arduous task. But there are some coaching advantages.

"It's usually when a kid is humbled by the fact that he's not going to the U of M, or anywhere on scholarship, that they start looking at other programs," said former Mustang's skipper Kevin Constantine, on the art of coaching in the juniors. "That's why coaching juniors is so easy. The players have already been humbled, they didn't get a scholarship. They know they have shortcomings and are eager to work at them."

The numbers are staggering though, as to just how many opportunities the junior levels have provided for our kids. Thousands of players who have come through their ranks, kids who possibly would've given up on the game had there not been somewhere in between the high school and college levels to go, have gone on to get an education. Highlighting speed, skill, discipline and basic fundamentals, the USHL and MJHL are two of the top developmental leagues in the nation. Kids from all over the world transition from high school to college in these leagues, and are both huge assets to our hockey's past, and to its future.

THE NORTH AMERICAN HOCKEY LEAGUE (NAHL)

The North American Hockey League is a developmental Junior A league affiliated with USA Hockey. The NAHL was founded in 1975 when the Michigan and Wolverine Junior Leagues merged to form the Great Lakes Junior Hockey League, which was later renamed in 1984 to the North American Hockey League. Most games are scheduled on the weekends to allow the students to pursue their educations. Each team plays a 58-game regular season schedule which then culminates with the annual Robertson Cup Championship Tournament. There, the players gain a lot of visibility from the numerous collegiate and professional scouts and coaches from across North America who are in attendance. The oldest and largest Junior A hockey league in the U.S., the NAHL spans west to Alaska, east to Ohio, and south to Texas and New Mexico. The League currently has 17 franchises, three of which are based in Minnesota: the Alexandria Blizzard, Fargo-Moorhead Jets and Southern Minnesota Express, which is based out of Owatonna.

The Southern Minnesota Express are led by head coach Pat Cullen, an International Falls native who was an All-American at Bemidji State University and had previously served as the head coach at Hamline University for five years. Under his tutelage the Express finished their inaugural season (2006) as the NAHL Central Division Regular Season Champions, NAHL Division Playoff Champions, and finished third in the NAHL Robertson Cup National Tournament. In their 2007 campaign, the Express were the NAHL Central Division Regular Season Runner-up, NAHL Division Playoff Champions and again finished third in the NAHL Robertson Cup National Tournament.

The Alexandria Blizzard are led by head coach and general manager Brad Willner, a former assistant coach at both St. Cloud State University and Providence College. As a player, Willner played professionally with the Albany River Rats (AHL) and Raleigh Ice Caps (ECHL) in 1995-96, before suffering a career ending injury. Willner played collegiate hockey for Lake Superior State University, winning two NCAA Championships (1992, 1994) and three Central Collegiate Hockey League (CCHA) championships (1992, 1993, 1995). He also earned Academic All-American Honors in 1995. Willner played junior hockey for the St. Paul Vulcans, which won the Gold Cup in 1991 as well.

The Fargo Moorehead Jets are led by head coach Chad Johnson, whose prior head coaching accolades include stints with the Junior A AWHL Bismarck Bobcats from 2001-05, the Helena Ice Pirates from 1999-00, and the Minot Muskies from 2000-01. The Grand Forks, ND, native was a stand-out at the University of North Dakota from 1990-93 before going to play professionally with the Fort Worth Fire of the Central Hockey League, and Quad City (Moline, IL) and Muskegon (MI) of the Colonial Hockey League (now United Hockey League).

THE GOLD MEDAL-WINNING 1960 U.S. OLYMPIC TEAM

Twenty years before the now famous "Miracle on Ice" Olympic team of 1980, which brought home the gold in Lake Placid, N.Y., there was another team making history on the other coast of the country, in Squaw Valley, Calif. They were the underdog 1960 U.S. Olympic men's hockey team, and with the help of some eight Minnesotans, they upset some of the best teams in the world that February, to give America it's first taste of hockey gold.

The U.S. held its preliminary try-out camp at Williams Arena, on the U of M campus, under the guidance of the 1956 silver-medal winning Olympic Coach, John Mariucci. After finalizing the roster, the team spent several months playing exhibition games against teams from all over the world.

The Olympic tournament got underway with the Russians and the Canadians being the overwhelming favorites to bring home the gold. The Americans, on the other hand, were not even expected to get past the first couple of rounds. The U.S. came out swinging though, and thanks to five John Mayasich goals, they defeated Australia, 12-1, and Czechoslovakia, 7-5, to advance into the medal rounds. Then, after beating the favored Swedes, 6-3, behind Roger Christian's hat-trick and his brother Billy's three assists, they went on to beat Germany, 9-1, setting the stage for a showdown with the mighty Canadians. There, behind former Gopher Jack McCartan's 39 saves in net, the U.S. edged Team Canada by the final score of 2-1.

Warroad's Christian Brothers

Then, on February 27th, in front of some 10,000 spectators who had jammed into Blyth Arena, in addition to the millions who tuned in on TV at home, the U.S. team squared off against the Soviets. Now, this was the era of the Cold War, and there were political ramifications surrounding the game, making it all the more dramatic.

The game was back and forth, and featured a lot of quick skating and hard hitting. The game would go back and forth early. Down 2-1 in the second, Warroad's Billy Christian decided to take over. After scoring the game-tying goal late in the second, Billy teamed up with his two wing-mates, brother Roger, and Tommy Williams of Duluth, to beat Russian goalie Nikolai Puchkov on a break-away wrister at 14:59 of the third. McCartan stood on his head for the last couple of minutes and the U.S. held on to advance to the gold-medal game against the Czechs.

Duluth's Tommy Williams

The U.S., which had earlier beaten the Czechs, weren't going to take anything for granted. Despite the Americans being noticeably fatigued, they came out strong and found themselves tied at three apiece after the first period. The U.S. squad fell behind, 4-3, after two, but then, behind Roger Christian, roared back for what would prove to be one of the greatest third periods of Olympic history. Roger struck first at 5:50, followed by Harvard's Bill Cleary, who took a Mayasich pass to put the U.S. ahead, 5-4. From there, it was all red, white and blue. Roger added two more goals that final period, to give the U.S. a stunning 9-4 win, and their first Olympic gold medal. Roger Christian led Team USA in scoring with eight goals, while Mayasich added seven of his own. The big win would do wonders for the growth and advancement of American hockey.

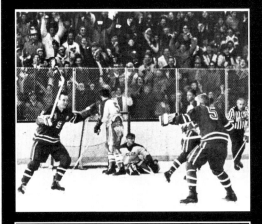
Roger Christian scoring against the Soviets...

THE MINNESOTA CONNECTION

Name	Hometown	College/Club
Roger Christian	Warroad	Warroad Lakers
William Christian	Warroad	Warroad Lakers
Paul Johnson	St. Paul	Rochester Mustangs
John Mayasich	Eveleth	Minnesota
Jack McCartan	St. Paul	Minnesota
Richard Meredith	Minneapolis	Minnesota
Robert Owen	St. Louis Park	Harvard
Tommy Williams	Duluth	Duluth Swans
James Claypool	Duluth	(Team Manager)

THE 1980 U.S. OLYMPIC HOCKEY "MIRACLE ON ICE"

The 1980 U.S. Olympic hockey team's gold medal run will forever remain etched in our memories as one of the greatest sporting achievements in American history. There have been numerous books written about the historic event, and it will forever remain as the team to which all others will have to measure up to. It put the sport, which at the time was perceived by many as merely a regional game found primarily in the North and East, into the national spotlight. Because of the icy miracle, the National Hockey League now has franchises in non-traditional hockey markets such as Florida, Texas, California, Arizona, Tennessee, Georgia and North Carolina. Looking back, it is still magical. To see the players throwing their sticks up into the crowd and crying to the chants of "USA! – USA!" while Al Michaels screams: *"Do you believe in miracles?...YES!"*, as they upset the heavily favored Soviets in the medal round, is arguably the greatest moment in the history of American sports.

A Dozen Home-Boys

The Americans, who, since the inception of the Winter Games, had won one gold medal (1960), four silver medals (1924, 1952, 1956 & 1972), and one bronze (1936), were eager to bring home some hardware to their native soil in 1980. Having finished fourth during the previous Olympics, in 1976, at Innsbruck, Austria, under Minnesota native and coach "Badger" Bob Johnson, the U.S. knew it would never have a better opportunity than the one they had in front of them in Lake Placid, N.Y.

The coach of that now fabled squad was Herb Brooks, who was no stranger to the USA Olympic hockey program. After being the last man cut from the gold medal team's roster in 1960, Brooks went on to play on the 1964 and 1968 Olympic teams, as well as on five other U.S. National Teams. Herbie, who had just finished leading the Golden Gophers to their third NCAA National Championship in 1979, would have the responsibility of selecting the 20 players to represent the United States. Brooks went with what he knew, local boys. While 12 of the 20 were native Minnesotans, nine of them were players whom Brooks had coached as Gophers, including: Roseau's Neal Broten, Grand Rapids' Bill Baker, White Bear Lake's Steve Janaszak, Rochester's Eric Strobel, Duluth's Phil Verchota, Minneapolis' Mike Ramsey, Babbitt's Buzz Schneider, St. Paul's Rob McClanahan and Richfield's Steve Christoff. The three other Minnesotans on the team were: Warroad's Dave Christian, who played at North Dakota, and Virginia's John Harrington and Eveleth's Mark Pavelich, both of whom played together at Minnesota-Duluth.

"Having played international hockey for so many years, it gives me an awfully warm feeling to be selected as head coach for the 1980 Olympics," Brooks said. "I'm extremely honored and humbled. To be picked when there are so many outstanding amateur hockey coaches in the nation, well, let's just say it's something I never really expected to happen."

In early September, the team began as challenging an exhibition schedule as had ever been organized for an American Olympic squad. Beginning with an initial European tour in early September, the team played a 61-game pre-Olympic schedule against foreign, college and professional teams, ultimately finishing with a 42-16-3 record. It was during this time together that the players were introduced to Brooks' new offensive game-plan called, the "weave." Brooks felt that if his club was going to compete against Europeans, they had better learn how to play like Europeans.

Entering the XIIIth Winter Olympic Games, the team was a decided underdog, an evaluation that seemed to be confirmed by a 10-3 defeat at the hands of the Soviets in the final exhibition game at Madison Square Garden in New York City. Though seeded seventh in the 12-nation pool, the Americans felt that they had something to prove. The Yanks took on Sweden in the opening game, as Bill Baker scored with 27 seconds remaining in the third period to give the U.S. a tough 2-2 tie. The goal acted as a catalyst for the young Americans, who then upset Czechoslovakia, and their amazing Stastny brothers, 7-3, thanks to goals from Pavelich, Schneider, Verchota and McClanahan. After beating both Norway and Rumania, now only West Germany (the team that knocked them out of the bronze medal in 1976), stood in the way of getting into the medal round.

Down 2-0 in the first, the Minnesota boys came through yet again as McClanahan and Broten each tallied to tie it up. McClanahan then scored again on another break-away in the third, while Phil Verchota lit the lamp late to give the U.S. a 4-2 win. This gave the Americans a round robin record of 4-0-1, and a date with the mighty Soviets – which were led by Vladislav Tretiak, the world's premier goaltender. The Soviets, which had just beaten the NHL All-Stars, 6-0, a few weeks earlier were the greatest hockey team ever assembled. They had outscored their opponents 51-11 through their first five games and were just another of a long line of dynasty teams which had won the last four Olympic golds, and five of the last six. In fact, the only team to beat them since 1956 was the U.S. squad, 20 years earlier in Squaw Valley.

Do You Believe in Miracles?...Yes!

The game had all the hype in the world, with political and social implications written all over it. The "Iron Range" line of Pavelich, Harrington and Schneider got the Americans on the board, when, down 1-0, Pavelich fed Schneider for a nice slap-shot which found the top corner. The Russians answered back three minutes later, only to see Mark Johnson tie it up with just seconds to go in the period on an open ice steal in front of the net. When they returned to the ice following the intermission, the U.S. team was shocked to see that Soviet coach Victor Tikhanov had replaced Tretiak in goal with backup keeper Vladimir Myshkin. While it would appear that the great bear was wounded, the Soviets came back to take the lead, having now out-shot the Yanks 30-10 through two periods. Johnson got his second of the game at 8:39 of the third to tie it at 3-3, setting up the heroics for the Iron Rangers.

Midway through the third, Schneider dumped the puck into the Russian zone and Harrington dug it out to his old UMD wingmate, Mark Pavelich. Pavelich then floated a perfect pass to the top of the circle, where team captain Mike Eruzione fired home "the shot heard 'round the world." The final 10 minutes of the game were probably the longest in U.S. hockey history, but the Americans held on as goalie Jim Craig played brilliantly down the stretch. Then, as the crowd counted down the final seconds, Al Michaels screamed "Do you believe in miracles,...Yes!" The Americans had made it into the gold medal game.

As the players went nuts on the ice, Herbie, ever the psychologist, quickly put his team back in their place. The next day at practice, Brooks put the team through a grueling workout, constantly reinforcing to them that they still had one game to go before they could celebrate. He wasn't their friend, he was their coach — and he demanded excellence from them.

Neal Broten

This was part of his ingenious master plan, to get the players to despise him, and force them to rally together. The rival Minnesota and East Coast kids now had a common goal to work towards.

In the final game the U.S. faced Finland, which had beaten the Czechs in the other semifinal. Down 1-0 in the second, Steve Christoff got the Americans on the board at 4:39 with a nice wrister down low. The Fins regained the lead, however, and went into the third up 2-1. After an emotional speech between the intermission from Brooks, reminding his players ever so eloquently that they would regret this moment for the rest of their collective lives if they let it slip away, the U.S. came out inspired and made history.

The hero this time would prove to be Phil Verchota, who took a Dave Christian pass in the left circle and found the back of the net at 2:25. With that, the Americans started to smell blood and immediately went for the jugular. Just three minutes later, Robbie McClanahan went five-hole with a Mark Johnson pass to give the U.S. a 3-2 lead. Johnson then added a short-handed back-hander just a few minutes later to give the U.S. a two-goal cushion. Jim Craig then hung on for the final few minutes of the game as Al Michaels this time screamed: *"This impossible dream, comes true!"* It was utter pandemonium in Lake Placid as the team threw their sticks into the crowd and piled on top of each other at center ice to the chants of "USA! — USA!"

Many of the players were visibly moved by what they had done, as evidenced during the singing of the National Anthem, where the entire team gathered on the top podium. Still wringing wet with their jersey's on, goaltender Jim Craig with an American Flag draped around him, they sang the Star-Spangled Banner. The country went crazy with a newly found sense of national pride. Sports Illustrated named the team, collectively as "Sportsmen of the Year," Life Magazine declared it as the "Sports Achievement of the Decade," and ABC Sports announcer, Jim McCay, went on to call the amazing achievement, "The greatest upset in the history of sports."

The Aftermath

A grateful nation, depressed by the Iranian hostage crisis, the Soviet invasion of Afghanistan, and mired in an economic recession, hailed the team as heroes. A visit to the White House followed, as well as appearances to cities across the land. The Wheaties box, magazine covers, awards, honors, speaking engagements and a whole lot of hoopla would follow for all the players.

The icy miracle was achieved by enormous ambition coupled with great passing, checking, speed, and sound puck-control. Shrewdly, Brooks refused to play the typical dump-and-chase style of hockey that was so prevalent in American hockey.

"I didn't want the team throwing the puck away with no reason," said Brooks. "That's stupid. It's the same as punting on first down. The style I wanted combined the determined checking of the North American game and the best features of the (faster, more wide open) European game."

"They were really mentally tough and goal-oriented," added Brooks of his team. "They came from all different walks of life, many having competed against one another, but they came together and grew to be a real close team. I pushed this team really hard, I mean I really pushed them. But they had the ability to answer the bell. Our style of play was probably different than anything in North America. We adopted more of a hybrid style of play — a bit of the Canadian school and a little bit of the European school. The players took to it like ducks to water, and they really had a lot of fun playing it. We were a fast, creative team that played extremely disciplined without the puck. Throughout the Olympics, they had a great resiliency about them. I mean they came from behind six different times to win. They just kept on moving and working and digging. I think we were as good a conditioned team as there was in the world, outside maybe the Soviet Union. We got hot and lucky at the right times, and it was just an incredible experience for all of us."

The Disney Movie "Miracle," which starred Kurt Russell as Brooks, came out just a few months after the coach's tragic death in the Summer of 2003 — educating an entirely new generation of kids about the fabled team as well as its inspirational legacy.

THE MINNESOTA CONNECTION

Name	Hometown	College
Bill Baker	Grand Rapids	Minnesota
Neal Broten	Roseau	Minnesota
Dave Christian	Warroad	North Dakota
Steve Christoff	Richfield	Minnesota
John Harrington	Virginia	UM-Duluth
Steve Janaszak	White Bear Lake	Minnesota
Mark Johnson	Minneapolis	Wisconsin
Rob McClanahan	St. Paul	Minnesota
Mark Pavelich	Eveleth	UM-Duluth
Mike Ramsey	Minneapolis	Minnesota
Buzz Schneider	Babbitt	Minnesota
Eric Strobel	Rochester	Minnesota
Phil Verchota	Duluth	Minnesota
Herb Brooks	St. Paul	Head Coach
Ralph Jasinski	Mounds View	Manager
Warren Strelow	Mahtomedi	Goalie Coach
Dr. V.G. Nagobads	Edina	Physician
Gary Smith	Minneapolis	Trainer
Bud Kessel	St. Paul	Equip. Mgr.

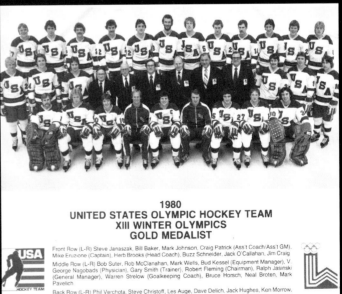

1980
UNITED STATES OLYMPIC HOCKEY TEAM
XIII WINTER OLYMPICS
GOLD MEDALIST

Front Row (L-R) Steve Janaszak, Bill Baker, Mark Johnson, Craig Patrick (Ass't Coach/Ass't GM), Mike Eruzione (Captain), Herb Brooks (Head Coach), Buzz Schneider, Jack O'Callahan, Jim Craig

Middle Row (L-R) Bob Suter, Rob McClanahan, Mark Wells, Bud Kessel (Equipment Manager), V. George Nagobads (Physician), Gary Smith (Trainer), Robert Fleming (Chairman), Ralph Jasinski (General Manager), Warren Strelow (Goalkeeping Coach), Bruce Horsch, Neal Broten, Mark Pavelich

Back Row (L-R) Phil Verchota, Steve Christoff, Les Auge, Dave Delich, Jack Hughes, Ken Morrow, Mike Ramsey, Dave Christian, Ralph Cox, Dave Silk, John Harrington, Eric Strobel

IN-LINE HOCKEY IN MINNESOTA

Early roller polo from the late 1800s...

Roller skating has had a long and storied history in America with roots that can be traced back for centuries. The four-wheeled version (quads: two in front and two in back) had been the mainstay prior the creation of in-line skates in the late 1970s. The design for four straight wheels (in a line) actually goes back much further though. In fact, the first record of in-line skates actually dates back to the early 1700s, when a Dutchman attempted to simulate ice skating on a road by fastening wooden spools to strips of wood which he attached to the bottom of his boots.

By the mid-1800s, an American inventor had developed the first "conventional" roller skates, with wheels arranged side by side. Soon, the sport of ice polo had evolved into roller polo, a short-lived fad that hung around until the early 1900s. So popular was roller polo, that in 1885, Minneapolis alone possessed 14 indoor roller polo rinks. Leagues soon sprang up throughout the East Coast as well as in the Midwest, with teams traveling by train to compete. As ice polo transformed into ice hockey, so too did roller polo emerge into roller hockey, just after the turn of the century. Ice hockey's modern ancestor was nothing like roller hockey as we know it today, but nonetheless, it gave hockey players something to do when there was no ice. Roller skating however, soon became a slice of American pop culture that had it all — exercise, entertainment and even romance. That's right, when the roller polo craze died off in the early 1900s, roller rinks became the ultimate cheap date.

In 1937 the Roller Skating Rink Operators Association created the United States Amateur Confederation of Roller Skating, in Detroit. By the late 1960s the organization began facilitating some of the country's first roller hockey tournaments. The game was still clumsy, due to the fact that the skates wouldn't permit the skater to maneuver very well. Unlike ice skates, roller skates were heavy, and awkward to try to play hockey in — not to mention the adventure of trying to stop in them without eating some pavement.

Still, kids in places such as Minnesota, New England and Canada, played many a game on the old tennis court with "quad" roller skates. (One of the hot-spots for organized "quad" roller hockey in the late '70s was in New York City, where the Fort Hamilton (Broooklyn) Roller Hockey League was producing such future NHL stars as Joey and Brian Mullen.) It was painful, but hey, it was hockey in the summertime. Then, somebody got smart and invented a training tool for hockey players and Nordic skiers alike, in what we now know as in-line skates. They were heavy, clunky and ugly — but they finally let hockey players train in the off-season with a product that would actually let them simulate a true skating motion.

The genius behind those first contraptions was Scott Olson, who can be considered as the pioneer of in-line skates. The genesis of in-line skates began in 1979, when Olson, a former St. Louis Park High School hockey star in the late 1970s, saw a pair of those first in-line skates while rummaging through a sporting goods store. Immediately seeing the potential as a valuable tool for hockey players who couldn't get ice time during the summer, he contacted the manufacturer of those skates (which were really just a set of wheels on a chassis — the buyer had to then rivet them onto a pair of old hockey boots), a California-based start-up company called Super Sport Skate Co., which marketed the product under the name of Ultimate Street Skates. Olson then became the company's Midwest franchisee of sorts, distributing the devises under his own company name called, "Super Street Skates." He then began selling the products on a grass-roots level out of his house and car.

Two years later, after deciding to manufacture his own skates designed specifically for hockey players, Olson launched his own in-line skate business out of his parents basement called "Ole's Innovative Sport Systems." Inspired by a 1966 Chicago Roller Skate Company in-line skate design patent intended to simulate ice skates, Olson set out to create a product that was maneuverable, light-weight and affordable for kids and adults everywhere. He started out by going around to sport shops such as Penn Cycle, in Bloomington, and buying pairs of molded boot skates (like the old Langs). He would then remove the steel blades, sell them as scrap iron, and use the boots to attach his blades to. He then decided to call his new, improved in-line creation, "Rollerblades."

Rollerblades became an instant hit with hockey players around the state, and soon Olson hired his brother, Brennan, to begin mass-producing "blades" in their new Edina office. Now, at the time, they were buying roller skate wheels from a small company called Kryptonic and taking them to the machine shop, where they were then shaved in half, to make an in-line sized wheel. Capitalizing on the fact that most every hockey player had an old pair of skates laying around in the basement (which could be easily converted into Rollerblades), the $35 cost was nothing when compared to buying a new pair of skates, which were hundreds of dollars. After a while, kids everywhere were bringing in their old skate boots to have a new set of blades attached, and for $15,

Minnesota hockey's first-family, the Naegele's: Bob Jr. & Bob III

they could keep rotating back and forth between in-line and ice hockey blades every other season. Parents really liked that idea too.

Soon, Olson wanted to construct the complete skate, boot and blade, together as one. So, he packed up and went to Italy, home of the world's premier plastic ski boot manufacturers, to design custom molded boots for his Rollerblades. By the early 1980s, the bike paths at Lake Calhoun were bustling with in-line skaters, and parking lots around the state were being transformed into pick-up hockey rinks during the summer. (Ironically, 3M couldn't figure out why it was suddenly selling a ton of electrical tape in the area, until they realized that the kids were using the rolls of tape as pucks.)

Before long the Olson's were assembling and selling Rollerblades across the country. As part of Olson's vision to market the products, he ventured to New York City, to play some pick-up games against those kids from Brooklyn who were using the old quad skates. There, the kids compared in-line skates versus the old-fashioned quad skates, and before long kids everywhere could be seen playing roller hockey and blading around the East Coast on Olson's Rollerblades. Business grew in the early '80s, but the market was underdeveloped and limited geographically. With some 25 employees and extremely limited resources, the company needed capital to expand and go big-time. It was at that time that Olson made the decision to sell his company to outdoor advertising magnate Bob Naegele Jr. (Naegele later led the ownership group to buy the Minnesota Wild NHL franchise.)

"Looking back, it was a dream come true to be able to start the craze that got it all going," said Olson. "Being a hockey nut, I was just happy to have brought a new hockey training tool to the people of Minnesota. Besides being able to cruise around as a means of transportation, to be able to play hockey during the off-season was awesome. It all happened so quickly from there, and I had no idea that it would lead to where it has gone today. It's been great to see so many kids having fun and being able to play and learn the game, and I am really honored to have played a part in that. In retrospect, I think Rollerblade really helped to advance the sport of hockey in America."

In 1985 Bob Naegele Jr. purchased Ole's Innovative Sport Systems, renamed it as Rollerblade, Inc., and supplied the leadership and resources necessary to take the company to the next level. Rollerblade was now not only a noun, but also a verb. "Blading" became all the rage throughout the country, making Rollerblade the undisputed leader of in-line skates and protective equipment. From the company's Minnetonka headquarters, he implemented a strategic marketing effort to position in-line skating as a new sport. His ideas, such as giving skates to rental shops along trendy Venice Beach, became a big success.

(Incidentally, after selling his company, Olson then started a new in-line skate company which manufactured interchangeable in-line-hockey skates called "Switchits." The skates, which could be converted from in-line skates to ice hockey skates with the flip of a switch, proved to be a huge hit. Then, after selling that company in 1992, Olson invented a new work-out contraption called the "RowBike" — which is an amalgam between a rowing machine and a bicycle on wheels.)

Meanwhile, Rollerblade's first big hit was the "Lightning," the skate that really got it all started. Soon Rollerblade was innovating such things as polyurethane boots and wheels, metal frames, dual bearings and heel brakes. For the next decade Naegele served as the chairman of Rollerblade Inc., repositioning the brand and fueling the explosive growth of in-line skating worldwide.

In the late '80s, in-line skating was dubbed as the sport of the '90s by the New York Times and Forbes magazine. One of the biggest boosts to the sport came in 1988, when Wayne Gretzky was traded from Edmonton to the Los Angeles Kings. Southern California instantly went hockey crazy, and Rollerblade was there to lead the way. From there, in-line skating spread like wildfire to warm-weather climates throughout the world. Soon Rollerblade owned an estimated 75 percent of the marketshare, as the business continued to grow like no other fad in history. In addition to roller-hockey, in-line racing, stunt competitions, marathons and good old fashioned exercise, the sport had evolved into a simple and efficient means of transportation. People everywhere could now be seen "blading" to work in suits and ties.

Rollerblade also really got involved at a grass-roots level in promoting the sports of in-line skating, roller hockey and extreme skating (a la the X Games). They even sponsored one of the first in-line tournaments with teams from across the US, Canada and Europe, called the World Roller Hockey Championships, which were held at St. Paul's Aldrich Arena in the late '80s.

Minnesota soon became the Mecca for in-line skates. In addition to Rollerblade, First Team Sports (Ultra Wheels) and Riedell — both Minnesota based company's, got into the action. (Riedell has manufactured skates of all sorts at its Red Wing plant for more than 60 years.) In the mid 1990s, according to the National Sporting Goods Association, in-line skating was the fastest growing sport in the U.S. and the world, rising at nearly a 50 percent annual growth rate. It was now a billion dollar industry as nearly 500 million pairs of in-line skates had been sold throughout the globe by 1995. In-line hockey was booming and people couldn't get enough of it.

By 1993 two professional leagues had emerged: Roller Hockey International (RHI) and the World Roller Hockey league (WRHL). While the WRHL was a TV-only league, the RHI hit the pavement with a dozen teams located mostly in warm-weather markets around the country. After a year, the two leagues merged under the name RHI. (This was nothing new to RHI owner Dennis Murphy, who also founded the upstart WHA and ABA.) The new and improved league featured 24 teams, and among them was the Minnesota Arctic Blast. The Blast entered the league in 1994, and played at the Target Center. Although they won the conference title that first year, the franchise folded after that first season. (The Arctic Blast came back in 1996, won their conference title, and promptly folded yet again after that season.) So did most of the others as well. By 1997 there were just 12 teams remaining, with no television deal to boot. Another pro team entered the mix in 1995, the Minnesota Blue Ox, which played their games at Aldrich Arena as well. They, too, folded after a season, but were reincarnated in 1998.

That season the Ox were led by several Minnesotans, including St. Cloud's Cory Laylin, Roseau's Billy Lund, Richfield's Dave Shute, Bloomington's Joe Bianchi, Edina's Charlie Wasley, Cottage Grove's Jay Moser, Wayzata's Brady Alstead, Inver Grove Heights' Eric Rud, Birchdale's Chris Imes, and Eagan's John Hanson, among others. The team, which played their games in the new Mariucci Arena, was coached by Minnetonka native Steve Martinson.

The game continued to grow, with new leagues of all ages, genders and abilities popping up around the world. The game needed some direction, and in 1994 it got it when Bob Naegele III, son of Rollerblade owner Bob Naegele Jr., and himself a college goalie at Brown University, formed the National In-line Hockey Association (NIHA). In addition to promoting and providing organization for the sport, NIHA also sponsored several major tournaments around the country, including the NIHA National Championship in Las Vegas. At about the same time, USA Hockey had created a program called USA Hockey In-line, which also aimed to provide structure, stability and administration to the game at the grass-roots level. USA Hockey later acquired NIHA to become the sole governing body of in-line hockey in America.

In addition to founding NIHA, Naegele also started another hockey business called In-line Sport Systems, which designed an innovative new rink product — Border Patrol. Border Patrol defined a new category, portable hockey rinks. Today the Minnesota-based company, renamed as Athletica, designs, manufactures and ships rinks all over the world so that people can play roller hockey comfortably and safely outdoors. In 1995 the Naegele family sold Rollerblade to Benneton, the famous Italian clothing manufacturer. That next year they purchased a small start-up roller hockey company based in Orange County, Calif., called Mission. Today, Mission produces some of the best hockey and in-line skates, as well as protective equipment, in the world. As for Mr. Naegele, he remains the principle owner of the NHL's Minnesota Wild, where he continues to make Minnesota proud.

All-Time State Tourney Appearances
Class AA/Tier I Single-Class (1945-2007)

Team	No.	1st	2nd	3rd	Cons
Alexander Ramsey	6	0	1	0	1
Alexandria	1	0	0	0	1
Anoka	5	1	1	1	1
Apple Valley	4	1	0	0	1
Austin	2	0	0	0	0
Bemidji	6	0	1	0	1
Blaine	6	1	0	2	1
Bloomington	3	0	1	0	0
Bloom Jefferson	16	5	0	3	1
Bloom Kennedy	7	1	1	0	1
Bloom Lincoln	1	0	0	0	0
Burnsville	8	3	1	1	0
Centennial	1	1	0	0	0
Champlin Park	1	0	0	0	0
Cloquet	4	0	0	0	2
Columbia Heights	1	0	0	0	0
Cretin-Derham Hall	2	1	0	0	0
Duluth Central	1	0	0	0	0
Duluth Denfeld	3	0	0	2	1
Duluth East	15	3	3	5	1
Eagan	1	0	0	0	0
East Grand Forks	3	0	0	0	0
Eastview	1	0	0	0	1
Eden Prairie	4	0	0	0	0
Edina	23	6	2	1	6
Edina East	5	3	1	0	0
Edina West	1	0	0	0	0
Elk River	6	1	0	1	1
Eveleth	13	5	2	4	0
Grand Rapids	14	3	5	2	2
Granite Falls	2	0	0	0	0
Greenway	8	2	0	2	2
Hallock	2	0	0	0	0
Hastings	6	0	1	1	1
Henry Sibley	7	0	0	1	0
Hibbing	9	2	0	4	2
Hill-Murray	21	2	6	2	2
Holy Angels	5	2	0	1	1
Hopkins Lindbergh	2	0	0	0	0
International Falls	16	6	2	4	0
Irondale	3	0	1	0	1
Kellogg	1	0	0	0	0
Lakeville North	1	0	0	0	0
Mariner	1	0	1	0	0
Minnetonka	4	0	0	1	1
Moorhead	10	0	6	2	0
Mounds View	5	0	0	0	0
Mpls Central	2	0	0	0	0
Mpls Henry	3	0	0	2	0
Mpls Roosevelt	8	0	0	0	1
Mpls South	4	0	0	1	0
Mpls Southwest	15	1	2	2	1
Mpls Washburn	6	0	1	0	2
Mpls West	2	0	0	0	0
North St Paul	4	0	0	0	1
Osseo	1	0	0	0	0
Owatonna	1	0	0	0	0
Park Center	1	0	0	0	0
Richfield	6	0	1	0	2
Robbinsdale	1	0	0	0	0
Rochester	4	0	1	0	0
Rochester Century	2	0	0	1	0
Rochester John Marshall	6	1	2	0	0
Rochester Mayo	7	0	0	0	0
Roseau	31	7	5	3	5
Roseville	3	0	1	1	0
South St Paul	27	0	2	6	2
Staples	1	0	0	0	0
St Cloud Apollo	1	0	0	0	0
St Cloud Tech	4	0	0	1	0
St Louis Park	4	0	0	0	0
St Paul Harding	8	0	1	0	2
St Paul Humboldt	2	0	0	0	1
St Paul Johnson	22	4	3	3	2
St Paul Monroe	1	0	0	0	0
St Paul Murray	6	0	0	0	2
St Paul Washington	3	0	1	1	0
Tartan	2	0	0	0	0
Thief River Falls	9	2	1	1	3
Warroad	9	0	3	1	0
Wayzata	2	0	0	0	0
White Bear Lake	17	0	0	0	5
Williams	3	0	2	0	0
Willmar	1	0	0	0	0
Winona	1	0	0	0	0
Woodbury	1	0	0	0	0

Source: http://www.minnhock.com/state-tournament-2000.htm

All-Time State Tourney Appearances
Class A/Tier II Dual-Class (1992-2007)

Team	No.	1st	2nd	3rd
Albert Lea	3	0	0	0
Alexandria	1	0	0	0
Benilde-St. Margaret's	2	2	0	0
Blake	4	0	0	0
Breck	5	2	0	1
Cambridge	1	0	0	0
Chisago Lakes	1	0	0	0
Detroit Lakes	2	0	0	0
Duluth Central	1	0	0	0
Duluth Marshall	4	0	2	1
East Grand Forks	4	0	1	0
Eveleth	2	2	0	0
Faribault	1	0	0	0
Farmington	2	0	0	0
Fergus Falls	7	0	0	1
Greenway	1	1	0	0
Henry Sibley	1	0	0	1
Hermantown	6	1	1	2
Hibbing	3	0	1	1
Hutchinson	3	0	0	0
International Falls	3	1	0	1
Lake Of The Woods	1	0	1	0
Litchfield	1	0	0	0
Little Falls	3	0	0	0
Mahtomedi	5	0	0	1
Mankato East	1	0	0	0
Mora	2	0	0	0
Mound-Westonka	2	0	0	0
Mpls Edison	1	0	0	0
Mpls Roosevelt	1	0	0	0
Mpls South	1	0	0	0
New Ulm	1	0	0	0
Orono	7	0	1	2
Princeton	2	0	0	0
Proctor	1	0	0	1
Red Wing	6	1	2	1
Rochester Lourdes	4	0	1	1
Rosemount	1	0	1	0
Sauk Rapids	1	0	0	0
Shakopee	1	0	0	0
Silver Bay	1	0	0	0
Simley	2	0	1	0
South St Paul	1	0	0	0
St Cloud Cathedral	3	0	0	0
St Louis Park	2	0	0	0
St Thomas Academy	4	1	0	1
Thief River Falls	1	0	0	0
Totino Grace	4	1	2	0
Wadena	1	0	0	0
Warroad	9	4	2	1

Source: http://www.minnhock.com/state-tournament-2000.htm

HIGH SCHOOL HOCKEY IN MINNESOTA

Simply known as the "Tourney," the Minnesota State High School Hockey Tournament is, in a word, amazing. In what has evolved into the largest high school sporting event in the country, it can also be compared on many levels to that of the Indiana Boys' Basketball Tournament and the Texas State Football Championship, in terms of popularity, attendance, revenues, community support, pride, and world-wide mystique. To play in the spectacle known simply as "March Madness," is probably the single greatest highlight of any young boy or girl's athletic life. And, with college and professional hockey futures hanging in the balance, it has evolved into a proving ground of sorts which can make-or-break young careers.

Although the State High School Tournament officially began in 1945, a lot of people don't realize that high school hockey in Minnesota goes back much, much further than that. The tradition and history that have made those three wonderful days in March so special today, has actually been a work in progress for more than a century. Its genesis from rovers — to red lines — to Cooperalls, is a journey that starts from its humble beginnings at the old St. Paul Auditorium. From there, it went to the Met Center, then back to the Civic Center, followed by a two-year hiatus at the Target Center, and lastly to its final resting place at the Xcel Energy Center in St Paul. The pinnacle of amateur hockey achievement in our state, the Tournament, in all of its glory, has become synonymous with Minnesota.

High school hockey's roots in Minnesota can be traced all the way back to the late 1890s, around the same time that the sport of hockey evolved from the game of ice polo. By then hockey had spread up from the Twin Cities, and also down by rail from Manitoba, to communities such as: Warroad, Roseau, Warren, Hallock, Argyle, Stephen, Thief River Falls, Crookston, Baudette, Eveleth and Duluth. As the sport grew in popularity throughout the state, industrial sponsored men's leagues began to emerge. With that, more and more rinks started to be constructed, spreading the game's popularity even further throughout the youth levels.

The first high schools to form varsity teams in Minnesota were St. Paul Mechanic Arts, St. Paul Central, St. Paul Academy, Minneapolis North, Minneapolis Central, Minneapolis East and Minneapolis West. By as early as 1899, in addition to playing one another, the high school squads played against several local men's senior league teams including, the St. Paul Hockey Club, St. Paul Athletic Club, Minneapolis Hockey Club, Mic Macs, Victorias, Laurels, and Chinooks, as well as the University of Minnesota, St. Thomas and Luther College. By 1900 two of the schools, St. Paul Central and St. Paul Mechanic Arts, were playing in a newly formed four-team men's senior amateur circuit along with the St. Paul and Minneapolis Hockey Club's, called the "Twin City Senior Hockey League." Many of the games were played in Minneapolis' first indoor

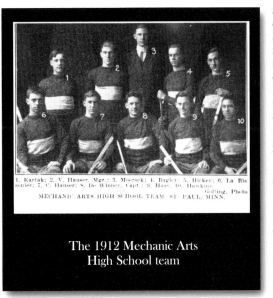

The 1912 Mechanic Arts
High School team

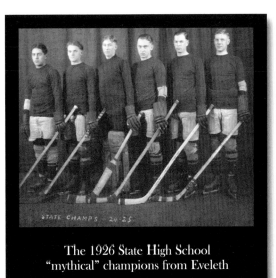

The 1926 State High School
"mythical" champions from Eveleth

arena, the old "Star Roller Rink" (located on 4th Avenue South and 11th Street), which had been retrofitted with natural ice for hockey that year. That next season of 1901-1902, the league expanded to six teams by adding the St. Paul Virginia's and St. Paul Mascots. To make it official, then world famous curler, Robert H. Dunbar, presented a silver cup to the league which was to be awarded annually to its champion. The Virginias went on to win the inaugural Dunbar Cup during that first season, while in 1903, the University of Minnesota, which had since joined the league, defeated both Minneapolis Central High School and the St. Paul Virginias on a frozen Como Lake in St. Paul to take the Cup. (The star of that Central team was a kid by the name of Bobby Marshall. Marshall, one of the first African Americans ever to play the game, would go on to star as an All-American Defensive End on the Gopher football team.)

That same year, several of the high school teams competed in the first-ever "Mythical" State Amateur Championship, which featured teams from St. Paul, Minneapolis, Duluth and Two Harbors. Soon, to meet all of the demand, another roller rink (located at Washington and Broadway Avenue North), was outfitted with natural ice. Electric lights were even installed on the 150' x 50' ice surface, so that the high school and senior teams could play all night long. In 1905 the Minneapolis Amateur Hockey Association constructed an outdoor hockey rink (located at the corners of Lake Street and Girard Avenue South), which featured not only a large warming house but also long bleachers for the large crowds. Before long high schoolers from around the Twin Cities were rooting against one-another at this new fan-friendly venue.

Hockey continued to flourish throughout the prep ranks of the state through the first decade of the new century. In 1908 Warroad and Roseau began their high school hockey rivalry, and in 1909 the St. Paul Public High School Championships were held for the first time. Mechanic Arts won the first three years, only to see Central win it from 1912-1914. (The two schools would share the crown exclusively on and off until 1933.) By 1914 the Minneapolis High School Hockey Conference (which included East, West, Central and North), as well as the St. Paul City Conference (which included Mechanic Arts, Central, Humboldt and Johnson), were up and running smoothly with teams maintaining their own outdoor rinks. Minneapolis West, coached by W.W. Bradley, dominated the Minneapolis High School Conference early on, winning 14 championships from 1908-1932. (During the late 1920's and early 1930s, the dominant West High School was led by Phil Perkins, Jack Flood, Laurie Parker, Burr Williams, Earl Barthelome and Manny Cotlow, who all amazingly went on to play professional hockey.) West's close proximity to the "lakes," combined with

The 1928 Virginia High School squad played a tough schedule against many of the area's local senior teams their nearness to the Minneapolis Arena proved to be factors in their early success. When the St. Paul champion met their Minneapolis counterparts for the Twin Cities Championship, the contests usually took place in front of large crowds at both the Hippodrome (on the State Fairgrounds in St. Paul), and also at the Coliseum (located on Lexington Avenue near University Avenue). Some of the really big games were held at the Minneapolis Arena, which had the advantage of having artificial ice - a real rarity back then.

The feeder programs for the high school kids were also growing. Countless youngsters who wanted to someday play for their hometown teams were taking up the game. Juvenile teams sprouted up, as well as organized youth leagues. In 1919 the first national youth hockey tournament for boys under high school age was sponsored by the Amateur Hockey Association of the United States (AHAUS).

As the decade of the 1920s began to unfold, the metro teams, tired of beating up on each other, began playing the northern teams more frequently. One of the first big games between the "North & South" took place in 1922, when St. Paul Central defeated Duluth Central, 5-3, in Duluth. On March 19, 1923, Eveleth beat Mechanic Arts, 9-2, in Eveleth, for what was billed as the second-coming of the State "Mythical" Championship — an event that hadn't taken place in some 20 years. The two teams then met again at the Minneapolis Arena on March 14, 1925, where Eveleth won again, 3-2. Although the games were unofficial state championship games, they nonetheless proved that there had been a shift of power in the game of hockey in Minnesota. The North had made a statement that they wanted some respect, and in time, they would be heard loudly.

No actual statewide amateur tournament was held until 1926, when the Minnesota Recreation Association conducted the first of several yearly tournaments in Hibbing. Later, the Minneapolis Park Board and the Minneapolis Arena held yearly tournaments at the Minneapolis Arena. That same year the Northeastern Minnesota High School League was formed with teams from Duluth (Central and Cathedral) and the Iron Range cities. Duluth, Eveleth, Virginia, Hibbing and Chisholm all had enclosed rinks during this era, which put them on an equal playing field with the metro schools. (Two Harbors, Cloquet and Buhl were also fielding competitive high school teams at the time as well.) But, when you factor in the fact that it was much colder that far up north from the Twin Cities, the northern schools probably got an extra month or so of valuable ice-time over the metro schools. In addition, many of the teams played in the Senior City League, which included high school and college players from local senior teams in Northeastern Minnesota.

As the sport branched out across the state, it also started to catch on in the suburbs. In 1925 natural ice was installed in the Hippodrome Arena at the Ramsey County

MR. HOCKEY MINNESOTA

Year	Player	High School	College
1985	Tom Chorske	Southwest	Minnesota
1986	George Pelawa	Bemidji	(Killed in auto accident)
1987	Kris Miller	Greenway	UMD
1988	Larry Olimb	Warroad	Minnesota
1989	Trent Klatt	Osseo	Minnesota
1990	Joe Dziedzic	Edison	Minnesota
1991	Darby Hendrickson	Richfield	Minnesota
1992	Brian Bonin	White Bear Lake	Minnesota
1993	Nick Checko	Bloom. Jeff.	Minnesota
1994	Mike Crowley	Bloom. Jeff.	Minnesota
1995	Erik Rasmussen	St. Louis Park	Minnesota
1996	Dave Spehar	Duluth East	Minnesota
1997	Aaron Miskovich	Grand Rapids	Minnesota
1998	Johnny Pohl	Red Wing	Minnesota
1999	Jeff Taffe	Hastings	Minnesota
2000	Paul Martin	Elk River	Minnesota
2001	Marty Sertich	Roseville	Colorado Coll.
2002	Gino Guyer	Coleraine	Minnesota
2003	Nate Dey	North St. Paul	St. Cloud
2004	Tom Gorowsky	Centennial	Wisconsin
2005	Brian Lee	Moorhead	UND
2006	David Fischer	Apple Valley	Minnesota
2007	Ryan McDonagh	Cretin	Wisconsin

Fairgrounds in White Bear Lake. (Incredibly, this was the only Twin Cities suburb to possess an indoor facility for the next 25 years.) White Bear Lake High School formed a varsity hockey team at that same time, thus becoming the first Twin Cities suburb to have a high school team. The Bears, who were led by future Gopher coach and NHL star Doc Romnes, played against the public schools of both Minneapolis and St. Paul, as well as the private schools of Cretin, St. Paul Academy and St. Thomas Academy.

In 1929 former St. Paul Athletic Club star, Nick Kahler, assembled a High School All-Star team called the Cardinals. The team, which played older, Senior teams, went on to win the Minneapolis Recreation League title that year. Members of the teams, most of whom were from South and West High Schools, included: Phil Perkins, Bill Oddson, Bubs Hutchinson, Red Malsed, Harry Melberg, John Scanlon, Evy Scotvold, Kelly Ness, Bill Cooley, Mack Xerxa and Bill Munns. One of the team's biggest games that year came against Eveleth High School. In a contest played at the Minneapolis Arena, the Cardinals edged Eveleth, which had not been defeated in the past three seasons of competition against Iron Range and Duluth schools, by the score of 2-1. An idea of the caliber of players that these teams possessed can be gathered from the fact that five of the 11 Minneapolis players and six of the 11 Eveleth skaters later played hockey professionally.

By the end of the decade hockey was sponsored by approximately 25 high schools in Minnesota. While most of the schools were both in the northeastern part of the state and in the Twin Cities area, high school hockey was slowly expanding. The 1930s, however, were a difficult time in America and Minnesota was no exception. While many public schools in the state were forced to drop their hockey programs during the Great Depression, due to financial hardship, other communities embraced the high school game as an inexpensive form of live entertainment. In addition, in many of the small towns during this era, where economies were more isolated and insulated from the rest of the world, the game flourished. Among the areas where high school hockey began to take off was northwestern Minnesota, where communities such as Roseau, Warroad, Thief River Falls, Hallock, Williams, Baudette, Crosby, Crookston, and even Detroit Lakes had begun building enclosed rinks. (Some of the schools, including Roseau and Hallock, used to also play the University of North Dakota, as well as in Senior leagues on a regular basis.)

High school hockey was finally taken off life support in the late 1930s, but went back on hiatus during the time surrounding WWII in the early 1940s. Here is how some of the local teams fared during this era: Cretin, led by John Quesnell, Doc Reardon, Bobby Dill, Bill Galligan, Bob Pates and Jim Mooney, posted a 45-10-2 record from 1936-39. In 1939 Humboldt, led by Bob Meyers, Joe Guertin,

GENE ALDRICH

Gene Aldrich (the namesake for whom Aldrich Arena on White Bear Avenue in St. Paul is named), was truly a pioneer, and someone to whom we should give sincere thanks. His dedication to young people and his belief that playing sports was something for all to enjoy, led him to try to innovate new ways of making athletics a great experience for everyone. In addition to working to keep ticket prices low so students could always attend sporting events, it was Aldrich who also suggested that cheerleaders and ice pageant shows perform skating routines between periods, and that high school bands should be in the stands rooting for their teams.

188

Elmer Monge and goalie Ray Gipple, winners of the St. Paul Public School title, defeated Minneapolis Marshall, winners of the Minneapolis City League title, before 2,600 fans at the St. Paul Auditorium by the score of 3-2 to win the Twin Cities Championship. Washington, under coach Frank Bergup, and led by Hal Younghans, Bob Graiziger, George Path and Joe Borsch, won back-to-back St. Paul City titles in 1939 and 1940 with a combined 25-1-5 record. Blake, which was coached by former Princeton goalie John Savage, and led by Jock and Tel Thompson, Bert Martin, Lindley Burton, Monty Wells and John Brooks, went undefeated during the 1937-38 season. Washburn won their second and third championships in 1937 and 1939, while Roosevelt captured their first title in 1940. And, Max Sporer's St. Paul Academy team, led by future Gophers Bob Carley and Harry Bratnober, sported a 33-2-0 record from 1941-43.

During this era, countless Minnesota high schoolers went on to play professionally at various levels, among those who cracked the NHL included: Bobby Dill (Cretin), Virgil Johnson (Minneapolis South), Cully Dahlstrom (Minneapolis South), Bill Moe (Minneapolis), Emil and Oscar Hanson (Minneapolis), Doc Romnes (White Bear Lake), Sam LoPresti (Eveleth), Frank Brimsek (Eveleth), Mike Karakas (Eveleth), Vic Des Jardins (Eveleth), John Mariucci (Eveleth), LeRoy Goldsworthy (Two Harbors), and Fido Purpur (Grand Forks, N.D.).

"TOURNEY-TIME!"

1945

As our boys returned home victoriously from battle following WWII, hockey was thrust to the front burner in Minnesota. People just couldn't seem to get enough of this rough and tumble high school game, which was in desperate need of some new leadership and direction. Enter the savior: Gene Aldrich.

In February of 1944, Aldrich, the longtime Director of Athletics for St. Paul's public schools, thought that a statewide high school hockey tournament would be a good idea. (There was an unofficial state tournament held in Roseau in 1942, when, then school superintendent C.D. Hollister organized a "northern school" high school hockey tournament, which was won by Thief River Falls.) Seeing how well the St. Paul schools were already drawing for their games, combined with the popularity of the game in northern Minnesota, Aldrich figured the interest and support would be there for a big-time tournament. With the complete approval of the State High School League and financial backing from St. Paul Book and Stationery owner Elmer Englebert, Aldrich began putting the pieces together for what would be the first of its kind in the United States. (Although the first "official" state tournament was claimed to have taken place in Massachusetts back in 1938, with only 500 people in attendance, Minnesota's was the first "real" state high school hockey tournament, sponsored by the schools and done to this magnitude.)

At the time, in 1945, there were only 26 high schools playing varsity hockey

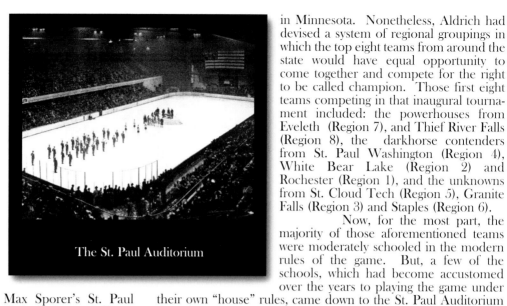

The St. Paul Auditorium

in Minnesota. Nonetheless, Aldrich had devised a system of regional groupings in which the top eight teams from around the state would have equal opportunity to come together and compete for the right to be called champion. Those first eight teams competing in that inaugural tournament included: the powerhouses from Eveleth (Region 7), and Thief River Falls (Region 8), the darkhorse contenders from St. Paul Washington (Region 4), White Bear Lake (Region 2) and Rochester (Region 1), and the unknowns from St. Cloud Tech (Region 5), Granite Falls (Region 3) and Staples (Region 6).

Now, for the most part, the majority of those aforementioned teams were moderately schooled in the modern rules of the game. But, a few of the schools, which had become accustomed over the years to playing the game under their own "house" rules, came down to the St. Paul Auditorium that winter, without even so much as a clue. For instance, Granite Falls and Staples had never played with blue lines before, and as a result didn't know what off-sides were. In addition, the boys weren't familiar with how to line up for the opening face-off either. So, before (and during) the game, referee John Gustafson gave the boys a few quick lessons on how the game was played down in the big city. There were other issues that first go-around as well, such as the formality of uniforms. The Granite Falls and Staples teams came to play in hodgepodge variety of non-matching long pants and sweatshirts, with perhaps the most storied feature of their outfits being the newspapers and magazines that the players had stuffed into their pant legs for shinguards. (Now that is truly old-time hockey!) It was a rough initiation for the teams, which also got their first taste of just how big a regulation sized rink was too.

With all the formalities out of the way, just after 2:00 PM on Thursday, February 15th, 1945, the Thief River Falls Prowlers and the White Bear Lake Bears hit the ice before a crowd of 856 onlookers. When that first puck was dropped, so began history. The Bears opened the scoring of that first match, when at 9:29 of the first period, defenseman George Kieffer made an end-to-end rush and flipped a shot past Prowler goalie Ralph Engelstad for the tournament's very first score. (Yeah, that's the same Ralph Engelstad who would donate about $100 million to the University of North Dakota around 50 years later to build a palatial hockey arena in his name.) Prowler's winger Wes Hovie tied it up only to see Bear's winger Bob Shearen score just 27 seconds later to regain the lead. But the Falls rallied behind Bob Baker's game-tying goal at the end of two, followed by his eventual game-winner at 3:56 of the third. Thief River Falls hung on to win that first game by the score of 3-2.

While the second game of the afternoon saw St. Cloud Tech beat Staples, 2-0, on goals by Chet Jaskowiak and Bill Clark, the first evening game saw Washington's Julius Struntz tally the first hat-trick of the tourney, en route to a 5-0 drubbing over Rochester. (Rochester made quite a showing, considering the fact that they didn't have a high school program until the early 1940s. Even more amazing is the fact that Rochester sits in the only county in the state of Minnesota that does not have a natural lake within its boundaries. However, they were able to play in the Mayo Auditorium, which featured artificial ice as early as the late 1930s.)

In the last game of

Front row from left: Pat Finnegan, Wally Grant, Neil Celley, Ron Drobnick, Andre Gambucci, Mel Peterson. Back row from left: George Campbell, Clem Cossalter, Milan Begich, Bice Ventrucci, Garfield Gulbranson, Ron Martinson, Coach Cliff Thompson.

The 1945 Innaugural State Champs from Eveleth

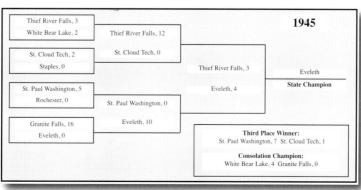

				1945
Thief River Falls, 3 White Bear Lake, 2	Thief River Falls, 12			
St. Cloud Tech, 2 Staples, 0	St. Cloud Tech, 0	Thief River Falls, 3		
St. Paul Washington, 5 Rochester, 0	St. Paul Washington, 0	Eveleth, 4	Eveleth State Champion	
Granite Falls, 16 Eveleth, 0	Eveleth, 10			

Third Place Winner:
St. Paul Washington, 7 St. Cloud Tech, 1

Consolation Champion:
White Bear Lake, 4 Granite Falls, 0

the day, as fate would have it, the underdog Granite Falls Granites were matched up against the mighty Eveleth Golden Bears. The Granites, which wound up borrowing uniforms and some equipment from nearby St. Paul Monroe High School (although goalie Gorman Velde decided to stick with his trusty football helmet), had no idea what they were in for. Eveleth, on the other hand, showed up like they owned the joint. They came in sporting jerseys from the Eveleth Junior College team, with breezers, skates and sticks that were given to them by the NHL's Chicago Blackhawks team, which then had its team training camp in nearby Virginia.

In what still stands today as the most lopsided win in Tournaments history, Eveleth went on to crush Granite Falls, 16-0. Falls didn't stand a chance against the Golden Bears, which usually played against amateur junior and senior teams from the Iron Range in 20-minute period games, rather than the typical 12-minute periods of high school games. Led by legendary coach Cliff Thompson, Eveleth was merciless. For the Granite Falls players, who had to have the off-sides rules explained to them throughout the game, it was a rude welcoming. Neil Celley, Wally Grant, Pat Finnegan and Milan Begich all had hat tricks for the Golden Bears, while Eveleth goalie Ron Drobnick had only one stop in the entire game. The half-ice shot still stands proudly today in the record book: "LEAST STOPS BY A GOAL-TENDER" — ONE, by Eveleth's Ron Drobnick."

The championship semifinals were both runaways. While Thief River Falls smoked St. Cloud, 12-0, on four Wes Hovie goals and three by Les Vigness, Eveleth beat up on Washington, 10-0. In that game, Pat Finnegan, Wally Grant and Neil Celley showed why they are still to this day regarded as the greatest ever high school hockey line in state history. While Celley and Finnegan each scored hat tricks, Wally Grant (who would later skate as a member of the famous "G" line at the University of Michigan), tallied four goals of his own.

In the championship game Eveleth battled Thief River Falls in a game of northern giants. When Eveleth's Pat Finnegan scored the game's first two goals within the first three minutes of the game, most thought it was over. But the Falls hung in there and actually rallied to take the lead behind Gene Brossa's goal at 4:12 of the first, followed by Watt Vigness' two goals in the second period to put the Prowlers ahead, 3-2. Grant decided to take the game into his own hands from there and was unstoppable after that, scoring yet another two goals in the third period to give Eveleth a 4-3 lead. That would prove to be enough for the Golden Bears. With Drobnick standing firm in goal, the Eveleth juggernaut rolled on to win the state's first-ever title by that final score of 4-3. For the undefeated Bears, it was simply business as usual — and a warm-up of things to come in the future.

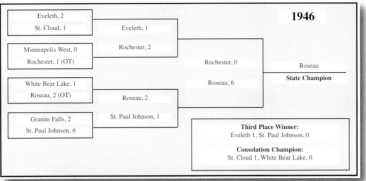

The 1946 State Champs from Roseau

Front Row: Ruben Bjorkman, James Oveson, Ray Baumgartner, Maurice Schille, Kenneth Wellen, Edwin Mellstrom.
Back Row: Coach O. Almquist, Lowell Ulvin, Robert Harris, George Peterson, Allan Sonsteng, Vernon Johnson, Thomas Buran.

The inaugural tournament proved to be a reasonably successful venture for Aldrich. In the end, some 8,434 spectators flocked to the St. Paul Auditorium, paying more than $4,000 in admissions fees — good for a $135.06 profit. From this meager beginning, the High School Tournament was born. Seeing how successful the event was, the Minnesota State High School League (MSHSL) decided to take full control of the tournament that next year and assumed complete responsibility for its financing as well.

1946
The 1946 Tournament saw the return of several teams, as well as the addition of a few new ones. Heavily favored Eveleth was back, along with Rochester, White Bear Lake, Granite Falls and St. Cloud. While Minneapolis West, St. Paul Johnson and Roseau, led by its bespectacled superstar, Rube Bjorkman, came in as tournament rookies.

In the opening round, Eveleth got a late goal by Tom Pavelich to barely sneak past a tough St. Cloud team, while Rochester's Allen Gilkenson scored at 3:25 of the first overtime period to beat West. While Roseau's Lowell Ulvin and White Bear's Bob Shearen each scored in the first period of the initial evening game, it was Bob Harris' overtime game-winner just three minutes into the extra session that gave Roseau a 2-1 victory. Then in the last game of the day, Johnson's three big guns of Jim Rentstrom, Jim Sedin and Orv Anderson each scored two goals apiece to lead the Governors past Granite Falls, 6-2.

In the semis, Rochester's Ray Purvis and Allen Gilkenson both hooked up for a pair of goals, as Rochester came up with the tourney's first big upset, knocking off the defending champions from Eveleth, 2-1. In the other semifinal contest Roseau's Rube Bjorkman, who wore goggles much like a WWII aviator, scored the 2-1 game-winner at 8:21 of the third period to beat Johnson. In the finals, Rochester hoped to make history, but was denied. The masked marvel, Bjorkman, took the game into his own hands, scoring a hat trick, en route to leading his Golden Rams to a 6-0 victory and their first state championship.

1947
The 1947 Tournament started out with a bang, as all of the opening round matchups were won by shutouts. Rube Bjorkman pulled off another hat trick in the first game, leading Roseau to a 5-0 win over St. Cloud. Eveleth also rolled into the semis, blanking Willmar, 6-0 on Dick Peterson's hat-trick. And, while Dave Riepke's three goals led Johnson to a 4-0 win over Rochester, West out-muscled South St. Paul, 6-0, with Bill MacFadden and Lloyd Lundeen tallying two goals each.

The amazing Bjorkman continued his antics, scoring

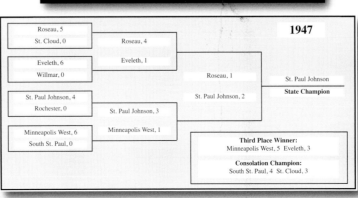

The 1947 State Champs from St. Paul Johnson

Front Row: Louis Cotronco, James Renstrom, David Reipke, Gene Nardini, Roy Bertelson, Orwin Halweg, Dan Sentasriero, Jack McGann.
Back Row: Gerald Swanson, Rueben Gustafson, Coach: Orville Anderson, Charles Rawlings, Don Eckert, Frank Paddock, Kenneth Dahl, Emery Barriette, James Sedin, Howard Ekstrom.

yet another hat-trick in the 4-1 drubbing of Eveleth in the first semifinal game. Johnson also advanced on goals by Jim Rentstrom, Howie Eckstrom and Dave Riepke, to earn a 3-1 victory over West.

Then, on Saturday, February 15, 1947, in front of a packed Auditorium of some 7,404 fans — many of whom arrived via street-cars to downtown St. Paul, Roseau took on Johnson in what would turn out to be one of the classics. Interestingly, it had become a North vs. South affair at the tournament, with the battle lines clearly drawn in the dingy-gray Auditorium ice sheet. Defending champion Roseau, which finished the season at 13-2-3 (having lost twice to Crookston Cathedral), had nine of its players back from the year before. Bjorkman, who centered Dan Baumgartner and Tom Buran, was the star, while defensemen Vernon Johnson and Lowell Ulvin, both 200-pounders, seemed to be an impenetrable force. Roseau coach Oscar Almquist, himself a legend in Minnesota hockey, had his boys ready to go. Johnson, on the other hand, came into the finals with an amazing 31-1 record, with its only blemish coming on a loss to Blake. Coach Rube Gustafson's Governors, chock full of Swedes and Italians, were led by the formidable first line of Dave Reipke, Jim Renstrom and Jim Sedin, with Orville Anderson and Howard Eckstrom played defense.

The game got underway with Johnson scoring at 2:58 of the second on a goal by center Orvin Halweg. Bjorkman then answered early in the third to tie it at one apiece. The game was tight from there on in, with Johnson goalie Jack McGahn playing big. The Johnson players were focused on stopping Bjorkman, a strategy that seemed to be working. Then, with just 1:18 to play, Johnson defenseman Howard Eckstrom dished to Dave Reipke at mid-ice. Reipke, rushing in, deked around the Roseau defenders, and flipped the game-winner over Roseau goalie Maurice Schille's left shoulder for the game-winner. Johnson had slain the giant.

1948

In 1948, for the first time ever, the defending champion did not make a return trip to the Tournament. That's because Johnson was knocked-off in the regional championships by newcomer Harding, from St. Paul. The favorite of the tourney, however, seemed to be Eveleth, which was led by All-Stater John Matchefts and a freshman phenom by the name of John Mayasich. Other contenders that year included Rochester and St. Cloud, (both making their fourth consecutive appearances), South St. Paul, and first-timer's Warroad, Minneapolis Washburn and St. Louis Park.

On February 19th, in the opening game of the tourney, St. Cloud, led by a pair of Jim Broker goals, beat Washburn 4-2. In the second game of the day, despite Rochester goalie Jack Nichols' 41 saves, Eveleth trounced Rochester, 7-2, thanks to multiple goals from John

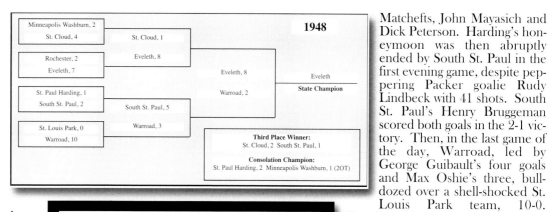

1948					
Minneapolis Washburn, 2 / St. Cloud, 4	St. Cloud, 1				
Rochester, 2 / Eveleth, 7	Eveleth, 8	Eveleth, 8	Eveleth		
St. Paul Harding, 1 / South St. Paul, 2	South St. Paul, 5	Warroad, 2	**State Champion**		
St. Louis Park, 0 / Warroad, 10	Warroad, 3				

Third Place Winner:
St. Cloud, 2 South St. Paul, 1

Consolation Champion:
St. Paul Harding, 2 Minneapolis Washburn, 1 (2OT)

Front Row: John Matchefts, James Stanaway, Robert Rozinka, Willard Ikola, John Drobnick, Tony Tassoni, John Mayasich, Wallace Perushek.
Back Row: Danny Voce, Edward Mrkonich, William Brascugli, Warren Juola, Richard Peterson, Ronald Ochis, Eugene Klune, Tom Ventrucci, C. R. Thompson (Coach).

The 1948 State Champs from Eveleth

Matchefts, John Mayasich and Dick Peterson. Harding's honeymoon was then abruptly ended by South St. Paul in the first evening game, despite peppering Packer goalie Rudy Lindbeck with 41 shots. South St. Paul's Henry Bruggeman scored both goals in the 2-1 victory. Then, in the last game of the day, Warroad, led by George Guibault's four goals and Max Oshie's three, bulldozed over a shell-shocked St. Louis Park team, 10-0. Despite giving up 10 goals, Park keeper Jim Mattson (who would later star for the Gophers), registered an amazing 49 stops — 20 of which came in the second period, a record which stood for several years.

John Matchefts' four goals easily led Eveleth past St. Cloud 8-1, in the semi's, while in the other semifinal, five different Warroad boys tallied for a 5-3 win over South St. Paul. On February 21st, before a sell-out Auditorium crowd, Eveleth hit the ice to battle fellow northerners Warroad. Eveleth jumped out early, only to see Warroad's Oshie brothers, Max and Buster, keep it close. But John Matchefts and Tony Tassoni each scored hat tricks, as powerhouse Eveleth went on to beat Warroad, 8-2, for their second title in four years.

1949

In 1949, because it was determined that the southern part of Minnesota was exhibiting less interest in hockey than that of the Twin Cities and northern Minnesota, the format was changed for determining the regional champions. The result was a change in three regions that ultimately made it possible for more suburban metro schools to enter the Tournament. The champions of those three new regions which entered the field that year included Minneapolis Central (Region One), Williams (Region Three), and St. Louis Park (Region Six). The other five finalists included the returning champs from Eveleth, Warroad, Minneapolis Washburn, White Bear Lake, and St. Paul Murray — first time winners of the St. Paul title.

Eveleth, led by John Mayasich's hat trick, started out right where they left off the year before, crushing White Bear, 6-0, despite Bear's goalie Dick Doyle's 42 saves. Buster Oshie led Warroad with three goals, while George Guibault and Sammy Gibbons each scored twice as Warroad advanced to the semis by beating Central, 7-1. The evening games were much tighter affairs, as Williams beat Washburn 2-0, on goals by Chet Lundsten and Sid Bryduck. Then, in the final game, Murray edged out St. Louis Park in a 2-1 overtime thriller, as winger Tom Wegleitner scored on a power play to give Murray the victory.

In the first semifinal game, Eveleth found itself in a rematch of the last year's title game against Warroad. Eveleth didn't even make it

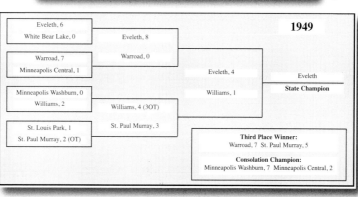

Front Row: John Matchefts, John Drobnick, Dan Voce, Ronald Castellano, Willard Ikola, John Mayasich, John Nelson, Tom Ventrucci, Robert McCarty.
Back Row: C. R. Thompson, Coach—Thomas Roberts, David Hendrickson, LaVerne Hammer, Edward Mrkonich, William Brascugli, Robert Halstrom, James Mudge, Jack Gornik, Mgr.

The 1949 State Champs from Eveleth

1949					
Eveleth, 6 / White Bear Lake, 0	Eveleth, 8				
Warroad, 7 / Minneapolis Central, 1	Warroad, 0	Eveleth, 4	Eveleth		
Minneapolis Washburn, 0 / Williams, 2	Williams, 4 (3OT)	Williams, 1	**State Champion**		
St. Louis Park, 1 / St. Paul Murray, 2 (OT)	St. Paul Murray, 3				

Third Place Winner:
Warroad, 7 St. Paul Murray, 5

Consolation Champion:
Minneapolis Washburn, 7 Minneapolis Central, 2

close, rolling over Warroad, 8-0, on yet another hat trick by John Mayasich. His wingmate, John Matchefts, added a goal and three assists to lead the Golden Bears in a laugher. The other semi would prove to be a barn-burner, as Williams and Murray battled for three overtimes. Down 3-2, Murray pulled their goalie with 55 seconds to go in regulation. Shortly thereafter, center Tom Wegleitner responded by scoring and sending the game into overtime. It was back and forth through two overtime periods until forward Chet Lundsten tallied early in the third extra session to give Williams a 4-3 victory.

Once again, the title would be given to a northern Minnesota team that year, as Eveleth found itself pitted against tiny Williams High School for all the beans. More than 7,000 fans jammed into the Auditorium's wooden seats to watch the Williams Wolves (a town of only 375 souls which was coached by Eveleth native Al Braga), try to make history. Coach Cliff Thompson's Eveleth team came out smoking in the championship game, as Ron Castellano opened the scoring late in the first. Williams kept it close through two though, as John McKinnon beat Eveleth goalie Willard Ikola on a penalty shot late in the second to make it 2-1. But then John Matchefts and Ron Castellano each scored to bust it open in third. John Mayasich added his seventh goal of the tournament at the 8:10 mark to give Eveleth a 4-1 victory, and their second consecutive championship.

1950
Riding a remarkable 47-game winning streak, Eveleth once again entered the 1950 Tournament as the heavy favorite. The juggernaut from the Iron Range flew through Region Seven by absolutely annihilating both Duluth Central, 23-0, and then Grand Rapids, 18-0, before finally beating International Falls, 5-1. The Falls also got into the tourney field via the "back door." (In those years, Regions Seven and Eight alternated in sending their second place teams to the tournament to represent the "geographically-nonexistent" Region Three.) Also joining the Bears and Broncos in the big dance were Williams, St. Paul Murray, St. Cloud, Minneapolis Central, Minneapolis South and South St. Paul.

John Mayasich got a pair of goals while Dan Voce added three of his own as Eveleth continued its domination by spanking Central, 6-0, in the opener. St. Cloud took care of South St. Paul in the afternoon game, 4-1, while Williams, led by Ray Beauchamp's four goals, beat South, 8-2. The best was saved until last though, as International Falls battled Murray into double-overtime. The two squads went into the extra session tied at one apiece, when, in the first overtime, Bill Wegleitner scored at 2:30 to give Murray a 2-1 lead. (At this point of the tourney's history, overtimes weren't sudden death.) But, not to be outdone, the Dougherty brothers, Bill and Dick, combined to tie it up less

Eveleth's Hall of Fame Coach, Cliff Thompson

than a minute later. Then, just after the opening face-off of the second overtime, the Dougherty's struck again, this time with Dick scoring on a pass from Bill to give Williams a 3-2 win.

In the first semifinal contest, Mayasich proved why he is still to this day the best player ever to hail from Minnesota, when he put on a clinic, scoring an amazing six goals in Eveleth's 7-0 shellacking of St. Cloud. The other semi saw Cinderella Williams beat International Falls by the score of 4-2, thanks to a couple of first period goals by Dick Lundgren and Sid Bryduck, as well as a pair in the second by senior forward Chet Lundsten.

Another capacity crowd gathered at the Auditorium to witness the championship game rematch between Eveleth and tiny Williams. Eveleth captain Willard Ikola, who was coming off of two consecutive shut-outs, knew he would have to play big in order to beat the Wolves. Mayasich opened the scoring by notching two quick goals for the Bears. Dan Voce then put Eveleth up 3-0, only to see Chet Lundsten score two of his own, followed by a Ray Beauchamp wrister over Ikola's sprawled out blocker to tie it up late in the third. Then, with only 20 seconds left in the game, Ron Castellano hit Mayasich on a quick centering pass at the top of the circle. Mayasich deked, and fired a low snapper into the back of the net to give Eveleth its third consecutive title, and its 50th consecutive victory.

1951
In 1951 Eveleth arrived in St. Paul with the title of "three-time defending state champion" in front of its name. The boys from the Range were somewhat of an enigma with the Twin Citians, who by now had heard of them much like they had heard about Paul Bunyan and Superman, with a sort of mythical god-like connotation. Led by All-Staters John Mayasich, Ron Castellano and Dan Voce, the Golden Bears came in with an amazing 66-game winning streak, fresh off of yet another undefeated 16-0 season in which they scored 179 goals, while yielding only 30.

In the opening game of the first round, Thief River Falls, which was riding a 16-game winning streak of its own, edged out St. Cloud, 3-2, on three first period goals by Alan Steenerson, Jack Erickson, and Darryl Lund. St. Cloud's sibling trio of Ron, Don and Dick Saatzer rallied their team back late to get to within one, but in the end they just couldn't beat Falls' keeper Bill Maruska for the equalizer. In Game Two, Johnson handed White Bear a big doughnut, beating them, 7-0, thanks to a couple of two-goal performances by both Bob Youngquist and Hugo Anderson. In the first evening game, Minneapolis Southwest, led by the Meredith brothers, Bob and Dick, edged St. Paul Murray 2-1. Then, in a replay of the last years' finals, Eveleth took on Williams in the nightcap. When Mayasich scored just 57 seconds into the game, people knew it was going to be ugly. He didn't stop there though, going on to score three more in that first period alone, as the Golden Bears hammered the Wolves, 12-0.

In the semis, Mayasich showed why he is the greatest, scoring an unbelievable tournament-record seven goals against Southwest. After a quick goal by Eveleth winger Dan Voce, Mayasich pumped in three quick ones of his own in the first period. Southwest came back to make it interesting behind three goals by the Meredith brothers. That was apparently all the wake up call Mayasich would need though, as he scored again in the second, and added another hat trick in the third. The Castellano's added one each as well for the Bears, as Eveleth cruised to an 11-5 victory. That put the Bears into the title match against Johnson, which had beaten Thief River Falls in the other semifinal contest by the score of 6-2, thanks to a

JOHN MAYASICH'S UNBELIEVABLE STATE TOURNEY RECORDS:

Most All Time Total Points:	46	(1948-1951)
Most All Time Total Goals:	36	(1948-1951)
Most Consec. Games Scoring a Goal:	12	(1948-1951)
Most All Time Hat Tricks:	7	(1948-1951)
Most Points One Tournament:	18	(1951)
Most Goals One Tournament:	15	(1951)
Most Points One Game:	8	(1951)
Most Goals One Game:	7	(1951)
Most Points One Period:	5	(1951)
Most Goals One Period:	4	(1951)

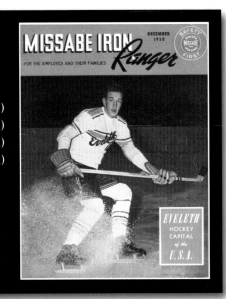

pair of goals each from Bob Youngquist and Ray Youngberg.

On Saturday, February 24th, 1951, in front of 7,163 Auditorium fans, Eveleth hit the ice to try and make it four-straight crowns. Johnson Coach Rube Gustafson knew that he would have to get a near perfect performance from his boys if they were going to have a chance. There was speculation before the game as to what kind of defense the Governors were going to throw at the Bears. Some teams had achieved a marginal level of success against them that season by running a "1-5" defense, in which one skater stayed at the blue line and the other four hung around the goalie. Or, perhaps he would just have the other four hang around Mayasich? Deciding to play it straight and take their chances, Johnson came out strong and held the Bears scoreless through the first on tough goaltending by Johnson keeper Warren Strelow. But, just a minute into the second, who else but John Mayasich beat Strelow to go up 1-0. Ten minutes later he scored again, and decided to add two more in the third just for good measure. His fourth and final goal of the game was a beauty, beating Strelow on a 20-foot blast from the point. Johnson's Bob Schmidt added a meaningless goal late, but to no avail, as Eveleth and Mayasich prevailed, 4-1. For Mayasich, who finished with 15 goals and three assists for 18 points, which is still a tournament record, it was sweet.

"I remember that St. Paul Johnson game was a tough one," recalled Mayasich, "and there was a lot of pressure on us to keep the winning streak going through that fourth year. When it was all over we couldn't believe what we had done, it was very special."

"When we were growing up, we didn't think about college hockey or the Olympics or the pros," he added. "We thought about making the high school team and getting to the state tournament. Eveleth had won the first state tournament in 1945, when I was in sixth grade, and that gave us something to strive for. In Eveleth you were expected to win and it was just assumed you would. As a result, we didn't take any time for sightseeing in St. Paul. All we did was watch and play hockey."

1952
Defending champion Eveleth made its return to the tournament via the "backdoor," fresh off of having their unprecedented 85-game winning streak snapped by Hibbing in the regional finals. In the opening game, Humboldt beat Winona 2-1. Winona forward Roger Neitze opened the scoring in the first, only to see Humboldt's Carl Weber tie it up in the second. Winona ran out of gas in the end though, as Humboldt's Bernie Weber got the game-winner with 3:45 left to go. Despite Dick Larson's 33 saves, Winona lost the game, 2-1. The afternoon match featured the Mayasich-less Golden Bears from Eveleth against Thief River Falls. Eveleth winger Mike Castellano's first period goal was matched by Falls' winger Jack Erickson's at 2:08 of the third to

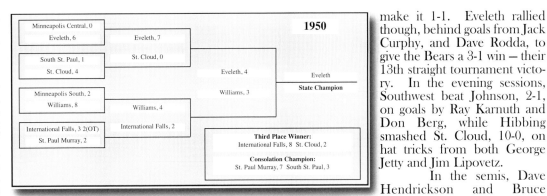

```
Minneapolis Central, 0                                        1950
Eveleth, 6          ──┐
                      ├── Eveleth, 7 ──┐
South St. Paul, 1   ──┤                │
St. Cloud, 4          ── St. Cloud, 0 ─┤
                                       ├── Eveleth, 4 ──┐
Minneapolis South, 2 ─┐                │               │
Williams, 8         ──┤                │               ├── Eveleth
                      ├── Williams, 4 ─┤               │  State Champion
International Falls, 3 2(OT) ─┐        │  Williams, 3
St. Paul Murray, 2  ──┤── International Falls, 2

                              Third Place Winner:
                              International Falls, 8  St. Cloud, 2

                              Consolation Champion:
                              St. Paul Murray, 7  South St. Paul, 3
```

Front Row: Robert McCarty, Dan Voce, Victor Rozinka, Willard Ikola, Ronald Castellano, John Mayasich.
Back Row: Coach C. R. Thompson, James Mudge, Bruce Shutte, Lavern Hammer, Leslie Curphy, Edward Mrkonich, John Drobnick, Francis Ritmanich, David Hendrickson, Mike Castellano, John Nelson, Tom Roberts, Mgr.

The 1950 State Champs from Eveleth

Front Row: John Mayasich (Co-Capt.), James Mudge, Dan Voce (Co-Capt.), Victor Rozinka, Ronald Castellano, Edward Mrkonich, Lavern Hammer.
Back Row: C. R. Thompson (Coach), David Hendrickson, Richard Tomassoni, Tom Roberts, Mike Castellano, Bruce Shutte.

The 1951 State Champs from Eveleth

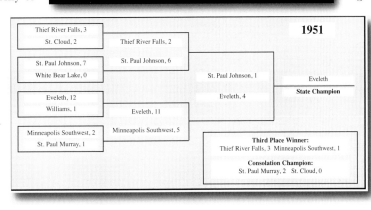

```
Thief River Falls, 3 ─┐                                      1951
St. Cloud, 2        ──┤── Thief River Falls, 2 ──┐
                      │                          │
St. Paul Johnson, 7 ──┐                          ├── St. Paul Johnson, 1 ─┐
White Bear Lake, 0  ──┤── St. Paul Johnson, 6 ──┘                         │
                      │                                                   ├── Eveleth
Eveleth, 12         ──┐                                                   │  State Champion
Williams, 1         ──┤── Eveleth, 11 ──┐          Eveleth, 4 ────────────┘
                      │                 │
Minneapolis Southwest, 2 ─┐            │
St. Paul Murray, 1  ──┤── Minneapolis Southwest, 5

                              Third Place Winner:
                              Thief River Falls, 3  Minneapolis Southwest, 1

                              Consolation Champion:
                              St. Paul Murray, 2  St. Cloud, 0
```

make it 1-1. Eveleth rallied though, behind goals from Jack Curphy, and Dave Rodda, to give the Bears a 3-1 win — their 13th straight tournament victory. In the evening sessions, Southwest beat Johnson, 2-1, on goals by Ray Karnuth and Don Berg, while Hibbing smashed St. Cloud, 10-0, on hat tricks from both George Jetty and Jim Lipovetz.

In the semis, Dave Hendrickson and Bruce Shutte each got two goals for Eveleth as they beat up on Humboldt, 6-1. The second semifinal featured Hibbing against Southwest, in what would prove to be a battle of solid goaltending. Both keepers, Don Vaia from Hibbing and Howie Cammack from Southwest, played big through two, as the score remained 0-0 going into the third. Finally, at 4:43 of the third period, Hibbing's George Jetty put the Bluejackets up 1-0 on a low wrister. Then, less than two minutes later, Hibbing's Jim Lipovetz made it 2-0 on a nice pass from Jack Petroske. Jim Blanchard scored for Southwest late, but Vaia held strong in net as Hibbing went on to win, 2-1.

The stage was now set for an all-northern Minnesota championship match, with the perfect storyline. Because Hibbing had beaten Eveleth just a week earlier in the regions, everyone figured that the Bears would be eager to exact some revenge on their Iron Range brethren. Mike Castellano opened the scoring for Eveleth at 9:15 of the first on a nice slapper from Palkovich. Then in the second, Hibbing fired back to take a commanding 3-1 lead on goals by Jack Petroske, George Jetty and Howard Wallene. At 1:21 of the third, Jetty tallied again for Hibbing, only to see Eveleth's Dave Hendrickson and Bruce Shutte each score to make it 4-3. But Don Vaia stood on his head, turning back 13 shots in the third period alone to get the win. For Hibbing, it was their first championship and it was sweet. For Eveleth, which had won five of the first seven tournaments, it was the end of a dynasty. (Incidentally, Eveleth's 85-game winning streak stands as the second longest ever in the history of high school hockey in the U.S.)

1953
Behind by Jack Stoskopf's two goals and one assist, and Billy Christian's one goal and two assists, Warroad kicked off the opening round of the '53 tourney by blanking Humboldt, 5-0. South St. Paul and Roseau got together for the second game of the day, with each team scoring two in the first. Both goaltenders, Henry Metcalf of South St. Paul, who posted 19 saves, and Roger Norberg of Roseau, who saved 12 of his own, played marvelously and forced the game into overtime. There, at 3:25 of the extra session, Bob Sharrow fed Dick Lick on a beautiful one-timer to give South St. Paul a 3-2 victory.

In the first evening

game, Southwest played Eveleth as tough as they had been played in several years at the Tournament. With the score tied at 0-0, Southwest's Jack Thomas beat Eveleth goalie Tom Yurkovich only nine seconds after the puck dropped in the second period. Eveleth winger Bob Kochevar tied it up at 8:20 in the third period, and then Gerald Palkovich got the game-winner with less than a minute to go in the game to give Eveleth a 2-1 win. Finally, Johnson, which was led by coach Rube Gustafson, and St. Louis Park got together for what would prove to be second longest game in the history of the tournament — four overtimes. Johnson opened the scoring in the game on Jack Hoistrom's rebound goal at 7:34 of the second period, only to see Park's Dennis Stedman tie it up at 7:32 of the third to send it into overtime. From there, both goalies, Gene Picha and Gerald Norberg, played fabulously. But, at 2:28 of the fourth overtime, with the players barely able to move from exhaustion, Johnson's Roger Bertelson slapped a 47-foot prayer that somehow got past Norberg's stick and found the back of the net. The Governors won the thriller, 2-1.

The opening semifinal contest featured something that hadn't been seen in the history of the Tournament — Eveleth got pummeled. Roy and Rod Anderson put the Governors up 2-0 in the first, and then Bob Wabman added three goals of his own, as Johnson beat the heck out of the Bears by the score of 7-1. In the other semi, Warroad and South St. Paul battled back and forth for the better part of two periods before Roger Christian finally beat Henry Metcalf at the 6:16 mark to give Warroad a 1-0 advantage. Jack Stoskopf made it 2-0 just two minutes after that, only to see Dick Lick bring it back to 2-1 a few minutes later. But Bob Lewis played great between the pipes as Warroad held on to beat the Packers, 2-1.

In the finals, Johnson, which won the title in 1947, found themselves pitted against the Christian brothers from Warroad, Billy and Roger. Johnson came out strong, taking the early lead on two first-period goals by Roger Bertelson, followed by two more in the second by Rod Anderson and Ray Karnuth. Warroad finally got on the board at 6:33 of the third when Roger Christian's pass found Jack Stoskopf's stick in front of the net. Johnson went on to win the contest, 4-1, behind some great goaltending from Gene Picha. The real hero of the game though, was Warroad's goalie Bob Lewis, who came up with an astonishing 39 saves in the losing effort. With the win, Johnson finally broke the five-year stranglehold of championships that the northern schools had enjoyed at the tourney.

1954
Bob Helgeland's hat-trick in the opener kicked off the tourney, as Thief River Falls continued their undefeated season with a 6-1 win over South.

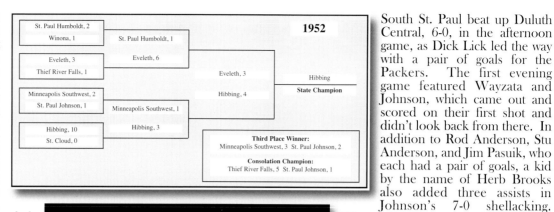

```
St. Paul Humboldt, 2
Winona, 1                St. Paul Humboldt, 1
                                               Eveleth, 3
Eveleth, 3                Eveleth, 6                            Hibbing
Thief River Falls, 1                           Hibbing, 4      State Champion

Minneapolis Southwest, 2
St. Paul Johnson, 1       Minneapolis Southwest, 1

Hibbing, 10               Hibbing, 3
St. Cloud, 0
```

1952

Third Place Winner:
Minneapolis Southwest, 3 St. Paul Johnson, 2

Consolation Champion:
Thief River Falls, 5 St. Paul Johnson, 1

Left to right: George Jetty, Herbert Sellors, Jack Petroske, William Webb, Frank Fields, Donald Holcomb, Donald Vaia, William Feno, Howard Wallene, James Lipovetz, Jerry Callengar, Martin Sundvall, Joe Ban, Stu. Mgr., Mauritz Uhrbom, Coach.

The 1952 State Champs from Hibbing

goalie Tom Beste on a low wrister. But, Bob Kochevar tallied with less than 30 seconds left in the second to put the game away. Johnson's Jack Hoistrom added one late, but the Governors came up short losing, 3-2.

On Saturday, February 27th, 1954, in front of 7,433 fans, Thief River Falls took the ice against Eveleth for the right to be called champion. The Prowlers were a disciplined team which was led by Lyle Guttu, Marv Jorde, Joe Poole, and the defensive tandem of Mike McMahon and Les Sabo, who loved to mix it up at the blue line. Eveleth, on the other hand featured Tom Beste, Jerry Judnick, Gene Klun, Bob Kochevar, Jerry Norman, Ed Oswald, and Dave Rodda. The game proved to be a defensive battle from the get-go, with both teams testing each other early. Finally, at 11:10 of the first, after peppering Eveleth keeper Tom Beste with a flurry of shots, Marv Jorde scored on a rebound to put the Prowlers up 1-0. The Falls just kept on coming after that, scoring three more goals in the second from both Lyle Guttu, who had a pair, and Jorde, who added one more of his own. Eveleth's Bob Kochevar did manage to score late, but Falls' goalie Jack Hoppe hung on down the stretch to lead his team to a 4-1 victory and their first state title.

(Incidentally, Harding went on to win the consolation title, 1-0, over Minneapolis South. What is significant about that is the fact that Dick Jinks scored his eighth goal of the tournament in that game, which was also the exact number of goals that his entire team scored during the whole tournament. That amazing individual performance is a record that still stands today.)

1955
Southwest, which lost to the Eveleth in both 1951 and 1953, was finally able to exact some

South St. Paul beat up Duluth Central, 6-0, in the afternoon game, as Dick Lick led the way with a pair of goals for the Packers. The first evening game featured Wayzata and Johnson, which came out and scored on their first shot and didn't look back from there. In addition to Rod Anderson, Stu Anderson, and Jim Pasuik, who each had a pair of goals, a kid by the name of Herb Brooks also added three assists in Johnson's 7-0 shellacking. Then, in the last game, Eveleth beat Harding, 5-2, on a pair of Jerry Judnick goals. Dick Jinks scored two for Harding, but the Bears peppered Harding goalie Ed Kohn with 36 shots to seal the deal.

Thief River Falls' forward Darryl Durgin netted a hat-trick, while Lyle Guttu added a pair in the first semifinal contest, as the Prowlers beat South St. Paul by the final of 8-1. Then, in the other semifinal game, Eveleth earned its sixth trip in seven years to the finals by beating Johnson, 3-2. In what proved to be a very tight game, Eveleth jumped ahead in the first on goals by Gene Klune and Dave Rodda. Johnson cut the deficit to 2-1 when Stu Anderson beat Eveleth

Front Row: Roger Johnson, Gary Shea, Jack Holstrom, Gene Picha, Duane Quatman, Glenn Peterson, William Johnson.
Back Row: Larry Paul, Jerry Gehrig, Robert Wahman, Rod Anderson, Roy Anderson, Roger Bertelson, Ray Karnuth, Rube Gustafson (Coach).

The 1953 State Champs from St. Paul Johnson

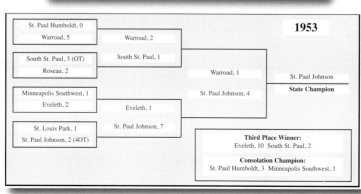

```
St. Paul Humboldt, 0
Warroad, 5                Warroad, 2
                                               Warroad, 1
South St. Paul, 3 (OT)    South St. Paul, 1                   St. Paul Johnson
Roseau, 2                                      St. Paul Johnson, 4   State Champion

Minneapolis Southwest, 1
Eveleth, 2                Eveleth, 1

St. Louis Park, 1         St. Paul Johnson, 7
St. Paul Johnson, 2 (4OT)
```

1953

Third Place Winner:
Eveleth, 10 South St. Paul, 2

Consolation Champion:
St. Paul Humboldt, 3 Minneapolis Southwest, 1

sweet revenge against their old foes from the Range in the tourney opener, as the Indians went on to tomahawk the Golden Bears, 4-1, thanks to three goals by Merv Meredith from Roger Rovick. In the afternoon match-up, Edina showed just how "green" they really were, getting nailed by the South St. Paul Packers, 4-0, on goals by Bob Sharrow, John Roth, Jack O'Brien and Bob Johnson.

The third game of the State High School Tournament would prove to be, arguably, the most famous of all-time. That's because the contest between Minneapolis South and Thief River Falls lasted an incredible 11 overtimes — the longest game ever to be played in Tournament history. South, the Minneapolis city champion, had seven players back from its tournament team of the year before, and felt good about its chances against the defending champs. The game started out innocently enough, with Dale Rasmussen putting South ahead 1-0 in the first on a slapper from just inside the left circle. The Falls' then came back to take a 2-1 lead on back-to-back goals by Loren Vraa and Glenn Carlson. Vraa's goal came off of Joe Poole's rebound in front of South goalie Roger Evenson, while Carlson's was a 30-foot blast from the left point. Then, at 6:03 of the third, Jerry Westby scored the tying goal for South on a deflected dribbler, to send the game into overtime.

As the teams began to play the five-minute overtimes, South's goalie Roger Evenson and Rod Collins of Thief River Falls both played tremendously. Time and again they stuffed everything that came their way. While Vraa and Poole both missed open goals in the first, South's Jim Westby missed a rebound from a Larry Alm shot in the second overtime that was a sure-goal. Finally, after nine overtimes, and no end in sight, Tournament officials decided to start the evening game between Johnson and Roseau at 11:33 pm. The two games then rotated in-between periods, giving the players a much needed rest between games. After Johnson's Ken Fanger scored at 6:32 of the first period to put the Govs ahead, 1-0, South and the Falls then came back out to play a 10th overtime. Still scoreless, the game's switched back one more time. Perhaps inspired, Roseau goalie John Almquist and Johnson goalie Tom Wahman both earned shut-outs for their second period games. Now, back to the 11th overtime. With both teams exhausted, South caught a break against the defending champs when Prowler's forward Duane Glass was called for a tripping penalty. Taking advantage of this rare power-play opportunity, South's Jim Westby struck again by slapping a rocket right through Collins' five-hole just as he was doing the splits, to end the unbelievable marathon at 1:50 of the 11th extra session. Both teams, fatigued, fell to the ice in disbelief. South's goaltender, Roger Evenson, who made a record 54 saves in the game, was wildly embraced by his teammates at the end of the

four and a half hour marathon.

The hero of the game was without question, Jim Westby. "I didn't aim," Westby later said. "If I had, I probably wouldn't have hit the goal. I just slapped it. I was all ready to tear in there for the rebound because I didn't think it would go in."

Incidentally, and completely overshadowed, Ken Fanger's first period goal was all that Johnson needed to hang on for the 1-0 win over Roseau. Then, in the first-ever "All-Metro" semis, Southwest's Merv Meredith, Eric Sundquist and Ed Noble secured a 3-1 win over South St. Paul, who's lone goal was scored in the third period by Bob Johnson. In the other semi, Herb Brooks put his Johnson squad up 1-0 at 9:07 of the first, only to see Dick Koob tie it back up for South in the second. Finally, in the third, Stu Anderson and Roger Wigens tallied for Johnson to give the Governors a 3-1 win, and a ticket to the finals.

St. Paul Johnson and Southwest then faced off for the right to be called champion that next night in front of a packed Auditorium crowd. The hero of the game would prove to be Herb Brooks, who got the Governors on the board at 2:32 of the first period. His teammate, Stu Anderson, then tallied less than seven minutes later, only to see Brooks score his second of the game just a minute and a half after that. Merv Meredith added one in the third, but it was too little — too late for Southwest, as they lost the game, 3-1. For the Governors, in seven Tournament appearances, it was their third state championship and second in three years.

1956

Eveleth opened up the three-day affair by keeping its first-round winning streak intact. Although Gary Fournelle's goal after the first minute of the game put White Bear Lake up by one, Eveleth's Jim Drobnick, Gus Hendrickson and Jerry Judnick, each beat Bear's goalie Gordon Mackenhausen, to give Eveleth a 3-1 win. Game Two was an exciting contest that saw Edina's Larry Johnson score just 32 seconds after the opening face-off. While Thief River Falls tied it up in the second on a goal from Cliff Strand, Johnson scored again in the third, only to see Falls' winger Jack Poole tie it five minutes later. With the game tied at two apiece, the game went into overtime. There, after Edina controversially had a goal disallowed because of a man in the crease in the first extra session, Prowler's center Cliff Strand hooked up with Duane Glass to beat Edina goalie Murray Macpherson at the 4:30 mark of the third sudden-death to win the game, 3-2. International Falls pulled off the tourney's the first upset in Game Three, beating the defending champs from Johnson, 3-1, thanks to a pair of Oscar Mahle goals. The late game, meanwhile, featured the day's only shut-out, as

1954

Minneapolis South, 1 / Thief River Falls, 6	Thief River Falls, 8
South St. Paul, 6 / Duluth Central, 0	South St. Paul, 1
St. Paul Johnson, 7 / Wayzata, 0	St. Paul Johnson, 2
St. Paul Harding, 2 / Eveleth, 5	Eveleth, 3

Thief River Falls, 4 / Eveleth, 1 → Thief River Falls **State Champion**

Third Place Winner: St. Paul Johnson, 5 South St. Paul, 3

Consolation Champion: St. Paul Harding, 1 Minneapolis South, 0

Front Row: Neil Aase (Student Manager), Marvin Jorde, Jack Hoppe, Lyle Guttu, Denni. Rolle (Coach).
Back Row: Loren Vraa, James Zavoral, Robert Heigeland, Bradley Teal, Mike McMahon, Lester Sabo, Joe Poole, Darryl Durgin, Jack Quesnell.
Not on picture – Rodney Collins.

The 1954 State Champs from Thief River Falls

Front Row: Karl Dahlberg, Herb Brooks, Roger Wigens, Tom Wahman, Jack Holstrom, John Patton.
Second Row: R. Gustafson (Coach), Rodney Anderson, Chuck Rodgers, Ken Fanger, Bill McKechnie, Ryan Ostebo, Stu Anderson, Tony Hudalla (Student Manager).

The 1955 State Champs from St. Paul Johnson

1955

Minneapolis Southwest, 4 / Eveleth, 1	Minneapolis Southwest, 3
South St. Paul, 4 / Edina Morningside, 0	South St. Paul, 1
Mpls. South, 3 (11OT) / Thief River Falls, 2	Minneapolis South, 1
St. Paul Johnson, 1 / Roseau, 0	St. Paul Johnson, 3

Minneapolis Southwest, 1 / St. Paul Johnson, 3 → St. Paul Johnson **State Champion**

Third Place Winner: South St. Paul, 2 Minneapolis South, 1

Consolation Champion: Thief River Falls, 3 Eveleth, 1

Roosevelt goalie Jerry Gangloff recorded 14 saves for a 4-0 Teddy victory over Washington. Four different Teddies scored in the game – Bart Larson, Bob Carlson, Doug Larson and John Hrkal.

Thief River Falls then did something that had never been done before in the first semi. Thanks to goals from Duane Glass, Jack Poole and Cliff Strand, the Prowlers handed Eveleth the only shut-out loss they had ever had in tournament play, winning the game 3-0. The second semifinal contest proved to be a classic, as International Falls hooked up with Roosevelt in a triple-overtime thriller. The Teddies jumped out to a quick lead, when Bob Carlson dug a puck out from behind the Broncos goal and stuffed it in past Falls' netminder Bob Laurion at 7:20 of the first. International Falls stormed back though, as Bill Cronkhite and Dave Frank each tallied to put the Broncos up 2-1. Roosevelt came back in the third to tie it up, behind a textbook three-on-two break-away in which the Larsons, Bart and Doug, fed Gary Olin on a nice top-shelf wrister. The score held at 2-2 through the third, and forced the contest into overtime. It remained that way until midway through the third extra session, when defenseman Elmer Walls, who wound up playing every minute of every game in the tournament, ended it all on a 35-foot prayer that somehow found its way over Jerry Gangloff's shoulder and into the top corner of the net. When it was all over, an exhausted I-Falls coach, Larry Ross, called it "the best high school hockey game he'd ever seen."

With that dramatic win, the stage was now set for a championship game of Herculean proportions. In what was billed as the "battle of the Falls'," Thief River Falls came out with something to prove. The Prowlers jumped all over the Broncos right out of the opening face-off, scoring just 10 seconds into the game when Glen Carlson and Duane Glass set up Cliff Strand on a nice one-timer. Thief River Falls made it 2-0 about six minutes later, when Jack Poole scored on another Glen Carlson assist. But the Broncos came right back when Oscar Mahle flipped one past Prowler goalie Rod Collins just 20 seconds later. Then, three minutes into the final period, Mahle scored his second goal of the game to tie it up at 2-2. The game went back and forth after that, with both squads mired in a physical and defensive battle. Finally at 9:55 of the second, Cliff Strand dished the puck to Jack Poole in front of the net, where he shoved it past goalie Bob Laurion for what would turn out to be the game-winner.

So compelling of a tale was that Thief River Falls championship season, that it even inspired a book by local author Mary Halverson Schofield, called "River of Champions." The book described how the boys persevered through so much adversity that year to win it all, including: nearly losing three of the boys who almost died in a blizzard the night before the St. Paul Johnson game, losing one of its star players to suspension just the day before

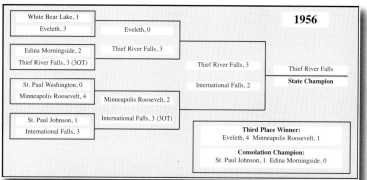

the playoffs began, and the fact that one of the boys had to scratch and claw his way through the tournament on novocaine, adrenaline and athletic tape because he was so hampered by injuries. The miraculous win was made possibly by Falls' goalie, Rod Collins, who Schofield remembered fondly. "The coach, Dennis Rolle, desperately needed a goalie," wrote Schofield. "So he took a bunch of kids, lined them up along a wall in the gym and hit tennis balls at them. Collins was the only one who didn't flinch."

1957

The 13th annual Tournament had a strange feeling to it in 1957. That was because for the first time since the event was held, Eveleth was not participating in it. While some were disappointed, there were eight teams in that year's field that were elated to not have to face them. Solid goaltending was the theme of this tournament, as there were a miraculous six shut-outs recorded in the three day affair. Murray was the exception to the rule in that opening round, scoring one goal against Roseau – which got a pair each from Ed Bulauco and Neal Johnson in the 5-1 win. The other three opening round games were all shut-outs, starting with South, which blanked Edina, 6-0, on two-goal performances by both Rick Alm and Jim Ekberg. International Falls got four goals from Dave Frank, another three from Oscar Mahle, and five assists from Bob Miggins as they spanked newcomer Hallock, 10-0. And lastly, Johnson beat South St. Paul, 3-0, on goals from Harold Vinnes, Jim Cocchiarella and Dave Brooks.

International Falls got two goals from Gene Steele and Oscar Mahle in the first, and another two in the third from Tom Neveaux and Dave Frank, as they beat South, 4-0, in the first semifinal game. The other semifinal contest would prove to be much more dramatic, as Roseau battled the Johnson juggernaut for a ticket to the finals. Johnson's Mark Skoog opened the scoring at 3:40 of the first period, only to see Roseau rally back for three quick goals in a span of three minutes – two by Dave Wensloff and another by Neal Johnson for a 3-1 lead. After Wensloff got his hat trick just 28 seconds into the second, Gary Ostedt, Harold Vinnes and Gary Schmalzbauer each scored for Johnson to tie it back up at 4-4. After a scoreless third, the game went into overtime. With back and forth play, Roseau's Arlyn Sjaaheim and Johnson's Tom Martinson played masterfully in net to force a second OT. Then, at 3:40 of the second overtime, Neal Johnson scored off of a perfect touch-pass from Dave Wensloff in front of the net to seal the deal for the Rams.

In the finals, Roseau would face International Falls. After a scoreless first period, the Falls got on the board when Dave Frank tallied at 1:25 of the second. Then, only 16 seconds later, Mahle scored on a nice wris-

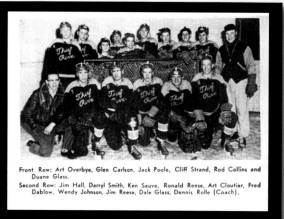

Front Row: Art Overbye, Glen Carlson, Jack Poole, Cliff Strand, Rod Collins and Duane Glass.
Second Row: Jim Hall, Darryl Smith, Ken Sauve, Ronald Reese, Art Cloutier, Fred Dablow, Wendy Johnson, Jim Reese, Dale Glass, Dennis Rolle (Coach).

The 1956 State Champs from Thief River Falls

Left to Right: Larry Ross (Coach), Ray Boyum, Robert Miggens, Tom Morse, John Kerry, Lester Etienne, David Frank, Oscar Mahle, James Wherley, Tom Neveaux (Capt.), Gene Steele, Lee Boyum, William Cronkhite, Richard Kalb, Tony Nagurski, Dennis Vance, Gary Thompson (Stu. Mgr.)

The 1957 State Champs from International Falls

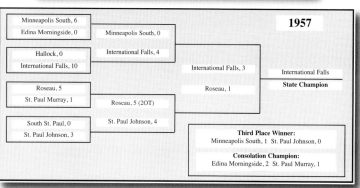

ter from the slot. Mahle then scored again 10 minutes later to give the Broncos a commanding 3-0 advantage. At 4:02 of the third, Jim Stordahl quieted the crowd when he scored on a Nystrom rebound to get to within two. But Bronco netminder Jim Wherley played big in the net from that point on, as the Broncos went on to win their first championship, 4-1.

1958

The festivities kicked off with Roosevelt taking on South St. Paul in the opener. The Teddies jumped out to a 1-0 lead on a Dick Wakefield score, only to see Ken Pedersen and Rich Brown score for the Packers in the second. Bud Bjerken then tied it back up for Roosevelt at 5:15 of the third to send the game into overtime. There, at 2:32 of the extra session, Pedersen scored on a Grannis assist to give the Packers a 3-2 win. Game Two was a rematch of the 1957 title game, only this time it had a much different outcome. Roseau's Bill Bulauca scored at 7:31 of the second to open the scoring. The score remained that way until 7:07 of the third, when the Rams got three unanswered goals from Don Ross, Larry Anderson and Larry Stordahl. Roseau goalie Dick Roth stopped all 13 shots he faced to hang on for the 4-0 shut-out.

Game Three would prove to be an upset, as St. Louis Park took on heavily favored Duluth East. After playing to a scoreless first, the Orioles' Bob Reith, Jim Boyce, Jack Burke and Don Brose all scored in a span of just seven minutes — pasting East goalie Paul Mehling. Tom Powell scored Duluth's only goal in the third, while Park's Lowell Nelson added one more for good measure in the 5-1 win. A couple of St. Paulites got together in front of their home town fans for the final game of the day. Murray's Lindel Hess and Jerry Groebner each scored in the first, only to see Harding's Dougie McLellan tally in the second, followed by Ron DeMike's goal with less than a minute to go in the third to force an overtime. It didn't last long though, as Dougie McLellan notched his second of the game just 48 seconds into the extra session to give Harding the 3-2 victory.

In the first semifinal contest, Roseau jumped out to a 4-1 first period lead over South St. Paul, thanks to goals by Keith Brandt, Jim Stordahl, Dave Wensloff and Larry Anderson. Stordahl and Wensloff each added another one in the second, only to see the Packers answer with goals from Grannis and Pedersen to make it 6-2 after two. Pedersen added another in the third, but it was too little too late as the Rams went on to beat the Packers, 6-3. The second semi pitted Harding against St. Louis Park. Goalies Arnie Johnson and Mike Storm each pitched shut-outs in the first, only to see Harding's Joe Schwartzbauer light the lamp at 4:56 of the second. Park's Bobby Reith answered with a goal of his own less than two minutes later to tie it, but Harding's Jim Olszewski got two quickies only 90 seconds apart after that to lead his team to a 3-1 win.

The finals featured last

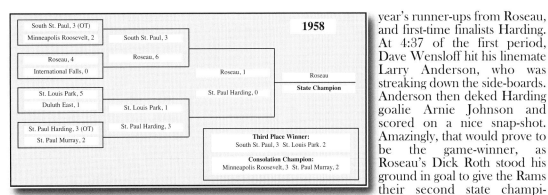

year's runner-ups from Roseau, and first-time finalists Harding. At 4:37 of the first period, Dave Wensloff hit his linemate Larry Anderson, who was streaking down the side-boards. Anderson then deked Harding goalie Arnie Johnson and scored on a nice snap-shot. Amazingly, that would prove to be the game-winner, as Roseau's Dick Roth stood his ground in goal to give the Rams their second state championship. It was a tough loss for Harding, which had outshot Roseau, 38-12.

1959

Roseau came out of the gates with something to prove in 1959, beating Thief River Falls, 7-2, in the Tournament opener. The Stordahl brothers were the heroes in this one, with Larry getting a hat-trick, and his brother Jim notching two of his own. Dan Cullen's four goals led International Falls to a 6-2 win over Robbinsdale in Game Two. Then, in the first evening game, South St. Paul's Doug Woog scored on a nice pass from Rich Brown early in the third to seal a 1-0 victory over Henry. Packer goalie Gary McAlpine stopped all 22 shots that came his way for the shut-out. In the late game, Washburn crushed Johnson, 6-0, on pairs of goals from Jim Councilman and John Simus, while goalie Jim Salmon came up with 23 saves for a shut-out of his own.

In the first semifinal game, Roseau's Stordahl brothers were once again the difference, as they each scored to give the Rams a 2-0 win over International Falls. The second semi pitted Washburn against South St. Paul. The game got underway with Bill Egan and Doug Woog each scoring in the first to give the Packers a 2-0 lead. Then, Rich Brown made it 3-0 for South just 41 seconds into the third, only to see Washburn storm back. In an amazing span of less than four minutes, Russ Hardin, Tom Gould, Larry Hendrickson and Jim Nyholm each got goals to rally Washburn ahead, 4-3, after two. The Packers didn't lie down though, as Doug Woog and Bill Egan each notched their second goals of the game in the third to once again put South St. Paul back on top. Washburn's Kenny Hanson tied it back up at 8:15 of the third and sent the game into overtime. After one scoreless overtime, Hanson took a pass from Russ Hardin at 2:12 of the second OT and slid it past the outstretched Gary McAlpine to give Washburn the dramatic 6-5 victory.

In the title match, Don Ross and Earl Johnson each scored in the first period to give Roseau a 2-0 lead going into the second. Washburn's Kenny Hanson, narrowed the gap by one when he scored on a nice slapper from the slot. Ross answered with his second and third goals of the game for Roseau though, and John Simus added one more for good measure as the undefeated 30-0 Rams went on to win the game, 4-2, for their second straight state title.

The 1958 State Champs from Roseau

Left to Right: Jackie McDonald (Stu-Mgr.), Richard Roth, Robert Lund, Dale Olson, Larry Anderson, Keith Brandt, Duane Espe, Donald Ross, Douglas Vacura, Ed Bulauca (Co-Capt.), Mitchell Vacura, James Stordahl, Larry Stordahl, David Wensloff (Co-Capt.), William Bulauca, Arvid Wallestad, Oscar Almquist (Coach).

The 1959 State Champs from Roseau

Left to Right: Jackie McDonald (Stu. Mgr.), Gerry Hovda, Richard Roth, Dale Olson (Co-Capt.), John Wahlberg, Earl Johnson, Darryl Heller, Keith Brandt, Kenneth Rygh, Errol Johnson, Donald Ross, James Stordahl (Co-Capt.), Douglas Vacura, Duane Espe, Vern Olson, Larry Stordahl, Francis Macioch (Asst. Coach), Oscar Almquist (Coach).

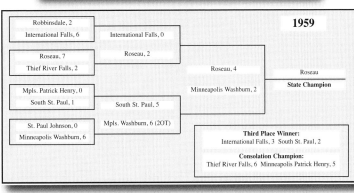

1960

Washburn opened the scoring of the opening match when Ken Hanson got an unassisted goal at 9:13 of the first. Duluth East forward Jim Ross tied it up on a nice pass from Bob Hoene early in the second, only to see Washburn jump ahead 3-1 on goals from Jim Nyholm and Jim Councilman. Ross tallied again for the Greyhounds at 6:49 of the second, which set off a Duluth scoring barrage. Within five minutes the Hounds got goals from Bill Sivertson, Bill Savolainen and another from Ross, this time on a sweet one-timer from Bill McGiffert at 10:53 of the third for the hat-trick. Duluth held on to win the game, 5-3, sending Washburn into the loser's bracket.

South St. Paul took on Thief River Falls in Game Two, as Arlan Hjelle kicked off the festivities for the Prowlers when he scored at 6:08 of the first. After a scoreless second, Doug Woog got the Packers on the board early in the third to make it 1-1, only to see Jim Wegge score for the Falls less than a minute later. The Packers then tied it back up at two with only 33 seconds left in the game to force the contest into overtime. There, 19 seconds into the second extra session, South St. Paul center Rich Brown beat Prowler goalie Wayne Halvorson for the 3-2 game-winner.

Don Laine and Jim Anderson each scored to make it 2-0 midway through the second in Henry's quarterfinal game against Eveleth, only to see Frank Judnick and Bill Stanisich tie it up in the third. Then, with just seconds to go in the final period, Henry's Jack Hanson beat Eveleth netminder Ray Kloiber on a break-away goal to seal the 3-2 victory.

The last quarterfinal contest of the day saw Washington's Jeff Sauer score an early pair of goals in the first and second periods against Edina. The Hornets came back to tie it up though on Franz Jevne and Paul Rosendahl's goals midway through the second frame. Washington's Don Norqual and Edina's Chuck Plain each added another in the third to send the game into overtime. There, it was Norqual finding the net once again, this time at the 3:51 mark, on a nice touch-pass from Jack Bunde for a Washington victory.

In the semis, South St. Paul's Doug Woog hooked up with Rich Brown to take a quick 1-0 lead over Duluth East. This apparently upset a few people from the Port City, as the Hounds howled back by scoring an amazing six straight goals. Bill Sivertson notched three, while Tom Weyl, Dave Steones and Mike Hoene each added one of their own. The Wooger scored again late in the third for the Packers, but it was too little - too late, as East went on to win the game by the final score of 6-2.

The other semifinal contest was a replay of the Twin Cities championship game between Washington and Henry. Henry's Terry McNabb scored at 6:20 of the first, only to see Washington's Bob Olson make it 1-1 late in that same period. After a scoreless sec-

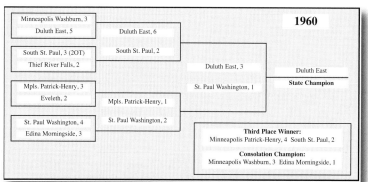

ond, Washington forward Bob Olson skated down on the Henry defensemen and set up his linemate Jeff Sauer, who beat Henry goalie Jack Toumie upstairs, for what would prove to be the game-winner at 4:24 of the third.

For the first time in a long time, the 1960 finals featured two teams that had never won it all — Duluth East and St. Paul Washington. Bill Sivertson opened the scoring for the Hounds, after pouncing on a Jim Ross rebound to beat Washington goalie John Fiandaca. Up 1-0, East kept the heat on when Sivertson fed Bill McGiffert out front at 5:24 to make it two-zip. Don Norqual rallied Washington back midway through the second though, when he made a cross-ice pass to a wide open Bill Olson, who put it past Duluth goalie Don Hilsen. The game remained tight from that point on, with Duluth keeper Don Hilsen playing solid between the pipes. After thwarting several scoring chances to keep his Hounds in the game, Hilsen finally breathed a sigh of relief when Mike Hoene added an insurance goal at 9:52 of the third to ice the game for the Hounds at 3-1, thus giving them their first ever state tourney championship.

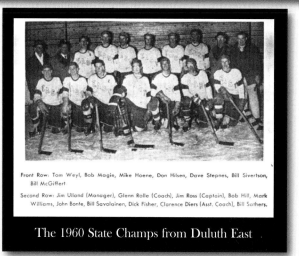

Front Row: Tom Weyl, Bob Magie, Mike Hoene, Don Hilsen, Dave Stepnes, Bill Sivertson, Bill McGiffert

Second Row: Jim Ulland (Manager), Glenn Rolle (Coach), Jim Ross (Captain), Bob Hill, Mark Williams, John Bonte, Bill Savolainen, Dick Fisher, Clarence Diers (Asst. Coach), Bill Sathers.

The 1960 State Champs from Duluth East

1961

North St. Paul opened up the tourney with a 4-1 win over Hallock thanks to a pair of goals by Dan Lindahl, as well as one each from both Bob Kohlman and Pat Goff. Roseau outlasted Roosevelt in the second game of the afternoon, as Ram's winger Dave Backlund scored the 3-2 game-winner on a beautiful pass from Jeff Vacura at 4:08 of overtime. Defending champion Duluth East narrowly beat St. Paul Johnson, 1-0, in the first evening game. With the game tied at 0-0 through regulation, Greyhound winger Bill Sivertson busted loose on a break-away and beat Governor goalie Bob Johnson at the 3:37 mark of the extra session to get the dramatic game-winner. Meanwhile, Duluth goalie Jon Birch stopped all 21 shots he faced for the shut-out. Then, in the night cap, South St. Paul, led by a pair of Doug Woog goals, pummelled Bloomington for 56 shots en route to an 8-1 victory.

Roseau then needed overtime to finish off North St. Paul in the first semifinal game. Rams winger Dick Ulvin proved to be the hero in this one as he notched his third goal of the game at the 5:25 mark of the third overtime by beating Polar goalie Jim Durose, thus giving his team an exhausting, 4-3 win. Then, in the other semifinal contest, South St. Paul's Doug Woog beat Duluth East goaltender Jon Birch midway through the first period on a pass from Brice Larson. East's Tom Weyl answered on an unassisted break-away that beat Packer keeper Gary McAlpine at 4:59 of the second, only to see South St. Paul's George Hocking tally at the 8:14 mark to give the Packers a thrilling 2-1 victory.

Steve Wilson (Student Manager), Jackie McDonald (Student Manager), Gary Johnson, Richard Rygh, David Johnson, Gary Grugel, Jerome Swenson, Paul Rygh, David Backlund, Paul Dorwart, David Peterson, Richard Ulvin, Robert Lillo, David Mattson, Jeffrey Vacura, Gordon Hipsher, Charles Oseid, Francis Macioch, (Assist. Coach); Oscar Almquist (Coach).

The 1961 State Champs from Roseau

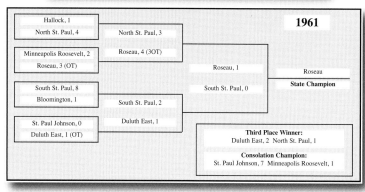

Roseau and South St. Paul got together in the finals, with Roseau's Dave Backlund striking first on a Paul Rygh centering pass midway through the first. The game went back and forth from there, with the Rams playing dump and chase in the last period to save their legs. Then, to really frustrate and tire out the Packers, Roseau iced the puck five times in a row during the final two minutes of the game. Oscar Almquist's Roseau Rams went on to shut-out the Pack by the final score of 1-0, winning their third championship in four years. Roseau's Gary Johnson needed to make only 14 saves in goal that night, but he stopped them all, including several from future Gopher coach Doug Woog, who, incredibly, failed to score for only the first time in nine tournament games.

1962

South St. Paul got a pair of goals from Joe Frank as well as a goal and two assists from Doug Woog, as the Packers went on to beat Edina, 4-2, in the opener. Game Two saw Roseau's Bob Lillo and Larry Skime each score a deuce as the Rams went on to beat St. Paul Monroe, 5-1. Greenway-Coleraine came out and smoked Washburn in the first evening game on four quick goals from Jack Stebe, Ron Rollins, Jim Barle and Rian Tellor, as the Raiders went on to clinch a 5-2 win, while Washburn's Bill Ronning scored a pair of goals in the loss. In the final quarterfinal game, the citizens of Minnesota got to witness the newest hockey phenom to come through the pipeline, International Falls' sensation, Keith "Huffer" Christensen, who opened the scoring early in the first for the Falls in its game against Richfield. While Glen Blumer added two more of his own in the second, goalie Mike Curran stopped all 20 shots that came his way as the Broncos cruised to a 4-0 win.

In a replay of the last year's title match, Roseau took on South St. Paul in the semifinal opener. Roseau's Larry Skime scored early in the first, only to see Joe Frank tie it right back up for the Pack. Dick Ulvin and Bob Lillo each scored for Roseau to put the Rams up 3-1, while Doug Woog assisted on a pretty Terry Abram goal for South St. Paul to narrow the gap. But when Lillo got his second goal of the game, it was all over. The Rams went on to beat the Packers 5-2.

The other semi saw Jack Stebe put Greenway up 1-0 at the 9:44 mark of the first, only to see International Falls' Jim Amidon get two goals and another from Matt Donahue, to take a 3-1 lead. Greenway's Jim Barle added one late in the third, but Falls' goalie Jim Lothrup stopped 12 third-period shots to preserve the 3-2 victory.

In the finals, International Falls met their northern neighbors from Roseau. Huffer Christensen came out and put his Broncos up 1-0 at the 3:49 mark of the first, only to see three more unanswered goals from Matt Donahue, Glen Blumer and

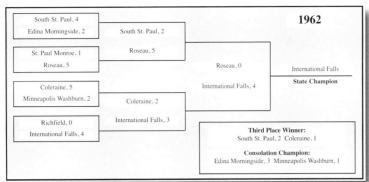

South St. Paul, 4 Edina Morningside, 2				**1962**
	South St. Paul, 2			
St. Paul Monroe, 1 Roseau, 5		Roseau, 0		
	Roseau, 5		International Falls	
Coleraine, 5 Minneapolis Washburn, 2		International Falls, 4	**State Champion**	
	Coleraine, 2			
Richfield, 0 International Falls, 4		International Falls, 3		

Third Place Winner:
South St. Paul, 2 Coleraine, 1

Consolation Champion:
Edina Morningside, 3 Minneapolis Washburn, 1

Left to Right: Larry Ross (Coach), Larry Roche, Don Milette,(Co-Capt), Jim Thompson (Co-Capt), Jim Amidon, Richard Haugland, Bob O'Leary, Charles Ketola, Matt Donahue, Glen Blumer, Bernard Woods, Les Eklund, Bob Hartje, Keith Christiansen, Mike Curran, Kevin Kennedy (Asst. Coach).

The 1962 State Champs from International Falls

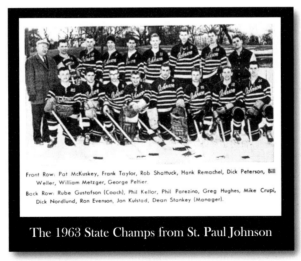

Front Row: Pat McKuskey, Frank Taylor, Rob Shattuck, Hank Remachel, Dick Peterson, Bill Weller, William Metzger, George Peltier.

Back Row: Rube Gustafson (Coach), Phil Kellor, Phil Parezino, Greg Hughes, Mike Crupi, Dick Nordlund, Ron Evenson, Jon Kulstad, Dean Stankey (Manager).

The 1963 State Champs from St. Paul Johnson

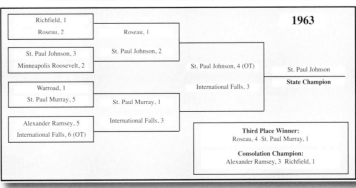

Richfield, 1 Roseau, 2				**1963**
	Roseau, 1			
St. Paul Johnson, 3 Minneapolis Roosevelt, 2		St. Paul Johnson, 2		
	St. Paul Johnson, 2		St. Paul Johnson, 4 (OT)	St. Paul Johnson
Warroad, 1 St. Paul Murray, 5		International Falls, 3	**State Champion**	
	St. Paul Murray, 1			
Alexander Ramsey, 5 International Falls, 6 (OT)		International Falls, 3		

Third Place Winner:
Roseau, 4 St. Paul Murray, 1

Consolation Champion:
Alexander Ramsey, 3 Richfield, 1

Bob O'Leary get by Rams goalie Gary Johnson through the second. Falls goalie Mike Curran, who would go on to play in the Olympics, held on and got the 4-0 shut-out as the Broncos dethroned Roseau to claim the title.

1963

Roseau beat Richfield, 2-1, in the opening game as Wendell Grand put Roseau in the black at 4:19 of the second. Richfield's Tim Olson answered three minutes later to tie it up, only to see Roseau freshman Bryan Grand hit Dick Anderson in front of the net for what would prove to be the game-winner at 7:59 of the third. In the second game of the day, Johnson's Rob Shattuck put the Governors on the board midway through the first, only to see Roosevelt's Chuck Gunderson and Jon Hall each tally to put the Teddy's up, 2-1, after two. But, thanks to two third period goals from Bill Metzger, the Governors rallied to beat Roosevelt, 3-2. Game Three saw St. Paul Murray's Jim Nylund score a natural hat-trick in a time-frame of less than nine minutes. Bill Carrol added two goals of his own as well, as Murray cruised past Warroad, 5-1, to reach the semis. In the evening game, International Falls took on Roseville's-Alexander Ramsey in what would prove to be a wild one. Down 4-1 midway through the second, Jim Amidon scored his second goal of the game to get the Bronco's rally started. Keith Bolin, Les Eklund and Amidon then scored in the third to give the Falls a 5-4 lead, only to see Ramsey's Jack Thoemke score with just 20 seconds left to send the contest into overtime. There, at 5:17 of the extra session, Falls forward Pete Fichuk slipped a shot past Ramsey goalie Gary Martinson to give the Broncos a dramatic 6-5 victory. Incidentally, Bob Boysen had a hat-trick and Jim Jaderston added a pair for Ramsey in the loss.

In the first semifinal game, Johnson narrowly got past a talented Roseau team by the final score of 2-1. After both teams went scoreless in the first, Governor's wing Rob Shattuck scored two quick goals, both on beautiful feeds from Mike Crupi. Roseau's Larry Skime scored a goal to get the Rams back in it in the second period, but Johnson's goalkeeper, Hank Remachel, who came up with 28 saves, held his ground to earn the win. The last semi was also a good game as International Falls met up with St. Paul Murray. The Broncos got on the board first in this one when Gary Wood scored a pair of goals in the second. Murray's John Zellner got his squad to 2-1 late in the third, but Falls' forward Bob Hartje put the final nail in the coffin with just over a minute to go in the game to clinch the 3-1 win.

The 1963 championship game would go down in the annals of hockey history as one of the best ever, with the defending champs from International Falls taking on St. Paul Johnson. The Broncos, despite being short-handed, struck first that night. Team captain Jim Amidon made it possible when he skated around four defenders to somehow find sophomore winger Gary Wood, who, from behind his own net, caught the pass and scored on a 30-foot bullet at 7:32 of the first. Johnson came right back though, as Mike Crupi tipped in a Shattuck shot only 45 seconds later. Then, just 17 seconds after that, Greg Hughes busted loose on a break-away to score again at 8:33, for a 2-1 Governor lead. The Falls, now rallying behind an injured Mike Crupi, scored just 89 seconds into the second on a long slapper by Bronco defenseman Dick Haugland to tie it up. (Incredibly, Haugland played the entire game with a ruptured appendix!) The play was fierce and physical by this point, as Bill Metzger scraped in front of the net for a rebound garbage goal at 5:08 to make the score 3-2. Then, with just 42 seconds left in the contest, who else but Jim Amidon grabbed a long rebound from just outside the blue line. As the crowd gasped, Amidon flew down the right side, floated to center ice and fired a rocket that found the back left side of the net, sending the game into overtime. With both teams going back and forth throughout the sudden death session, finally, at the 4:31 mark, Mike Crupi, back from his doctor's exam, took the puck in the corner and slid it over between a defender to Shattuck, who one-timed it past Falls goalie Larry Roche for the exhilerating 4-3 game-winner.

1964

The opening game of the tourney proved to be a revenge match between Duluth East and International Falls, which the Hounds beat in the Region Seven finals, thus forcing the Broncos to come in through the "back door" as the Region Three champions. Duluth got on the board first that morning when John McKay beat Larry Roche on a low slapper to make it 1-0. The Broncos came right back though, as Tim Sheehy tied it up at 1-1 at 9:20 of the first. The score remained tied until midway through the second, when Falls' winger Marshall Sether beat East goalie Ed Barbo for what would prove to be the game-winner.

Richfield powered past Roseau in the second game of the day, behind pairs of goals each from Ken Doerfler, Mike Burg and Dick Metz. Then, in the first evening game, Henry went on to tally twice in all three periods with five different players scoring goals. Dick Subject got two for Henry, while Scott Tarbox got the lone Bloomington goal in the 6-1 loss. The last game of the day was a laugher, as the defending champs from Johnson blanked Alexander Ramsey, 4-0. Bill Weller opened the scoring at 10:15 of the first, while Rob Shattuck added two and Mike Crupi got another. Johnson goalie Rich Peterson had to make only 12 saves for the shut-out.

In the semifinal opener, International Falls played a dandy against Richfield. Keith Bolin struck first for the Broncos at 3:19 of the first period. Both

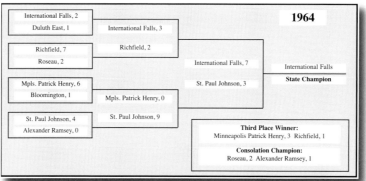

			1964	
International Falls, 2				
Duluth East, 1	International Falls, 3			
Richfield, 7	Richfield, 2			
Roseau, 2		International Falls, 7	International Falls	
Mpls. Patrick Henry, 6		St. Paul Johnson, 3	State Champion	
Bloomington, 1	Mpls. Patrick Henry, 0			
St. Paul Johnson, 4	St. Paul Johnson, 9			
Alexander Ramsey, 0				

Third Place Winner:
Minneapolis Patrick Henry, 3 Richfield, 1

Consolation Champion:
Roseau, 2 Alexander Ramsey, 1

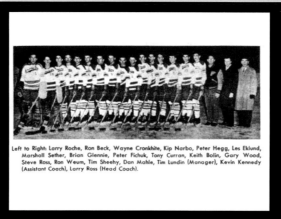

Left to Right: Larry Roche, Ron Beck, Wayne Cronkhite, Kip Narbo, Peter Hegg, Les Eklund, Marshall Sether, Brian Glennie, Peter Fichuk, Tony Curran, Keith Bolin, Gary Wood, Steve Ross, Ron Weum, Tim Sheehy, Dan Mahle, Tim Lundin (Manager), Kevin Kennedy (Assistant Coach), Larry Ross (Head Coach).

The 1964 State Champs from International Falls

keepers played well through the second as the score remained 1-0 into the third. Tim Sheehy made it 2-0 for the Falls just a minute into the last period, only to see Barry Bloomgren pull Richfield to within one at 5:58. Then, at 11:06, Tony Curran fed Sheehy in the slot for his second goal of the game. Richfield rallied late in the game, when Dick Metz scored with less than 30 seconds left, but it was not to be as the Broncos held on for the 3-2 win.

The other semi was an onslaught, as Johnson mauled Henry, 9-0. Mike Crupi, Bill Weller and Greg Hughes each had two goals in the win, while George Peltier, Gary LaMotte and Rob Shattuck each had one apiece. Meanwhile, Govs goalie Rich Peterson made just 18 saves for his second consecutive shut-out.

Then, in a rematch of the last year's finals, International Falls didn't waste much time in letting Johnson know just how they felt about losing the title to them the year before. Greg Hughes got Johnson on the board first on an assist from Rob Shattuck at 6:26 of the opening period. Broncos center Pete Fichuk came right back though, scoring on a nice wrister just a minute later. Shattuck again fed Hughes for another goal at 10:30 of the first, only to see Fichuk answer with his second goal of the period to tie it back up at 2-2. That's when the Falls said enough is enough and brought out the heavy artillery. Led by goals from Keith Bolin, Les Eklund, Gary Wood and a pair from Tony Curran, the Broncos went on to blow out the Governors, 7-3, for their third title.

1965

Johnson battled Alexander Ramsey in the opener as Ramsey's Bob Olein scored first, only to see Johnson's Bert DeHate and Gary LaMotte give their team a 2-1 first-period lead. Ramsey tied it back up on a Jerry Christensen goal, only to see Skip Peltier and Bert DeHate each tally to give the Govs a 4-2 win.

Thief River Falls, on goals from Monte LeMoine and John Olson, jumped out to a quick two-goal lead over Bloomington in Game Two. Gordon Henry and Ron Wheeler tied it right back up for the Bears just three minutes later though. Then, after a scoreless second, Bloomington's Gene Carr scored at 2:44 of the third, as the Bears rolled to a 4-2 victory. Game Three, meanwhile, was all South St. Paul. The Packers went up 4-0 against Southwest, on goals from Jim LeMay, Roger Klegin, Larry Palodichuk, and his brother Al Palodichuk. Southwest added one late, but Packer goalie Jim Quirk held on for the easy 4-1 win. The last game of the day saw northern powers, International Falls and Roseau, got toe-to-toe. Roseau's Jerry Klema opened the scoring just 30 seconds into the game, while Gary Wood and Dan Mahle came

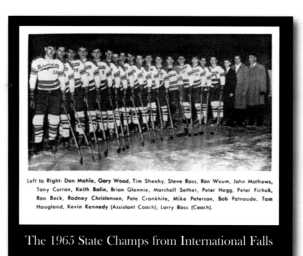

Left to Right: Dan Mahle, Gary Wood, Tim Sheehy, Steve Ross, Ron Weum, John Mathews, Tony Curran, Keith Bolin, Brian Glennie, Marshall Sether, Peter Hegg, Peter Fichuk, Ron Beck, Rodney Christensen, Pete Cronkhite, Mike Peterson, Bob Patnaude, Tom Haugland, Kevin Kennedy (Assistant Coach), Larry Ross (Coach).

The 1965 State Champs from International Falls

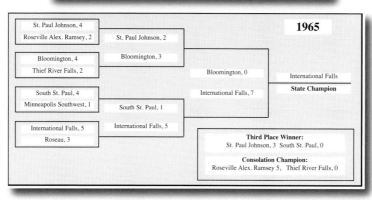

			1965	
St. Paul Johnson, 4				
Roseville Alex. Ramsey, 2	St. Paul Johnson, 2			
Bloomington, 4	Bloomington, 3			
Thief River Falls, 2		Bloomington, 0	International Falls	
South St. Paul, 4		International Falls, 7	State Champion	
Minneapolis Southwest, 1	South St. Paul, 1			
International Falls, 5	International Falls, 5			
Roseau, 3				

Third Place Winner:
St. Paul Johnson, 3 South St. Paul, 0

Consolation Champion:
Roseville Alex. Ramsey 5, Thief River Falls, 0

right back to put the Broncos ahead, 2-1. After playing a scoreless second, Austin Wallestad and Tom Billberg gave Roseau a 3-2 lead, only to see the Broncos roar back on goals from Keith Bolin, Dan Mahle and Pete Fichuk to win, 5-4.

The first semifinal proved to be one of the biggest upsets in tourney history, as Bloomington, which got two goals from Jack Nichols and another from Gordy Henry, went on to beat St. Paul Johnson, 3-2. While Roger Dupre and Bert DeHate each scored for Johnson in the loss, what made the game even more dramatic was the fact that while Governor goalie Jim Resch had only eight saves in the game, Johnson's boys peppered Bloomington keeper Terry Smith with 38 shots. Then, in the other semifinal game, International Falls' high-scoring center Tim Sheehy got a hat-trick to lead the Broncos over South St. Paul for a 5-1 win. Pete Fichuk and Tony Curran got the other two goals for the Falls, while Terry Abram managed the only Packer goal of the day.

Many thought that destiny would be on the side of the underdog Bloomington Bears in the title game, but oh were they wrong. The championship tilt proved to be a flop, as International Falls crushed the young cubs by the ugly final of 7-0. Dan Mahle got the hat-trick and Pete Fichuk and Tony Curran each added a pair in the Bronco win. Amazingly, the game could've been even worse had it not been for the unbelievable netminding of Bloomington's goalie, Terry Smith, who set a championship game record by making 45 saves.

1966

South St. Paul met White Bear in the opener, and thanks to a pair of Chuck Mortel goals, the Packers went on to beat the Bears by the final of 3-1. In the other afternoon game, the defending champs from International Falls took on Bloomington Kennedy. Tim Sheehy got the Broncos on the board first when he scored back-back goals late in the first and then early in the second. Jon Hammer got Bloomington on the board at 10:45 of the second to make it 2-1, but when John Mathews beat Bloomington goalie Bob Vroman late in the third to make it 3-1, it was all over. Game Three had Roseau going against Greenway-Coleraine, as Bryan Grand, who was making his fourth consecutive appearance in the tourney, scored all four of Roseau's goals to give the Rams a 4-2 win over Greenway. Kent Nyberg got both of Greenway's goals in the loss. The last quarterfinal game of the day featured Johnson vs. Roosevelt. Glenn Goski scored for Johnson at 5:11 of the second and Gary Johnson added another in the third as the Governors cruised to a 2-0 victory behind 25 saves from goalie John Anderson.

Both semifinals played out to be two of the best ever,

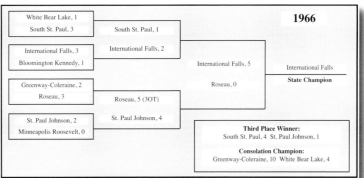

with International Falls and South St. Paul going at it first. The two-time defending champs from International Falls entered the 1966 tournament with a spotless 25-0 record, while averaging better than seven goals per game, yet holding their opponents to just one. They were led by Tim Sheehy, who had amassed 53 goals and 40 assists during that season. Coming out swinging, the Packers scored at 7:27 of the first when Terry Lawrence's long-range slapper was deflected in by Jon Bonk. Behind for only the second time all season, the Broncos lunged back into the game by scoring just seven minutes later in the first. The Falls then caught the Pack during a line-change, and made them pay when Rod Christensen fed Peter Hegg out front for an easy back-hander that beat South St. Paul goalie Jim Quirk. Then, striking while the irons were still hot, International Falls tallied just 10 seconds later when Sheehy stuffed in a Dan Mahle missed breakaway rebound in front of the net, as the Broncos hung on for a tough 2-1 win.

Johnson and Roseau hooked up in the other semifinal, as Governor winger Phil DeHate scored the first of his two first period goals at the 1:36 mark. Ryan Brandt and Mike Baumgartner each got one as well for Roseau that period to make it a 2-2 tie after one. Than, just 16 seconds into the second, Johnson's Ron Peltier scored on a couple of nice passes from Bert DeHate and his brother, Skip Peltier, to regain the lead. Roseau's Rockford Ammerman tied it back up in the third, only to see Doug Peltier put Johnson back on top at 4:42. Then with the Govs up 4-3, Mike Lundbohm scored at 8:28 to send the game into overtime. Finally, at 7:06 of the third extra session, it finally came to an end when Rocky Ammerman beat Johnson goalie John Anderson on a nice wrist-shot from the top of the circle to get the dramatic 5-4 game-winner, despite his team being out-shot, 54-25.

So, after all that, it was Roseau and International Falls for all the beans. The fans expected another thriller, but what they got instead was a blow-out. The Broncos, which peppered goalie Jim Nelson with 44 shots, got goals from Rod Christensen, Ron Weum, Steve Ross, Dan Mahle and John Mathews to squash Roseau, 5-0, for their third straight state championship. It's amazing to think that the Bronco dynasty would have had an unprecedented five consecutive championships, had it not been for the overtime loss to St. Paul Johnson back in 1963.

1967

The International Falls dynasty officially came to an end in 1967, when Greenway-Coleraine knocked them off in the Region Seven championships. The Raiders, riding high, took on Roosevelt in the opener, with the Teddies drawing first blood on a goal by Rich Bakke at 5:23. That would be all the scoring the Teddie's would be doing though, as the Raiders lit up Roosevelt goalie

The 1966 State Champs from International Falls

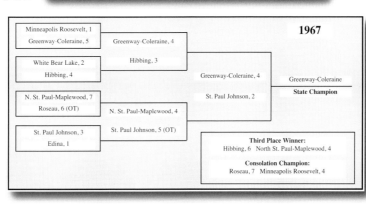

The 1967 State Champs from Greenway-Coleraine

Steve Price with five unanswered goals from George Delich, Jeff Kosack, Mike Holland, Jim Stephens and Ken Lawson, en route to cruising to a 5-1 victory.

Game Two was highlighted by an amazing six-goal first period between Hibbing and White Bear Lake. Nick Novak opened the scoring with a goal at 3:16, followed by a pair of Mike Barbato tallies at 4:29 and 7:23 to give Hibbing a quick 3-0 lead. White Bear came back just a minute later though, when Steve Hall beat Blujacket goalie Andy Micheletti upstairs. Dick Mlaker gave Hibbing a 4-1 lead, only to see Bears' forward Dennis Putney make it 4-2 at the 10:59 mark to seal the deal.

The third game of the day between North St. Paul and Roseau proved to be the third highest scoring game in tournament history. The Polars started the scoring just 90 seconds into the game when Craig Sarner beat Roseau goalie Jim Nelson. Al Hansen and Keith Ebert then scored to give North a commanding 3-0 lead. From there, Rams forward's Mike Lundbohm and Bruce Falk each scored a pair, only to see Dave Opsahl score two quick ones early in the third to give the Polars a 6-4 lead. Fifteen seconds later, Rams defenseman Lyle Olson made it 6-5, and five minutes after that Rocky Ammerman tied it up to send the game into OT. There, seven minutes into the extra session, North's Keith Ebert took a pass from Sarner and slid it under the pads of Rams' goalie Jim Nelson to give his Polars the dramatic 7-6 upset.

In the last game of the day St. Paul Johnson's Peltier brothers, Ron and Doug, scored all three goals in a 3-1 victory over Edina. Tom Carlsen managed Edina's lone goal as Governor goalie Terry Del Monte posted just 11 saves in the quarterfinal win.

In the first semi, Greenway took on Hibbing in another wild one. Bill Baldrica scored late in the first to give the Bluejackets a 1-0 lead. His linemate, Bob Collyard, made it two-zip just after the four-minute mark of the second, only to see Mike Adams get one just 20 seconds later for Hibbing. That's when the people of St. Paul became formally introduced to a lightning quick 140-pound centerman by the name of Mike Antonovich, who tied it up at 7:48 of the second on a nice assist from Ken Lawson. Mike Metzer tallied early in the third to give Greenway its first lead of the day, but Bill Baldrica struck again to tie it back up with just a minute left. Sixteen seconds later, Ken Lawson put a dagger in the collective heart of Hibbingites everywhere, when he flipped the puck past Bluejacket goalie Andy Micheletti to give his Raiders a 4-3 win. (Incidentally, while these two teams were clearly two of the best in the state, they were both beaten soundly by Duluth Cathedral, which, because they were private, and won the Independant State Title, couldn't compete in the public school's state tournament.)

The other semifinal game had the Polars of North St.

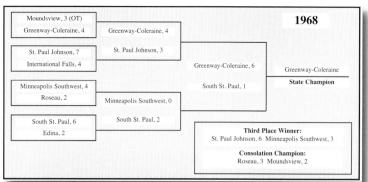

			1968	
Moundsview, 3 (OT)				
Greenway-Coleraine, 4	Greenway-Coleraine, 4			
St. Paul Johnson, 7	St. Paul Johnson, 3			
International Falls, 4		Greenway-Coleraine, 6		Greenway-Coleraine
Minneapolis Southwest, 4		South St. Paul, 1		**State Champion**
Roseau, 2	Minneapolis Southwest, 0			
South St. Paul, 6	South St. Paul, 2			
Edina, 2				

Third Place Winner:
St. Paul Johnson, 6 Minneapolis Southwest, 3

Consolation Champion:
Roseau, 3 Moundsview, 2

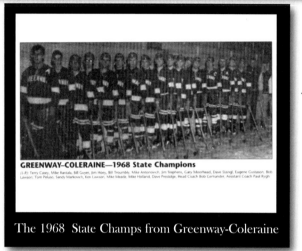

GREENWAY-COLERAINE—1968 State Champions
(L-R) Terry Casey, Mike Rantala, Bill Goyer, Jim Hoey, Bill Trisumbly, Mike Antonovich, Jim Stephens, Gary Moorhead, Dave Stangl, Eugene Gustason, Bob Lawson, Tom Peluso, Sandy Markovich, Ken Lawson, Mike Meade, Mike Holland, Dave Prestidge, Head Coach Bob Germander, Assistant Coach Paul Rygh.

The 1968 State Champs from Greenway-Coleraine

Front Row: Larry Thayer, Skip Thomas, Jim Knutson, Bob Krieger, Jay Larson, Tim Mc-Glynn, Bill Fee, Rick Fretland, Doug Hastings.
Back Row: Ed Zins (Asst. Coach), Ray Book (Student Manager), Jeff Field, Tim Carlson, Bruce Carlson, Steve Curry, Bill Nyrop, Mark Fretland, Willard Ikola (Coach).

The 1969 State Champs from Edina

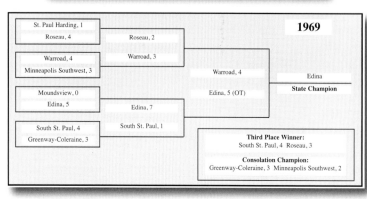

			1969	
St. Paul Harding, 1				
Roseau, 4	Roseau, 2			
Warroad, 4	Warroad, 3			
Minneapolis Southwest, 3		Warroad, 4		Edina
Moundsview, 0		Edina, 5 (OT)		**State Champion**
Edina, 5	Edina, 7			
South St. Paul, 4	South St. Paul, 1			
Greenway-Coleraine, 3				

Third Place Winner:
South St. Paul, 4 Roseau, 3

Consolation Champion:
Greenway-Coleraine, 3 Minneapolis Southwest, 2

Paul going up against legendary coach Rube Gustafson's St. Paul Johnson Governors. Govs center Ron Peltier lit the lamp at 1:46 of the opening period, only to watch Terry Wasiluk tie it up just 21 seconds later on an assist from Al Hansen. Hansen then got a goal of his own at 3:19, while Johnson's Doug Peltier tied it back up at 11:08 of the first. The Polars regained the lead just 17 seconds into the second on a goal by Dave Opsahl, only to see Johnson's George Fincel tie it up yet again. Then, early in the third, Craig Sarner beat Johnson goalie Terry Del Monte to regain the lead. But, as it had been all game, Johnson came right back on an Ed Giannini goal midway through the third. The score remained tied from there on in, and went into sudden death. That's where Ron Peltier took over, scoring his second goal of the game only 34 seconds into the extra session to give his Governors a 5-4 win.

So, the finals were set, it would be Greenway vs. Johnson, as Ron Peltier set up Russ Zahradka at the 4:33 mark of the first period to get things started for the Govs. Greenway roared back though, as Ken Lawson, Jeff Kosak and Jim Macneil all got second period goals to give the Raiders a 3-1 lead. The game remained tight through the second and into the third, until, with just over a minute left in the contest, Johnson's Glenn Goski beat Del Monte to get his team to within one. The Raiders pressed hard, but with just 10 seconds left in the game, the bespectacled wonder, Mike Antonovich, nailed an empty-netter to ice the game for Greenway, 4-2.

1968

As fate would have it, No. 1 ranked Mounds View, which was led by a pair of big, mobile twins named Bart and Brad Beutow, played the defending champs from Greenway in the opener. In a fabulous back and forth, wide-open game which wound up going into overtime, Dave Stangl took a Mike Antonovich pass and beat Mounds View goalie Mike Schuett at 5:31 of the extra session to give his Raiders a 4-3 victory.

St. Paul Johnson then beat International Falls in the second game of the afternoon, as the Governors got a hat-trick from Doug Peltier, a pair from Scott Frantzen, and goals from Steve Schwietz and Ed Giannini, to cruise to a 7-4 win. Pat DeMarki scored twice for the Falls in the losing effort.

Southwest, which got a pair of goals from Jack Gravel, went on to beat Roseau, 4-2, in the first evening game, as Ram's winger Earl Anderson put a pair of his own past Southwest goalie Brad Shelstad in the loss.

The last game of the day then saw South St. Paul roll over Edina, 6-2, thanks to Joe Bonk's hat-trick and Dale Abram's pair of goals in the third. Hornet center Bob Krieger also scored a pair of goals in the loss.

Greenway struck first in the semis on goals from Tom Peluso and Sandy Markovich to give the Raiders a 2-0 lead over Johnson through two periods. Governor winger John Horton made it 2-1, only to see Greenway's Ken Lawson and Jim Stephens each tally to make it a three-goal game. Ed Giannini and Horton then both tallied for Johnson to cut the deficit to one, but Greenway goalie Terry Casey held off a late Johnson rally to preserve a 4-3 win for the Raiders.

South St. Paul played Southwest in the other semifinal contest, with the Packers winning, 2-0. Terry Madland scored first on a nice assist from Dick Todd, while Dale Abram found the back of the net with just under a minute to go in the second for the other. South St. Paul goaltender Mark Kronholm made 22 saves in earning the shut-out.

The finals were hyped from every angle by the press, with the most obvious angle being Greenway's attempt to repeat as state champs. But another interesting sidebar was the fact that this was South St. Paul coach Lefty Smith's final game for the Packers, because he had recently been named as the University of Notre Dame's head hockey coach. Greenway opened the scoring at the four minute mark, when Dave Stangl beat Packer goaltender Mark Kronholm. South St. Paul evened it up early in the second though, on George Tourville's wrister from Joe Bonk. That would unfortunately be as close as Lefty would get that day, however, as Greenway exploded for five unanswered goals in the third. Both Mike Antonovich and Tom Peluso each had a couple of tallies, while Jim Stephens added another in the 6-1 win.

1969

For its 25th anniversary, the Tournament changed venues. Because the new Civic Center was being constructed alongside of the old St. Paul Auditorium, the tourney temporarily moved to Bloomington, where it resumed play in the newly constructed Met Center — home of the NHL's expansion North Stars.

Harding took on Roseau in Game One, with Mike Broten opening the scoring for the Rams at 4:51 of the first period. The teams pounded on each other from there until Dennis Trooien scored a power-play goal with just 16 seconds to go in the second. At 6:06 of the third, Roseau got what would prove to be the game-winner from young centerman by the name of John Harris. (Harris, in addition to winning an NCAA hockey championship with the Gophers in 1974, would go on to become Minnesota's most prolific amateur golfer, later starring on the PGA's Champions Tour.) Anderson and Smedsmo would each add goals later in the third as Roseau cruised to a 4-1 victory.

The second game of the afternoon pitted Southwest against a young Warroad team which was led by a kid named

Henry Boucha. While Southwest jumped out to a quick 2-0 lead on a pair of goals from Dixon Shelstad, it was Boucha who led the rally back and ultimately beat Southwest goalie Brad Shelstad for what would prove to be the 4-3 game-winner.

Mounds View and Edina played the first evening game, with Edina blasting some 40 shots at Mustang goalie Terry Moores. Five of them found the back of the net for the Hornets, with budding superstar Bobby Krieger getting the first one only a minute into the game. Mark Fretland added a pair of goals, as did his freshman brother Rick, while Bruce Carlson added another to make the final 5-0. Hornet's keeper Doug Hastings stopped all 14 shots he faced en route to earning the shut-out.

The best was saved for last though when it came to the final quarterfinal contest of the day. That's because South St. Paul and Greenway played a thrilling back and forth game that came right down to the wire. Junior center Paul Hanson put the Packers up first, when he beat Greenway goalie Mike Rantala at 2:15 of the first. Greenway answered back in the second by scoring three straight goals in a span of less than two minutes apart. Mike Antonovich got the first one, followed by Jim Hoey and Tom Peluso. Then, at 1:22 of the third, the Packers' Gene Mortel got one, followed by Mike Neska's just five minutes later to tie it up. Both teams played a furious final few minutes, but with just 19 seconds left in the game, Packer winger Scott Sandison beat Rantala through the five-hole to give his team a dramatic 4-3 come-from-behind win.

Region Eight rivals Roseau and Warroad then got together for an all-northern semifinal shoot-out. Henry Boucha put the Warroad Warriors up 3-1 at 7:01 in the third, only to see Mike Broten tally his second of the game just two minutes later. Roseau pressed hard to get the equalizer in the final minutes, but couldn't get the puck past Warroad goaltender Jeff Hallett, whose 14 saves were enough for the 3-2 win.

The last semi was a blow-out as Edina came out and scored the first six goals of the game against South St. Paul, en route to a 7-1 victory. Bruce Carlson and Bobby Krieger each had three points, while Tim Carlson, Mark Fretland, and Jim Knutson also tallied for Willard Ikola's Hornets. Meanwhile, Edina's Doug Hastings registered 25 saves in the win.

The stage was now set for one of the most emotionally-charged championship games of all-time, Edina vs. Warroad. The sentimental favorite Warriors were led by Henry Boucha, who had been playing nearly every minute of his team's games up to that point. Edina, on the other hand, was the "cake-eating" team that everybody loved to hate — the New York Yankees of Minnesota hockey, as it were. They were pompous, but they

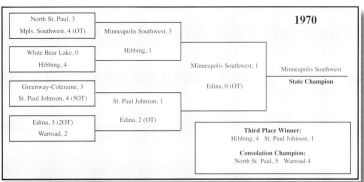

1970

North St. Paul, 3			
Mpls. Southwest, 4 (OT)	Minneapolis Southwest, 3		
White Bear Lake, 0	Hibbing, 1	Minneapolis Southwest, 1	
Hibbing, 4		Edina, 0 (OT)	**Minneapolis Southwest**
Greenway-Coleraine, 3			**State Champion**
St. Paul Johnson, 4 (5OT)	St. Paul Johnson, 1		
Edina, 3 (2OT)	Edina, 2 (OT)		
Warroad, 2			

Third Place Winner:
Hibbing, 4 St. Paul Johnson, 1

Consolation Champion:
North St. Paul, 5 Warroad 4

Front Row: James Barry (Asst. Coach), Roger Werner (Student Manager), Gary Fredrickson, Brad Richards, Dan Caspersen, Bob Williams, Bill Shaw, Doug Robbins, Tom Mitchell, Brad Shelstad, Meyers Peterson (Ath. Director).

Back Row: Larry Larson (Asst. Coach), Ron Sundby, Jay Idzorek, John Taft, Paul Miller, Ray Eliason, Bob Lundeen, James Moore, Greg Page, Doug Falls, Dave Peterson (Coach).

The 1970 State Champs from Mpls. Southwest

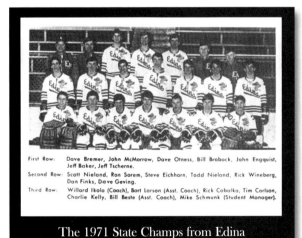

First Row: Dave Bremer, John McMorrow, Dave Otness, Bill Broback, John Engquist, Jeff Baker, Jeff Tscherne.

Second Row: Scott Nieland, Ron Sorem, Steve Eichhorn, Todd Nieland, Rick Wineberg, Dan Finks, Dave Geving.

Third Row: Willard Ikola (Coach), Bart Larson (Asst. Coach), Rick Cobalka, Tim Carlson, Charlie Kelly, Bill Beste (Asst. Coach), Mike Schmunk (Student Manager).

The 1971 State Champs from Edina

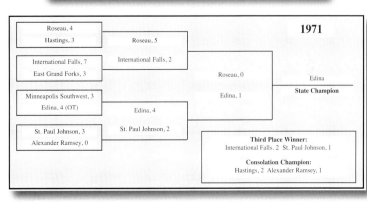

1971

Roseau, 4			
Hastings, 3	Roseau, 5		
International Falls, 7	International Falls, 2		
East Grand Forks, 3		Roseau, 0	
Minneapolis Southwest, 3		Edina, 1	**Edina**
Edina, 4 (OT)	Edina, 4		**State Champion**
St. Paul Johnson, 3	St. Paul Johnson, 2		
Alexander Ramsey, 0			

Third Place Winner:
International Falls, 2 St. Paul Johnson, 1

Consolation Champion:
Hastings, 2 Alexander Ramsey, 1

were good, having come into the game with an impressive 25-1 record. The Hornets had outscored their opponents that year by the insane margin of 142 to 19, while goalie Jim Hastings posted a whopping 13 shut-outs.

The game got underway with Edina setting the tempo early. Just 22 seconds after the opening face-off, Rick Fretland buried a long-range wrist-shot over Jeff Hallett's outstretched glove. The Warriors came back to tie it up on a power-play goal at 7:32, when Hangsleben and Kvarnlov set up Leo Marshall out front for the equalizer. But, just two minutes later, Eddie Huerd whacked in a rebound that bounced past Hastings to give Warroad a 2-1 advantage. Threatening to blow the game wide open, John Taylor came down on a three-on-one and let a blast loose that nailed the pipe. Edina then rallied, thanks to a couple of pairs of brothers. First the Carlson brothers, Tim and Bruce, hooked up to tie the game only 47 seconds into the second. Then, Rick Fretland added his second of the game just a minute later, on a nice back-hander from his brother Mark from behind the net to give Edina a 3-2 lead.

Then something happened that will forever be remembered in the annals of tournament history. Henry Boucha came down the ice and fired the puck into the Edina net. He followed his own rebound towards the backboards, and just as he got behind the goal, he got checked head first into the boards. Boucha went down in a heap and didn't get up. The record crowd stood in shock as Warroad coach Dick Roberts rushed onto the ice to check on his star player. Boucha was eventually helped off the ice from the controversial play and taken to the hospital where it was determined that he had ruptured his eardrum.

With their leader now out of the game, Warroad tried to get it together. But, when Edina's Tim McGlynn scored on a 20-footer only minutes later to go up 4-2, things started to look grim. Then, after an inspirational pep-talk from their coach, the courageous Warriors came back behind a pair of Frank Krahn goals to tie it back up in the second. The first came on a 20-foot blast from Bobby Storey, while the second came on a Al Hangsleben tip-in at 10:41.

The third period was fast and furious, but both keepers kept their teams in it to force a sudden-death overtime. The Warriors got the early break, but couldn't capitalize. Then Edina took over, as defenseman Skip Thomas fired a prayer of a slap-shot through traffic that somehow found the back of the Warroad net just over two minutes into the extra session. The Hornets had done it. The first suburban high school team ever to win a title, Edina had beaten Warroad, 5-4, in one of the greatest title matches in tourney history.

1970
Down 3-0 from North St. Paul winger Dan Leigh's pure hat-trick, Southwest came back in the third period of Game One to put together one of the best

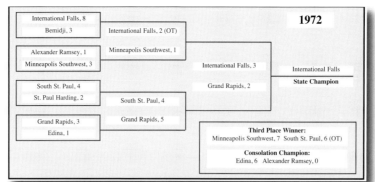

rallies in tourney history. After Dan Casperson scored just 26 seconds into the third, Paul Miller got the next two goals to force overtime. There, who else but Miller, scored on a low snap-shot just a minute into the extra session for not only the second pure hat-trick of the afternoon, but also for the 4-3 game-winner.

Hibbing pummeled White Bear Lake, 4-0, in Game Two, thanks to yet another pure hat-trick from junior winger Ron Brager. Future Gopher All-American Mike Polich got the other goal as sophomore goaltender George Milinovich came up with 20 saves to earn the shut-out.

The third quarterfinal contest between Greenway and Johnson turned into a gut-wrenching thriller, that just seemed to go on and on. The game started on a bad note when Johnson captain Mark Kroll broke his collarbone on the game's first shift. Johnson forward Neal Barrette opened the game's scoring at 9:27 of the first when he tipped in Les Auge's (another future Gopher All-American) slapper from the point. Greenway's Bob Lawson evened it back up just a minute later when he knocked in a Tom Peluso shot in front of the net that beat Johnson goalie Doug Long. Johnson center Tom Holm put the Governors back up on top one more time at 7:50 of the second, only to see the Raiders answer with two quick ones from Bob Lynch and Joe Miskovich in the opening minutes of the third to regain the lead. But Johnson's third-line centerman Jim Metzger came to the rescue midway through the third when he deflected defenseman Bill Nyquist's shot past Greenway keeper Mike Rantala. The 3-3 score held up through regulation as the teams went into sudden death. Johnson missed two power-play opportunities during the first and second overtime periods, but couldn't pull the trigger. Meanwhile, Johnson defensemen Les Auge and Bob Peltier guarded their blue line like it was a baby. The game raged back and forth, finally going into a fifth extra session. Finally, at the 3:24 mark of fifth OT, Johnson center Fran McClellan flipped in a Bob Peltier missed shot to notch the 4-3 game-winner. Johnson's goalie Doug Long, who made a tournament record 61 saves in the four-hour grudge match, was then mobbed by his teammates.

The 15,000-plus fans figured that they had definitely gotten their money's worth that night, seeing such a fantastic overtime game. Little did they know, but there was another one starting right before their eyes. The last game of the day featured the defending champs from Edina against the Warriors from Warroad in a rematch of the 1969 finals. Bobby Krieger would prove to be the hero in this one, as he opened the scoring not even a minute after the first face-off. Sophomore center Steve Eichorn then made it 2-0 for Edina at 3:40 of the second, when he beat Warroad's Jeff Hallett on a couple of nice set-up passes from Marty

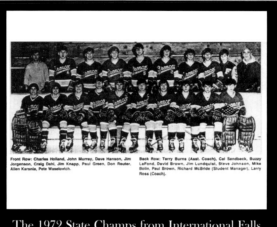

The 1972 State Champs from International Falls

The 1973 State Champs from Hibbing

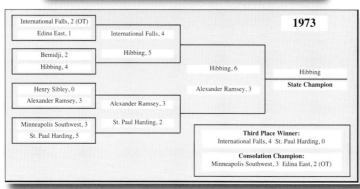

204

Rogers and Bill Nyrop. Down but not out, the Warriors came right back in the third, as Jerome Hodgson took an Ed Boucha pass and drilled it past Hornet netminder Larry Thayer. Lyle Kvarnlov added another goal just 15 seconds later to tie it up and ultimately send the game into overtime. There, already a minute and a half into the second OT, Bobby Krieger scored his second goal of the game by beating Hallett for the 3-2 game-winner.

Southwest went on to beat Hibbing in a tough and physical semifinal contest which featured seven penalties. The Indians got two goals late in the first from Dan Casperson and Paul Miller, and another in the second from Brad Richards as they rolled to the 3-1 win.

The other semi had Edina going against Johnson in yet another overtime match. Edina's Bruce Carlson put the Hornets on the board first at 4:20 of the opener, only to see Govs center Fran McClellan even it up just two minutes later. Fast-forward to the third overtime, still tied at one, when, finally at 4:34 of the third extra session, Edina's Bruce Carlson stuffed a Billy Nyrop pass by Johnson goalie Doug Long for the 2-1 game winner.

With that, an Edina repeat seemed eminent. The only thing standing in their way was coach Dave Peterson's Southwest Indians. The game was back and forth all night, as each team took its chances. Shelstad had his hands full all game, especially trying to keep tabs on the water-bug, Bobby Krieger, who came at the keeper time and time again. His biggest chance came with just 10 seconds left in regulation, when Krieger stole the puck, flew in all alone, deked across the crease, and flipped a back-hander towards the top shelf. Shelstad, calm and collected, stoned him yet again. After both goalies posted shut-outs through regulation, the championship match went into sudden death. Finally, at the six-minute mark of overtime, Jay Idzorek started a rush towards the Edina end and dished over to his defenseman, Bob Lundeen, who took an open shot from the right point. Bill Shaw, parked out in front of the net, saw the blast coming right towards him. Trying to deflect it with his stick, it instead flew right into his chest, and ricocheted into the top corner of the net for the dramatic, and bizarre 1-0 game-winner.

1971
Hastings and Roseau hooked up in the opener, as Roseau's Mike Broten tallied two goals early in the first, followed by another from defenseman Gary Ross to give the Rams a 3-0 lead. After a scoreless second, Hastings roared back to tie it in the third behind three straight goals from Gary Wytaske (on an assist from future North Star Dean Talafous), Ron Regenscheid and Jerry Meier. Then, with just over a minute to go in the game, Roseau's Mitch Brandt beat Hasting's goalie Ron Savage for the 4-3 game winner.

International Falls

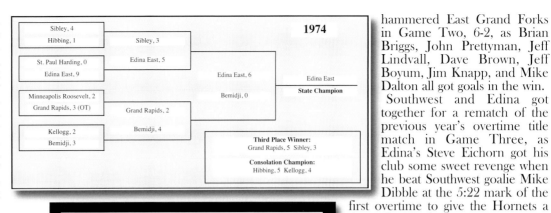

			1974	
Sibley, 4 / Hibbing, 1	Sibley, 3			
St. Paul Harding, 0 / Edina East, 9	Edina East, 5	Edina East, 6	Edina East	
Minneapolis Roosevelt, 2 / Grand Rapids, 3 (OT)	Grand Rapids, 2	Bemidji, 0	State Champion	
Kellogg, 2 / Bemidji, 3	Bemidji, 4			

Third Place Winner:
Grand Rapids, 5 Sibley, 3

Consolation Champion:
Hibbing, 5 Kellogg, 4

First Row: Jon Hughes, Bill Thayer, Charlie Petersen, Jerry Johnson, Steve Nichols, Tim Pavek, Steve Sherman.
Second Row: Coach Willard Ikola, Larry Johnson, Andy Overman, Mike Mastor, Matt Ikola, Dave Finks, Assistant Coach Ed Zins.
Third Row: Student Manager Adam White, Craig Norwich, Jim Anderson, Tom Brower, Bob Frawley, Steve Polsfuss, Student Manager John Senior.

The 1974 State Champs from Edina East

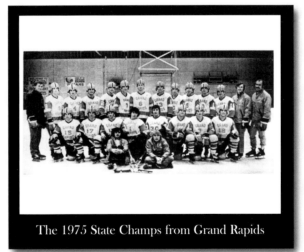

The 1975 State Champs from Grand Rapids

			1975	
Minneapolis Southwest, 5 / Roseau, 3	Mpls. Southwest, 2 (OT)			
Bloomington Lincoln, 4 / Hopkins-Lindbergh, 2	Bloomington Lincoln, 1	Minneapolis Southwest, 1	Grand Rapids	
Duluth East, 1 / Hill Murray, 3	Hill Murray, 0	Grand Rapids, 6	State Champion	
Henry Sibley, 3 / Grand Rapids, 8	Grand Rapids, 2			

Third Place Winner:
Hill Murray, 5 Bloomington Lincoln, 2

Consolation Champion:
Duluth East, 4 Hopkins-Lindbergh, 3

hammered East Grand Forks in Game Two, 6-2, as Brian Briggs, John Prettyman, Jeff Lindvall, Dave Brown, Jeff Boyum, Jim Knapp, and Mike Dalton all got goals in the win.

Southwest and Edina got together for a rematch of the previous year's overtime title match in Game Three, as Edina's Steve Eichorn got his club some sweet revenge when he beat Southwest goalie Mike Dibble at the 5:22 mark of the first overtime to give the Hornets a dramatic 4-3 win.

The last quarterfinal had St. Paul Johnson blanking Alexander Ramsey, 3-0, as Bob Peltier and Scott Klinkerfues, who each netted a pair, took care of the offense, while Governor goalie Doug Long made 14 saves in earning the shut-out.

It was then Roseau and International Falls going at it in the first semifinal, with Roseau coming out and scoring four quick ones from Jeff Tangan, Kent Lanlie and a pair from John Harris, to beat Bronco goalie Peter Waselovich. Falls' forwards Dave Brown and Jeff Boyum halved the deficit in the second, but Merlin Nelson's late goal iced it for the Rams, who went on to win the game, 5-2.

Edina now had to get by Johnson if they wanted to get back to the finals for the third time in three years. The Hornets jumped out to a quick 2-0 lead on goals from John Enquist and Tim Carlson. Then, Governor center Bob Peltier made it 2-1 at 2:43 of the second, only to watch the Hornet's Steve Eichorn tip in a Ron Sorem shot to make it 3-1. Johnson rallied behind Stan Blom's unassisted goal midway through the third, but Edina's Bill Brobak beat Doug Long on a nice wrist shot to make the final 4-2 in favor of the Hornets.

The championship game between Willard Ikola's Edina Hornets and Terry Abrams' Roseau Rams had a lot of hype going in. The record crowd of 15,319 at the Met Center was treated to a defensive gem that night, as Hornet's junior center Rick Wineberg got the game's only goal at 8:57 of the first, when he deked and beat Roseau goalie Tim Delmore on a low slapper. Dave Otness and Charlie Kelly got the assists, while junior goalie Dave Bremer posted just 19 saves to earn the shut-out. The 1-0 victory gave the Hornets their second title in three years.

1972
International Falls beat Bemidji, 8-3, in the opener behind Craig Dahl's hat trick and Don Reuter's two goals. Bemidji's Gary Sargent, a future North Star, added a pair of goals in the loss.

Southwest beat Alexander Ramsey, 3-1, in Game Two, as Mark Narum opened the scoring for the Rams at 9:06 of the first, only to see Murray Johnson tally twice in the second to beat Ramsey goalie Dave Miller for what would prove to be the game-winner.

South St. Paul played Harding in Game Three, as the

Packers pounded Knight's goalie Gary Flash with 50 shots on goal, including a 23-shot barrage in the third period alone, for the 4-2 victory. After falling behind 2-0, the Pack roared back for four straight on goals from Warren Miller, John Shewchuck, Rich Keogh and Tom Waldhauser.

Grand Rapids then upset the defending champs from Edina in the last quarterfinal contest of the day by the final score of 3-1. Led by Rapids defenseman Kelly Cahill's monster checks on several Hornet players, the Indians got goals from Jim Stacklie, Don Madson and Doug Christy, who hammered a Madson pass from behind the cage past Edina goalie Jeff Tscherne at 8:19 of the third. (For Gus Hendrickson, who starred for Eveleth High School in 1958, beating Eveleth folk-hero Willard Ikola was quite an accomplishment. "I remember going to church when I was a little kid and seeing Ike sit there," said Hendrickson. "I never took my eyes off of him — you'd have thought I was praying to the wrong guy all those years!")

International Falls and Southwest hooked up in the first semi, as the Broncos opened the scoring at 13:25 of the first when Allen Karsnia scored on a Craig Dahl rebound out front. Southwest came back to tie it when Tom Pontinen pounced on a rebound at 4:25 of the second. With the score remaining tied 1-1 through regulation, the game went into sudden death. The Bronco's third line of Buzzy LaFond, Jim Jorgenson and Paul Brown would prove to be the heroes in this one. LaFond started out the rush by dumping the puck behind the Indian net. Jorgenson then dug out the puck and fed it out front to Brown, who buried it past Indian keeper Peter Waselovich at 2:07 of the extra session to give his team a dramatic 2-1 win.

Grand Rapids then beat South St. Paul, 5-4, in the other semi. Greg Stanley opened the scoring for Grand Rapids early in the first, followed by Ken Yackel's shot from Roger Rothstein in the slot at 6:43. Jim Stacklie gave the Indians a 2-1 lead on a power-play goal midway through the second, followed by Mark Wenda's hard slap-shot goal from the right circle. Doug Christy and Tom Clusiau made it 4-2 for the Indians, only to see Dan Bonk and John Shewchuck, who nailed a 40-footer, each score to tie it up late in the third. Then, with just minutes to go in the game, Indians forward Greg Stanley found the back of the net to give Rapids the 5-4 win.

International Falls and Grand Rapids then met for the championship in front of some 16,000-plus screaming fans. The Broncos erupted for three third period goals in this one, and then had to hang on for dear life as the Indians mounted a fierce rally. After both teams played to a scoreless first period, Rapids winger Dan Madson scored an unassisted power-play goal with just less than a minute left in the second to give his club a 1-0 lead. The Broncos tied it

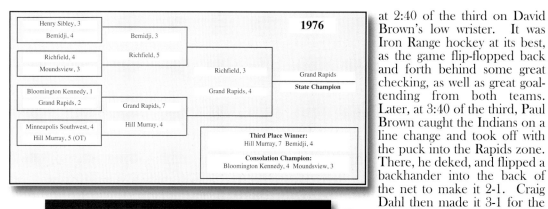

				1976
Henry Sibley, 3				
Bemidji, 4	Bemidji, 3			
Richfield, 4	Richfield, 5			
Moundsview, 3		Richfield, 3		**Grand Rapids**
Bloomington Kennedy, 1		Grand Rapids, 4		**State Champion**
Grand Rapids, 2	Grand Rapids, 7			
Minneapolis Southwest, 4	Hill Murray, 4			
Hill Murray, 5 (OT)				

Third Place Winner:
Hill Murray, 7 Bemidji, 4

Consolation Champion:
Bloomington Kennedy, 4 Moundsview, 3

Row 1: Jeff Nelson, Paul Diekmann.
Row 2: Brad Nordberg, Mark Schroeder, Erin Roth, Bill Hoolihan, Dan Lempe, Dave Madson, Pete DeCenzo, Doug Bymark.
Row 3: Don Carlson, Jim Jetland, Don Lucia, Tom Madson, Scott Kleinendorst, Al Cleveland, Dave Welliver, Jim Leone, Ed Gregerson.
Row 4: Jim Nelson, Rick McDonald, Gary DeGrio, John Acheson, Don Schroeder, Lee Thies, Bill Rothstein, Dave Akre, Lynn Ellington. Not pictured: Buzz Christensen.

The 1976 State Champs from Grand Rapids

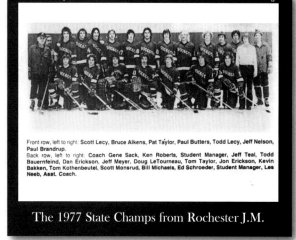

Front row, left to right: Scott Lecy, Bruce Aikens, Pat Taylor, Paul Butters, Todd Lecy, Jeff Nelson, Paul Brandrup.
Back row, left to right: Coach Gene Sack, Ken Roberts, Student Manager, Jeff Teal, Todd Bauernfeind, Dan Erickson, Jeff Meyer, Doug LeTourneau, Tom Taylor, Jon Erickson, Kevin Bakken, Tom Kothenbeutel, Scott Monsrud, Bill Michaels, Ed Schroeder, Student Manager, Les Neeb, Asst. Coach.

The 1977 State Champs from Rochester J.M.

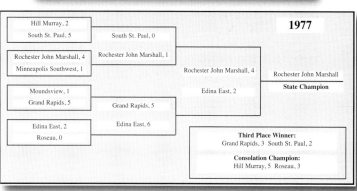

				1977
Hill Murray, 2				
South St. Paul, 5	South St. Paul, 0			
Rochester John Marshall, 4	Rochester John Marshall, 1			
Minneapolis Southwest, 1		Rochester John Marshall, 4		**Rochester John Marshall**
Moundsview, 1		Edina East, 2		**State Champion**
Grand Rapids, 5	Grand Rapids, 5			
Edina East, 2	Edina East, 6			
Roseau, 0				

Third Place Winner:
Grand Rapids, 3 South St. Paul, 2

Consolation Champion:
Hill Murray, 5 Roseau, 3

at 2:40 of the third on David Brown's low wrister. It was Iron Range hockey at its best, as the game flip-flopped back and forth behind some great checking, as well as great goaltending from both teams. Later, at 3:40 of the third, Paul Brown caught the Indians on a line change and took off with the puck into the Rapids zone. There, he deked, and flipped a backhander into the back of the net to make it 2-1. Craig Dahl then made it 3-1 for the Broncos at the 10:45 mark, on a beautiful goal that followed his own rebound. Rapids winger Doug Christy added one with 28 seconds left, as the Indians attacked six-on-five, but the gritty Waselovich stood tall in the end and preserved the 3-2 victory for his school's sixth state title.

1973

International Falls and Edina played to a scoreless first and second period in the opener before Bronco winger Buzzy LaFond finally scored at 8:35 of the third to put the Broncos up 1-0. Junior defenseman Craig Norwich then scored five minutes later to even it up, as the score stayed that way through the end of regulation. Then, at 2:19 of the game's second overtime, Falls' senior centerman David Brown took a Gary Beck pass and flipped it past Edina goalie Frank Zimmerman for a dramatic 2-1 Broncos win.

Game Two was also an exciting affair with Hibbing and Bemidji mixing it up. After Bemidji got two first period goals from Dick Howe and Andy Kannenberg, the Bluejackets stormed back behind Joe Micheletti's hat-trick to earn a 4-2 victory.

Ramsey made quick work of Sibley in Game Three, as Bob Richards scored a pair of goals and Tim Fitzsimmons added another in the 3-0 blanking. Meanwhile, Rams goalie Dave Tegenfeldt made 17 saves to earn the shut-out.

In the last quarterfinal of the day, Harding and Southwest played a dandy. Harding center Paul Holmgren got his Knights on the board just 30 seconds into the game when he beat Southwest goalie Gene Tierney on an unassisted break-away goal. The Indians came right back though, scoring two straight in the second on goals by Tom Pontinen and Mark Johnson. Harding's Tom Glancey answered at 12:54 of the second to tie it back up, only to see Indian center Tom Paulson score at 11:25 of the third. Then, with less than two minutes to go, Harding defenseman Nick Schwartz beat Tierney for what would prove to be the game-winner, as the Knights rolled into the semis with a 5-3 win.

The Hibbing Bluejackets, coached by George Perpich, and the International Falls Broncos, coached by Larry Ross, were both well disciplined Iron Range teams. Meeting for the third time that season, Hibbing was anxious to exact a little revenge for its 8-3 drubbing in the Region Seven finals, which forced the Jackets to come through the Region Three back door by beating Roseau. In a game that was very fast paced with a lot of hard hitting, the Falls jumped out to a quick 2-0 lead on Steve Johnson's 20-footer, followed by Kevin Nagurski's tip-in. Hibbing's Dave Herbst then added a pair of goals late in the first and early into the second to even the score at 2-2. The score remained that way until 1:31 of the third, when Joe Micheletti beat Bronco goalie Pete Waselovich. Up 3-2, Hibbing poured it on, as George Perpich Jr. got a pair of goals within a 30 second span to give the Jackets a commanding three-goal lead. The Broncos, visibly tired from their double-over-time win the night before, just wouldn't lie down though. They came right back on goals from Buzzy LaFond and Paul Brown with less than five minutes to go. The Broncos eventually pulled Waselovich for the game's final minute, but Hibbing keeper Tim Pogorels stood on his head, finishing the game with 22 hard fought saves to lead the Jackets to a thrilling 5-4 win.

The other semi had Harding and Ramsey playing to a scoreless first. Then, in the second, Ramsey took a quick two-goal lead on tallies from Ken Porten and Mike Green. Harding came right back when future NHLer Paul Holmgren fed Tom Glancey to bring the Knights to within one. Center Mike DiSanto then evened it up three minutes later, only to see Rams right wing Tom Williams beat Harding goalie Gary Flasch with less than two minutes to go in the game. Harding pulled their keeper in the waning minutes, but Ramsey hung on for a tough-fought 3-2 win.

The championship was now set with Hibbing and underdog Ramsey ready to battle. Hibbing's Tom Schleppegrell fed Mike Crea only 85 seconds into the game to get his squad on the board first. Ramsey center Pat Graizinger answered back with only five seconds to go in the first to make it 1-1. Ramsey then took the lead early in the second when Tom Fitzsimmons scored on a Mike Bailey pass. Then, Joe Micheletti tied it up on a short-handed goal to start a rally. First Micheletti fed George Perpich for a goal at 3:31 of the third, and then added one himself only nine seconds later. Perpich scored again just 14 seconds after that, only to see Micheletti notch his hat-trick less than a minute later. The amazing barrage of artillery was unbelievable as Hibbing went on to win the game by the final of 6-3.

1974

Sibley jumped all over the defending champs from Hibbing in the first quarterfinal game, as John Albers, Doug Spoden, Tim Salscheider and Mark Prettyman all tallied in the 4-1 upset victory.

Edina East came out and absolutely destroyed Harding in the afternoon game, pummeling Knight goalie Ted Vanderbeek with 49 shots on goal. Both Tim Pavek and Steve Poltfuss had

hat tricks, while Bill Thayer added a pair in the 9-0 onslaught.

Roosevelt and Grand Rapids got together in the first evening game, which would have to be settled in overtime. Mark DeCenzo's goal just 41 seconds into the game gave the Indians an early 1-0 lead, but the Teddies went ahead 2-1 just four minutes later on goals from future NHL star Reed Larson and also by Brian Young. Rapids tied it back up just 20 seconds into the third when Tim McDonald tipped in a Mike Johnson shot to send the game into overtime. There, Indians center Evin Roth took a Dan Lempe pass at the 1:40 mark of the extra session and fired it past goalie Richard Bain for the 3-2 game-winner. Bemidji edged Kellogg in the last quarterfinal of the day, as the Lumberjacks got goals from Dick Howe, Jimmy Conway and Brian Nelson. Kellogg rallied in the third to get to within one, but Bemidji's goalie Jeff Wizner held on for the 3-2 win.

Sibley and Edina met in the first semifinal, as Sibley's Bob Baumgartner got two first period goals to give the Warriors an early 2-0 lead. Edina, which hadn't been down by more than one goal that entire season, started to get worried. After a scoreless second, Doug Spoden made it three-nil, when he out-muscled two Edina defenders to slip a sweet back-hander past Hornet keeper John Hughes, just two minutes into the third. With the scent of upset now rancid, Edina geared up for what would prove to be one of the greatest third period comebacks of all time. Somehow pulling five straight unanswered goals out of their magic hat from Dick Pavek, Billy Thayer, Bob Frawley and a pair from Chas Peterson, the Hornets rolled to a fabulous 5-3 victory.

Bemidji knocked off Grand Rapids in the other semifinal, thanks to goals from Rod Beck, Jim Conway, Mike Fairchild and Bill Isrealson. The Indians got a couple of goals late from John Rothstein, but it wasn't enough as the Lumberjacks cruised to a 4-2 victory.

The next night Willard Ikola's Edina Hornets completed their perfect 24-0 championship season when they romped all over Bemidji by the final score of 6-0. Jerry Johnson opened the scoring just 30 seconds into the game and was followed by goals from Bob Frawley, Dave Finks, Jim Anderson, Andy Overman and Bill Thayer. Sophomore sensation Jon Hughes posted just 12 saves that night, as he earned the coveted championship shut-out.

1975

A significant event took place in 1975 that had never happened before in Tournament history. Private schools, which in the past played in their own annual "Private or Independant School Tournament," were finally admitted to the Minnesota State High School League. Terry Skrypek's Hill-Murray Pioneers were the first team to make it into the tournament field that year, coming in with an undefeated record and plenty to prove.

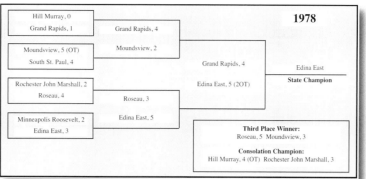

The 1978 State Champs from Edina East

Front Row: Mike Vacanti, Steve Ikola, Brad Reynolds, Scott Hampson, Tom Kelly Capt., Scott Johnson, Bill Peterson, Gary Aulik. Middle Row: Ed Zins, Ass't. Coach, John Donnelly, Mark Gagnon, Steve Brown, Mike Lauen, Rocky Smith, Greg Hampson, Willard Ikola, Head Coach. Back Row: Rolf Jensen, Stu. Mgr., Tom Carroll, Tom Johnson, Brad Benson, Kent Simmons, Ted Pearson, Fred Field Stu. Mgr.

The 1979 State Champs from Edina East

Front Row L to R: Tony Johnson, Greg Hampson, Tom Carroll, John Donnelly, Mike Lauen, Mark Gagnon, Mike Vacanti.
Second Row L to R: Coach Ed Zins, Jeff Davis, Bob Panchot, Ted Vaaler, Tom Paden, Steve Brown, Kent Simmons, Ted Pearson, Coach Willard Ikola.
Third Row L to R: Rolf Jensen, Tom Sullivan, Brad Benson, Bob Smith, Tom Paugh, Jeff Helgemoe, Jim Maley.

1979 Bracket

- Hill Murray, 3 / Edina East, 4 → Edina East, 12
- Grand Rapids, 4 / Roseau, 6 → Roseau, 4
  - → Edina East, 4 (OT)
- Irondale, 6 / Minneapolis Washburn, 4 → Irondale, 4
- Rochester John Marshall, 5 / St. Paul Harding, 3 → Rochester John Marshall, 7
  - → Rochester John Marshall, 3
- → Edina East, State Champion

Third Place Winner: Roseau, 9 Irondale, 7

Consolation Champion: Grand Rapids, 6 Minneapolis Washburn, 2

Southwest and Roseau commenced Tournament play, with the Indians going on to beat the Rams, 5-3, thanks to a late third period rally that was highlighted by Mark Gherity's game-tying and game-wining goals. Rams center Mike Burgraff added a pair of goals in the loss.

Game Two had Bloomington Lincoln going against Hopkins-Lindbergh. The Bears opened the scoring when Bart Larson beat Hopkins-Lindbergh goalie Bill Perkl at 5:53 of the first on a low slapper. The Flyers then came back in the second to take the lead on a pair of goals from Joe Lawless and Scott Whitney, only to see the Bears retort with three unanswered tallies in the second and third periods by Tim Harrer, Dave Gunderson and Bart Larson, to win the game, 4-2.

Hill-Murray beat Duluth East, 3-1, in the first evening game, thanks to goals from Tom Conroy, Mike Hurt and Mike Regan. The Hounds mounted a rally in the second as Phil Verchota hit Steve Mars on a nice give-and-go, but it wasn't enough as the Pioneers peppered East's sophomore goaltender, Walt Aufderheide, and hung on for their first win.

Grand Rapids scored early and often in Game Four, as they were led by Pete DeCenzo's hat-trick and John Rothstein's two goals and three assists to beat Sibley, 8-3. The Rapids pelted Warrior's goalie Pat Farrington with an amazing 51 shots en route to the win.

Southwest and Bloomington met in the first semifinal, and after a scoreless first, Bloomington center Terry Houck put the puck past Indian goalie Dan Mott at 5:38 of the second to take a one goal lead. John Meredith answered for Southwest midway through the third to tie it up and ultimately send the game into overtime. There, at 7:49 of the extra session, Southwest winger Steve Lindmeier beat Bloomington keeper Mickey Pickens on assists from Bob Bonin and Jeff Blake, to score the 2-1 game-winner.

The other semi between Grand Rapids and Hill-Murray was a rough and physical contest that featured some eight penalties ranging from elbowing, to slashing to interference. Indians winger Erin Roth was the hero in this one, scoring the game's only two goals, both coming midway through the second on assists from DeCenzo and Rothstein to beat Pioneer goalie Steve Janaszek. Meanwhile, Indians goalie Dan Clafton posted just 12 saves in the shut-out victory.

With that, the finals were set between Grand Rapids and Minneapolis Southwest. Southwest's John Meredith scored the game's first goal late in the first, giving his Indians a 1-0 lead that would last until the seven-minute mark of the second. That's when Grand Rapids brought out the heavy artillery. At 7:54 John Rothstein blasted one by Southwest goalie Dan Mott to even it up at one apiece. Then, less than three minutes later, Dan Lempe added a pair of

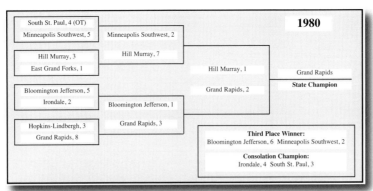

1980

South St. Paul, 4 (OT) / Minneapolis Southwest, 5	Minneapolis Southwest, 2			
Hill Murray, 3 / East Grand Forks, 1	Hill Murray, 7	Hill Murray, 1		
Bloomington Jefferson, 5 / Irondale, 2	Bloomington Jefferson, 1	Grand Rapids, 2	Grand Rapids	
Hopkins-Lindbergh, 3 / Grand Rapids, 8	Grand Rapids, 3		**State Champion**	

Third Place Winner:
Bloomington Jefferson, 6 Minneapolis Southwest, 2

Consolation Champion:
Irondale, 4 South St. Paul, 3

Front Row, L. to R.: Jon Casey, Robert Madson, John DeCenzo, Scott Billeadeau, Thomas Rothstein, Michael Brill, Shawn Edwards, Jeffrey Hovanec, Todd Grina, Jeff Storlie.
Second Row, L. to R.: Ted Brill, Asst. Coach, Todd Lempe, Bruce LaRoque, Pat Bowe, Steve LaRoque, Tony Kellin, Jim Malwitz, Brian Crippa, Glenn Palso, Will Sarkela, Athletic Director.
Back Row, L. to R.: Lynn Ellingson, Ass't. Coach, Rod (Buzzy) Christensen, Coach, Eric Lempe, David Casey, Don Carlson, Trainer, Bob Dunnell, Manager. Not Pictured, Chris LaVasseur.

The 1980 State Champs from Grand Rapids

Front Row, L. to R.: Steve Nornes, Rob Ohno, Dan Beaty, Joe Wech, Chris Robideau, Scott Schoening, Kirk Nelson, Tom Kelly, Terry Sullivan, Steve Bianchi.
Back Row, L. to R.: Asst. Coach John Bianchi, Craig Havlicek Mgr., Chris Gram, Scott Myklebust, Jim Becker, Jim Gess, Tony Mazzu, Paul Gess, Kyle Kranz, Lee Fjellman, Randy Thompson, Mgr., Coach Tom Saterdalen.

The 1981 State Champs from Bloomington Jefferson

1981

Bloomington Jefferson, 4 / Grand Rapids, 3 (OT)	Bloomington Jefferson, 4			
Apple Valley, 4 (OT) / North St. Paul, 3	Apple Valley, 1	Bloomington Jefferson, 3		
South St. Paul, 2 / Edina West, 1	South St. Paul, 3	Irondale, 2	Bloomington Jefferson	
Irondale, 7 / Roseau, 3	Irondale, 5		**State Champion**	

Third Place Winner:
South St. Paul, 3 Apple Valley, 1

Consolation Champion:
Grand Rapids, 5 Edina West 2

goals, followed by Dennis Doyle's wrister at 13:33. Roth then scored at 4:46 while DeCenzo added another one five minutes later, as Grand Rapids went on to take the lopsided 6-1 championship finale.

1976

After seven years, the bicentennial Tournament of 1976 said good-bye to Bloomington's Met Center, and hello to its old stomping grounds in downtown St. Paul, where she was originally groomed some 31 years prior. On March 4th, the tourney officially christened the new St. Paul Civic Center, a plush 16,188-seat arena, complete with see-thru plexiglas dasher-boards.

Bemidji edged out Sibley in Game One, as John Fairbanks got the first of his two goals just three minutes into the game. Sibley answered with three straight from Tom Cascalenda, Greg Cosgrove and Tim Fangel, only to see the Lumberjacks rally to score three unanswered goals of their own in the third from Fairbanks, Eric Niskanen and Lee Hanson to rally for a 4-3 win.

A couple of future 1980 Olympic stars got together in Game Two, with Richfield's Steve Christoff and Mounds View's Robbie McClanahan squaring off for a trip to the semis. Richfield, which got a pair of goals each from Christoff and Tom Szepanski, held on to fend off a late Mustang charge that included goals from McClanahan, Brad Michaelson and Jeff Lundgren, to earn a 4-3 victory.

It was Bloomington Kennedy meeting up with Grand Rapids in the third game of the day, as Kennedy's Dave Dillon scored first with just five seconds to go in the opening period. Indians center Pete DeCenzo then added a pair of goals in the second and third to ice the game for Rapids, 2-1. The first came on an Al Cleveland tip-in, while the second came off a nice set-up pass from Don Lucia. (Lucia would later go on to become the head coach of the Golden Gophers.)

Southwest and Hill-Murray met in the final quarterfinal, in what would turn out to be a wild one. With Southwest up 4-2 going into the final period, the Pioneers mounted a comeback which began with a Jeff Lukas tally to get to within one. Then, with their goalie Len Eagon pulled, Hill-Murray was able to get the equalizer with just 53 seconds remaining on the clock to force overtime. There, at 4:11 of the OT, Pioneer winger Mike Hurt came down and stuffed a Steve Pierce rebound past Indians goalie Mike Senescall to get the dramatic, 5-4, game-winner.

The first semi saw Bemidji and Richfield do battle. While Dan Dow opened the scoring for the Lumberjacks at 2:50 of the first, Richfield's Jan Lasserud and Bemidji's Lee Hanson each exchanged a pair of goals to make it 3-2 for Bemidji. Then, midway through the second and into the third, Spartan wingers Steve Christy, Tom Szepanksi and

Tommy Scudder all tallied to give Richfield the 5-3 come-from-behind win.

The last semifinal of the day featured yet another wild one between Grand Rapids and Hill-Murray. Indians goalie Jim Jetland had to make only 13 saves compared to his counterpart from Hill, Len Eagon, who faced 42 shots that night. Rapids jumped out to a quick 3-0 lead on goals by Dan Lempe, Tom Madsen and Al Cleveland, only to see Hill-Murray answer with two goals from Pat Regan and Steve Pierce to get it close. Dave Akre and Mark Schroeder each scored in the second, while Al Cleveland got his hat trick on a pair of back-to-back power-play goals late in the third to give Grand Rapids the 7-4 win.

Coach Jim Nelson's Grand Rapids Indians were now set to face Larry Hendrickson's Richfield Spartans for all the beans. Don Lucia set up Brad Nordberg to open the scoring at just 1:25 of the first, when he beat Geof Haraway on a pretty goal. Rapids then made it 2-0 when Al Cleveland tallied at 7:42 of the second. But Richfield came back behind its star player, Steve Christoff, who beat Jetland with just over a minute to go in the second. Erin Roth scored for Rapids midway through the third, only to see Christoff get another one at 12:21 to make it 3-2. Dan Lempe and Dave Akre hooked up just a minute later to make it 4-2 for Grand Rapids on an empty netter, only to see Christoff hit Jan Lasserud on a sweet one-timer to get it to 4-3 with just nine seconds left. Richfield's six attackers tried in vain to tie it up, but Jetland hung on to preserve the 4-3 win.

1977

Hill-Murray and South St. Paul got together in Game One, as Packer winger Keith Peterson's hat trick proved to be the difference in the 5-2 victory.

Game Two saw Rochester John Marshall come flying out of the gates against Southwest, as Scott Lecy and Todd Bauernfeind each scored in the first six minutes to make it 2-0. The Indians came back on a Kurt Madgyra goal with 29 seconds remaining in the second that beat JM goalie Paul Butters, but Lecy added his second of the game late in the third to ice it for the Rockets, 4-1.

Game Three was a blow-out, with the defending champs from Grand Rapids making quick work of Mounds View. Mark Roy, Scott Kleinendorst, Al Cleveland and Bill Rothstein (who netted a pair), all tallied for the Indians as they routed the Mustangs, 5-1, to advance to the semis.

The last quarterfinal of the day saw the rather inauspicious debut of one of the greatest lines in Minnesota hockey history, Roseau's Neal Broten, Aaron Broten and Butsy Erickson. Edina East got two goals from Bret Bjerken and John Donnelly in the third to blank the Rams 2-0. Hornet goalie Steve Carroll posted 22 saves in the shut-out.

The first semifinal contest had South St. Paul going up against Rochester. The game

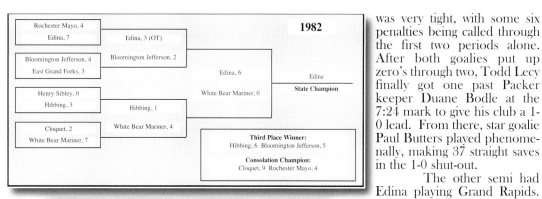

				1982	
Rochester Mayo, 4 / Edina, 7	Edina, 3 (OT)				
Bloomington Jefferson, 4 / East Grand Forks, 3	Bloomington Jefferson, 2	Edina, 6	Edina	
Henry Sibley, 0 / Hibbing, 3	Hibbing, 1	White Bear Mariner, 0	**State Champion**	
Cloquet, 2 / White Bear Mariner, 7	White Bear Mariner, 4			

Third Place Winner:
Hibbing, 6 Bloomington Jefferson, 5

Consolation Champion:
Cloquet, 9 Rochester Mayo, 4

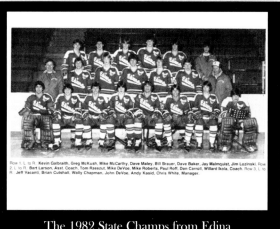

Row 1, L. to R.: Kevin Galbraith, Greg McKush, Mike McCarthy, Dave Maley, Bill Brauer, Dave Baker, Jay Malmquist, Jim Lozinski. Row 2, L. to R.: Bart Larson, Asst. Coach, Tom Rzeszut, Mike DeVoe, Mike Roberts, Paul Roff, Dan Carroll, Willard Ikola, Coach. Row 3, L. to R.: Jeff Vacanti, Brian Cutshall, Wally Chapman, John DeVoe, Andy Kasid, Chris White, Manager.

The 1982 State Champs from Edina

Front Row, L. to R.: Tim Galash, Jeff Borndale, Mark Horvath, Tom Follmer, Mark Krois, Nick Belde, Scott Faust, Pat Heffernan, Mike Schwietz.
Back Row, L. to R.: Assistant Coach Bill Lechner, Diane Yarusso (stat), Trisha Driscoll (stat), Jim Jirele, Jeff Thomas, Jim Boryczka, Tom Graske, Paul Syfko, Mark Stonich, Mike Roth, Todd Norman, Mark Nowicki, Bob Leier, Tony Curella, Brian Zelenak, Head Coach Terry Skrypek. Missing: Managers John Rather and Joe Giannini.

The 1983 State Champs from Hill-Murray

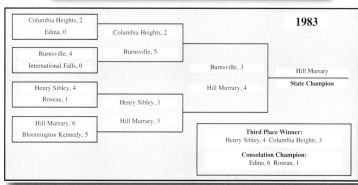

				1983	
Columbia Heights, 2 / Edina, 0	Columbia Heights, 2				
Burnsville, 4 / International Falls, 0	Burnsville, 5	Burnsville, 3	Hill Murrary	
Henry Sibley, 4 / Roseau, 1	Henry Sibley, 1	Hill Murrary, 4	**State Champion**	
Hill Murrary, 6 / Bloomington Kennedy, 5	Hill Murrary, 3			

Third Place Winner:
Henry Sibley, 4 Columbia Heights, 3

Consolation Champion:
Edina, 6 Roseau, 1

was very tight, with some six penalties being called through the first two periods alone. After both goalies put up zero's through two, Todd Lecy finally got one past Packer keeper Duane Bodle at the 7:24 mark to give his club a 1-0 lead. From there, star goalie Paul Butters played phenomenally, making 37 straight saves in the 1-0 shut-out.

The other semi had Edina playing Grand Rapids. The Indians, which had come into the tournament averaging seven goals per game, were the odds-on favorites to three-peat, despite the fact that Edina had been ranked No. 1 for most of that season in the polls. The two teams got started by trading a pair of goals each through the first as Mel Pearson tallied twice for Edina, and Gary DeGrio and Mark Roy scored for the Indians. Grand Rapids came out big in the second, scoring two straight within a minute's time on goals from Scott Kleinendorst and Steve Swentkofske. The Hornets remained calm though, and rallied behind a pair of Steve Pepper goals to score four straight in a time span of just less than six minutes. Indians' center Kurt Kleinendorst closed the gap with just over a minute to play, but his team couldn't pull their goalie because the Hornets kept dumping the puck into their zone. Edina held on to get the upset victory by the final of 6-5.

And so, in front of a record championship crowd of 17,083 at the new Civic Center, it was 24-1 Edina vs. 24-2 Rochester for all the marbles. Rochester came out the gates ready to go as Scott Lecy took the opening face-off draw, skated into the Edina zone, slipped a perfect pass over to his linemate Bruce Aikens, and watched him beat Hornet goalie Steve Carroll up high for a 1-0 lead. The Rockets took a 2-0 lead at 7:24 when Lecy took a long outlet pass from defenseman Paul Brandrup for a breakaway. He came in on Carroll, faked left, and went top-shelf on the other side. Edina came back just five minutes later on a Dave Terwilliger garbage goal out front, and then tied it up at 12:01 of the second when Tom Kelly's power-play blast from the blue-line rifled through traffic and into the back of the John Marshall net. Just a minute into the third, it was Lecy again for the Rockets, as he this time stuffed in a rebound in the crease. Up 3-2 with just a minute to go, Rochester got an insurance goal on a wild six-on-five play. Edina, which had pulled their goalie, was pressing hard to try and tie it up. Then, on a crucial face-off in the Rochester end, Lecy won the draw, passed it over to Brandrup for the give-and-go, and took the return pass the length of the ice for the open-net breakaway goal to seal it.

1978

For the first time in tourney history, players were required to start wearing face-masks in 1978 — a controversial decision that was met with much debate. Grand Rapids needed just a first period goal from Bill Rothstein to beat Hill-Murray, 1-0, in the opener, as Jim Jetland recorded 24 saves in earning the shut-out victory. Mounds View got goals from Steve Klein, Pat Conlin, Jeff Ness, Harry Geist and Pete Eastman, as they went on to beat South St. Paul, 5-4, in Game Two, while Packer winger Tom Sadowski had a pair of goals in the loss. A pair of Aaron Broten goals late in the third clinched a 4-2 Roseau win over the defending champs from Rochester in Game Three, and Willard Ikola's protégé, Steve Ikola, beat Roosevelt goalie John Berke with just 54 seconds left to get the game-winner in Edina's 4-3 Game Four victory.

Grand Rapids and Mounds View hooked up for the first semi, and thanks to goals from Tom Rothstein, Scott Kleinendorst, Irwin Frizzell and Don Schroeder, the Indians beat the Mustangs, 4-2.

The other semifinal contest had Edina going up against the Roseau Rams. Roseau, led by the amazing line of Aaron and Neal Broten and Butsy Erickson (a line that would later be reconnected at the U of M), came into the game with a perfect 23-0 record, having scored an amazing 10 or more goals in 11 games that season. Edina's Mark Gagnon opened the scoring on a short-handed goal midway through the first, only to see Neal Broten tie it up just two minutes later. Hornet winger Mike Lauen then beat Ram netminder Dean Grindahl at 10:59 of the first to regain the lead. After a Jeff Goos tying goal, Edina went ahead at 7:13 of the second when Tom Kelly fired a prayer from center ice that bounced off of Grindahl's shoulder and into the back of the net. Butsy Erickson then tied it up off an Aaron Broten rebound just three minutes later, only to see Lauen score again — this time grabbing a Broten rebound shot that had caromed off the pipe the length of the ice. Lauen added another goal late in the third to complete his hat-trick and ice the game for the Hornets by the final of 5-3.

Edina then faced another northern power in the finals, Grand Rapids, which had won it all in both 1975 and 1976, and finished third in 1977. Edina's Steve Ikola got the Hornets on the board first, when he took a couple of sweet passes from John Donnelly and Tom Kelly to beat Indian's goalie Jim Jetland at the 10:00 mark. Bill Rothstein answered by scoring a power-play goal with just over a minute to go in the period to make it 1-1. Rapids then made it 2-1 just 29 seconds into the second on defenseman Irwin Frizzell's shot from the point, only to see the stubborn Hornets rally behind a Mark Gagnon shot out front just 25 seconds later. The Indians resumed the lead on a Gary DeGrio unassisted wrister from the high slot that beat Edina goalie Gary Aulik. Edina tied it up at 2:44 of the third on Greg Hampson's 30-foot slapper, and then took a 4-3 lead at 9:40 when Scott Johnson tipped a long shot from Donnelly past Jetland. Bill Rothstein then jammed in a loose puck in front of the cage just 14 seconds later

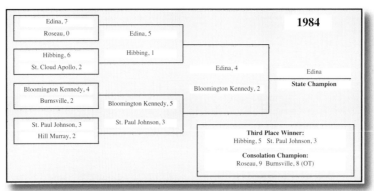

1984

Edina, 7 / Roseau, 0	Edina, 5		Edina	State Champion
Hibbing, 6 / St. Cloud Apollo, 2	Hibbing, 1	Edina, 4		
Bloomington Kennedy, 4 / Burnsville, 2	Bloomington Kennedy, 5	Bloomington Kennedy, 2		
St. Paul Johnson, 3 / Hill Murray, 2	St. Paul Johnson, 3			

Third Place Winner:
Hibbing, 5 St. Paul Johnson, 3

Consolation Champion:
Roseau, 9 Burnsville, 8 (OT)

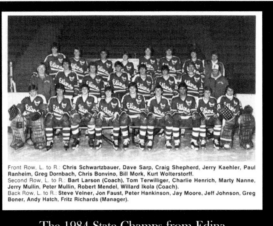

Front Row, L. to R.: Chris Schwartzbauer, Dave Sarp, Craig Shepherd, Jerry Kaehler, Paul Ranheim, Greg Dornbach, Chris Bonvino, Bill Mork, Kurt Wolterstorff.
Second Row, L. to R.: Bart Larson (Coach), Tom Terwilliger, Charlie Henrich, Marty Nanne, Jerry Mullin, Peter Mullin, Robert Mendel, Willard Ikola (Coach).
Back Row, L. to R.: Steve Velner, Jon Faust, Peter Hankinson, Jay Moore, Jeff Johnson, Greg Boner, Andy Hatch, Fritz Richards (Manager).

The 1984 State Champs from Edina

Front Row, L to R: Matt Larson, Kurt Hammond, Kevin Featherstone, Steve Treichel, Steve Ferrera, Mike Mageau
Middle Row L to R: Scott Bloom, Mike Travalent, Herm Finnegan, Greg Gelineau, Kevin Gorg, Scott Schulze, Scott Benson, Don Granato
Back Row, L to R: Coach Tom Osiecki, Mgr. Paul Lewis, Mike Luckraft, Kelly Ramswick, Kevin Schrader, John Borrell, Mark Osiecki, Mgr. Steve Kisch, Coach Bruce Anderson

The 1985 State Champs from Burnsville

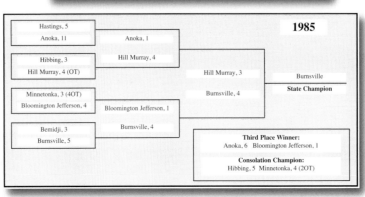

1985

Hastings, 5 / Anoka, 11	Anoka, 1		Burnsville	State Champion
Hibbing, 3 / Hill Murray, 4 (OT)	Hill Murray, 4	Hill Murray, 3		
Minnetonka, 3 (4OT) / Bloomington Jefferson, 4	Bloomington Jefferson, 1	Burnsville, 4		
Bemidji, 3 / Burnsville, 5	Burnsville, 4			

Third Place Winner:
Anoka, 6 Bloomington Jefferson, 1

Consolation Champion:
Hibbing, 5 Minnetonka, 4 (2OT)

to tie the game at four, and send it into overtime. After playing a scoreless first OT, Edina's Tommy Carroll, who came into the game as a substitute, got the game-winner by shooting his own rebound past Indian's goalie Jim Jetland at 1:06 of the second extra session. Edina, despite being outshot 52 to 23, held on for the 5-4 victory behind goalie Gary Aulik's championship game record 48 saves.

1979

The Hornets barely etched out a big and quick Hill-Murray team, 4-3, in the opener, thanks to goals from Steve Brown, Mike Laven, John Donnelly and Mark Gagnon.

Game Two was a clash of the titans, with Roseau battling Grand Rapids, and their young goaltender by the name of Jon Casey, who would one day play for the North Stars. Glen DaMota's hat-trick and Aaron Broten's two goals and two assists led the way for the Rams in this one, as they hung on to win a very tough 6-4 nail-biter.

Game Three saw Washburn jump out to a 2-0 lead over Irondale, only to see the Knights rally back behind future Gopher Scott Bjugstad's hat trick, and Mark Bader's two goals, to win the game by the final score of 6-4.

The last quarterfinal of the day pitted Rochester John Marshall against St. Paul Harding. Rochester jumped out to a 4-1 lead after the first, thanks to goals from Rick Ruesink, Pete Segar, Doug LeTourneau and Dirk Anderson. Harding then rallied back on a pair of second period goals from Jeff Thole and another from Bill Taleen, But, Todd Lecy's goal at 5:30 of the third period iced it for the Rockets as goalie Paul Butters hung on for the 5-3 win.

Edina and Roseau got together yet again for the first semifinal contest. These two teams had created a great rivalry over the past several years, and the 16,000-plus fans in attendance were eager to see them beat up on each other. Edina then came out and annihilated the Rams, 12-4. Five of the goals came on power-play situations, meaning that there were a lot of players sitting in the penalty box throughout this wild one. The Hornets got a hat-trick from Mark Ganon, and a pair of goals each from Tom Carroll and Mike Laven to lead the way.

The other semifinal game was also a high scoring affair, as Irondale met up with Rochester. The two teams methodically scored back-and-forth against each other in this one, with Rochester finally winning the contest, 7-4. The Rockets got a hat-trick from Todd Lecy and a pair of goals from Doug LeTourneau, while Mike Kelly scored two and added an assist for Irondale in the loss.

With that, the stage was now set for a rematch of the 1977 state championship game pitting Edina vs. Rochester. Lecy picked up right where he left off, scoring for Rochester just a minute into the game. Greg Hampson answered at the 4:56 mark of the first to make it 1-1. The score remained tied until the midway point of the second, when Brad Benson beat Rochester goalie Paul Butters on a nice break-away goal. The Rockets responded with two power-play goals midway through the third from Scott Monsrud and Doug LeTourneau to make it 3-2. But, with just over a minute to go in the game, and their goalie sitting on the bench, Edina's Tom Carroll found the back of the net to send the game into overtime. It didn't take long to settle the score in sudden death either. That's because at 3:27 of the extra session, Edina left winger Mike Laven deked and beat Rochester goalie Paul Butters on a nice pass from Mark Gagnon for the spine-tingling game-winner. The Civic Center's record crowd of 17,469 went berserk as the Edina players mobbed their goalie, Mike Vacanti, who had 29 saves in the 4-3 victory. The win gave Willard Ikola's Hornets their third title in just six years.

1980

Southwest and South St. Paul hooked up in the opener, as the Indians got on the board first when Dan May scored a short-handed goal at 4:08 of the first. The Packers evened it up three minutes later on a Gary Mausolf goal, only to see Southwest fire back with three straight tallies from Charlie Lundeen, Doug Hackett and Dan Burns. After playing to a scoreless second, South St. Paul came out and got it to 4-3 on a pair of power-play goals from Steve Zweig. Then, with just 28 seconds to go in the game, and the Packers goalie pulled, South St. Paul defenseman Phil Housley beat Southwest goalie Greg Dick to tie it up at 4-4. The Packers just kept the pressure on after that, as May scored his second goal of the game just 47 seconds into the extra session to give his squad a dramatic 5-4 win.

Game Two had the undefeated Hill-Murray Pioneers going against East Grand Forks. Thanks to a pair of goals from Pat Foley and another from Rob Schwietz, the Pioneers hung on to beat the Green Wave by the final of 3-1.

Bloomington Jefferson and Irondale met in the first evening game, and thanks to centerman Jay North's hat-trick, Jefferson went on to beat the Knights, 5-2.

The last quarterfinal featured Hopkins Lindbergh going against Grand Rapids. The Indians jumped out to a quick 2-0 lead within the game's first four minutes on goals from Jim Malwitz and Tom Rothstein that beat Hopkins' goalie Duffy Loney. The Flyers made it 2-1 at 11:38 on a Todd Bjorkstrand wrister that slipped past Rapids' netminder Jon Casey upstairs, followed up by a Pat Reichel power-play goal just over a minute later to tie it up. But, Grand Rapids took over from there, scoring six more goals in the second and third from Scott Billedeau, Jeff Hovanec, Todd Grina, Tom

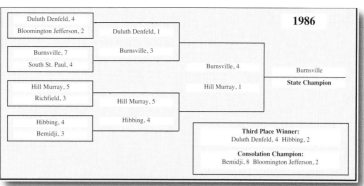

1986

Duluth Denfeld, 4 / Bloomington Jefferson, 2	Duluth Denfeld, 1	
Burnsville, 7 / South St. Paul, 4	Burnsville, 3	Burnsville, 4
Hill Murray, 5 / Richfield, 3	Hill Murray, 5	Hill Murray, 1
Hibbing, 4 / Bemidji, 3	Hibbing, 4	

Burnsville
State Champion

Third Place Winner:
Duluth Denfeld, 4 Hibbing, 2

Consolation Champion:
Bemidji, 8 Bloomington Jefferson, 2

Front Row L to R: Noel Manley, Marc Linsenman, Jon McDermott, Carl Anderson, Rob Granato, Brad Hendrickson. Middle Row L to R: Scott Bloom, Mike Gresser, Matt Larson, Matt Leegwater, Tom Dennis, Steve Ferrera, Mike Engfer, Steve Treichel. Back Row L to R: Coach Tom Osiecki, Manager Pete Heunisch, John Sundby, Dan Brettschneider, Mark Osiecki, Scott Schulze, Lance Werness, Manager Brian Ferrell, Coach Bruce Anderson.

The 1986 State Champs from Burnsville

dug the puck out of the corner, then skated around a Pioneer defender and lifted a backhander past goalie Jeff Poeschl to make it 1-0. Hill-Murray tied it up at 6:35 of the second when Mark Kissner grabbed Sean Regan's blue line blast rebound and stuffed it into the back of the net. Six minutes later, Indian winger Todd Lempe got what would prove to be the game-winner when he deflected a Shawn Edwards shot past Poeschl to make it 2-1. Hill-Murray tried like hell to tie it up, but Casey played huge in earning the 2-1 championship victory. For the Pioneers, which out-shot the Indians by a two to one margin (32 to 16), it was, incredibly, their fifth straight tourney defeat at the hands of Grand Rapids.

1981

The Jaguars jumped out to a 1-0 lead against Grand Rapids in the opener, thanks to defenseman Rob Ohno's power-play goal from Steve Bianchi at 10:04 of the second period. The Indians tied it up with just 15 seconds to go in the period when Bruce LaRoque beat Jefferson netminder Chris Robideau. Rapids then added a pair of goals from Eric Lempe and Tony Kellin to go up 3-1, only to see Bloomington answer with a pair of their own from Dan Beaty and Bianchi, who beat Indians goalie Paul Kaczor on a break-away with just 11 seconds to go in the game. The game then went into sudden death, where, just 49 seconds later, Bloomington's Steve Nornes assisted on Jim Gess' 4-3 game-winning goal.

North St. Paul and Apple Valley met for Game Two, in what would prove to be another overtime thriller. While Mike Anderson led the way for the Polars with a pair of tallies, it was Apple Valley's Bruce Heglund who finally got the overtime game-winner just 29 seconds into the extra ses-

---

Rothstein and a pair from Todd Lempe to cruise to an 8-3 win.

Hill-Murray and Southwest got together for the first semi and showed why there was no love loss between these two teams. In a game that included an incredible 14 penalties, Hill-Murray pounded the Indians by the final score of 7-2. Mark Kissner and Tom Xavier each netted a pair, while Pioneer goalie Jeff Poeschl registered 26 saves in the win.

Grand Rapids and Bloomington met for the other semi, in a penalty-laden affair that kept the referees busy all night. Bloomington jumped out first on a low slapper by Tim Sullivan that beat Jon Casey at 10:48 of the first. But the Indians roared back for three unanswered goals from Tom Rothstein, Jim Malwitz and Shawn Edwards, who got an empty netter, to beat Jefferson by the final of 3-1. Jaguar goalie John Columbo had 23 saves in the game, while Jon Casey came up with 22 of his own for the win.

Grand Rapids drew first blood in the finals against Hill-Murray, when at 13:45 of the first John DeCenzo, the team's scoring leader,

The 1987 State Champs from Bloomington Kennedy

1987

Burnsville, 4 / Roseville, 1	Burnsville, 5	
Hill Murray, 1 / Warroad, 5	Warroad, 3	Burnsville, 1
Edina, 3 / Greenway-Coleraine, 8	Greenway-Coleraine, 2	Bloomington Kennedy, 4
Bloomington Kennedy, 7 / South St. Paul, 3	Bloomington Kennedy, 4	

Bloomington Kennedy
State Champion

Third Place Winner:
Greenway-Coleraine, 4 Warroad, 3

Consolation Champion:
South St. Paul, 4 Hill Murray, 3

Front Row: L to R: Chris Lind, Marko Kreus, Mark Wallinga, John Carlson, Kent Landreth, Jason Miller, Mike Parent, Thane Vennix. Second Row: Coach Jerry Peterson, Coach Mark Hultgren, Joe Decker, Pat McGowan, John Manuel, Dan Bauer, Kyle McLean, Rick Weiss, Terry Burnham, Coach Wade Anderson. Third Row: Steve Cronkhite, Dave Stansberry, Tex Golding, Chad Pittelkow, Tom Hanson, Kevin Kalli.

sion to give the Eagles a 4-3 win.

Edina West and South St. Paul met for the third quarterfinal of the day, as Wes Olson put the Cougars up 1-0 at 9:41 of the first on a power-play goal from Mike O'Connor and Tom Frisk. The Packers came back on a power-play goal of their own that was set up by Phil Housley, who dished to Dave Sobaski in front of the net to tie it up at 1-1 just 11 seconds into the second period. The very physical game raged back and forth, with a whopping 10 penalties between the two clubs occurring in the first two periods alone. Then, with just five seconds left in the contest, future NHL All-Star Phil Housley skated in, deked, and beat Edina goalie Jim Lozinski upstairs for the game-winner.

The last quarterfinal game of the day had Irondale and Roseau going toe-to-toe. Roseau's Larry Goos opened the scoring at 2:27 of the first, only to see Irondale charge back for four straight goals from Mark Bader, Steve Hoppe, Mike Bjugstad and Steve Checco. Roseau answered with two more from Shawn Hallie and Keith Beito, but Irondale's Dana Hildreth and Steve Witucki responded with a pair of their own to give the Knights a 7-3 win.

The Apple Valley Eagles and Bloomington Jaguars met in the first semifinal match, as the Jaguars, which got goals from Joe Wech, Chris Gram and a pair from Dan Beatty, went on to beat the Eagles by a 4-1 margin. The other semi had Irondale and South St. Paul going at it in a wild one. The Packers came out and appeared to have this one in the bag after three goals by Tom Stiles, Phil Housley and Larry Housley. But, Irondale, which got second and third period goals from Loren Bayer, Lou Hedberg, Ken Brovold, Dave Kirwin and Steve Hoppe, rallied back to win the game by the final score of 5-3.

So, it would be the Jaguars and Knights in the title game. Irondale opened the scoring at 9:44 of the first when defenseman Dave Kirwin beat Bloomington keeper Chris Robideau on an unassisted slapper to make it 1-0. The Jags answered back with two of their own, when Jim Becker and Paul Gess tallied late in the first period to take a 2-1 lead. The Jags added another goal less than a minute into the second on a Tony Mazzu goal from Steve Bianchi and Dan Beatty to take a two goal lead. Irondale pressed hard in the last seconds of the game, finally getting one back on the six-on-five advantage with just four seconds to go, but the Jags held on to win the game and the title by the final of 3-2.

1982

Rochester Mayo and Edina (Edina-West was consolidated into Edina-East to form one combined school after eight years as two separate programs), played in a wild Game One, with the Hornets coming up victorious. Edina's John DeVoe started it out by scoring at 8:08 of the first, only to see Mayo come right back to score three quick ones for a 3-1 lead. Edina, led by Dave Maley's two goals, then promptly

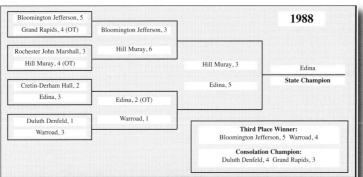

```
Bloomington Jefferson, 5
Grand Rapids, 4 (OT)        Bloomington Jefferson, 3                                    1988
Rochester John Marshall, 3   Hill Muray, 6
Hill Muray, 4 (OT)                                    Hill Muray, 3
Cretin-Derham Hall, 2                                 Edina, 5          Edina
Edina, 3                     Edina, 2 (OT)                              State Champion
Duluth Denfeld, 1            Warroad, 1
Warroad, 3
```

Third Place Winner:
Bloomington Jefferson, 5 Warroad, 4

Consolation Champion:
Duluth Denfeld, 4 Grand Rapids, 3

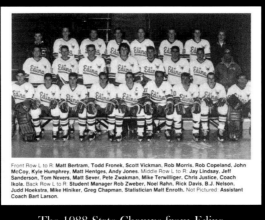

The 1988 State Champs from Edina

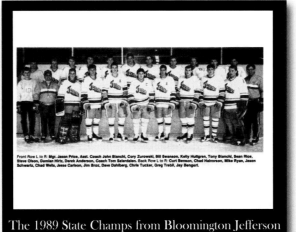

The 1989 State Champs from Bloomington Jefferson

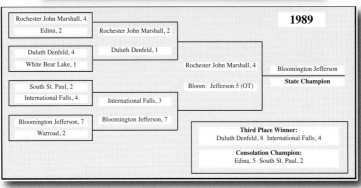

```
Rochester John Marshall, 4
Edina, 2                    Rochester John Marshall, 2                                  1989
Duluth Denfeld, 4           Duluth Denfeld, 1
White Bear Lake, 1                                   Rochester John Marshall, 4
South St. Paul, 2                                    Bloom. Jefferson 5 (OT)   Bloomington Jefferson
International Falls, 4       International Falls, 3                             State Champion
Bloomington Jefferson, 7    Bloomington Jefferson, 7
Warroad, 2
```

Third Place Winner:
Duluth Denfeld, 8 International Falls, 4

Consolation Champion:
Edina, 5 South St. Paul, 2

responded by scoring six unanswered goals to win the game, 7-3.

Game Two saw Bloomington beating East Grand Forks, 4-3, thanks to Steve Bianchi and Kyle Kranz' one goal and one assist. Meanwhile, Hibbing blanked Sibley, 3-0, on a pair of Gary and Greg Hooper goals to claim Game Three.

The last quarterfinal had Cloquet taking on White Bear Mariner in another blow-out. White Bear's Brydges had a hat trick while his teammate McLeod added a pair in the 7-2 drubbing. For Cloquet, it was a tough loss. The Lumberjacks were making their first-ever appearance in the tourney, and to top it off, they were missing their star player, Corey Millen, a future NHLer, who had broken his ankle in the sectional playoffs.

Edina then met Jefferson in the first semifinal contest, as the two teams skated to a scoreless first period. Hornets winger Paul Roff opened the scoring at 6:01 of the second period when he knocked in Jeff Vacanti's rebound to make it 1-0. The Jags answered at 8:17 when Kyle Kranz's 15-foot one-timer from Terry Sullivan found the roof of the net. The teams skated into the third when Roff got his second goal of the game at the 5:50 mark on a nice wrister from just outside the circle. With Jefferson's goalie pulled in favor of a sixth attacker, and less than a minute left in regulation, Scott Myklebust zipped a pass over to Kranz, who beat Galbraith on a beautiful slapper at the 14:39 mark to send the game into overtime. There, with just 57 seconds left in the eight-minute session, Edina's Dan Carroll passed the puck up to Mike DeVoe, who touch-passed it to Wally Chapman, who in turn ripped a 30-foot slapper off the side of the crossbar and into the net for the dramatic 3-2 game-winner.

The other semi saw much less dramatics, as White Bear Mariner beat Hibbing 4-1, on goals from Baker, Schultz, and a pair from Anderson. Mariner goalie Bohrer made 28 saves in the semifinal win, to give his team its first ever trip to the finals.

The Mariners and Hornets then met for the title, in what turned out to be a laugher. The 18,985 fans at the Civic Center could be seen leaving early and often in this one as Edina gave Willard Ikola his sixth state title by scoring six unanswered goals to blank White Bear, 6-0. Edina goalie Kevin Galbraith posted just seven saves in the title game shut-out, something that hadn't happened in Tournament history since 1974. Scoring for the Hornets were: Dan Carroll, Mike McCarthy, Jeff Vacanti, Dave Maley, Bill Brauer and Paul Roff.

1983

Two significant events happened in 1983 that gave the Minnesota State High School Tournament a lot of great local, as well as national exposure. First, WCCO-TV began televising the Tournament throughout the state, giving everyone at home the chance to follow the games. Secondly, Sports Illustrated's famed scribe, E.M Swift, wrote a wonderful feature story about the Tournament, entitled: "The Thrill of a Lifetime." The 11-page article, complete with eight color illustrations, let the entire world know about our little secret up here in the great northwoods, and instantly put Minnesota high school hockey on par with the likes of Indiana basketball and Texas football.

Edina, which joined most of the other schools at the tournament by switching from the traditional hockey socks and breezers to those hideous "long-pant" incarnations called *"Cooperalls,"* met Columbia Heights in the first quarterfinal game, as the Hylanders got goals from Joe Mickelson and D.J. Haller to earn a 2-0 first round upset over the Hornets. Columbia Heights goalie Reggie Miracle recorded 29 saves in the shut-out.

Game Two saw yet another shut-out, as Burnsville blanked International Falls, 4-0. Future NHLer Todd Okerlund (who was also the son of pro wrestling's famed "Mean-Gene" Okerlund), led the Braves with a pair of goals and an assist, while goalie John Olson posted just 13 saves in net.

The third game of the day was also a blow-out, as Henry Sibley beat Roseau, 4-1, on a pair of goals from Tom Genz. Brent Nagel and Steve Fleming also tallied for the Warriors, while defenseman Tom Pederson got Roseau's lone goal at 6:38 of the third period.

The final quarter featured the undefeated Hill-Murray Pioneers against the Bloomington Kennedy Eagles in a contest that came down to the wire. Kennedy got on the board first when Larry Leeman scored just 26 seconds into the game, while Tim Cline evened it up just seven minutes later. Pioneer right wing Tony Curella made it 2-1 at 9:02, only to see Eagles winger Dallas Miller beat Pioneer goalie Tim Galash with only a minute to go in the first. Hill-Murray, down 3-1, came out swinging in the second and put up four straight goals from Nick Bede, Jeff Borndale, Curella and Mark Horvath to take the lead. Kennedy responded with a pair of tallies from Jim Hartman and Pat Swetela to tie it up yet again, but with only 43 seconds left in the game, Tony Curella notched his hat-trick by beating Eagle keeper Jeff Miles for the 6-5 game-winner.

Burnsville beat Columbia Heights in the first semifinal game when Dave MacNulty, after being dragged down on a breakaway, broke a 2-2 tie on an exciting penalty shot with less than five minutes to go in the game. (It was the first successful penalty shot in the state tournament since 1960.) The Braves then added two more empty netters in the final minute of the contest to capture the 5-2 win.

Henry Sibley and Hill-Murray met for the second semifinal, in a game that

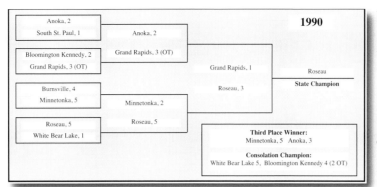

was all Hill-Murray. Center Mark Horvath had a pair of power-play goals in this one, while Jeff Borndale added another in the 3-1 win.

The finals then saw Hill-Murray and Burnsville go at it, as Braves center Louie Molnar opened the scoring at 4:32 of the first on a Dave Thon assist. Hill came back on Mark Krois' put-in eight minutes later, only to see Burnsville's Todd Skime tally on a power-pay goal at 4:11 of the second. Down 2-1, the Pioneers roared back to take the lead on goals from Tom Graske and Mark Krois at the end of the second period. Burnsville tied it up on Tom Campbell's goal from Todd Okerlund at 6:36, as the teams skated down the home-stretch locked at three-apiece. Then, after a flurry of activity from both teams, Hill-Murray center Jim Jirelle got the goal of a lifetime with just 3:12 remaining in the game, when he knocked in Scott Fausts' rebound past Braves goalie John Olson. The Braves tried to mount a rally, but Pioneer goalie Mike Schwietz stood on his head for the last three minutes to give his club a dramatic 4-3 win as well as its first state title.

The 1990 State Champs from Roseau

1984

Edina pulverized Roseau in the opener, 7-0, on goals from sophomore sensation Pete Hankinson, Jerry Kaehler, Marty Nanne (as in the son of North Star's legend Louie), Tom Terwilliger, and also a pair from future NHLer Paul Ranheim. Edina keeper Chris Schwartzbauer posted 23 saves in the shut-out.

Hill-Murray and Johnson met in Game Two, with the Governors winning a back-and forth slug-fest by the final of 3-2. Jim Hau led the way for Johnson with a pair of goals, while Tom Graske and Steve Rohlik each scored for the Pioneers in the losing effort.

The third game of the afternoon was another blowout, with Hibbing eliminating St. Cloud Apollo, 6-2. Apollo jumped out to a quick 2-0 lead in the first on goals from Mike Hiltner and Erik Halstrom, but the Bluejackets roared back for six unanswered goals in the second and third. Tallying for Hibbing that night were: Antonio Catani, Nick Andrich, Richie Bryant, Pat Iozzo, John Schwartz and Tom Hanson.

The last quarterfinal of the day saw Kennedy edge out Burnsville in a tight 4-2 contest. The two teams exchanged a pair of goals through the second period, but when Eagle's center Tracey Leeman beat Burnsville goalie Andy Luckraft at 7:03 of the third to give his team a 3-2 lead, it was all but over. Kennedy's John Reuder added an empty-netter with 24 seconds to go to put the final nail in Burnsville's coffin.

Johnson and Kennedy played a wild semifinal opener, with Kennedy jumping out to a quick 3-0 lead on goals from Dallas Miller, Jeff Kuester and Dan Tousignant. The Governors got two of their own in the second from Jim Hau and Mitch Converse, but when Miller and Kuester each tallied again for the Eagles late in the third, it

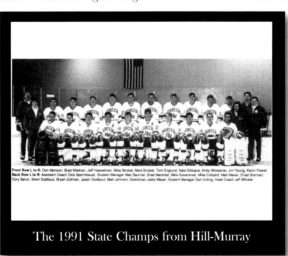

The 1991 State Champs from Hill-Murray

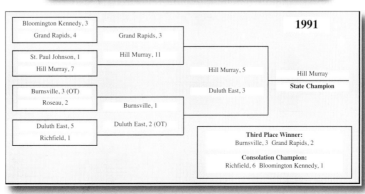

sealed Johnson's fate at 5-3.

Edina and Hibbing met in the other semi, and thanks to goals from Tom Terwilliger, Jay Moore, Paul Ranheim, Marty Nanne and Bill Mork, the Hornets whipped Hibbing, 5-1, to earn a return trip to the finals. Meanwhile, Edina goalie Chris Schwartzbauer came up with 23 saves in the win.

In the championship game Edina picked up where they left off, going up 1-0 midway through the first on a goal from Jeff Johnson. They then made it 2-0 at 4:31 of the second when Greg Dornbach beat Bloomington goalie Bruce Wilson on a nice wrister from the circle. Kennedy marched back to tie it up late in the second on goals from Dallas Miller and Jeff Jungwirth, only to see the Hornets put it away in the third on a pair of goals from Marty Nanne and Paul Ranheim. For Willard Ikola's 21-4-1 Hornets, this was their unprecedented seventh state championship.

1985
Anoka and Hastings hooked up for one of the wildest tourney openers of all-time. The Tornadoes came out and got two quick ones from Dave Boitz and Mike Bunker. Hastings then made it 2-1 at 4:43 when Brad Stepan beat Anoka goalie Tony Moore on a short-handed goal. The Tornadoes then stormed ahead in the second on goals from Tod Hartje and Jeff Foss, as well as a hat-trick from Bill Carlson. Hastings then answered with four of its own from Jeff Pauletti, Gary Ruedy and a pair from Rob Williams. Anoka responded by scoring three more from Jeff Reiman, Pat Sullivan and another from Hartje, to seal the amazing 11-5 victory. All in all, the Tornadoes peppered Raiders' goalie Dave Fries with 46 shots on goal. Incredibly, four records were set in this game, including: Most Assists by One Team in One Period — 10, Most Goals in a Period by Two Teams — 8, Fastest Two Goals at the Start of a Game by One Team — 1:16, and Fastest Four Goals by One Team — 2:02.

Hill-Murray and Hibbing met in Game Two, and after back and forth first and second periods, Pioneer winger Tommy Quinlan beat Bluejackets goalie John Hyduke on a nice wrister to tie the game up at 3-3 with just a minute to go in the third. Then, just 34 seconds into overtime, Hill-Murray forward Nick Gerebi got the game-winner on an unassisted break-away goal.

In Game Two, Jefferson and Minnetonka played what would turn out to be the longest state tournament contest since 1955, when Minneapolis South defeated Thief River Falls, 3-2, in 11 overtimes. The game got started innocently enough when Skipper defenseman Jim Wilharm scored on a power-play goal at the 3:25 mark of the first period. Jefferson answered only 28 seconds later when Brock Rendall beat Tonka goalie Dale Roehl to tie it up at 1-1. The scoring went back and forth through the second and early into the third with each team scoring a pair of goals

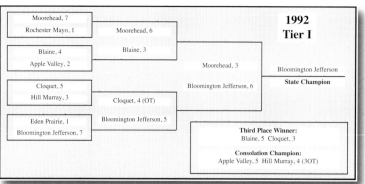

The 1992 State Champs from Bloomington Jefferson
Tier I

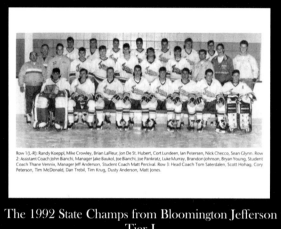

The 1992 State Champs from Greenway-Coleraine
Tier II

to make it 3-3. Fred Holmner started it out at 1:01 for Minnetonka, followed by Jags center Kurt Svendsen at 3:06, and Tonka center Tom Walsh at 13:03. Pat Beaty got the equalizer at 1:44 of the third, only to see both goalies pucker up and force the game into overtime. The teams raged back and forth in the extra sessions, until finally, after the third overtime, Tournament officials decided to postpone the game until morning. So, after a good night's rest, the two teams picked up where they left off from the night before. Finally, at 2:21 of the fourth sudden death session, Brock Rendall took a pass from Mark Brandt and beat Roehl down low to get the dramatic game-winner.

Now, back to Friday night, for the fourth quarterfinal between Burnsville and Bemidji. Thanks to a pair of Herm Finnegan goals that beat Bemidji goalie Steve Peters, Burnsville won a close 5-3 victory. George Pelawa added two of his own in the Lumberjack loss.

Both semifinals ended in 4-1 finals. Tray Tuomie had a hat trick for Hill-Murray in their 4-1 win over Anoka in the first semifinal game. Meanwhile, Burnsville got goals from Scott Bloom, Kevin Featherstone, Kelly Ramswick and Don Granato in their 4-1 victory over Jefferson in the other one.

From there, Burnsville went on to win its first championship by virtue of a 4-3 triumph over Hill-Murray in the title game. Hill-Murray's Mark Johnson put his Pioneers on the board first when he beat Braves goalie Kevin Gorg just 26 seconds into the game. Burnsville answered with a goal from Herm Finnegan at 9:00, only to see Pioneer center Phil Zelenak make it 2-1 just three minutes later. Burnsville then answered with a pair of goals in the second and third from Mike Luckcraft and Scott Bloom to go up 3-2. Hill rallied to tie it up on a goal from Tom Graske, only to see Bloom notch the game-winner late in the third. Gorg then simply stood on his lips down the stretch to seal the deal.

1986
Duluth Denfeld and Bloomington Jefferson played the opening quarterfinal game, as Minnesota got its first look at Denfeld's future NHL goaltender, Robb Stauber. It was his brother, Bill, however, who opened the scoring for the Hunters just 10 seconds after the opening draw, when he beat Jefferson keeper Bobby Hanson — arguably the school's best-ever to play between the pipes. Darren Matetich then tallied just 90 seconds later to give Denfeld a 2-0 lead, only to see Jefferson answer back at 2:57 of the second when Todd Olson beat Stauber from the top of the circle. Denfeld center Mike Vuconich made it 3-1 at the 6:36 mark, followed by Kevin Maas' goal six minutes later. Another future NHLer, Tommy Pederson, added one late for the Jaguars, but it wasn't nearly enough as Duluth went on to win the game by the final of 4-2.

Burnsville and South St. Paul met for Game Two, in what would prove to be a wild one. Led by Scott Bloom's hat-trick and two assists, as well as Jon McDermit's pair of goals, the Braves went on to beat the Packers, 7-4, to advance onto the semifinals.

Richfield, led by star winger Danny Palmer, and Hill-Murray then hooked up in a rough Game Three, which saw some 10 penalties get called. Pioneer center Tray Tuomie got the first goal of the day when he beat Richfield goalie Damian Rhodes, yet another future NHLer, at 2:55 of the first. The Spartans came right back though, on a pair of goals from Brian Provost and Trent Jutting to take the lead midway through the first. The score remained 2-1 until just 33 seconds into the second, when future Gopher Nick Gerebi found the back of the net to tie it up. Steve Rohlik's goal at 11:46 of the period gave Hill-Murray the lead back at 3-2. Pioneer winger Tom Quinlan then went on to add a pair of insurance goals in the third, as Hill rolled to a 5-3 win.

The last quarterfinal game of the day pitted Hibbing and Bemidji, as the Lumberjack's opened the scoring when George Pelawa, a specimen at 6-foot-3 and 240-plus pounds, beat Hibbing goalie Jim Monacelli at 6:14 of the first. The Bluejackets tied it up only three minutes later on a John Schwartz wrister, only to see Bemidji get the lead back just 23 seconds later when Pelawa set up Rob Sauer out front. Hibbing regained the lead midway through the second on goals from Pete Wohlers and John Schwartz, only to see Sauer get his second of the day on a short-handed breakaway to tie it back up at 3-3. Wohlers iced the game at 7:29 of the third, however, when he put his third goal of the game past Bemidji goalie Steve Peters, for the hat-trick, as Hibbing hung on for the 4-3 win. (Tragically, Pelawa, who was drafted by the Montreal Canadiens, was killed in an automobile accident just before he was set to attend UND on a scholarship that next summer.)

Burnsville went on to beat Duluth Denfeld, 3-1, in the first semifinal, as Jason Francisco got Duluth up 1-0 just one minute into the game, only to see Burnsville rally back on three unanswered third period goals from Mike Gresser, Dan Bretschnieder and Lance Werness.

Hill-Murray then beat Hibbing, 5-4, in the other semi, as the Pioneers got goals from Tom Quinlan, Sean Fabian, Todd Valento, Steve Rohlik and Tray Toumi. Meanwhile, Hibbing's Doug Torrell tallied a pair of goals in the loss.

So, the stage was now set for a rematch of epic proportions, Burnsville vs. Hill-Murray for the state crown. The Braves had beaten the Pioneers 4-3 the year before in the finals, and Hill desperately wanted to get some pay-back. The game got underway under a cloud of penalties, four alone in the first, which set the tone early. The Pioneers got on the board first when Tom Quinlan and Tray Tuomie set up Steve Rohlik on

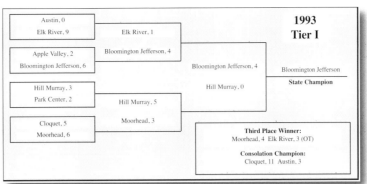

The 1993 State Champs from Bloomington Jefferson
Tier I

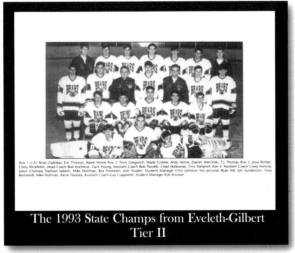

The 1993 State Champs from Eveleth-Gilbert
Tier II

Greg Knox opened the scoring at the 9:45 mark of the first to give Warroad a 1-0 lead. Hill-Murray then answered back when Sean Fabian scored an unassisted power-play goal at 1:05 of the second. It was all Warriors from there though, as Warroad went on to tally four unanswered goals from Mike Flick, Jared Baines and a pair from Scott Peterson to win the game by the final of 5-1.

Greenway's Kenny Gernander tallied a hat trick en route to leading his team to an 8-3 spanking of Edina in Game Three. The Raiders also got goals from Corey Schoenrock, Chris Rauzi, Andrew Parker, Derek Vekich and Justin Tomberlin, as well as three assists from Craig Miskovich. Greenway goalie Jeff Stolp made just 13 saves in the win.

a nice one-timer at 11:43 of the first. Matt Larson tied it up at 2:59 of the second, and then Scott Bloom took a Lance Werness pass at 9:55 to beat Horvath on a low wrister and give the Braves a 2-1 lead. Bloom then took over, first setting up Jon McDermott at 5:39 of the third, followed by an empty netter of his own with just 45 seconds to go. Braves goalie Tom Dennis hung on for the 4-1 victory, as head coach Tom Osiecki's Braves joined the elite fraternity of back-to-back state champions.

1987

The Braves opened the 1987 state tourney right where they left off — in the winner's column. Burnsville and Roseville met in the opener, with Burnsville scoring the game's first four goals on shots from Jon Lindquist, Dan Brettschneider, Paul Kivi and Rob Granato. Raiders center Scott Marshall finally got his team on the board at 1:08 of the third, but the damage had been done as Burnsville cruised to a 4-1 final.

Warroad and Hill-Murray met for Game Two, in what proved to be another blow-out. Winger

Kennedy pounded South St. Paul in the final quarterfinal contest of the day. Jason Miller netted the hat-trick, while the Eagles also got goals from Pat McGowan, Chad Pittelkow, Joe Decker and Tom Hanson in the 7-3 win. Gary Lewandowski added a pair of goals for the Packers in the loss.

The Bloomington Kennedy Eagles, whose only loss during the regular season was to Greenway-Coleraine, now had its chance to exact a little revenge against the Raiders in the first semifinal game. There, thanks to Jason Miller's two goals, the Eagles did just that and went on to win by the final of 4-2.

Burnsville and Warroad met in the other semifinal. Warroad's Larry Olimb led the Warriors to a quick 3-1 lead in the first, only to see Burnsville rally back behind a pair of Lance Werness goals, as the Braves hung on to win the game, 5-3

Burnsville then hit the ice against its rivals from Kennedy in an attempt to make it three straight state titles. The Braves jumped out to a quick 1-0 lead when Lance Werness

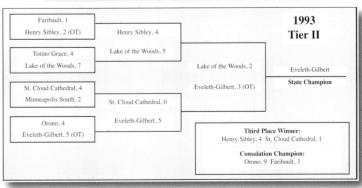

took a Rob Granato pass and buried it into the back of the Kennedy net. From there, it was all Kennedy though, as the Eagles scored four unanswered goals from Pat McGowan, Joe Decker, Chad Pittelkow and Jason Miller to upset the Braves, 4-1, and win their first-ever state title. The emotional leader of that Kennedy team was a 5-foot-8, 140-pound junior center spark-plug by the name of Dave Stansberry, whose "Rudi-like" moxy made him the tournament's biggest fan-favorite.

1988

Bloomington's Tony Bianchi got the second fastest goal in tournament history when he beat Grand Rapids goalie Brett Nelson just 16 seconds into the opening game on a break-away through the slot. Troy Cusey evened it up for the Indians just over a minute later on a nice slapper from the top of the circle, only to see Jags winger Todd Witcraft regain the lead for his club at 9:35 on a one-timer out front. Tommy Pederson then took a Chris Tucker pass and beat Nelson on a power-play goal from the left side at 5:43 of the second to make it 3-1 for Jefferson. The Indians then proceeded to mount a three goal rally, with Tom Murphy swatting a John Brill rebound past Jefferson keeper Derek Anderson just 49 seconds into the third, followed by a goal from John Murphy that was assisted by Chris Marinucci and Jeff Neilsen at 4:14, and finally Murphy's second of the game during a scrum out front at 11:40 to take the lead. But Jefferson didn't quit. With the Bloomington goalie on the bench, Jeff Saterdalen poked in a Tony Bianchi rebound to get the game-tying goal with just 17 seconds left on the clock to send it to OT. There, at the 5:05 mark, Jefferson's Chris Tucker would emerge as the hero as he took a Tommy Pederson pass and rifled it home from the point past Nelson for the dramatic 5-4 win.

Game Two was just as exciting, as Rochester John Marshall and Hill-Murray also found themselves in sudden death. Rochester opened the scoring on a Matt Brumm power-play goal at 5:13. The Pioneers came back on a pair of goals from Mike Hurley, who scored from the high slot, and Tim Carroll, who tallied on a break-away. The next goal saw Doug Zmolek slide the puck over from the point to an awaiting Pat Ferschweiler, who beat Pioneer goalie Scott Cardinal on a nice one-timer. Hill took a 3-2 lead at 8:59 of the second when Greg Hagen caught Rochester goalie Jeff Kruesel way out of the net for an easy score. Then, with just 13 seconds to go in the game, and with their goalie pulled, Rochester pressed into the Pioneer zone. There, winger Gene Rebelatto came in across the crease and beat Cardinal on a beautiful backhander to send the game into overtime. There, the game raged back and forth until the 6:41 mark of the first extra session, when Hill-Murray defenseman Brian Krois unloaded a blast from just inside the blue line that found the top-shelf to give his club a thrilling 4-3 win.

Edina and Cretin met in

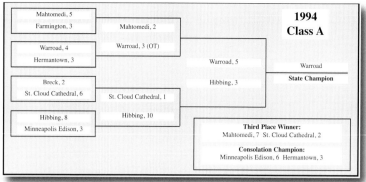

Third Place Winner:
Mahtomedi, 7 St. Cloud Cathedral, 2

Consolation Champion:
Minneapolis Edison, 6 Hermantown, 3

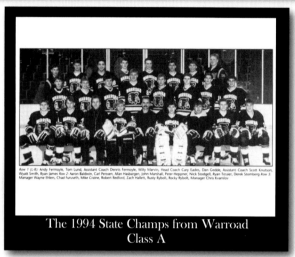

The 1994 State Champs from Warroad
Class A

the third game of the day, as Greg Chapman, Kyle Humphrey and Scott Fronek all scored in the first period to give the Hornets a commanding 3-0 lead. Cretin came back on defenseman Tony Lancette's goal late in the first. Then, late in the third, Chris Weinke beat Edina goalie Matt Bertram to get to within one. But that was as far as they got that night, as Edina hung on for the 3-2 win. (Inidentally, Weinke would go on to play pro baseball until 1998, before winning the Hesiman Trophy as the quarterback at Florida State University — later playing in the NFL as well.)

Warroad then beat Duluth Denfeld in the final game of the day, as Larry Olimb, Jim Fish and Joey Biondi all tallied in the 3-1 victory over the Hunters.

Hill-Murray then squared off against Bloomington Jefferson in the first semifinal contest, and thanks to goals from Tim Carrol, Mike Hanson, Mark Tollefsbol, Jim Scott and a deuce from Todd Montpetit, the Pioneers hung on to beat the Jags, 6-3.

Edina and the undefeated Warroad Warriors played a defensive gem in the second semi, with John McCoy getting the Hornets on the board first when his wrister beat Warroad goalie Chad Erickson just 42 seconds into the game. After a scoreless second, Vince Huerd knocked in a Dan Marvin rebound at 4:21 to tie the game up at 1-1. The score remained that way until the 2:51 mark of overtime, when Mike Hiniker jammed in a loose puck out front into the side of the net for the 2-1 game-winner.

Edina then met Hill-Murray in a title game full of action and drama. John McCoy got Edina into the black at 4:41 of the first, only to see Pioneer forward Mark Tollefsbol tie it up three minutes later. Edina center Robbie Morris worked a nice give-and-go with Chris Justice to make it 2-1 less than two minutes after that, only to see Hill-Murray's Mike Hurley tie it back up at 2-2 off a pretty little backhander with just a second to go in the first. Edina then got a tough poke-in goal from Noel Rahn at 1:04 of the second, followed by Morris' second of the day on a break-away just six minutes later. The Pioneers got one back from Greg Hagen less than a minute into the third, but Hornets centerman Chad Vandertop iced it at 5:46 when he beat Scott Cardinal down low. With the 5-3 victory, Willard Ikola's Hornets cruised to their eighth state title.

1989

The state's top rated squad, Edina, lost to Rochester John Marshall in the opening quarterfinal game, 4-2. JM's Doug Zmolek and Edina's Dan Plante each had a pair of goals respectively.

The Duluth Denfeld Hunters then defeated White Bear Lake, 4-1, in Game Two, thanks to a pair of goals from Troy Skorich and a pair of

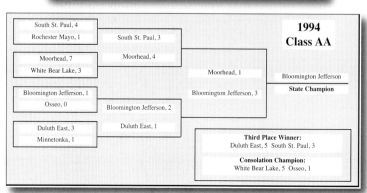

The 1994 State Champs from Bloomington Jefferson
Class AA

Third Place Winner:
Duluth East, 5 South St. Paul, 3

Consolation Champion:
White Bear Lake, 5 Osseo, 1

216

assists from Greg Christenson.

In Game Three, International Falls upended South St. Paul, 4-2, on a two-goal performance from Marty Olson.

In the last quarterfinal, Bloomington Jefferson pounced all over Warroad as Sean Rice and Dave Dahlberg each netted a pair of goals for the Jags, while Joey Biondi, who averaged three points per game that season for Warroad, added a goal and an assist in the loss.

In the first semifinal game, Denfeld, despite going up 1-0 on a break-away goal from Greg Christenson, fell to Rochester John Marshall, 2-1, thanks to scores from both Eric Means and Jon Hilken. In the other semi, Jefferson got two goals from Sean Rice, and one each from Dave Dahlberg, Bill Swanson, Chad Halvorson, Chris Tucker and Jason Schwartz to pound International Falls, 7-3.

So, the finals were set; it would be Bloomington Jefferson and Rochester John Marshall for all the marbles. Rochester's Jeff Fogarty opened the scoring at 6:10 of the first when he beat Jefferson goalie Derek Anderson on a shot from out front. Jefferson's Jason Schwartz got the equalizer with just 14 seconds to go in the first, while Chris Tucker got the go-ahead goal on a breakaway at 6:42 of the second. Rochester's Doug Zmolek answered back late in the second though, as the future NHL star netted a pair of goals to give his Rockets the lead once again. Tucker tied it up one more time at 7:41 of the third, only to see Jeff Fogarty tally for Rochester to go up, 4-3. Then, at 11:01 of the third, Tony Bianchi took a Chris Tucker pass, deked, and found the back of the net to make it 4-4. The game roared back and forth for the final minutes, as neither team was able to get the go-ahead goal. Deadlocked, the two went in to sudden death. There, at 3:29 of the extra session, Chris Tucker took a Jesse Carlson pass and skated it all the way into the zone and beat Rochester goalie Sam Person on a beautiful wrister to win the Jag's second state title in dramatic fashion. Ironically, it was the first overtime title game since 1979, when Edina East beat Rochester John Marshall by the same 5-4 margin.

1990

Down 1-0, Matt Bender and Steve Magnusson each scored in the third to rally Anoka past South St. Paul in the opening game of the 1990 state tourney by the final of 2-1.

Game Two was a wild one, as Bloomington Kennedy got beat by Grand Rapids 3-2 in overtime. While future UMD star and Hobey Baker winner, Chris Marinucci, had a goal and an assist, it was Jeff Wilson who played hero by beating Kennedy goalie Ben Schiebe just four minutes into sudden-death.

Minnetonka outlasted Burnsville in the third quarterfinal, as the Braves lost the lead on four different occasions in the 5-4 defeat. Justin McHugh, Mike Pankoff, Hoby Mork, Pat Ward, and Eric Haagenson all

Red Wing, 3				**1995**
Hutchinson, 1	Red Wing, 1			**Class A**
Totino Grace, 4	Totino Grace, 2			
Chisago Lakes Area, 1		Totino Grace, 2		
Detroit Lakes, 1		International Falls, 3	International Falls	
International Falls, 5	International Falls, 3		**State Champion**	
Blake, 3	Warroad, 2			
Warroad, 6				

Third Place Winner:
Warroad, 7 Red Wing, 2

Consolation Champion:
Hutchinson, 5 (OT) Blake, 4

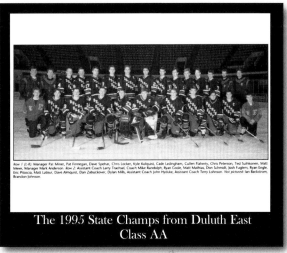

The 1995 State Champs from International Falls
Class A

Rochester Mayo, 5				**1995**
White Bear Lake, 4	Rochester Mayo, 4			**Class AA**
St. Paul Johnson, 2	Moorhead, 5 (2OT)			
Moorhead, 5		Moorhead, 3		
Edina, 3		Duluth East, 5	Duluth East	
Champlin Park, 2	Edina, 2		**State Champion**	
Duluth East, 5	Duluth East, 6			
Bloomington Jefferson, 0				

Third Place Winner:
Edina, 6 Rochester Mayo, 2

Consolation Champion:
Bloomington Jefferson, 7 White Bear Lake, 2

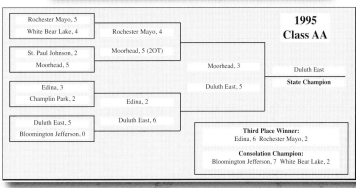

The 1995 State Champs from Duluth East
Class AA

tallied for the Skippers in the win.

The last game of the day saw Roseau crush White Bear Lake, which was led by another future Hobey Baker winner, Brian Bonin, who would go on to star for the Gophers. The Rams proved to be too tough in this one though, as winger Chris Hites notched a pair, while Dale Genderson, Chris Gotziaman and Jason Hanson each tallied as well to lead the Rams to a 5-1 victory.

Grand Rapids secured its championship berth with a 3-2 semifinal victory over Anoka, as Troy Cusey, Jeff Wilson and Kelly Fairchild all tallied for the Indians. Roseau, meanwhile, led by goals from Chris Gotziaman, Dale Lund, Chris Hites as well as a deuce from Jamie Byfuglien, then advanced to the finals with a 5-2 win over Minnetonka in the other semi.

The all-north finals got underway with the No. 2 ranked Roseau Rams vs. the No. 1 ranked Grand Rapids Indians. Interestingly, it was the first time since 1972, when International Falls edged Grand Rapids, 3-2, that two northern Minnesota schools matched up against each other for the state title. The Indians drew blood first when Troy Cusey fired home a Tony Retka pass at 9:23 in the first period. That lead held up for only 42 seconds into the second period, however, until Roseau's Chris Gotziaman beat Rapids goalie Chad Huson on a break-away goal to tie it up. Todd Hedlund got the go-ahead goal for the Rams at 1:56 of the third, while Gotziaman scored his second goal of the game at 14:00 to secure the 3-1 final for Roseau. It was a big win for the Rams, giving them their fifth ever state championship.

1991

Burnsville knocked off the defending champs from Roseau in the opener, as Chris Loken, Chad Hall and Rolf Simonson each tallied for the Braves in the 3-2 upset. Hill-Murray pounded on St. Paul Johnson in Game Two in a penalty-fest, as the Pioneers cruised to a 7-1 win behind winger Matt Mauer's hat-trick. In the first evening game, Grand Rapids got goals from Matt Blade, Kirk Nielsen, Dave Holum and Troy Cusey to hold off Bloomington Kennedy, 4-3. The last quarterfinal game of the day, meanwhile, was all Duluth East, which, behind Kevin Rappana's two goals and two assists, defeated Richfield 5-1. Richfield's lone goal came from future NHLer Darby Hendrickson.

The first semifinal of Day Two was a goalie's nightmare. The Pioneers absolutely annihilated Grand Rapids in that opener by the unconscionable score of 11-3. Leading the charge for Hill-Murray was the identical twin tandem of Mike and Mark Strobel, who between them tallied seven points. In addition, Matt Mauer and Jeff Hasselman each added a pair for good measure.

The other semi was a much different affair, as Duluth East needed overtime to defeat Burnsville, 2-1. Derek Locker opened the scoring for the Hounds late in the second, only to see Chris Porter tie it up for the Braves midway through the third. It remained that way until 6:58 of sudden death, when Greyhound forward Rusty Fitzgerald played hero by beating Burnsville goalie Jeff Rathburn on a nice feed from Shawn Proudlock.

The championship tilt was another dandy, as Duluth East met up with Hill-Murray. After skating to a scoreless first, Duluth's Derek Locker opened the scoring at 2:35 of the second. Adam Vork made it 2-0 for the Hounds just a minute later, only to see Nate Gillespie cut the deficit to one at the 7:12 mark. Locker tallied again just 25 seconds later to give his club a commanding 3-1 lead midway through the second. That's when the Pioneers kicked it into overdrive, getting four unanswered goals down the stretch from Bryan Zollman, Jeff Hasselman and a pair from Mike Strobel. Hill-Murray goalie Kevin Powell came up with 27 saves down the stretch as the Pioneers hung on for a 5-3 victory and their second state title.

1992

In 1992, following the recommendations of the state's High School Hockey Coaches Association, the Minnesota State High School League Board of Directors decided to try a two-year experiment of sorts, by changing the event's format to feature two "tiers," or classes, which include a total of 16 teams. They figured that instead of dividing the schools based on enrollment, as was the case with all other activities, they suggested that the divisions should be based on performance and ability. With that, the coaches in each section then ranked all the teams based on their performances following the regular season. Based on their recommendations, the top-eight sectional teams were then placed in the Tier I, or upper division, with the remaining teams going into the Tier II division. Then, a post-section tournament, so to speak, was created, with the winners of each tier going on to represent their section at the state tournament.

Never in the Tournament's 48-year history, had anything ever been met with so much controversy. The hockey purists went crazy, and started to scramble to try and save their tournament. Like "New Coke" in years past, people were concerned that another tournament would dilute the "Classic," which had long been the model for success in the eyes of the nation. While the die-hards stuck to the "If it ain't broken, then don't fix it," scenario, many others, particularly from the small, non-traditional hockey hot-beds of the state, said "Hey, what about us? We'd like our kids to be able to have a shot at the post-season as well."

The new format, with all of its good intentions, was intended for those schools in

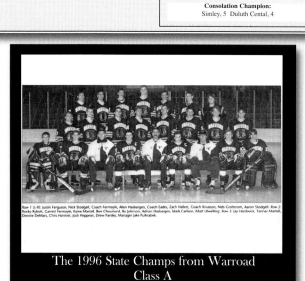

The 1996 State Champs from Warroad
Class A

the state that seemingly never had a prayer of making it to the big tournament. It wasn't supposed to "compete" with the original, rather, it was supposed to be another venue for some more kids to have a chance to play in the post-season. However, under the new format, two things came to the front burner that would prove to be controversial. First, the second tier lessened the chances of watching the classic big-school/small-school "David vs. Goliath" match-ups that, in part, made the tournament such a unique experience in so many people's eyes. Secondly, it also allowed for team's with poor regular season records to get hot in the playoffs and make it to the tourney. And, in 1992, during the inaugural run of the new tiered format, that very scenario played out, when Greenway-Coleraine, a past state champ and perennial power, and Rosemount, a team that had won but two games all year, made it to the Tier II finals. Despite the fact that Greenway crushed Rosemount in the title game, the system showed some obvious flaws, that would need to be tweaked in the years to come.

1992 (Tier I)

In the first ever game of the Tier I quarterfinals, Moorhead pummeled Rochester Mayo by the final of 7-1. Leading the charge for the Spuds were John Haberlach and Jim Jacobson, who each netted a pair of goals, while Ryan Kraft added a goal and three assists as well. Game Two pitted Blaine against Apple Valley in a much closer affair. Chad Marlow's two goals paced the Bengals in this one, as Blaine went on to a 4-2 win. The first evening game saw one of the state's biggest future NHL stars in action, Cloquet's Jamie Langenbrunner. His power-play goal at 2:25 of the third gave his Lumberjacks a 3-2 lead, as they hung on to beat Hill-Murray by the final score of 5-3. The night game, meanwhile, proved to be a laugher as Joey Bianchi's hat-trick and Tim McDonald's two goals led Bloomington Jefferson past Eden Prairie by the final of 7-1.

Moorhead and Blaine hooked up in the first semifinal contest, in what would prove to be a much closer game than the final 6-3 score would indicate. With the score tied at 2-2 in the second, Moorhead got a goal from Ryan Kappes at 4:01, only to see Blaine tie it up just a minute later on Jim Garbe's one-timer from just inside the circle. Tied at three, the Spuds took over and went on to win it in the third, thanks to a pair of goals from future NHLers, Jason Blake and Ryan Kraft.

The other semi came down to sudden death, as Jefferson's Nick Checco tied it at 4-4 with less than a minute to go in the game against a very tough Cloquet team. This set the heroics for Tim McDonald, who got the third of his three goals of the game at the 3:03 mark of overtime to give his Jaguars a dramatic 5-4 victory over the Lumberjacks.

In the finals, Moorhead

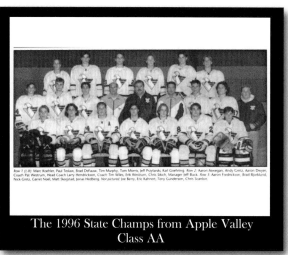

The 1996 State Champs from Apple Valley
Class AA

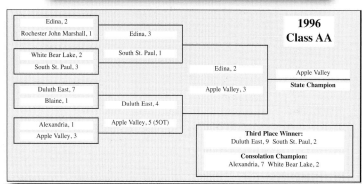

opened the scoring at 3:31 when Greg Salvevold took a Jason Blake pass and beat Jefferson goalie Randy Koeppl downstairs. Cort Lundeen tied it up for the Jags six minutes later, while Matt Jones made it 2-1 for Bloomington less than two minutes after that. Moorhead's Jason Blake tied it up at two apiece on a power-play goal early in the second, only to see Jefferson's Joey Bianchi go nuts. After Nick Checco gave Jefferson the lead at 7:22 of the second, Bianchi took a couple of sweet passes from yet another future NHLer, Mike Crowley, to tally a pure hat trick in less than five minutes, giving his Jags a commanding 6-2 lead. (Incidentally, that feat surpassed the previous tournament record set by Eveleth's John Mayasich back in 1951.) Moorhead added one late, but couldn't get back into it as top-ranked Bloomington Jefferson rolled to a 6-3 victory and the state championship. (With the win, Joey Bianchi, son of Jaguars assistant coach John Bianchi, became the third Bianchi sibling to win a state title, as brother Steve won it in 1981, and Tory in 1989.)

1992 (Tier II)

While the Tier I tournament remained at the Civic Center, much of the Tier II tournament was held at the Target Center in Minneapolis. There, Cambridge goalie Christian Conrad blanked New Ulm, 4-0, in the first quarterfinal behind a pair of goals from Jason Hall and three points from Jason Ziebarth. Greenway downed Alexandria in Game Two, 6-2, thanks to Jeff Antonovich's three points; while Orono stopped Mahtomedi in Game Three, 4-1, thanks to goals from Tim Sweezo, Scott Greenlay, Jason Prodahl and Adam Peterson. Rosemount then outlasted Minneapolis Roosevelt, 2-1, in overtime to round out the quarters. The Teddies jumped out to a 1-0 lead in this one, only to see Rosemount come back on Chris Hvinden's third period equalizer and Matt Hanson's game-winner just 20 seconds into the extra session.

Greenway beat Orono, 5-3, in the first semifinal behind a pair of Mike Vekich goals. Meanwhile, Dan Peschel added a pair of goals for Orono in the loss. Rosemount then pounded Cambridge in the second semi, 7-1, thanks to Chris Hvinden's four-goal outburst.

Greenway kept it going in the Finals, pummelling Cinderella Rosemount, 6-1, for the inaugural dual tiered tourney title. Winger Tim Kalisch opened the festivities with a pair of goals in the first period, while goalie Jason Koski stopped 17 of 18 shots in the big win.

1993 (Tier I)

Elk River welcomed the tourney first-timer's from Austin in the opening quarterfinal contest by giving them a 9-0 beating. Eight different Elk's scored in this one, including a pair from Clay Thompson. The defending champs from Bloomington Jefferson made quick work of Apple Valley in the second afternoon game, as John De St. Hubert notched

two goals and two assists to lead the Jags to a 6-2 win over the Eagles. Hill-Murray went up 3-0 on Park Center in Game Three, only to see the Pirates rally to score two goals in the final minute of the game to make it interesting. Jason and Brent Godbout figured into all of the scoring for the Pioneers, while Jason Bliven and Damian Ellis each had a goal and an assist in the 3-2 loss for Park. The night game was a slug-fest, as Moorhead and Cloquet duked it out for the right to go to the semis. Cloquet jumped out to a 4-3 lead early into the third, thanks to the unbelievable performance of Sergei Petrov and Jamie Langenbrunner, who scored four goals and four assists, respectively. At 1:32 of the third future NHLer Matt Cullen got his third assist of the game when he fed Louis Paquin out front for a goal, only to see Cloquet answer back at the 10:05 mark. Then, with less than five minutes to go in the game, Ryan Kraft tied it at 5-5, followed by Josh Arnold's goal at 11:37, which put the Spuds up for good, 6-5.

The first semifinal contest had Elk River jumping out to a quick 1-0 lead over Bloomington Jefferson on Woody Glines' goal at 3:58. The Jags came right back though, and went on to win the game 4-1 thanks to a pair of goals each from Nick Checco and Tim McDonald. The other semi saw Moorhead jump out to a quick 3-1 lead just seven minutes into the game on goals from Greg Salvevold, Josh Arnold and Ryan Kraft. Hill-Murray then pulled off one of the greatest comebacks in tourney history, getting goals from Mike Goveronski, Aaron Laszlo, Brent Godbout and two from Jason Godbout, to rally back for a 5-3 win.

Then, in the finals, it was Jefferson by a landslide. Joey Bianchi opened the scoring at 3:55 of the first, and was followed by three second period goals from Ian Peterson, Nick Checco and Mike Crowley. Jaguar goalie Randy Koepple turned away all 13 shots that came his way en route to earning the coveted championship shut-out. The win give the Jags their second straight title and a perfect 28-0 season.

1993 (Tier II)

Eveleth-Gilbert, making just its first trip back to the tourney in 33 years, edged Orono in overtime, 5-4, in the opener. Josh Studier got the game-winner at the 1:18 mark of the extra session. Eveleth's Zach Young and Orono's Bryan Benedict each had a pair of goals in the contest as well. Game Two saw Henry Sibley edge Faribault, 2-1, behind Curt Thesing's game-winning goal at the 3:28 mark of double overtime. The third quarterfinal featured Lake of the Woods overcoming a 3-0 first period deficit to beat Totino Grace, 7-4. Leading the charge for Lake of the Woods was Mark Amundson, who tallied four goals and a pair of assists in the big come-back win. Game Four featured St Cloud Cathedral beating Minneapolis South, 4-2, behind Nathan Young's three points and goalie

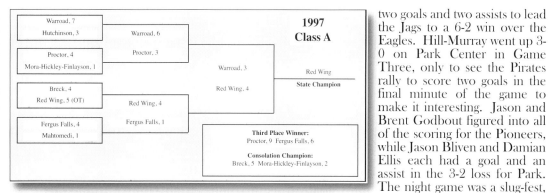

1997 Class A

Warroad, 7 / Hutchinson, 3 → Warroad, 6
Proctor, 4 / Mora-Hickley-Finlayson, 1 → Proctor, 3
Warroad, 3
Breck, 4 / Red Wing, 5 (OT) → Red Wing, 4
Fergus Falls, 4 / Mahtomedi, 1 → Fergus Falls, 1
Red Wing, 4

Red Wing
State Champion

Third Place Winner:
Proctor, 9 Fergus Falls, 6

Consolation Champion:
Breck, 5 Mora-Hickley-Finlayson, 2

The 1997 State Champs from Red Wing
Class A

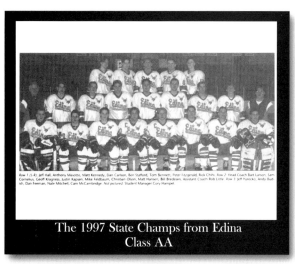

The 1997 State Champs from Edina
Class AA

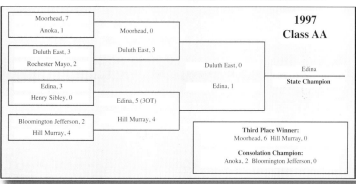

1997 Class AA

Moorhead, 7 / Anoka, 1 → Moorhead, 0
Duluth East, 3 / Rochester Mayo, 2 → Duluth East, 3
Duluth East, 0
Edina, 3 / Henry Sibley, 0 → Edina, 5 (3OT)
Bloomington Jefferson, 2 / Hill Murray, 4 → Hill Murray, 4
Edina, 1

Edina
State Champion

Third Place Winner:
Moorhead, 6 Hill Murray, 0

Consolation Champion:
Anoka, 2 Bloomington Jefferson, 0

Chad Koenig's 22 saves.

Lake of the Woods kept it going in the semifinals, narrowly beating Henry Sibley, 5-4, behind goalie Troy Ricci's 29 saves in net. With the score tied at one apiece heading into the third, Lake of the Woods got goals from Mark Amundson, Ryan Usiski and Pete Gens, with Ryan Nosan notching the game-winner at the 14:34 mark. Eveleth then blanked St Cloud Cathedral, 5-0, in the other semi-final. Terry Gretprich notched a pair of goals in the contest, while Eric Thorson stopped all 24 shots he faced for the shut-out.

In the Tier II finals, Eveleth went on to beat Lake of the Woods, 3-2, in double overtime. Chad Hutskowski and Wade Grahek each scored for Eveleth in the first and second periods and then Zach Young got the thrilling game-winner at 2:05 of the second extra session to finally bring the Golden Bears back to the promised land — a feat they had last accomplished back in 1951 when they had won four straight titles.

1994 (Class AA)

In 1994, the league's Board of Directors chose to re-format the tournament once again, opting this time to eliminate the Tier I & II system, and instead implementing a Class A and AA system. The new format would classify participating schools by enrollment, as it was for every other sport, instead of by performance. In addition, schools could now choose, at the beginning of the year, which level they wanted to participate in. That way, some of the smaller Class A programs which wanted to play against the bigger Class AA school's could move up if they so chose.

The 50th Tournament got underway with South St. Paul beating Rochester Mayo, 4-1, thanks to a tremendous individual effort from Packer sophomore winger Ryan Huerta. Game Two saw Moorhead, behind Ryan Kraft, Josh Arnold, Rob Gramer and Matt Cullen, pound on White Bear Lake 7-3, despite a solid performance from Bears winger Jesse Rooney. The first evening game saw the defending champs from Bloomington Jefferson win a hard-fought 1-0 win over Osseo, whose goalie Matt Jeffers, turned away a record-tying 20 shots in the first period alone. The last game of the day was a dandy, as Duluth East, which was led by Dave Spehar and Clint Johnson, beat a very talented Minnetonka team, 3-1.

In the first semi, led by All-Stater's Mike Crowley and Joey Bianchi, Bloomington Jefferson edged out Duluth East 2-1, thanks to another outstanding performance from goalie Jeff Heil. Then, in the second semifinal, Moorhead barely hung on to beat South St. Paul by the final score of 4-3. Moorhead's lethal combo of Ryan Kraft, Josh Arnold and Matt Cullen all figured into the mix, which gave the Spuds a return trip to the finals. The Spuds, which finished second in 1992 and third in 1993, were eager to knock off the two-time defending champs from Bloomington.

In the championship game, Moorhead standout right

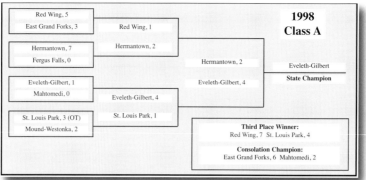

					1998 Class A

Red Wing, 5				
East Grand Forks, 3	Red Wing, 1			
Hermantown, 7	Hermantown, 2			
Fergus Falls, 0		Hermantown, 2		
Eveleth-Gilbert, 1		Eveleth-Gilbert, 4	Eveleth-Gilbert
Mahtomedi, 0	Eveleth-Gilbert, 4		**State Champion**
St. Louis Park, 3 (OT)	St. Louis Park, 1		
Mound-Westonka, 2			

Third Place Winner:
Red Wing, 7 St. Louis Park, 4

Consolation Champion:
East Grand Forks, 6 Mahtomedi, 2

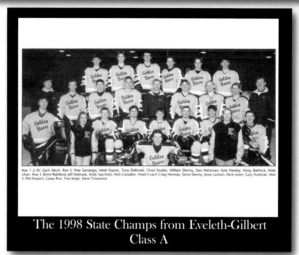

The 1998 State Champs from Eveleth-Gilbert
Class A

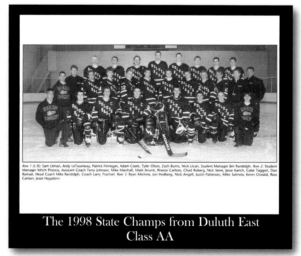

The 1998 State Champs from Duluth East
Class AA

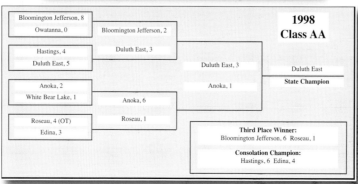

					1998 Class AA

Bloomington Jefferson, 8				
Owatanna, 0	Bloomington Jefferson, 2			
Hastings, 4	Duluth East, 3			
Duluth East, 5		Duluth East, 3		
Anoka, 2	Anoka, 6		Duluth East
White Bear Lake, 1		Anoka, 1	**State Champion**
Roseau, 4 (OT)	Roseau, 1		
Edina, 3			

Third Place Winner:
Bloomington Jefferson, 6 Roseau, 1

Consolation Champion:
Hastings, 6 Edina, 4

wing Ryan Kraft put the Spuds ahead late in the first period by stuffing in a rebound for his eighth goal of the tournament. Jaguars junior wing Mark Parrish, who would go on to NHL stardom, then tied the tilt with a 25-foot slapper at the 4:30 mark of the second period. Both goalies played outstanding hockey through the second, as the score remained dead-locked until just shy of six minutes into the third period. That's when senior defenseman Derek Camuel barreled past both Moorhead defenders on a breakaway to score what would prove to be the game-winner. Mike Crowley, who would be named as the state's Mr. Hockey for the season, added an insurance goal late in the period as Jeff Heil hung on down the stretch for the 3-1 win.

With the dramatic victory, the Jags had established themselves as one of the state's all-time great dynasties, joining just Eveleth (1948-51) and International Falls (1964-1966) as the only other team to have won at least three titles in a row. Over those three years, the Jaguars, which finished the season at 26-1-1, put together 49 consecutive victories, sandwiched between a pair of ties and a 59-game unbeaten streak. (In fact, those 49 straight victories still rank in the top-10 all-time in American high school hockey history.)

1994 (Class A)

The Class A Tournament was played at both the Civic Center in St. Paul, and also at Mariucci Arena on the U of M campus. Hibbing pounded Minneapolis Edison, 8-3, in the opener behind Derek Gabardi's hat-trick and Joe Lolich's two goals. Mahtomedi beat Farmington, 5-3, behind Brandon Sampair's hat trick in Game Two. One of the highlights of the game was the outstanding play of Farmington's third-line center Amber Hegland, who became the first girl to play in the boys' ice hockey tournament. (No stranger to competing with the boys, Amber also played cornerback on the Tigers football team which competed in the 1991 Prep Bowl.) St. Cloud Cathedral advanced past Breck, 6-2, in Game Three, behind Jorgen Larsson's hat-trick and Benji Wolke's two goals. Warroad then edged past Hermantown, 4-3, in the last quarterfinal game, thanks to Zach Hallett's game-winner at the 12:33 mark of the third period.

The first semifinal saw Hibbing crush St Cloud Cathedral, 10-1, as Eric Rewertz and Joe Lolich each scored a pair of goals in the victory. The other semi was much closer as Warroad got past Mahtomedi, 3-2, in overtime thanks to future NHLer Wyatt Smith's thrilling game-winner at the 1:34 mark of the extra session.

Warroad kept rolling from there, beating rival Hibbing by the final score of 5-3 in the finals. The Warriors, which were led by

Wyatt Smith's two goals, got the game-winner from Ryan James, who iced the victory on a break-away goal with just over three minutes left in the game. For Hockey Town USA, the victory had finally given the program something it was unable to do in nine previous tournament appearances — a state championship.

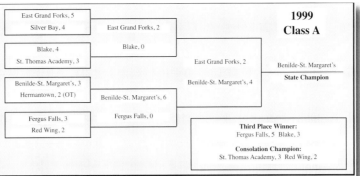

East Grand Forks, 5 / Silver Bay, 4	→ East Grand Forks, 2			**1999 Class A**	
Blake, 4 / St. Thomas Academy, 3	→ Blake, 0		East Grand Forks, 2		
Benilde-St. Margaret's, 3 / Hermantown, 2 (OT)	→ Benilde-St. Margaret's, 6	Benilde-St. Margaret's, 4		Benilde-St. Margaret's **State Champion**	
Fergus Falls, 3 / Red Wing, 2	→ Fergus Falls, 0				

Third Place Winner: Fergus Falls, 5 Blake, 3
Consolation Champion: St. Thomas Academy, 3 Red Wing, 2

1995 (Class AA)

Rochester Mayo and White Bear Lake hooked up in the opener, and thanks to Mayo junior winger Matt Leinbek's pure hat-trick in the second, the Spartans came back from a 2-0 defect to beat the Bears by the final of 5-4. Tony Grosso got the game-winner for Rochester, while Bears winger Whitey Schwartzbauer scored a pair in the loss. After falling behind 2-1, Moorhead's Matt Cullen notched a goal and two assists in leading the Spuds past St. Paul Johnson in Game Two. The third game of the day saw John Farrell play hero for the Edina Hornets. Farrell got the go-ahead goal at 11:13 of the first to make it 2-1, and then scored the game-winner at 5:54 of the third to give his Hornets a 3-2 win over a tough Champlin Park team. The last game of the day saw Duluth East exact a little revenge against Bloomington Jefferson, when, after losing 2-1 to the Jags in the 1994 tourney semifinals, they came out and spanked the three-time defending champs, 5-0. While Greyhounds' phenom Dave Spehar opened the scoring by tallying a pure hat-trick in the first nine minutes of the game, senior goalie Cade Ledingham made 18 saves for the shut-out.

The first semifinal proved to be a classic as Moorhead and Mayo banged heads for all of regulation and then part of two overtimes, before Spuds' star winger Matt Cullen beat Spartan keeper Marc Ranfranz just 11 seconds into the second extra session. While Matt and Mark Cullen combined for five points in the win, Mayo forwards Tony Grosso and Jason Notermann each tallied a pair of goals in the loss. Meanwhile, the other semi was all Duluth East, as Ryan Engle opened the scoring against Edina in the game's first 15 seconds. Spehar then made it 2-0 just six minutes later and just kept on rolling after that, notching his second straight hat-trick as the Hounds rolled over Edina by the final score of 6-2.

The championship tilt featured the state's three top-scoring players: Dave Spehar, who had 102 points for the season, teammate Chris Locker, who tallied 92, and Moorhead's Matt Cullen, who finished with 88 total points. In the title game, it was Dave Spehar once again getting the Hounds on the board first, when he beat Moorhead goalie Jason Gregoire at the 3:39 mark of the first. Matt Cullen answered for the Spuds late in the first period, and then made it 2-1 on a nice wrister just 14 seconds into the second. Duluth East came right back though, thanks to Chris Locker's goal late in the second to tie it up. Moorhead made it 3-2 at 5:21 of the third, when Cullen set up Joel Jamison on a nice one-timer, only to see Greyhound junior center Ted Suihkonen get the equalizer

The 1999 State Champs from Benilde St. Margaret's Class A

just 40 seconds later. From there, it was all Spehar, as he electrified the sell-out crowd by proceeding to get pulled down from behind on a break-away to earn a penalty-shot. Moorhead's Rory Kortan had tripped the speedy centerman to set up the dramatic scenario, which would prove to be just the third successful penalty shot in tournament history. With the Hounds now up by one, Spehar made a little history. Just four minutes later, Dave Almquist went behind the net and floated a backhander to Spehar, who fired it home for his third straight hat-trick of the tournament, tying the legendary John Mayasich of Eveleth who had also done the feat back in the 1951 tourney. The Hounds went on to win it, 5-3.

1995 (Class A)

Warroad topped Blake, 6-3, in the quarterfinal opener on Wyatt Smith's hat-trick and Allen Hasbargen's two goals. International Falls spanked Detroit Lakes in Game Two, 5-1, on a pair of goals each from Barrett Olson and Jon Austin. Red Wing beat Hutchinson, 3-1, in Game Three behind a pair of points each from Jay Barry and Brendan O'Rourke. The last quarterfinal then saw Totino Grace top Chisago Lakes, 4-1, behind Jake Searles' two goals.

International Falls narrowly escaped past Warroad in the first semi, 3-2, behind Jon Austin's two goals and Todd Sether's 17 saves in net. The other semi was also a tight one as Totino Grace skated past Red Wing, 2-1, behind future NHLer Johnny Pohl's third period tally at the 9:58 mark.

The Falls then hung on to beat Totino-Grace in the Class A final, 3-2, thanks to Jon Austin's 35-foot game-winning slapper from the top of the circle that beat Eagle goalie Aaron Ratfield with just eight seconds left in the game.

1996 (Class AA)

Rochester John Marshall and Edina met in the first game of the 1996 state tournament, in what would prove to be a defensive gem. Rochester's Bryce Beckel opened the scoring at 2:40 of the first, only to see Edina's Dan Carlson tie it up at 13:14. The score remained that way until the final two minutes of the game, when Hornet forward Peter Armbrust beat Rocket goalie Derek Link for the game-winner. Game Two was also a good game, as South St. Paul rallied from a 2-1 deficit in the third to beat White Bear Lake, 3-2. Packer center David Bonk got the tying goal midway through the final period, while Klint Nateau got the dramatic game-winner with just 56 seconds to go in the game. The defending champs from Duluth East steam-rolled over Blaine, 7-1, in the first evening game. Dave Spehar's four goals and two assists led the charge for the Hounds, while Andy Wheeler also notched a pair and Chris Locker added one of his own for good measure.

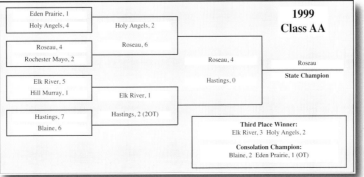

The 1999 State Champs from Roseau Class AA

Eden Prairie, 1 / Holy Angels, 4	→ Holy Angels, 2			**1999 Class AA**	
Roseau, 4 / Rochester Mayo, 2	→ Roseau, 6		Roseau, 4		
Elk River, 5 / Hill Murray, 1	→ Elk River, 1	Hastings, 0		Roseau **State Champion**	
Hastings, 7 / Blaine, 6	→ Hastings, 2 (2OT)				

Third Place Winner: Elk River, 3 Holy Angels, 2
Consolation Champion: Blaine, 2 Eden Prairie, 1 (OT)

The night game was all Apple Valley, which, thanks to goals from Brad Defauw, Aaron Westrum and Chris Sikich, rallied from a 1-0 deficit early in the first to earn a 3-1 win over Alexandria.

Edina kept it going into the next round, easily beating South St. Paul, 3-1, in the first semifinal game. Edina's Brad and Dan Carlson led the way with a goal and an assist apiece.

Meanwhile, the second semifinal game would prove to be one of the tournament's all-time classics. Duluth East and Apple Valley went back and forth all night in this one, as the lead exchanged hands on numerous occasions. Down 3-2 midway through the third, Dave Spehar tied the game at 3-3, only to see Eagle's center Erik Westrum, a future NHLer, tally to give his team the lead yet again. Then, with Apple Valley leading 4-3 late in the third period, Spehar set up Chris Locker on a nice give-and-go to tie the game with just 38 seconds left in regulation. Five overtimes later, Eagles' defenseman Aaron Dwyer took a Chris Sikich pass from the top of the circle and slid it past Greyhound goalie Kyle Kolquist to give Apple Valley an incredible 5-4 victory, thus putting an end to the wild marathon. Apple Valley goalie Karl Goehring made 65 saves that night, including 17 in the fourth overtime alone, to break the old record of 61 saves held by St. Paul Johnson's Doug Long in 1970. (In addition, the 93 minute and 12 second game is recorded as the longest ever in state tournament history, surpassing the 1955 classic when South St. Paul needed 87:50 to defeat Thief River Falls, 3-2, in 11 overtimes.)

Despite playing into the wee hours of the morning, the fatigued Eagles came back to defeat Edina in the title game that next night, giving the school its' first state title. Edina's Peter Fitzgerald got the Hornets on the board first, when he lit the lamp at the 2:12 mark of the first. Chris Sikich tied it up just four minutes later when he fired home a slapper from the right circle, followed by Aaron Fredrickson's goal at 3:22 of the second to make it 2-1 for the Eagles. Five minutes later, Edina's Dan Carlson scored a short-handed goal to tie it back up at 2-2, setting the stage for Apple Valley's Matt Skogstad, who, on the power-play, found the back of the net at 14:21 of the second. Eagle goalie Karl Goehring then stood tall for the final period, as Apple Valley hung on for the thrilling 3-2 victory.

1996 (Class A)

Litchfield/Dassel-Cokato opened the Class A tourney by edging Mora in a double overtime thriller, 5-4, on Troy Urdahl's game-winner at the 5:29 mark of the second extra session. Red Wing beat Duluth Central, 3-1, in the second game behind Johnny Pohl's hat-trick. Game three saw Breck take out Simley, 5-2, behind goalie Jake Erb's 25 saves in net. Warroad then pounded Detroit Lakes, 6-0, in the quarterfinal finale. Leading the way for the Warriors were Tanner Martell and Matt

Ulwelling, who netted a pair of goals each in the big win, while goalie Aaron Stodgell made 10 saves en route to earning the shut-out.

Red Wing beat Litchfield, 4-1, in the first semifinal behind Tom Moore's two goals and Johnny Pohl's one goal and two assists. The other semi featured yet another shut-out from Warroad as they blanked Breck, 5-0. Kaine Martell notched a pair of goals and Aaron Stodgell turned away all 16 shots he faced as the Warriors cruised into the finals.

Warroad then went on to annihilate the No. 3 ranked Red Wing Wingers by the final of 10-3 in the Class A final. The Warriors were leading 6-0 before Warroad goalie Aaron Stodgell gave up his first goal of the tournament to Johnny Pohl, at the 13:31 mark. Matt Ulwelling and Zach Hallett netted a pair of goals each in the lopsided win.

1997 (Class AA)

Moorhead pounced on Anoka in the opening game of the 1997 tourney, beating the Tornadoes, 7-1. Brian Nelson led the charge by scoring an amazing four goals, while Mark Cullen added a goal and four assists in the win. The second game saw Duluth East hold off a late charge from Rochester Mayo to win by the final score of 3-2. Matt Mathias, Nick Anderson and Pat Finnegan all scored for the Hounds, while senior winger Brian Buskowiak tallied both goals for the Spartans. Game Three was all Edina as Tom Bennett, Sam Cornelius and Dan Carlson each scored for the Hornets, while junior goalie Jeff Hall stopped all nine shots he faced to earn the 3-0 shut-out. Hill-Murray and Bloomington Jefferson squared off in the nightcap, in what would prove to be no love-fest. Hill-Murray went up 3-0 early, only to see Bloomington's John Konrad score a couple of quick goals late in the third to get it to 3-2. The Jags pressed in the final minutes of the game but couldn't beat Pioneer goalie Jason Carey, as Hill added an empty netter and cruised to a 4-2 victory.

Duluth East rolled over Moorhead in the first semifinal game of the day, as Gabe Taggart opened the scoring with a power-play goal at 9:54 of the first. Senior centerman Matt Mathias then scored a pair of goals down the stretch and goalie Kyle Kolquist stopped all 12 shots that came his way to earn the 3-0 shut out.

Hill-Murray and Edina got together for a penalty-laden second semifinal game, with the Hornets holding on for an amazing 5-4 triple-overtime victory. This one went back and forth all night as the Pioneers went up 1-0 on Rick Brosseau's goal just a minute into the game. Edina's Tony Massotto then netted the first of his two first period goals to get the equalizer. Edina went up 4-2 into the third when Justin Kapsen tickled the twine, only to see the Pioneers come right back on a pair of goals from Tony Rockenbach and Steve Jones to tie it up at four apiece. The teams then battled

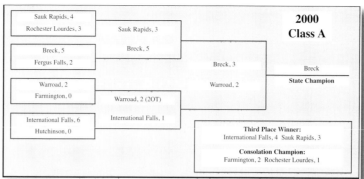

2000 Class A

Sauk Rapids, 4 / Rochester Lourdes, 3 → Sauk Rapids, 3
Breck, 5 / Fergus Falls, 2 → Breck, 5 → Breck, 3
Warroad, 2 / Farmington, 0 → Warroad, 2 (2OT)
International Falls, 6 / Hutchinson, 0 → International Falls, 1 → Warroad, 2 → **Breck State Champion**

Third Place Winner: International Falls, 4 Sauk Rapids, 3
Consolation Champion: Farmington, 2 Rochester Lourdes, 1

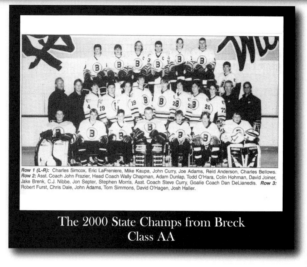

Row 1 (L-R): Charles Simcox, Eric LaFreniere, Mike Kaupa, John Curry, Joe Adams, Reid Anderson, Charles Bellows. Row 2: Asst. Coach John Frazier, Head Coach Wally Chapman, Adam Dunlap, Todd O'Hara, Colin Hohman, David Joiner, Jake Brenk, C.J. Nibbe, Jon Septer, Stephen Morris, Asst. Coach Steve Curry, Goalie Coach Dan DeLianedis. Row 3: Robert Furst, Chris Dale, John Adams, Tom Simmons, David O'Hagen, Josh Haller.

The 2000 State Champs from Breck
Class AA

Row 1 (L-R): Steve Witkowski, Scott Foyt, Matt Hendricks, Ben Griffith, Matt Moore, Trevor Frischmon, Karl Herschberger. Row 2: Asst. Coach Steve Guider, Asst. Coach Sean Goodsell, Adam Taylor, Ben Kelly, Brandon Bochenski, Dan Holmgren, Dan Grassman, Dan Ubl, Co-Head Coach Scott Bjugstad, Co-Head Coach Steve Larson. Row 3: Scott Romfo, Tony Nelson, Chad Smith, Andy Johnson, Marcus Rymer, Chris Brown, Doug Witkowski, Mike Johnson, Roy Peterson.

The 2000 State Champs from Blaine
Class AA

2000 Class AA

Duluth East, 4 / Roseau, 1 → Duluth East, 4
Edina, 2 (OT) / Hill Murray, 1 → Edina, 2 → Duluth East, 0
Hastings, 4 (OT) / Bloomington Jefferson, 1 → Hastings, 3
Blaine, 4 / Rochester Mayo, 1 → Blaine, 4 → Blaine, 6 → **Blaine State Champion**

Third Place Winner: Hastings, 4 (2OT) Edina, 3
Consolation Champion: Roseau, 4 Rochester Mayo, 1

it out for three overtimes until Edina's Sam Cornelius got the game-winning goal at the 5:26 mark of the third extra session.

This set up a final which featured a couple of teams which had been there before, the 1996 state runner-ups from Edina and the undefeated Duluth East Greyhounds. This one would prove to be a defensive battle from the start, with both goalies playing outstanding between the pipes. At the 13:20 mark of the first period, Hornets senior winger Dan Carlson took a pass from Ben Stafford and proceeded to score what turned out to be the game-winning goal. Edina goalie Jeff Hall then stood on his head the rest of the game and stopped all 20 shots that came at him for the coveted championship shut-out. The anti-climactic 1-0 win gave the Hornets their ninth boys' hockey championship trophy, two more than any other school in state history.

1997 (Class A)

The defending champs from Warroad downed Hutchinson, 7-3, in the quarterfinal opener as Josh Hepner and Mark Carlson each notched a pair of goals for the Warriors. Game Two saw Red Wing outlast Breck, 5-4 in overtime, thanks to Johnny Pohl's game tying goal late in the third period which was then followed by Travis Trembath's game-winner just 51 seconds into sudden death. Proctor beat Mora, 4-1, in the third contest behind Dom Talarico's hat-trick and Jay Dardis' three helpers. Fergus Falls rounded out the quarters by topping Mahtomedi, 4-1, behind Chris Swanson's goal and assist.

Warroad kept it going in the semis, doubling up on Proctor, 6-3, as Matt Ulwelling, Tanner Martell and Jackson Harren notched a pair of goals each in the big win. Meanwhile, in the other semi, Red Wing was all over Fergus Falls, beating the Flyers, 4-1, behind Tom Moore's hat-trick and Johnny Pohl's three assists.

Then, in a rematch of the 1996 Class A championship game, Red Wing and Warroad once again squared off for the title. This year, however, had a different outcome, as the undefeated Wingers finally exorcised some demons by winning their first title in three consecutive tourney appearances. Red Wing got off to a quick start with three first-period goals, one each by the brother's Pohl – Mark and Johnny, and another by Tom Moore. Warroad answered with goals from Jackson Harren and Chris Heppner in the second, but at 1:22 of the third, Red Wing junior forward Mark Bang took a Mark Pohl pass and beat Warroad goalie Justin Ferguson for what would turn out to be the game-winner. The Wingers held on down the stretch behind goalie Joe Edstrom's 16 saves for the 4-3 victory.

1998 (Class AA)

Bloomington Jefferson and Owatonna got together in the opening quarterfinal game of

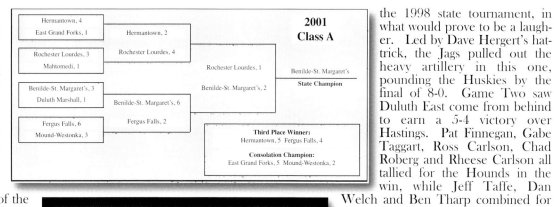

2001 Class A

Hermantown, 4 / East Grand Forks, 1 → Hermantown, 2
Rochester Lourdes, 3 / Mahtomedi, 1 → Rochester Lourdes, 4
Hermantown, 2 / Rochester Lourdes, 4 → Rochester Lourdes, 1
Benilde-St. Margaret's, 3 / Duluth Marshall, 1 → Benilde-St. Margaret's, 6
Fergus Falls, 6 / Mound-Westonka, 3 → Fergus Falls, 2
Benilde-St. Margaret's, 6 / Fergus Falls, 2 → Benilde-St. Margaret's, 2
Rochester Lourdes, 1 / Benilde-St. Margaret's, 2 → Benilde-St. Margaret's **State Champion**

Third Place Winner: Hermantown, 5 Fergus Falls, 4

Consolation Champion: East Grand Forks, 5 Mound-Westonka, 2

Row 1 (L-R): Manager Brannon Garvert, Mike Tyree, Ricky Hopkins, Jake Schuman, Ryan Hopkins, Paul Bergsten, Tony Grannes. Row 2: Jimmy Mulder, Blake Friesen, John Paulson, Chris Wickersham, Garrett Gruenke, Luke Gaskins, Brian Sefton, Joe Graw. Row 3: Tony Cleveland, Danny Charleston, Josh Pauer, Ian Schaser, Eric Clark, Justin Green, Greg Battani.

The 2001 State Champs from Benilde-St. Margaret's Class A

the 1998 state tournament, in what would prove to be a laugher. Led by Dave Hergert's hat-trick, the Jags pulled out the heavy artillery in this one, pounding the Huskies by the final of 8-0. Game Two saw Duluth East come from behind to earn a 5-4 victory over Hastings. Pat Finnegan, Gabe Taggart, Ross Carlson, Chad Roberg and Rheese Carlson all tallied for the Hounds in the win, while Jeff Taffe, Dan Welch and Ben Tharp combined for eight points for the Raiders in the loss. Anoka got two first period goals from Rick Talbot and never looked back in its 2-1 win over White Bear Lake in Game Three. The final game of the night between Roseau and Edina went back and forth three different times before finally going into overtime. With Edina up 3-2 after two, Roseau's David Lunbohm notched the equalizer at 2:33 of the third. The score remained that way until 4:14 of sudden death, when Phil Larson took a Lunbohm pass and sent it past Hornets' goalie Jeff Hall for the dramatic game-winner.

The first semifinal featured Jefferson and Duluth East skating to a scoreless first period. Jake Heisler finally got the Jags on the board at 10:34 of the second, only to see Duluth East's Kevin Oswald and Nick Angell each tally in the third to go up 2-1. Todd Koehnen got the equalizer for Jefferson at 11:10 of the final session, which sent the game into overtime. There, just two minutes and 22 seconds later, Kevin Oswald tallied his second goal of the evening to give the Greyhounds a dramatic 3-2 victory.

The other semi was a blow-out as Anoka romped all over Roseau by the final of 6-1. While the Rams opened the scoring early in the first, the Tornadoes roared back for six unanswered goals, highlighted by Rick Talbot's hat-trick.

The finals pitted the new kids on the block from Anoka, and the old stand-bys from Duluth East, in what would prove to be the last ever game in the old Civic Center. (The NHL's Minnesota Wild announced their plans to build a new arena on that site, the Xcel Energy Center, and as a result, the tournament would move to the Target Center in Minneapolis for a two-year hiatus before returning to St. Paul to play in the new arena.) The Hounds came in to the game riding a 22-game winning streak, and were eager to win their second title in four years. Gabe Taggart opened the scoring for Duluth East at the 7:31 mark when he came in on Danny Scott, deked and fired a nice wrist shot into the back of the net. Both teams had numerous opportunities in the second, but it was Ross Carlson's 19th goal of the season that put the Greyhounds ahead 2-0. Anoka's Jerrid Reinholz then answered back just 20 seconds later to make it 2-1. The third period was wide open, as Chad Roberg took a couple of passes from the Carlson brothers, Ross and Rheese, to go up 3-1 at 3:43 of the third. Greyhound goalie Adam Coole stopped the remaining 23 shots he faced that night as the Hounds went on to

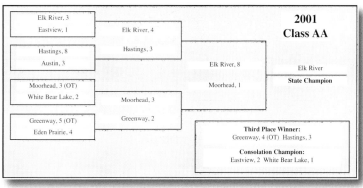

Row 1 (L-R): Manager Jami Boutin, Cheerleader Lacy Johnson. Row 2: Cheerleader Toni Salzman, Cheerleader Amarae Mills, Dustin Hall, Matt Jackson, Ian Holen, Brent Solei, Cheerleader Amanda Duckowitz, Cheerleader Cassie Cook. Row 3: Manager Heather White, Assistant Coach Rob Loftus, Assistant Coach Joel Wesloh, Barnabas Birkeland, Ben Gustafson, Tim Madsen, Brandon Longley, Eric McFee, Kiel DeShaw, Carl Foss, Manager Dana Lefebvre, Assistant Coach Paul Berning, Head Coach Tony Sarsland. Row 4: Chris Nothe, Andy Holmes, Nate Droogsma, Nick Micek, Joel Hanson. Row 5: Kelly Plude, Trevor Stewart, Andy Olsen, Derek McChesney. Not pictured: Goalie Coach Dave Larson, Cheerleader Courtney Stiff.

The 2001 State Champs from Elk River Class AA

2001 Class AA

Elk River, 3 / Eastview, 1 → Elk River, 4
Hastings, 8 / Austin, 3 → Hastings, 3
Elk River, 4 / Hastings, 3 → Elk River, 8
Moorhead, 3 (OT) / White Bear Lake, 2 → Moorhead, 3
Greenway, 5 (OT) / Eden Prairie, 4 → Greenway, 2
Moorhead, 3 / Greenway, 2 → Moorhead, 1
Elk River, 8 / Moorhead, 1 → Elk River **State Champion**

Third Place Winner: Greenway, 4 (OT) Hastings, 3

Consolation Champion: Eastview, 2 White Bear Lake, 1

beat Anoka, 3-1, to take the title.

1998 (Class A)

Eveleth-Gilbert opened the festivities by blanking Mahtomedi, 1-0, on Tony Dolinsek's third period goal and goalie Pete Samargia's 19 saves in net. Hermantown got after Fergus Falls in Game Two, beating the Flyers, 7-0, thanks to Nick Dolentz's two goals. Hawks goalies Chris Oppel and Allen Knowles combined for 19 saves in the win. Game three saw the defending champs from Red Wing beat East Grand Forks, 5-3, behind a pair of goals each from Johnny Pohl and Tom Moore. St. Louis Park then edged Mound-Westonka, 3-2, in overtime to round out the quarters. Leading the way for St. Louis Park was Dan Halvorson, who netted the game-winner at the 7:29 mark of the extra session.

The first semifinal game featured Eveleth-Gilbert beating St Louis Park, 4-1, behind Andy Sacchetti's two goals and Pete Samargia's 24 saves in net. The other semifinal saw the Hermantown Hawks, behind goalie Chris Oppel's 26 saves, upset Red Wing, 2-1, to advance on to the Finals. Hermantown got a pair of third period goals from B.J. Knapp and Chris Barron en route to the big comeback victory.

Eveleth-Gilbert then went on to beat Hermantown in the all-northern Minnesota Class A finals. Hermantown took the early lead on Jon Francisco's quick slapper from the slot at 3:04 of the first period, only to see Eveleth come right back in the second on a pair of goals from Steve Denny and Jeff Dolinsek. The score remained 2-1 until the third, when, after Pat Andrews tied it up at 8:18 of the final period, Kyle Hawley got what would prove to be the game-winner with just 4:38 left in regulation. Jeff Dolinsek then added an empty-netter for insurance as the Golden Bears cruised to a 5-3 victory.

1999 (Class AA)

Holy Angels and Eden Prairie got together in the first state tournament game ever played in the Target Center. The Eagles got on the board first when Brian Rasmussen scored a short-handed goal at 14:12 of the first period. That would be all the scoring Eden Prairie would do that day however, because Holy Angels would come back four unanswered goals from Casey Garven, Justin Hauge, Josh Singer and Adam Kaiser to roll to a 4-1 win. The second quarterfinal pitted Roseau versus Rochester Mayo in a game where Mike Klema looked like a man among boys. Klema not only scored two goals in the game, he was also a physical presence on the ice, as the Rams beat up on the Spartans by the final of 4-2. The first evening game of the day was all Elk River, as the Elks, behind a pair of Joey Bailey goals, cruised to a 5-1 win over Hill-Murray. In the final quarterfinal of the day, Hastings and Blaine played one of the most wide-open games in tourney history. Future NHLer Jeff Taffe opened the scoring just 22 seconds into the first,

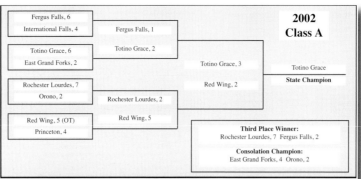

while Adam Holmgren got the first of his three goals just 33 seconds later. Hastings notched the next three tallies to make it 4-1 going into the second, when the scoring frenzy reached epic proportions. At the start of the second period, the teams actually set a new state tournament record for the fastest three goals ever scored. (Blaine's Trevor Frischmon at 3:11, Hasting's Matt Van Der Bosch at 3:19 and Blaine's Erik Johnson at 3:27.) Blaine then came out and scored three straight in the third to regain the lead, only to see Dan Welch score a pair down the stretch to seal the wild 7-6 victory for Hastings.

Roseau scored early and often against Holy Angels in the first semifinal game, as the Mike Klema show continued to dominate. Klema scored an unbelievable four goals in this one as the Rams went on to beat the Stars by the final of 6-2. The other semi saw a much closer contest between Elk River and Hastings. Carson Ezati opened the scoring at the 8:57 mark of the first when he beat Hasting's keeper Matt Klein out front. After playing to a scoreless second, Hastings' junior center Adam Gerlach found the back of the net at 1:56 of the third to tie it up. Both teams had plenty of opportunities down the stretch, but neither could capitalize, as the game went into overtime. Then, finally, at the 10:15 mark of the second extra session, Travis Kieffer took a couple of passes from Cody Swanson and Jeff Taffe, and buried the puck past Elk River goalie Mitch Glines for the thrilling 2-1 win.

The finals were now set with Roseau and Hastings ready to do battle. Both teams looked sharp in the first, and each missed a couple of solid scoring chances early on. At 6:40 of the second period Josh Olson finally put Roseau on the board, and from there on out the Rams didn't look back. Both Dan and Mike Klema, as well as Matt Erickson, all scored goals after that as the Rams went on to cruise to a 4-0 victory. Ram's goalie Jake Brandt stopped all 19 shots that came his way that night en route to earning the coveted shut-out. And with that, Roseau, the smallest school in the AA Tournament, with just 339 students, won its sixth state championship, proving that David could still indeed beat Goliath in the two class format.

1999 (Class A)

East Grand Forks opened the 1999 Class A tourney by slipping past Silver Bay, 5-4, behind Shawn Bartlette's hat-trick. Game two saw Blake rally to sneak by St. Thomas Academy, 4-3, behind a pair of goals from Jon Reigstad. Benilde-St. Margaret's then edged past Hermantown, 3-2 in overtime, in the third quarterfinal game. Down two zip, BSM rallied behind future Gopher Troy Riddle's natural hat-trick, which included the game-winner at the 2:50 mark of the extra session. The final quarterfinal game was yet another close contest with Fergus Falls beating Red Wing, 3-2. Fergus got a

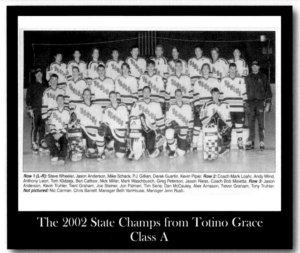

The 2002 State Champs from Totino Grace
Class A

The 2002 State Champs from Holy Angels
Class AA

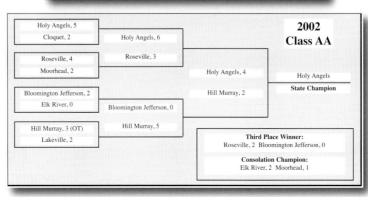

pair of third period goals in this one from Cory Donnay and Josh Anderson to rally back and earn the "W."

East Grand Forks blanked Blake, 2-0, in the opening semi thanks to goalie Tommy White's 21 saves. Jon Hussey and Patrick Knutson each tallied for EGF in the win. The other semi was a blow-out as Benilde-St. Margaret's clobbered Fergus Falls, 6-0. Troy Riddle and his brother Jake combined for six points in this one, while goalie Jake Schuman posted 14 saves in the shut-out.

Then, in the Class A championship, Benilde St. Margaret's came back from an early 2-1 deficit to beat the East Grand Forks Green Wave by the final score of 4-2. Troy Riddle proved to be the hero in this one, scoring not only the game's opening goal, but also what proved to be the game-winner at the 4:08 mark of the third period as well. It was the first ever state title for the Red Knights.

2000 (Class AA)
The 2000 Class AA tourney opened with Duluth East beating Roseau by the score of 4-1, behind a pair of goals from Zach Burns. Game two was a barn burner as Edina edged Hill-Murray, 2-1, in double overtime. Steve Eastman finally got the go-ahead goal at the 5:28 mark of the second extra session to send the Hornets into the semis. The third quarterfinal contest was also an overtime thriller, with Hastings outlasting Bloomington Jefferson, 4-3, on Adam Welch's game-winner at the 1:30 mark of the extra frame. Blaine then took care of Rochester Mayo in the last quarterfinal, 4-1, behind future NHLer Brandon Bochenski's three points.

Duluth East beat Edina, 4-2, in the first semifinal, behind a pair of goals and an assist from Nick Licari. Meanwhile, Blaine edged past Hastings, 4-3, in the other semi thanks to Matt Hendricks' two goals and Bochenski's two assists. Blaine just kept on rolling from there, pummelling Duluth East, 6-0, in the Finals. Blaine got a pair of goals each from Matt Moore and Trevor Frischmon, while goalie Steve Witkowski blocked all 21 shots that came his way en route to leading his squad to its first ever state title.

2000 (Class A)
Sauk Rapids rallied from a 3-0 deficit to defeat Rochester Lourdes in the opener, 4-3. Nathan Raduns had a pair of goals, while John Schultz got the game-winner at the 13:45 mark of the third period. Game two then saw Breck eliminate Fergus Falls, 5-2, behind Todd O'Hara's hat-trick. Warroad blanked Farmington, 2-0, in Game three thanks to Cory Monshaugen, who scored both Warrior goals. Meanwhile, goalie Brian McFarlane stopped all 16 shots that came his way for the shut-out. The last quarterfinal was a blow-out as International Falls crushed Hutchinson, 6-0. Mitch LaVern tallied two goals and goalie Jayme Fischer posted 12 saves en route to earning his shut-out.

Breck topped Sauk

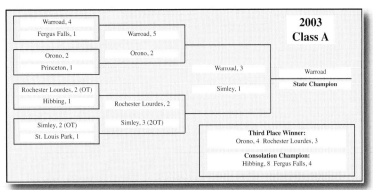

Rapids, 5-3, in the opening semifinal. Josh Haller, Joe Adams, Jake Brenk, Adam Dunlap and Eric LaFreniere each tallied in the victory. Meanwhile, in the other semifinal, Warroad snuck past International Falls by the score of 2-1 in a double overtime thriller. After a scoreless first and second, Ryan Hilfer put the Falls on the board at the 4:18 mark of the third period. Tony Selvog then got the game tying goal just a minute and a half later, followed by the game-winner at the 2:06 mark of the second extra session.

Breck went on to beat Warroad in the Finals by the score of 3-2, earning their first ever state title after four appearances in the big dance. Josh Haller, Joe Adams and Jake Brenk each tallied in the win, while John Curry came up with 18 saves in goal. Selvog and Nick Marvin each scored for the Warriors in the loss.

2001 (Class AA)
Elk River beat Eastview in the opening round quarterfinal, 3-1, behind goals from Joel Hanson, Trevor Stewart and Nate Droogsma. Game two saw Hastings punish Austin by the final score of 8-3. Jesse Polk had a pair of goals while the Welch boys, Adam and Casey, combined for four points. The third quarterfinal was much closer as Moorhead topped White Bear Lake in overtime, 3-2, behind Jeff Bernstrom's game-winner at the 3:31 mark of the extra session. The final quarterfinal was also a tight one with Greenway edging Eden Prairie, 5-4, in overtime. A pair of future Gophers led the way in this one as Andy Sertich and Gino Guyer combined for four points, with Sertich getting the equalizer in the third and Guyer getting the game-winner in sudden death.

The first semifinal featured Elk River downing Hastings, 4-3, behind Trevor Stewart's pair of third period goals which proved to be the difference in this one. Meanwhile, the other semi saw Moorhead sneak past Greenway in overtime, 3-2, with Wade Harstad getting the game-winner at the :42 mark of the extra frame. Moorhead netminder Chad Beiswenger came up with 28 saves in the victory as well.

Elk River then went on to crush Moorhead in the Finals by the score of 8-1. Kelly Plude had a hat-trick and Eric McFee added a pair of goals in this one, while goalie Brent Solei stopped 16 of the 17 shots that came his way en route to leading the Elk's to the title.

2001 (Class A)
Hermantown opened the 2001 Class A tourney by upending East Grand Forks by the score of 4-1. B.J. Radovich scored a pair of goals for the Hawks while Nate Buck turned away 19 of the 20 shots he faced in net. Game two saw Rochester Lourdes beat Mahtomedi, 3-1, behind Brandon Harrington's goal and assist. The third quarterfinal featured Benilde-St. Margaret's defeating Duluth Marshall, 3-1, thanks to Ricky and Ryan Hopkins, who each had a goal

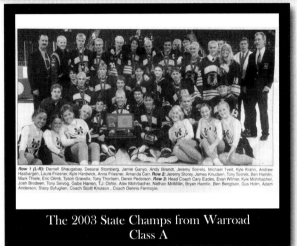
The 2003 State Champs from Warroad
Class A

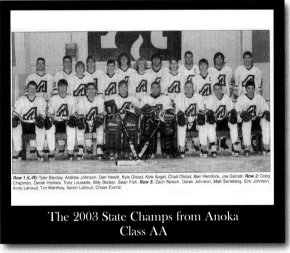
The 2003 State Champs from Anoka
Class AA

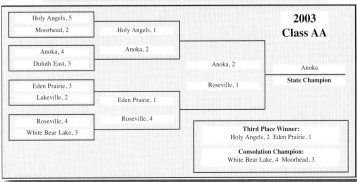

and an assist in the win. Game Four then saw Fergus Falls doubling up on Mound-Westonka, 6-3, thanks to Ryan Miller's third period pure hat-trick and Ryan Kantrud's two goals.

Rochester Lourdes beat Hermantown in the first semifinal contest by the final score of 4-2. Brandon Harrington had a pair of goals and an assist in the win. The other semi saw Benilde-St. Margaret's beat up on Fergus Falls, 6-2. Danny Charleston had a pair of goals in this one while Ricky Hopkins added three points to boot.

Benilde-St. Margaret's cruised from there, beating Rochester Lourdes in the title game, 2-1. Ian Schaser opened the scoring for BSM in the first, followed by Ricky Hopkins just a few minutes later. Lourdes winger Matt Rink made it 2-1, but that was as close as they would get as goalie Jake Schuman stopped 20 of 21 shots to secure the victory for BSM.

2002 (Class AA)
Holy Angels beat Cloquet/Esko/Carlton, 5-2, in the opening quarterfinal contest to kick off the Class AA state tourney. Tyler Howells had a pair of goals and Jimmy Kilpatrick added four points for Holy Angels in the win. Game Two saw Roseville double up on Moorhead, 4-2, on goals from Andrew Carroll, Nick Klaren, Collin Cody and Neal Schneider. The third quarterfinal was highlighted by Bloomington Jefferson's goalie, Jeremy Earl, who turned away all 18 shots he faced en route to a 2-0 shut-out victory over Elk River. Game four was a thriller as Hill-Murray edged Lakeville, 3-2, in overtime. Tony Rawlings was the hero in this one, scoring the game-winner at the 2:53 mark of sudden death.

Holy Angels went on to down Roseville in the first semifinal, 6-3. Dan Kronick was on fire in this one, scoring four goals, while goalie Ben Luth stopped 19 shots in the big win. The other semi was a blow-out as Hill-Murray spanked Bloomington Jefferson by the final score of 5-0. Forward Brian Kaufman tallied twice, Garrett Regan added three points, and goalie Tony Ciro turned away all 18 shots that came his way for the shut-out. Then, in the finals, Holy Angels got past Hill-Murray, 4-2, to claim the championship. The Pioneers got on the board first, but Holy Angels rallied with goals from Dan Kronick, Kevin Krmpotich, Tyler Howells and Kevin Rollwagen. Luth came up big in net as well, turning away 20 of the 22 shots he faced en route to the title victory.

2002 (Class A)
The 2002 Class A tourney opened with Fergus Falls outlasting International Falls, 6-4, behind Ryan Miller's three goals and two assists. Totino Grace beat East Grand Forks in the second quarterfinal, 6-2, thanks to Dan McCauley's hat-trick. Game three saw Rochester Lourdes take out Orono by the final of 7-2. Brandon Harrington led the charge in this one with a pair of goals, while goalie Dan Smith turned away 14 of the 15 shots he faced in net. The last quar-

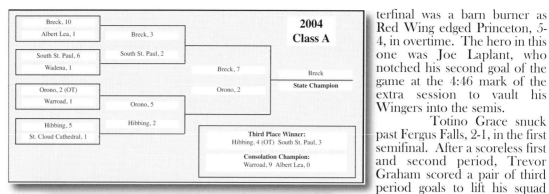

					2004 Class A

terfinal was a barn burner as Red Wing edged Princeton, 5-4, in overtime. The hero in this one was Joe Laplant, who notched his second goal of the game at the 4:46 mark of the extra session to vault his Wingers into the semis.

Totino Grace snuck past Fergus Falls, 2-1, in the first semifinal. After a scoreless first and second period, Trevor Graham scored a pair of third period goals to lift his squad into the finals. The other semi saw Red Wing dump Rochester Lourdes, 5-2, behind Tom Pohl's hat-trick and Joe Laplant's two goals and two assists.

From there, Red Wing squared off against Totino Grace in the finals, ultimately coming up on the losing end of a tight 3-2 hockey game. Totino Grace jumped out to a two goal lead in this one on goals from Nick Miller and Trevor Graham, only to see Red Wing tie it up in the second on goals from Aaron Underwood and John Loquai. Graham then got his second goal of the game, on the power-play, at the 11:50 mark of the third period. The goal would prove to be the game-winner as Totino Grace held on to win the title.

2003 (Class AA)
Holy Angels jumped out to a quick 3-0 lead in the opener thanks to a goal and an assist each from Jimmy Kilpatrick and Nick Ames, and hung on to beat Moorhead in Game One, 5-2. Game two was tight as Anoka got past Duluth East, 4-3, on a pair of late third period goals from Andrew Johnson and Ben Hendrick. Eden Prairie edged Lakeville in the third quarterfinal contest, 3-2, thanks to Dave Watters, Nate Hanson and Matt Rau, who each notched a pair of points in the win. Game Four was also close as Roseville topped White Bear Lake, 4-3, behind a pair of third period goals by Brandon Svendson which sealed the deal.

Anoka snuck past Holy Angels in the first semifinal game, 2-1. Aaron LaHoud and Zach Nelso each scored in the first period to give the Tornadoes a 2-0 lead in this one. Holy Angels forward Kevin Huck made it close, but Anoka goalie Kyle Olstad stood strong and didn't let in any goals in either the second or third periods en route to earning the victory. The other semi saw Roseville breeze past Eden Prairie, 4-1, on goals from Andy Carroll, Blake Twardowski, Mike Sertich and Kellen Chamblee. Raiders goalie Jerad Kauftmann stopped 15 of 16 shots to boot as Roseville advanced on to the Finals.

There, Anoka skated past Roseville by the final score of 3-1. Roseville jumped out to an eary 1-0 lead on a Carroll goal, only to see Anoka tally three unanswered goals en route to winning the championship. The Johnsons, Andrew and Derek, each scored, as did Craig Chapman. Goalie Kyle Olstad came up with 15 saves as well en route to leading his Tornadoes to their

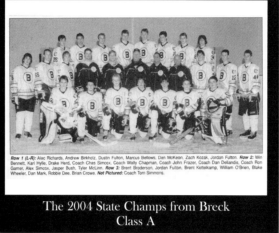

Row 1 (L-R): Alec Richards, Andrew Birkholz, Dustin Fulton, Marcus Bellows, Dan McKeon, Zach Kozak, Jordan Fulton. Row 2: Win Bennett, Karl Hylle, Drake Herd, Coach Chas Simcox, Coach Wally Chapman, Coach John Frazer, Coach Dan Deliandis, Coach Ron Garner, Alex Simcox, Jasper Bush, Tyler McLinn. Row 3: Brent Broderson, Jordan Fulton, Brent Kettelkamp, William O'Brien, Blake Wheeler, Dan Mark, Robbie Dee, Brian Crowe. Not Pictured: Coach Tom Simmons.

The 2004 State Champs from Breck
Class A

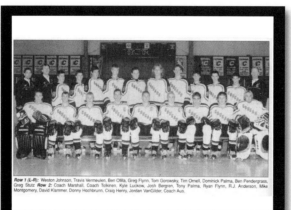

Row 1 (L-R): Weston Johnson, Travis Vermeulen, Ben Ollila, Greg Flynn, Tom Gorowsky, Tim Ornell, Dominick Palma, Ben Pendergrass, Greg Stutz. Row 2: Coach Marshall, Coach Tolkinen, Kyle Luckow, Josh Bergren, Tony Palma, Ryan Flynn, R.J. Anderson, Mike Montgomery, David Klammer, Donny Hochbrunn, Craig Henry, Jordan VanGilder, Coach Aus.

The 2004 State Champs from Centennial
Class AA

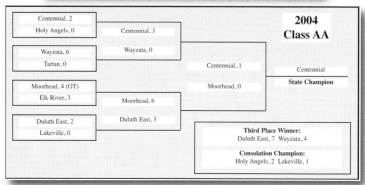

					2004 Class AA

first ever state title.

2003 (Class A)

Warroad downed Fergus Falls in the Class A opener, 4-1, behind a pair of Tony Selvog goals. Orono edged Princeton in Game Two, 2-1, thanks to a goal and assist each from Glenn Ylitalo and Pat Dynan. Rochester Lourdes needed overtime to get past Hibbing in the third quarterfinal contest, winning the game by the score of 2-1 thanks to John Brunkhorst's game-winner at the 1:46 mark of the extra session. Game Four was also an extended-play thriller with Simley edging St. Louis Park, 2-1, on Adam Hoaglund's game-winner at the 1:46 mark of sudden-death.

Warroad beat Orono in the first semifinal, 5-2, behind future University of North Dakota star T.J. Oshie's two goals and one assist. The other semi, meanwhile, was much closer as Simley narrowly got past Rochester Lourdes by the final of 3-2 in double overtime. Mike Bailey scored a pair of goals in this one, while Adam Hoaglund notched the game-winner at the 8:00 mark of the second extra session to send the Spartans to the Finals.

There, however, Warroad was simply too touch as they went on to beat Simley by the final score of 3-1. Tied at 1-1 until midway through the third, Warroad senior center James Knudsen got the game-winner at the 11:23 mark. Gabe Harren then added an insurance goal a few minutes later as the Warriors cruised to their third state title in school history.

2004 (Class AA)

Centennial opened the 2004 Class AA tourney by blanking Holy Angels, 2-0. Tom Gorowsky had a goal and an assist, while goalie Greg Stutz turned away all 22 shots that came his way. Game Two was another shut-out as Wayzata beat up on Tartan, 6-0. Kevin Kolkind and Joey Miller each had a pair of goals while goalie Jason Krueger made 16 saves as well. In addition, future Ohio State All-American linebacker James Laurinaitis had a pair of assists to boot. Game Three was much tighter as Moorhead edged Elk River, 4-3, in overtime. Matt Becker scored a pair of goals in this one, and Cory Loos got the game-winner at the 1:43 mark of the extra session. The final quarterfinal was yet another shut-out as Duluth East smoked Lakeville, 2-0, on goals from Mark Hennessy and Brian Lasky, while Hounds goalie Jake Maida made 21 saves in the win.

Centennial breezed past Wayzata in the semifinals, 3-0, as goalie Greg Stutz turned away all 16 shots that he faced in this one. Leading the charge for the Cougars was Tim Ornell, who had a pair of goals, as well as Tom Gorowsky, who added a trio of assists in the victory. The other semi saw Moorhead doubling up on Duluth East by the final score of 6-3. The Spuds jumped out to a 5-0 lead in this one and hung on from there thanks to a pair of goals from Cory Loos and a trio of

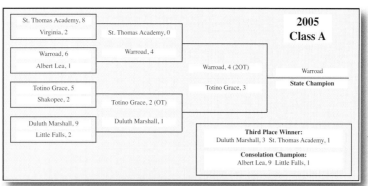

The 2005 State Champs from Warroad
Class A

assists from Brian Gifford. Hounds forward Rob Johnson had a pair of goals in the loss.

Centennial goalie Greg Stutz then went on to make history in the Finals, becoming the first keeper in the tourney's 61 year history to post three straight shut-outs en route to winning the championship. Junior Mike Montgomery shelfed what turned out to be the game-winner at the 4:04 mark of the second period on assists from Travis Vermeulen and R.J. Anderson.

2004 (Class A)

Breck opened the 2004 Class A tourney in style, crushing Albert Lea, 10-1. Leading the charge for the Mustangs was future first round NHL draft pick, Blake Wheeler, who netted a hat-trick in the lopsided win. Game Two then saw South St. Paul take care of Wadena, 6-1, behind a pair of goals each from Mike Pilot and Louie LaManna. The third quarterfinal was a tight one as Orono upset Warroad, 2-1, in overtime behind Glenn Ylitalo's game-winner at the 4:02 mark of the extra session. The last quarterfinal contest saw Hibbing dump St Cloud Cathedral, 5-1, thanks in large part to the Walters boys, Drew and Shea, who combined for a whopping eight points in the victory.

Breck outlasted South St. Paul in the first semifinal, 3-2, behind Blake Wheeler's three assists. Meanwhile, the Fultons, Dustin and Jordan, each scored for the Mustangs, while Robbie Dee came up with the game-winner late in the third. The other semi saw Orono take out Hibbing by the final score of 5-2. Down 2-0 early, Orono rallied back behind Pat Dynan's hat-trick to earn a spot in the Finals.

In the championship game, however, Breck dominated, beating Orono by the final of 7-2. Blake Wheeler tallied yet another hat-trick in this one, while goalie Alec Richards came up with 24 saves as well. It was Breck's second title as they finished their stellar season with a 28-1-2 overall record.

2005 (Class AA)

Duluth East opened the 2005 Class AA tourney with a 3-2 victory over White Bear Lake. Leading the way for the Hounds were Chris Anderson, Mike Schumacher and Keegan Flaherty, who each tallied in the win. Moorhead blanked Rochester Century in Game Two, 3-0, behind goalie Spencer Duetz's 14 saves and Matt Becker's two points. Meanwhile, Century goalie Alex Kangas turned away a whopping 42 shots in the loss. Game Three saw Holy Angels edge past Bloomington Jefferson, 3-2, behind Tyler Hawkins' two goals. The last quarterfinal featured Tartan beating Elk River, 4-3, thanks to Mike Wallgren's game-winner at the 15:50 mark of the third period.

Moorhead skated past Duluth East in the first semifinal, 4-1, behind goals from Ryan Clukey, Chris VandeVelde, Drew Fisher and Cory Loos. Incidentally, Duluth goalie Chris Sall came up with an astonishing 48 saves

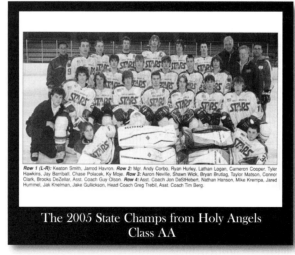

The 2005 State Champs from Holy Angels
Class AA

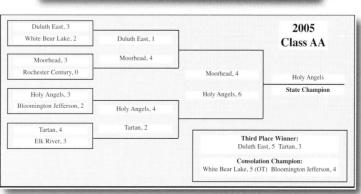

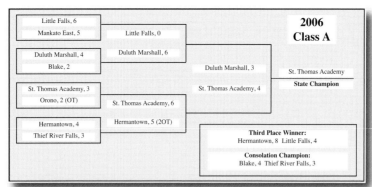

in the loss. The other semi saw Holy Angels double up on Tartan, 4-2, behind a pair of third period goals from Lathan Logan. Also chipping in was future Gopher Jay Barriball, who had a goal and an assist in the big win.

Holy Angels kept on rolling from there, downing Moorhead in the title game by the final of 6-4. Leading the charge for the Stars was Barriball, who had a pair of goals and an assist in the finale. Goalie Keaton Smith also came up with 37 saves en route to leading the Academy to their second ever championship. Ironically, it was the sixth time the Spuds would finish as runner's up in the big dance.

2005 (Class A)

St Thomas Academy came roaring out of the gates in Game One, whipping Virginia by the score of 8-2. Leading the charge for the Cadets were Jordan Schroeder and J.C. Blaisdell, who tallied a pair of goals each in the win. Warroad topped Albert Lea in Game two, 6-1, on a pair of goals from Aaron Marvin and a pair of assists from T.J. Oshie. Game Three featured Totino Grace beating Shakopee by the final of 5-2. Leading the way for TG was Brian Schack, who had a pair of goals and an assist in the victory. Duluth Marshall came out swinging in the last quarterfinal contest, crushing Little Falls, 9-2. Starring for the Hill Toppers was Scott Kozlak, who tallied four goals in the big win.

Warroad blanked St Thomas Academy in the first semifinal, 4-0, thanks to goalie Mark Thiele, who turned away all 16 shots he faced that afternoon. Kyle Krahn scored a pair of goals for the Warriors, while Ben Bengtson added a goal and an assist to boot. The other semi was a tight one as Totino Grace edged past Duluth Marshall, 2-1, in overtime. Tied at one apiece after three, Erik Bredesen proved to be the hero in this one, scoring the game-winner at the :32 mark of the extra session.

It took double overtime for Warroad to get past Totino Grace in the finals, winning their fourth overall title by the score of 4-3. The undefeated Warriors got the game-winner from sophomore Aaron Marvin at the 11:37 mark of sudden-death. Goalie Mark Thiele had 33 saves, while Josh Brodeen, Kyle Hardwick and Bob Anacabe each tallied as well in the win.

2006 (Class AA)

Blaine winger Ryan Johnson scored the opening goal of the 2006 Class AA tourney for Blaine, but the star of this game was Matt Olson, who tallied a pure hat-trick en route to leading his Bengals past Lakeville North by the score of 7-2. Game Two saw Cretin-Derham Hall defeat Eagan, 5-2, thanks in large part to the efforts of Ben Kinne, who scored two goals and added three assists in the win. Teammate Chris Hickey also added a pair of goals and an assist to boot. The third quarterfinal contest saw Hill-Murray edge Minnetonka by the final score of 5-4. Nick Larson had three goals, including the game-winner to lead the

Pioneers to victory. Grand Rapids then rallied in Game Four to beat Roseau, 7-4, behind Patrick White's amazing four goal performance.

Blaine had its 22-game undefeated streak ended by Cretin Derham Hall in the opening Class AA semifinal, losing by the final of 4-2. Raider's winger Chris Hickey had two goals, including the game winner, while freshman Tommy Zimmerman and Ryan Kurtz added one apiece in the win. The Raiders out-shot the Bengals, 17-2, in the second and cruised from there behind goalie Ben Hause, who made 18 saves en route to leading his team to the Finals.

The other semi saw Grand Rapids edge past top-ranked Hill-Murray, 3-2. Junior Zach Morse got the Thunderhawks on the board first when he tallied at 6:36 on a shot from the right point which slipped past Hill-Murray goalie Joe Phillippi. Senior Brian Arrigoni tied the score for the Pioneers, but Kyle Welliver and Patrick White's goals extended the lead to 3-1. White's game-winner then came when he faked a backhand shot and then went to his forehand at 14:59 of the second period. Junior Nick Larson scored at 9:21 in the third period to pull the Pioneers within one, but that was as close as they would get. Hill-Murray out-shot Grand Rapids 24-14, but came up just short in the end.

Cretin-Derham Hall Raiders then went on to crush Grand Rapids in the Finals, 7-0, to earn its first-ever state championship title. Juniors Ryan McDonagh and Chris Hickey led the Raiders in scoring with two goals apiece, while goalie Ben Hause stopped all eight shots that he faced in earning the coveted shutout. Senior Corvin Kieger added one goal and two assists as well.

2006 (Class A)

Little Falls opened the 2006 Class A tourney by defeating Mankato East/Loyola, 6-5. Ben Hanowski and Zack Beattie each scored a pair of goals for the Flyers as they held off a late rally to advance to the semis. Duluth Marshall doubled up on Blake in Game Two, 4-2, as three different Hill Toppers scored over a four minute span of the first period. Sophomore Jared Festler scored three unanswered goals for Blake, but Duluth Marshall goalie Jason Paul made 24 saves to lead his team in to the next round. Game Three was a thriller as St. Thomas Academy topped Orono, 3-2. Down 2-1 with just under a minute to go, senior forward J.C. Blaisdell got the equalizer to send it to overtime. There, defenseman Tony Mergens slapped home a Blaisdell rebound at the 4:06 mark of the extra session to give his Cadets the victory. The last quarterfinal match-up saw Hermantown rally past Thief River Falls, 4-3, thanks to senior Karl Gilbert's natural hat-trick that came in the final ten minutes of play. The game-winner, meanwhile, came with just 37 seconds left on the clock.

Row 1 (L-R): Jack Baer, Tony Mergens, Conor Rooney, Mike Joyce, Jordan Schroeder, Pepper Skytee, Marc Haverkamp. Row 2: Jon Schreiner, Ryan Brodd, Mike Mulally, Derick Fiebiger, Tim McManus, Rob Vannelli, JC Blaisdell, Mgr. Pat Sutherland. Row 3: Tom Hickey, Anders Lee, Jack Geiser, Jeff Urick, Coach Tom Vannelli, Coach Mike Vannelli, Coach Greg Vannelli, Dewey Herzog, Nick Larson, Coach Jerry Meybrey, Aaron Crandall.

The 2006 State Champs from St. Thomas Academy
Class A

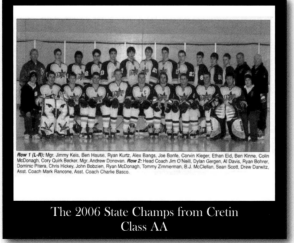

Row 1 (L-R): Mgr. Jimmy Keis, Ben Hause, Ryan Kurtz, Alex Bangs, Joe Bonfe, Corvin Kieger, Ethan Eid, Ben Kinne, Colin McDonagh, Cory Quirk Becker, Mgr. Andrew Donovan. Row 2: Head Coach Jim O'Neill, Dylan Gergen, Al Davis, Ryan Bohrer, Dominic Pitera, Chris Hickey, John Bobzien, Ryan McDonagh, Tommy Zimmerman, B.J. McClellan, Sean Scott, Drew Darwitz, Asst. Coach Mark Rancone, Asst. Coach Charlie Basco.

The 2006 State Champs from Cretin
Class AA

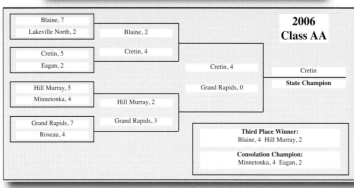

Duluth Marshall blanked Little Falls, 6-0, in the opening semifinal behind Rob Bordsen's hat-trick. Junior winger Bob Gutsch added two goals and one assist while Hill Topper goalie Jason Paul earned the shut-out with 17 saves. In addition, he also fended off a whopping nine Flyer power plays. The other semi was much tighter as St. Thomas Academy snuck past Hermantown, 6-5, in double overtime. Senior center Jack Baer got the game-winner at the 3:29 mark of the second extra session, beating goalie Nathan Hardy to give his Cadets a ticket to the Finals. STA had a 5-2 third period lead, only to see Hermantown rally and tie it up at 5-5 with goals from Jared Rodlund and Ryan Hill. Karl Gilbert got the equalizer when he tallied his second goal of the game at 12:36 of the third period.

The Finals were a barn-burner as St. Thomas Academy rallied to beat Duluth Marshall for the Class A crown, 4-3. Trailing 3-1 going into the third, STA scored three unanswered goals in just over two minutes to take the title. Following goals from Anders Lee and J.C. Blaisdell, Jack Baer scored his second game-winner in as many days, this one coming on a break-away with 5:43 remaining on the clock. The Hill Toppers rallied back in the final minutes and thought they had the equalizer when junior Bob Gutsch's shot off the post magically came to rest behind St. Thomas Academy goalie Aaron Crandall. It wasn't meant to be, however, as the Cadets hung on for the big win.

2007 (Class AA)

Making their record-setting 31st appearance at the state tourney, Roseau opened the Class AA quarterfinals by spanking Woodbury, in its first tournament appearance, 7-2. Leading the charge for the Rams were Nick Oliver, Kurt Weston and Aaron Ness, who each had three points in the win. Game Two saw Rochester Century edge past Hill-Murray in overtime, 6-5. Sophomore forward Joe Faupel scored the last four goals of the game, including the game-winner at 3:20 of the extra session, while teammate Garrett Grimstad had five assists to boot. Game Three saw Grand Rapids upset No. 1 seed Edina, 3-1, behind Patrick White's two goals and Zach Morse's two assists. Burnsville then advanced to the semifinals by upsetting Blaine, 4-2, in the last quarterfinal game of the night. Blaze forward Jake Hendrickson notched the game-winner at 1:05 of the third period, while Tyler Barnes, Chad McDuff and Zach King all scored as well.

The Roseau Rams defeated the Rochester Century Panthers, 3-1, in the first semifinal behind Dustin Moser's first period goal and assist. Seniors Kurt Weston and Ryan Larsen also tallied for the Rams, while sophomore goalie Mike Lee came up with 22 saves in net. The other semi saw Grand Rapids

eke past Burnsville in overtime, 4-3, thanks to sophomore Sam Rendle's game-winner with just over a minute to go in the extra session. Up 3-0 in the third period, the Blaze rallied back in a big way in this one. Thunderhawks goalie Reidar Jenson stood strong in the end though, registering 15 saves en route to leading his team to the Finals.

The all-northern Minnesota final between Grand Rapids and Roseau brought an old-school flavor to the Class AA Finals. When it was all said and done, however, this one was all Roseau, as they crushed the Thunderhawks, 5-1. The Rams were led by sophomore Tyler Landman, who notched a pair of third period goals, and senior Kurt Weston, who added three assists. Roseau netminder Mike Lee played solid the entire game and finished with 28 saves as he led his club to its seventh state title.

2007 (Class A)

St. Thomas Academy opened the Class A tourney by beating Orono, 5-2. The Cadets were led by James Saintey, who scored a pair of goals and an assist, and Jon Schreiner, who added four assists as well. Duluth Marshall, in their third consecutive appearance at the tourney, edged the Blake Bears, 4-3, in Game Two. Hilltopper's goalie Jesse Behning faced just 13 shots in the win, while his team dished out 27 shots of their own. The top-seeded Hermantown Hawks beat Little Falls in Game Three, 6-3, behind junior Drew LeBlanc's hat-trick and two assists. The last quarterfinal saw the Warroad Warriors down the Albert Lea Tigers, 3-1, thanks to junior Bryce Ravndalen's two goals and Aaron Marvin's three assists.

In a rematch of the 2006 state championship game, the first semifinal contest was a classic as Duluth Marshall upset St. Thomas Academy, 3-2, in double overtime. Hilltopper's junior Dano Jacques was the star in this one, recording a natural hat-trick, while teammate Jack Connolly added two assists in the big win. The other semi was also a tight one as Hermantown knocked off Warroad, 4-3. Warroad jumped out to an early 3-1 lead, only to see the Hawks rally back with three unanswered goals, highlighted by the game-winner off of the stick of Ryan Schmidt at the 7:05 mark of the third period.

Duluth Marshall, making their second straight appearance in the title game, was hoping to finally bring home the title this year. Rival Hermantown had their own agenda though and took out the Hill Toppers by the final score of 4-1. Brett Granmo got the Hawks on the board first, only to see Marshall senior Jack Connolly tied it up less than a minute later. The game was tight, but Hermantown blew it open in the second, scoring a pair of goals, and then adding another in the third for good measure — an empty netter by senior Ryan Schmidt. Hermantown goalie Nathan Hardy played huge, coming up with 32 saves, and preserving his team's undefeated record. It was the school's first state title.

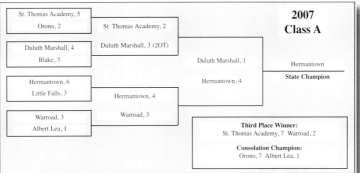

		2007
St. Thomas Academy, 5 / Orono, 2	St. Thomas Academy, 2	Class A
Duluth Marshall, 4 / Blake, 3	Duluth Marshall, 3 (2OT)	Duluth Marshall, 1 / Hermantown, 4
Hermantown, 6 / Little Falls, 3	Hermantown, 4	Hermantown / State Champion
Warroad, 3 / Albert Lea, 1	Warroad, 3	

Third Place Winner:
St. Thomas Academy, 7 Warroad, 2

Consolation Champion:
Orono, 7 Albert Lea, 1

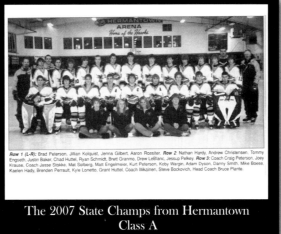

Row 1 (L-R): Brad Peterson, Jillian Kolquist, Jenna Gilbert, Aaron Rossiter. Row 2: Nathan Hardy, Andrew Christensen, Tommy Engseth, Justin Baker, Chad Huttel, Ryan Schmidt, Brett Granmo, Drew LeBlanc, Jessup Pelkey. Row 3: Coach Craig Peterson, Joey Krause, Coach Jesse Stokke, Mat Solberg, Matt Engelmeier, Kurt Peterson, Koby Wargin, Adam Dyson, Danny Smith, Mike Boese, Kaelen Hady, Brenden Perrault, Kyle Lonetto, Grant Huttel, Coach Illikainen, Steve Bockovich, Head Coach Bruce Plante.

**The 2007 State Champs from Hermantown
Class A**

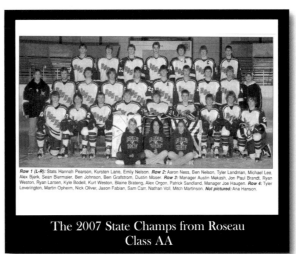

Row 1 (L-R): Stats Hannah Pearson, Kursten Lane, Emily Nelson. Row 2: Aaron Ness, Ben Nelson, Tyler Landman, Michael Lee, Alex Bjerk, Sean Biermaier, Ben Johnson, Ben Grafstrom, Dustin Moser. Row 3: Manager Austin Mekash, Jon Paul Brandt, Ryan Weston, Ryan Larsen, Kyle Bodell, Kurt Weston, Blaine Brateng, Alex Orgon, Patrick Sandland, Manager Joe Haugen. Row 4: Tyler Leverington, Martin Opheim, Nick Oliver, Jason Fabian, Sam Carr, Nathan Voll, Mitch Martinson. Not pictured: Ana Hanson.

**The 2007 State Champs from Roseau
Class AA**

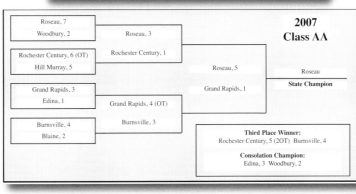

		2007
Roseau, 7 / Woodbury, 2	Roseau, 3	Class AA
Rochester Century, 6 (OT) / Hill Murray, 5	Rochester Century, 1	Roseau, 5 / Grand Rapids, 1
Grand Rapids, 3 / Edina, 1	Grand Rapids, 4 (OT)	Roseau / State Champion
Burnsville, 4 / Blaine, 2	Burnsville, 3	

Third Place Winner:
Rochester Century, 5 (2OT) Burnsville, 4

Consolation Champion:
Edina, 3 Woodbury, 2

SHATTUCK-ST. MARY'S

Zach Parise

Shattuck-St. Mary's, located in Faribault, is a Minnesota prep power-house. The school has had a long and storied hockey history that goes all the way back to the 1920s. It was the first school to have organized hockey in southern Minnesota, due in large part to the fact that many of the school's faculty and students were from out East and were already familiar with the game. In the programs early days, it regularly played against many of the state's private schools and colleges which had started programs of their own, including Blake, De La Salle, Cretin, St. Paul Academy, St. Thomas Academy, Pillsbury Academy, St. Paul Luther, St. Olaf and Carlton.

Three of the program's early stars, Marty Falk, Wally Taft and Bud Wilkinson, would all go on to star for the University of Minnesota. Wilkinson was so good as a goaltender that in 1932 he led Shattuck to an undefeated season and in the process, he went unscored upon over the entire season. (Incidentally, with the Gophers, Wilkinson would earn All-American honors in both football and hockey before going on to became a nationally acclaimed football coach at the University of Oklahoma, where he would lead his Sooners to five straight undefeated seasons.)

Shattuck's hockey program fell into hard times in the 1980s and even had to partner with a local co-op program with Faribault High School in order to field a full team. With just two players on the roster in 1989, the school embarked on a visionary plan to make hockey a priority. That next year a massive recruiting campaign was kicked off to turn the program around. It would be a transformation like none other. By 1993 SSM had outgrown the local high school hockey league and expanded its season to include a full schedule of USA Hockey games and tournaments. In 1996 the school fielded its first girls' team and the boys' top midget team skated to its first ever National Championship tournament.

Three years later, the boys' prep team, led by former Los Angeles King's head coach, Andy Murray, began what would become a tradition of excellence by winning its first Tier I Boys' U-18 National Championship title, or Midget Triple-A. The boys' prep team has since won three more National Championships in 2001, 2003 and 2005. Further, in 2005 and 2006 the girls' prep team won back-to-back Tier I Women's U-19 National Championships as well.

Today, SSM's hockey program is made up of eight teams playing a seven-month schedule of between 50-70 games per season. The teams travel throughout North America to play in tournaments and are as good or better than Canada's top teams. Under the direction of Tom Ward, the school's Director of Hockey, and former North Star's great, J.P. Parisé, who serves as the Director of Player Evaluation, the school's program is based on the conviction that its players must be good students, good citizens and also great athletes. Four midget teams, two bantam teams and two girls teams make up our highly competitive program. SSM alumni have gone on to compete at the highest levels of junior, collegiate and professional hockey. From NHL superstar Sydney Crosby, to Zach Parise, to Jack Johnson to Ty Gretzky — the program's past players reads like a who's-who of the hockey world.

One of the premier hockey programs on the planet, Sports Illustrated said it best: *"Shattuck-St. Mary's is to high school hockey what Harvard is to law school."*

SHATTUCK'S NHL DRAFT PICKS

Name	Current League	NHL Draft Status
Joe Corvo '95	NHL	Los Angeles Kings (83rd selection of the 1997 entry draft)
Peter Ratchuk '96	DEL	Colorado Avalanche (25th selection of 1996 entry draft)
Noah Clarke '97	AHL	Los Angeles Kings (250th selection of 1999 entry draft)
Ryan Malone '99	NHL	Pittsburgh Penguins (115th selection 1999 entry draft)
Ryan Caldwell '99	AHL	New York Islanders (202nd selection of 2000 entry draft)
Cliff Loya '99	ECHL	Chicago Blackhawks (207th selection of 2000 entry draft)
Ben Eaves '00	AHL	Pittsburgh Penguins (131st selection 2001 entry draft)
Patrick Eaves '02	NHL	Ottawa Senators (29th selection of 2003 entry draft)
Brady Murray '02	WCHA	Los Angeles Kings (152nd selection of the 2003 entry draft)
Chris Porter '02	WCHA	Chicago Blackhawks (282nd selection of the 2003 entry draft)
Zach Parisé '02	NHL	New Jersey Devils (17th selection of 2003 entry draft)
Brian Salcido '03	AHL	Anaheim Mighty Ducks (141st selection of 2005 entry draft)
Casey Borer '03	WCHA	Carolina Hurricanes (69th selection of 2004 entry draft)
Matt Smaby '03	WCHA	Tampa Bay Lightning (41st selection of 2003 entry draft)
Drew Stafford '03	WCHA	Buffalo Sabres (13th selection of 2004 entry draft)
Matt Ford '03	WCHA	Chicago Blackhawks (256th selection of the 2004 entry draft)
A.J. Thelen '03	CCHA	Minnesota Wild (12th selection of 2004 entry draft)
Spencer Dillion '03	USHL	Florida Panthers (267th selection of 2004 entry draft)
Jonathan Toews '05	WCHA	Chicago Blackhawks (3rd selection of 2006 entry draft)
Taylor Chorney '05	WCHA	Edmonton Oilers (36th selection of 2005 entry draft)
Michael Gergen '05	WCHA	Pittsburg Penguins (61st selection of 2005 entry draft)
Sydney Crosby	NHL	Pittsburg Penguins (1st selection of 2005 entry Draft)
Jack Johnson	CCHA	Carolina Hurricanes (3rd selection of 2005 entry draft)
Kyle Okposo	WCHA	New York Islanders (7th selechon of 2006 entry draft)
Tyler Ruegsegger '06	WCHA	Toronto Maple Leafs (166th selection of 2006 entry Draft)
Nigel Williams	WCHA	Colorado Avalanche (51st selection of 2006 entry draft)
Jamie McBain	WCHA	Carolina Hurricanes (63rd selection of 2006 entry draft)

THE UPPER MIDWEST HIGH SCHOOL ELITE LEAGUE

The High School Elite Hockey Development Program and the Upper Midwest High School Hockey Elite League are among the nation's very best. Intended primarily as a high-level supplement to the high school season, the league features five teams from Minnesota, one North Dakota/Minnesota combo team and Wisconsin's top prep team. Shattuck's top team and other top Midget AAA teams also participate in some of the league's action as well. The program's director, Dr. John G. Russo, a former player at the University of Wisconsin, has had a long coaching career that has included stops at Iowa State, Farmington, St. Louis Park, Breck, Mpls. South and Blake High Schools.

As for the program's success, all nine Minnesota high school players who were selected in the 2004 NHL Entry Draft played in the program. Not bad for a program just a few years old. In addition, 14 players who have played in the program were ranked in the NHL's Central Scouting Mid-Term Draft Ranking. Fully 17 of the 21 players named to the Star Tribune's 2004 All-Metro team, including the player of the year (Tom Gorowsky) played in the program, as did 36 of the players in the 2004 Class AA and A State Tournaments.

The league's games are filled with coaches and scouts from scores of NCAA Division I programs throughout the country, as well as from the ranks of the USHL, NAHL and NHL. The results speak for themselves. The league has given countless Minnesota kids even more opportunities, and that is what it is all about.

MINNESOTA'S PRIVATE/CATHOLIC HIGH SCHOOL TOURNEY

In addition to the boys state high school tournament, back in the 1960s and early '70s there were state tournaments held for private, Catholic and independent schools as well. Teams from both parties played against each other during the regular season, but only the public schools participated in the state tournament. Because the State High School League didn't allow those schools to compete in its state tournament until 1974-75, the private, Catholic and independent schools would field their own, which was held at the Mpls. Auditorium, Wakota Arena and at Aldrich Arena. The top teams, including the likes of Duluth Cathedral, Hill and later Hill-Murray, St. Paul Academy, St. Agnes, Cretin, Blake, St. Thomas Academy and Benilde, would often beat the top public schools during the regular season. In the early '60s the Central Catholic Conference and the Minnesota Independent School League hosted an eight team post-season tournament called the Minnesota Prep School Tournament.

By 1964 the Minnesota Prep School Tournament was replaced by the State Catholic Tournament, which paired the top six teams from the Central Catholic Conference against out-state powers Duluth Cathedral and Crookston Cathedral. The winner would then face the MISL champion in the Twin City private school title game, with tournament sites being alternated between Duluth and the St. Paul Auditorium.

According to the outstanding website, mnpuck.com, the tournament would occasionally allow Michigan's top Catholic school champs from Marquette to compete as well. The dominant team of this era by far was Duluth Cathedral, which won the first five tournaments (1965-69) and regularly whipped the state's top public school teams. Up north, the Hill-Toppers would crush Duluth East, Greenway and Hibbing, and even ended International Falls' three-year, 58-game winning-streak. The Toppers were led by Steve "Pokey" Trachsel, who went on to play for UM-Duluth; Kevin Hoene, who played at Notre Dame; Steve Sertich, who played at Colorado College, and Phil Hoene, who played at UM-Duluth and then in the NHL.

The early 70s, however, were all about Hill, which won the new Independent State Tournament in 1970 and 1972 (as Hill-Murray), and Blake, which won it in 1971 and 1973. Hill was led by defenseman Dave Langevin, who would go on to play for UMD and then win four Stanley Cups with the New York Islanders in the early '80s. Several other Hill players would go on to play D-I hockey as well, including Pat Conroy, who played at Notre Dame, as well as Dick Spannbauer and Bill Klatt, who each played for the Gophers.

In 1974 St. Paul Academy won what would be the last Independant School title. That next year, the MSHSL allowed the Independent schools to participate in the public state tourney after some eligibility and recruiting issues were cleared up. They have been skating together ever since.

Cathedral's Phil Hoene

Cathedral's Pokey Trachsel

MINNESOTA HOCKEY COACHES ASSOCIATION HALL OF FAME

2006
Whitey Aus
Peter Aus
Bruce Johnson
Mike Thomas

2005
Skip Peltier
Brad Shelstad
Ken Staples
Chuck Grillo

2004
Bryan Grand
Jeff Whisler
Bill Vukonich
Tom Saterdalen

2003
Del Genereau
John Gilbert
Doug Woog

2002
John Bartz
Terry Skrypek
Terry Cullen

2001
Rod Anderson
Bart Larson
Bill McGann

2000
Jon Bittner
Ted Brill
Jim Nelson

1999
John Bianchi
Gene Olive
Eddie Zins

1998
John Broderick
Roger Koster
Roger "Bud" Leak
Jim Pohl

1997
John Matchefts
Don Saatzer
Bob Utecht

1996
Don Clark

Gordy Genz
Gus Hendrickson
Dick Holmsten
Rudy Kogi
Dick Roberts

1995
Bill Halbredher
Rod Magnuson
Tom Osiecki
Jerry Peterson
Don "Whitey" Willer
Warren Strelow

1994
Arnie Bauer
Bernie Braoderick
Bob Turner
Gene Aldrich

1993
Bill Frantti
Jim Baxter
Ed McGowan
Duddley Otto

1992
John Neihart

Al Godfrey
Dave Hendrickson
Carl Thorsen
Tom Wegleitner
John Rossi
Bob Gernander
Charles "Lefty" Smith
Bob Johnson
Lou Cotroneo
Don Olson
Wes Hoscheid

1991
Rube Gustafson
Oscar Almquist
Larry Ross
Willard Ikola
Al Maki
Rob Bjorkman
Dennis Rolle
Glenn Rollie
George Perpich
Gene Sack
John Mariucci
Leo Goslin
Carl Carlson
Ron Costellano

WOMEN'S HOCKEY IN MINNESOTA

The history of women's hockey goes back for more than a century in North America, with the first recorded women's hockey games taking place in 1891, in Ontario and also in Ottawa. Soon Lord Stanley of Preston (Canada's sixth Governor General and namesake of the NHL's Stanley Cup), was regularly hosting mixed skating parties that often featured pick-up games on Ottawa's Rideau rink. Before long, organized women's circuits throughout Canada called "Bakers Leagues," had popped up.

The ladies' game soon spread to the States after the turn of the century to both the East Coast and also into Minnesota and Upper Michigan's Copper Country. In 1916, according to U of M yearbooks, some 30 women tried out for the first-ever Gopher women's team. The Gopher women's program sported at least two squads per year, with 15 ladies on each roster. Although most of their competition came against other U of M teams, there was an annual cup awarded for the school's championship team. In addition, each woman who tried out had to have at least a C average in their studies to be considered. The teams often practiced their stick handling skills in the gymnasium, until after the Christmas break when they would venture outdoors to practice on the skating rink at Northrop Field. While Gopher men's hockey coach Emil Iverson helped to coach them on occasion, the majority of the women's teams' coaches were fraternity boys who were also playing intramurally. The women played through the 1920s, often-times drawing big crowds to see their games.

The women wore long dresses and overcoats, always remaining "lady-like" on the ice. But, while they wanted to play like the boys, they surely didn't want to take a beating like the boys. In fact, in 1927, to protect her face from flying pucks, Queen's (Canada) goaltender Elizabeth Graham became the first recorded hockey player ever to wear a face mask — more than three decades before Montreal Canadiens' Hall of Fame goalie Jacques Plante, then considered the originator of sporting a cage.

This came at an empowering time for women, who were now in the midst of the women's suffrage movement which challenged society for equality in education, work and play. In addition to fighting for equal rights (Incredibly, women were finally allowed the right to vote in only 1926...), women were having to prove to the world that they could do anything men could do. Male doctors were even claiming that the women's unique anatomy, coupled with their moral obligation to bear children, was not suitable for vigorous physical activity, especially with something as rough as hockey. But large numbers of women pressed on and continued to compete for the love of the game.

In 1929 the University of Minnesota women finally got a home of their own, when a hockey rink was constructed behind the old library on campus. These were the heydays for women's hockey, as the Gophers now were playing teams from Duluth and the Iron Range, as well as from nearby Carleton College. In addition, the Gopher women played against other women's club teams, co-ed fraternity and sorority teams, and even some men's

Women's hockey at the Goodrich Rink in St. Paul during the 1920s

teams. While other women's sports were emerging on campus, it was thought that many of the school's most talented female athletes were hockey players.

But, when the Great Depression hit in the early 1930s, the women's program at the U of M came to a halt. The game continued to flourish in Canada though, as the Rivulettes, a women's squad from Preston, Ontario, posted an unbelievable win-loss record of 348-2 throughout the 1930s, often-times beating local men's teams.

During the war years of the '40s, women's hockey continued to blossom. With most of the men overseas, women began working, supporting their families, and enjoying a new independence they had not known before. While women's baseball flourished during this time (a pro league called the AAGPBL was started in the Midwest, that included the Minneapolis Millerette's, and was featured in the movie "A League of Their Own"), other women's team sports, including hockey, were often-times the only game in town. But, after the war ended, men's hockey began to boom, which meant less ice-time for the ladies, and as a result, the growth of the women's game slowed way down.

In 1956, a nine-year-old girl by the name of Abby Hoffman forever changed the game of hockey for women. The young defenseman from Brantford, Ontario, made headlines across Canada that year when she brought the issue of gender equity to the front burner in a rather unique way. You see, Abby had been playing on the boy's team that entire season, while disguised as a boy. Because the kids dressed at home, and she wore her hair short, nobody seemed to notice. At the end of the season Abby was selected to play in the Timmy Tyke minor hockey tournament, which also included a post-season swimming party at the local pool. Busted! Still determined to play in the league (because there were no girl's youth teams back then), Abby and her family took their case all the way to the Ontario Supreme Court. There, the court ultimately ruled against her, and as a result she was banished from the league. Life went on for Abby though, as she later went on to become a Canadian Olympic track and field star. In 1982, in remembrance of her struggle to "just play hockey," the Ontario Women's Hockey Association created a national women's tournament in her honor called the Abby Hoffman Cup.

By the late 1960s women's-only programs began forming throughout the U.S. and Canada, and by the early '70s, teams had popped up in Sweden, Finland, Japan, China, Korea, Norway, Germany and Switzerland. By now, several U.S. college varsity and club teams had formed throughout the East Coast, and also in the Midwest. The U of M re-established a club team during the early '70s as well. The girl's game was developing quickly, but still had a long way to go at this point. Soon special protective chest and pelvic gear was designed especially for women, as their game began to evolve into its own style.

In the mid 1970s, in addition to community-based grass-roots programs, girls ice hockey was starting to be included in the athletic programs of sev-

The 1925 Lady Gophers hockey team

eral Minnesota school districts. Inspired by Billie Jean King, who defeated professional male tennis champion Bobbie Riggs in a "Battle of the Sexes" tennis match broadcast around the country, little girls everywhere saw that they were capable of achieving anything. In 1974, the first state peewee and bantam tournaments were held with White Bear Lake winning the peewee title and Mounds View taking the bantam crown. (The peewee tournament lasted from 1974 to 1976, until being resuscitated in 1989; while the bantams lasted from 1974 to 1978. Midgets, which was for 16-19 year-olds was later added as well.) While most of the programs folded within only a few years, a few stayed together and continued to play into the early 1980s. Many of those same girls who got their start at the youth level went on to star on women's midget, senior and club teams around the state.

In 1980, USA Hockey, the governing association of amateur ice hockey in the United States, organized the first-ever girls peewee and midget national championships, with Wayzata taking home the national midget title. Women's senior A and B divisions were added to the championship the following year. In addition, several colleges and universities on the East Coast were now offering women's hockey as part of their sports curriculum's.

In the late 1970s a woman by the name of Lynn Olson, the venerable "godmother" of women's hockey in Minnesota, was instrumental in starting the Minnesota Women's Hockey League. With no age limit per se, high school aged girls as well as middle-aged women in their 40s and 50s all came together in the new league to have a little fun and play some competitive hockey. Several teams, including the Blue Js, Rink Rats, Shooting Stars and Gold Diggers, emerged as the teams to beat in the league. Into the early '80s, as the sport continued to grow, a new elite midget team from Wayzata, called the Checkers, burst onto the Minnesota hockey scene. (One of the people who helped a lot in the development of the girls game at this level was Dr. Bob May, who, in addition to helping start the Checkers, also coached at North Dakota.) In 1980 the Checkers came home with the national Open B Division women's title. Then, led by Laura Halldorson (the future Gopher women's hockey coach), and Jill Pohtilla (the Augsburg women's hockey coach), the Checkers went on to win a couple of USA Hockey National Midget Championships in the early 1980's in both the 15-and-under, and later in

The 1995 Girls State Champs from Apple Valley

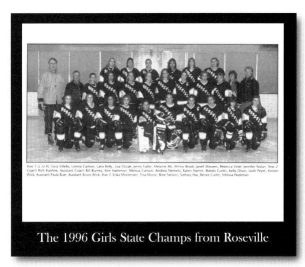

The 1996 Girls State Champs from Roseville

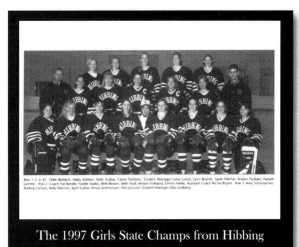

The 1997 Girls State Champs from Hibbing

The 1998 Girls State Champs from Apple Valley

the 19-and-under categories. In 1987 a new powerhouse team called the Thoroughbreds took the women's game to a new level. The elite team from Minneapolis dominated league play and often times played against the best amateur club teams from around the nation.

By 1982 there were 116 teams registered in the women's division of USA Hockey, covering the spectrum from squirts through seniors. In 1984 Providence College won the inaugural Eastern College Athletic Conference Women's Championship, which later came to serve as the equivalent of the women's college hockey national title. In 1986 the Minnesota Women's Hockey Association was formed, which then became a part of the Minnesota Amateur Hockey Association (MAHA) and USA Hockey. This really opened the door for women everywhere to get involved in hockey.

In 1986, Women's Hockey in Minnesota (WHAM) became the Minnesota Women's Hockey Association, and their alliance with USA Hockey and Minnesota Hockey was initiated. In the 1990's the MWHA incorporated and became known as the Minnesota Girls' and Women's Hockey Association (MGWHA), when they helped form and organize the leagues for girls hockey teams in Minnesota. The current name of "Women's Hockey Association of Minnesota" was instituted when Minnesota Hockey took over the role of organizing the girls' teams within the Districts of Minnesota Hockey and WHAM became the organizer of adult women's hockey. (With over 900 players playing in seven divisions, WHAM encourages girls and women of all age groups and skill levels to compete. With players ranging in ages from 17 to 75, all skill levels are represented from the beginner to the Olympian, and all for the love of the game.)

International women's hockey was growing too, as the U.S. defeated Sweden, 5-0, to win the bronze medal in the first-ever Women's World Invitational Tournament held in North York and Mississauga, Ontario, in 1987. Furthermore, in 1988, Minnesota hosted the USA Hockey Girls National Tournament (they would host it again in 1992). That next year the girl's and women's section of USA Hockey was established for the purpose of overseeing the development of girls' hockey throughout the country. In addition to legislating rules and regulations, the division would also help run national tournaments and developmental training camps as well. The director of the new program, Lynn Olson, who would hold

233

the position for the next six years. One of the first big hurdles Olson faced was the issue of recognition: "When I first started, the girls program was not really recognized," said Olson. "That's the way I felt and so did a lot of the rest of the country and we were very happy to see that USA Hockey was appointing a director to help establish a better program. We grew from 150 teams to over 700 teams; just the visibility that was created and the credibility of being a part of USA Hockey helped establish that."

There would be other issues as well, including the fact that at that time, there were a lot of men who simply were not comfortable with the idea of girls playing hockey: "I believe USA Hockey is firmly behind the program but not everybody at the amateur level is necessarily interested in promoting it because it takes time away from their sons," added Olson. "It has been a problem over the years, but it's getting better."

Although the sport went through somewhat of a lull in popularity during the late '80s, it really picked up speed in the early '90s. In 1990 Minnesota had 29 amateur youth teams in the state. That same year, Minnesota led the nation in the total number of registered women's hockey players, with just less than 6,000. By this time the age classification for girls hockey was broken down into 10-and-under, 12-and-under, 15-and-under and 19-and-under, or midget.

In 1990 the first-ever IIHF Women's World Championships were held in Ottawa. There, after blowing a 2-0 lead, the U.S. lost to Team Canada by the final score of 5-2 in the championship game. While body checking was allowed in the contest, it was later ruled illegal.

Something else interesting happened in the development of the game in 1990, when, as part of a gender equity requirement set forth by state and federal laws, schools were required to give equal athletics opportunities to both boys and girls. That next year, according to a Minnesota Department of Education survey, only 35 percent of Minnesota's high schools were in compliance with these new gender equity regulations. In an attempt to become compliant, many state schools introduced the game of ringette (a game similar to hockey that uses a straight, bladeless stick to slide a rubber ring across a gym floor and into a goal). While the game was pretty well received, most girls wanted to play the game of ice hockey.

It is interesting to note that in 1991, Edina's Jen Hanley became the first female goalie in the state to play regularly for a boy's varsity team. Her big break came on March 2nd, 1991,

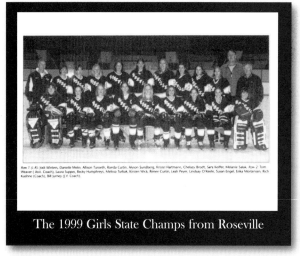
The 1999 Girls State Champs from Roseville

Row 1 (L-R): Jodi Winters, Danielle Molin, Allison Tunseth, Ronda Curtin, Alyson Sundberg, Kristel Hartmann, Chelsey Brodt, Sara Keiffer, Melanie Salak. Row 2: Tom Weaver (Asst. Coach), Laura Suppes, Becky Humphreys, Melissa Turbak, Kirsten Wick, Renee Curtin, Leah Peyer, Lindsay O'Keefe, Susan Engel, Erika Mortensen, Rich Kuehne (Coach), Bill Jumey (J.V. Coach).

The 2000 Girls State Champs from Park Center

Row 1 (L-R): Kori Brown, Kelly Irlbeck, Courtney Canniff, Krissy Wendell, Jennifer Kern, Nicole Marcella, Sarah Munson, Amy Jones. Row 2: Coach Tom Nault, Manager Heidi Christ, Coach Jamey Canniff, Kara Anderson, Jessica Page, Steph Johnson, Erin Baldwin, Melissa Lindemann, Jessica Horn, Lindsey Kern, Coach Amy Kiecker-Olson, Manager Tina Maassen, Coach John Donovan. Row 3: Christine Munson, Erin Ficken, Katie Crass, Robin Ryan, Cindy Zierke, Kelly Turnau.

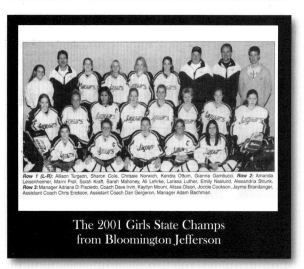
The 2001 Girls State Champs
from Bloomington Jefferson

Row 1 (L-R): Allison Turgeon, Sharon Cole, Chrissie Norwich, Kendra Ottum, Gianna Gambucci. Row 2: Amanda Leisenheimer, Marni Prall, Sarah Kraft, Sarah Mahoney, Ali Lehrke, Larissa Luther, Emily Naslund, Alexandria Strunk. Row 3: Manager Adriana Di Piacledo, Coach Dave Irvin, Kaytlyn Mount, Alissa Olson, Joccie Cookson, Jayme Brandanger, Assistant Coach Chris Erickson, Assistant Coach Dan Gergeron, Manager Adam Bachman.

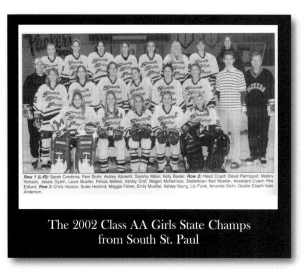
The 2002 Class AA Girls State Champs
from South St. Paul

Row 1 (L-R): Sarah Cimotrna, Pam Stohr, Ashley Albrecht, Sammy Miller, Kelly Bester. Row 2: Head Coach David Palmquist, Mallory Yorkson, Jessie Dyslin, Laura Mueller, Felicia Nelson, Ashley Graf, Megan McNamara, Statistician Neil Mueller, Assistant Coach Pete Edlund. Row 3: Chris Hanson, Susie Hosford, Maggie Fisher, Emily Mueller, Ashley Young, Liz Funk, Amanda Stohr, Goalie Coach Kate Anderson.

when Willard Ikola, after 33 years of coaching, started her in the nets against rival Richfield in a game at the sold-out Met Center. Hanley, who had gone undefeated during the season, led the Hornets to a 4-2 victory that night, earning herself a lot of national attention. She later attended both Hamline and St. Thomas Universities, before going on to play on the U.S. Women's National Team. Hanley would later serve as the head coach for the Burnsville girls high school team as well.

By 1992 there were 39 girls and women's teams registered with MAHA and USA Hockey in Minnesota, and a record 25 teams took part in the five divisions of the MAHA State Hockey Tournament that year as well. After that season, the Minnesota State High School League took a survey called "Girls Really Expect A Team!" or (GREAT!) to gain a more accurate assessment of which sports high school girls were most interested in playing. Nearly 8,000 girls signed a petition saying that they would love to play high school hockey if it were only offered. Their wish was about to be granted.

It is interesting to note that Mitzi Witchger was the founder of GREAT! A tireless promoter of Minnesota girls hockey, Witchger pushed hard for Title IX gender equity for girls sports and devoted countless hours to help grow girls hockey at the high school level. Perhaps her biggest accomplishment, however, was starting sanctioned girls high school hockey in 1993, when there were no interscholastic teams at the time. (As of 2007, according to WHAM, more than 125 girls' teams from over 140 Minnesota high schools compete to play in the three day televised state high school tournament.) Thanks Mitzi!

On November 19, 1994, South St. Paul and Holy Angels played the first ever girls' high school hockey game in state history. Later that year, in response to the overwhelming outcry for more organization in the sport, eight teams representing 11 state schools hit the ice for the inaugural girls state tournament, which, incidentally was not yet sanctioned by the MSHSL. Blaine/Coon Rapids would go on to beat Anoka/Champlin Park, 3-0, for the "unofficial" 1994 state title. That same year, there were 78 amateur youth teams registered in the state, up from 29 only four years earlier.

Something else dramatic happened that year for women's hockey as well, when Farmington's Amber Hegland played third-line center for the Tigers' boys state tournament team, thus becoming the first girl ever to play in the boys' state tournament. Amber, who had skated since she was two, and played on boys' teams since she was five, also played cornerback on the Tigers' varsity football team as well.

In 1995, after seeing how the experiment would fare, the Minnesota State High School League's Representative Assembly took a giant leap of faith by voting to become the first such organization in the country to sanction girls' ice hockey as a varsity sport. The news was viewed as a major advancement for women's sports everywhere.

"Now the younger girls will have role models and know that they can get better," said Lynn Olson. "It will give them more encouragement to start playing."

Twenty-four varsity teams took to the ice that season, while an additional 12 schools featured junior varsity teams, giving more than 1,000 girls in Minnesota the chance to play hockey at various high school levels. Then, on February 24, 1995, with the eyes of the nation upon them, the MSHSL sponsored the first-ever girls' state high school hockey tournament.

Held at the 3,500-seat Aldrich Arena in Maplewood, the inaugural tournament field included teams from Stillwater Area, Apple Valley, South St. Paul and Henry Sibley. The 22-0-1 undefeated Apple Valley Eagles, which came into the tournament as the favorite, faced Stillwater in the opener. Stillwater's Jenny Ginkel then made history by scoring the first ever goal of the tourney, just 92 seconds into the first period. But the Eagles screamed back behind the play of senior defender and Star Tribune Girls' Hockey Player of the Year, Jamie DeGriselles. (DeGriselles would go on to star and coach at the University of New Hampshire.) Despite being a defenseman, she led the Eagles with 43 goals and 35 assists for 78 points that season. In addition to DeGriselles' great play, freshman Michelle Sikich, who tallied 70 points that season, netted a hat-trick in the third period to rally Apple Valley to a 6-4 win.

Meanwhile, South St. Paul, behind Kelly Kegley's two goals and goalie Jenny Retka's whopping four saves in net, defeated Henry Sibley in the other semifinal game, 4-0 to advance to the championship game.

There, in front of a standing-room-only crowd in the title game, freshman goaltender Jenny Jannett posted an 18-save shut-out to lead Apple Valley to a 2-0 victory over the Packers for the first girl's high school hockey championship. Michelle Sikich and Betsey Kukowski each tal-

The 2002 Class A Girls State Champs
from Benilde St. Margaret's

The 2003 Class AA Girls State Champs
from South St. Paul

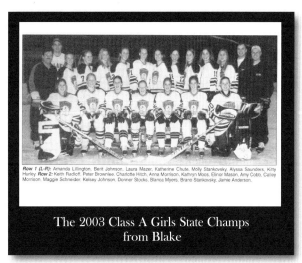

The 2003 Class A Girls State Champs
from Blake

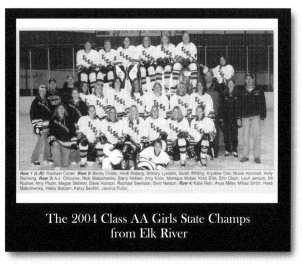

The 2004 Class AA Girls State Champs
from Elk River

lied for the Eagles in the big win.

As high school hockey grew, so too did the college game. In 1995 Augsburg College made history by becoming the first fully funded women's varsity hockey program not only in the state, but in the nation. At the same time, the Minnesota Legislature was making strides to help the girl's game grow as well. Believe it or not, a lot of the women at the state capital like to skate themselves, and many even play in a league of their own on Sunday nights. They wanted to do their best to see to it that girls everywhere had the same opportunities that the boys did. So, in 1995 the legislature passed a bill requiring that 15 percent of all ice time in both public and private rinks be reserved for girls, increasing to 30 percent in 1996 and 50 percent in 1997. Arena owners throughout the state could no longer get away with giving the girls undesirable time-slots either at the crack of dawn or in the middle of the night, and report that they had filled their quota. In addition, the Minnesota Amateur Sports Commission, the governing body that runs all amateur sports in the state, received funds through the legislature called the Mighty Ducks Bill, which was earmarked for either the construction of dozens of new arenas or for the renovation of existing ones. In 1995, 23 grants totaling nearly $3 million were awarded to 23 communities throughout the state. In all, more than $20 million was awarded for the sole purpose of giving more kids the chance to play hockey in Minnesota.

The University of Minnesota women's team also turned varsity in 1996, due in part to rising gender equity issues at the collegiate level. Both the Big 10 Conference, as well as the NCAA were enforcing strict rules about equity and making sure that member schools were providing an equal number of sports for both male and female athletes. This was one way the school saw fit to satisfy them both. Former Colby College coach Laura Halldorson took over as the team's first head coach that year, as the team hit the ice at Mariucci Arena. One of their biggest problems for the team right out of the gates though was a lack of competition. Other than Augsburg, there weren't any other varsity programs in the area, so many of the team's games that year were played on the East Coast, against the more established programs.

In addition to the U.S. National Women's Championships being held in Bloomington in 1996, it is interesting to note that the number of girls programs had nearly doubled that year to 47 teams now playing throughout the state. Roseville, Blaine/Coon Rapids, Burnsville and the Blake School rounded out the 1996 high school tournament field, as Roseville, led by the fabulous Curtin sisters, Ronda and Renee, went on to beat Burnsville for the second annual girl's high school championship.

Roseville opened the tourney by beating Blaine/Coon Rapids, 6-2, as the Curtins scored an incredible 10 points between them. Burnsville blanked Blake in the other semi, 5-0, behind goalie Laura Kelly's whopping three saves in net. Nicki DiCasmirro scored a pair of goals for the Blaze, while Laura Slominski added a goal and an assist to boot. Then, in the Finals, it was all Roseville, as the Raiders beat Burnsville by the final score of 5-2. Leading the way for Roseville were, of course, the Curtins, who tallied another five points between them en route to leading their squad to the title.

By now women's ice hockey had become one of the fastest growing sports in the world, growing from 5,573 women who were registered with USA Hockey in 1991, to more than 23,000 by 1997. (While there were just 35 teams in Minnesota in 1986, in 1997 there were 332 teams — broken down like this: 235 youth + 68 high school + 17 junior varsity + 12 college. Those 332 teams in Minnesota represented more than one-third of all the teams in the country at the time.) That same year, in addition to the Gophers and Augsburg, which had varsity teams, there were numerous club teams which were playing in the Midwestern Collegiate Women's Hockey Alliance, including: Carleton, Gustavus Adolphus, Mankato State, UM-Duluth, St. Catherine's, St. Thomas, St. Cloud State, St. Mary's and St. Olaf.

With some 68 schools now offering girls high school programs in the state, in 1997 the tournament moved to the bigger State Fair Coliseum. In addition, the field also expanded from a four to an eight-team format, as Hibbing, Roseville, Blaine, Eagan, Owatonna, Stillwater, Mounds View and Hopkins battled it out for the right to be called champion. Hibbing went on to win it all that year by doing something that had never been done, they beat the 51-0 (all-time) Roseville Raiders in the first quarterfinal game. Led by Beth Wolff's goal with just 18 seconds left in the game, the Bluejackets scored three unanswered third period goals to win 4-3. After knocking off Blaine in the semis 4-2, thanks to Amber Fryklund's hat-trick, the Hibbing Blue Jackets then met Eagan in the finals. Eagan, which was led by the state's most exciting player, seventh-grader

The 2004 Class A Girls State Champs from Benilde St. Margaret's

The 2005 Class AA Girls State Champs from South St. Paul

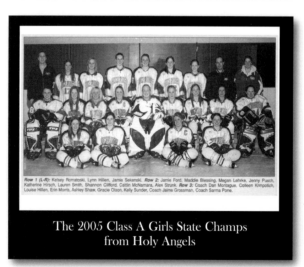

The 2005 Class A Girls State Champs from Holy Angels

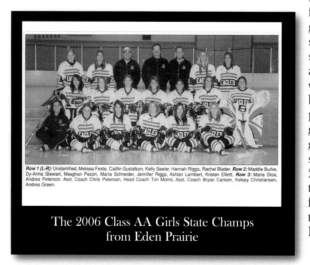

The 2006 Class AA Girls State Champs from Eden Prairie

Natalie Darwitz, advanced to the title game by first beating Owatonna, and then Mounds View. In the 9-3 quarterfinal win over Owatonna, Darwitz scored four goals and had three assists, while against Mounds View, which was led by All-Stater Laura Tryba, she scored each of her team's three goals in a 3-2 win. In the championship game, however, Darwitz could only muster a pair of goals, as Hibbing, behind Amber Fryklund's four scores and Haley Walters' one goal and two assists, went on to beat the Wildcats, 6-3, for their first title. The tournament drew record crowds at the Coliseum, as some 13,000 fans came to cheer on the ladies.

The number of Minnesota high schools with varsity girls hockey teams jumped to 85 in 1995, as the defending state high school champs from Hibbing were joined in the tournament field by Anoka, Apple Valley, Bloomington Jefferson, Burnsville, Mounds View, Roseville and South St. Paul. After beating Burnsville, 2-1, in the Section Two finals to advance to the tournament, Apple Valley, led by Bethany Petersen, defeated Anoka, 3-1, in the quarters, and then Mounds View, 8-2, in their semifinal game to get to the title game. Both Jenna Boutain and Michelle Sikich each tallied hat-tricks in the big semifinal win. Meanwhile, Hibbing, which beat Bloomington Jefferson, 3-1, in the quarters, narrowly squeaked by Roseville, 4-3, in the semis to make it to the finals. Leading the charge for Hibbing was Amber Fryklund, who scored a pair of goals in both the quarterfinal and semifinal games.

In the finals, Apple Valley, which was eager to avenge an earlier 3-2 regular season loss to Hibbing, played the Blue Jackets tough throughout regulation. In a defensive gem, both goalies, Apple Valley's Jenny Jannett and Hibbing's Natalie Lamme, played tremendously as the teams headed into sudden death overtime with the score tied at 0-0. Then, at 1:25 of the extra session, Apple Valley sophomore winger Leslie Stoen flipped a rebound past Lamme for the game-winner. For Jannett, whose 14 saves were enough to garner a coveted shut-out, stopping Beth Wolff's breakaway shot late in the third period, as well as numerous Amber Fryklund blasts (one of which hit the pipe), proved to be the difference in the game. (Incidentally, Fryklund would go on to become the all-time leading scorer at Bemidji State University from 2000-03.) One of the highlights of the tournament was the fact that for the first time ever, it was broadcast live throughout the state on television by KMSP-TV.

The 1998 hockey season was a

huge one for women's hockey everywhere. For starters, the Lady Gophers shocked the hockey world by finishing fourth at the American Women's College Hockey Alliance National Championships. Minnesota concluded its first regular-season with a 21-5-3 record and was invited to compete in the AWCHA national tournament in Boston. The Gophers drew top-ranked New Hampshire in the semifinal game, however, and wound up losing to the eventual national champion Wildcats, 4-1. In the third-place game, the Lady Gophers got blanked by Northeastern, 4-0, to finish a very successful inaugural campaign with a 21-7-3 record and a fourth-place national trophy to boot.

As for individual honors and accolades, Forward Nadine Muzerall wound up leading the nation in scoring with 32 goals and 32 assists for 64 points, and was rewarded with one of the 11 nominations for the prestigious Patty Kazmaier Award — women's college hockey's Hobey Baker equivalent. In addition, Nadine Muzerall and Brittny Ralph were named to the Women's Hockey News All-America Second Team, while head coach Laura Halldorson was honored as the American Hockey Coaches Assoc. National Coach of the Year.

Beyond that, there was an extremely significant event which really put women's hockey on the map in 1998, the amazing gold-medal run of the women's Olympic team in Nagano, Japan. Led by Minnesotan's Jenny Schmidgall (Potter) of Edina, and Alana Blahoski of St. Paul (both of whom scored five points in the Games), as well as Karyn Bye, from River Falls, Wis. (who finished as the third-leading scorer in the tournament with five goals and three assists in six games), Team USA defeated Team Canada, 3-,1 to win the first-ever Olympic gold medal in women's hockey history. The upset victory was sweet for the Americans, who had finished as runner-ups to their north-of-the-border neighbors in all five of their

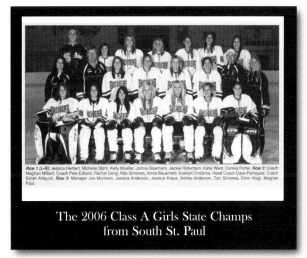

The 2006 Class A Girls State Champs
from South St. Paul

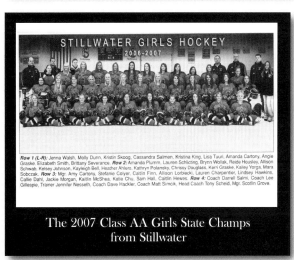

The 2007 Class AA Girls State Champs
from Stillwater

The 2007 Class A Girls State Champs
from Blake

previous Women's World Championship meetings.

The game, which was televised throughout the world, was back and forth through the first period. Then, behind second and third period goals from both Gretchen Ulion and Shelley Looney that beat renowned Canadian goalie Manon Rheaume (who had played on several men's pro teams), the U.S. went up 2-1. Finally, with just eight seconds remaining in the game, Sandra Whyte intercepted a loose puck and tallied an empty-netter to clinch the 3-1 victory. It was an accomplishment that would thrust women's hockey into the national spotlight. Following the telecast, USA Hockey was inundated with thousands of phone calls from curious girls around the country who wanted to start playing hockey, as well as adult women who wanted to start their own leagues. In addition, a huge media blitz followed the historic win, including appearances on numerous national morning variety shows as well as a cover shot on the Wheaties box.

While the game did not have the same global implications of the 1980 Lake Placid "Miracle on Ice" men's game, it did represent just how far women's hockey had come. Fully each of the women on that team had been told at least once in her life that she couldn't play hockey, and most had to scrape by for years on unappreciative boy's teams because there was simply no other alternative.

For Karyn Bye, who grew up playing hockey on boys teams (she kept a short haircut and had just her initials on the back of her uniform, instead of her name, so she could play undetected as a girl), it was a dream come true. As a young girl, Bye even wrote to the Olympic Committee to find out more about the women's Olympic team, to which they replied by simply sending her information about field hockey. "I just wanted to show everyone how thankful I am to be an American and to be on the first women's ice hockey team to win the

MS. HOCKEY WINNERS

Year	Player	High School
1996	Winny Brodt	Roseville
1997	Annamarie Holmes	Apple Valley
1998	Laura Slominski	Burnsville
1999	Ronda Curtin	Roseville
2000	Krissy Wendell	Park Center
2001	Renee Curtin	Roseville
2002	Ashley Albrecht	South St. Paul
2003	Andrea Nichols	Hibbing
2004	Erica McKenzie	Hastings
2005	Gigi Marvin	Warroad
2006	Allie Thunstrom	North St. Paul
2007	Katharine Chute	The Blake School

THE LET'S PLAY HOCKEY GIRLS HIGH SCHOOL GOALIE OF THE YEAR

Year	Player	High School
1999	Katie Beauduy	Blaine
2000	Shari Vogt	River Lakes
2001	Jody Horak	Blaine
2002	Amber Hasbargen	Warroad
2003	Robin Doepke	Chaska
2004	Emily Brookshaw	Hill-Murray
2005	Johanna Ellison	Colquet/Esko/Carlton
2006	Alannah McCready	Centennial
2007	Ashley Nixon	Blaine

Ashley Albrecht

Winny Brodt

La Toya Clarke

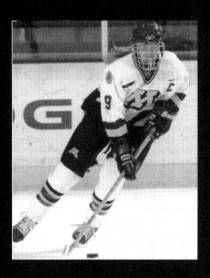

Ronda Curtin

Ambria Thomas

Tracy Engstrom

Kelly Stephens

Jody Horak

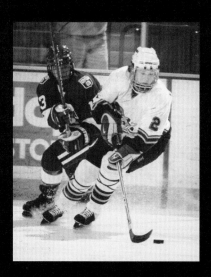

Courtney Kennedy

Shannon Kennedy   Erica Killewald   Lindsay Wall

Nadine Muzerall   Andrea Nichols   Brittny Ralph

Kris Scholz   Laura Slominski   Gigi Marvin

THE PATTY KAZMAIER MEMORIAL AWARD

Krissy Wendell

In 1998, the USA Hockey Foundation created a new, national level award designed to recognize the accomplishments of the most outstanding player in women's intercollegiate ice hockey each season. The Patty Kazmaier Award is presented by the Foundation to the player who represents the highest standards of personal and team excellence. It is the equivelant to the Hobey Baker Memorial Award in men's hockey.

KAZMAIER RECIPIENTS

Year	Recipient	School
2007	Julie Chu	Harvard University
2006	Sara Bauer	University of Wisconsin
2005	Krissy Wendell	University of Minnesota
2004	Angela Ruggiero	Harvard University
2003	Jennifer Botterill	Harvard University
2002	Brooke Whitney	Northeastern University
2001	Jennifer Botterill	Harvard University
2000	Ali Brewer	Brown University
1999	A.J. Mleczko	Harvard University
1998	Brandy Fisher	New Hampshire

SUE RING-JARVI

The matriarch of Gopher women's hockey, Sue Ring-Jarvi was the founder of the women's hockey club team at the University of Minnesota. Ring-Jarvi served as captain of the club program, was the club president from 1974-76, and then acted as club advisor from 1977-79.

Committed to growing the program from the ground up, she personally recruited more than 40 women to take part in the U of M women's hockey club program. Ring-Jarvi was also the best player on the team, scoring 115 points on 65 goals and 50 assists in just 38 games during the 1978-79 season alone. As U of M hockey club president, Ring-Jarvi organized fundraisers for the club program, which enabled them to travel and compete. Through her efforts the sport of women's hockey exploded in the state of Minnesota. While playing at the U of M, she also convinced her club teammates to put on clinics for girls and women in the Twin Cities area.

In 1977, Ring-Jarvi formed the Women's Hockey Association of Minnesota (WHAM), and in 1980 she formed the Minnesota Blue J's club team, which went on to become THE local powerhouse team in the Midwest. Ring-Jarvi has organized many tournaments, most notably the Women's Hockey Invitational and Dream Team Tournaments. In 1994 she received her coach's certification at the U of M, and, in 1999, she received a first level referee license. In addition, Ring-Jarvi also served as the coach of the girl's hockey team at Mounds View High School from 1995-98.

gold medal," said Bye, the 1995 USA Hockey Women's Player of the Year (from the University of New Hampshire), after the game. "Just holding this medal in my hand, I can picture all the sprints we ran, all the hard work we did, and it was all worth it. It's just unbelievable."

The Gopher women's team made it back to the Final Four in '99 for their second time in a row. There, the 28-4-3 Lady Gophers took on a top ranked University of New Hampshire team in the semis on their home ice at Mariucci Arena. The Gophers, led by several Minnesota stars including: Jenny Schmidgall of Edina, Winny Brodt of Roseville, and Laura Slominski of Burnsville, jumped out to an early 2-0 lead on a pair of goals by Nadine Muzerall. But, UNH rallied to tie it and then send it into overtime. After a back-and-forth exchange by both teams, Melisa Heitzman finally beat Gopher goalie Erica Killewald at the 12:37 mark of the extra session. It was a heart-breaking loss for the Gophers, which, in only their third season were already one of the game's elite teams. They did rally that next night, however, to beat Brown University, 3-2, on third period goals from both Tracy Engstrom and Nadine Muzerall, to earn third place honors.

It is important to note that St. Cloud State launched their hockey program in 1998, behind head coach Kerry Brodt-Wethington. The team, which would play its games at the

National Hockey Center, won its first ever WCHA game on October 22, 1999, when they beat Ohio State University, 3-2. Lindsay Jerke, from Coon Rapids, was named as the team's first captain.

Meanwhile, the 1999 Girls High School Tournament once again featured sell-out crowds and plenty of excitement. The '99 tournament field included: Bloomington Jefferson, Burnsville, Duluth, Mankato, Mounds View, Park Center, Roseville and South St. Paul. Led by the 1999 Ms. Hockey Award winner Ronda Curtin, who scored 91 points that year, the undefeated 21-0-1 Roseville Raiders roared into the finals to win their second state title. (Ironically, Curtin's next door neighbor growing up was Winny Brodt, also a Ms. Hockey Award winner.)

Kathleen Ridder Drops the Innaugural Puck at Ridder Arena on Nov. 2, 1997...

Curtin scored a pair of hat-tricks in the quarterfinal and semifinal wins over both Burnsville and Duluth to lead her squad to the big dance.

In the other bracket, Krissy Wendell, the first-ever prep player in the nation to score 100 goals in the regular season, led her undefeated Park Center Pirates into the first round of the tournament to face South St. Paul. There, the Packers, which were led by freshman sensation Ashley Albrecht and Erika Hockinson, recorded one of the biggest upsets in tourney history. Despite a pair of Wendell goals late that beat Packer goalie Sarah Ahlquist, South St. Paul

The two-time National Champion
Lady Gophers (2003 & 2004)

Natalie Darwitz

at the incomprehensible 100-4-3.

During the summer of 1999, the Thoroughbreds (19 & under midget all-stars) made their sixth straight appearance at the USA Hockey National Championships, this time in Washington DC, where they earned the silver medal after losing to the Connecticut Polar Bears in the title game. In addition, the Blue J's, the state's top women's senior team, won the USA Hockey Nat. Championships, also in Washington D.C., by beating the Massachusetts-based Nighthawks, 7-0, in the finals. The J's, who were led by Olympic star Alana Blahoski, St. Cloud State coach Kerry Brodt, and former Thoroughbred Joy Woog, outscored their opponents that year by the amazing margin of 32-3. Additionally, many of the women from both of these teams came together during the summer of '99 to play in the first "Minnesota Dream Team" Tournament. The event, which featured 23 of the state's top high schoolers, 23 of the top college players, and 23 of the top senior women's players, mixed up the teams with all age groups for a weekend of competition. The event, arguably, brought together one of the greatest single women's talent pools in the history of the sport.

Another exciting advancement for women's hockey happened in 1999 as well. The Minnesota Intercollegiate Athletic Conference (MIAC) was awarded a supplemental grant of $440,000 from the U.S. Olympic Committee and the NCAA to help develop women's hockey as a sport on the varsity level. While the current conference members at the time included Augsburg, Gustavus Adolphus, St. Benedict's, St. Catherine's, St. Mary's and St. Thomas, with the news, Bethel, Concordia (Moorhead), Hamline, St. Olaf and Carleton all announced their intentions to move forward with advancing their programs from club status to varsity as well. The MIAC would be the second conference in the nation, and the first in the Midwest, to offer a championship in women's hockey. It would also be the first to offer women's hockey completely at the NCAA Division III (non-athletic scholarship) varsity level. While most of these schools had competed in recent years in the Midwestern Collegiate Women's Hockey Alliance (MCWHA), the MIAC would finally be their own conference with similar Division III schools.

Incidentally, after winning the 1999-2000 MIAC regular-season and playoff championships, Augsburg's Lady Auggies finished the season as the national runner-ups in the inaugural AWCHA Division III national

hung on to win the game, 3-2. The Packers then faced Bloomington Jefferson, which had beaten Mounds View, 4-3, in the other semifinal behind Bethany Peterson's three-point afternoon. In a back-and-forth thriller, Packer winger Erika Hockinson missed an empty netter that would have won the game, only to see the Jag's Jessica Brandanger come right back and score the equalizer with just seconds left to send the game into overtime. Two overtimes later, Jaguar senior winger Lindsey Christensen slid the game winner past Ahlquist to give Jefferson a ticket to the finals.

In the title game, Curtin exploded for four goals, as the Raiders went on to crush the Jaguars, 8-2. Curtin's 10-point performance over the three games, solidified her as the best female hockey player in state history up to that point. As Minnesota's all-time leading-scoring hockey player, boys or girls, with more than 400 total points, she would go on to play for the University of Minnesota. Her sister, Renee (the second leading scorer in the state that year), who scored four goals and two assists in the tournament as well, would also wear the Maroon and Gold. With the win, Raiders coach Rich Kuehne's four-year record now stood

Gopher Coach Laura Halldorson

Krissy Wendell & Natalie Darwitz

championship series against Middlebury (VT.), held in Boston, Mass. (The AWCHA sponsored the Division III national championships in both 2000 and 2001, and then the NCAA began a Division III women's national tournament in 2002.)

As for things on the D-I collegiate level, in 1999 the long anticipated Western Collegiate Hockey Association Women's League finally came to fruition. The upstart circuit hit the ice with seven charter members: Bemidji State University; University of Minnesota; University of Minnesota-Duluth; Minnesota State University, Mankato; Ohio State University; St. Cloud State University; and the University of Wisconsin. The teams would play a 24-game league schedule followed by a three-day conference tournament, which was to be held at the Bloomington Ice Gardens that March. The new league, a division of the American Women's College Hockey Alliance (AWCHA) gave the sport a lot more credibility throughout the Midwest and would do wonders in growing the game beyond the East Coast. The WWCHA would now be the second D-I women's conference in the nation, along with the East Coast Athletic Conference (ECAC).

The 2000 girls high school state tourney was historic in the sense that it would be the last time the state's two greatest players of all time would compete against each other, Park Center's Krissy Wendell and Eagan's Natalie Darwitz. Both would go on to stardom as teammates with the Golden Gophers as well as with several U.S. Olympic and National teams. The quarterfinals opened with Hibbing/Chisholm skating past Bemidji, 3-2, behind Andrea Nichols' two goals. Game Two saw Anoka spank Austin, 6-1, thanks to a pair of goals each from Heather Talbot, Jamie Hewitt and Amber Sharratt. Krissy Wendell then made her presence felt in Game Three by scoring five goals en route to her Park Center Pirates crushing Chaska, 8-2. Natalie Darwitz, meanwhile, tallied a pair of goals and a pair of assists in Game Four, but it wasn't enough to get her Eagan Wildcats past Bloomington Jefferson. Allison Lehrke scored a pair of goals for the Jaguars in the 5-4 victory.

Park Center continued to dominate in the semis thanks to Wendell, who scored four goals and added three assists in her team's 7-2 win over Bloomington Jefferson. The other semi saw Anoka edge past Hibbing/Chisholm, 3-2, behind goals from Amber Sharratt, Melissa Christensen and

UM-Duluth Coach Shannon Miller

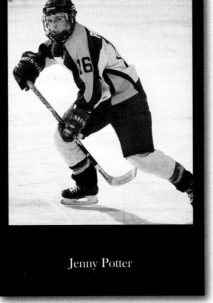
Jenny Potter

Becca Levine. From there, Wendell scored a hat-trick in the finals as her Park Center squad blanked Anoka, 6-0. Katie Crass scored twice and Erin Ficken added one of her own, while goalie Amy Jones turned away all 19 shots she faced in leading the Pirates to their first ever state title.

Meanwhile, the 2000 Gophers rolled through the WCHA Playoffs, beating Mankato and Wisconsin, 10-0 and 5-0, to set up a rematch with the UMD Bulldogs in the WCHA tournament championship game. There, Duluth came out smoking and cruised to a tough 2-0 victory. Both teams were selected to participate in the AWCHA National Tournament in Boston, however, and as luck would have it they would go on to face each other one more time, with a national championship game berth hanging in the balance. It would be historic. With the Gophers down 2-0 early in the second period, Nadine Muzerall scored two consecutive goals to tie the score and set up Tracy Engstrom's thrilling power-play game-winner at 6:45 of the third.

From there, the Gophers went on to face Brown in the Finals. Down 1-0 early, Minnesota roared back with four unanswered goals from Courtney Kennedy, Laura Slominski, Muzerall and Winny Brodt to capture their first AWCHA National Championship, 4-2. Kennedy got on the board first when she dramatically chipped in her own rebound while falling down in front of the net at 4:47 of the second period. Slominski would score with just over a minute left in the period to make it 2-1. Then, early in the third, Muzerall got what would prove to be the game-winner, while Brodt's tally less than a minute after that would put it out of reach. Brown added another goal late in the third, but it was too little too late as Erica Killewald, who stopped 34 of 36 shots that night in goal, hung on down the stretch to give her team the amazing victory. The Gophers had officially arrived. Following the final buzzer the team went ballistic at center ice as they celebrated their incredible achievement.

The team finished with an impressive 32-6-1 record that year and fought hard for everything they got. Leading the team in scoring was Nadine Muzerall, who tallied 49 goals and 28 assists for 77 points. Following her were Ambria Thomas and Laura Slominski, who each scored 62 and 59 points, respectively. As for post-season honors and accolades, Winny Brodt was selected as the WCHA Defensive Player of the Year and joined Muzerall on the WCHA all-conference

The Three-Time NCAA D-I National Champion Lady Bulldogs (2001, 2002 & 2003)

Caroline Ouellette   Erika Holst   Erin Olson

Jessica Koizumi   Michaela Lanzi   Noemie Marin

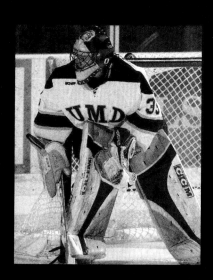

Rita Schaublin   Samantha Hough   Tawni Mattilla

Abby Cooper   Ashley Stewart   St. Cloud State Coach Jeff Giesen

Fiona McLeod   Kristy Oonincx   Laura Fast

Rickie Lee Doyle   Roxanne Stang   Laura Gieselman

first team.

Meanwhile, the University of Minnesota Duluth Lady Bulldogs, which hit the ice in 1999, wasted little time in making a name for themselves in the world of Women's Division I Hockey. Shannon Miller, the head coach of Team Canada at the 1998 Winter Olympics, was named as the team's first head coach and immediately injected an international flavor to the program's roster. In February of that season the Bulldogs clinched the Women's WCHA Regular Season Championship title with a sweep of Minnesota State-Mankato and then defeated Minnesota, 2-0, behind goalie Tuula Puputti's shut-out, at the WCHA playoffs. The team then advanced on to the AWCHA Final Four to compete for the National Championship in Boston, MA. There, the Bulldogs lost to Minnesota, 3-2, in the opener, and then fell to Dartmouth, 5-4, in the third place game to finish fourth in the country with an impressive 25-5-3 record. Jenny Schmidgall, who led the nation in scoring (41-52-93), and teammate Maria Rooth were also nominees for the Patty Kazmaier Award, emblematic of the nation's top collegiate women's hockey player.

The 2001 girls state tourney opened with Blaine beating rival Blake by the final of 3-1. Leading the charge for the Bengals was Andrea Jensrud, who scored a pair of goals in the win. South St. Paul blanked Moorhead, 4-0, in Game Two, behind Ashley Albrecht's two goals and goalie Kerry Rollwagen's 10 saves in net. Bloomington Jefferson also got a shut-out in Game Three as they held Forest Lake scoreless in a 5-0 rout. Joccie Cookson had a pair of goals in this one, while goalie Larissa Luther stopped all 19 shots that came her way. The last quarterfinal of the day featured Chaska edging past Owatonna, 2-1, behind a goal and an assist each from Crystal Wasem and Katie Ward.

Blaine blanked South St. Paul, 1-0, in the first semifinal behind Kristina Bunker's second period goal from Krista Johnson. Goalie Jody Horak played huge in net, turning away all 26 shots that came her way. The other semi saw Bloomington Jefferson beat Chaska, 4-1, on a pair of goals from Sharon Cole. The title game was close as Bloomington Jefferson hung on to beat Blaine, 2-1. The Bengals jumped out to an early 1-0 lead on Tiffany Hagge's goal in the first period, only to see the Jaguars rally back behind goals from Allison Turgeon and Joccie Cookson to take the lead for good. Goalie Larissa Luther made 19 saves in net en route to leading her squad to their first ever state championship.

Not that they needed any, but the Gophers got a lot of

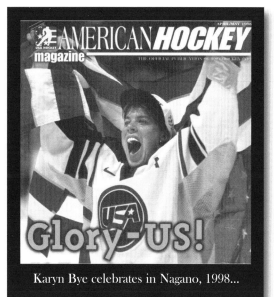

Karyn Bye celebrates in Nagano, 1998...

extra incentive in 2000 when it was announced that the NCAA would be hosting its first Women's Ice Hockey Championship... and that Mariucci Arena had been chosen as the site of the inaugural Frozen Four. Minnesota would earn the WCHA Tournament's top seed heading into the tourney, but wound up getting spanked by Ohio State, 4-0, in the semifinal, followed by a disastrous 4-3 loss to Wisconsin in the third-place game. The result was the fact that the defending national champs now had to sit back and watch the Frozen Four being played on their home ice. Ouch!

The team did wind up with a solid 23-9-2 overall record though, good for a No. 5 national ranking and their first WCHA Women's League title. La Toya Clarke led the team with 53 points, while Ambria Thomas and Nadine Muzerall added 49 and 46, respectively. Muzzy would finish her illustrious career in Gold Country with a record 235 career points in 139 career games. Individually, several Gophers were recognized with post-season honors, including senior defender Courtney Kennedy, who was selected as the initial First Team All-America selection in Gopher women's hockey history. Kennedy, the WCHA Player of the Year, was also named as one of just three finalists for the prestigious Patty Kazmaier Award, while Laura Halldorson shared her first WCHA Coach of the Year honor with St. Cloud State's Kerry Wethington.

Meanwhile, the Lady Bulldogs from Duluth would make history by becoming the state's first team to ever win an NCAA Women's Hockey National Championship in 2001. The post-season journey began in March, when the team won their second consecutive WCHA Playoff Championship by defeating Ohio State, 3-0, in Rochester, MN. Maria Rooth earned tournament MVP honors while forward Erika Holst and defenseman Navada Russell were named to the all-tournament team. From there, the team advanced on to the Frozen Four, where they won the inaugural NCAA Division I National Championship by defeating St. Lawrence University, 4-2. It would mark the first ever NCAA team championship in UMD history. Maria Rooth was named Most Valuable Player of the tournament while her teammates Tuula Puputti and Brittny Ralph were named to the all-tournament team as well. That June the team was honored by President George W. Bush as the first ever women's hockey team to be invited to the White House.

In 2002 the girls state tournament made a giant leap by establishing a two-class system, Class AA and A, depending on the size of enrollment for each school. The Class AA tourney opened that year with White Bear Lake sneaking past Lakeville in

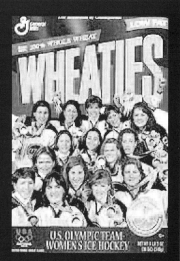

the quarterfinal opener, 3-2, in overtime, thanks to Melissa Mondo's game-winner at the 2:44 of the extra session. Game Two saw Burnsville skate past Cloquet/Esko/Carlton, 3-1, behind a pair of goals from Melissa Mackley. South St. Paul rolled past Moorhead in the third game of the day, 4-1, thanks to Maggie Fisher's hat-trick. Game Four then saw Bloomington Jefferson crush Anoka, 6-1, behind a pair of goals from Sharon Cole.

The first semifinal featured White Bear Lake edging past Burnsville, 3-2, in double overtime. Nina Erickson scored a couple of goals in this one but it was Melissa Mondo who was the hero when she beat Becky Kilpatrick at the 3:03 mark of the second extra session to send her team to the Finals. The other semi was a blow-out as South St. Paul beat up on Bloomington Jefferson, 7-1, thanks to Liz Funk's hat-trick and Pam Stohr's two goals. The Packers kept on rolling from there, edging past White Bear Lake in the championship game, 2-1. Ashley Young put South St. Paul up 1-0 in the first, only to see Mondo answer back in the second to tie it back up at one apiece. Then, at the 5:12 mark of the third period, Ashley Albrecht notched what would prove to be the game-winner past Bears goalie Laura Brennan, who came up with a whopping 28 saves in the loss.

Meanwhile, in the 2002 Class A tourney, just four teams would qualify under the new format. In the opening semifinal game, Hibbing/Chisholm doubled up on Willmar thanks to Andrea Nichols' hat-trick. The other semi was a blow-out as Benilde St. Margaret's blanked Farmington, 5-0, thanks to Rachel Drazen's two goals and goalie Katie Jetland's 10 saves in net. Benilde St. Margaret's then went on to beat Hibbing/Chisholm in the Finals by the score of 2-1. Carrie Thompson opened the scoring for BSM, only to see Andrea Nichols tie it up early in the second period. Then, with just 30 seconds to go in the second, Devon Nichols got what would prove to be the game-winner for Benilde St. Margaret's as they hung on down the stretch behind Jetland's 24 saves in the crease.

Back in the collegiate ranks, the 2001-02 Lady Gophers found themselves ranked No. 1 not only in the conference, but in all the national polls. They would retain that No. 1 ranking for eight consecutive weeks and rode that wave right into the WCHA Playoffs, where they won the WCHA regular season title for the second year in a row. In addition, on March 9th the Gophers also established another first in Minnesota women's hockey history when they defeated Wisconsin, 3-2, for the WCHA Final Five Championship.

From there, Minnesota headed to New Hampshire, where they faced off against Brown as the top seed in the NCAA Frozen Four. After a scoreless first period, Kelly Stephens scored midway through the second period to make it 1-1. Brown tallied again on a power-play goal that period though and the Gophers could not find the back of the net

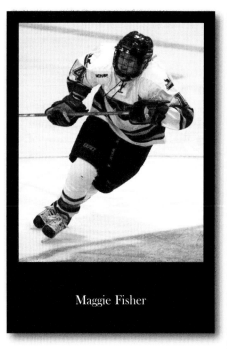

Maggie Fisher

Megan Jedinak

Shari Vogt

for the rest of the evening. It was a tough loss. Minnesota's Cinderella season then came to an end that next night when they skated to a 2-2 tie with Niagara in the third-place game. The team finished the season with a 28-4-6 record, while First Team All-American Ronda Curtin was recognized as one of just three Patty Kazmaier finalists in the nation.

The Lady Bulldogs from Duluth would make some more history in 2001-02 by winning their second straight NCAA National Championship. Making the feat even more amazing is the fact that five of the team's top players traveled to Salt Lake City that February to compete with their respective national teams at the 2002 Winter Olympic Games. When it was all said and done, Caroline Ouellette won a gold medal for Team Canada, while 2002 Olympic silver medalist Jenny Potter earned a silver for Team USA. In addition, Maria Rooth and Erika Holst won bronze medals for Sweden; Hanne Sikio and Tuula Puputti skated for fourth-place Finland; and Kristina Petroyskaia placed fifth with Team Russia.

When all of the players came back to school, the team rolled into the post-season with a vengeance. The team would go on to beat Brown University, 3-2, in the Frozen Four Finals, held in Durham, NC. The star of the game was Tricia Guest, who tallied the game-winner at the 15:04 mark of the third period. UMD goalie Patricia Sautter came up with 33 saves for the big win as well. In addition, forward Joanne Eustace and defenseman Larissa Luther were selected to the 2002 NCAA All-Tournament Team. For the season, Maria Rooth earned All-American honors for the second straight season and was also named as one of the top 10 candidates for the Patty Kazmaier Award for the third consecutive year. And, that May the back-to-back champs got to go back to the White House to catch up with the President.

Meanwhile, a major event happened in 2003, when the girls state tourney left the State Fairgrounds and moved to Ridder Arena, the new home of the University of Minnesota's Lady Gophers. It was a brand new state-of-the-art women's-only hockey facility that could seat a few thousand adoring fans up close and personal.

The 2003 Class AA tourney opened with Cloquet/Esko/Carlton blanking Anoka, 4-0. The Lumberjacks got a pair of goals from Michelle Maunu, while goalie Johanna Ellison made 27 saves in the shut-out. Game Two saw Apple Valley beat Elk River, 3-2, on a trio of second period goals from Jenna Scanlon, Kallie Tabor and Anne Schema. Game Three had Eden Prairie downing Owatonna, 5-3, thanks to Megan McCarthy's hat-trick. Game Four was a battle between North St. Paul and South St. Paul, which entered the tourney on a 55-game winning streak. The Packers then added to that total by rallying to beat the Polars, 7-2, behind a pair of hat-tricks each from Maggie Fisher and Ashley Young.

Cloquet/Esko/Carlton beat Apple Valley in the first semifinal, 3-1, on goals from Jenna Roberts, Tamara Price and Liz Palkie.

Kelly Hart

Lumberjacks netminder Johanna Ellison came up with 23 saves en route to leading her squad to the Finals. The other semi saw South St. Paul shut-out Eden Prairie, 3-0, thanks to yet another Maggie Fisher hat-trick. Packer goalie Sarah Crnobrna had to stop just seven shots in the big win. From there, South St. Paul edged Cloquet/Esko/Carlton in overtime, 2-1, for their second straight state title. Leading the way for the Packers was senior defender Sammy Miller, who beat Johanna Ellison at the 1:11 mark of the extra session.

Hibbing/Chisholm opened the 2003 Class A tourney by beating Farmington by the final score of 6-2. Andrea Nichols was the star of this one, scoring five goals and assisting on the other, en route to leading her club to the Finals. The other semifinal game featured Blake blanking Willmar, 3-0, Kelsey Johnson, Amy Cobb and Alyssa Saunders each tallied for the Bears, as they went on to face Hibbing/Chisholm in the Finals. There, they rallied from a 1-0 deficit to beat the Bluejackets by the final score of 3-2 and take the state title. Blake senior captains Kathryn Moos and Kelsey Johnson led the charge, scoring two goals and two assists, respectively.

As for the Lady Gophers, the 2002-03 season was one of the most significant in the program's short history. First, the Gophers said goodbye to Mariucci Arena and moved into their new home, Ridder Arena, right next door. The state-of-the-art facility would be the first ever women's only college hockey arena in the country. Named after longtime contributors Bob and Kathleen Ridder, the bowl-shaped arena seats 3,000 people and includes a club room as well as nine luxury suites. Second, while the Gophers returned 13 letter-winners from the year before, this season was special in that it had without question the single-greatest recruiting class in women's college hockey history. Leading the way were a pair of Minnesota high school hockey legends, Krissy Wendell and Natalie Darwitz, who starred at Park Center and Eagan High Schools, respectively. Both of the ladies played on the silver medal-winning U.S. Olympic team in Salt Lake City that past year as well.

The team played well that season and wound up getting invited to participate in the Frozen Four, which was being held up in Duluth. There, the Gophers stunk up the joint and wound up getting pulverized by Harvard, 6-1. To make matters worse, they then fell to Dartmouth, 4-2, in the third place game to wind up in fourth. The Maroon and Gold ended the 2002-03 campaign with a 27-8-1 overall record

Lisa Peters

and a 19-4-1 mark in the WCHA. As for individual honors and accolades, it was all about All-Americans Natalie Darwitz and Krissy Wendell, who were named as two of the top 10 candidates for the Patty Kazmaier Award.

Believe it or not, UMD would make it a three-peat in 2002-03, winning their third straight National Championship title. The team got rolling that February when they beat Bemidji State to clinch the WCHA regular season title. A few weeks later the team won the WCHA Final Five title with a big win over rival Minnesota. From there, the team made history when they defeated Harvard in double overtime, 4-3, thanks to Nora Tallus' thrilling game-winner at the 4:19 mark of the second extra session. Making the moment even more special was the fact that the game was played at the DECC, in Duluth, in front of 5,167 fans — the largest crowd in NCAA women's hockey history. Forward Jenny Potter and Hanne Sikio were named to the All-Tourney team, while Caroline Ouellette was named as the tournament's MVP. As for post-season honors and accolades, Jenny Potter earned First Team All-American honors for the second time in her career and was named as a Patty Kazmaier Finalist as well.

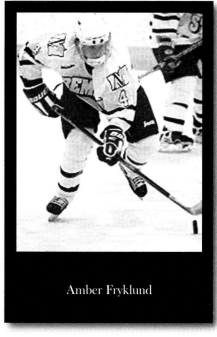

Amber Fryklund

Meanwhile, Lakeville kicked off the 2004 Class AA state tourney by blanking Chisago Lakes in overtime, 1-0, on Molly McDonald's game-winner which came at the 3:15 mark of sudden death. Lakeville goalie Christine Seiler made 18 saves en route to earning the shut-out. Game Two featured Elk River downing Anoka, 5-3, behind Erin Olson's two goals and Jessica Pullar's four points. The third quarterfinal contest saw Eden Prairie rally back from a 1-0 deficit to beat the two-time defending champs from South St. Paul, 3-1. Megan McCarthy, Meghan Pezon and Katie Jaeger all tallied for Eden Prairie in the historic win. Game Four was a tight one as North St. Paul edged past Eagan, 6-5. Allie Thunstrom had a hat-trick for the Polars, while Janelle Philipczyk tallied four goals for the Wildcats in the loss.

The Polars kept rolling in the semis, beating Eden Prairie by the final score of 3-2. North St. Paul jumped out to a 3-0 lead in this one on goals from Allie Thunstrom, Jenny Schmidt and Caitlin Hogan, and then fended off a late Eagle rally to advance to the Finals. Elk River snuck past Lakeville in the other semi, 3-2, behind Jessica Pullar's pair of goals and goalie Rachael Carter's 14 saves in net.

From there, Elk River topped North St. Paul in an overtime thriller to capture their first ever state title. With just under a

Lill Raynard

minute to go in the extra session, senior Anya Miller got the game-winner to give her club the championship trophy. Erin Olson had a pair of goals for the Elks, while Amy Plude chipped in with a trio of assists as well.

Benilde St. Margaret's blanked Hibbing/Chisholm in the 2004 Class A opener, 3-0, behind a goal and an assist each from Elizabeth Burg and Carrie Thompson. Goalie Sarah Windhorst led the Red Knights with 13 saves en route to earning the coveted shut-out. The other semi saw New Prague double up on Alexandria, 4-2. With the score tied at two apiece, Jenna Kilpatrick came through with a pair of goals to lead the Trojans into the Finals. There, Benilde St. Margaret's beat New Prague by the final score of 6-2 to earn their second Class A title in three years. Ashley Duffy and Carrie Thompson each tallied a pair of goals, while netminder Sarah Windhorst turned away 10 of the 12 shots she faced for the big win.

With the theme of "Get It Done," the Lady Gophers dominated in 2003-04, winning the WCHA regular season championship for the third time in five years with a 19-3-2 conference mark. Then, after beating Ohio State in the first game of the WCHA Final Five playoffs, 5-1, the Gophers rallied back from three goals down to beat rival Duluth for the title. It was one of the most emotional come-backs in program history. Minnesota then squared off against Dartmouth in the 2004 Frozen Four semifinal game at Providence, R.I. The Big Green tallied first but the Gophers came back behind three goals from Krissy Wendell and two more from Kelly Stephens to win the game, 5-1. Jody Horak played huge in net, garnering 21 saves. With the win, the team would now face Harvard for all the marbles.

The Crimson took an early 1-0 lead in the first period of this one, only to see the Gophers rally back to tie it on Darwitz's top-shelf goal at 4:51 of the second. Harvard went ahead on a power-play, 2-1, midway through the second period, but from there on out the best line in college hockey: Darwitz, Wendell and Stephens, dominated the action on both ends of the ice. Minnesota tied the game when Andrea Nichols scored on a perfect slot pass from LaToya Clarke to make it 2-2 heading into the third. The final frame was all Maroon and Gold as the Gophers poured in four goals in the third period for the 6-2 win. Just how fast did the Gophers come out the gates that period? Well, Darwitz scored only nine seconds into the period to set an NCAA record for the fastest goal coming out of an intermission. From there, Stephens added her third goal of the Frozen Four just 32 seconds later at :41 of the third. Fittingly, Darwitz and Wendell each added one apiece for good measure to seal the deal and give the 30-2-2 Gophers their first ever NCAA championship for any women's team sport at the University of Minnesota.

Wendell, the tournament's Most Outstanding Player, was named as a first-team All-American and as the WCHA Player of the Year. Furthermore, Darwitz and Lyndsay Wall earned first-

Augsburg's Lauren Chezick earned AHCA Division III All-American honors and MIAC Player of the Year honors in 2002-03, and earned All-MIAC first-team honors all four years of her career (2001-05) — becoming just the sixth women's hockey player in conference history to do so. Chezick rewrote the record books while at Augsburg, establishing career records for points (137) and assists (82), while ranking second in school history for goals (68). Chezick played in 102 career games, setting single-season school records for points (57) and assists (32) in the 2002-03 campaign as a member of the top scoring forward line in school history.

team All-WCHA honors as well. From there, the party was on. The new media darlings of Minnesota were everywhere, from throwing out first pitches at Twins baseball games to meeting with the governor. But the biggest thrill by far came on May 19, 2004, when the team got to go to the White House and meet President Bush, where they presented him with his very own Gopher jersey.

Meanwhile, in 2004 UMD got knocked out of the post-season hunt with a 4-2 loss to the Gophers, ultimately finishing the season with a 20-12-2 overall record. In addition, Jenny Potter finished her illustrious career in Duluth by finishing second in the Patty Kazmaier Award voting. Incredibly, it was the two-time All-American's fourth straight finalist nomination. Potter would finish her illustrious career at UMD as the program's all-time leading scorer with 108 goals and 148 assists for 265 points.

As for some other college news, Minnesota State Mankato, which finished the season with a 10-21-3 overall record, had its first two-time All-WCHA First Team honoree in goaltender Shari Vogt. Head coach Jeff Vizenor earned WCHA Coach of the Year honors that year as well for helping to turn the program around.

As for the youngsters, the 2005 Class AA tourney commenced with Cloquet/Esko/Carlton edging Centennial, 2-1, thanks to Maria Lammi's game-winner at the 10:41 mark of the third period. Game Two saw Wright County defeat Rochester Mayo by the final score of 2-1, with Michelle Moen tallying the game-winner on a power-play at the 9:05 mark of the third period. The third quarterfinal contest was a blow-out as Wayzata crushed Cretin-Derham Hall, 6-0. Breanna Johnson and Kassie Brandenborg each tallied a pair of goals each in this one, while Jessica Laurinaitis added a goal and an assist to boot. Game Four was a tight one as South St. Paul beat Anoka, 4-3, behind goals from Ashley Young, Maggie Fisher and Felicia Nelson.

Cloquet/Esko/Carlton blanked Wright County in the first semifinal game, 3-0, thanks to goals from Whitney Anderson, Danielle Scheuer and Tiffani Rodd. Meanwhile, goalie Johanna Ellison turned away all 24 shots she faced in net to preserve the shut-out. The other semi was a blow-out as South St. Paul rolled over Wayzata, 7-2. Felicia Nelson had a hat-trick in this one, while Ashley Young added five points of her own en route to leading her Packers to the Finals. There, they defeated the Cloquet/Esko/Carlton Lumberjacks by the final of 5-1. Annie Bauerfeld led SSP with a pair of goals, Ashley Young chipped in with three points and Maggie Fisher added two of her own in the victory. In addition, junior goalie Danika Porter made 12 saves as the Packers clinched their third title in just four years.

Hibbing/Chisholm kicked off the 2005 Class A tourney with a 2-1 win over Alexandria. Claire Collier and Kayla Hagen each tallied in the win, while goalie Brittany Krause turned away 16 of the 17 shots she faced en route to leading her squad to the

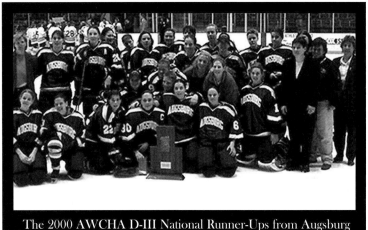

The 2000 AWCHA D-III National Runner-Ups from Augsburg

Finals. The other semi saw Holy Angels defeat New Prague, 5-1, behind Lauren Smith's two goals and three assists. New Prague goalie Daerda Culshaw made a whopping 32 saves in the loss. The Finals then saw Holy Angels edge past Hibbing/Chisholm, 5-3. Leading the charge for the Stars were Jennifer Pusch, who had a hat-trick, and Jaime Sekenski, who tallied a pair of goals to boot. Goalie Alex Strunk came up with 25 saves en route to leading her club to its first state title.

For the first time ever, the 2006 Class AA tourney featured games being played at the Xcel Energy Center in St. Paul as well as at Ridder Arena on the University of Minnesota's main campus. With the growth and popularity of girls hockey, it was only fair that they too get to play their games in the nation's finest hockey facility, the Xcel Center, home of the NHL's Minnesota Wild. The quarterfinals, semifinals and finals would be held at the "X," with the consolation games being held over the river at Ridder.

Speaking of Ridder, the Gophers, led by the nation's top goalie, Jody Horak, made it back-to-back national titles 2004-05. Co-captains Kelly Stephens and Krissy Wendell each tallied four points against Bemidji State in the opener of the newly expanded WCHA Championships, which were held at Ridder Arena that year. Minnesota rolled over Ohio State in the next game, 7-1, behind Darwitz's hat-trick, which then set up a date with Wisconsin in the title game. This went down to the wire but the Gophers came out on top, 3-2, in a real thriller. After a scoreless first period, Darwitz notched her 100th point of the season to make it 1-0. Bobbi Ross then made it 2-0 when she stuffed in a rebound out front. But, with just over a minute remaining in the game, the Badgers did the unthinkable. With their goalie pulled, Wisconsin made it 2-1 with just 50 seconds to go and then got the equalizer with just 24 seconds showing on the clock. The Gophers were stunned. Down but not out, the best line in college hockey came together to score the overtime game-winner. After Wisconsin got called for two penalties in the extra session, Darwitz and Stephens set up Wendell, who put away the game winner to give the Gophers the thrilling victory and the coveted WCHA crown.

From there, the Gophers hosted an NCAA Regional game against Providence College at Ridder Arena. Down 1-0 early, the Gophers rallied with six unanswered goals to beat the Friars, 6-1, to advance on to the Frozen Four in Durham, N.H. Bobbi Ross and Kelly Stephens both scored a pair of goals in that one, while Becky Wacker and Erica McKenzie each tallied one apiece. Minnesota went on to score five goals in the first period and cruised

Led by coach Mike Carroll, a former two-time All-American goalie at MSU-Mankato, the Lady Gustie's have emerged as the powerhouse team in the MIAC. In nine seasons, Carroll has compiled an overall record of 172-48-11. The winningest coach in program history, Carroll's Gusties have advanced to the NCAA National Tournament in five of the last seven years. Carroll has directed the Gusties to five MIAC regular season titles (2000-01, 2001-02, 2004-05, 2005-06, 2006-07) and has been named the MIAC Coach of the Year four times (2002, 2004, 2005, 2006). In addition, Carroll has also guided a pair of AHCA D-III Player's of the Year in Sarah Moe (2002) and Andrea Peterson (2007).

past Dartmouth in the opening round of the Frozen Four, 7-1. Darwitz set a record by scoring just 13 seconds into the game and the Gophers never looked back in this one. Darwitz scored again less than two minutes later and Wendell got into the act shortly after that. Wall and Stephens also scored in that first frame, while Wendell added her second goal of the game in the third, followed by an empty netter by Janelle Philipczyk with about a minute to go to seal the deal. With that, the Gophers found themselves back in the NCAA Finals against the Harvard Crimson. It was going to be a rematch of epic proportions between college hockey's two biggest heavyweights.

This one was all about Natalie Darwitz, who figured in all four Gopher goals and wound up ending the season with an NCAA-record 114 points. The game started out slow for the Maroon and Gold. In fact, the Gophers did not get a shot on goal until nearly six minutes had passed. They got on the board first though, when Wendell put back Darwitz's rebound out front to make it 1-0 late in the first period. The Crimson quickly tied it less than a minute into the second session, only to see Lyndsay Wall's slap-shot put the Gophers back up 2-1 about seven minutes later. Harvard tied it up again at 10:33 on a power-play goal, but Ashley Albrecht put Minnesota back on top yet again about eight minutes after that on a slap-shot of her own that beat Harvard Goalie Ali Boe. Harvard would tie it up for the third and last time midway through the third period on yet another power-play goal. In fact, it was Wendell, of all people, who was called for a checking penalty with 7:32 remaining in the third period, which allowed Harvard defender Caitlin Cahow to go five-hole on Gopher Goalie Jody Horak just over a minute later. With the game tied at three apiece the game seemed destined for overtime. However, with just over a minute to go in the game, Natalie Darwitz took over. Kelly Stephens came in on Boe and fired a shot, only to have Darwitz pound home the rebound out front. The goal, which proved to be the game-winner, made it 4-3 at the 18:52 mark of the third. The Gophers hung on from there and then danced like fools when the final buzzer sounded, signifying their back-to-back NCAA National Championships.

When it was all said and done the Gophers finished with an amazing 36-2-2 overall record. As for honors and accolades, once again it all started and stopped with Krissy Wendell and Natalie Darwitz, who had proven themselves to be the best of the very best. While both were one of the three finalists for the prestigious Patty Kazmaier Award, it was Wendell who actually wound up finally bringing home the hardware. No matter. They were both clearly the best Division I women's hockey players in the

Augsburg's Tiffany Magnuson

Augsburg's Annie Annunziato

country. As for the numbers: Darwitz wound up with 42 goals and 72 assists for an NCAA record 114 points, while Wendell tallied 43 goals and 61 assists for 104 of her own. Meanwhile, Darwitz, Wendell and Lyndsay Wall were each named as First Team All-Americans, while Goalie Jody Horak earned second team honors. The trio were also named to the All-WCHA first team, while Horak and Kelly Stephens earned second team honors. Stephens, who tallied an amazing 76 points, was understandably overshadowed by her two linemates. No worries, it was the greatest line in the history of women's college hockey.

In 2005-06 the St. Cloud State Lady Huskies finally turned the corner. Even without their graduated star forward, Roxy Stang, the program's all-time leading scorer, the team went on to win a school-best 18 games that season. In addition, SCSU hosted a first round WCHA playoff game for the first time, where they defeated Ohio State in a best-of-three series to advance to the WCHA Championships. Leading the way for SCSU were Kristy Oonincx, Hailey Clarkson, Denelle Maguet, Laura Fast and Ashley Stewart, who all scored a boat load of goals that season. From there, the team cracked the top-10 in the national polls, officially putting them on the hockey map. The team would go on to get beaten by Wisconsin, 9-0, but certainly made a big leap with regards to earning some respect from the Gophers and Bulldogs, which have owned the WCHA since the very beginning.

As for the preps at the state tourney, the 2006 Class AA quarterfinal opener featured Coon Rapids beating Rochester Mayo/Lourdes by the final of 4-2. Down 2-0, the Cards rallied on a pair of goals from Christine Knop, as well as one apiece from Terra Rasmussen and Amalee Windmeier. The defending champions from the Academy of Holy Angels fell to Roseville Area, 4-3, in Game Two thanks to the stellar play of Erin Cody and Frances Dorr, as well as goalie Briana Brausen. The undefeated Eden Prairie Eagles defeated Stillwater Area, 6-1, in Game Three behind strong showings from Andrea Green and Meghan Pezon, who each scored two goals in the big win. The last quarterfinal saw the Cloquet/Esko/Carlton Lumberjacks beat Moorhead in double overtime thanks to Sadie Lundquist's game winner midway through the second extra session.

Coon Rapids beat Roseville Area, 3-2, in the opening

MIAC TITLES WON OR SHARED (1999-2007)		
School	No.	Last Title
Gustavus Adolphus College	6	2007
University of St. Thomas	2	2004
Augsburg College	2	2000*
St. Mary's University	2	2000*

*Shared championship

semifinal contest. Jennifer Yelle tallied the game-winner at the 6:15 mark of the third period on a rush with Michelle Rust to send the Cards to the Finals. Meanwhile, Eden Prairie beat Cloquet-Esko-Carlton, 3-1, in the other semifinal on sophomore Andrea Peterson's game-winner which got past goaltender Paige Thunder at the 3:10 mark of the third period.

From there, Eden Prairie stayed perfect by defeating Coon Rapids, 6-1, in the Class AA title game. Eden Prairie jumped out to a 1-0 lead on Maria Schneider's goal at the 12:03 mark of the first period and cruised from there. Meaghan Pezon scored at 3:22 and was followed by Melissa Feste, who had two goals and two assists in the game. Andrea Green and Ashlan Lambert also got into the action, while Kelly Seeler and Maria Stoa each had three assists in the big win.

The opening 2006 Class A semifinal game saw Warroad defeat New Prague, 5-2, thanks to Holly Roberts and eighth-grader Brook Story, who each had a pair of goals in the game. The other semi saw South St. Paul doubling up on Alexandria, 4-2. Leading the charge for the Packers were Annie Bauerfeld, who had a hat-trick, as well as Rita Simones and Jackie Robertson, who both chipped in with two assists.

Then, in the Finals, top-ranked South St. Paul rallied to beat Warroad in overtime, 3-2, to win their second consecutive state title and fourth overall for head coach Dave Palmquist. Down 2-0 early in the third period, the Packers came back to tie it up on goals from Katelyn Crnobrna and Jonnie Bloemers. Bloemers then carried the momentum from her game-tying goal into overtime, where she got the game-winner on a backhander at the 3:20 mark of sudden death. Senior Holly Roberts scored both of Warroad's goals in the heart-breaking loss.

Meanwhile, the Lady Gophers lost to Wisconsin in the 2005 WCHA Playoffs, 4-1, and then lost to the Badgers yet again when it mattered most. Minnesota opened up the post-season with a trip out east, where they blanked Princeton, 4-0, in the NCAA Regionals. Leading the charge for the Maroon and Gold was goalie Brittony Chartier, who stopped all 33 shots that came her way. With the win, the team headed back to Minneapolis, where they would face New Hampshire in the opening round of the NCAA Women's Frozen Four, which just so happened to be

JILL POHTILLA

Jill Pohtilla grew up in Plymouth and went on to graduate from Wayzata High School in 1981. Pohtilla then played volleyball and softball at Augustana College (Sioux Falls, S.D.) for three years before transferring to the University of Minnesota, where she graduated in 1987 with degrees in psychology and biology. Pohtilla would then go on to teach and coach volleyball, softball and hockey at the high school level. On the ice, Pohtilla has played hockey on all levels for nearly three decades, and was a member of the four-time national champion Minnesota Checkers womens hockey team.

Pohtilla was hired in 1995 as Augsburg's first women's hockey coach, and in that capacity she has worked hard to build the sport among colleges and universities in Minnesota. She was instrumental in developing the Midwestern Collegiate Women's Hockey Alliance (MCWHA), and later, was part of the formulation of women's hockey as a varsity championship sport in the Minnesota Intercollegiate Athletic Conference (MIAC) — just the second conference in the nation (and first at the exclusively Division III level) to sponsor the sport.

Pohtilla has also been active on the national women's hockey scene. In 1997, 1998, 2004, 2005 and 2006, she was selected by U.S. Olympic women's hockey head coach Ben Smith to teach and coach at the U.S. Olympic Women's Hockey Development Camp in Lake Placid, N.Y., leading teams of 15-16 and 17-18 year olds. In addition, Pohtilla served as the president of the Minnesota Girls and Womens Hockey Associations in 1990.

One of the winningest coaches in the history of collegiate women's hockey, Pohtilla sports a career record of 160-122-23 entering her 13th season behind the Lady Auggie bench. She is also ranks fifth all-time in coaching victories among active coaches in all NCAA divisions, while standing second among NCAA D-III coaches in both all-time wins and winning percentage (.575).

DR. BOB MAY

Dr. Bob May, who coached high school hockey at Minneapolis Roosevelt in the early 1950s, went on to serve as the head coach at the University of North Dakota for two seasons from 1957-59. There, May led the Sioux to a NCAA Division I National Championship in 1959, beating Michigan State, 4-3, in Troy, NY. In addition, May's Sioux placed second in 1958 as well. May would finish his short but illustrious career at UND with a record of 44-17-2 (.714).

From there, May would then go on to become a pioneer in the development and advancement of women's hockey in Minnesota. May was very active with the Checkers, Minnesota's first dominant women's club team in the 1970s. In 1980 the Checkers won the National Open B Division women's title. From there, the Checkers, which were led by Laura Halldorson, who would go on to serve as the Gopher Women's Hockey Coach, and Jill Pohtilla, who would go on to serve as the Augsburg Women's Hockey Coach, went on to win a couple of USA Hockey National Midget titles in the early 1980's, in both the 15-and-under and later in the 19-and-under categories.

taking place at Mariucci Arena. It was the team's fifth straight Frozen Four appearance. There, Bobbi Ross led the Gophers into the Finals with an amazing four-goal performance in a tight 5-4 victory. Ross scored the game-winner with just under two minutes to go in the game on a nice give-and-go from Whitney Graft. Next up were the rival Wisconsin Badgers for all the marbles. Would it be yet another title for the Lady Gophers? Sadly, the Badgers came out smoking in this one and blanked Minnesota, 3-0, to win the National Championship.

As for the prepsters, the 2007 Class AA high school tourney opened with the North Metro Stars defeating the Burnsville Blaze 4-3, in double overtime. Leading the charge for the Cinderella Stars was sophomore Breana Anderson, who scored both the game-tying goal and then the game-winning goal at 11:16 of the second overtime. Game Two saw Benilde St.-Margaret's blank the Grand Rapids/Greenway Lightening, 2-0, behind Kate Bacon and Samantha Press, who each tallied, while goalie Amanda Nagel stopped all 17 shots that came her way. Game Three featured the Stillwater Area Ponies downing Bemidji by the final of 3-1, thanks to Allison Schwab and Callie Dahl, who each had a goal and an assist in the win. The last quarterfinal was a blow-out as Roseville Area beat Rochester Mayo, 6-2, with a record 48 shots on goal. The Raiders were led by senior winger Erin Cody, who had four goals and one assist in the victory.

Led by Alecia Anderson's hat-trick, the North Metro Stars then beat Benilde-St. Margaret's, 5-2, in the first semi. Despite out-shooting their opponents 35-15, the Red Knights came up short against Stars' eighth-grade goalie, Kayla Krueter. The other semi saw the Stillwater Area ponies defeat Roseville, 4-2, thanks to a pair of goals from Allison Schwab. Then, in the Finals, the Ponies cruised to a 4-1 victory of the North Metro Stars to claim their first ever Class AA title. The Ponies were led by sophomore Callie Dahl, who had a goal and two assists, while senior goalie Amanda Plumm recorded 22 saves in the big win.

A new format was implemented for the Class A tourney in 2007, which now included quarterfinal contests. No longer would just four teams be playing for the smaller schools, a sign of just how far the game had grown over the past several years.

Game One of the Class A tourney saw Blake shut-out the Breck Mustangs, 4-0, on Sally Komarek's goal and two assists. Senior goalie Rachel Bowens-Rubin was perfect in net, meanwhile, stopping all 20 shots she faced. Game Two was a thriller as Hibbing/Chisholm beat the Alexandria Cardinals, 1-0, on Ariel Hakala's game-winning goal with just 23 seconds remaining in overtime. In their first-ever tourney appearance, Crookston blanked Marshall, 5-0, in Game Three. The Pirates were led by the outstanding play of goalies Jennifer Meyer and Birgetta Martin, who combined for the shut-out. The last quarterfinal saw Farmington beat Austin, 5-2, thanks to Erin Johnson's one goal and four assists, and Rachel Ripley's two goals and two assists.

Blake then defeated Hibbing/Chisholm, 4-1, in the first semifinal to advance to the title game. The Bears were led by sen-

iors Laura Komarek and Katharine Chute, who each scored two goals, while senior goalie Rachel Bowens-Rubin made 21 saves in net. The other semi saw Farmington double up on Crookston, 4-2, behind Erin Johnson's two goals and one assist.

The Finals were tight, but in the end the Blake Bears edged past Farmington, 2-1, to earn their second state title. Margaret Chute got Blake on the board first, only to see Farmington eighth grader Krystal Bauman tie the game at 1-1 early in the second period. Chute's older sister, Katharine, then got what would prove to be the game-winner at 2:38 of the third period when she beat Farmington goalie Erin McNamara to give the Bears the championship. Incidentally, as a team, the Bears tied a tournament record for "Fewest Goals Against in a Tournament," with just two — a testament to the abilities of Blake goalie Rachel Bowens-Rubin.

Meanwhile, back on campus, the Gophers got Badgered for the second straight season in 2007. Minnesota opened up the WCHA playoffs by beating up on Bemidji, 5-1 and 4-1, behind the scoring of Brittany Francis and Bobbi Ross, who combined for a whopping 11 points. The WCHA semifinals came down to the wire as the Gophers beat Duluth, 3-2, in overtime with Gigi Marvin netting the thrilling game-winner midway through the extra session. Then, on March 4, 2007, the team faced off against Wisconsin in the WCHA finals. Down 1-0 early, Brittany Francis and Bobbi Ross hooked up late in the first period to tie it at one apiece. The game roared back and forth, but the Badgers were too tough down the stretch and went on to win the game by the final of 3-1. With that, the team fell to a program-worst 23-12-1 record on the season and missed an NCAA championship berth. The team ended up ninth in the pair wise, but only the top eight could advance on to the NCAA regionals.

Then, in August of 2007, Gopher Coach Laura Halldorson shocked the hockey world by announcing her resignation after 11 seasons behind the Gopher bench. Halldorson, who led her teams to three national titles, would leave the program she started with an outstanding career record of 278-67-22. The Gophers also won four WCHA titles during her tenure as well. Among her many honors and accolades, she was named as the national coach of the year in 1998, 2002 and 2004. Associate head coach Brad Frost was named as the team's interim head coach for 2007-08, with Laura Slominski remaining as the team's top assistant.

"After 20 years in this career, it is time for me to retire from coaching college women's hockey," said Halldorson. "It has been a great journey, and I have especially enjoyed my 11 years here at the University of Minnesota. The players and staff who have been involved in this program over the past decade definitely hold a special place in my heart, and I look forward to keeping in touch with them. I am proud of the history and tradition of Gopher Women's Hockey; and with the recent success we have had in recruiting, the future is very bright. As the saying goes, 'It's been a great run!' Go Gophers!"

INDEX

Aase, Ron 150
Abbott, John S. 94
Abbott, Leon 177,178
Abel, B.J. 146
Abel, Taffy 19,20,22,38,46
Abrahamson, Brett 114
Abrahamson, Chuck 169
Abrahamson, John 160
Abram, Dale 202,203
Abram, Terry 199,201,205
Acton, Keith 65
Adam, Kevin 160
Adams, Joe 225
Adams, Mike 202
Adams, Wes 22,50
Adlys, Bernie 155
Agar, George 26
Ahearn, Kevin 91
Ahlin, Rudy 25,39,48
Ahlquist, Sarah 240,241
Aikens, Bruce 209
Ailsby, Lloyd 26
Akre, Dave 209
Albers, John 207
Alberts, Andrew 48
Albrecht,Ashley 237,238,240,245,246,249
Aldrich, Gene 42,188,189,231
Aldrich, Steve 166
Alexander, Johnny 137
Alexander, Mike 153,154
Alley, Jim 95
Alley, Steve 48,49
Alm, Larry 29,195
Alm, Rick 196
Almquist, Dave 221
Almquist, John 195
Almquist, Oscar 24,25,39,42,45,46, 167,191,199,231
Alstead, Brady 185
Ames, Nick 226
Amidon, Jim 199,200
Ammerman, Rockford 201,202
Amundson, Brock 172
Amundson, Mark 219,220
Anacabe, Bob 228
Anderson, Alecia 251
Anderson, Breana 251
Anderson, Chad 161
Anderson, Chris 227
Anderson, Colin 134
Anderson, Derek 216,217
Anderson, Dick 199
Anderson, Dirk 210
Anderson, Don 25
Anderson, Earl 48,202
Anderson, Hugo 192
Anderson, Iver 20,25
Anderson, Jim 198,207
Anderson, John 201
Anderson, Jon 100,102
Anderson, Josh 225
Anderson, Keith 142
Anderson, Larry 197
Anderson, Mike 112,114,115,211
Anderson, Nick 222
Anderson, Orville 190,191
Anderson, R.J. 227
Anderson, Ric 150
Anderson, Rod 194,231
Anderson, Roy 194
Anderson, Russ 48
Anderson, Stu 194,195
Anderson, Tom 148
Anderson, Wendell 43,49,96,98
Anderson, Whitney 248
Andolsek, Ludwig 136
Andrea, Paul 27
Andrews 23
Andrich, Nick 213
Angel, Nick 223
Angell, Nick 118
Annunziato, Annie 249
Anthony, Nick 117,118
Antonovich, Jeff 219
Antonovich, Mike 48,91,92,97,202,203
Antoskiewicz, Henry 129
Arbour, John 91
Armbrust, Peter 221
Armstrong, Bob 38
Armstrong, Larry 40,95
Armstrong, Murray 97
Armstrong, Ray 18
Arnason, Tyler 139,142
Arnold, Bob 95
Arnold, Josh 219,220
Aronson, Steve 171
Arrigoni, Brian 228
Ash, Bob 27
Aufderheide, Walt 208
Auge, Les 48,98,100,204
Aulik, Gary 210
Auran, Mike 173
Aus, Peter 160,161,169,231
Aus, Whitey 160,169,231
Austin, Jon 221
Austin, Ken 95,175,176
Awada, George 141,142
Awaijane, Tom 163
Awrey, Don 27
Backes, David 48,146,148,149
Backlund, Dave 198,199
Backstrom, Niklas 82,85-89
Bacon, Kate 251
Bader, Larry 49
Bader, Marc 212
Bader, Mark 210
Baer, Jack 229
Bagley, Don 95
Bahr, Mark 178
Bailey, Joey 224
Bailey, John 26
Bailey, Matt 142
Bailey, Mike 207,227
Bain, Richard 207
Baines, Jared 215
Baker, Bill 48,49,98-100,102,105-107,183
Baker, Damian 164
Baker, Robert 49
Bakke, Hal 28
Bakke, Rich 201
Baldi, Ernest 36
Baldrica, Bill 202
Baldwin, Dale 152,154
Baldwin, Howard 68
Ball, Terry 27,91
Ballard, Keith 48,118-123,127
Balvin, Brenton 161
Bang, Mark 223
Barbato, Mike 202
Barber, Don 67
Barbo, Ed 200
Barle, Jim 199
Barnes, Tyler 229
Baron, Mark 132
Barrett, Freddy 64
Barrette, Neal 204
Barriball, Jay 125,126,228
Barron, Bob 18
Barron, Chris 224
Barron, Frank 15
Barry, Jay 221
Barthelome, Earl 187
Bartholdi, Herb 95
Bartholome, Earl 26,46
Bartlette, Shawn 224
Bartness, Gary 129
Bartoli, Ed 26,27
Bartz, John 231
Basch, Charles 136
Bates, Bob 30
Bauer, Arnie 164,231
Bauerfeld, Annie 248,250
Bauernfeind, Todd 209
Bauman, Krystal 251
Baumgartner, Bob 207
Baumgartner, Dan 191
Baumgartner, Mike 48,201
Baumgartner, Steve 161,162
Bawlf, Fred 18
Baxter, Jim 231
Bayer, Loren 212
Beattie, Zack 228
Beatty, Dan 211,212
Beaty, Pat 214
Beauchamp, Ray 192
Beauduy, Katie 237
Beaulieu, Andre 61,167,176
Beaupre, Don 62,63,64,65,66,67
Beck, Gary 206
Beck, Rod 207
Beckel, Bryce 221
Becker, Jim 212
Becker, Matt 227
Beckett, Glen 154
Bede, Nick 213
Begich, Milan 190
Behning, Jesse 229
Behrendt, Jack 95
Beiswenger, Chad 225
Beito, Keith 212
Belisle, Omer 155
Bell, Harry 26
Bell, Scott 93,110,111,164
Bellows, Brain 64-71
Belzberg, Morris 68
Bend, Lin 26
Bender, Matt 217
Benedict, Bryan 219
Bengtson, Ben 228
Bennett, Tom 222
Benowicz, Cleve 17
Benson, Brad 211
Bentley, Doug 26
Benysek, Ladislav 78,88
Berg, Don 193
Berg, Reggie 112,114-116,142
Berge, Mick 149
Bergland, Tim 48
Bergloff, Bob 100
Bergstrom, Terry 150,154
Bergup, Frank 189
Berke, John 210
Berkhoel, Adam 48
Bernardi, Joe 20
Bernstrom, Jeff 225
Bertelson, Roger 194
Bertogliat, Jesse 111
Bertram, Matt 216
Bessone, Amo 46
Bessone, Peter 46
Beste, Tom 194
Beutow, Bart 202
Beutow, Brad 140,202
Bianchi, Joe 185,218-220
Bianchi, John 219,231
Bianchi, Steve 211,212,219
Bianchi, Tony 110,111,216,217,219
Bierman, Bernie 40
Bigham, Eric 164
Bigness, Watt 190
Bilben, Derek 174
Billberg, Tom 201
Billedeau, Scott 211
Billings, Osborne 95
Biondi, Joey 216,217
Birch, Jon 198
Bischoff, Grant 31,100,102,103
Biskup, Greg 154
Bittner, Jon 231
Bjerken, Bret 209
Bjerken, Bud 197
Bjork, Bernard 136
Bjorklund, Scott 165,166
Bjorkman, Rob 231
Bjorkman, Rube 32,49,95,96,190,191
Bjorkstrand, Todd 211
Bjornson, Kris 153
Bjugstad, Mike 212
Bjugstad, Scott 48,49,66,127,210
Blade, Matt 217
Blahoski, Alana 237,241,245
Blair, Gerald 51
Blair, Wren 27,51,53,54,56,58
Blais, Dean 34,97,98,217
Blaisdell, J.C. 228,229
Blake, Bob 24,25,46
Blake, Jason 48,49,127,178,218,219
Blake, Jeff 208
Blanchard, Jim 193
Blanche, Rich 176
Blaylock, Wally 166
Blitz, R.S. 94
Bliven, Jason 219
Bloemers, Jonnie 250
Blom, Stan 158
Bloom, Scott 102,214,215
Bloomgren, Barry 200
Blouin, Sylvain 89
Blue, Darren 147
Blue, John 100
Blumer, Glen 199
Bochenski, Brandon 48,127,225
Bodle, Duane 209
Boehm, Ron 27
Boeser, Bob 165
Boeser, Jeff 170
Boeser, Robert 49
Boitz, Dave 214
Boivin, Leo 51
Bolin, Keith 199-201
Bombardir, Brad 81,88,89
Bonin, Bob 208
Bonin, Brian 48,110-114,127,128,188,217
Bonk, Dan 206
Bonk, David 221
Bonk, Joe 202,203
Bonk, Jon 201
Boo, Jim 178
Boogaard, Derek 81,83,87,89
Bookler, Ron 148
Booten, Lowell 30
Bordsen, Rob 229
Boreen, Merrill 229
Borer, Casey 143,230
Borndale, Jeff 213
Borsch, Joe 189
Boucha, Henry 33,34,46,48,91,92,179,203,204
Bouchard, Dick 26
Bouchard, Pierre Marc 79-81,83,85,87,88,89
Boulianne, Jude 155
Boutain, Jenna 236
Boutette, Pat 130,131,134
Boutilier, Paul 67
Bowens-Rubin, Rachel 251
Boyce, Jim 197
Boyd, Bill 22
Boyd, Bob 91
Boysen, Bob 199
Boyum, Jeff 205
Brackenbury, Curt 92
Bradford, Jack 17
Bradley, Drey 153,154
Bradley, W.W. 187
Braga, Al 192
Brager, Ron 204
Brandanger, Jessica 241
Brandenborg, Kassie 248
Brandrup, Paul 209
Brandt, Jake 224
Brandt, Keith 197
Brandt, Mark 214
Brandt, Mitch 205
Brandt, Ryan 201
Brandy, Joe 170
Braoderick, Bernie 231
Brasar, Per-Olov 61
Brascugli, Pete 39
Bratnober, Harry 189
Brauer, Bill 212
Brausen, Briana 250
Breckheimer, Ted 25
Bredesen, Erik 228
Breen, Dennis 19,22
Bremer, Dave 205
Brenk, Jake 225
Brennan, Laura 246
Brenneman, John 27
Bretschneider, Dan 215
Bretto, Joe 25,48
Brettschneider, Dan 144,145
Briggs, Brian 205
Briggs, Kellen 122-125
Brill, John 93,110,216
Brill, Ted 231
Brimsek, Frank 37,45,46,48,136,189
Brink, Andy 110
Brink, Milt 25,39,42,46,48
Brobak, Bill 205
Brodeen, Josh 228
Broderick, John 231
Brodt, Vic 142
Brodt, Winny 237,238,240,242
Brodt-Wethington, Kerry 240,241
Brodzinski, Mike 137,138,141
Broker, Jim 191
Brooks, Dave 49,97,104
Brooks, Herb 7,29,46,49,60,67,97-99, 104-109,121,122,161,175,176,182,183, 137,140,141,143,194-196
Brooks, John 189
Brooks, Lee 142
Brookshaw, Emily 237
Bros, Ben 18
Bros, Chet 95
Bros, Ken 95
Bros, Thayer 94
Brose, Don 144,145,147,197
Brossa, Gene 190
Brosseau, Rick 222
Broten, Aaron 46,48,100-102,209,210
Broten, Mike 203,205
Broten, Neal 8,46,48,49,60,62,64-71,73,99- 101,105-107,113,127,128,182,183,209
Broten, Paul 48,101,103
Brovold, Ken 212
Brown, Brad 89
Brown, Charles 49,151,154,155
Brown, Chris 160,164
Brown, Dave 205,206
Brown, Fred 26
Brown, George 46
Brown, Harold 26
Brown, Harry 175
Brown, Joe 95
Brown, Paul 206,207
Brown, Rich 26,197,198
Brown, Robert 92
Brown, Steve 210
Brown, Walter 46
Bruggeman, Henry 191
Brumm, Matt 216
Brunette, Andrew 77-81,88,89
Brunkhorst, John 227
Bryant, Richie 213
Bryduck, Sid 191,192
Buchholz, Mark 162
Buck, Nate 225
Buck, Roger 31
Budge, Rich 150
Budish, Jeff 169
Buetow, Brad 99,164
Bulauca, Bill 197
Bulauco, Ed 196
Bullock, Nelson 26
Bunde, Jack 198
Bunker, Mike 214
Buran, Tom 201
Burg, Dick 29,97
Burg, Elizabeth 248
Burg, Mike 200
Burgraff, Mike 208
Burhans, Ledge 150
Burke, Jack 197
Burns, Brent 80,86,87,88,89
Burns, Charlie 54,56,57
Burns, Dan 211
Burns, Terry 154
Burns, Zach 225
Burton, Lindley 189
Bush, Walter Jr. 49,50,175
Bush, Walter 27,28,45-47,51,175,176
Buskowiak, Brian 222
Busniuk, Ron 91,92,131
Butters, Bill 48,91,92,98,108,160
Butters, Paul 100,209-211
Bye, Karyn 237,245
Byfuglien, Dustin 48
Byfuglien, Jamie 217
Byrne, Pat 21
Caffery, Terry 57
Cahill, Kelly 206
Cain, J. Lawrence 45
Caldwell, A. 129
Caldwell, Ryan 230
Callinan, Jeff 110,111
Campbell, D. Kelly 45
Campbell, Gene 29,43,49,96
Campbell, Tom 213
Camuel, Derek 220
Cardinal, Scott 216
Cardwell, Steve 91,92
Carley, Bob 95,189
Carlsen, Harold 95
Carlsen, Tom 202
Carlson, Arley 29
Carlson, Bill 214
Carlson, Bob 196
Carlson, Brad 222
Carlson, Brothers 175
Carlson, Bruce 203-205
Carlson, Carl 231
Carlson, Dan 221-223
Carlson, Glen 195,196
Carlson, Jack 48,63,90,92
Carlson, Jeff 90,92
Carlson, Jesse 217
Carlson, Mark 223
Carlson, Neal 161
Carlson, Rheese 223
Carlson, Ross 223
Carlson, Steve 48,90,92
Carlson, Tim 203-205
Carlston, Scott 134
Carlton, Brian 152
Carman, Mike 126
Carmichael, Dale 137
Carney, Keith 85,86,88,89
Carpenter, Bobby 46
Carr, Gene 200
Carrol, Bill 199
Carroll, Andrew 135,226
Carroll, Dan 212
Carroll, Mike 249
Carroll, Pat 147
Carroll, Steve 127,144,145,148,209
Carroll, Tim 216
Carroll, Tom 210,211
Carter, Rachael 247
Carter, Ryan 48,146
Carvo, Joe 230
Cascalenda, Tom 208
Casey, Jon 48,65-71,127,210,211
Casey, Terry 203
Casperson, Dan 204,205
Castellano, Mike 193
Castellano, Ron 192
Catani, Antonio 213
Cavanagh, Joe 46
Ceglarski, Len 46
Celley, Neil 39,42,44,190
Ceryance, Frank 39
Cesky, Jara 160
Chadwick, Bill 46
Chambers, Jack 18
Chamblee, Kellen 226
Chapman, Craig 226
Chapman, Greg 216
Chapman, Wally 212
Chaput, Vic 150
Charleston, Danny 226
Chartier, Brittony 250
Chase, John 46
Checco, Nick 110-113,141,188,218,219
Checco, Steve 212
Chet, Ben 95
Chezick, Lauren 248
Chiasson, Ray 46
Chorney, Taylor 230
Chorske, Tom 48,100,188
Chouinard, Eric 81
Chouinard, Marc 82-85,88,89
Christensen, Jerry 200
Christensen, Keith 49,135,199
Christensen, Lindsey 241
Christensen, Matt 131,132,134
Christensen, Melissa 242
Christensen, Rod 201
Christensen, Stacy 166
Christensen, Greg 217
Christian, Bill 28,33,46,49,181 193,194
Christian, Dave 33,34,46,48,49, 93,105-107,182,183
Christian, Gordon 28,33,49
Christian, Roger 28,33,46,49,181,194
Christiansen, Keith 46,91,129-131,133-135
Christianson, Huffer 179
Christoff, Steve 48,49,98-100,103,105, 127,182,183,208,209
Christopher, Des 147
Christy, Doug 206
Christy, Steve 208
Chrystal, Bob 26
Chucko, Kris 123,124
Churla, Shane 68,69,71
Chute, Katharine 237,251
Chute, Margaret 251
Ciccarelli, Dino 62-67,73
Ciro, Tony 226
Clafton, Dan 208
Clark, Andy 165
Clark, Bill 189
Clark, Don 21,39,45-47,49,231
Clark, James 36
Clarke, Bob 68,70,71
Clarke, George 19,20,22
Clarke, La Toya 238,245,248
Clarke, Noah 230
Clarke, Nobby 20,22,25,38
Clarkson, Hailey 250
Clausen, George 95
Clauson, Jim 172,173
Claypool, James 46,181
Clayton, Bert 18
Clayton, Harry 18
Cleary, Bill 46
Cleary, Bob 46
Cleveland, Al 208,209
Climie, Matt 155,157
Cline, Tim 213
Cloutier, Dan 80
Clukey, Ryan 227
Clusiau, Tom 206
Clymer, Ben 48,113,114,119
Cobb, Amy 247
Cobb, George 27
Cocchiarella, Jim 196
Cody, Collin 226
Cody, Erin 250,251
Cole, Sharon 245,246
Collier, Claire 248
Collins, Bill 27,54
Collins, Rod 195,196
Collyard, Bob 48
Collyard, Bob 202
Columbo, John 211
Colwill, Les 26
Comstock, Blaine 33,49,132,151,154,155
Conacher, Lionel 38
Conlin, Pat 165,166,210
Connelly, Wayne 53,91
Connolly, Jack 229
Conrad, Christian 219
Conroy, Anthony 49
Conroy, George 21,22,25
Conroy, Pat 231
Conroy, Tom 208
Conroy, Tony 18-22,25,46
Considine, Guy 169
Constantine, Ben 95,97
Constantine, Kevin 179,180
Constantine, Sandy 39
Converse, Mitch 213
Conway, Bill 95
Conway, Dick 18,170
Conway, Jack 95
Conway, Jim 207
Cook, Bill 38
Cook, Brendan 157
Cook, Brian 140,142
Cook, Bun 38
Cook, Fred 18
Cook, Robin 155
Cookson, Joccie 245
Cooley, Bill 188
Cooper, Abby 244
Cooper, Derek 148
Cooper, Jon 174
Coppo, Paul 46
Cornelius, Sam 222,223
Cornwell, Tim 164
Cosgrove, Greg 208
Cossalter, Clem 44
Costellano, Mike 44
Costellano, Ron 44,231
Cotlow, Manny 187
Cotlow, Manny 25
Cotroneo, Lou 165,231
Cotton, Harold 51
Councilman, Jim 197,198
Courchaine, Bill 173
Couture, Gerry 26
Craig, Jim 106
Cramp, Ken 95
Crandall, Aaron 229
Crass, Katie 242
Crea, Mike 207
Crisp, Terry 27
Crnobrna, Katelyn 250
Crnobrna, Sarah 247
Cronkhite, Bill 196
Crosby, Sydney 230
Crowley, Mike 48,111-113,115,127, 141,188,219,220
Crupi, Mike 199,200
Cullen, Dan 197
Cullen, Jon 142,143
Cullen, Mark 48,221,222
Cullen, Matt 48,139,141-143,219,220,221
Cullen, Pat 155,164,180
Cullen, Ray 54
Cullen, Terry 231
Culshaw, Daerda 249
Cunniff, John 46
Cunningham, Bob 27
Cunningham, Jim 48,178
Curella, Tony 213
Curphy, Jack 193
Curran, Lefty 179
Curran, Mike 46,49,91-93,199
Curran, Tony 200,201
Currie, Bob 26
Curry, John 225
Curtin, Renee 236,237,241
Curtin, Ronda 236-238,240,241,246
Cusey, Troy 216,217
Cutter, Frank 94
Dahl, Callie 251
Dahl, Craig 137,140-143,156,160,165,205,206
Dahlberg, Dave 217
Dahlen, Ulf 67
Dahlquist, Chris 48,68,70
Dahlstrom, Cully 24-26,46,48,189
Daigle, Alexandre 81-83,88,89
Dale, Jack 29,49,97
Dalton, Mike 205
Damberg, Roy 39
Damerow, Chad 168
Damjanovich, Aaron 161
DaMota, Glen 210
Dardis, Jay 223
Darwitz, Natalie 236,241,242,247-250
Davis, Bob 38
Day, Erik 113
De Paul, Billy 25
De St. Hubert, John 219
DeAngelis, Mike 131,133
DeBus, Steve 112-114
DeCenzo, John 211
DeCenzo, Mark 207
DeCenzo, Pete 208
Decker, Joe 215,216
Dee, Robbie 227
DeFauw, Brad 48,222
DeGrio, Gary 209,210
DeGriselles, Jamie 235
DeHate, Bert 200,201
DeHate, Phil 201
Deis, Tyler 148
Del Monte, Terry 202
DeLeo, Frank 39
Delich, George 202
Delmonte, Armand 26
Delmore, Tim 205
Delveaux, Todd 166
DeMarchi, Matt 120-122
DeMarki, Pat 202
DeMike, Ron 197
Demitra, Pavol 85,86,88,89
Denis, Jean 26
Denney, Corb 23
Dennis, Tom 215
Denny, Steve 224
DePaul, Bill 39
DePaul, Robert 136
DePaul, Roland 95
DePaul, Walter 136
Derrett, Brian 26
Des Jardins, Vic 20-23,25,38,46,189
Deschamps, Buzz 27
Desmond, Richard 46
Detlefsen, Keith 164
Detlefson, Keith 163
DeVoe, John 212
DeVoe, Mike 212
DeWolf, Josh 141
Dey, Nate 143,188
Dibble, Mike 205
DiCasmirro, Nate 139,142
DiCasmirro, Nicki 236
Dick, Greg 211
Dill, Bob 25,30,46,48,51,73,188,189
Dillion, Spencer 230
Dillon, Barry 150,154
Dillon, Dave 208
Dilworth, Dan 49
DiSanto, Mike 207
Doepke, Robin 237
Doerfler, Ken 200
Dolan, Tom 36
Dolentz, Nick 224
Dolinsek, Jeff 224
Dolinsek, Tony 224
Donaghue, Mike 155
Donahue, Matt 199
Donnay, Cory 225
Donnelly, John 209,210
Dornbach, Greg 214
Dornhoefer, Gary 27
Dorr, Frances 250
Dougherty, Bill 192
Dougherty, Dick 26,43,46,49,96,97,192
Dowd, Jim 74,77,78,88,89
Doyle, Dennis 208
Doyle, Dick 191
Doyle, Larry 45
Doyle, Mike 142
Doyle, Rickie Lee 244
Drazen, Rachel 246
Dreher, Bill 165
Driscoll, Charles 18
Driscoll, John 50,51
Drobnick, Jim 195
Drobnick, Ron 42,190
Droogsma, Nate 225
Drouin, Jude 54,56,57
Drury, Herb 18,22,38
Dryden, Ken 56
Duchene, Luien 26
Duchesne, Gaetan 71
Dudley, Harold 169
Dudulowicz, Aggie 26
Duetz, Spencer 227
Duffus, Parris 93
Duffy, Ashley 248
Dufour, Marc 27
Duhamel, Benoit 161
Dunbar, Robert H. 187
Dungan, Tod 169
Dunlap, Adam 225
Dunlop, Alex 18
Dunlop, Fosdale 18
Dupre, Roger 201
Dupuis, Pascal 79-82,84,88,89
Durgin, Darryl 194
Durose, Jim 198
Dustin, Bobby 110
Dwyer, Aaron 222
Dynan, Pat 227
Dziedzic, Joe 48,102,110,111,188
Dzikowski, Ken 134
Eagles, Mark 154
Eagon, Len 208,209
Earl, Jeremy 226
Eastman, Derek 142
Eastman, Pete 210
Eastman, Steve 225
Eaves, Ben 127,230
Eaves, Patrick 127,230
Ebert, Keith 202
Eckstrom, Howard 191
Edstrom, Joe 223
Edwards, Shawn 211
Edwards, Troy 155
Egan, Bill 197
Eggleton, Al 95
Eichorn, Steve 204,205
Eidsness, Rory 136,141
Eilefson, Brent 169
Ekberg, Jim 196
Eklund, Les 199,200
Eldredge, W.B. 95
Eldridge, Beaupre 94
Eldridge, Chester 167
Eldridge, Chick 167
Elik, Todd 68

Elliott, Babe 18,20,22
Ellis, Damian 219
Ellison, Aro 39
Ellison, Johanna 237,246-248
Elston, Fred 94
Engelstad, Ralph 189
Engle, Ryan 221
Englebert, Elmer 189
Englestad, Cal 95
Engstrom, Tracy 238,240,242
Enquist, John 205
Erb, Jake 222
Erb, Jamie 155
Erickson 118
Erickson, Art 25,39
Erickson, Bryan 48,127
Erickson, Butsy 100,101,178,209
Erickson, Chad 34,48,131,216
Erickson, Dennis 97
Erickson, Jack 192,193
Erickson, Luke 157
Erickson, Matt 224
Erickson, Nina 246
Eriksson, Rolie 58,61,62
Erredge, Matt 165
Eseau, Lenny 137
Espe, David 100
Essay, Ken 172
Essel, Bill 148
Essling, Victor 36
Eustace, Joanne 246
Evans, John 159
Evanson, Roger 195
Everett, Doug 46
Fabian, Erik 124
Fabian, Sean 100,103,215
Fahey, Trevor 27
Fairbanks, John 208
Fairchild, C. 18
Fairchild, Kelly 48
Fairchild, Mike 207
Falk, Bruce 151,154,202
Falk, Marty 95,230
Falk, Willard 158
Falkman, Craig 29,49,91,92,97
Fangel, Tim 208
Fanger, Ken 195
Farichild, Kelly 217
Farrell, John 221
Farrell, Mike 48
Farrington, Pat 208
Fast, Laura 244,250
Faupel, Joe 229
Faust, Scott 213
Featherstone, Kevin 214
Federenko, Brad 134
Fermoyle, Andy 145,147
Fermoyle, Pat 174
Fernandez, Manny 74,77,79,81,83,84,85,88,89
Ferreira, Jack 68
Ferry, Paul 155
Ferschweiler, Pat 216
Fest, Melissa 250
Festler, Jared 228
Fiandaca, John 198
Fichuk, Pete 199,200,201
Ficken, Erin 242
Fidler, Mike 62
Fiebelkorn, Jed 110
Fincel, George 202
Finger, Jeff 138
Finks, Dave 207
Finnegan, Gilbert 44
Finnegan, Herm 137,214
Finnegan, Pat 39,42,44,190,222,223
Fischer, David 188
Fischer, Jayme 225
Fish, Jim 216
Fishback, Dan 134
Fisher, Drew 227
Fisher, Maggie 246-248
Fitzgerald, Ed 18,20,22,49
Fitzgerald, Peter 222
Fitzgerald, Rusty 48,134,218
Fitzpatrick, Sandy 27
Fitzsimmons, John 136,141
Fitzsimmons, Tim 206
Fitzsimmons, Tom 207
Flaherty, Keegan 227
Flaman, Harvey 135
Flasch, Gary 206,207
Fleming, Bob 29,45,47
Fleming, Jake 121,123,124
Fleming, Steve 213
Fletcher, James 30
Fletcher, Justin 142,143
Flick, Mike 215
Flood, Jack 24,25,187
Fogarty, Jeff 217
Foley, John 18
Foley, Pat 211
Ford, Matt 230
Forgie, Tom 26
Forlid, Steve 144
Foss, Jeff 214
Foster, Kurtis 86,88,89
Foussard, Henri 50
Fox, Aaron 145
Fox, W.W. 29
Foy, Matt 83
Francis, Brittany 251
Francisco, Jason 215
Francisco, Jon 121,134,224
Francisco, Pat 134
Frank, Dave 196
Frank, Joe 199
Frantti, Bill 231
Frantzen, Scott 202
Fraser, Ian 26
Frawley, Bob 207
Frawley, Charles 162
Frazee, Jeff 125,126
Fredrickson, Aaron 222
Fretland, Mark 203,204
Fretland, Rick 203,204
Frider, Jeff 161
Fries, Dave 214
Frisch, Ryan 141
Frischmon, Trevor 224,225
Frisk, Tom 212
Fritsinger, Bill 137
Frizzel, Irwin 152
Frizzell, Irwin 210
Fronek, Scott 216
Frost, Brad 251
Fryberger, Bob 47
Fryberger, Dates 49,47
Fryberger, Jerry 47
Fryer, Cam 134
Fryklund, Amber 236,247
Ftorek, Robbie 46
Fullerton, James 46
Fulton, Dustin 164,227
Fulton, Eric 155
Fulton, Jordan 227
Funk, Liz 246
Fusco, Mark 46
Fusco, Scott 46
Gabardi, Derek 220
Gaborik, Marian 6,74,76-88,89
Gabriel, Milo 30
Gaffaney, Brian 142
Gager, Eric 153,154
Gagliardi, John 165,166
Gagner, Dave 67-71
Gagnon, Mark 211
Gainey, Bob 68,71
Galash, Tim 213
Galbraith, Kevin 212
Galbraith, Perk 20,22,38
Gallant, Gord 91
Galligan, Bill 25,30,95,188
Gambucci, Andre 38,44,49
Gambucci, Elio 38
Gambucci, Gary 29,46,48,90,92,97
Gambucci, Jimmy 98
Gambucci, Serge 45,46
Gambucci, Sergio 136
Gangloff, Jerry 196
Ganon, Mark 210
Garbe, Jim 218
Gardiner, Chuck 21
Garrett, Emy 20,21,22,25
Garrett, John 92
Garrison, John 46
Garrity, Jack 46
Gartner, Mike 67
Garven, Casey 224
Gasparini, Gino 140
Gasperlin, Ray 136
Gasseau, Sandy 140
Gaulrapp, James 149
Gavey, Aaron 88
Gavin, Stew 69,71
Gawryletz, Travis 135
Gehrke 22
Geisbauer 141
Geisler, Beau 131,134,135
Geist, Harry 210
Genderson, Dale 217
Genereau, Del 172,173,231
Gens, Pete 220
Genz, Gordy 164,231
Genz, Tom 213
George, Todd 145
Gerebi, Nick 214,215
Gergen, Michael 230
Gerlach, Adam 224
Gernander, Bob 176,231
Gernander, Ken 48,100,102,111,215
Gervais, Jean-Guy 157
Gess, Paul 212
Getchell, Aaron 166
Geving, Dave 176
Gherity, Mark 208
Giannini, Ed 202,203
Gibbons, A.R. 94
Gibbons, Dennis 154
Gibbons, Mike 151,153,154
Gibbons, Sammy 191
Gibbs, Barry 54,57
Gibbs, Howie 95
Gibson, Doc 46
Gieselman, Laura 244
Giesen, Jeff 244
Gifford, Brian 227
Gilbert, Jean 27
Gilbert, John 35,231
Gilbert, Karl 228,229
Gilbert, Tom 48
Gilbertson, Stan 48
Giles, Curt 62,63,131-135
Gilkenson, Allen 190
Gill, Adam 168
Gillies, Colton 80
Gilmour, Doug 65
Ginkel, Jenny 235
Gipple, Ray 189
Glancey, Tom 206,207
Glass, Duane 195,196
Glines, Mitch 224
Glines, Woody 219
Godbout, Brent 219
Godbout, Jason 219
Goehring, Karl 116,222
Goepfert, Bobby 127,138,141,143
Goff, Pat 198
Gogfrey, Al 231
Goheen, Moose 17,18,20-22,25,38,46,48,49
Goldsworthy, Bill 53,54,57-59,169
Goldsworthy, Leroy 48,189
Goldsworthy, Sean 169
Goldthorpe, Goldy 91,92,175
Goligoski, Alex 124-126
Goodman, Mike 20-22,38
Goos, Jeff 210
Goos, Larry 212
Gordon, Andrew 142,143
Gordon, Ben 124
Gordon, Jack 55,56,57,58
Gordon, Kevin 173
Gordon, Malcolm 46
Gordon, Ronald 136,141
Gorence, Tom 48,98,178
Gorg, Kevin 214
Gorowsky, Tom 188,227
Goski, Glenn 201,202
Goslin, Leo 231
Gosselin, Guy 48,49,133
Gottsleig 22
Gotziaman, Chris 217
Gould, Fred 95
Gould, Tom 197
Goulet, Jason 141,142
Goulet, Marty 156,157
Goveronski, Mike 219
Graft, Whitney 251
Graham, Trevor 226
Grahek, Wade 220
Graiziger, Bob 25,95,178,189
Graizinger, Pat 207
Gram, Chris 212
Gramer, Rob 220
Granato, Don 214
Granato, Rob 215,216
Grand, Bryan 150,151,154,199,201,231
Grand, Wendell 199
Granmo, Brett 229
Grannis, Dave 197
Grant, Danny 53,54,56,57
Grant, Wally 39,42,44,45,46,190
Grant, William 22
Graske, Tom 213,214
Gravel, Jack 202
Gravel, John 27
Gray, Russell 95
Green, Andrea 250
Green, Chuck 173
Green, Mike 207
Green, Norm 68,69,71-74
Greenlay, Scott 219
Gregoire, Jason 221
Gregory, Rick 165,166
Gresser, Mike 215
Gretprich, Terry 220
Gretzky, Wayne 43,73
Griffin, Dan 49
Griffith, Steve 49,164
Grillo, Chuck 140,231
Grimstad, Garrett 229
Grina, Todd 211
Grindahl, Dean 210
Groebner, Jerry 197
Gronstrand, Jari 67
Gross, Dave 148
Grosso, Tony 221
Gruba, Tony 142
Gruden, John 48
Gruye, Ross 174
Guertin, Joe 188
Guest, Tricia 246
Guibault, George 191
Gund, George 61,68
Gund, Gordon 61,68
Gunderson, Chuck 199
Gunderson, Dave 208
Gunderson, Dick 165,166
Gustafson, Reuben 95
Gustafson, Rube 191,194,202,231
Gustason, Gary 155
Gutsch, Bob 229
Guttu, Lyle 194
Guyer, Gino 120,121,123,124,188,225
Haaganson, Eric 217
Haakstad, Lyman 134
Hackett, Doug 211
Hagen, Greg 216
Hagen, Kayla 248
Haider, Bill 30
Haider, Frank 30
Hakala, Ariel 251
Halbrehder, Bill 130,231
Hale, Charles 36
Hale, Larry 26
Haley, Joe 36
Hall, Chad 217
Hall, Glenn 53
Hall, Jason 219
Hall, Jeff 222,223
Hall, Jon 199
Hall, Wayne 27
Halldorson, Laura 233,235,237,241,245,251
Haller, D.J. 213
Haller, Josh 225
Hallett, Jeff 203,204
Hallett, Zach 220,222
Hallie, Shawn 212
Halstrom, Erik 213
Halvorson, Chad 217
Halvorson, Dan 224
Halvorson, Wayne 198
Halweg, Orvin 191
Hammer, Jon 201
Hamner, Craig 178
Hampson, Greg 210,211
Hampson, Ted 56,57,61
Hampton, Rick 61,62
Hangsleben, Al 204
Hangsleben, Allan 34,48
Hankinson, Ben 48,100,102,111,116
Hankinson, Casey 48,111,113,114,116
Hankinson, Peter 100,102,111,116,213
Hanley, Jen 234
Hanna, Adam 165,166
Hanowski, Ben 228
Hansen, Al 202
Hansen, John 154
Hansen, Robert 162
Hanson, Bob 165,166,214
Hanson, Dave 92,178
Hanson, Emil 158,189
Hanson, Emory 24,25
Hanson, Jack 198
Hanson, Jason 217
Hanson, Joe 158
Hanson, Joel 149,225
Hanson, John 185
Hanson, Julius 158
Hanson, Keith 48
Hanson, Ken 197,198
Hanson, Lee 208
Hanson, Lewis 158
Hanson, Matt 219
Hanson, Mike 216
Hanson, Nate 226
Hanson, Oscar 23-25,158,189
Hanson, Paul 203
Hanson, Tom 213,215
Hanus, Tim 139,140,142
Haraway, Geof 209
Hardin, Russ 197
Harding, Austie 46
Harding, Josh 84-86,89
Hardwick, Kyle 228
Hardy, Nathan 229
Hargesheimer, Phil 24
Harkness, Ned 46
Harren, Gabe 227
Harren, Jackson 223
Harrer, Tim 48,100,208
Harrington, Brandon 225,226
Harrington, Chris 122,123,165
Harrington, John 49,105-107,130,132-134, 165,166,182,183
Harris, Bob 95,190
Harris, John 98,203,205
Harris, Nick 171
Harris, Rob 49
Harris, Ted 54,56-58
Harstad, Wade 225
Hart, Kelly 247
Hartigan, Mark 127,139,141,142
Hartje, Bob 199
Hartje, Tod 93,214
Hartman, Brian 154
Hartman, Denny 166
Hartman, Jim 213
Hartman, Matt 143
Hartsburg, Craig 62,64
Hartzell, Kevin 177,178
Hasbargen, Amber 237
Hasselman, Jeff 217,218
Hastings, Doug 203
Hastings, Jim 204
Hau, Jim 213
Hauer, Brett 48,49,131,133
Hauge, Justin 224
Haugen, Jerry 166
Haugland, Dick 200
Haun, George 164
Hause, Ben 228
Hauser, Adam 48,114-120
Haverlach, John 218
Hawkins, Tyler 227
Hawley, Kyle 224
Hayek, Peter 48,100
Hayward, Brian 69
Heaslip, Mark 48
Heatley, Murray 91
Hedberg, Lou 212
Hedican, Bret 48,49,138,140,143
Hedlund, Todd 217
Heffelfinger, Walter 15
Hegg, Peter 201
Hegland, Amber 220,234,235
Heglund, Bruce 211
Heidman, Cliff 129
Heikkinen, Wally 135
Heil, Jeff 220
Heisler, Jake 223
Heisler, Rod 151,154
Heitzman, Melisa 240
Helgeland, Bob 194
Helmer, Chad 166
Henderson, Matt 48
Hendrick, Ben 226
Hendricks, Matt 142,143,225
Hendrickson, Dan 113
Hendrickson, Darby 48,49,74,77,80,81,88, 89,103,110,113,188,217
Hendrickson, Dave 44,193,231
Hendrickson, Gus 195,206,231
Hendrickson, Jake 229
Hendrickson, Keith 134
Hendrickson, Larry 175,197,209
Hengen, Billy 143
Hennessy, Mark 227
Henning, Lorne 66
Henry, Alex 88,89
Henry, Gordon 200,201
Henry, Jim 33,34
Hensen, David H. 49
Hentges, Mark 127,171
Hepner, Josh 223
Heppner, Chris 223
Herbst, Dave 207
Hergert, Dave 223
Hergesheimer, Wally 26
Herzig, Tom 132,134
Hess, Lindel 197
Hewitt, Jamie 242
Hextall, Dennis 57,58
Heyliger, Vic 44,46
Hickey, Chris 228
Hildreth, Dana 212
Hilfer, Ryan 225
Hilgert, Ken 127,148
Hilken, Jon 217
Hill, Bill 20,38
Hill, Bob 131
Hill, James J. 16
Hill, Ryan 229
Hill, Sean 48,49,87
Hilsen, Don 198
Hiltner, Mike 213
Hiniker, Mike 216
Hirsch, Tom 48,49
Hirsch, Tyler 124,125
Hites, Chris 217
Hjelle, Arlan 198
Hoaglund, Adam 227
Hocking, Geroge 198
Hockinson, Erika 240,241
Hodge, Kimball 17
Hodge, Ray 17
Hodgins, Bill 95
Hodgson, Jerome 205
Hodgson, Ted 26
Hoene, Bob 198
Hoene, Kevin 231
Hoene, Mike 198
Hoene, Phil 48,231
Hoey, Jim 203
Hoffman, Abby 232
Hofmann, Lenny 168
Hogan, Caitlin 247
Hoistrom, Jack 194
Hokanson, Gary 101
Holcomb, Dwight 162
Holcomb, John 162
Holen, Alec 162
Holland, Mike 202
Holm, Tom 204
Holmes, Annamarie 237
Holmgren, Adam 165,166,224
Holmgren, Paul 48,92,176,178,206
Holmner, Fred 214
Holmsten, Dick 231
Holst, Erika 243,245,246
Holt, Charles Jr. 46
Holum, Dave 141,217
Hooper, Gary 212
Hooper, Greg 212
Hooton, Brock 143
Hopkins, John 150
Hopkins, Ricky 225,226
Hopkins, Ryan 225
Hoppe, Jack 194
Hoppe, Steve 212
Horak, Jody 237,238,245,248,249
Horn, Dan 144,148
Horner, Jack 154
Horsch, Mitch 178
Horton, John 203
Horvath, Mark 213
Hoscheid, Wes 231
Hosfield, Mike 163
Houck, Terry 208
Hough, Samantha 243
Housley, Larry 212
Housley, Phil 46,48,49,176,178,211,212
Hovanec, Jeff 211
Hovie, Wes 189,190
Howe, Dick 206,207
Howe, Mark 46
Howe, Mike 123-125
Howell, Harry 61
Howells, Tyler 226
Hubbard, Stanley 43,45,178
Huck, Fran 92
Huck, Kevin 226
Huerd, Eddie 204
Huerd, Vince 216
Huerta, Ryan 220
Hughes, Brenton 27
Hughes, Greg 200
Hughes, Howie 26,27
Hughes, John 207
Hughes, Terry 148
Hull, Brett 9,67,69,73,127,130,133-135
Hultgren, Kelly 127,141,142
Humphrey, Kyle 216
Hunt, Grady 156,157
Huntley, Dan 173
Hurley, Mike 216
Hurt, Mike 208
Huson, Chad 217
Hussey, Jon 225
Hutchinson, Bubs 188
Hutskowski, Chad 220
Hvinden, Chris 145,219
Hyduke, John 214
Idzorek, Jay 205
Iglehart, Stewart 46
Ikola, Willard 38,40,44,45,46,49,192,203, 205-207,210-212,214,216,231,234
Ilitch, Mike 46
Imes, Chris 33,49,93,127,185
Iozzo, Pat 213
Irmen, Danny 122-125
Irvine, Ted 27
Irwin, Geoff 149
Isrealson, Bill 207
Iverson, Kay 95
Jackman, Tim 146,148,149
Jackson, Don 48
Jacobson, Jim 218
Jacques, Dano 229
Jaderston, Jim 199
Jaeger, Katie 247
Jagaros, Greg 144
Jagunich, Andrew 39
Jagunich, Glee 25,39
James, Ryan 221
Jamieson, Moose 21,22,38
Jamison, Joel 221
Janaszak, Steve 48,49,98-100,105,183,208
Jannett, Jenny 235,236
Jappe, Herman 129
Jarvis, Blaine 157
Jasinski, Ralph 177
Jaskowiak, Chet 189
Jedinak, Megan 246
Jeffers, Matt 220
Jenewein, Scott 148
Jenke, Lee 174
Jenkins, Dick 177
Jennings, Bill 46
Jensen, David 48,100
Jensen, Joe 142
Jensen, Paul 49
Jensen, Steve 48,49
Jenson, Reidar 229
Jensrud, Andrea 245
Jeremiah, Eddie 46
Jerke, Lindsay 240
Jerome, Dave 153
Jetland, Jim 100,209,210
Jetland, Katie 246
Jetty, George 193
Jevne, Franzq 198
Jinks, Dick 194
Jirelle, Jim 213
Johannson, Jim 49
Johannson, John 48
Johannson, Ken 29
Johnson Erik 125,126
Johnson, Aaron 160
Johnson, Ade 19,20,38,39
Johnson, Andrew 226
Johnson, Arnie 197
Johnson, Bob 34,49,61,70,71,97,100, 105-107,127,195,198,231
Johnson, Breanna 248
Johnson, Brian 134
Johnson, Bruce 231
Johnson, Bucky 95
Johnson, Chad 180
Johnson, Ching 19-22,38
Johnson, Cliff 129
Johnson, Clint 220
Johnson, Craig 48,49,102,103,110
Johnson, Derek 226
Johnson, Earl 197
Johnson, Ed 150
Johnson, Eric 142
Johnson, Erik 224
Johnson, Erin 251
Johnson, Gary 199,201
Johnson, Hodge 24,25,39
Johnson, Jack 230
Johnson, Jeff 214
Johnson, Jerry 207
Johnson, Jim 27,48,68,73,91,132,178
Johnson, Joel 161
Johnson, Justin 118,120,121,123,124
Johnson, Kelsey 247
Johnson, Ken 150
Johnson, Krista 245
Johnson, Larry 195
Johnson, Luke 100,102
Johnson, Mark 46,48,105-107,182,183,206,214
Johnson, Matt 88,89
Johnson, Mike 207
Johnson, Murray 205
Johnson, Neal 196
Johnson, Paul 181,205
Johnson, Paul 26,46,49
Johnson, Rob 227
Johnson, Robert 46
Johnson, Ryan 228
Johnson, Scott 155,210
Johnson, Tyler 174
Johnson, Vernon 191
Johnson, Virgil 24-26,46,48,189
Johnsson, Kim 85-89
Johnston, Brian 162
Jones, Amy 242
Jones, Joe 18
Jones, Matt 219
Jones, Monty 134
Jones, Steve 222
Jonsson, Peter 157
Jorde, Marv 26,29,194
Jorgenson, Jim 206
Jorgenson, Mark 47
Joseph, Burton 95
Joseph, Shane 146,148
Joslyn, Paul 94
Joyce, Ted 165
Judnick, Frank 198
Judnick, Jerry 194,195
Jund, Joe 26
Junger, Fred 95
Jungwirth, Jeff 214
Juola, Ted 39
Justice, Chris 216
Jutting, Trent 215
Jutting, Troy 146-149
Juzda, Bill 34
Kabel, Robert 26
Kaczor, Paul 211
Kaehler, Jerry 213
Kahler, Nick 18,20,22,24,42,46,158,188
Kairies, Red 175
Kaiser, Adam 224
Kaiser, Carl 26
Kaiser, Matt 171
Kalinski, Jon 149
Kalisch, Tim 219
Kangas, Alex 227
Kannenberg, Andy 206
Kantrud, Ryan 226
Kaplan, Lou 90
Kappes, Ryan 218
Kapsen, Justin 222
Karakas, Mike 24,25,38,45,46,48,189
Karakas, Tom 25,26,95
Karn, George 164
Karner, Jim 155
Karnuth, Ray 193,194
Karr, John 61,67
Karsnia, Allen 206
Kasher, Mike 25,39
Kaufman, Brian 226
Kaufmann, Evan 124,125
Kauftmann, Jerad 226
Keating, Mickey 26
Kegley, Kelly 235
KeLeo, Frank 39
Kelley, Dick 95
Kelley, John 46
Kelley, Snooks 46
Kellin, Tony 211
Kelly, Charlie 205
Kelly, Laura 236
Kelly, Mike 210
Kelly, Tom 209,210
Kelzenberg, Todd 148
Kenady, Chris 48
Kennedy, Courtney 238,242,245
Kennedy, Shannon 239
Kennett, O.J. 155
Kenny, Charles 18
Keogan, Murray 131
Keogh, Rich 206
Keon, Dave 92
Kern, Tom 127,144,148
Keseley, Jon 163,164
Kessel, Bud 183
Kessel, Phil 124,125
Keys, Jeff 170
Kieffer, George 189
Kieffer, Travis 224
Kieger, Corvin 228
Killewald, Erica 239,240,242
Kilpatrick, Becky 246
Kilpatrick, Jenna 248
Kilpatrick, Jimmy 226
King, Don 30
King, Zach 229
Kinne, Ben 228
Kinney, Pat 151
Kirrane, Jack 46
Kirwin, Dave 212
Kiryluik, Merv 134
Kisio, Kelly 68
Kissner, Mark 211
Kivi, Paul 215
Klages, John 160
Klaren, Nick 226
Klasinski, Paul 178
Klatt, Bill 91,92,95,97,231
Klatt, Trent 48,72,102,103,110,118,188
Klava, Jerod 163
Klegin, Roger 200
Klein, Matt 224
Klein, Steve 210
Kleinendorst, Kurt 127,209
Kleinendorst, Scott 48,209,210
Kleisinger, Len 150
Kleist, Paul 15
Klema, Dan 224
Klema, Jerry 200
Klema, Mike 224
Klingfus, Josh 155
Klinkertues, Scott 205
Kloiber, Ray 198
Klune, Gene 44,194
Knapp, B.J. 224
Knapp, Jim 205
Knibbs, Bill 27
Knipscheer, Fred 127,139,140-142
Knoke, Mike 100
Knop, Christine 250
Knowles, Allen 224
Knox, Greg 215
Knudsen, James 227
Knudson, Joe 154
Knutila, Benny 129
Knutson, Jim 203
Knutson, Patrick 225
Koalska, Matt 48,118-123
Kochevar, Bob 44,194
Koehnen, Todd 223
Koenig, Chad 220
Koepple, Randy 219
Kogi, Rudy 231
Kohlman, Bob 198
Kohlman, Curley 25
Kohn, Bill 113,114
Kohn, Ed 194
Koivu, Mikko 80,84-86,88,89
Koizumi, Jessica 243
Kolkind, Kevin 227
Kolquist, Kyle 222
Komarek, Laura 251
Komarek, Sally 251
Konik, George 27
Konrad, John 166,222
Koob, Dick 195
Korn, Jim 48
Kortan, Rory 221
Kosack, Jeff 202
Koski, Jason 219
Koster, Roger 231
Kosti, Rick 131-133
Kozlak, Scott 228
Kraft, Ryan 111-114,118,218-220
Krahn, Frank 204
Krake, Skip 27
Kramer, Dave 144
Kranz, Kyle 212
Kraska, Erik 172
Krause, Brittany 248

Krawchuck, Gary 152
Krensing, Mike 134
Krieger, Bob 202-205
Krivokrasov, Sergei 74,88
Krkal, John 196
Krmpotich, Dan 171
Krmpotich, Kevin 226
Krogen, Cory 164
Krois, Brian 216
Krois, Mark 213
Kroll, Mark 204
Kronholm, Mark 203
Kronick, Dan 226
Krueger, Jason 227
Kruesel, Jeff 216
Krueter, Kayla 251
Krug, Jason 148
Kruzich 133
Kryzanowski, Ed 33,34
Kuba, Filip 74,79,81,84,88,89
Kucler, Joe 25
Kuehne, Rich 241
Kuester, Jeff 213
Kuhlman, H.J. 95
Kukowski, Betsey 235
Kukulowicz, Aggie 26
Kulyk, Glenn 134
Kunkle, Charles 45
Kurpis, Ray 178
Kurtz, Ryan 228
Kurvers, Tom 48,127,128,131-134
Kvarnlov, Lyle 204,205
Kyle, Robert 165
La Batte, Phil 95
Laaksonen, Antti 74,78,80,88,89
Labafle, P.K. 18
LaBatte, Phillip 49
Labossiere, Gordon 57
LaFleur, Brian 113
LaFond, Buzzy 206,207
LaFond, Paul 150
LaFontaine, Pat 46
LaFrance, Guy 26
LaFreniere, Eric 225
LaHoud, Aaron 226
Lahti, Matt 36,39,167
Laine, Don 198
Lakso, Bob 131,132,134
Lalond, W. 17
LaManna, Louie 227
Lambert, Ashlan 250
Lamier, Henry 36
Lamme, Natalie 236
Lammi, Maria 248
LaMotte, Gary 200
Lampman, Bryce 48
Lampton, Dave 95
Lancette, Tony 216
Landman, Tyler 229
Lane, Myles 46
Lang, Jim 144
Langen, Bill 39
Langenbrunner, Jamie 9,48,49,180,218,219
Langenbrunner, Ryan 165,166
Langerstrom, Cornell 17,18
Langevin, Dave 46,48,130,134,231
Langfeld, Josh 48
Langrell, Laurie 26
Langway, Rod 46
Lanlie, Kent 205
Lanzi, Michaela 243
Larkin, Art 18
Larkin, Wayne 26
LaRoque, Bruce 211
Larsen, Ryan 229
Larson, Bart 196,208,231
Larson, Brice 198
Larson, Dick 193
Larson, Doug 196
Larson, Frank 95
Larson, Matt 215
Larson, Nick 228
Larson, Phil 223
Larson, Reed 46,48,49,93,98,99,176,207
Larson, Rick 166
Larson, Ritchie 142
Larson, Steve 160
Larsson, Jorgen 220
Lasch, Ryan 143
Lasky, Brian 227
Lasserud, Jan 208,209
Laszlo, Aaron 219
Lauen, Mike 48
Laurinaitis, James 227
Laurinaitis, Jessica 248
Laurion, Bob 196
Laven, Mike 210,211
LaVern, Mitch 225
LaVigne, Bill 39
LaVigne, Foxy 36
LaVigne, Hart 36
Lawless, Joe 208
Lawrence, Terry 201
Lawson, Bob 204
Lawson, Ken 202,203
Lawton, Brian 66
Laylin, Cory 102,110,185
Lea, Bruce 26
Leak, Roger 231
LeBlanc, Drew 229
LeBrun, Al 27
LeCaine, Bill 26
Lecy, Scott 209
Lecy, Todd 210
Ledingham, Cade 221
Ledingham, Walt 130,131,134
Lee, Anders 229
Lee, Brian 188
Lee, Mike 229
Leeman, Larry 213
Leeman, Tracey 213
Lehrke, Allison 242
Leigh, Dan 204
Leimbek, Matt 115,116
Leinbek, Matt 221
Leitza, Brian 139,141
Lemaire, Jacques 6,74,77,78,81,82,84,86,88
LeMay, Jim 200
Lemieux, Dennis 151,154
LeMoine, Monte 200
Lempe, Dan 132,134,207-209
Lempe, Eric 211
Lempe, Todd 211
Lenardon, Bill 135
Leonard, Leo 18
Leopold, Jordan 48,49,115-121,126-128
Leplant, Joe 226
Lescarbeau, Bucky 153
Lescarbeau, Todd 153,154
Leschyshyn, Curtis 74
Lessard, Junior 127,128,131,133-135
LeTourneau, Doug 210,211
Levandoski, Joe 26
Levine, Becca 242
Lewandowski, Gary 215
Lewis, Bob 194
Lewis, Herbie 20,21,22,38
Licari, Nick 225
Lick, Dick 193,194
Lievers, Brett 141,142
Lillo, Bob 199
Lilyholm, Len 29,49,91,92,97
Lindahl, Dan 198
Lindbeck, Rudy 191
Lindberg, Chris 133
Lindegard, Jerry 95
Linder, Joe 46
Lindmeier, Steve 208
Lindquist, Jon 215
Lindvall, Jeff 205
Link, Derek 221
Linnerooth, Chuck 163
Lipovetz, Jim 193
Liska, Mark 154
Locker, Chris 221,222
Locker, Derek 218
Lockhart, Tom 46
Logan, Lathan 228
Loken, Chris 217
Lolich, Joe 220
Loney, Duffy 211
Long, Doug 204,205,222
Long, Joe 164
Loos, Cory 227
LoPresti, Pete 48,58,61,62
LoPresti, Sam 25,37,45,46,48,129,136,189
Loquai, John 226
Lothrup, Kim 199
Loya, Cliff 230
Lozinski, Jim 212
Lucia, Don 115-117,119,122,126,143,208,209
Lucia, Tony 125,126
Luckcraft, Mike 214
Lukas, Jeff 208
Lunbohm, David 223
Lund, Bill 142,185
Lund, Dale 217
Lund, Darryl 192
Lundblad, Brady 166
Lundbohm, Mike 201,202
Lundeen, Bob 49,205
Lundeen, Charlie 211
Lundeen, Cort 219
Lundeen, Lloyd 190
Lundgren, Dick 192
Lundgren, Jeff 208
Lundgren, Victor 36
Lundquist, Sadie 250
Lundsten, Chet 191,192
Luth, Ben 226
Luther, Larissa 245,246
Lyke, Brian 148
Lynch, Bob 204
Lynch, George 136
Lynn, Vic 26
Lyons, Mike 114
Maas, Kevin 214
MacAdam, Al 61,62,64
MacDonald, I.D. 95
MacFadden, Bill 190
Machek, Victor 39
MacInnes, Alex 95
MacInnes, John 46
MacIntosh, Ian 26
Macioch, Frank 165
MacIver, Norm 127,131,134
Mack, Jason 153
Mackenhausen, Gordon 195
Mackey, Kevin 168
MacKinnon 122
Mackley, Melissa 246
MacLean, Kevin 93
MacLellan, Brian 67
MacNulty, Dave 213
Madgyra, Kurt 209
Madland, Terry 203
Madsen, Tom 209
Madson, Dan 206
Magnus, Jim 95
Magnuson, Rod 231
Magnuson, Tiffany 249
Magnusson, Steve 110,217
Maguet, Denelle 250
Mahle, Dan 200,201
Mahle, Oscar 29,195,196
Mahoney, Bill 65
Mahoney, Mike 27
Maida, Jake 227
Maki, Al 231
Malawski, Jeff 172,173
Maley, Dave 212
Malone, Ryan 138,142,143,230
Malsed, George 158
Malsed, Red 188
Malwitz, Jim 211
Maniago, Cesare 27,50,51,53,55,57,58
Mann, Vic 95
Marcetta, Milan 54
Marcotte, Jacques 26
Marin, Noemie 243
Marinucci, Chris 48,127,128,131,133,134,216,217
Mariucci, John 24,26,32,38,40,41,43-46,48,49, 51,95-97,100,108,119,127,136,137,189,231
Markovich, Sandy 203
Marlow, Chad 218
Maroney, Dennis 26
Mars, Steve 208
Marshall, Bobby 15,18
Marshall, Jason 80,88,89
Marshall, Leo 204
Marshall, Scott 215
Martell, Kaine 222
Martell, Ken 178
Martell, Tanner 222,223
Martens, Luke 157
Martin, Bert 189
Martin, Birgetta 251
Martin, Jim 153
Martin, Paul 48,117,118,120-122,188
Martini, Joey 172,174
Martinson, Gary 199
Martinson, Ron 44
Martinson, Steve 48
Martinson, Tom 196
Maruk, Dennis 61,66
Maruska, Bill 192
Marvin, Aaron 228,229
Marvin, Cal 32,34,35,45,46
Marvin, Dan 216
Marvin, Gigi 237,239,251
Marvin, Nick 225
Marvin, Willie 142
Marzitelli, Frank 90
Masnick, Paul 26
Mason, Bill 173
Mason, Bob 48,49,133
Massier, Murray 26
Massotto, Tony 222
Masterton, Bill 29,52,53,58
Matchefts, John 44-46,49,191,192,231
Matetich, Darren 214
Mather, Bruce 46
Mathews, John 201
Mathias, Matt 222
Matschke, John 97
Matschke, Julie 24,25
Mattilla, Tawni 243
Mattson, Jim 96,97,191
Mattson, Paul 144
Mauer, Matt 217
Maunu, Michelle 246
Maus, Dick 165
Maus, Eddie 165
Mausolf, Gary 211
Maxner, Wayne 27
Maxwell, Brad 62,65
Maxwell, Bryan 61
May, Bob Dr. 251
May, Bob 233
May, Dan 211
Mayasich, Fred 26
Mayasich, John 28,38,43,44-46,49,96, 97,127,181,191,193,219,221
Mazzu, Tony 212
McAlpine, Chris 48,102,103,117
McAlpine, Gary 197,198
McBain, Jamie 230
McCabe, Bob 30
McCabe, Chuck 95
McCartan, Jack 46,48,49,91,92,97,181
McCarthy, Eugene 165
McCarthy, Megan 246,247
McCarthy, Mike 212
McCauley, Dan 226
McClanahan, Rob 48,49,100,105,106,182,183,208
McClellan, Fran 204
McComb, Dave 27
McCormick, Joe 19,22
McCormick, John 130
McCoy, Bob 25
McCoy, John 216
McCoy, Tom 49,97
McCready, Alannah 237
McDermott, Jon 215
McDonagh, Ryan 188,228
McDonald, Gord 135
McDonald, Lane 46
McDonald, Molly 247
McDonald, Tim 218,219
McDuff, Chad 229
McElmury, Jim 48,49,91,150,151,154,155
McElroy, T.J. 143
McFarlane, Brian 225
McFee, Eric 225
McGahn, Jack 191
McGann, Bill 231
McGee, Vernon 165
McGiffert, Bill 198
McGill, Jack 26
McGlone, Bill 24,25
McGlynn, Dick 91
McGlynn, Tim 204
McGowan, Ed 231
McGowan, Everett 18
McGowan, Pat 215,216
McHugh, Justin 110,111,217
McInnes, Alex 39
McIntosh, Bruce 48,49,91,97
McKay, John 200
McKechnie, Walt 53
McKenzie, Erica 237,249
McKenzie, John 92
McKinnon, Corey 161
McKinnon, Dan 32,33,49
McKinnon, John 22,192
McLachlan, Murray 97
McLaughlin, Kyle 142
McLellan, Dougie 197
McLellan, Fran 205
McLennan, Jamie 74,89
McLeod, Bruce 130,147
McLeod, Fiona 244
Mclnnes, Alex 25
McMahon, Mike 27,91,194
McNabb, Terry 198
McNair, Harvey 18,175
McNamara, Erin 251
McNamara, John 148
McNeely, Harry 50
McNeill, Mike 48
McNight, maqtt 135
McNulty, Bob 27,50,51
McPherson 18
McQueston, Harry 26
McQuire, Mickey 22,38
McRae, Basil 69,71
McRae, Bud 26
McTigue, Bernie 38
Means, Eric 103,111,147,217
Mehling, Paul 197
Meier, Jerry 205
Melanson, Rollie 66
Melberg, Harry 188
Melde, Dan 163
Mellor, Tom 91
Melnyk, Walter 26
Meloche, Gilles 61-66
Melson, Taj 138,141,142
Melynchuk, Jerry 26,29
Menzies, Mark 172
Meredith, Bob 192
Meredith, Dick 26,29,43,96,97,192
Meredith, John 98,208
Meredith, Merv 195
Meredith, Richard 49
Meredith, Wayne 29,49
Mergens, Tony 228
Metcalf, Henry 193,194
Methven, Bruce 157
Metz, Dick 200
Metzer, Mike 202
Metzger, Bill 199,200
Metzger, Jim 204
Meyer, Jennifer 251
Meyer, Scott 138,141
Meyers, Bob 30,188
Michaels, Al 106
Michaelson, Brad 208
Micheletti, Don 98,99
Micheletti, Andy 202
Micheletti, Joe 48,206,207
Micheletti, Pat 48,100,102,127
Mickelich, Bill 25
Mickelson, Joe 213
Mickey, Larry 27
Miggins, Bob 196
Mikol, Jim 27
Mikulan, Ray 26
Milani, Tom 130,134
Milbury, Mike 46
Miles, Jeff 213
Mileti, Nick 92
Milford, Jake 27
Milinovich, George 204
Milks, Hib 38
Millen, Corey 48,49,100,212
Miller, Anya 248
Miller, Art 26
Miller, Dallas 213,214
Miller, Dave 205
Miller, Jason 31,100,102,215,216
Miller, Jim 163
Miller, Joey 227
Miller, Kris 93,188
Miller, Nate 114,116,119,142
Miller, Nick 161,226
Miller, Paul 205
Miller, Ryan 157,226
Miller, Sammy 247
Miller, Shannon 242,245
Miller, Warren 48,98,206
Mills, Andy 102
Mills, Dylan 114
Minser, Fred 18
Miracle, Reggie 213
Miskovich, Aaron 114-116,188
Miskovich, Craig 215
Miskovich, Joe 204
Mitchell, Chad 174
Mitchell, Willie 77,79,81,88,89
Mlaker, Dick 202
Modano, Mike 67,68,69,70,71,72
Moe, Bill 46,189
Moen, Jeff 110,111,112
Moen, Michelle 248
Mohns, Doug 22,57
Molin, Sacha 141,142
Molnar, Louie 213
Molock, Max 167
Monacelli, Jim 215
Mondo, Melissa 246
Monshaugen, Cory 225
Monsrud, Scott 154,211
Montebello, Tony 154
Montgomery, Mike 227
Montpetit, Todd 216
Mooney, Jim 188
Moore, Alfie 22
Moore, Dominic 85
Moore, Gregg 134
Moore, Jay 214
Moore, Larry 163
Moore, Matt 225
Moore, Skeeter 134
Moore, Tom 222-224
Moore, Tony 214
Moores, Terry 203
Moos, kathryn 247
Morelli, Reg 26
Morin, Stephane 93
Morin, Travis 149
Moritz, Roy 18
Mork, Bill 214
Mork, Hoby 217
Morque, Chris 155
Morris, Robbie 216
Morrison, George 91
Morrison, Jack 49
Morrow, Ken 46
Morse, Zach 228,229
Mortel, Chuck 201
Mortel, Gene 203
Moseley, Fred 46
Moser, Dustin 229
Moser, Jay 185
Mott, Dan 208
Motzko, Joe 48,139,142,143
Mouillierat, Kael 149
Moy, Rodger 31
Mrcronich, Ed 44
Mrozik, Rick 48
Muckler, John 54,69
Mueller, Dylan 169
Mullen, Joe 46
Muloin, Wayne 27
Munns, Bill 95,188
Munson, Beef 24,25
Murdoch, Murray 21
Murphy, Tom 216
Murphy, Ed 18
Murphy, John 151,154
Murphy, Larry 68
Murphy, P.I. 39
Murray, Andrew 155-157,230
Murray, Brady 230
Murray, Hugh, Sr. 46
Murray, Muzz 25
Muscatelli, Tito 39
Musty, Mike 166
Muzerall, Nadine 237,239,240,242,245
Myklebust, Scott 212
Myrum, George 162
Naegele, Bob III 184,185
Naegele, Bob Jr. 184,185
Naegele, Bob 74
Nagel, Amanda 251
Nagel, Brent 213
Nagle, Galen 153
Nagobads, Dr. V.G. 183
Nagurski, Critter 160
Nagurski, Kevin 207
Nanne, Lou 29,46,49,60,61,66,67,73,96,97,213
Nanne, Marty 213,214
Napier, Mark 65
Narum, Mark 205
Nash, Butch 40
Naslund, Ron 49
Nateau, Klint 221
Naymark, Len 31
Neale, Harry 91,92
Neihart, John 164,231
Neilsen, Jeff 216
Neiman, Leroy 73
Neitze, Roger 193
Nelso, Zach 226
Nelson, Brett 216
Nelson, Brian 207,222
Nelson, Felicia 248
Nelson, Hub 25,46
Nelson, Jim 201,202,209,231
Nelson, Lowell 197
Nelson, Merlin 205
Nelson, Steve 169
Nelson, Tom 134
Nemanich, Tony 45
Neska, Mike 203
Ness, Aaron 229
Ness, Jeff 210
Ness, Kelly 188
Neveaux, Tom 196
Nevin, Bob 57
Newman, Tom 110
Newson, Tom 18
Newton, Mike 134
Nichols, Andrea 237,239,242,246-248
Nichols, Devon 246
Nichols, George 22,25
Nichols, Jack 191,201
Nicklin, Percy 38
Nielsen, Jeff 48,74,75,88
Nielsen, Kirk 48,217
Nielson, Jeff 102,110-112
Nierengarten, Willard 165
Nilan, Bob 25
Niskanen, Eric 208
Niskanen, Matt 135
Nixom, Ashley 237
Noah, John 33,49
Noble, Ed 195
Nodl, Andreas 143
Noga, Matt 141,142
Nolander, Don 95
Norberg, Gerald 194
Norberg, Roger 193
Nordberg, Brad 209
Norman, Jerry 97,194
Nornes, Steve 211
Norqual, Don 198
North, Jay 211
Northrop, George 94
Norwich, Craig 48,206
Nosan, Ryan 220
Notermann, Jason 221
Novak, Aaron 155
Novak, Nick 202
Nummelin, Petteri 85,88
Nyberg, Kent 201
Nyholm, Jim 197,198
Nyhus 96
Nylund, Jim 199
Nyquist, Bill 204
Nyrop, Bill 46,48,205
Nystrom 97,197
O'Brien, Jim 125,126
O'Connor, Mike 212
O'Connor, Ted 51
O'Donnell, Sean 74,88,89
O'Hara, Todd 225
O'Leary, Bob 199
O'Neil, Jerry 150
O'Rourke, Brendan 221
O'Shea, Danny 54,92
O'Shea, Steve 154
O'Sullivan, Patrick 85
Oberstar, Paul 136,141
Oddson, Bill 25,188
Odnokon, Mark 134
Ohno, Rob 211
Okerlund, Todd 48,49,100,213
Okposo, Kyle 125,230
Olds, Wally 49,91,97
Olein, Bob 200
Oleksuk, Bill 134
Olimb, Larry 31,93,100,102,103,110, 113,127,188,215,216
Olin, Gary 196
Olive, Gene 231
Oliver, Murray 57,58,64
Oliver, Nick 229
Oliver, Scott 172
Olson, Barrett 174,221
Olson, Bill 198
Olson, Bob 198
Olson, Dave 173
Olson, Don 25,168,231
Olson, Ed 46,95
Olson, Erin 243,247,248
Olson, Greg 148
Olson, Gus 20,21,23,25
Olson, John 200,213
Olson, Josh 224
Olson, Lyle 202
Olson, Lynn 233-235
Olson, Marty 217
Olson, Matt 228
Olson, Scott 184
Olson, Tim 199
Olson, Todd 214
Olson, Wes 212
Olsson, Anders 157
Olstad, Kyle 226
Olszewski, Jim 197
Ooninex, Kristy 244,250
Oppel, Chris 224
Opsahl, Al 49,95
Opsahl, Dave 202
Ordway, Jack 18
Ordway, John 50
Ornell, Tim 227
Oshi, Buster 191
Oshi, Max 191
Oshie, T.J. 227,228
Osiecki, Mark 48,93
Osiecki, Tom 215,231
Oss, Arnold C. Jr. 49
Ostedt, Gary 196
Ostwald, Ed 44
Oswald, Ed 194
Oswald, Kevin 223
Otness, Dave 205
Ottenbriet, Harry 26
Otto, Duddley 231
Otto, Joel 48,49,127,151,153-155
Ouellette, Caroline 243,246,247
Ouellette, Gerry 27
Overman, Andy 207
Owen, Ed 95
Owen, George 46
Owen, Robert 49,181
Page, Pierre 67,68
Pagel, Rico 113,115,116
Palazzari, Aldo 48
Palazzari, Doug 44-48
Palkie, Liz 246
Palkovich, Gerald 193,194
Palm, Trent 135
Palmer, Danny 215
Palmer, Ding 46
Palmer, Port 18
Palmquist, Dave 250
Palodichuk, Al 200
Palodichuk, Larry 200
Panagabko, Pete 27
Pankoff, Mike 217
Papike, Joe 25,39,48
Papike, Vance 39
Paquin, Louis 219
Paradise, Bob 167
Paradise, Dave 141,142
Paradise, Dick 91,92
Paradise, Robert 46,48,49
Parent, Bernie 54
Parise, J.P. 27,54,56-,230
Parise, Jordan 124,143
Parise, Zach 48,127,230
Park, Richard 78,81,88,89
Parker, Andrew 215
Parker, Jeff 48
Parker, Laurie 95,187
Parkyn, Dr. H.A. 94
Parrish, Mark 7,48,49,85,87-89,138,141,142,220
Passolt, Jeff 136,140
Passolt, John 144
Pasuik, Jim 194
Pateman, Eric 147
Pates, Bob 188
Path, George 189
Patrick, Craig 46
Patterson, George 18,24
Paul, Jason 228,229
Pauletti, Jeff 214
Paulson, Babe 95
Paulson, John 169
Paulson, Tom 206
Pavek, Dick 207
Pavek, Tim 207
Pavelich, Mark 48,49,105-107,131-134,182,183
Pavelich, Tom 190
Payne, Steve 62,63,64,65
Pearson, Mel 27,209
Pearson, Mike 97
Pechet, Mitch 26
Peckham, Marc 144
Pedersen, Ken 197
Pederson, Tom 48,100,102,213,214,216
Pelawa, George 188,214,215
Pellerin, Scott 74,88
Pelletier, Marcel 27
Pelowski, Mark 173
Peltier, Bob 204,205
Peltier, Doug 97,202
Peltier, George 200
Peltier, Ron 201,202
Peltier, Skip 200,201,231
Peluso, Mike 48,114,133,134
Peluso, Tom 203,204
Pepper, Steve 209
Perkins, Phil 25,187,188
Perkl, Bill 208
Pernula, Nick 171
Perpich, George Jr. 207
Perpich, George 206,207,231
Perpich, John 98,136,137
Perreault, Jeff 172
Persian, Steve 166
Person, Sam 217
Peschel, Dan 219
Peters, Bob 127,150,152,153,155-157,163
Peters, Colin 142
Peters, Lisa 247
Peters, Steve 152,214,215
Petersen, Bethany 236
Petersen, Brett 163
Petersen, Toby 48
Peterson, Adam 219
Peterson, Andrea 250
Peterson, Bethany 241
Peterson, Chas 207
Peterson, Dave 180,205
Peterson, Dick 44,190,191
Peterson, Ian 219
Peterson, Jerry 231
Peterson, John 95
Peterson, Keith 209
Peterson, Leonard 36
Peterson, Rich 200
Peterson, Scott 215
Petroske, Jack 49,96,193
Petrov, Sergei 219
Petroyskaia, Kristina 246
Pezon, Meaghan 247
Pezon, Meghan 250
Philipczyk, Janelle 247,249
Phillippi, Joe 228
Phillips, John 25,39
Phillips, Sam 39,168
Phippen, Pat 98,178
Picha, Gene 194
Pickens, Mickey 208
Pickering, Hayden 95
Pierce, Steve 208
Pietrangelo, Fank 93
Pilot, Dave 144
Pilot, Mike 227
Pitlick, Lance 48,100,102,110
Pitt, Nathan 172
Pittelkow, Chad 215,216
Plager, Bob 27
Plain, Chuck 198
Plante, Dan 216
Plante, Derek 9,27,48,127,131-134
Pleau, Larry 46
Pleban, Connie 44-46,127,129,130
Pleban, Pete 24,25,39
Plude, Amy 248
Plude, Kelly 225
Plumm, Amanda 251
Podein, Shjon 48,132,178
Poeschl, Jeff 211
Pogorels, Tim 207
Pohl, Jim 231
Pohl, Johnny 48,114,116-121,188,221-224
Pohl, Mark 223
Pohl, Tom 226
Pohtilla, Jill 233,250,251
Polich, John 48
Polich, Mike 48,98,100,204
Polk, Jesse 225
Pollesel, Ed 26
Poltfuss, Steve 207
Pomplun, Shawn 155
Pomroy, Gordy 129
Pond, Frank 95
Pontinen, Tom 206
Poole, Jack 195,196
Poole, Joe 26,194,195
Port, Tim 173
Porten, Ken 207
Porter, Chris 218,230
Porter, Danika 248
Porter, Tom 168,169
Possin, Mike 165,166
Potter, Jenny 246-248
Potter, Tim 148
Potulny, Grant 117-124

Potulny, Ryan 122-125,127,143
Pouliot, Benoit 80
Powell, Ernie 130,132
Powell, Kevin 218
Powell, Tom 197
Pratt, Dan 136,141
Pratt, Tracy 27
Preissing, Tom 48
Prelesnik, Ed 167
Prelesnik, John 25,39
Prelesnik, Louis 167
Prelesnik, Tony 25,39,167
Prentice, Dean 57
Press, Samantha 251
Prettyman, John 205
Prettyman, Mark 207
Price, Steve 202
Price, Tamara 246
Primeau, Reginald 26
Prodahl, Glen 148
Prodahl, Jason 219
Propp, Brian 68,69
Proudlock, Shawn 218
Provost, Brian 215
Pryor, Chris 48
Pudlick, Mike 141,142
Pullar, Jessica 247
Puputti, Tuula 245,246
Purpur, Fido 25,26,46,127,189
Purslow, Chris 142
Purvis, Ray 190
Pusch, Jennifer 249
Putney, Dennis 202
Quesnell, John 188
Quinlan, Tom 214,215
Quirk, Jim 200,201
Radivojevic, Branko 88
Radovich, B.J. 225
Raduns, Nathan 225
Rahn, Noel 216
Raleigh, Don 26
Ralph, Brittny 237,239,245
Ramsey, Alexander 205
Ramsey, Mike 46,48,49,81,83,99,100, 105,107,182,183
Ramswick, Kelly 214
Ranfranz, Marc 221
Ranheim, Craig 169
Ranheim, Paul 127,213,214
Rantala, Mike 203,204
Rappana, Kevin 217
Rasmussen, Brian 224
Rasmussen, Dale 195
Rasmussen, Erik 48,112,113,117,188
Rasmussen, Terra 250
Rasmussen,Willaim 50
Ratchuk, Peter 230
Ratfield, Aaron 221
Rathburn, Jeff 218
Rau, Matt 226
Rauzi, Chris 215
Ravndalen, Bryce 229
Rawlings, Tony 226
Raymond, A. 18
Raymond, Mason 135
Raynard, Lill 247
Readmen, Steve 173
Reardon, Doc 188
Rebelatto, Gene 216
Reeder, Konrad 143
Regan, Garrett 226
Regan, Mike 208
Regan, Sean 211
Regenscheid, Ron 205
Reichart, Bill 26,29
Reichart, William 49
Reichel, Dave 136,141
Reichel, Pat 211
Reichmuth, Isaac 123,133
Reid, Tom 54,57
Reigstad, Jon 224
Reiman, Jeff 214
Reinholz, Jerrid 124,223
Reipke, Dave 191
Reith, Bob 197
Remachel, Hank 199
Remole, Jerry 95
Rendall, Brock 214
Rendle, Sam 229
Rentstrom, Jim 190,191
Resch, Glenn 130
Resch, Ian 154
Resch, Jim 201
Reszka, Marcus 168,169
Retka, Jenny 235
Reuder, John 213
Reuter, Don 205
Rewertz, Eric 220
Rheaume, Manon 237
Rhodes, Damian 48,215
Ricci, Troy 220
Rice, Adam 169
Rice, Sean 217
Richards, Alec 207
Richards, Bob 206
Richards, Brad 205
Richards, Dan 154
Richards, Todd 48,100,113
Richards, Travis 48,49,100,102,103,110
Richardson, Billy 26
Riddell, Riley 156,157
Ridder, Bob 31,39,41,45-47,49,50,247
Ridder, Kathleen 240,247
Riddle, Jake 225
Riddle, Troy 117-123,224,225
Riepke, Dave 190,191
Riley, Bill 46
Riley, Jack 46
Riley, Joe 46
Riley, Scoff 173
Ring-Jarvi, Sue 240
Rink, Matt 226
Rintoul, Ryan 145,148
Ripley, Rachel 251
Ripley, Vic 22
Risebrough, Doug 74,75,84
Ritz, Gordon 27,50
Roberg, Chad 223
Roberts, Dick 95,204,231
Roberts, Don 140,159,162,163
Roberts, Gordy 46,62,93
Roberts, Holly 250
Roberts, Jenna 246
Roberts, Jim 53
Roberts, Maurice 46
Robertson, Jackie 250
Robertson, W.J. 15
Robideau, Chris 212
Robideaux, Scott 172,173
Robitaille, Randy 88
Roce, Jerry 169
Roche, Larry 200
Rockenbach, Tony 222
Rodd, Tiffani 248
Rodda, Dave 44,193,194
Rodden, Ed 20,38
Rodlund, Jared 229
Roehl, Dale 214
Roest, Stacy 74,77,88,89
Roff, Paul 212
Rogers, Marty 204,205
Rogers, Owen 135
Rohlik, Steve 213,215
Rohloff, Jon 48
Rolle, Dennis 95,196,231
Rollie, Glenn 231
Rollins, Ron 199
Rollwagen, Kerry 245
Rollwagen, Kevin 171,226
Roloson, Dwayne 77-79,81-83,85,88,89
Rolston, Brian 83- 89
Romnes, Doc 22,24,25,27,40,46,48,95,170,188,189
Rompre, Robert 49
Rondeau, Dick 46
Ronning, Bill 199
Ronning, Cliff 80,88,89
Rooney, Bill 148
Rooney, Jesse 220
Rooth, Maria 245,246
Rosendahl, Paul 198
Ross, Barrie 27
Ross, Bobbi 249,251
Ross, Don 49,197
Ross, Gary 49,155,205
Ross, Jim 198
Ross, Larry 46,96,196,206,231
Ross, Ray 26
Ross, Steve 201
Ross, W.A. 94
Rossi, John 231
Roth, Dick 197
Roth, Erin 207-209
Rothstein, Bill 209,210
Rothstein, John 134,207,208
Rothstein, Roger 206
Rothstein, Tom 210,211
Rounelle, Gary 195
Rovick, Roger 195
Roy, Mark 209
Rozzini, Gino 26
Rud, Eric 185
Rudberg, Lawrence 129
Ruedy, Gary 214
Ruegsegger, Tyler 230
Ruisink, Rick 210
Russ, Clyde 95
Russ, Lloyd 95
Russell, Navada 245
Russo, John G. 230
Rust, Michelle 250
Rutledge, Wayne 27
Ryan, Pat 95
Ryan, Simon 165
Rybar, Joe 134
Ryman, Marsh 41,95
Saatzer, Dave 148
Saatzer, Dick 192
Saatzer, Don 192,231
Saatzer, Ron 192
Sabo, Les 194
Sabol, Shaun 48,178
Sabourin, Gary 27,53
Sacchetti, Andy 224
Sack, Gene 231
Sadowski, Tom 210
Saintey, James 229
Salcido, Brian 230
Sall, Chris 227
Salmon, Jim 197
Salscheider, Tim 207
Salvevold, Greg 219
Samargia, Pete 224
Sampair, Brandon 138,142,220
Sampson, Ed 49
Sampson, Gary 49,161
Samuelsson, Ulf 71
Sandalack, Alex 26
Sandelin, Scott 48,127,133
Sanden, Dave 177
Sanders, Frank 49,91,92,97
Sanders, Jack 25
Sanders, Roy 18
Sanderson, Marv 150
Sandison, Scott 203
Santerre, Gino 141
Sargent, Gary 48,62,151,154,176,205
Sarner, Craig 48,49,91,92,97,202
Sarsland, Tryg 165
Saterdalen, Jeff 138,140,142,216
Saterdalen, Tom 231
Sauer, Jeff 198
Sauer, Kurt 48
Sauer, Rob 215
Saugestad, Ed 127,140,152,158,159
Saunders, Alyssa 247
Saunders, Ken 26
Sautter, Paricia 246
Savage, John 189
Savage, Ron 205
Savolainen, Bill 198
Scanlan, Jim 152,154
Scanlon, Chuck 154
Scanlon, Jenna 246
Scanlon, John 95,188
Schack, Brian 228
Schade, Fred 95
Schaeffer, Butch 48
Schaeffer, Gordon 95,158
Schaeffer, Paul 25,39
Schartin, Ray 30
Schartin, Toy 30
Schaser, Ian 226
Schaublin, Rita 243
Scheid, Chris 142
Schema, Anne 246
Scheuer, Danielle 248
Schiebe, Ben 217
Schille, Maurice 191
Schleppegrell, Tom 207
Schlieff, George 172
Schmaltzbauer, Gary 29,49,97,196
Schmidgall, Jenny 237,240,245,247
Schmidt, Chad 166
Schmidt, Clarence 34,48
Schmidt, Ryan 229
Schneider, Buzz 49,100,105-107,182,183
Schneider, Maria 250
Schneider, Neal 226
Schoenrock, Corey 215
Scholz, Kris 239
Schreiner, Jon 229
Schroeder, Don 210
Schroeder, Jordan 228
Schuett, Mike 202
Schultz, Fred 165
Schultz, John 225
Schultz, Nick 74,77,81,88,89
Schultz, Wayne 27
Schulz, Charles 46,49,109
Schumacher, Al 168
Schumacher, Mike 227
Schuman, Jake 225,226
Schwab, Allison 251
Schwabe, Evan 134
Schwartz, Gus 170
Schwartz, Jason 217
Schwartz, John 213,215
Schwartz, Mike 160
Schwartz, Nick 206
Schwartzbauer, Chris 213,214
Schwartzbauer, Joe 197
Schwartzbauer, Whitey 221
Schweitz, Mike 213
Schwietz, Rob 211
Scissons, Jeff 134
Scofield, Tyler 157
Scott, Danny 223
Scott, Jim 216
Scott, Phil 95
Scotvold, Evy 188
Scudder, Tommy 209
Seaborn, Jim 20,21,38
Searles, Jake 221
Sedin, James 49,95,96,191
Seeger, Walter 18
Seeler, Kelly 250
Segar, Pete 210
Seiler, Christine 247
Sekenski, Jaime 249
Sekeras, Lubomir 74,80,88,89
Selman, Bill 130
Selvog, Tony 225,227
Senden, Stuart 116,117
Sendin, Stuart 114
Senescall, Mike 208
Serratore, Frank 93,156,178,179
Serratore, Tom 156,157
Sertich, Andy 122-125,225
Sertich, Marty 127,128,188
Sertich, Mike 132,133,135,226
Sertich, Steve 49,231
Sether, Marshall 200
Sether, Todd 174,221
Shack, Joe 26
Sharpley, Glen 61
Sharratt, Amber 242
Sharrow, Bob 193
Shattuck, Rob 199,200
Shaver, Al 72
Shaver, Wally 72
Shaw, Bill 205
Shea, Pat 22,25
Shearen, Bob 189,190
Sheehy, Neil 48
Sheehy, Tim 46,48,49,91,200,201
Shelanski, Brett 173
Shelstad, Brad 98,202,203,205,231
Shelstad, Dixon 203
Sheppard, James 80
Sheridan, John 178
Shero, Fred 27
Sherritt, Gordon 26
Shewchuck, John 206
Shikowsky, Chad 173
Shinabarger, Tom 155
Shock, Ron 53
Short, Steve 48,176
Shushinsky, Maxim 88
Shute, Dave 185
Shutte, Bruce 44,193
Sikich, Chris 222
Sikich, Michelle 235,236
Sikich, Zach 171
Sikio, Hanne 246,247
Simones, Rita 250
Simonson, Rolf 217
Simpson, Joe 24
Simus, John 197
Sinden, Harry 27
Singer, Josh 224
Sirianni, Rob 155,157
Sivertson, Bill 198
Sjaaheim, Arlyn 196
Sjerven, Grant 139,141
Skarda, Randy 48,100,102
Skime, Larry 199
Skime, Todd 213
Skogstad, Matt 222
Skoog, Dave 196
Skorich, Troy 216
Skoula, Martin 86,88,89
Skramstad, Alvin 36
Skrypek, Terry 170,171,207,231
Slominski, Laura 236,237,239,240,242,251
Smaagaard, Garrett 124
Smaby, Matt 230
Smedsmo 48,203
Smith, Bobby 60-65,68-71,73
Smith, Charles 231
Smith, Dan 168,226
Smith, Gary 58,183
Smith, Greg 62
Smith, Keaton 228
Smith, Lauren 249
Smith, Lefty 127,203
Smith, Rick 91
Smith, Stanford 26
Smith, Terry 201
Smith, Wyatt 34,48,112-116,118,142,220,221
Smoleroff, Darryl 165,166
Snuggerud, Bo 171
Snuggerud, Dave 48,49,93,100,103
Sobb, Jeff 155
Solei, Brent 225
Somers, Artie 21,22
Somers, Bob 175
Sonmor, Glen 40,49,58,62-65,67,90,92, 93,97,99,127,175
Sorem, Ron 205
Soumi, Al 39
Spannbauer, Dick 231
Speak, Andy 173
Spehar, Dave 113-116,142,188,220-222
Sperling, Jac 77
Spoden, Doug 207
Sporer, Max 189
St. Vincent, Frank 95
Stacklie, Jim 206
Stafford, Ben 223
Stafford, Drew 230
Stahura, Kurt 164
Stang, Roxanne 244,250
Stangl, Dave 202,203
Stangl, Jim 148
Stanisich, Bill 198
Stanley, Edward 45
Stanley, Greg 206
Stansberry, Dave 216
Staples, Ken 231
Stapleton, Tim 134
Stauber Brothers 47
Stauber, Robb 48,102,110,127,128,214
Stedman, Dennis 194
Steege, Brandon 110
Steele, Gene 196
Steenerson, Alan 192
Steichens, Jim 175
Steones, Dave 198
Stephanson, Ken 27
Stephens, Jim 202,203
Stephens, Kelly 238,246,248-250
Stephens, Win Jr 175
Steve, Jack 199
Stevens, Judd 124
Stevenson, Grant 146,148,149
Stevenson, Jeremy 88
Stewart, Ashley 244,250
Stewart, Bill 46
Stewart, Black Jack 40,41
Stewart, Cam 74,88
Stewart, Jason 141
Stewart, Nels 38
Stewart, Trevor 225
Stiles, Tom 212
Stinar, Dale 172
Stoa, Maria 250
Stoa, Ryan 125,126
Stodgell, Aaron 222
Stoen, Leslie 236
Stohr, Pam 246
Stolp, Jeff 103,110,215
Stordahl, Jim 197
Stordahl, Larry 49,97,197
Storey, Bobby 204
Storm, Mike 197
Story, Brook 250
Stoskopf, Jack 193,194
Stoyko, Bob 27
Strand, Cliff 136,195,196
Strelow, Warren 183,193,231
Strewart 22
Strobel, Art 26
Strobel, Eric 49,99,100,105,182,183
Strobel, Mark 217
Strobel, Mike 217,218
Strodahl, Larry 29
Strom 96
Strot, Brett 93,102
Struck, Carl 17,18
Strunk, Alex 249
Struntz, Julius 189
Stuart, Mark 48
Stuart, Mike 48
Studier, Josh 219
Sturgeion, Roger 93
Stutz, Greg 227
Subject, Dick 200
Suihkonen, Ted 221
Sullivan, Pat 136,141,214
Sullivan, Terry 212
Sullivan, Tim 211
Summers, Danny 26
Sundberg, Harry 175
Sundquist, Eric 195
Suomi, Al 48
Suomi, John 95
Sushinsky, Maxim 74
Sutton, Andy 88
Svendsen, Kurt 214
Svendson, Brandon 226
Swanson, Bill 217
Swanson, Cody 224
Swanson, John 143
Swanson, Wallace 158
Sweezo, Tim 219
Swenson, Duane 169
Swentkofske, Steve 209
Swetela, Pat 213
Szabo, Peter 142
Szepanski, Tom 208
Tabor, Kallie 246
Taffe, Jeff 48,115-119,188,223,224
Taft, John 48,49
Taft, Wally 230
Taggart, Gabe 222,223
Takko, Kari 67
Talafous, Dean 48,205
Talarico, Dom 223
Talbot, Heather 242
Talbot, Rick 166,223
Taleen, Bill 210
Tallackson, Barry 118,120-124
Tallus, Nora 247
Tanabe, David 48
Tangan, Jeff 205
Tannahil, Don 92
Tarbox, Scott 200
Tassoni, Tony 191
Taylor, Jack 18
Taylor, Jake 122
Taylor, John 204
Taylor, Matt 18
Taylor, Ted 27
Teal, Jeff 48
Teasdale, Frank 94
Techar, Bill 144,148
Tegenfeldt, Dave 206
Tellor, Rian 199
Terris, Marc 162
Terwilliger, Dave 209
Terwilliger, Tom 213,214
Tharp, Ben 223
Thayer, Bill 207
Thayer, Larry 205
Thayer, Mac 95
Thelen, A.J. 80,230
Thesling, Curt 219
Thibeault, Gilles 26
Thiele, Mark 228
Thoemke, Jack 199
Thole, Jeff 210
Thomas, Ambria 238,242,245
Thomas, Jack 194
Thomas, Mike 231
Thomas, Skip 204
Thompson, Carrie 246,248
Thompson, Clay 219
Thompson, Cliff 39,40,42,46,95,129,190,192
Thompson, Jock 189
Thompson, Norm 130
Thompson, Tel 189
Thompson, Terry 173
Thompson, Tiny 20,22,23
Thomson, Jim 150
Thorsen, Carl 231
Thorson, Eric 220
Thunder, Paige 250
Thunstrom, Allie 237,247
Thygeson, Walt 129
Tierney, Gene 206
Tinordi, Mark 69,71
Tjarnqvist, Daniel 84,88
Todd, Dick 203
Todd, George 95
Toenjes, Bill 30
Toews, Jonathan 230
Tok, Mike 134
Tollefsbol, Mark 216
Tomberlin, Justin 215
Tomiuk, Nick 26
Toomey, Sean 48,134
Toplin, Arthur 94
Torrel, Doug 134,215
Toth, Andy 25,39,95
Toumi, Tray 215
Toumie, Jack 198
Tourville, George 203
Tousignant, Dan 213
Trachsel, Jim 166
Trachsel, Pokey 231
Travica, Dan 161
Trebil, Dan 48,111,113
Trebil, Ryan 114
Trembath, Travis 223
Trew, Bill 172
Trieble, Al 30
Trooien, Dennis 203
Trot, Charles 15
Trumble, Hal 46
Tryba, Laura 236
Tscherne, Jeff 98,206
Tucker, Chris 216,217
Tuomie, Tray 214,215
Turcotte, Ed 172
Turgeon, Allison 245
Turner, Bob 231
Turner, Jack 26
Turner, Vern 38
Tutt, Thayer 45,46
Twardowski, Blake 226
Ulseth, Steve 47,100,113,127,178
Ulvin, Dick 198,199
Ulvin, Lowell 190,191
Ulwelling, Joe 163,164
Ulwelling, Matt 222,223
Urdahl, Troy 222
Usiski, Ryan 220
Utecht, Bob 231
Vacanti, Jeff 212
Vacanti, Mike 211
Vaia, Don 193
Vairo, Lou 178
Valento, Todd 215
Valicevic, Chris 168
Van Bockel, Ryan 171
Van Buskirk, Tony 36
Van Der Bosch, Matt 224
Van, Allan 30,49,95
Van, Howie 30
Van, Wylie 30
Vanbiesbrouck, John 46
Vandell, Roland 136
Vanderbeek, Ted 207
Vandertop, Chad 216
VandeVelde, Chris 227
Vanek, Thomas 120,121,123
Vannelli, Len 90
Vannelli, Mike 125,126
Vannelli, Tom 98
Veilleux, Stephane 85,86,88
Vekich, Derek 215
Vekich, Mike 219
Verchota, Phil 49,100,105,106,182,183,208
Vermeulen, Travis 227
Viger, Fred 36
Vigness, Les 190
Vigness, Watt 190
Villalta, John 161
Vinnes, Harold 196
Vinnes, Harrold 169
Vizenor, Jeff 248
Voce, Dan 44,192
Vogt, Shari 237,246,248
Vork, Adam 218
Voss, Doug 160
Vraa, Loren 195
Vroman, Bob 201
Vuconich, Mike 214
Vukonich, Bill 231
Wabman, Bob 194
Wacker, Becky 249
Wagner, Steve 146,149
Wahman, Tom 195
Waibel, Jon 118,120,121,123
Wakefield, Dick 197
Waldhauser, Tom 206
Walker, Howard 34
Walker, Willis 94
Wall, Lindsay 239,248,250
Wallene, Howard 193
Wallestad, Austin 154,201
Wallgren, Mike 227
Wallin, Richard 82
Walls, Elmer 196
Walsh, Tom 214
Walters, Drew 227
Walters, Haley 236
Walters, Shea 227
Walton, Mike 90,91
Walz, Wes 76-80,84,85,88,89
Wambach, Rene 161
Wanvick, Woody 129
Wanvig, Kyle 88
Ward, Katie 245
Ward, Larry 148
Ward, Pat 217
Warner, Jim 48
Warren, A.H. 22
Warren, Chuck 158
Waselovich, Peter 205-207
Wasem, Crystal 245
Wasiluk, Terry 202
Wasley, Charlie 185
Watson, Bill 127,128,131-134
Watson, Joe 27
Watson, Leland 95
Watson, Sid 46
Watt, Jim 48
Watters, Dave 226
Watters, Gordon 95,96
Weasler, Dean 142
Weber, Bernie 193
Weber, Carl 193
Weber, Travis 120-122
Weber, Vic 150
Wech, Joe 212
Wegge, Jim 198
Wegleitner, Bill 192
Wegleitner, Tom 95,191,192,231
Weidenborner, Cy 18,22,49
Weiland, Cooney 20-22,127
Weinhandl, Mattias 85
Weinkauf, Mike 144,148
Weinke, Chris 216
Welch, Adam 225
Welch, Casey 225
Welch, Dan 116,119,120,223,224
Welch, Russ 178
Weller, Bill 200
Wellington, 22
Welliver, Kyle 228
Wells, Monty 189
Wenda, Mark 178,206
Wendell, Krissy 118,237,240,242,247-250
Wenkus, Eric 171
Wensloff, Dave 196,197
Werner, Leonard 165
Werness, Lance 31,215
Westby, James 49,97
Westby, Jerry 195
Westby, Jim 195
Weston, Kurt 229
Westrum, Aaron 222
Westrum, Erik 48,114-118,222
Westrum, Pat 92,93
Wethington, Kerry 245
Weum, Ron 201
Weyl, Tom 198
Wharram, Ken 176
Wheeler, Andy 221
Wheeler, Blake 124-126,227
Wheeler, Ron 200
Wherley, Jim 197
Whisler, Jeff 231
White, Patrick 228,229
White, Todd 83,85,88,89
White, Tommy 225
Whiteside, Cy 26
Whitney, Scott 208
Wick, Mark 172
Wiemer, Jason 88
Wigens, Roger 195
Wild, Justin 166
Wild, Paul 95
Wilharm, Jim 214
Wilkinson, Bud 40,95,230
Willer, Don 231
Willey, Kevin 165.166
Willey, Lyle 26
Williams, Blake 166
Williams, Burr 25,187
Williams, Butch 48,177
Williams, Nigel 230
Williams, Rip 129,177
Williams, Rob 214
Williams, Thomas 181,207
Williams, Tommy 28,46,48,49,51,54
Williamson, Dean 100,102,179
Williamson, Murray 28,29,46,51,91,97, 127,175-177,179
Willner, Brad 180
Wilson, Bruce 214
Wilson, Jeff 217
Windhorst, Sarah 248
Windmeier, Amalee 250
Wineberg, Rick 205
Wink, Jack 136
Winsor, Ralph 46
Winter, Cletus 136
Winter, Travis 157
Winters, Coddy 16,20,38,46
Wirtz, William 46
Witchger, Mitzi 234
Witcraft, Todd 216
Witucki, Steve 212
Wizner, Jeff 207
Wohlers, Pete 215
Wolff, Beth 236
Wolke, Benji 220
Wong, Mike 48
Wood, Gary 199,200
Wood, Gordon 94
Woodey, Ron 175
Woods, Barry 173
Woog, Doug 29,46,97,100,102,103,110-112, 114,115,119,175,176,178,197-199,231
Woog, Joy 241
Worsley, Gump 54,55,57
Worters, 22,38
Woytowich, Bob 27
Wright, Lyle 18,46
Wytaske, Gary 205
Xavier, Tom 211
Xerxa, Mack 188
Yackel, Ken 26,43,46,48,49,96,97,206
Yelle, Jennifer 250
Ylitalo, Glenn 227
Young, Ashley 246,248
Young, Bill 162
Young, Brian 207
Young, Erik 116
Young, John 93
Young, Nathan 219
Young, Tim 58
Young, Zach 219,220
Youngbauer, Walt 95
Youngberg, Ray 193
Younghans, Hal 189
Younghans, Tom 48,167
Youngquist, Bob 192,193
Yurkovich, Tom 29,49,194
Zahradka, Russ 202
Zelenak, Phil 214
Zellner, John 199
Zenzens, Con 15
Zenzens, Gus 15
Zholtok, Sergei 78,79,81,88,89
Ziebarth, Jason 219
Zimmerman, Frank 206
Zimmerman, Tom 228
Zins, Eddie 231
Zmolek, Doug 48,68,102,103,110,114,216,217
Zollman, Bryan 218
Zweig, Steve 211
Zyuzin, Andrei 83,88,89
Zywiec, Frank 176

List of Works Cited:

1. *Ross Bernstein: Interviews from over 100 Minnesota sports personalities and celebrities
2. "Gopher Hockey by the Hockey Gopher," by Ross Bernstein, Minneapolis, MN, 1992
3. "Fifty Years • Fifty Heroes" A Celebration of Minnesota Sports, by Ross Bernstein, Minneapolis, MN, 1997
4. "Hubert H. Humphrey Metrodome Souvenir Book": by Calvin Griffith, Jim Klobuchar, Halsey Hall, Muriel Humphrey Brown, Charles O. Johnson, Patrick Reusse, Joe Soucheray - compiled by Dave Mona. MSP Publications.
5. "An Investment of 26 Years Yields Nothing but Memories," Star Tribune Article by Curt Brown, March 11, 1993.
6. "The Official National Hockey League 75th Anniversary Commemorative Book": by Dan Diamond, NHL Pub., 1991.
7. "USA Hockey," by Kevin Allen, Triumph Books, Chicago, IL, 1997.
8. "A Thinking Man's Guide to Pro Hockey": by Eskenazi, Gerald, E. P. Dutton, 1972.
9. "The Hockey Encyclopedia": by Fischler, Stan, and Shirley Fischler, Macmillan, 1983.
10. "NHL The World of Professional Hockey": by Jay Greenberg, On Frarik, and Gary Ronberg, Rutledge Press, 1981.
11. "The Pictorial History of Hockey" by Joseph Romain, & Dan Diamond, Gallery Books, 1987.
12. "The Sporting News Hockey Guide & Register": Sporting News Publishing, 1984-90.
13. "Sid!" by Sid Hartman & Patrick Reusse - Voyager Press, 1997
14. "Broten Lived Out a Dream" by Dan Barriero, Star Tribune, Oct. 16, 1996
15. The U.S. Hockey Hall of Fame Handbook
16. "One Goal - A Chronicle of the 1980 US Olympic Hockey Team": by John Powers and Art Kaminsky: Harper Row, 1984
17. The US Olympic Hockey Guide -1996
18. North Stars article by Curt Brown, Star Tribune, March 11, 1993
19. "An Investment of 26 Years Yields Nothing But Memories" Star Tribune, 1981.
20. North Stars Media Guides (1970s -90s)
21. "Don Roberts Bids Farewell to Gustavus Adolphus," by Jim Rueda, Mankato Free Press
22. "The Christian Story": Christian Brothers, Inc. Press Release Information
23. "Minnesota Trivia," by Laurel Winter: Rutledge Hill Press, Nashville, TN, 1990
24. "NCAA Championships": The Official 1996 National Collegiate Championships & Records, by the NCAA
25. The Phoenix Coyotes Media Guide: 1997
26. The U.S. Olympic Comm. Olympian Report
27. The Star Tribune Minnesota Sports Hall of Fame insert publication
28. "Hockey": The Illustrated History, by Dan Diamond
29. "One Hundred Years of Hockey": by Brian McFarlane
30. "The Official NHL Stanley Cup Centennial," by Dan Diamond
31. "Can You Name That Team?" by David Biesel
32. Duluth News Tribune and Herald: UMD Hockey article, March 25, 1984
33. The Sporting News: UMD Hockey article - April 2, 1984
34. "Ivory Tower": John Mariucci article - "The Coach Behind the Comeback," by Peter Vanderpoel, 1953
35. "Hockey Chicago Style: The History of the Blackhawks," by Paul Greenland: Sagamore Publishing
36. "Dallas Stars" - Professional Team Histories
37. "Scoreboard," by Dunstan Tucker & Martin Schirber, St. John's University Press, Collegeville, MN, 1979.
38. "The Great American Hockey Dilemma," by Murray Williamson, Ralph Turtinen Publishing Co., Wayzata, MN, 1978.
39. "The Flakes of Winter," by Stan Fischler, Warwick Publishing Co, Toronto, Canada, 92.
40. "Icy Pleasures," by Paul Clifford Larson, Afton Historical Society Press, Afton, MN 98.
41. "Great Book of Hockey," by Stan & Shirley Fischler, Publications International, Ltd., Lincolnwood, IL, 1997.
42. "Awesome Almanac MN," by Jean Blashfield, B&B Pub. Inc., Fontana, WI, 93.
43. "Hockey America," by Kevin Hubbard & Stan Fischler, Masters Press, Indianapolis, 97.
44. "Minnesota State High School Hockey Tournament History," Art Solz Jr., Minneapolis, MN, 1968.
45. "The Goldy Shuffle: The Bill Goldsworthy Story," by Richard Rainbolt & Ralph Turtinen, Denison Pub., Minneapolis, 1971.
46. "Skate for Goal!," by Gary L. Phillips, Afton Press, Afton, MN 1982.
47. "The Blazing North Stars," by Stan Fischler, Prentice Hall Pub., Englewood Cliffs, NJ, 1972.
48. "Hockey Hall of Fame," by Dan Diamond and Joseph Romain, Doubleday Pub., NY, 1988.
49. "NHL Hockey: An Official Fans Guide," by

50. "Total Hockey," by Dan Diamond, Total Sports Publishing, NY, 1998
51. "The Encyclopedia of Sports," by Frank Menke, AC Barnes Pub., Cranbury, NJ, 1975.
52. "Sad and Mad," by Curt Brown, Star Tribune, March 11, 1993.
53. "Going for Gold," by Tim Wendel, Lawrence Hill Pub. Co. Westport, CT., 1980
54. "The Internet Hockey Database," by Ralph Slate
55. "My lifetime in sports," by George Barton, Stan Carlson Pub., Minneapolis, 1957.
56. "The Story of Hockey," by Frank Orr, Random House, NY, 1971.
57. "Hockey legends of all time," by Morgan Hughes, Pub. Intl., Lincolnwood, IL, 1996.
58. Sports Illustrated: Stars article, May 25, '81
59. Sports Illustrated: Stars article, June 1, 1981
60. "Ice Polo in Minnesota," 1883-1901, by DonClark
61. "Minn. Indoor Rinks," 1894-1982, by Don Clark
62. "Early Eveleth Hockey," First Fifty Years, 1903-1952, by Don Clark
63. "Early St. Paul Hockey," 1896-1942, by Don Clark
64. "Early Minneapolis Hockey," 1895-1942, by Don Clark
65. "Early Duluth Hockey," by Don Clark
66. "Hockey in the U.S.," by Don Clark
67. "USAHA - United States Amateur Hockey Association," 1920-1926, by Don Clark
68. "American Hockey Association," 1927-1942, by Don Clark
69. "Central Hockey League," 1931-1932, 1934-1935, by Don Clark
70. "Minnesota Amateur Hockey Association - The Early Years," by Don Clark
71. "The Great American Hockey Dilemma," by Murray Williamson (Ralph Turtinen Pub, 1978).
72. "Times have changed," by John Millea, Star Tribune, January 3. 1999.
73. "Something Wild is going on here," by John Millea, Star Tribune, December 6, 1998.
74. "Melting away" by Roman Augustoviz, Star Tribune, January 17, 1999.
75. "Heritage on ice," by Patrick Reusse, Star Tribune, February 28, 1999.
76. "Hockeytown Indeed," by Tim Klobuchar, Star Tribune, February 28, 1999.
77. "Tradition, meet reality," by Rachel Blount, Star Tribune, February 14, 1999.
78. "Too Many Men on the Ice," by Joanna Avery & Julie Stevens, Polestar Pub., Victoria, B.C., 1997.
79. "Girls Hockey in Minnesota, Where to from here?", by Dr. Robert H. May, T. S. Denison Publishing, Minneapolis, 1978
80. "NHL Hockey: An official Fans Guide," by Triumph Books, Chicago, IL, 1997.
81. "Hockey Hall of Fame," by Dan Diamond and Joseph Romain, Doubleday Pub., NY, 1988.
82. "Best of Hockey," by Morgan Hughes, Publications Int., Lincolnwood, IL, 1998.
83. "NHL Hockey - An official fans guide," Triumph Books, Chicago, IL, 1997.
84. "Hockey's young superstars," by Eric Dwyer, Polestar Press, Vancouver, BC, 1992.
85. "Great Moments in Hockey," by Brian Kendall, Penguin Pub., Toronto, 1994.
86. "The Official NHL Stanley Cup Centennial Book," by Dan Diamond, Firefly Books, Buffalo, NY, 1992.
87. "Legends of Hockey," by Opus Productions, Penguin Books, Toronto, Ont., 1996.
88. "Heritage on ice," by Patrick Reusse, Star Tribune, February 28, 1999.
89. "Hockeytown Indeed," by Tim Klobuchar, Star Tribune, February 28, 1999.
90. "The Official Notional Hockey League 75th Anniversary Commemorative Book," by Diamond, Dan, NHL Publications, 1991.
91. "A Thinking Man's Guide to Pro Hockey," by Eskenazi, Gerald, E. P. Dutton, 1972.
92. "The Hockey Encyclopedia," by Stan and Shirley Fischler, MacMillan, 1983.
93. "NHL: The World of Professional Hockey," by Greenberg, Jay, Frank Orr, and Gary Ronberg, Rutledge Press, 1981.
94. "The Pictorial History of Hockey," by Romain, Joseph, and Dan Diamond, Gallery Books, 1987.
95. "The Story of Hockey," by Frank Orr, Random House, NY, 1971.
96. "Professional Sports Teams Histories," by Michael LaBlanc, Gale Research Pub., Detroit, MI, 1994.
97. "The Great Book of Hockey," by Stan and Shirley Fischler, Publications International, Ltd., 1996.
98. "The Encyclopedia of Sports," by Frank Menke, AC Barnes Pub., Cranbury, NJ, 1975.
99. "The Encyclopedia of North American Sports History," by Ralph Hickock, 1992.
100. "Fischler's Illustrated History of Hockey Book," by Stan Fischler, Warwick Publishing, Toronto, Ontario, 1993.
101. "Skating by C.G. Tebbutt," Published by

Longman, Green and Company, London , 1892.
102. "Municipal Hockey In Minneapolis," by W.W. Fox, Assistant Director of Recreation from article in "Parks and Recreation."
103. "Hockey in the US: The Canadian Influence," by Don Clark and Roger A. Godin
104. "My lifetime in sports," by George Barton, Stan Carlson Pub., Minneapolis, 1957.
105. "Organizations that Wield the Shinny Sticks on Ice," St. Paul Globe, January 25, 1888.
106. "Polo on Ice," Duluth News-Tribune, January 14, 1893.
107. "Ice Follies 20th Anniversary Brochure"
108. "Minnesota State Fair: The history and heritage of 100 years," Argus Publishing, 1964.
109. "The Origins Of American Hockey," By Kevin Allen
110. "The Eveleth Hockey Story," By G. P. Finnegan, Postmaster, Eveleth
111. "Eveleth: Where It All Began," By Bruce Brothers
112. "Eveleth Hockey," by Chuck Muhich, State Sports News, November 15, 1953.
113. "Wren Blair - in Living Color," By Paul Rimstead the Canadian magazine
114. "The Islanders sew it Up," by E.M. Swift, Sports Illustrated, 1980.
115. "Skates, Sticks, & Men," The Story of Amateur Hockey in the US by S. Kip Farrington, Jr., 1972.
116. "The Official NHL Stanley Cup Centennial Book," by Dan Diamond, Firefly Books, Buffalo, NY, 1992.
117. "Death Ended Masterton's Dream of Big Time Hockey," St. Paul Dispatch 1/15/68
118. "Masterton Dies of Head Injuries," St. Paul Dispatch 1/15/68
119. "NHL: The World of Professional Hockey," by Frank Orr
120. "Glen Sonmor: The scrapper who led Gophers, the Fighting Saints and the Stars has mellowed," by Bruce Brothers, Minnesota Hockey Magazine, 1988.
121. "Glen Sonmor - full speed ahead!", by Charley Hallman, 1972 Saints program.
122. "More Bad Boys," by Stan Fischler, McGraw Hill Pub., Whitby, Ontario, 1995.
123. "Jon Casey: Always Proving Himself" - From Grand Rapids to Grand Forks to the pro's, it's been a constant battle, by Kent Youngblood.
124. "Hockey's young superstars," by Eric Dwyer, Polestar Press, Vancouver, BC, 1992.
125. "The Islanders sew it Up," by E.M. Swift, Sports Illustrated, 1980.
126. "The First 50 Years of Tournament Dominated by Dynasties," By Mike Cook.
127. "State Tournament: Premier Event Of Its Kind Nationwide," By Larry Larson.
128. "You think state tourney is great now? You shoulda been there..." By John Gilbert.
129. "From Humble Beginnings, Tournament Becomes Showcase," by J.G. Preston.
130. "Aldrich dream still growing" by Charley Hallman, St. Paul Pioneer Press/Dispatch, March 10, 1998.
131. "It's Becoming More Difficult to Attain Unbeaten Status," By Mike Fermoyle, St. Paul Pioneer Press Dispatch.
132. "The Thrill of a Lifetime," by E.M Swift, Sports Illustrated, March 7, 1983.
133. "The Warroad Lakers 1946-47 to 1996-97," by Roger A. Godin (Total Hockey)
134. "Marvin 'godfather' of Warroad hockey," by John Gilbert
135. "Lakers a Major Part of "Hockeytown USA," by Jess Myers
136. "Hockey Legends' Favorite State Tournament Memories," by J.G. Preston
137. "Fighting Saints - were they ever!" by John Gilbert
138. "Curling Club provided foundation for wealthy Duluth hockey tradition," by John Gilbert (MN Hockey Magazine, 11/89)
139. "Duluth's 1st college team had to wait for uniforms, competition," by Gary Bartness
140. "Rip Williams, now 80, Mr. Hockey in Duluth," By Jess Myers
141. "SCSU Hockey: Reestablishing the Tradition," by Kimberly Knutson.
142. "SCSU hockey: Old slapshots never die; they just fade away," by Kimberly Knutson and Greg Erickson.
143. "St. Cloud builds arena, tradition, respect," by Bruce Brothers.
144. "For Brose Hockey Is All About Goals," by Paul Allan, MSU Sports Information Director
145. "Saugestad 'cabin fever' to supplant hockey for a spell," by Dave Wright, MN Hockey, summer 1990.
146. "Beaulieu Brought Goals to St. Mary's," By Dave Wright
147. "Concordia Sports - The First One Hundred Years" by Vernon Finn Grinaker, Concordia Website.
148. "In-line skates: 'Not-so-new' product continues on a roll in Minnesota," by Judd Zulgad.
149. "Sports Leagues & Teams," by Mark Pollak, McFarland and Co. Publishing, Jefferson, NC, 1996.

150. "Too Many Men on the Ice," by Joanna Avery & Julie Stevens, Polestar Pub., Victoria, B.C., 1997.
151. "A Woman's Game," by Shirley Fischler Total Hockey, 1998.
152. "US women have golden moment in Nagano," by Rachel Blount, Star Tribune, Feb. 18, 1998.
153. "Precious Mettle," by Rachel Alexander, American Hockey, April/May 1998.
154. "Emotion pours out in victory, defeat," by Sharon Raboin, USA Today, 02/18/98.
155. "Curtin Call: Roseville senior is '99 Ms. Hockey," by Shane Frederick, Feb. 25, 1999.
156. "MIAC get's grant," Women's Hockey News, Vol. 2, 1999.
157. "Move from boys' ranks leads to record year for Krissy Wendell and her Pirates teammates," By Dave Pedersen.
158. "Rainy River Community College: A 30-Year History," by Dan Huntley, 1999.
159. " 'U' takes a step forward in second season," by Rachel Blount, Star Trib, Mar. 28, '99.
160. "Southern Minnesota's Pride on Ice: Rochester's Mustangs," By Mark Dayton.
161. "The Great American Hockey Dilemma," by Murray Williamson (Ralph Turtinen Publishing, 1978).
162. "Up from the Minor Leagues of Hockey," by Stan and Shirley Fischler, 1970.
163. "Hull says he's willing to make sacrifices for Stars," by Helene Elliott, Sporting News (Oct. 19, 1998)
164. "Shooting from the lip" Sports Illustrated article, 11/2/98 by Johnette Howard
165. "Hockey Showdown, The Canada-Russia Hockey Series," by Harry Sinden and Will McDon ough, Toronto: Doubleday, 1972.
166. "Golden Ice," by Stan Fischler, McGraw Hill Ryerson Ltd., Scarborough, Ontario, 1990.
167. "Going for Gold," Tim Wendel, Westport, CT: Lawrence Hill & Co., 1980.
168. "One Goal," by John Powers and Arthur Kaminsky, NY: Harper & Row Pub., 1984.
169. "USA Hockey," by Kevin Allen, Triumph Books, Chicago, IL, 1997.
170. "Minnesota NHLers: Remembering Their Roots," (www.nhlpa.com), March 2, 1999
171. University of Minnesota Men's Athletics Media Guides: Hockey
172. University of Minnesota Women's Athletics Media Guides: Hockey
173. Bemidji State Media Guides: Hockey
174. Moorhead State Media Guides: Hockey
175. UMD Media Guides: Hockey
177. Mankato State Media Guides: Hockey
178. St. Cloud State Media Guides: Hockey
179. Augsburg College Media Guides: Hockey
180. Bethel College Media Guides: Hockey
181. Carlton College Media Guides: Hockey
182. Concordia College Media Guides: Hockey
183. Hamline University Media Guides: Hockey
184. Macalaster College Media Guides: Hockey
185. St. John's Media Guides: Hockey
186. St. Mary's Media Guides: Hockey
187. St. Olaf College Media Guides: Hockey
188. St. Thomas College Media Guides: Hockey
189. Minnesota State High School League Hockey Tournament Programs: 1945-1999
190. "Eveleth Hockey - First Fifty Years (1903-1952)," By Don Clark
191. "Eveleth Hockey," By Don Clark
192. "Gopher Hockey," by Don M. Clark
193. "St. Paul Hockey 1896-1942," by Don Clark
194. "Ice Polo In Minnesota 1883-1901," by Don M. Clark
195. "Early Ice Games," By Don Clark
196. "Hockey - World Encyclopedia," 1967
197. WCHA Yearbook, 40th Anniversary Edition, 1991-92
198. NHL Guide and Record Book, 1991-1992
199. "Ice Hockey, U.S. Records, Olympics and World Championships 1920-86," By Don Clark
200. "Minn. Hockey History," By Don Clark
201. "Early Minneapolis Hockey - 1895-1942," by Don Clark
202. "Minneapolis Municipal Hockey," by W.W. Fox, Director Of Municipal Athletics
203. "The Origins of American Hockey," by Kevin Allen
204. "Early St. Paul Hockey 1896-1942," by Don Clark
205. Spalding Ice Hockey Guide, 1912
206. "A Chronological History of Minnesota Hockey," by Don Clark
207. "Ice Polo In Minnesota 1883-1901," By Don M. Clark
208. "United States Amateur Hockey Association," by Don Clark
209. MAHA Handbooks: 1952, 54, 58, 64
210. "Minnesota Amateur Hockey Association - The Early Years," By Don M. Clark
211. Spalding Ice Hockey Guide: 1921
213. "Eveleth Hockey-First Fifty Years" (1903-1952) By Don Clark
214. The United States Hockey Hall Of Fame: A Brief History